The Design of
Operating Systems for
Small Computer Systems

The Design of Operating Systems for Small Computer Systems

STEPHEN H. KAISLER

Physical Research Scientist
U.S. Central Intelligence Agency

A Wiley-Interscience Publication

JOHN WILEY & SONS

New York • Chichester • Brisbane • Toronto • Singapore

Copyright © 1983 by John Wiley & Sons, Inc.

Library of Congress Cataloging in Publication Data:

Kaisler, Stephen H. (Stephen Hendrick)
  The design of operating systems for small computer
systems.

  "A Wiley-Interscience publication."
  Includes bibliographical references and index.
  1. System design.   2. Operating systems (Computers)
I. Title.
QA76.9.S88K34   001.64´25   82-6912
ISBN 0-471-07774-7   AACR2
Printed in the United States of America

10 9 8 7 6 5 4 3 2 1

Preface

The explosive growth of minicomputer and microcomputer systems technology has opened up new areas of operating system design. New operating system designs appear regularly. They range in complexity from a simple real-time executive monitor to advanced systems that rival that mighty behemoth, OS/360. This trend has allowed continuous research and development of techniques and provided a steady stream of improvements and features in commercially available operating systems. Where once the thought of tinkering with the operating system was greeted with horror, today almost every frustrated and would-be systems programmer can design and build his or her own operating system. This capability has resulted from better high-level languages, better machines, and most important, a better understanding of the essential functions and structures of operating systems.

Operating systems design has generally proceeded in a hook-or-crook fashion. Most books on operating system principles discuss the general concepts and theory with a few examples from large systems. They may include some code segments that depict high-level simplified structures that illustrate the general concept. However, any would-be system designer has a treacherous road to follow in converting the concepts to working reality. This text provides a detailed examination of features and concepts in the design of operating systems. The major trade-offs in space, time, and functional flexibility are analyzed and described for each feature of an operating system. The design of a specific operating system—a real-time executive multiprogramming system—is described and discussed.

It is my intention to provide a "how-to" handbook on the design of operating systems for small computer systems. It is expected that the reader possesses sufficient knowledge of hardware, high-level languages, and data structures to design and implement an operating system. The basic principles are supplemented by topical modules that discuss advanced concepts, provide case studies, and summarize the classical literature in operating system design.

STEPHEN H. KAISLER

Silver Spring, Maryland
September 1982

v

Acknowledgments

This text would not have been possible without the help and encouragement of many friends, students, and colleagues. I would like to acknowledge the assistance of friends and colleagues at International Computing Co. and Logicon, Inc. who provided encouragement and material for the text. I would like to thank students in CS267/268 at George Washington University who waded through initial drafts and who provided both critical reading and many helpful comments for improving the text. Friends and colleagues in the U.S. Government provided considerable support and encouragement. Lastly, I would like to thank the wonderful and professional people at John Wiley & Sons, particularly the editorial staff, for working so hard to make this text a reality.

S.H.K.

Contents

2. Device Management   43

6. File Management   424

1

Introduction

1.1 OBJECTIVE OF THE TEXT

This text is concerned with the design of operating systems (OSs) for small computer systems. By small computer, I mean those machines and associated peripherals that are manufactured by minicomputer vendors. I chose this approach to defining small computers to avoid an extended debate over other computer characteristics, such as memory size, processing speed, and amount of software.

The state of the art in computer systems technology has advanced through almost four generations since the first computer was constructed and operated in the early 1940s. Progress in both hardware and software has been extremely rapid. It is sufficient to say that many large-scale minicomputers of today possess computational power equivalent to that of some of the smaller mainframes, and many microcomputer systems are rapidly approaching the sophistication and computational power of the smaller minicomputers. As technology advances, the user's perception of what a small computer can and should do changes.

No application is developed in a vacuum. Many factors affect the design, development, and implementation of a computer-based system. Among them are financial and personnel resources, the nature of the application, and the complexity of the problem to be solved. The variety of applications for which computers are used has generated a wide range of requirements for the system software, which controls the hardware and provides the operational environment in which applications are developed. In most cases, the user is quite happy to "live" with the OS software provided by the vendor, usually because there is no alternative means of support. Recently, more users have become oriented to the idea of creating their own systems software or tailoring the available software to meet their perceived unique needs.

1

This text is intended for the computer science professional who is developing OS software for small computers. It is also intended for the home hobbyist and frustrated systems programmers who wish to create system software in their own images. At the same time, this text will be helpful to applications programmers who want to understand more about the internal structure and operation of the OS.

I presume at least a working knowledge of one ALGOL-like structured language, as my PDL (see appendix A) resembles superficially ALGOL and Pascal. I also presume at least a senior undergraduate comprehension of computer system technology with regard to data structures, programming techniques, and computer hardware.

I have surveyed the available technical literature concerning OS design. Most of this literature is concerned with academic or theoretical questions. Translation of theory to reality is often a difficult task without pragmatic guidelines to follow. Many excellent textbooks on OS design focus on the critical issues while neglecting the basic structural aspects, and many papers in the literature take the "here's what we did" approach without discussing in detail exactly what decisions are to be made, which structures defined, and which modules coded.

My approach in this text is to concentrate on the analysis of a general-purpose, multiprogramming OS for a small computer. I intend to concentrate on identifying design parameters, evaluating trade-offs in design, and making decisions relative to structures and algorithms useful in OS design. An extensive OS skeleton is presented to illustrate the points discussed in the text.

In each chapter, the text is supplemented by code skeletons and commentary which correspond closely to many current systems. These code skeletons illustrate the various internal aspects of OS structure and algorithms. By this method I hope to enrich the information that you derive from this text while allowing you to skip topics that are not of interest.

1.1.1 Setting the Stage

Chapter 1 is intended to set the environment in which OSs are to be designed. To this end, section 1.2 presents a thorough discussion of the baseline hardware characteristics. The descriptions contained in section 1.2 are drawn from a survey of hardware components manufactured by a variety of minicomputer vendors.

Section 1.3 discusses some alternative viewpoints regarding OS design of and section 1.4 covers one possible OS taxonomy.

Section 1.5 presents some of the major concepts that have affected the design of modern OSs. My intent is to present only a set of baseline concepts that can be used throughout the rest of the text. Finally, section 1.6 presents a brief discussion of the major points covered in the remaining chapters of the book.

1.2 Computer System Components

A computer system is composed of a variety of components, which include the central processing unit, unit record devices for input/output, mass storage devices, and communication devices. Each device has specific attributes that govern its handling and usage. An understanding of device characteristics is essential to the development of an OS. This section describes the attributes of specific device classes using the PDP-11 peripherals as examples. Examples from other manufacturers are included where they represent significant variations in hardware component design. (*Note*: I discuss only minicomputer manufacturers in this section.)

1.2.1 Computer System Configurations

A computer system is a complex of both hardware and software components. In its simplest form, it may be composed of a central processor unit (CPU) with main memory, a small disk, and a teletype. The system may be supported by a small real-time OS. A more complex system, evidenced by recent introductions by major minicomputer manufacturers, may include a diverse array of peripherals coupled with a functional approach to systems architecture. Additional hardware units may include a communications processor (such as Data General's Data Communications Processor). At the far end of complexity, multiple computer configurations emphasize resource sharing, enhanced systems power, and survivability in the face of failing components.

The connection of components in a computer system is currently represented by the following major architectures. These architectures utilize a different central element for interfacing with other elements of the system and attempt to provide optimum flexibility and economy.

1. **Bus central.** A passive or active data/control bus is used to connect all functional elements in the system. The PDP-11 family utilizing the UNIBUS is representative of this approach (see figure 1.1).

2. **Memory central.** The main memory is used as a connector between the CPU and the peripherals. Most minicomputers utilize this approach (see figure 1.2).

3. **CPU control.** All peripherals and main memory are arrayed around the CPU. This approach is common to most microcomputer systems currently available (see figure 1.3).

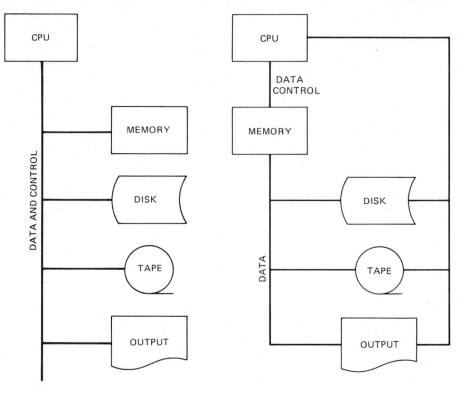

Figure 1.1   **Bus central architecture.**   Figure 1.2   **Memory central architecture.**

1.2.2   Central Processing Unit/Main Memory

The CPU provides the arithmetic and control logic for decoding and executing instructions. It also contains the logic for interfacing to the input/output bus (UNIBUS) as well as other features depending on the model. Most minicomputer systems are implemented as a family of computers varying in speed, memory size, and other features. In the following paragraphs, we use the PDP-11/70 as our model. Some of the CPU features are:

Word size.   The PDP-11/70 has a 16-bit word composed of two 8-bit bytes. This 16-bit word allows direct addressing of 32K 16-bit words or 64K 8-bit bytes (K = 1024).

Asynchronous operation.   The CPU runs independently of the main memory, thus allowing the highest possible speed of execution.

General registers.   The PDP-11/70 provides two sets of general registers (labeled R0 through R5). In addition, a stack pointer register (R6) and program counter (R7) are included. These registers can be used as accumulators, index

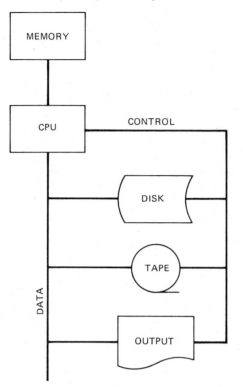

Figure 1.3   CPU central architecture.

registers, and autoincrement/autodecrement registers. Each register is 16 bits in length.

Processor modes.   The PDP-11/70 provides three modes of operation, known as kernel, supervisor, and user. These modes provide hardware protection for a multiprogramming environment by providing three distinct sets of stacks and memory management registers. The kernel mode has access to all instructions and all memory, including the device registers.

Vectored interrupts.   The PDP-11/70 implements a scheme known as vectored interrupts, in which each device class has a unique two-word interrupt vector in lower memory. When an interrupt occurs, the current program counter (PC) and processor status word (PSW) are pushed onto the stack, and the new PC and PS are fetched from the interrupt vector.

Power fail and auto restart.   The PDP-11/70 provides hardware detection of power failure and automatic error recovery in the OS.

Processor bus.   The PDP-11/70 is connected to memory and the peripherals via the UNIBUS. This provides a uniform approach to communications, control, and input/output. Each device, including memory, is assigned an address on the UNIBUS. The closer a peripheral is to the CPU, the higher its priority when interrupts are serviced. The memory is closest to the CPU on the UNIBUS.

Instruction set. The PDP-11/70 provides a flexible instruction set of more than 400 instructions which operate on registers and memory locations. Unlike other machines, as device registers are assigned memory addresses, there are no I/O instructions. Rather, almost all instructions may operate directly on the device registers. Instruction classes include arithmetic operations, logical operations, program control, and branches.

Stack architecture. The PDP-11/70 implements a hardware stack in an area of memory set aside by the programmer. Specific instructions allow for dynamic establishment, modification, and deletion of the stack and its contents. On the PDP-11, a stack starts at the highest location reserved for it and expands linearly downward to the lowest address. The lower bound of the stack is stored in the stack limits register.

Memory management unit. The memory management unit (MMU) provides the hardware facilities for memory management and protection. This feature allows several programs to exist simultaneously in memory and to be executed concurrently. The MMU provides a virtual addressing capability (extended address space) via the page management approach.

Floating-point processor. The PDP-11/70 provides a hardware assist for performing floating-point operations via the floating-point processor (FPP). The FPP contains special 32-bit registers and a complete set of instructions. It is attached as a peripheral device on the UNIBUS.

System console. The PDP-11/70 provides a front panel console and switches for examining the status of the machine. From the console, the operator can display any memory location and its contents, change the contents, or perform debugging operations.

Main memory is treated as a peripheral on the PDP-11 to the extent that it communicates with the CPU over the UNIBUS as does every other peripheral. Memory is situated adjacent to the CPU on the UNIBUS, and thus has the highest priority. It is therefore guaranteed the most immediate service when it has data ready. The memory units are read/write, random access, and store 16 bits per word consisting of two 8-bit bytes. Each memory control unit can handle either full-word or byte addressing. The PDP-11/70 can accommodate up to 2M bytes of memory using the MMU. Each memory byte is accompanied by a parity bit; odd-parity checking is used. If a parity error occurs, the processor is interrupted and control is transferred to a service routine through the interrupt vector table.

1.2.3 Mass Storage Memory—Disks/Drums

In a multiprogramming general-purpose computer system, main memory is a short-term, relatively scarce commodity. Many programs compete for residency to obtain access to the CPU. Long-term storage is provided by devices whose size is several orders of magnitude larger than main memory. A minicomputer with 256K bytes of main memory might be supported by mass storage devices of 2.5M, 25M, or 200M bytes, representing increases in magnitude of 1, 10, or 100.

Typically, mass storage devices in minicomputers have been disk drives or magnetic tapes. Recently, a move toward bulk semiconductor memories has been proposed as a high-speed replacement for the fixed-head disk. These devices form a storage hierarchy characterized by increasing size and slower access speeds. The hierarchy can be represented as follows:

STORAGE HIERARCHY

Level		Size	Speed
0.	CPU and cache/ registers	2K–16K bytes	100 nsec–1 μsec
1.	Main memory	16K–2M bytes	200 nsec–1 μsec
2.	Extended memory	128K–4M bytes	1–4 μsec
3.	Disk devices	256K–400M bytes	4 μsec–70 msec
4.	Magnetic tape	256K–infinity	10 μsec–2 msec

Within levels 3 and 4, a large range of devices exists: from floppies to high-speed disk packs, from cassettes to high-speed vacuum tape drives. Disk drives provide large quantities of directly accessible storage. The industry has provided the following types of drives to meet the varying storage requirements of computer system designers.

1. Fixed-head disks offer a single disk platter that is physically locked into the drive unit. These disks usually have at least one head per track and may have multiple heads per track for greater efficiency. These devices provide fast access (4–8 μsec) but limited storage (256K–2M bytes).

2. Moving-head disks provide a single disk platter that is usually removable from the disk drive unit. A disk arm moves in or out relative to the center of the disk. These devices feature larger storage (2.5M–10M bytes) with slower access time (17–70 msec).

3. Disk pack drives feature a set of disks stacked together as a single mountable unit. The number of disks varies but 11 seems to be common to the 2314-compatible devices. Each disk is bracketed by an arm containing read/write heads for its upper and lower surfaces. All disk arms move in unison and only one head may transfer data at any one time. These devices offer large amounts of economical storage (25M–600M bytes) at speeds comparable to moving-head disk cartridges (35 msec).

Disk Structures and Parameters

A disk is a circular platter consisting of concentric rings of decreasing radii known as tracks. Each track is divided into blocks of data known as sectors. The number of sectors per track varies between 12 and 64. Each sector contains a fixed number of words; the usual range is 64-128-256. Disk controllers are usually limited to accessing a minimum of one sector. The maximum depends on the vendor but may be as high as 65K words (DEC's RP06).

In disk packs, the set of tracks situated vertically through the pack is known as a cylinder. No physical arm movement is necessary to switch tracks; rather, a new read/write head is energized at the end of each track. Flores [flor72] provides a detailed description of these disk drives.

Disk units are characterized by several parameters which generally affect the design of efficient accessing algorithms. Disk devices are random access devices; that is, one can get to a block of data by specifying its cylinder, track, and sector addresses. Accessibility is not instantaneous. The read/write heads have to be positioned over the proper sector before a data transfer can occur. The average time from data request to data transfer is a function of two time parameters. Seek time is the time required to position the access mechanism over the proper track. One method for implementing a disk-access service policy is known as shortest-seek-time-first [wilh76]. Rotational latency is the delay incurred to reach the desired block/sector on the track. The average value of r is given as half the time required for one rotation of the disk.

Many studies have been performed which attempt to optimize data allocation and retrieval from disk devices [full74, piep75, teor72, wilh76]. An excellent book by Wiederhold [wied77] presents a detailed discussion of file and database design relative to physical device characteristics. Many algorithms exist for implementing both allocation and service policies; the reader is directed to the references for notes on several of the more readable and comprehensible papers.

Physical Attributes for Disk Devices

In PDP-11 series machines, each generic disk device is represented by a set of control and status registers containing the information necessary to communicate with that device. The number of registers is dependent on the device type. For example, an RK-11 disk cartridge require six registers, whereas an RP04 disk pack drive has more than 20. A variety of information concerning the status of the drives is available through these registers. An OS designer can choose to use or ignore as much of the data as he or she desires.

Fixed-head disks have predefined and preedited formats associated with the recording surfaces. Data are written in blocks in a fixed number of characters and in a fixed code. I/O instructions for rotating memories tend to be generic across all sizes and models. Commonly implemented instructions are:

GATHER-READ/SCATTER-WRITE	Read/write a set of scattered disk blocks
SCATTER-READ/GATHER-WRITE	Read/write a set of contiguous disk blocks to a scattered set of memory blocks
READ/WRITE BLOCK	Transfers contiguous disk blocks to/from one or more contiguous memory blocks
STATUS	Retrieves a value from one of the device registers (e.g., current sector, parity error, etc.)

Moving-head disks are provided with additional instructions to control the movement of the read/write heads. These include:

SEEK-INWARD/OUTWARD	Given a specified cylinder number, moves the heads to the desired cylinder
MOVE CYLINDERS INWARD/OUTWARD	Moves the heads toward/away from the disk center the specified number of cylinders

The following is a summary of some commonly used physical data in managing disk devices.

WORD COUNT	Total number of words to be affected by a given function
DRIVE SELECT	Logical drive number of the controller
CYLINDER ADDRESS	Cylinder address of the first data word
SECTOR ADDRESS	Sector number for a data block
FUNCTION	Function to be performed on the disk drive
DRIVE READY	Indicates that device is available for a new function
BUS ADDRESS	Memory address for data transfer
DATA LATE	Indicates that data were not supplied/accepted correctly by the controller during a read/write operation
PARITY ERROR	Indicates that the controller has detected a parity error in a data word during a transfer operation

1.2.4 Sequential Memory—Magnetic Tape Systems

Magnetic tape devices form the highest level of the storage hierarchy. In most systems, it is considered backup storage to the on-line disk files. In this function, duplicates of files on disk are copied to tape for preservation in case of disk hardware failures. Tapes also serve as archival data storage for large amounts of data.

A magnetic tape is a sequentially accessible device. Although magnetic tapes were once used as mass storage devices, the long traversal time does not make magnetic tapes suitable for on-line file devices. Magnetic tape drives vary in type from cassettes to high-speed vacuum drives, and also vary in the number of bits per inch (bpi) that can be written on the tape. The tape density ranges from 800 to 6250 bpi for industry-compatible tapes. Characters are written on the tape in either seven-track or nine-track format. Each vertical frame on the tape represents a character of 6 bits plus parity (seven-track) or 8 bits plus parity (nine-track). Tape speeds vary from 12.5 to 125 in. per second.

A tape drive is connected to the computer system by a tape controller. Each controller can support up to eight drives. Each drive, depending on speed, can support a data transfer rate of 36,000 (TM11) to 72,000 (TU16) characters per second. The capacity per reel varies from 5 to 40 million characters depending on recording format and method (NRZI or phase-encoded).

During system operation, the controller monitors the status and operation of each drive. Whenever service is required from the CPU, an interrupt is generated. Reading can generally be performed while the tape is moving forward or backward. Writing can be performed only while the tape is moving in a forward direction. During write operations, parity is generated character by character and checked on the read operation. In addition, at the end of each physical record, a cyclic redundancy character (CRC) and/or longitudinal parity character (LPC) are generated to check for errors.

The primary parameters for a tape drive include the tape speed and density. Where the user is concerned, the major parameter is the time required to access a particular record on the tape. Access time is a function of the number of records intervening between the current record and the desired record. Beyond this characteristic, other considerations are imposed by logical file structures determined by the OS.

Physical Attributes of Tape Devices

A tape can be considered as a single-track, reversible, fixed-head disk with an indefinite track length. Reflecting strips, detectable by the drive electronics, mark the beginning and the end of the tape. The tape is divided into logical units called files. Each file is further subdivided into records. Files are terminated by a special file marker; they may contain a variable number of records. Records are separated by interrecord gaps and may contain a variable number of characters. A generic set of instructions for a tape drive includes:

READ FORWARD/REVERSE	Reads one block of tape into memory while moving the tape in the forward/reverse direction
SET STATUS	Set of instructions that allows the controller to set density on-life/off-line and parity for reading/writing
WRITE FORWARD/REVERSE	Writes one block of data on the tape from core while moving in the forward/reverse direction. Reverse writing is commonly associated with preformatted tape (such as DECTAPE or LINCTAPE)
REWIND	Moves the tape to the beginning tape marker at rewind speed
FAST FORWARD	Moves the tape to the end of the logical tape
SKIP N RECORDS FORWARD/REVERSE	Moves the tape in a forward/reverse direction to the next file marker
WRITE FILE MARKER	Writes a file marker on the tape
STATUS	Retrieves the status of the tape from the device registers

Each tape system is represented by a set of control and status registers which contain the information necessary to communicate with that device. Examples of some of the registers you might encounter are:

STATUS BITS	Indicate end of file, parity error, end of tape, bad tape, seven or nine-track, write block, and ready, among others
DENSITY SELECT	Specifies the density of a specific drive
MEMORY ADDRESS	Specifies the destination/source of a read/write operation

WORD COUNT REGISTER   Specifies the number of words to be read/written in the next operation

FRAME COUNT   Specifies the number of records to be passed during a skip operation

1.2.5   Peripheral Devices—Unit Record Equipment

A peripheral device is a unit that is not part of the central processor but which provides an interface between the computer system and the user. Peripheral devices can be broadly segregated into three classes: unit record equipment, communications, and data acquisition and control devices.

A raw peripheral device is electronic or electromechanical in nature; it contains merely enough components to interface it to the computer system. Control logic is provided by a component known as the device controller, which may handle many devices of a similar type. The device controller provides the standard interface between the memory bus/CPU and the devices. Device controllers are specific to the class of device they manage. By inserting a device controller between the devices and the CPU–memory complex, we move some of the control intelligence away from the CPU and thus reduce its processing burden. Distributing system intelligence in this manner reduces the possibility of single-point failures and enhances the modularity and maintainability of the resulting system.

The device controller performs a variety of functions: it selects a particular device for activation; establishes operating information such as word count, control parameters, and memory address; initiates the I/O operation; tests the status of the device; and interrupts the CPU to signal completion of an I/O event. Device controllers also perform format conversion (e.g., from card code to ASCII). Some device controllers may perform certain functions related to error detection and handling in devices. The recent surge in the use of microprocessors as the basis for device controllers has meant better logic, better response, and easier maintenance (particularly through the use of built-in diagnostics).

In this section we describe briefly the characteristics of the major unit record peripherals: card readers, teletypes, video display units, and printers. Flores [flor72] provides an exhaustive survey and analysis of peripheral devices which includes detailed discussions of device handlers. Soucek [souc76] has written a book for scientists and engineers which provides a tremendous amount of detail on minicomputers and microprocessors.

Card Readers

At one time, card readers were probably the most widely used form of communication with a computer and they are likely to remain with us well into the future. The predecessors to the computer, electromechanical accounting machines, were dominated by card equipment. One of the earliest forms of long-term memory was the punched card, which was embodied in the NCR Card Random Access Machine (CRAM).

The punched card defines the concept of a unit record—one data record is equivalent to one physical item. This concept has pervaded the development of peripheral devices to the extent that the definition is stretched to include video display units. A punched card usually consists of 80 columns and 12 rows. The top two rows are called the field punches and are represented by the 11 and 12 bits. In combination with multiple bits punched in rows 0 through 9, data can be encoded on the card in Hollerith format.

A punched card is moved past a series of mechanical feelers or photocells that sense the absence or presence of holes in the card and convert them to bit values. These sensors are the essence of the card reader. Card readers have speeds that range from 100 to over 2000 cards per minutes.

Line Printers and Teleprinters

Line printers are output devices. The printer mechanism will either print a line or a character at a time (see the discussion of teletypes below). The speed of line printers ranges from about 10 lines per minute to well over 5000 lines per minute. Two types of printing technology are available: impact and nonimpact.

Printers generally use fanfold paper, although teleprinters such as teletype devices use paper rolls. The horizontal spacing is usually 10 to 12 characters per inch and the vertical spacing is three to four lines per inch. The character set ordinarily contain a 64- or 96-character font (including lower case). The number of characters per line seems to be standardized at 80 (card compatible) or 132 columns. Among the status indications that may be returned from a printer are on-line/off-line, out of paper, parity error, and ready.

A variation on the stand-alone, output-only printer is the teleprinter. Whereas a printer is usually connected directly to the computer system, a teleprinter may be connected directly or through an associated communications subsystem. Associated with the printer mechanism is a keyboard for data entry. The keyboard is arranged in "QWERTY" format and usually transmits up to 34 nonprintable control characters, 52 upper-/lower case letters, 10 numerical, and 20 or so special characters. Given its simplicity and low cost, the teletype-like device appears to be the most common I/O device on minicomputer and microcomputer systems. The teleprinter often does double duty as both the operator's console and the interface for applications programmers and systems users.

Video Display Units

A video display unit (VDU) consists basically of a keyboard for the manual input of characters, a cathode ray tube (CRT) screen which displays the characters held in the terminal's character store, and other electronic circuits. In many instances alphanumeric VDUs have replaced teleprinters as the primary human–machine interface in small computer systems. This fact is due largely to greater transmission speed, comparable cost, larger display area, and special functions provided by the terminal.

VDUs can generally be classified in one of the following categories:

1. Dumb terminals, which offer a limited number of functions and usually feature teletype compatibility
2. Quasi-intelligent terminals, which offer extended functions such as editing and formatted data entry
3. Programmable terminals, featuring software support in varying degrees of sophistication

The first two classes usually have control and display generation residing in the CPU or the input/output processor (IOP). Programmable terminals include a self-contained microprocessor and local memory which provides storage for the terminal software system. This distribution of system intelligence often relieves the CPU or IOP of a significant processing burden as well as providing the system user with a flexible display tool.

VDUs, unlike teleprinters, normally have a buffer or memory store for supporting the refreshing of the screen image. Transmission between the computer system and the terminal can occur in one of three modes irrespective of connection method. In half-duplex mode, each character is displayed and transmitted as it is keyed in. In full-duplex operation, each character is transmitted as it is entered and is subsequently reflected back to the terminal from the computer for display. In block-mode operation, the entire contents of the buffer (or portions thereof) are transmitted to the computer while the entire buffer is displayed on the screen.

VDU terminals can possess a number of special features which can significantly increase the processing load on the CPU or IOP. The ability to display images in color so as to identify conditions or types of data will require additional control information to be supplied to the terminal. Another feature is reverse video, which displays a negative image of the data, that is, black on white instead of white on black. Another feature provides for variable brightness levels that allow visual separation of information by varying the intensity level of the display. A character or group of characters may be set blinking in order to attract the user's attention. VDUs operating in line mode usually implement a scrolling feature whereby lines of data can be moved up or down as a new line is added or an existing one is removed. Each of these features requires an increase in complexity of the terminal control software included in the OS.

Nominally, a screen is blank when the system is initialized. To indicate the current position on the screen, a character called a cursor is displayed where the next character is to be keyed in or where a character will be deleted or removed. The cursor is usually a horizontal bar located below the normal character position so as not to obscure any characters. The cursor can be set blinking to attract attention or be suppressed altogether. It is nondestructive in that it does not delete existing characters over which it passes.

Usually associated with the cursor are editing and formatting controls. Special keys are provided to position the cursor in the following manner:

Move the cursor left/right one space
Move the cursor up/down one line
Home the cursor to the first position, top line
Home bottom the cursor to the first position, last line
Tab the cursor forward/backward to a previously set stop
Return (move) the cursor to the first position of the next line
Backspace the cursor one space to the left (may delete any character)
Line feed the cursor to same position, next line

The editing features consist of a set of functions for manipulating elements of a screen image. Among the more common functions performed relative to the cursor are:

INSERT   Permits character to be added to existing lines by shifting the locations initially occupied to the right with data being lost if they move off the end of the line

INSERT LINE   Allows a new line to be added above or below the current position of the cursor

DELETE   Removes characters from an existing line with the remaining text closing up the gap after the characters are deleted

LINE DELETE   Allows lines of text to be removed

CLEAR DISPLAY   Erases all displayed data on the screen and returns the cursor to the home position

SET BLINK   Initiates blinking of data inserted at the position occupied by the cursor

CLEAR BLINK   Terminates blinking at the position occupied by the cursor

1.2.6.   Data Acquisition and Control Devices

One of the first uses of mini- and microcomputers was in the process control function. Process control presents two implications for computer peripherals: acquirng data from and transmitting control signals to the external, possibly nondigital environment.

Whether for instrument control or data recording or both, data from the external device must be captured and reformatted into a form amenable to computer processing. This fact requires both transmitting and receiving channels for I/O to the instrument. Once the data are captured, they are processed and displayed for the system operator. At the same time, the computer system may issue instructions to the instrument or device to modify certain state variables in the process. A major problem with automated instrumentation is that the device and computer often may be so specialized that unique programming support is required for error detection and handling, data-handling functions, and real-time synchronization.

Recently, several manufacturers have introduced standardized interfaces for connecting a wide variety of devices to computer systems. The following paragraphs examine two data acquisition and control systems as representative examples.

Hewlett-Packard's Interface Bus

The Hewlett-Packard Interface Bus (HP-IB) is an interdevice connection scheme which corresponds to IEEE Standard 488. The definition of the HP-IB provides four primary elements:

Mechanical specification such as cables and connectors
Electrical specifications such as signal voltages and current levels
Functional specifications such as commands and protocols
Operational characteristics and specifications for a wide variety of instruments manufactured by HP

The HP-IB is a byte-serial, bit-parallel, party-line bus structure which is organized to provide communication among a group of up to 15 instruments. Devices connected to the bus are classified as talkers, listeners, or controllers. Data and messages are transferred asynchronously on the bus and are coordinated through a handshaking mechanism. When the system is configured, each device is assigned an address. An "attention" line, if true, requires all devices to listen to the data lines and, if false, allows addressed devices to actively send or receive data. Several listeners may be active simultaneously but only one talker can be active at a time. A specific talker address is placed on the data lines, which forces other talkers to be "locked out."

In addition to the attention line, four other control lines are provided in the HP-IB. The "interface clear" line operates as a reset function by placing the interface system in a quiescent state. The "remote enable" line allows the controller to select local or remote control of each device. The "service request" line indicates to the controller that some device on the bus wants attention. Finally, the "end or identify" line allows a device to indicate the end of a multiple-byte transfer sequence.

Digital Equipment's Lab Peripheral System

DEC's LPS-11 Lab Peripheral System provides a modular, real-time subsystem for interfacing devices to the PDP-11 family of computers. The LPS-11 is composed of four elements, which are briefly described below.

Analog-to-Digital (A/D) Converters.   An A/D converter enables a user to sample analog signals at a specified rate. These signals are converted to their digital value and stored in memory via a direct memory access option. The system includes eight channels, with each channel having a throughput rate of approximately 40 kHz. The throughput rate is dependent on the number of bits used in the conversion.

Programmable Real-Time Clock.   A programmable real-time clock with five programmable frequencies allows the user several methods for measuring and counting intervals or events. The clock can be synchronized with the CPU's real-time clock to count external events, measure intervals of time between events, or provide interrupts at selected intervals. The clock operates in one of four programmable modes: single interrupt, repeated interrupts, external event timing, or event counting from a zero base. Frequencies range from 100 Hz to 1 MHz, plus additional external event and line frequency inputs.

Display Controller.   The display controller allows the user to display data in a 4096 by 4096 dot array wherein each point is individually addressed. The display controller may be used with a variety of graphic devices, oscilloscopes, or storage scopes. The display controller includes two 12-bit digital-to-analog (D/A) converters for generating the x, y addresses of any point in the array.

Digital I/O Option.   The digital I/O option provides two 16-bit buffered registers for input and output. In program transfer mode, data are moved to/from the output/input registers and subsequently to/from the external device under program control. In external interrupt mode, an external device may initiate an interrupt and then transfer a stream of data to the computer system.

1.3 PERSPECTIVES ON OPERATING SYSTEMS

Barron [barr71] argues that he cannot tell you what an OS is but that he can recognize one when he sees it. His comment points out the dual problem of distinguishing the components that make up an OS as well as what services it should provide to the user. A dichotomy arises from the different (and often conflicting) viewpoints held by the user and the system designer.

In developing an OS, the system designer selects a methodology for design and implementation. Sometimes the methodology is influenced by the environment in which the system will be used. More often, methodology is influenced by the designer's philosophy or view of a system. Several philosophies have been described in the literature and are discussed briefly in the following sections.

1.3.1   Operating System Objectives

An OS cannot be all things to all users (to paraphrase Abraham Lincoln). Thus early in the design, the systems designer must establish goals for the system. The primary goal, of course, is to allow users to accomplish computational or data processing tasks. Sayers [saye71] has enumerated a list of goals in a comprehensive survey of OSs. Another study by Hoare and Perrott [hoar72] defined the attributes of OSs through a user survey. These goals include:

1. **Reliability.**   The system should be as reliable as the hardware on which it runs. It should be capable of detecting, diagnosing, and recovering from most major errors due to user mishandling. It should protect users from their errors, or at least minimize damage to the environment.

2. **Protection.**   The system should isolate users from the effects of each other's executions. It should minimize the ability to which one user can tamper with another's programs or data. To some extent, the system should protect both itself and the users from errors caused by users.

3. **Predictability.**   The system should be responsive to user requests in a predictable fashion. The time necessary to execute user programs should not vary too widely. The result of user commands should be the same regardless of the sequence in which commands are submitted (as long as system rules are obeyed).

4. **Convenience.**   An OS is forced on the users because it makes their job much easier and relieves them of the burden of allocating and managing various resources. Since the users are in close contact with the system, the system should be designed with basic human engineering factors in mind.

5. **Efficient.**   The system should be reasonably efficient in allocating resources. It should maximize the utilization of system resources by the users. The system should not utilize large quantities of resources since these resources are then unavailable to satisfy users' requests.

6. **General services.**   The system provides exactly the services the user wants. The user should not be penalized for not using additional services if they are not applicable to the task. At the same time, if a system does not provide services that allow a user to accomplish useful work, it will not be accepted.

7. **Flexibility.**   The system's operations can be tuned in response to the

behavior of the users. Resources can be increased/decreased to improve efficiency and accessibility.

8.   **Extensibility.**   New features can be added to the system in an evolutionary fashion. Since user needs change, no application environment is static. Therefore, the OS will have to change if it is to remain a viable tool.

9.   **Transparency.**   The user can remain blissfully ignorant of those things that exist beneath the interfaces to the system. At the same time, it permits the user to learn as much about the system as desired. Most users operate in a happy medium between these two extremes.

Any OS to be developed should adhere to these objectives. The degree to which individual objectives are compromised depends on the particular methodology selected by the system designer.

1.3.2   Resources Managed by the Operating System

The primary reason for the existence of an OS is the allocation and management of various system resources. The objective of resource management is to effect efficient resource utilization among users and relieve them of the burden of handling resources. But what are the resources managed by an OS? Various authors have described a host of categories with varying levels of definition. In this text the following resource categories are considered as the basis of an OS.

Processor Time

The most important resource in the computer system is access to the central processor and, thereby, execution time. Without it, no computation can proceed. The simplest strategy is to let a single user have access to the machine until his or her computation is completed. In fact, many minicomputer and microcomputer systems are utilized in just this fashion. But most computations spend half their existence waiting for I/O operations to complete. Economic necessity forces the system to be shared among multiple simultaneous users. Thus a more complex sharing mechanism is required to use processor time efficiently while exploiting I/O device parallelism.

Memory Management

The second scarcest resource on minicomputer and microcomputer systems is main memory. Generally, most small systems are configured with 32K to 128K bytes. Scheduling access to main memory operates hand in hand with processor scheduling. As a program can execute only if it is main memory, it should be in main memory only if it is ready for a crack at the processor. As memory is scarce, the system must pack it as effectively as possible. Various strategies for utilizing memory and sharing it among multiple users have been proposed. Their objective is to reduce the wasted space arising from the different sizes and flavors of user programs. However, most memory allocation schemes are rather complex and generate significant overhead while their contribution to overall system efficiency is often hard to measure quantitatively.

Peripheral Devices

Most peripherals are allocated to one user at a time. For certain common devices, such as the card reader and line printer, severe inefficiencies may result if the program has an extended execution time. Fast random access devices are shared among multiple users through the file management system. Delay on these devices is tolerable because of their speed and the gaps between a program's I/O requests. That mode is not feasible on record-oriented devices because they must be physically loaded and unloaded for each use.

Proper allocation of devices has strong implications for the efficiency and performance of the system. Since most minicomputer systems contain one line printer, execution can be brought to a halt. Thus OSs generally include a SPOOLing mechanism within the I/O management services. Device allocation strategies need to be minimally aware of deadlock problems. However, since it is usually easy to restart a program on a small system, the extensive overhead is often not worth the utility. Moreover, on most minicomputer systems, one or more users act as their own operators and can deal effectively with that problem as well as the OS.

Finally, attempting to develop an optimal device allocation strategy is both difficult and expensive. The balancing of multiple resources in an OS is extremely difficult due to the interaction of many factors. It is difficult to isolate and measure the effect of any one policy in such a system. Knowing that performance is inadequate does not help in isolating the specific problem. Most monitoring techniques are expensive, need to be executed continuously, and can only identify general manifestations of problems. In most minicomputer systems, the utility is not worth the cost.

Software Resources

Software resources consist of the functions available to the user for managing data and controlling program execution. Among such resources are I/O and file management services, system scheduling services, system libraries, and utilities. The most common method for allowing multiple users access to software resources is to make all programs reentrant. This is clearly preferable to creating multiple copies of the software, which consumes scarce memory resources.

However, in most minicomputer systems, there is a greater need for efficiency and correctness in the software because of the scarcity of the previously mentioned resources.

1.3.3   Views of Operating Systems

Current minicomputer OSs exhibit several different implementation philosophies. One such view is the programmed operator approach. The system functions are viewed merely as extensions to user programming language. The extensions to the programming language are provided as subsystems which are collections of modules. The subsystems implement one or more operators; there is usually little or no interaction between the subsystems. The system responds to requests from the user but otherwise remains a passive entity. This view implements a philosophy of minimal intrusion upon the user [hoar72]. Several commercial low-end minicomputer systems observe this philosophy.

Another view is represented by the monitor/manager approach. A monitor is a collection of procedures and data structures that is shared among processes, although only one process can use it at a time. If a process finds the monitor occupied with another user, the requestor may or may not be enqueued in a wait status. If the monitor is unoccupied, the requesting process is allowed access to the resource. The OS is viewed as a collection of resources, each protected by a monitor. Where multiple copies of a resource exist, each unit has an associated reentrant monitor that allows multiple processes to be active. Monitors are usually implemented by resource semaphores [hoar74, dijk71]. An alternative version, modified for greater flexibility by dynamic data structures, has been used as a facility in the Project SUE system.

A concept associated with monitors is that of managers as introduced by Jammel and Stiegler [jamm77]. A manager combines the ideas of a monitor with those of a process; that is, it is a dynamic entity. A manager allows each request to proceed immediately; it is blocked only when it awaits orders or responses. The manager concept also allows adaptive algorithms to be implemented where the system dynamically responds to its environment. To date, it is not clear if any commercial system has a concept equivalent to the manager concept.

Another approach consists of the abstract machine methodology. An OS running on a configuration of computer hardware implements an abstract machine. The OS provides the user with a set of capabilities which are significantly different from, and extensions of, the simplistic features of the hardware. In effect, the abstract machine acts as an interpreter to map user-perceived functions into hardware operations.

The concept of the abstract machine has been extended to a multiple-layer approach. Dijkstra [dijk68] pioneered this approach in the T.H.E. multiprogramming system. Each layer in an OS represents an abstract machine which, building on the capabilities of lower-level machines, further extends the functional environment for the user. Chandrasekaran and Shankar [chan76] have constructed an abstract machine model for a communications switching system. However, their model can be redefined to apply to OSs as well. Each level of abstraction is described in terms of the object realized (i.e., made accessible to the user) and possible hidden decisions. An application of their model is shown in table 1.1.

This work represents one of the few efforts toward systematic formal specifications. It should be realized that most OSs tend to be haphazard collections of features thrown together to reflect the whims of the OS designer(s). Without formal specification of OS functions, objects, and decisions, one cannot begin to comprehend the interaction between components. Further research is required to develop an understanding of the properties of abstract machines for formally specifying OS functions.

Table 1.1   Abstract Machine Approach to OSs

Level	Abstract Machine	Object	Decision
1	Hardware	Interrupts Descriptions	Hardware
2	Devices	I/O devices Communication lines	Device handling
3	Page management	Pages	Paging policies
4	Process management	Processes	Processors Scheduling
5	Memory management	Memory segments	Memory mapping
6	I/O management	Records	I/O functions Buffering
7	File and directory management	Files Directories	Structure Implementation
8	Message management	Interprocess messages	IPC primitives Message synthesis and distribution
9	User job/program management	Jobs and programs	Accounting Resource allocation
10	Checkpointing Journaling	Checkpoints System logs	Snapshot policy Dump/recovery
11	Operator command management	Operator functions	Operator interface implementation
12	User command management	OSCL functions	Command syntax and semantics
13	System utilities	Utilities	Functions and structures

A final approach is represented by the virtual machine (VM) methodology. The VM can be considered an extension of the abstract machine methodology. A VM provides an efficient facsimile of one or more complete computer systems which yields a multienvironment system [gold73]. A VM is usually implemented through a virtual machine monitor (VMM) software program executing on real hardware which provides a set of virtual resources (some of which may not be physically present). Under the control of the VMM, different users may then execute different OSs and thus select their own programming environment. Goldberg [gold73] cites the following advantages to the VM approach:

Improving and testing OS software

Running different OSs or different versions of an OS

Running with a virtual configuration which is different from the real system

Adding hardware enhancements to a configuration that is different from the real system

To date, few truly virtual machines have been implemented because most computer systems cannot support them. Goldberg discusses a proposal for virtualizable architectures which will support the design and development of VMs. However, user demand has not been strong enough to bring the VM approach to effective reality.

Other methodologies exist for describing OSs. We have mentioned only a few of the current approaches. The reader should note that the field of system design is in a state of flux. Requirements for fault-tolerance, distributed systems, performance, and information protection are having a significant impact on the functions and capabilities a user requires from an OS.

1.3.4 The Problem of Duality

Lauer and Needham [laue78] have proposed that OSs may be roughly divided into two categories: message oriented and procedure oriented. A message-oriented system has a small static number of large processes. These processes share a limited amount of data through an explicit set of message channels. A procedure-oriented system has a large number of small processes which are rapidly changing. These processes communicate through direct sharing and synchronization of data variables. These models are developed in more detail in the following paragraphs.

The Message-Oriented Model

A message-oriented system is characterized by a facility for passing messages between processes (see section 3.5). Processes can send, receive, wait for, and examine the status of messages. A process waiting for a message is activated when the message arrives from the sender. Normally, the process is placed on the ready-to-run queue to await its turn. However, if the receiver's priority is greater than the currently executing process, that process is suspended and the receiver is placed in execution. The basic architecture meets this description since interrupts may be thought of as messages from devices to their software corollaries—the device handlers.

These systems establish specific communication paths for specific types of communication among particular pairs of processes. The paths are usually dedicated at system initialization. The number of processes and their connections remains relatively static throughout the life of the system. As connections are static and dedicated, creating new processes is exceedingly difficult. Processes may be deleted, although it is unlikely that this will be done since each process operates in a relatively static well-defined context. This architectual style is found in data acquisition, process control, command and control, and, of course, communications systems where processes are associated with system resources (see also the CAP descriptions).

Lauer and Needham note a number of features that characterize this architectural style:

1. Synchronization among processes and queueing for congested resources is implemented in the message queues attached to processes associated with those resources (see section 7.9).

2. Data structures manipulated by more than one process are passed in messages between the processes.

3. Peripheral devices are treated as processes where an operation on a device is the result of a message sent to the device.

4. Priorities are statically assigned when the system is designed.

5. Processes operate on one message at a time.

6. Processes are relatively isolated in function.

The Procedure-Oriented Model

A procedure-oriented system experiences rapid change of context through efficient system call facilities. Process cooperation is achieved through locks (see section 5.8), semaphores (see section 7.10), or events (see section 3.4). Under this architecture, a process attempts to claim a resource, and may be forced to wait on a queue until some other process releases it. A processor is preempted when a resource, which is claimed by a higher-priority process, is released.

This architectural style places system resources under the protection of monitors, semaphores, and so on, which encode the necessary data structures for managing the resource. Creation and deletion of processes in this environment is relatively easy; communications channels come and go as necessary.

Each process has one function to perform but may "wander" all over the system (via service requests) to accomplish it. HYDRA [wulf74] is an example of this type of system.

Lauer and Needham note the following features which characterize this architectural style:

1. Synchronization of processes and queueing for congested resources is handled by queues of processes waiting on semaphores associated with those resources.
2. Data are shared directly among processes.
3. Processes usually hold resources for relatively short periods of time.
4. Peripheral devices are treated as resources that are held by a process while an I/O operation is executed.
5. Processes have dynamic priorities which are associated either with functions or resources.
6. A global naming scheme is required for system resources so that all processes may easily access them.

How the Duality Arises

Lauer and Needham suggest that these two models are "duals" of each other (in the linear programming sense) because they preserve the functionality across architectural style. The following table (drawn up by Lauer and Needham) demonstrates some of these features:

Message-Oriented	Procedure-Oriented
Processes	Monitors
Process creation	Monitor allocation
Channels	External identifiers
Ports	Global names
Send message; await reply (immediate)	Procedure call
Send message; await reply (delayed)	Fork and join
Send reply	Return from procedure
Selective wait for messages	Event mechanisms

The concept of duality implies that a program written in one system can be transformed directly into the other by replacing each construct with its correspondent. The semantic content of the program remains invariant. Lauer and Needham offer one simple caveat: any program that would be transformed in this manner must obey the rules of their canonical models. This is not as difficult as it seems, as the imposition of their canonical rules it no different than following structured programming practices.

As many readers know, it is not easy to change the structure of an OS once implementation has begun. Few systems reflect the duality espoused by Lauer and Needham. Careful inspection of the code skeletons in this text will reveal instances of both approaches with little violation of the basic principles. What is obvious is that dual subsystems are logically indentical to each other and, therefore, should have nearly identical performance given identical scheduling strategies. Many of the structures in the text can be transformed into their duals. Two interesting and thought-provoking questions arise from this approach: Are there subsystems or constructs that have no dual counterpart? If no dual exists, is this structure a good thing to use in OS design?

Lauer and Needham feel that these questions are open questions that need significant study. Their impact on OS design could be tremendous.

1.4 TYPES OF OPERATING SYSTEMS

Many schemes have been proposed for classifying OSs. Classification allows one to get a better feeling for what an OS does. We have chosen to classify them from the viewpoint of the user, since user perception will directly affect the usage of a given system. Clearly, there is no single right way to classify OSs since many systems possess features and capabilities that overlap several categories.

Considerable work has been done in the area of classifying OSs. Kurzban et al. [kurz75] presented a very lucid discussion of several types of operating systems. Sayers [saye71] performed a comprehensive study of the charcteristics of OSs. Abernathy, et al. [aber73] surveyed the design goals, salient features, and possible conflicts among goals. Other references include Barron [barr71], Colin [coli71], and Wilkes [wilk68].

1.4.1 Batch Operating Systems

In the early stages of computer development, the computer was dedicated to a single user for the time interval as necessay to set up and execute the problem. The most time-consuming procedures were job setup and takedown. The introduction of batch monitors automated the procedure of setting up a computer for a job execution. The prime purpose of the batch operating system was to enhance the efficiency of the machine by executing sequences of jobs without human intervention.

The batch monitor was implemented as a small nucleus of code plus a nonresident portion. Each language compiler or utility program was written as a subroutine of the monitor. The compiler translated user programs into object programs which were also treated as subroutines of the monitor.

The workload was presented to the batch monitor as a stream of jobs. Each job was separated from the next by a "job description" record that provided basic information on the user's identity and the compiler that he or she wanted to use. Each job included a program and some data to be processed and was followed by a "terminator" record, which signaled to the monitor that it should reinitialize itself for the next user's workload.

To execute a job, the batch monitor interpreted the job description record and loaded the appropriate compiler from its mass storage (usually magnetic tape). The compiler translated the user's program into an object deck which was stored in memory or on mass storage. If it was stored in memory, the operation was referred to as compile, load, and go. If it was stored on tape, another control card was required to request execution of the object deck. The object deck was loaded into memory in place of the compiler and control transferred to it. In this manner, a large segment of main memory could be shared among different subsystems, although only one such subsystem could be resident and executing at any time.

The batch monitor approach, while improving the utilization and utility of the computer system, suffered from some serious weaknesses. An operator was required to load card decks, mount tapes, and monitor the state of the machine. The monitor had no control over the executing program. If the object program executed an illegal instruction of "halted," the machine had to be restarted from the operator's console. If the program entered an infinite loop, the operator was required to detect it and take action to cancel the job and restart the system.

The popularity of batch monitors encouraged the development of standard file management systems and automatic control of peripherals. Despite their productivity, batch systems were still limited by the slowest component. Interaction with the user was discouraged since the whole system had to wait for any input. Nevertheless, many successful batch OSs were developed during the late 1950s and early 1960s. IBSYS, the IBM OS for the IBM 7090/7094 computers, is particularly notable because of its widespread influence on other systems.

Today, many OSs retain the basic principles underlying batch processing. A user, sitting at a terminal, can construct a job command file and submit it to the BATCH subsystem. This feature is available in the recent systems available from Data General (AOS) and Digital Equipment (VMS).

1.4.2 Real-Time Executives

One of the earliest applications of minicomputers was in the process control and monitoring environment. The process control system is characterized by the need to acquire a digital or analog sensor input, analyze it, and then initiate a signal to cause an action that changes the process it is controlling. All this must occur in real-time, where real time is explicitly the reaction time of a given process. Among the many instances where real-time digital control has made an appearance are laboratory data acquistion systems, biomedical sensors, and automotive engine performance.

A real-time computer system generally includes many of the same peripherals found in larger program development systems. However, the time constraints associated with process control place different requirements on the OS software. These requirements led to the development of real-time executives. A real-time executive is viewed as a lean, performance-oriented beast which provides a minimal set of services. Most minicomputer vendors provide a real-time executive which is a scaled-down version of a larger disk-oriented OS.

Several features characterize the design considerations for a real-time executive. Among them are:

Management of analog/digital sensor data

High reliability

A wide variety of I/O facilities

Small memory requirements

Simplified processing algorithms

Dedicated to one or few functions

An excellent tutorial on minicomputer real-time executives was delivered at the 1974 Fall Computer Conference. This tutorial presents a detailed discussion of the design and implementation of real-time executives.

J.D. Schoeffler, *Minicomputer Real time Executives,* IEEE Computer Society, JH2627-8C, 1974.

1.4.3   Multiprocessing Systems

Multiprocessing systems are composed of two or more central processing units executing instructions in parellel. Each processor may be operating in batch, multiprogramming, or time-sharing mode. Two or more CPUs may be either tightly or loosely coupled, Mackinnon [mack74] defined these types of tightly coupled systems:

1. Homogeneous multiprocessors, where the CPUs are identical or from the same family (such as the Univac 1100 series)
2. Nonhomogeneous multiprocessors, where the arithmetic and logical units are special-purpose functional units (as in the GRI-99 or DCC CP-9000)
3. Array processors (such as the ILLIAC IV)
4. Pipeline processors (such as IBM 360/91, CRAY-1, etc.)

Loosely coupled mutiprocessor systems share communications facilities or direct access devices. Two CPUs may be connected together via a synchronous line in a loosely coupled mode where each CPU appears to the others as some sort of communications terminal. Another approach is for two CPUs to share a mass storage device through a dual-pointing capability. In this case, each CPU accesses the disk over its own I/O bus although the device is shared between the two CPUs. The distinguishing characteristic is that there is no direct control of the resource of one processor by the other; each CPU operates independently. Generally, loosely coupled multiprocessing systems operate in a master–slave relationship. Two recent examples produced by major manufacturers are Digital Equipment's VAX 11/780 and Data General's Eclipse M/600.

IBM has advocated both loosely and tightly coupled systems architectures for nearly 20 years. An early example was the IBM 7090–IBM 1401 complex operating in a master–slave relationship. More recently, various models of the IBM System/370 family have been configured as multiprocessors. Papers by Arnold et al. [arno74] and MacKinnon [mack74] have explored these concepts. The reader is also referred to the discussion in Liebowitz and Carson [lieb77] relative to multiprocessors in a distributed processing environment.

1.4.4 Time-Sharing/Multiprogramming Systems

Time-sharing systems (TSSs) are an attempt to give each user a personal computer while efficiently utilizing the resources of a relatively expensive machine. The range of time-sharing systems varies widely over the capabilities and features provided by the system. A key distinction between multiprogramming systems and TSSs is that all user interactions occur through an on-line terminal such as a teletype or CRT. Furthermore, the requirements of human engineering imply that a response time appropriate to human attention spans is maintained. Finally, it must appear to the user that there is unrestricted access to the computer.

The techniques embodied in the design of batch OSs led to inefficiencies in computer system usage as machines became bigger and faster. It was found that better utilization of equipment could be obtained by sharing the resources of a computer system among several users simultaneously. As most computer systems are peripheral-limited, maintaining several user programs in memory allowed one program to use the central processor while another program was waiting for a data transfer from a peripheral device. This approach is known as multiprogramming.

Multiprogramming systems are characterized by the concept of concurrency. That is, more than one program can be executing within the computer system at the same time. Since there is only one central processor, only one program may be executing at any instant. Programs alternate in their usage of the CPU according to some policy and thus exist in different stages of execution (completion). However, each program has its own portion of the total system resources for the duration of its execution. It is up to the OS to determine which program is ready to execute and allow it to access the CPU.

The concepts of multiprogramming and time sharing are complementary.

Most minicomputer systems couple multiprogramming capabilities with an interactive time-sharing capability. At a minimum, it involves a foreground/background approach to multiprogramming.

In previous types of OSs, efficient operation of the machine through management of critical resources was the essential design motivation. In TSSs, this motivation must be tempered by consideration of user characteristics and needs. An essential feature of time sharing is the operation of the computer in a conversational mode. Wilkes [wilk68] distinguishes between the following types of conversation, which have a significant impact on the flexibility and complexity of the OS:

1. Fully conversational mode, where it is possible for a program to talk to the user and the user to talk to it while the program is being executed.

2. Semiconversational mode, where the program may talk to the user but the only control over the program that the user has is the capability to abort it.

Watson [wats70] has classified time sharing into the following categories by the nature of access they allow the user:

1. **On-line file maintenance and retrieval systems.** These are highly specialized and are characterized by a limited range of queries to a common information base. Examples are the MEDLARS System of the National Library of Medicine and the Wizard of Avis car reservation system.

2. **Special-purpose time-sharing systems.** These usually allow their users the ability to prepare and execute programs in a limited number of languages (generally one). Examples are the RAND Corporation's JOSS System and IBM's QUIKTRAN System.

3. **General-purpose time-sharing systems.** These emphasize rapid response to many users while providing access to a file system and concurrent utilization of a wide variety of on-line software facilities. They are characterized by their allowing users the ability to integrate additional facilities. Examples are the MULTICS Systems at MIT and the major operating systems AOS from Data General Systems and VMS from Digital Equipment.

4. **Multiprogramming batch systems.** These allow on-line access which tends to emphasize a maximum rate throughout rather than rapid response. They may serve a limited number of users and provide some or all of the facilities available in the batch environment. Examples are Univac's 1100 Series Operating System, Honeywell's GECOS, and IBM's OS/360 with Time Sharing Option (TSO).

In this text, we are concerned with the design problems and considerations relevant to the development of a general-purpose interactive multiprogramming system.

Given these distinctions, the creation of a time-sharing system is basically a software task that can be achieved with simplicity and flexibility if supported by the proper hardware components. Among these hardware requirements are memory management and protection units (although this need can be circumvented by designing an interpretive system at some loss to response time) and privileged/unprivileged (e.g., supervisor/user) modes of operation. This last feature is derived from the fact that object programs should not be able to interfere with the operation of the supervisor. In effect, a "firewall" is erected between each user and the supervisor, and between each user and every other user attached to the system. Thus the failure of one user program is not apparent to any other user.

The range of users accessing a TSS may vary from the inexperienced to the sophisticated. Unlike multiprogramming systems, however, users will adapt their behavior to the system in a manner that takes advantage of its good features and circumvents its bad ones. In addition, a TSS will attract only those users to whom it can give a reasonable response which is in accord with their expectations. This fact places TSS designers at a disadvantage since measurements of the performance and response times of users on a particular system are not directly applicable to another system.

The components and general principles for constructing a TSS have been described quite lucidly in the literature [wilk68, wats70]. Wilkes has described the states through which a program passes while in a TSS. A user is connected to the TSS via a "logging-in" sequence which establishes a session. At this point, the session is placed in command status; that is, anything the user types will be interpreted as a system command. The system loads the program into memory while the session is in the "waiting command" state. When the program is scheduled for execution, it enters the working state. When a program is given control of the CPU, it is said to be in the execution state. The program generally cycles between the working and execution states until it needs to perform an I/O operation. Three types of I/O operations with corresponding states are possible. If the program tries to read a line from the user console, any line in the input buffer will be transferred to the program and it will continue to run. If no line is available, the program enters the input wait state until the user has typed in a complete line. A program may go into the output wait state when the output buffer overflows due to an excessive number of output lines. The program may also enter a file wait state if it cannot access a file that is being used by another program. Once the wait condition has been satisfied, the program automatically enters the working state. Finally, when the program is terminated, it is placed in the dead state by the supervisor.

TSSs incorporate the features of the systems mentioned in previous sections. But, as Watson [wats70] notes, they introduce an extra dimension to these features through several intrinsic and technological problems and requirements. The intrinsic problems are associated with the design and implementation of a set of software modules which provide the foregoing capabilities on a given computer system.

Watson has discussed many of these problems in his excellent book, *Timesharing Systems Designs Concepts*, although his examples are oriented toward large mainframe-based systems. Nevertheless, these problems are relevant to the design of TSSs for smaller computer systems. Solutions to several of these problems are discussed in later sections. In the next few paragraphs, some of the significant problems are summarized.

File Systems and Information Sharing.   The file system provides each user with a private storage for information. At the same time, it must also support the sharing of information among various users while providing protection mechanisms to ensure the privacy of each user's data.

Communication with the System.   Systems communication involves terminal design, data transmission to and from the computer, and the command and programming languages one uses to solve problems.

Reliability and Recovery.   The user expects the system to operate correctly when it is available. Should failure occur, the user expects recovery to be as smooth and fast as possible. Isolation of users one from another places stringent requirements on error-detection and error-handling procedures.

Resource Allocation and Contention.   The TSS hardware/software complex is composed of a limited number of resources which must be shared among many users. The scheduling and allocation of resources is at best a difficult problem since it involves the principle of fairness while attempting to avoid deadlock. The basic rationale behind multiprogramming is full utilization of system resources. Thus while several programs are waiting for I/O activity to complete, another program can be executing. The sharing of resources is extended to the sharing of the CPU main memory, devices, and files among programs of equivalent rank.

SPOOLing (Simultaneous Peripheral Operation On-Line).   SPOOLing is the use of direct access secondary storage as intermediate storage for system input and output. SPOOLing frees the system from excessive I/O wait times and helps neutralize the speed discrepancy between the slow unit record peripherals and the fast CPU. Each program's I/O is stored on a disk file. Input is read by the program when it is executed; output is printed by the system after the program has terminated.

System Overhead, Utilization, and Response Time.   These problems are intimately connected since the time spend performing system functions means less time available to the user for problem solving. Overhead may be good or bad when it is directed to enhancing the utilization of the system or ensuring efficient scheduling of resources. Overhead time should not be substantially greater than the CPU time allocated to executing user programs. Large overhead times are not bad when they include time spent executing system I/O utilities on behalf of user programs. Response time is a function of the number of users on the system and their processing demands, but for proper evaluation, must be weighed against initial design decisions (such as the number of concurrent users, size of time/memory quanta, etc.).

1.4.5 Distributed Network Operating Systems

The emergence of distributed processing and computer networking technology as a viable method for providing computing resources has led to the development of network operating systems (NOSs). Kimbleton and Mandell [kimb76] view the NOS as a mediating agent which provides ease of access to resources and control of resource access among the various hosts of the network.

Kimbleton and Mandell suggest that five major issues must be considered in developing an NOS:

Provision of a uniform user viewpoint of resources

Modular expansibility

Control of host–network interaction

Allocation of global network resources to distributed, independent processes

Implementation mode

These issues pose a significant problem. If one is developing an NOS from scratch, it is much easier to accommodate the support mechanisms for interprocess communication necessary to satisfy these issues. Realistically, most NOSs are designed to augment and interface with existing, emplaced host OSs. Thus an NOS must implement a variety of specialized host interfaces.

Kimbleton and Mandell [kimb76] suggest that an NOS has four global objectives:

User communication

Data migration

Network job execution

Control

These objectives form the basis for developing a set of network primitive operators upon which an NOS is built. The elements of these objectives are summarized in the paragraphs below.

User Communication

Users (and their subordinate processes) need to communicate in a distributed network. Communication involves five categories of services: creation, coordination, forwarding, alerting, and event processing. Utilizing these services, users in a distributed network can participate in teleconferencing sessions. Both ARPANET and TENEX [thom75] provide conferencing capabilities.

Data Migration

Data migration provides the basic capability required to permit a process executing on one host to access data residing in one or more remote hosts. The simplest approach requires that the executing process request a copy of the file containing the data it needs for its computation. The file is then transferred from the remote host to the local host in its entirety. Several minicomputer systems currently implement facilities oriented to this approach. These facilities require the computers to be either tightly (bus to bus) or loosely coupled. References include [dec78], [dgc75], and [dick74].

The development of a general data migration capability at the subfile level requires three categories of primitives: selection, translation, and transformation. ARPANET is currently pursuing research on these topics. It is apparent that these machanisms need to interface with both the file and I/O managers of the host in order to effect a significant retrieval/update capability.

Network Job Execution and Control

A network job consists of a set of processes, executed sequentially or simultaneously, at one or more hosts of the network. Execution of a network job requires four major capabilities: process assignment and control, process monitoring, a NOS control language, and interprocess communications support. Together, these capabilities must satisfy the objectives of user interaction with the user's processes and synchronization among processes (if desired). Several excellent papers have discussed concepts associated with distributed processing (NJE by another name)—among them [suns76] and [wald72].

Impact of Distributed Processing on OS Design

The future of distributed processing systems (DPSs) appears to be quite bright at this point. The current DPS philosophy emphasizes resource sharing among multiple hosts. DPSs are adaptable to the implementation of new functions as the applications environment evolves. At the same time, by adding new hosts or additional resources to a given host to expand both capacity and function, a DPS can also evolve. Furthermore, a DPS appears to provide more reliable computing services than a single processor.

Further detailed discussion of computer networking and distributed processing technology is beyond the scope of this text. We want to point out that any

OSs designer should be aware of the requirements for distributed processing so that they may be accommodated in the design. A good overview of distributed processing is provided in an IEEE CompCon tutorial by Liebowitz and Carson [lieb77]. Another good tutorial on computer networks is found in Cotton et al. [cott76]. Retz [retz75] discusses design considerations for the packet-switching environment. Akkoyunlu et al. [akko74] discuss the IPC facilities required for a network OS.

1.5   MAJOR CONCEPTS AFFECTING OPERATING SYSTEM DESIGN

Since the beginning of the computer age (circa 1950s), hardware and software technology has experienced phenomenal growth. Suffice it to say that in the short span of 30 years, the technology has experienced three or four generations where the software tended to lag behind the corresponding hardware generation. Recently, hardware improvements in the central processor, memory, and peripherals have tended to stabilize. Many of the features found on large mainframes (say, IBM or Univac) have now migrated to minicomputers and, indeed, to some microcomputers. The distinction between microcomputers and minicomputers is often blurred except for size and cost differences.

Each hardware generation introduced new facilities and concepts which signaled major changes in the way OSs are designed. Other concepts arose from the need to obtain greater efficiency from the system software. A survey of modern minicomputer OSs will reveal a diverse and sophisticated set of capabilities many of which are becoming standard features as new systems are developed. As an aspiring system designer, you should be aware of the major concepts that affect current system design. Indeed, you should realize that many of these concepts are essential to the design and implementation of a modern mini- or microcomputer OS.

This section presents a brief description and analysis of many of the major concepts that have been described (or proposed) in the small computer systems, and exposure to them is both beneficial and instructive. You will encounter many of these concepts in the system described in later chapters of this text.

1.5.1   Relocatability

Relocatability is an important aspect of modern OSs. It allows the instruction and data segments of a program to be individually and dynamically allocated a set of addresses in memory independent of the compilation procedure. A relocatable program address space is generated relative to zero. The act of relocation, where actual physical addresses are assigned to logical addresses, may be performed at different times, including:

1. Link time, when separate modules are mapped together to form an executable program
2. Load time, when an executable load module (whose addresses are relative to zero) is loaded into memory
3. Execution time, when the address translation hardware performs the actual address mapping

The first case is exemplified by the Data General RDOS Relocatable Loader (assuming no memory management). The reader should refer to the DGC manuals [dgc75]. The second case is exemplified by the DEC Relocatable Loader for the lower PDP-11 series machines. The third case is exemplified by many of the current minicomputer systems using some variation of memory management hardware (refer to [dec78]).

1.5.2 Reentrancy

A program is termed reentrant when a single copy of the instruction segment can be shared by multiple users. Reentrancy has two aspects: the instruction segment cannot modify itself and the local data for each user is stored in a user's data segment. On the PDP-11 family of machines, this concept is referred to as position-independent code (PIC—see [dec75] for a discussion of PIC). This concept has also been implemented on the HP-3000 series machines utilizing a stack architecture.

In the system described in the text, each user process is assigned a process data block (PDB), which provides storage for local variables and the user stack. Each time a process is scheduled for execution, a pointer to the process control block (PCB) is set up prior to giving the process control of the CPU. The PCB contains the address of the PDB. This represents a software-implemented reentrant capability as opposed to the hardware implementations mentioned above. Another variation suitable for simpler systems is described in Data General's FORTRAN IV library manual [dgc75].

1.5.3 Interrupts

Interrupts are a hardware mechanism that forces the CPU to cease its current activity and deal with an external event. Interrupts were developed primarily to increase the efficiency of central processor scheduling. One motivation was to allow intelligent devices to proceed with I/O operations independently of the central processor. Then the device need only signal the CPU via interrupt when the data transfer was completed. Another motivation arose from events internal to the CPU—namely, the occurrence of faults such as integer overflow, divide-by-zero, exceeding memory bounds, and so on, as well as the associated supervisor trap mechanism. A final motivation occurs in multiprocessor systems, where each processor must signal the other when accessing shared resources. Interrupts are explored in more detail in section 2.2.

1.5.4 Channels and I/O Processors

The concept of a channel has existed in large-scale mainframes for many years. Indeed, it is the mainstay of most I/O processing in such systems. With the notable exception of the Interdata family of machines (which bear a striking resemblence to System/360s), the concept of channels and I/O processors has only recently emerged in minicomputer systems. Even then, they are only supplied with top-of-the-line machines, such as the Hewlett-Packard 3000, the Digital Equipment VAX-11/780, and Data General's M/600 ECLIPSE Systems.

A channel is usually a small self-contained processor executing a special program known as the channel command program. They are usually expensive, so there are fewer channels than devices. Channels generally exist in two varieties: multiplexor and selector. A multiplexor channel is byte (or word) oriented and is connected to unit record peripherals. A selector channel provides block data transfers between the peripherals and memory. It is usually connected to high-speed magnetic tape systems and disk mass storage systems.

An I/O channel fetches the instructions of its channel command program from memory. In contrast, an I/O processor has a local memory in which the I/O programs are stored. The I/O processor retrieves I/O parameters from a memory shared with the CPU but then executes its I/O program out of its local memory. Otherwise, the functions performed by an I/O channel and an I/O processor are exactly the same.

Note. The data channel that appears in the architecture of most minicomputers does not correspond to a selector channel. The data channel is not a processor but merely a high-speed conduit between memory and the mass storage devices.

1.5.5 Linkage Editors and Loaders

The concepts of linkage editor and loader are crucial to the design and implementation of OSs. They allow independently compiled modules and databases (e.g., parameter files) to be mapped together into an executable module which is loaded into memory.

A linkage editor is a program provided by the system designer which binds the independent logical spaces of each subroutine and module into one composite logical space—the executable module. Linking consists of at least the following steps:

Collect all modules from user and system libraries.

Resolve all external references between modules.

Report undefined references.

Construct overlay structure (if supported).

Determine and construct load module type.

A loader copies the executable module into memory at the behest of the OS. During this copying, the loader may perform the address translation of a relocatable module. A loader may exist in binary or relocatable form. During a binary load, the executable module had been mapped to physical addresses at linkage time and thus no relocation is possible. The program is bound permanently to those physical addresses. On the other hand, a relocating loader loads the program into any section of main memory. The allocation of memory to a given program is fixed for the duration of that program's execution.

Two excellent tutorials on the structure and design of linkers and loaders can be found in

L. Presser and J.R. White, Linkers and Loaders, *ACM Computing Surveys,* Vol, 4, no. 3, 1972.
R.M. Graham, *Principles of Systems Programming,* Wiley, New York, 1975.

1.5.6   Systems Programming Languages

From time immemorial it seems, OSs were implemented in assembly language. Usually, this resulted from the inefficiencies of the available programming languages relative to assembly code. Many languages were not suitable for writing OSs (although it was once argued that SNOBOL would make a good OS implementation language).

However, in the last five years or so, numerous systems programming languages (SPLs) have been developed and implemented. Many manufacturers have begun using high-level SPLs to implement compilers and OSs. Indeed, the system presented in this text is described in a program design language (see Appendix A) drawn from an ALGOL variant. Most SPLs obtain an efficiency on the order of $2:1$ verses assembly language. Usually, the system designer need drop into assembly language only to deal directly with the hardware (which usually represents less than 1% of the OS).

A systems programming language should provide the systems designer with features that relate to OS problems. Among these features are:

1.   The SPL should support parallel operations; thus at a minimum, it should be reentrant.

2.   The SPL must support a modular structure (i.e., subroutines) as well as intermediate communications such as global variables and parameters.

3. The SPL must be self-documenting and able to produce understandable programs.
4. The system code must be modifiable without excessive difficulty (a feature not present in assembly languages).
5. The system code must be reasonably efficient.

A number of papers have discussed other features related to systems programming languages. The reader is urged to consult Clark and Horning [clar73], Friedman and Schneider [frie73], Habermann [habe73], Kosinski [kosi73], Sammet [samm71], and Wulf et al. [wulf71].

Additional references include:

V. Basili, *SIMPL-X: A Language for Writing Structural Programs,* Dept. of Computer Science, University of Maryland, TR-223, 1973.

W.A. Wulf, BLISS: A Language for Systems Programming, *CACM,* Vol. 14, no. 12, 1971.

M. Richards, BCPL: A Tool for Compiler Writing and Systems Programming, *AFIPS Proceedings, SJCC, 1969,* Vol. 34, pp. 557–566.

S. Zilles, Procedural Encapsulation: A Linguistic Protection Technique, Proceedings of the SIGPLAN/SIGOPs Interface Meeting, *SIGPLAN Notices,* Vol, 8, no. 9, 1973.

R.J. Lipton, *Research on a High-Level Language Approach to Operating Systems Design,* Dept. of Computer Science, Yale University, AD/A-023866, 1976.

1.5.7   Microprogramming and Writable Control Store

Microprogramming is a technique used to implement the control functions of a computer at the hardware register level. Microprogramming involves the same instruction fetch, decode, address generation, data fetch, and execution operations as in normal programming, However, the objects of the instructions' effects are machine registers. Generally, a machine instruction, as viewed by the user, is composed of multiple microinstructions.

Microprogramming provides the system designers with several advantages of which the OS designer should be cognizant. The first advantage is parallel control of multiple hardware resources. A second advantage is emulation, whereby a different instruction set is interpreted by the firmware routines. Typical of this approach are most models of the IBM System 360/370 series, which are microprogrammed to yield different performance characteristics and data path size.

Associated with microprogramming is the concept of the writable control store (WCS). Basically, a user may insert new microprograms in the WCS to provide new machine instructions that supplement the manufacturer-implemented set. Two machines that support a writable control store are Data General's Eclipse Series [dgc75] and Hewlett-Packard's HP-1000 series based on the 21MX processor. Under the DGC approach, the user can implement up to 16 new instructions as microprocedures that are accessed by the XOP instruction. HP provides a full microprogramming package which executes under the RTE-IV OS. It supports the assembly of microprograms, debugging, full WCS support utilities, and the capability to perform dynamic WCS overlap.

Some excellent references include:

R. F. Rosen, Contemporary Concepts in Microprogramming and Emulation, *ACM Computing Surveys,* Vol. 1, no. 4, 1969.

S.S. Husson, *Microprogramming: Principles and Practices,* Prentice-Hall, Englewood Cliffs, NJ, 1970.

M.J. Flynn and R. Rosin, Microprogramming: An Introduction and Viewpoint, *IEEE Transactions on Computers,* Vol, C-20 no. 7, 1971.

A.K. Agrawala and T.S. Rauscher, *Foundations of Microprogramming,* Academic Press, New York, 1976.

A.B. Salisbury, *Microprogramable Computer Architectures,* Elsevier, North-Holland, New York, 1976.

1.5.8 Structured and Modular Programming

The concept of structured programming is concerned with improving the organization of programs. In this manner it is hoped that the data and control structures are clearly and correctly described. Several benefits have been claimed for structured programming:

Programs are easier to understand, therefore easier to modify and document.
Programs are more economical to run.
Programs are easier to debug.

Some people confuse structured programming with goto-less programming. Although gotos do lend confusion to a program if improperly used, they sometimes cannot be avoided when the basic machine instruction contains the JMP instruction (a goto by any other name).

Structured programming is credited to several authors—most notably Dijkstra and Wirth. Several good reference texts are available, including:

N. Wirth, *Systematic Programming: An Introduction,* Prentice-Hall, Englewood Cliffs, NJ, 1973.

O-J. Dahl, E.W. Dijkstra, and C.A.R. Hoare, *Structured Programming,* IEEE CompCon Tutorial, IEEE Catalog 75CH1049-G, 1975.

Modular programming is a concept that emphasizes the breaking of a complex task into smaller and simpler subtasks. Each program consists of modules having limited scope—typically one or two pages of language statements. Several benefits accrue from modular programming:

Modules are easier to design, write, and test.

Interactions between modules can be easily controlled.

Understanding and functional description are enhanced.

Structured and modular programming are often associated with the concepts of stepwise refinement and top-down programming. These concepts recursively apply modular programming techniques until an atomic module is achieved. The reader will note the use of structured and modular programming techniques throughout this text. Several good references on modular programming include:

N. Wirth, Program Development by Stepwise Refinement, *CACM,* Vol. 14, no. 4, 1971.

D.L. Parnas, On the Criteria to Be Used in Decomposing Systems into Modules, *CACM,* Vol, 15, no. 12, 1972.

G.J. Myers, *Composite Design: The Design of Modular Programs,* IBM Technical Report TR 00.2406, Poughkeepsie, NY, 1973.

1.6 PREVIEW OF COMING ATTRACTIONS

This chapter has served to establish the environment in which OSs are developed. This environment consists of hardware, software processes, and people. In the remaining chapters of this text we describe various approaches to implementing the components of an OS. We also provide detailed examples written in a program design language which are drawn from several existing OSs. This section presents a short synopsis of each of the remaining chapters.

Chapter 2 discusses the management of devices that are attached to the computer system. Devices can be operated via either programmed I/O or interrupt mechanisms. At the lowest level of an OS is the interrupt service routine (ISR), which recognizes interrupts by type and dispatches control to the appropriate software mechanism. Coupled with the ISR are device handlers which are responsible for initiating device operations, monitoring the status of the device, and in certain cases, scheduling the next I/O operation to be performed by the device. The intent of device handlers is to provide a standardized interface to the user—a virtual machine that masks the eccentricities and pecularities of each device class and of specific devices within a class. Rounding out this chapter are detailed examples of device handlers for most of the devices mentioned in section 1.2.

Chapter 3 discusses the management of tasks and processes. Tasks and processes are examined using a detailed example. Depending on the complexity of the system, a variety of functions is supported for managing tasks and processes; each is described with a detailed example. An essential element of a multiprocessing system is the coordination and synchronization of processes and tasks. Two well-known methods—events and messages—are discussed.

Chapter 4 discusses the management of main memory—a resource often as critical as processor time. An enduring debate in systems design is the trade-off between memory space and processor time allocation. The OS supports several major functions: allocating, sharing, mapping, protecting, and extending memory. Each of these functions is discussed with detailed examples drawn from the literature or actual experience.

Chapter 5 discusses the fundamental concepts of I/O management. The movement of bytes (words) or aggregate units (blocks) of data. The I/O control system provides a further virtualization of the system capabilities by logically organizing data as records or blocks. These logical units may be accessed by various methods. A particular problem in I/O management is the impedance mismatch between the speeds of the CPU and the peripheral devices. This problem is solved by a technique known as buffering. Various strategies for the allocation and management of buffers are described. Detailed examples are given for access devices, sequential and unit record devices, and specialized devices.

Chapter 6 discusses the structure of the file management system. Files are collections of records or blocks of data. They may be either temporary, such as a CRT keystroke or permanent, such as a file on a mass storage device. Files on mass storage devices may be organized in several ways. Beyond the simple allocation of file space are the concomitant problems of volume sharing, file protection and sharing, and user directory management.

Chapter 7 discusses the fundamental concepts of user environment management. The user interface to the OS is again a process of virtualization since the user is provided with programming languages, system services, and the operator control language. Usually, these languages are extensible in the sense that the user can add new functions to the OS. Also covered here are the system utilities, including the management of the system clock, error management, queue management, and edit/conversion routines. Generally, these routines are buried in the internals of the OS, yet they represent an essential set of functions for its implementation.

2

Device Management

In section 1.2 the basic hardware components of a computer system were described in sufficient detail to acquaint the systems designer with their characteristics. At the lowest level of the OS the designer faces the problem of developing a set of software modules to service each class and type of device. These modules should present common interfaces to all classes of devices while masking individual characteristics. This chapter discusses the principles of device management and describes a set of device handlers for servicing the generic classes of devices normally found in a minicomputer system.

2.1 CONCEPTS OF DEVICE MANAGEMENT

Device management routines are the lowest level of software in the OS. A device handler resides closest to the hardware. It must "know" the intimate characteristics of the device it services and must be able to respond to conditions originating in the device. The multitude of devices that can be connected to modern minicomputer systems poses a problem of considerable complexity for the OS designer: how to present a uniform interface to all other system routines so that a particular device handler may be configured into the system at any time. As the typical cost of a minicomputer system (with disks, printers, terminals, and tapes) devotes over 60 percent of the price to I/O and mass storage devices, a primary goal of OS design is to use these devices in the most efficient manner.

The characteristics of most hardware components of the computer system have been explored in section 1.2. A detailed survey of device characteristics can be found in *Peripheral Devices* by Ivan Flores [flor72]. In addition, most minicomputer manufacturers usually publish handbooks and manuals describing the operational and programmatic aspects of their peripheral devices. Notable examples are the *PDP-11 Peripherals Handbook* by Digital Equipment [dec78] and the *Peripherals Manual* published by Data General [dgc75]. The reader should consult the appropriate manufacturers' publications for his or her local system.

It is not my intent to dwell on device characteristics any more than is necessary to understand the general construction of a handler for each type of device. Specific instructions for each device are suitably masked by calling a subroutine which implements that operation.

2.1.1   Basic Functions of Device Management

The following are the basic functions of device management that any operating system must perform:

1. **Status tracking.**   The system needs to keep track of the status of the device at all times. The device status is maintained in a database known as the device control block. At the most elementary level, a device is configured in the system or it is not. Its presence or absence is indicated by the presence or absence of a device control block.

2. **Device access.**   In a multiuser environment, the system must implement a policy for determining which user gets the device, for how long, and when he or she can use it.

3. **Device control.**   Each device responds to specific control instructions based on device-dependent parameters. Some devices recognize only a limited subset of commands (e.g., one cannot "READ" the line printer). The device handler must map a generic set of control instructions to the specific commands that are associated with each device.

4. **Device allocation.**   In some cases, a device must be physically assigned to a process for the duration of I/O operations. The device is "connected" to the program through an artifice known as a channel (see section 5.3).

5. **Space allocation.**   Mass storage devices require additional management functions to allocate space among multiple users. In many systems, these functions are associated with the device handler.

2.1.2   The Device Control Block

A device is described to the OS by a database known as the device control block (DCB). The DCB describes the characteristics of the device as they relate to a generic set of functions that are supported by the OS. When a device is configured in the system, a DCB is created and inserted into the device list.

There are two classes of devices usually found in computer systems: unit record peripherals and mass storage devices. The structure of the device DCB varies for each class.

Unit Record Peripheral DCB

A unit record peripheral is usually a character or line-oriented device. Characters are received by the device handler in a serial fashion. The structure of the DCB for unit record peripherals is shown in table 2.1.

Device Control Block: Mass Storage Device

A mass storage peripheral is usually a block-oriented device. Data are received by the device handler in fixed-size blocks after the appropriate address has been provided to the device controller. One device controller can manage several units of the same class. The structure of the DCB for mass storage units is depicted in table 2.2.

2.1.3   Device Characteristics

There are several characteristics which are common to many of the devices that are usually configured in an OS.

Device Name

Each device has a name, represented as a character string, by which the user can reference that device. In this system, each device name is 4 bytes in length and has the following structure:

Position	Contents	Usage
1, 2	Device	Must be the first characters in the device name
3, 4	Unit id	Two-character mnemonic indicating a specific device

The designer is free to make the device name as long as necessary. In this case, a simple approach was taken which satisfies the needs of the system environment. Up to 63 units per device class can be configured under this naming approach, as the unit identifier is usually treated as an octal digit.

Some of the more common device mnemonics are CR for card reader, LP for line printer, DK for fixed-head disk, DP for moving-head disk, and MT for magnetic tape drives. Thus the specification for a line printer might be "lp00," indicating unit 0 of the line printer device class. Note that line printers are treated as a generic class of devices. Individual differences among line printers would be found in the device handlers for each distinct unit type.

Table 2.1   Device Control Block: Unit Record Peripheral

Entry	Usage
device-name	Contains the system name for the device (e.g., one line printer may be known as "1p0")
device-attributes	Contains the bits that define the attributes of this device
device-switch-ptr	Contains a pointer to the switch table containing the addresses of the device-specific I/O routines
device-buffer-size	Declares the size of the buffer required for the device
device-record-size	Contains the size of the physical record for the device
device-unit	Address of the device on the I/O bus

Table 2.2   Device Control Block: Mass Storage Peripheral

Entry	Usage
device-name	Contains the system name of the device (e.g., for a moving-head disk drive, "dl0")
device-attributes	Describes the physical characteristics of the device related to I/O operations
device-switch-ptr	Used to map generic I/O functions to specific device I/O routines
device-record-mask	Mask for the physical record size
device-request-in-progress	Indicates whether or not the device is currently processing an I/O request
device-service-rs	Address of a resource semaphore that controls access to the device
device-unit	Address of the specific device on the controller
device-timeout	Holds the device timeout interval
device-failures	Counts the consecutive number of device failures during the processing of one I/O request

Device Attributes

Each device is characterized by a set of attributes that describe the current status of the device. These attributes are maintained in the DEVICE-ATTRI-BUTES entry of the DCB. The structure of the DEVICE-ATTRIBUTES entry is shown in table 2.3.

Note that the line printer would always be marked "read-protected" while the card reader would always be marked "write-protected." A magnetic tape drive could be marked either read- or write-protected by the user who assigned

Table 2.3 Structure of the Device Attributes Word

Bit Number	Usage
15	Write-protect bit
14	Read-protect bit
13	Direct access device
12	Device available bit
11	Output buffering standard bit
10	Input buffering standard bit
9–2	Unused
1, 0	Status of direct access device

the tape drive. In many systems, the system log journal tape is often assigned in "read-protect" mode during normal operations to prevent users from accessing sensitive system data.

The interpretation of device attributes depends on the physical characteristics of the device unit and the logic contained in the device handler.

Device Switch List

One of the motivations for utilizing DCBs is to present a uniform interface to the I/O manager. Each I/O request is translated into a call to a routine in the device handler which performs the physical I/O operation. The translation is performed by looking up the routine address in a "switch list" based on the operation code. The structure of the generic switch list appears below. Devices that cannot accommodate certain functions will have negative values in the slots associated with those functions.

device-switch-list of

    fd-read-sequential,

    fd-write-sequential,

    fd-read-random,

    fd-write-random,

    fd-read-line,

    fd-write-line,

fd-open,

fd-close,

fd-next-buffer,

fd-flush-buffer.

The interpretation of a command is specific to the device. The switch list contains the address of the appropriate routine in the device handler. These addresses are established when the OS is mapped together to form an executable module. Note also that for some devices a particular entry may be undefined (has a value of −1), indicating that the command is illegal or not implemented for a particular device.

Device Record Size

For certain unit record peripherals, the physical record size of the device is determined by its physical characteristics. For example, the card reader has a physical (and logical) record size of 80 bytes, while the line printer has a record size of 132 bytes. For some devices, the system manager, when configuring the DCB, may want to specify a fixed record size. The manager may also want to specify the number of buffers for input and output. These specifications are maintained in the device-record-size entry of the DCB. Its structure is show in table 2.4.

2.2   CONCEPTS OF DEVICE CONTROL

One may visualize each peripheral device as a processor external to the CPU. Each peripheral either is a source of input, a sink for output, or both. Each device can communicate with the CPU in one of two ways: via a communications register, which is usually one of the CPU registers, or via a communications (or I/O) bus, which is linked to memory.

Under the register scheme, the CPU has a distinct set of I/O instructions which act with well-defined device registers (e.g., TEST BUSY EQUAL TO

Table 2.4   Structure of the Device Record Size Entry

15–14	Number of output buffers to allocate
13–12	Number of input buffers to allocate
11–0	Physical record size for the device

ZERO). The control procedure discovers the state of the peripheral by reading the device register contents, and then initiates device operations by writing suitable information into the register. Under the I/O bus scheme, each device has a numerical address on the bus. A message (e.g., a device command) is placed on the bus with the device's address prefixed to it. The device controller recognizes those messages intended for it, intercepts them on the bus, and processes them in an appropriate manner. The bus usually consists of control lines, address lines, and data lines. Further discussion of these features is more suited to a hardware text. The reader interested in I/O architectures is referred to [beiz71], [bell71], [dgc75], [dec78], and [flor72].

Devices may operate autonomously from the CPU or they may not. The former concept is concerned with the interrupt mechanism, the latter with programmed I/O techniques. These two methods of peripheral control are discussed in the following sections.

2.2.1 Concept of Programmed Input/Output

Programmed I/O focuses on the movement of data between the central processor registers and the I/O devices. It usually depends on the availability of basic I/O instructions in the central processor (although the PDP-11 is an exception). Programmed I/O control involves:

Setting and clearing various device flags
Setting up device control registers
Interpreting the values of control registers
Transferring data to/from a CPU register

Direct access to the control registers and flags of a device makes programmed I/O very flexible. However, it is also very inefficient in the use of I/O devices, the main memory, and the CPU.

The steps for reading or writing data are about the same. The following sequence of steps shows how a word would be written to a device under programmed I/O.

1. Transfer output word from memory to CPU register.
2. Read device busy flag.
3. If device is busy, go to step 2.
4. Transfer word from register to device data buffer.
5. Issue start device command.
6. Increment memory address.
7. Decrement word count.
8. Read device busy flag.

   9. If device is busy, go to step 8.

  10. If word count not equal to zero, go to step 4.

  11. Issue clear device command.

The reasons that cause programmed I/O to be inefficient should be clear. First, central processor activity is reduced to the speed of the device because the CPU must wait for the device to complete each transfer operation. Second, the central processor spends a large part of its time waiting for data from devices. Third, using this approach, only one device can be serviced at a time, as the processor must devote its entire attention to that device. Finally, during the data transfer period, the memory is effectively idle.

One cannot lightly dismiss programmed I/O operations. Many low-end minicomputers and microcomputers do not have an interrupt system. Thus knowledge of programmed I/O is essential to the implementation of even a rudimentary OS on these machines.

2.2.2 Concept of Interrupt Management

An interrupt is a signal to the CPU that forces it to divert its attention from its current activity. The value of an interrupt facility lies in the ability of the processor to respond automatically to conditions outside the system, or within the processor itself. It is possible to have several types of interrupts. The most common, of course, are interrupts caused by peripherals demanding service when an I/O operation is completed. Another source of interrupts is the memory management unit, which may signal page faults and addressing errors. Within the processor, interrupts may be generated as the result of arithmetic errors. Finally, on some minicomputers a program can generate a software interrupt through execution of a special instruction.

An interrupt results in a subroutine jump to an interrupt service routine (ISR). This routine must save the current state of the processor before attending to the cause of the interrupt. When the ISR has finished execution, it must transfer control to the interrupted process without leaving a trace of its operation.

There are two major types of interrupt mechanisms to be considered: polled interrupts and vectored interrupts.

Polled Interrupts

Examples of polled interrupt machines are members of the Data General Nova family of minicomputers. In the Nova, the interrupt system consists of an interrupt request line to which each peripheral is connected, an Interrupt-On flag in the CPU, and an interrupt priority mask. The Interrupt-On flag controls the status of the interrupt system. If the flag is set to one, interrupts are said to be enabled, and the CPU will respond to them as they occur. If the flag is zero, the CPU will not respond to any interrupts.

When a peripheral device completes its operation, it places a request on the interrupt request line. It also sets its Busy flag to zero and its Done flag to one (see *DGC Peripherals Manual*). If the Interrupt-On flag is one and interrupt request appears, the CPU performs the following steps:

1.   The Interrupt-On flag is set to zero so that no further interrupts can disturb it.

2.   The current value of the program counter is placed into memory location 0.

3.   Depending on the type on interrupt, control is transferred to the routine whose address is stored in memory locations 1, 2, or 3, which refer to an I/O device, the real-time clock, or the stack, respectively.

4.   The ISR saves the contents of the processor registers, determines which device requested the interrupt, and services the interrupt. It determines the device identifier in one of two ways:

   (a)   Using the INTERRUPT-ACKNOWLEDGE instruction to poll the interrupt request line and return the device code of the interrupting device

   (b)   Scanning the device list and using I/O-SKIP instructions to test the Done flag of each device

5.   After servicing the device, the ISR restores the values of the processor registers, sets the Interrupt-On flag to one, and exits to the interrupted process by jumping to the address in memory location 0.

There are two modifications to this procedure. First, the interrupt priority mask determines the priority of service when multiple interrupts occur simultaneously. Each I/O device is connected to a bit in the interrupt priority mask. If a bit is set to one, all devices at that level are prevented from requesting an interrupt when they complete an operation. To implement a multiple priority interrupt routine, each ISR, when it receives control, must establish a new priority mask via the MASK-OUT instruction. At its completion, of course, the ISR must restore the previous priority mask.

Second, the priority of service may be modified by the ordering of the device list. Normally, faster devices such as disks will be placed near the top of the list. You should note that it is essential that the list be scanned from the beginning each time in order to ensure that the critical devices are always serviced first.

Vectored Interrupts

An example of a vectored interrupt machine is the Digital Equipment PDP-11 series. In the PDP-11, a set of low address memory locations are reserved for the interrupt vector. Each entry in the interrupt vector corresponds to a specific peripheral device class. Additional entries are reserved for the memory management unit, stack faults, and arithmetic faults. An interrupt vector entry consists of two words: the address of the interrupt service routine and a new processor status word.

The PDP-11 is organized around a unified bus which contains data, address, and control lines. When a device completes an I/O operation, it places an interrupt request on the bus request line. When the processor relinquishes control of the bus, and an interrupt is pending, the following sequence of operations occurs:

1. The device at the highest priority level receives control at its interrupt vector address (IVA). The device interrupt request specifies the IVA.

2. The processor stores the current PSW and program counter into temporary CPU registers.

3. The address of an interrupt service routine defining the new PC and the new processor status (PS) are loaded into the PS and PC registers, respectively. Loading an address into the PC register transfers control to the ISR (see *PDP-11 Processor Manual*).

4. The interrupt service routine is executed.

5. Upon completion of the ISR, control is returned to the interrupted process via the Return From Interrupt (RTI) instruction.

On the PDP-11, multiple interrupts are handled through a nesting procedure. The system stack is used to store the old PC and PS values, and the contents of the CPU registers. If a higher-priority interrupt occurs, the current ISR is itself interrupted while the new interrupt is serviced. The requisite information is just pushed down on top of the system stack. This facility is controlled by the priority status of the CPU. The PDP-11 supports up to eight priority levels (numbered zero to seven). When an ISR gains control, it issues an "SPL 7" command to lock out all interrupts. After saving the machine state in an appropriate manner, it issues an "SPL n" command to establish the processor priority level for handling this interrupt. Thus interrupts having a higher-priority level than n, usually specified by a device register, may then interrupt the ISR. More details concerning this procedure can be found in the appropriate DEC manuals.

Each type of device has its own ISR and PSW. As each interrupt is uniquely identified, there is no need to have an interrupt status register, and hence no interrupt analysis routine is required. This approach may generate significant savings in time to process an interrupt. However, this savings is offset by the potentially large amounts of memory required to store the interrupt vectors.

Servicing Nonexistent Devices

One problem that most OSs designers will face at some point is the case of the nonexistent device. On most minicomputers, attaching a peripheral to the processor requires that certain device registers and signals be "strapped" onto the system's I/O bus. If this strapping is incorrect, spurious interrupts may occur that are attributed to a nonexistent device. If a spurious interrupt is not handled properly, control of the processor may take a random flying leap into memory, execute some random sequence of data, and eventually crash the system. To prevent this catastrophe, the system designer should provide a routine that dismisses interrupts for nonexistent devices. The address of this routine would be inserted into each interrupt vector for those devices that have not been configured in the system. In the PDP-11, this routine would merely execute an RTI instruction. Alternatively, the system designer may have the routine perform a diagnostic analysis of the cause before dismissing the interrupt.

Interrupt Servicing

At the beginning of an interrupt, different machines will service the interrupt signal in different ways. Here we assume a vectored interrupt machine. The address of the location that was interrupted is stored in INTERRUPTED-ADDRESS, and the interrupt service routine is executed.

A common interrupt service routine is depicted in module 2.2.1. The procedure first saves all the registers in use by the executing process. Next, it increments the number of interrupts. The map status register is saved so that the system state may be entered. This step is necessary because I/O instructions may be executed only from a state in which they are enabled. For interrupts, this is always assumed to be the system state. The address of the current process is saved in PENDING-PROCESS because the result of the interrupt may be to make another process, for example one with higher priority, ready for execution.

Finally, the contents of the INTERRUPT-VECTOR-ADDRESS point to the ISR for the device. This routine is executed to perform device-specific actions.

MODULE 2.2.1

```
procedure start-interrupt
     save-registers( )
     increment interrupt-lock-count
     read-map-status( ) → map-status
     set-map-state(system-state)
     p → pending-process
     call(memory(interrupt-vector-address))
endproc
```

Interrupt Termination

Module 2.2.2 depicts a common interrupt termination routine. This routine serves as the exit from interrupt servicing. It sets the current process to the value of the pending process and restores the register values. If the map state is zero, the computer was executing under OS control; then it just returns to the interrupted routine. However, if the system was in user state, it must restart the clock (i.e., reenable interrupts). The system must also restore the map status and state (which places the map in the appropriate user map). The system can then just transfer control to the interrupted routine.

MODULE 2.2.2

```
procedure finish-interrupt
    pending-process → p
    restore-registers( )
    read-map-state( ) → map-state
    if map-state equals zero
        then
            call (interrupted-address)
    endif
    decrement interrupt-lock-count
    if interrupt-lock-count not equal to zero
        then
            start-clock( )
    endif
    set-map-status(map-status)
    set-map-state(map-state)
    call(interrupted-address)
endproc
```

2.2.3   User Device Handler Implementation

A device handler can be integrated into the OS in three ways. First, the device handler may be permanently "wired" into the OS structure. Most minicomputer systems contain real-time clocks in their hardware suites. The structure of the multiprogramming OS is built around the ability to track events and divide time equitably among different processes. A real-time clock handler is usually embedded directly in the kernel (or nucleus) of the OS to provide the most efficient service.

The second approach involves the selection of device handlers during system generation (see section 7.4). The system manager specifies the devices to be configured in the OS. The SYSGEN program gathers the appropriate device handlers during the linkage editing phase of system generation. However, for a given version of the OS, the hardware suite is static until a new system generation is performed.

Finally, device handlers may be dynamically introduced into the OS during normal operations. For example, the user is allowed to specify the characteristics of a special device and the modules needed to handle its interrupts. The user may then integrate the device into the system interrupt structure (e.g., the device list) and proceed to utilize the device. When operations are finished, the device may be removed from the interrupt structure. Of course, the device has been physically and electronically connected to the system all the while. Any signals it may have generated while its device handler was not present are treated (and ignored) as spurious transients.

Data General Corporation has provided a scheme whereby users may dynamically configure devices into their Real-Time Disk Operating System. In fact, this scheme is successfully used by their FORTRAN runtime library to interface the DGC 8020 Floating Point Processor into the system interrupt structure [dgc75]. This scheme is described in the following paragraphs.

The RDOS Run-Time Device Handler Implementation Scheme

RDOS allows the user to integrate a device handler dynamically into the OS interrupt structure. The user must specify the following data structures and parameters for the device:

A DCB, including a processor state save area

The address of the interrupt service routine for the device

An interrupt service mask which determines which devices, if any, may interrupt the currently interrupting device.

To introduce a device into the system, the user issues the DEFINE-INTERRUPT system command (our notation) as follows:

SYSTEM(DEFINE-INTERRUPT, DEVICE-CODE, DCB-ADDRESS)

where DEVICE-CODE is the physical address of the device on the I/O bus

DCB-ADDRESS is the address of the device control block

The interrupt service routine address and mask are contained within the DCB. The DEVICE-CODE cannot correspond to the address of any device configured during system generation. The effect of this command is to place the DCB address in the interrupt vector table. Whenever an interrupt for this device is received, the interrupt executive retrieves the DCB address and dispatches control to the interrupt service routine.

In a corresponding fashion, the user may remove a device handler from the system interrupt structure by issuing the following system command (our notation):

SYSTEM(REMOVE-INTERRUPT, DEVICE-CODE)

where   DEVICE-CODE   is the physical address of the device on the
                                I/O bus

The effect of this command is to clear the entry for the device in the interrupt
vector table. RDOS does not allow the user to remove devices that were configured during system generation. This precautionary measure prevents the user
from removing devices on which other users may depend. Clearly, the system
cannot allow any user to remove a disk device such as the one on which the
nonresident OS modules are stored.

2.3   TERMINAL MANAGEMENT

The terminal is the point of physical interface between the user and the system.
Terminals may be VDUs or teletype-like devices. At least one terminal is present in each system—the operator's console. Most manufacturers recommend
that the operator's console be a hard-copy device in order to record error
messages that may occur during system operation.

Most terminals are split into two devices: an input device—the keyboard—
and an output device—the screen or printer. Both input and output must be
shared between processes; this, of course, is accomplished by resource semaphores. Output is multiplexed in both space and time by using the two-dimensional features of the VDU. Input can be easily multiplexed in time through use
of virtual input devices termed lines. That is, a completed line entered by the
user is directed to one and only one process.

On input, a queue of characters is associated with the keyboard. This queue
contains characters that were typed while the keyboard was active but have not
yet been requested by a process. Characters are echoed when they are typed by
the user to provide immediate reassurance that the system is active. Some
systems echo characters only when they are extracted from the queue in
response to a request for input.

In most systems, processes may request input from the terminal in three
modes. In character-at-a-time mode, a single character is returned in response
to each request. Most operator's consoles manage input in this way. Line-edit
mode is used for processing commands and user data. Page-edit mode is used
primarily for editing files; it is simply a driver for editing facilities supporting
textual manipulation.

When processing commands to the system, it is often useful to specify indirect sources of input, for example, programmable function keys, macro files,
or command language procedures. The processing of such input is distributed
among the low-level keyboard driver, the terminal input and line handlers, and
the high-level command line interpreters.

On output, the terminal (e.g., a VDU) is usually treated as a cursor-addressable, two-dimensional, right-ragged array indexed by line number and character position. Individual lines may have contrast types, such as reverse video or blinking. In general, the system maintains a fixed number of text lines in memory. Most systems make a range of text-editing features available to processes, such as:

Cursor motion by characters, words, lines, or pages

Deletion of characters, words, lines, or pages

Joining and splitting lines

Character overwrite and insertion

String location and substitution

Text selection and transfer (mark, pick, put)

In the multiple-process environment, simultaneous activities compete for the user's attention. This presents a number of problems.

1. The physical display may not be large enough to accommodate all the information produced by the concurrent activities.
2. The user must be able to organize work so that related information is arranged logically on the screen.
3. Different processes may provide different viewing options, depending on the nature of the information or their internal state.

Most systems solve these problems by hierarchically decomposing the screen into rectangular areas called windows. This "boxing function" may be implemented in software (e.g., SMALLTALK) or in firmware (e.g., the Delta Data 7000). The size, relative position, and video characteristics of a window usually depend on the application.

The features described in these introductory paragraphs give you some idea of the complexity associated with the terminal manager. Where features are implemented in software, this software is usually an applications program interfaced between the user and the OS. In many cases, these features are included as part of a transaction management or text-editing system where the terminal is dedicated to the specific application. In this section we concentrate on the fundamental operations associated with terminal I/O. Substantial information regarding terminal management can be found in [mart73].

In summary, we view a terminal as merely a source or sink of characters. From the point of view of the process, it merely requests a "chunk" of data from the terminal handler via the normal READ/WRITE functions. Upon receipt of a request for a chunk, the terminal handler assembles the input stream in a line buffer maintained for the process and transfers it to the process when a termination character is seen. The notion of a chunk can be as elaborate as you desire. And, of course, we must still be able to read character by character.

2.3.1   Terminal Concepts

The terminal management routines utilize two databases in handling a teletype or VDU. These are the TTY device control block (TTYDCB) and the TTY switch table. Note that in the following sections we use the generic acronym TTY to mean either a keyboard-printer or a VDU.

The TTYDCB, having three entries, is shown in figure 2.1. The device name is specified in the standard format. For a TTY, it would have the form "TTY0." The device status has the same format as described in section 2.1.3. The third entry is the address of the TTY switch table, which defines the permissible functions for the terminal. The structure of the TTY switch table is shown in figure 2.2. Note that the only functions allowed to the terminal are the stream I/O functions.

Conceptually, the terminal is treated as two separate devices: the input keyboard and the output display. This treatment is necessitated by the fact that each element has a separate address on the I/O bus and is connected to the I/O bus by separate cables. Consequently, in performing I/O operations on a terminal, a user program must assign two channels. The input channel is usually referred to by the device name "TTI0"; the output channel is referred to by the device name "TTO0."

Normally, there is only one operator terminal per system. Both the OS modules and user programs must be allowed access to the terminal. Obviously, if indiscriminate reading and writing were allowed, conflicts among messages would occur. To prevent such conflicts, the terminal is protected by two sets of resource semaphores: one each for input and output.

TTY Resource Semaphores

There are two resource semaphores contained in each of the input and output sets. They are (for input):

TTI-ACCESS   A semaphore that controls access to one of the device handler routines

TTI-INPUT-RS   A semaphore maintaining a circular queue of characters read from the keyboard

In addition, a third semaphore is required for output buffering, known as TTY-OUTBUF-RS. This semaphore controls access to the output buffer and prevents the messages from different users from being intermixed. Thus when a user is granted access to the TTY-OUTPUT-BUFFER, he or she is guaranteed the ability to enter the entire message into the queue.

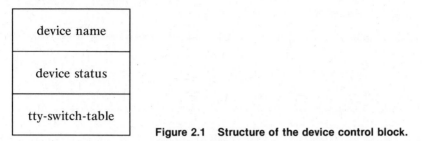

Figure 2.1   Structure of the device control block.

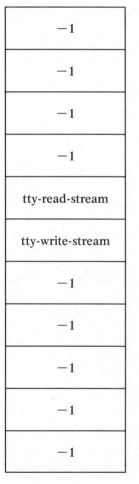

Figure 2.2   Structure of the TTY device switch table.

2.3.2   Terminal Input/Output Functions

As mentioned above, terminal I/O can be managed on a character-by-character basis or through stream I/O. In the first case, no channel is required. Access to the terminal is directly through the device handler. In the second case, a process must open channels giving the file names associated with the input and output devices. Thus some system overhead associated with the initial file processing algorithms will be experienced, but more flexibility in program construction will be attained. The major procedures used to implement terminal I/O functions are described in the following paragraphs.

Getting a Character

The user may read one character at a time from the operator's terminal. The format of the system request is

    SYSTEM(GET-CHARACTER, EVENT-NR)

    SYSTEM(VALUE1, EVENT-NR) → CHARACTER

where   EVENT-NR   is used to signal the user when the character is available for processing

            CHARACTER   is a location in the user's program which receives the ASCII value of the next input character

The procedure for processing this system request is depicted in module 2.3.1. The system requests access to the input queue. It retrieves the first character in the queue, if any, and stores it as the value of the event. The user retrieves the value of the character by requesting the event value. If no character is present in the input queue, the process will block until the next character is entered at the terminal.

Putting a Character

The use may transmit one character at a time to the terminal for display on the output device. The format of the command is

    SYSTEM(PUT-CHARACTER, CHARACTER)

where   CHARACTER   is the character to be displayed at the terminal

The procedure for executing this command is depicted in module 2.3.2. Normally, the output character is inserted into a circular queue so that the calling task is not delayed. If the buffer is full, the calling task will be delayed until a character has been transmitted.

MODULE 2.3.1

```
procedure get-character
        request(tti-access)
        request(tti-input-rs) → event-data[p]
        release(tti-access)
        subprocess-ok()
endproc
```

MODULE 2.3.2

```
procedure put-character
    character[usp] → request-update-data[p]
    request(tto-access)
    request(tty-outbuf-rs)
    release(tty-output-rs, request-update-data[p])
    release(tto-access)
    os-exit()
endproc
```

Terminal Stream Input

The user may read data from the terminal under the control of the I/O manager. To do so, the user issues a standard stream read request (see chapter 5). The user process is coupled to the device handler by the I/O manager. The procedure for handling stream input is depicted in module 2.3.3.

Each input character is echoed to the display as it is read. Special symbols are used to edit the input stream. The interpretation of these characters and execution of their respective functions is handled in the module. Note that such support was not available for input performed on a character-by-character basis.

Initially, the routine requests access to both input and output buffers. It must be granted access to the output buffer so that it can echo characters as they are entered at the keyboard. It also sets up a data storage area for characters as they are received. If a user has issued a request, the data will be transferred directly to the user's program space. Otherwise, the entire string is assembled in system space and transferred to the caller (most likely a system routine).

The processing of an input stream is cyclic. That is, each character is examined as it is received. If the character has a special meaning, the appropriate operation is performed. Errors will cause the terminal alarm to be sounded and the loop to be reentered. The system signals the user when it is expecting input by sounding the terminal alarm. It then cycles, reading characters until a stream termination character is encountered.

To process each character as it is read, the terminal handler must be cognizant of at least the following special characters:

BACKSPACE

A backspace character is used to erase the preceding character in the stream. The GET-CHARACTER-AND-DECREMENT function removes the last character in the buffer. If the buffer is empty, the procedure rings the bell to indicate an error (e.g., attempting to erase something that is not there). When echoing a character erasure, the system inserts a back-arrow into the display buffer. Module 2.3.3 depicts this operation.

BACKLINE

The user, at any time, may erase the contents of the input buffer up to the last line termination character. To do so, the user types an "end-of-line" or backslash character. The procedure resets the buffer pointer to the beginning of the buffer, thus effectively erasing the most recently entered contents. It echoes the string "⟨cr⟩⟨lf⟩0" on the display to notify the user that the line has been canceled.

CARRIAGE RETURN

The carriage return signals the end of the input stream. In the display, the string "⟨cr⟩⟨lf⟩0" is inserted to signify to the user that a stream has ended. The carriage return, line feed, and null characters are inserted into the input buffer. The stream is then copied to user space if the user has issued an outstanding request. Access to the I/O devices is released, and the system exits to the user.

ESCAPE

Whereas backline simply erases the current buffer contents and allows the user to try again, escape signifies that the user wishes to terminate the entire input operation. The length of the input stream is set to zero, and a null character is placed in the line buffer. The contents of the line buffer are then copied to user space if an outstanding request was issued by a user process. Access to the I/O device is released, and control is returned to the caller.

NONE OF THE ABOVE

The input character is not a special character. The three tests in this section validate the input character and determine that it will not overflow the line buffer. Invalid characters are rejected by the procedure. If neither of the conditions above holds, the character is inserted into the line buffer and echoed in the display stream.

MODULE 2.3.3

```
procedure tty-read-stream
    request(tti-access)
    request(tto-access)
    request-map[p] → user-map
    if user-map not equal to system-map
        then
                address(tty-line-buffer) * 2 → tty-line-address
        else
                request-data-address[p] * 2 → tty-line-address
    endif
    tty-line-address → tty-start-address
    request-size[p] * 2 → number-of-bytes
    number-of-bytes − 1 + tty-line-address → tty-line-limit
    request(tty-outbuf-rs)

ringbell:
    release(tty-outbuf-rs, bell)
    while true
        do
        request(tty-input-rs) → inchar
        case inchar of
        backspace:
            get-character-and-decrement(tty-start-address, ringbell)
            release(tty-output-rs, back-arrow)
            exitcase
        backline:
            tty-string-out('⟨cr⟩⟨lf⟩ 0'
            tty-start-address → tty-line-address
            exitcase
        carriage-return:
            tty-string-out('⟨cr⟩⟨lf⟩⟨0⟩')
            write-character-and-increment(tty-start-address,
                                            carriage-return)
            write-character-and-increment(tty-start-address, 0)
            string-size(tty-start-address) + 1 → str-temp
```

```
            str-temp/2 → event-status[p]
            if user-map not equal to zero
                  then
                  request-data-address[p] → user-data-address
                  move-to-user-space(user-map, tty-line-buffer, user-
                        data-address, event-status[p])
            endif
            release(tto-access)
            release(tti-access)
            io-exit( )
            exitcase
      escape:
            tty-string-out('ESCAPE ⟨cr⟩⟨lf⟩⟨0⟩')
            write-character-and-increment(tty-start-address, 0)
            clear event-status[p]
            if user-map not equal to zero
                  then
                        move-to-user-space(user-map, tty-line-buffer,
                              request-data-address[p], 1)
                  else
                        clear request-data-address[p]
            endif
            release(tto-access)
            release(tti-access)
            io-exit( )
            else
      none-of-the-above:
            if inchar less than blank
                  then
                  goto ringbell
            endif
            if inchar greater than or equal to max-character-code
                  then
                  goto ringbell
            endif
            if tty-line-address is greater than or equal to tty-line-limit
                  then
                  goto ringbell
            endif
            write-character-and-increment(tty-line-address, inchar)
            release(tty-outbuf-rs, inchar)
      endcase
   enddo
endproc
```

Terminal Stream Output

In comparison to stream input, the procedure for displaying a stream on a terminal is relatively simple. When the stream is passed to the device handler, it is assumed to be in absolute format. That is, the user has properly edited it for content and length. Thus this procedure makes no provision for the extensive editing functions found in stream input.

This procedure, depicted in module 2.3.4, copies the string from user space (if a user process issued a request) into the tty-line-buffer. A maximum of 134 characters will be copied since this corresponds to the standard width of the DECwriter type terminals. The procedure scans the line buffer and examines each character. When a null character is detected, the end of the stream has been reached and the operation is terminated. If the character is a top-of-form code, the procedure transmits the string "⟨cr⟩⟨lf⟩⟨lf⟩⟨vt⟩⟨0⟩" which forces the terminal to eject a page. If the character is determined to be a carriage return, the string "⟨cr⟩⟨lf⟩⟨0⟩" is printed to force a new line on the terminal. Otherwise, the character is inserted directly into the output buffer.

MODULE 2.3.4

```
procedure tty-write-stream
    request(tto-access)
    if request-map[p] not equal to zero
        then
        request-map[p] → user-map
        request-data-address[p] → user-data-address
        map-string-in(user-map, user-data-address, tty-line-buffer,
                                                                 134)
        address(tty-line-buffer) * 2 → tty-line-address
        else
        user-data-address * 2 → tty-line-address
    endif
    request(tty-outbuf-rs)
    while true
        do
        get(tty-line-address) → outchar
        if outchar not equal to zero
            then
            if outchar equals top-of-form
                then
                tty-string-out('⟨cr⟩⟨lf⟩⟨lf⟩⟨vt⟩⟨0⟩')
                else
                if outchar equals carriage-return
```

```
                              then
                              tty-string-out('〈cr〉〈lf〉〈0〉')
                              else
                              release(tty-output-rs, outchar)
                        endif
                  endif
                  increment tty-line-address
            endif
            enddo
      release(tto-access)
      set one to event-status[p]
      io-exit( )
endproc
```

2.3.3   Console Input/Output Processes

At the device interface, two processes handle the transmission of characters to and from the console.

The TTY Input Process

A process for reading characters from the console is depicted in module 2.3.5. This procedure uses programmed I/O to read characters from the device. One pass through the process code corresponds to the act of reading one character from the device. The process repeatedly tests the TTY-READY flag for a character appearing in the buffer. If no character is availabe, the process delays for a clock cycle and test the flag again. When a character appears, the TTY-READY flag becomes true and the DO loop is exited.

To process the input, the procedure READ-TTY is called to obtain the character from the device buffer. The parity bit is stripped from the character and the character is inserted into the input buffer. Both the READ-TTY and STRIP-PARITY routines are assembly language modules specific to the actual computer system. The process then repeats to obtain the next character.

MODULE 2.3.5

```
process input-tty-process
      clear tty-ready
      while tty-ready equals 0
            do
            sense-tty-input(tty-ready)
```

```
            if tty-ready equals 1
                then
                        exitdo
            endif
            request(time-interrupt)
            enddo
        read-tty( ) → character
        strip-parity(character) → character
        release(tty-input-rs, character)
        repeat
endprocess
```

The TTY Output Process

A process for writing a character to the console is depicted in module 2.3.6. A
character is obtained from the system output buffer after requesting exclusive
access to it. The process tests the TTY-OUT-READY flag until it becomes true.
When the device is ready, the parity bits are added to the character and it is
transmitted to the device buffer. The process repeats for the next character.

MODULE 2.3.6

```
process output-tty-process
        request(tty-output-rs) → character
        release(tty-outbuf-rs)
        clear tty-out-ready
        while tty-out-ready equals zero
            do
            request(time-interrupt)
            sense-tty-output(tty-out-ready)
            enddo
        add-parity(character) → character
        write-tty(character)
        repeat
endprocess
```

2.4 LINE PRINTER MANAGEMENT

In most minicomputer systems, there is only one line printer. Thus the line
printer must be treated as a scarce resource. Normally, the line printer is shared
among multiple users via a technique known as SPOOLing (see section 1.4.4).

In systems with small memory and few users, SPOOLing may not be practical. One way to protect the line printer is to use resource semaphores.

Two resource semaphores are required to control the line printer in a small multiuser system. The semaphore LPT-CONTROLLER is used to allocate the line printer to one of several processes within the system. LPT-ACCESS mediates access to the line printer by the device handler or the process, as the case may be. As processes request access to the line printer, they are queued using a first in, first out (FIFO) policy.

2.4.1   Writing an Output Line

The line printer is a sequential unit record device. A procedure for printing one line of output is depicted in module 2.4.1. This procedure requests access to the line printer. The calling process is allowed to proceed when the line printer is free. If the request was submitted from user space, the line to be written is copied into a temporary buffer in system space. Otherwise, the data may be fetched directly from the memory associated with a system process. In either case, a character pointer is constructed for the data stream.

In this example, the data stream is printed two characters at a time using programmed I/O. The following characters are of special importance to the device handler:

1. A top-of-form character causes the current word to be printed (via FLUSH). The page is ejected by the hardware.
2. A carriage return forces the current word to be printed. The page is vertically tabbed one line.

Otherwise, the character is printed. You are invited to augment this module to recognize other characters for control purposes.

Characters are fetched from the data stream until a null character is encountered. As each character is fetched, the byte pointer is incremented by one. Thus the user can pack several "print lines" into a single data stream. Once the data stream has been printed, the line printer is released and successful execution is signaled to the caller.

MODULE 2.4.1

```
procedure lpt-write-line
    request(lpt-access)
    if request-map[p] not equal to zero
        then
        request-map[p] → user-map
        request-data-address[p] → user-data-address
```

```
                request-size[p] → data-size
                move-from-user-space(user-map, user-data-address,
                    lpt-buffer, data-size)
                address(lpt-buffer) * 2 → lpt-address
                else
                request-data-address[p] * 2 → lpt-address
            endif
            set one to lpt-flag
            while lpt-flag equals one
                do
                getchar(lpt-address) → lpt-character
                if lpt-character equals zero
                    then
                            exitdo
                endif
                if lpt-character equals top-of-form
                    then
                    flush( )
                    lpt-word-out(top-of-form-command)
                    else
                    if lpt-character equals carriage-return
                        then
                        flush( )
                        lpt-word-out(end-of-line-command)
                        else
                        lpt-character-out(lpt-character)
                    endif
                endif
                increment lpt-address
                enddo
            set one to event-status[p]
            release(lpt-access)
            io-exit( )
        endproc
```

Transmitting One Word

The procedure for transmitting one word to the line printer is depicted in
module 2.4.2. Under programmed I/O, this procedure waits until the line
printer is ready. However, it delays for a fixed period before signaling a timeout
condition. Most minicomputer systems are rather simple; they cannot detect
such conditions as paper jam or end-of-paper. Usually, it is left up to the
operator to visually detect the problem. If a timeout condition is detected, access to the line printer is released.

MODULE 2.4.2

```
procedure lpt-word-out(lpt-data)
    for time-count from 0 to time-limit
        do
        sense-lpt-status( ) → lpt-status
        if lpt-status equals one
            then
                send-lpt-word(lpt-data)
                exitproc
            else
                request(time-interrupt)
        endif
        enddo
    set er-timeout to event-status[p]
    release(lpt-access)
    io-exit( )
endproc
```

Transmitting a Character

Characters are fetched from the data stream one at a time. In this example, the line printer is assumed to be a word-oriented device. Thus two characters must be packed into one word before transmission to the line printer. The procedure to transmit a character is depicted in module 2.4.3.

Flushing the Current Word

When an end-of-line or top-of-form is detected, the current word must be forced out before a control word is transmitted. This action is known as "flushing." If the word buffer contains only one character, it is packed with a space before printing. The procedure to flush a buffer is shown in module 2.4.4.

MODULE 2.4.3

```
procedure lpt-character-out(character)
    set-parity(character) → character
    if flag equals zero
        then
        character → lbyte(lpt-word)
        increment flag
```

```
        else
            character → rbyte(lpt-word)
            lpt-word-out(lpt-word)
            clear flag
        endif
endproc
```

                              MODULE 2.4.4

```
procedure flush
    if lpt-flag not equal to zero
            then
            lpt-character-out(space)
    endif
endproc
```

2.5   MAGNETIC TAPE MANAGEMENT

Magnetic tapes are mass storage devices that are assigned to a single user. On magnetic tape, you can generally store any number of files, separated by end-of-file marks, that are composed of any number of records. The essential aspect of tape operation is that it is sequential. That is, from any point on the tape, you may search forward or backward over any number of records or files. However, all intervening records must be examined or at least recognized by the hardware.

As a magnetic tape is accessible by only one program at a time, the OS provides you with a set of functions by which you directly manage tape operations. For the duration of the assignment, the tape belongs to you to do with as you wish. In disk systems, the OS must allocate and manage space because the device is shared among many users. Because there is no sharing of a magnetic tape subsystem, the OS provides you with considerably more flexibility. As there is no directory on a magnetic tape, you are responsible for knowing the contents of the tape. It may be that you format the tape to implement a directory, but this approach is a function of individual user programs.

Two types of functions are generally supported for magnetic tape devices: standard I/O and file management functions and direct control functions. A user process associates a channel with a tape drive via the OPEN request. When you open a tape file, you specify a file number on the tape. The act of opening the channel forces the tape to be positioned at the beginning of the file. You may now read or write records via the standard I/O functions. When all processing has been completed, you release the tape drive by issuing a CLOSE request.

This scenario allows you to process only one file with each OPEN/CLOSE request pair. However, most tapes contain several files. You may want to process more than one file. To do so, you need a way to manipulate the tape to access other files. This capability is provided by the direct tape control functions.

2.5.1   Invoking the Magnetic Tape Functions

The functions for direct management of a tape subsystem are invoked through the tape function request. The format of this request is:

SYSTEM(TAPE-FUNCTION, EVENT-NR, CHANNEL, FUNCTION, COUNT)

where   EVENT-NR   is used to signal a user process when the specified function has been completed

               CHANNEL   is the number of the channel that has been opened to the physical device

               FUNCTION   is the function code

               COUNT   is a numeric value specific to the function

The user may execute nine different functions when controlling the magnetic tape subsystem. These are specified as:

Function Code	Function
1	Rewind the tape
2	Skip tape files forward
3	Skip tape files backward
4	Skip tape records forward
5	Skip tape records backward
6	Erase tape
7	Initialize tape
8	Release tape
9	Write a file mark

In addition to these functions, the standard requests for OPEN and CLOSE of a file are supported through the system service request mechanism. The user can store/retrieve data on the tape using the standard sequential read and write requests.

The procedure for executing a tape function is depicted in module 2.5.1. The tape function code is used to transfer control to the appropriate module of the tape management subsystem. Each function will set the event status for that request. Upon completion of the function, a normal exit is taken from the OS.

MODULE 2.5.1

```
procedure tape-function
    request-tape-function[p] → function-code
    case function-code of
        1:   rewind-tape( ) → result
             exitcase
        2:   skip-tape-files( ) → result
             exitcase
        3:   backspace-tape-files( ) → result
             exitcase
        4:   skip-tape-records( ) → result
             exitcase
        5:   backspace-tape-records( ) → result
             exitcase
        6:   tape-erase( ) → result
             exitcase
        7:   initialize-tape( ) → result
             exitcase
        8:   release-tape( ) → result
             exitcase
        9:   write-tape-file-mark( ) → result
    endcase
    set-return-and-exit(result)
endproc
```

2.5.2   Tape Management Database

Each tape drive in the system has a DCB associated with it. The DCB contains specific information about the status of that device and its structure is depicted in table 2.5. The DCB-LINK is used to link the DCB into the standard device list.

Normally, up of to eight tape drives may be attached to a magnetic tape controller. A distinction must be made between the drive number and the unit number. The drive number is the physical index of a given tape drive in the string of drives attached to the controller. The unit number is the logical drive number and is usually selected by a thumbwheel mounted on the tape drive's control panel. Thus logical unit number six may actually be physical drive number three (i.e., fourth from the controller where numbers run from zero to seven).

You are allowed to store any number of files on the tape (actually the practical limit is the value of a one-word integer). Each file may be of variable length. Two entries in the DCB keep track of the current file number and current record number within a file. Both file and record numbers begin at zero. In

Table 2.5   Device Control Block: Magnetic Tape Subsystem

device-name	File name of the device, (e.g. "MT00")
device-status	Status bits for this subsystem
unit-number	Logical index for a tape drive when indexed from the file system
drive-number	Physical index of the tape drive in the string of drives attached to the controller
file-name	Entry recording the current file in a directory-based tape management system
drive-rs-address	Address of the resource semaphore which controls access to the tape drive
file-number	Current file on the tape
record-number	Current record number in the file
reel-id	Current reel in multireel file
retries	Count of the number of error retries during error recovery attempts
tape-switch-table	Address of the tape function table

some systems, you are allowed to declare a multireel tape file. A command is often provided to switch to the next reel when the current tape has been exhausted. Although an entry is provided for a REEL-ID, we will not discuss multireel tape files in any more detail.

The DEVICE-NAME entry stores the string representation of the device name, for example, "MT00." The FILE-NAME entry can be used for those systems where each file has a header record describing the name and contents of the file. Although not used here, this approach has been utilized in several synchronous preformatted tape drives based on the DECtape principle.

2.5.3   Opening a Tape Channel

You access a tape through the system service request OPEN. This request associates a channel with a specific tape drive. The procedure for opening a channel is depicted in module 2.5.2. This procedure is called from the routine OPEN-DEVICE-CHANNEL in section 6.7.3.

The calling procedure has verified the existence of the specified tape drive and located its DCB. The address of the DCB is stored in the DCB pointer within the process control block. The device status is checked to see if the channel is already open on the drive. If so, an error code is returned to you.

When you open a channel to a file, you specify the tape drive name followed by a file number. As the tape may be positioned anywhere along its length, the tape must be moved to point to the proper file. If the file number is zero, the tape is rewound to the load point. Otherwise, the tape is backspaced to the beginning of the current file and the distance (in files) to its new position is calculated. The position is adjusted to point to the proper file. Setting the request size to zero indicates that the tape should be backspaced to the nearest file mark.

Next, the procedure establishes access to the device through the tape controller. This procedure allocates the controller to you and selects the drive number as the current drive for the controller. If the device was off-line, an error condition is returned to you. You must, however, physically enable a tape drive by properly setting the ONLINE/OFFLINE switch on the tape drive control panel before the controller can execute any commands. The procedure then sets up the attributes word of the DCB based on the open mode bits. The channel is declared open and the controller is released.

MODULE 2.5.2

```
procedure open-tape(→result)
    dcb-address → request-dcb-address[p]
    if channel-open-bit of device-status[dcb-address] not equal to zero
        then
        er-file-open → event-status[p]
        er-file-open → result
        exitproc
    endif
    ccb-address → request-channel-address[p]
    clear request-size[p]
    if file-mgr-extension[pdb] equals zero
        then
        tape-rewind( ) → result
        if result less than zero
            then
                exitproc
        endif
        else
            backspace-tape-files( )
            file-mgr-extension[pdb]-file-number[dcb-address]
                → nbr-files-to-move
            adjust-tape-position(nbr-files-to-move) → result
            if result less than zero
                then
                    exitproc
            endif
    endif
    establish-access-to-device( ) → result
```

```
            if result less than zero
                then
                        exitproc
            endif
            if write-protect-bit of file-mgr-open-mode[pdb] not equal to zero
              then
              if input-mode-bit of file-mgr-open-mode[pdb] not equal to zero
                  then
                  release-device( )
                  set input-mode-bit of channel-attributes[ccb-address]
              endif
              if output-mode-bit of file-mgr-open-mode[pdb] not equal to
                zero
                  then
                  set output-mode-bit of channel-attributes[ccb-address]
              endif
            endif
            set channel-open-bit of device-status[dcb-address]
            release-device( )
            set one to event-status[p]
            set one to result
endproc
```

2.5.4 Closing a Tape Channel

The procedure for closing a channel to a tape drive is depicted in module 2.5.3. This procedure is called from the routine CLOSE-DEVICE-CHANNEL, which is described in section 6.8.3. This routine is invoked by the system service request CLOSE.

If the tape was not protected when you close the channel, a file mark is written to indicate an end-of-file. A second file mark is written immediately after the first to indicate the current extent of data on the tape. The tape drive is then backspaced over the second file mark so that it is positioned at the end of the file just written. The tape drive is reset to available status.

Note that closing a tape channel leaves the tape positioned exactly at the location of the last I/O operation that was executed. This allows you to read or write successive files on the tape without having to reinitialize the tape each time it is accessed.

MODULE 2.5.3

```
procedure close-tape(→result)
      dcb-address → request-dcb-address[p]
      if channel-open-bit of device-status[dcb-address] equals zero
```

```
            then
                set er-channel-closed to event-status[p]
                set er-channel-closed to result
                exitproc
            endif
            if write-protect-bit of channel-attributes[ccb-address]
                                                    not equal to zero
                then
                    set one to request-size[p]
                    write-tape-file-mark( ) → result
                    if result less than zero
                        then
                            reset-tape( )
                            exitproc
                    endif
                    write-tape-file-mark( ) → result
                    if result less than zero
                        then
                            reset-tape( )
                            exitproc
                    endif
                    backspace-tape-records( ) → result
                    if result not equal to er-end-of-file
                        then
                            reset-tape( )
                            exitproc
                    endif
            endif

entry reset-tape:
    clear device-available-bit-of device-status[dcb-address]
    set one to event-status[p]
    set one to result
endproc
```

2.5.5 Tape Input/Output Operations

A magnetic tape consists of a linear sequence of files each composed of a linear
sequence of records. Once a tape is positioned at the beginning of a file, the user
must read through all intervening records (from record 0) in order to reach the
nth record. A tape may be accessed only by using a sequential access method
(see section 5.7). The sequential access method translates READ or WRITE requests into calls to the READ-TAPE and WRITE-TAPE routines.

Reading a Tape

_____

The procedure for reading a tape is depicted in module 2.5.4. This procedure accomplishes the following basic tasks:

1. It obtains control of the tape drive (i.e., access to the controller).
2. It attempts to read a record
3. It checks the end-of-device condition.
4. It releases access to the controller.

A special check is required for detecting the end-of-device because there may be no file mark recorded on the tape. On multireel files, a module would be called to switch tapes to the next reel. Most systems treat an end-of-device indication as an end-of-file condition and leave processing of it to the user. A case where the end-of-device error becomes important is when the user writes a file and dismounts the tape without the proper closing procedure. Since no file mark has been written, any procedure reading the tape would encounter garbage after processing all the valid records.

MODULE 2.5.4

```
procedure read-tape(→result)
    establish-access-to-device( ) → result
    if result less than zero
        then
            exitproc
    endif
    read-record( ) → result
    if result equals er-end-of-device
        then
            release-device( )
            set er-end-of-device to event-status[p]
            exitproc
    endif
    release-device( )
    event-status[p] → result
endproc
```

Reading a Record

_____

The procedure for reading a record from a tape file is depicted in module 2.5.5. On input, this is where the action is. The value of REQUEST-SIZE[P] indicates the number of words to be read from tape. This value is returned as the event value if the read operation was successful.

The procedure calls the tape-reading procedure to transfer data from the tape to memory. TAPE-READ is a small assembly language procedure containing the device-specific hardward instructions necessary to initiate the data transfer. If the result is less than zero, the word count was decremented properly to zero and a successful read was accomplished. If the result is greater than or equal to zero, the read operation was not successfully completed. The procedure must test for different error conditions, including:

1. **End-of-file.**   The number of words read prior to the file mark is lost (possibly). The system automatically sets up the parameters to continue reading of the next file. The last operation is not required but is performed for the convenience of the user.

2. **End-of-device.**   An end-of-device error code is returned to the user who has responsibility for further processing.

3. **Tape error condition.**   Any other type of tape error (such as a late frame or parity error) results in a general tape error. Since the tape error may be transient, the operation will be retried n times, where n is specified by RETRY-LIMIT (typically 10). If the number of retries is exhausted, the error is declared a permanent hardware error and the device is taken off-line. Only the simple treatment of a hardware error is shown here; a more complex treatment would involve a careful diagnosis of the myriad characteristics of the tape drive that are device specific.

Finally, assuming none of the three tests was true, the status of the event, set by TAPE-READ, is returned to the user. This status word may be the hardware status word maintained by the device controller. The reader is referred to the appropriate vendors' manuals for interpretation of this status word.

MODULE 2.5.5

```
procedure read-record(→result)
     set one to event-status[p]
     clear retries[dcb-address]
     request-size[p] → event-data[p]

read-restart:
     tape-read(request-data-address[p]) → result
     if result less than zero
          then
                event-status[p] → result
                exitproc
     endif
```

```
            sense-end-of-file( ) → result
            if result equals one
                  then
                        clear record-number[dcb-address]
                        increment file-number[dcb-address]
                        er-end-of-file → event-status[p]
                        event-status[p] → result
                        exitproc
            endif
            sense-end-of-device( ) → result
            if result equals one
                  then
                        er-end-of-device → event-status[p]
                        event-status[p] → result
                        exitproc
            endif
            sense-tape-error( ) → result
            if result equals one
                  then
                        if retries[dcb-address] less than retry-limit
                              then
                              increment retries[dcb-address]
                              backspace-record( )
                              goto read-restart
                              else
                              er-hardware → event-status[p]
                              take-device-offline( )
                              event-status[p] → result
                              exitproc
                        endif
            endif
            event-status[p] → result
            increment record-number[dcb-address]
    endproc
```

Writing a Tape

The procedure for writing a tape is depicted in module 2.5.6. This routine assumes that a "write ring" has been physically inserted into the tape. In a similar fashion, this procedure performs these basic operations:

1. It obtains control of the tape drive (i.e., access to the controller).
2. It attempts to write a record.

3.   It checks the end-of-device condition.
4.   It releases access to the controller.

As with the READ-TAPE routine, a separate check is made for the end-of-device condition. If this test becomes true, the system might call a routine to switch tape reels if a multireel file had been declared. Alternatively, the standard processing is to backspace the tape one record and report the error to the user.

MODULE 2.5.6

```
procedure write-tape(→result)
    establish-access-to-device( ) → result
    if result less than zero
        then
                exitproc
    endif
    write-record( ) → result
    if result equals er-end-of-device
        then
                set er-end-of-device to event-status[p]
                exitproc
    endif
    release-device( )
    event-status[p] → result
endproc
```

Writing a Record

The procedure for writing a tape record is shown in module 2.5.7. The structure of the routine is similar to that for reading a record; most comments from the previous discussion will apply here as well. The procedure TAPE-WRITE is an assembly language routine containing the actual hardware instructions necessary to initiate the transfer of data from memory to tape.

Since reading and writing are similar operations, rather than reproduce the previous discussion, we will use this opportunity to examine the instruction level events in writing a tape. When the TAPE-WRITE procedure is executed, the following steps are performed:

1.   The memory storage location where data reside is loaded into the tape drive controller's memory address register.
2.   The number of words to be written is loaded into the tape drive controller's word counter.

3. The desired transport is selected.
4. The WRITE function is loaded into the tape drive controller's command register.
5. A START command is issued to the controller, which initiates the WRITE sequence.
6. Once the WRITE command is initiated, a word is fetched from memory and stored in the memory data register.
7. The tape is moved past the heads and the two bytes of the word are written in successive tape frames.
8. The word counter is decremented by one.
9. Repeat of steps 6 through 8 until the word counter reaches zero.
10. After the last word is written, any additional bytes such as a cyclic redundancy check are written.
11. The busy flag is set to zero; the done flag is set to one and a program interrupt is generated.

A similar sequence is performed when executing the READ-TAPE operation. The reader is referred to the appropriate hardware manuals for a detailed explanation of tape commands and status words.

MODULE 2.5.7

```
procedure write-record(→result)
    set one to event-status[p]
    request-size[p] → event-data[p]
    clear retries[dcb-address]

write-restart:
    tape-write(request-data-address[p] → result
    if result less than zero
        then
                event-status[p] → result
                exitproc
    endif
    sense-end-of-device( ) → result
    if result equals one
        then
                set er-end-of-device to event-status[p]
                event-status[p] → result
                exitproc
    endif
    sense-tape-error( ) → result
    if result equals one
        then
```

```
                    if retries[dcb-address] is less than retry-limit
                        then
                        increment retries[dcb-address]
                        backspace-record( )
                        goto write-restart
                        else
                        set er-hardware to event-status[p]
                        take-device-offline( )
                        event-status[p] → result
                        exitproc
                    endif
            endif
        increment record-number[dcb-address]
        event-status[p] → result
endproc
```

Selecting the Retry Limit

The retry limit is the number of times that the device handler will attempt to execute a command before conceding failure. Selecting a retry limit takes some
practice and depends on the environment in which the system is used. Anyone
who has used a minicomputer extensively knows the frustration of attempting to
cancel a magnetic tape operation by hitting the "BREAK" key on the console
when the tape begins to rewind unexpectedly. Usually, this behavior is the result
of a hardware error; the device handler then begins several attempts to retry the
operation. For a particularly long tape record (e.g., several thousand words),
this can take several seconds. What the user notices, however, is that he or she
cannot stop the retry sequence. This occurs because the handler is executing
while the "BREAK" function is handled by the process manager—one level
above in the hierarchy. The user must wait until the retry sequence is complete.
Thus, selecting a small or large number of retries determines the amount of
time required before the user regains "control" of the device.

In a real-time system, the user wants to keep the number of retries small.
If an error occurs, the user wants to be notified immediately so that corrective
action can be taken. In a general-purpose environment, a larger number of
retries can be specified, especially if tape drives are heavily used and the
possibility of transient errors is greater.

2.5.6   Tape Control Functions

The functions invoked by the TAPE-FUNCTION command are properly known
as control functions because they affect the status or position of the tape. Each
of these functions is discussed in the following paragraphs.

Rewinding a Tape

The procedure for executing the REWIND function is depicted in module 2.5.8. The procedure is straightforward; it performs three steps: it obtains access to the tape controller; it executes the rewind procedure; and it releases the device.

Rewinding the tape is an explicit hardware function. Thus TAPE-REWIND is a procedure that sets up the REWIND command in the controller and initiates it. The hardware automatically senses the beginning-of-tape mark, stops the tape, and generates the interrupt.

MODULE 2.5.8

```
procedure rewind-tape(→result)
    establish-access-to-device( ) → result
    if result less than zero
        then
                exitproc
    endif
    tape-rewind( )
    release-device( )
    set event-status[p] to result
endproc
```

Skipping Tape Files

The procedures for skipping tape files forward and backward are shown in modules 2.5.9 and 2.5.10, respectively. The procedure for accomplishing either function is relatively the same. The skipping of files begins at the current position of the tape. Thus if you are positioned in the middle of the file, this file is considered as one of the files to be skipped. The device handler only recognizes the limits of a file by its end-of-file mark. As no information is kept in the file about its current number, the user may skip too many files and run off the end of the device.

In each case, the procedure obtains control of the device. The count specified in the system service request (stored in REQUEST-SIZE[P]) is the number of files to be skipped. On skipping forward, the procedure skips all records from its current position. After each record is skipped, the result is totaled in a DO loop. When a negative result occurs, either an end-of-file has been detected or some tape error has occurred. An end-of-file causes the decrementing of the skip counter (NUMBER-OF-FILES) and a repeat of the process. Any other error causes the device to be released, and the operation status (an error code) to be returned to the user.

On backspacing, one must test each execution of the backspace command to see if an end-of-file mark was encountered. This must be done because the EOF marker is really just another tape record, albeit one having a special interpretation. Any error except an end-of-file causes the device to be released and the error code to be returned to the user. At the end of the procedure, we skip forward one record over the the end-of-file we just crossed and position the tape at the first record of the file for reading or writing.

MODULE 2.5.9

```
procedure skip-tape-files(→result)
    establish-access-to-device( ) → result
    if result less than zero
        then
            exitproc
    endif
    request-size[p] → number-of-files
    clear request-size[p]
    while number-of-files greater than zero
        do
        set one to result
        while result greater than zero
            do
                skip-record( ) → result
            enddo
        if result not equal to er-end-of-file
            then
                release-device( )
                event-status[p] → result
                exitproc
        endif
        decrement number-of-files
        enddo
    release-device( )
    event-status[p] → result
endproc
```

MODULE 2.5.10

```
procedure backspace-tape-files(→result)
    establish-access-to-device( ) → result
    if result less than zero
        then
            exitproc
    endif
```

```
        request-size[p] → number-of-files
        set one to request-size[p]
        while number-of-files greater than or equal to zero
                do
                while true
                        do
                        backspace-record( ) → result
                        if result not equal to er-end-of-file
                                then
                                release-device( )
                                set result to event-status[p]
                                exitproc
                                else
                                if result equals er-end-of-file
                                        then
                                                exitdo
                                endif
                        endif
                        enddo
                decrement number-of-files
                enddo
        skip-record( )
        release-device( )
        set one to event-status[p]
        set one to result
endproc
```

Skipping Tape Records

You may request that tape records be skipped in a forward of backward sequence. Records may be skipped only within the context of the current tape file.
The count parameter specifies the number of records to skip. If an end-of-file is
reached in either direction, the function execution is aborted. The procedures
for executing these functions are depicted in modules 2.5.11 and 2.5.12, respectively. The algorithms are straightforward in that each performs the following
steps:

  Obtains control of the device
  Skips a record either forward or backward
  If an error results, aborts the function execution
  Decrements number of records to be skipped

Repeats the operation until the record count goes to zero
Releases the device

Two procedures, SKIP-RECORD and BACKSPACE-RECORD, which are depicted in modules 2.5.13 and 2.5.14, respectively, effect the actual tape movement. In SKIP-RECORD, the assembly procedure TAPE-SKIP (not shown) is called to set up the device registers and start the I/O operation. The procedure must check the end-of-device condition since there may not have been an end-of-file mark at the end of the tape. If an end-of-file is encountered, the file number is incremented by one and the record number is set to zero. Prior to exit, the record number that indicates the next record to be read is incremented by one.

In BACKSPACE-RECORD, the procedure first checks for the tape load point. If it is found, the file number and record number are set to zero prior to exit. Otherwise, an assembly language procedure, TAPE-BACKSPACE (not shown), is called to set up the device registers and start the I/O operation. The procedure checks for an end-of-file condition. If found, the record number is set to -1 to prevent further attempts to backspace. It is impossible to initialize the record number to a positive value because there is no way to keep track of the records in the preceding file.

MODULE 2.5.11

```
procedure skip-tape-records(→result)
    establish-access-to-device( ) → result
    if result less than zero
        then
            exitproc
    endif
    request-size[p] → number-of-records
    while number-of-records greater than zero
        do
            skip-record( ) → result
            if result less than zero
                then
                    release-device( )
                    event-status[p] → result
                    exitproc
            endif
            decrement number-of-records
        enddo
    release-device( )
    event-status[p] → result
endproc
```

MODULE 2.5.12

```
procedure backspace-tape-records(→result)
    establish-access-to-device( ) → result
    if result less than zero
        then
                exitproc
    endif
    request-size[p] → number-of-records
    while number-of-records greater than zero
        do
                backspace-record( ) → result
                if result less than zero
                    then
                            release-device( )
                            event-status[p] → result
                            exitproc
                endif
                decrement number-of-records
        enddo
        release-device( )
    event-status[p] → result
endproc
```

MODULE 2.5.13

```
procedure skip-record(→result)
    set one to event-status[p]
    tape-skip( ) → result
    if result less than zero
        then
                event-status[p] → result
    endif
    sense-end-of-device( ) → result
    if result equals one
        then
                er-end-of-device → event-status[p]
    endif
    sense-end-of-file( ) → result
    if result equals one
        then
                er-end-of-file → event-status[p]
                increment file-number[dcb-address]
                clear record-number[dcb-address]
```

```
            event-status[p] → result
            exitproc
      endif
      increment record-number[dcb-address]
      event-status[p] → result
endproc
```

MODULE 2.5.14

```
procedure backspace-record(→result)
      set one to event-status[p]
      sense-tape-load-point( ) → result
      if result equals one
            then
                  clear record-number[dcb-address]
                  clear file-number[dcb-address]
                  er-end-of-device → event-status[p]
                  event-status[p] → result
                  exitproc
      endif
      tape-backspace( ) → result
      sense-end-of-file( ) → result
      if result equals one
            then
                  decrement file-number[dcb-address]
                  set −1 to record-number[dcb-address]
                  er-end-of-file → event-status[p]
                  event-status[p] → result
                  exitproc
      endif
      decrement record-number[dcb-address]
      event-status[p] → result
endproc
```

Erasing a Tape

The tape erasure function effectively makes all data beyond the current point inaccessible (logically). It does not physically write zeros (or any other character) on the tape. To accomplish erasure, it writes an end-of-file mark at the current location and then backspaces over the end-of-file mark. Any subsequent READ commands will detect the end-of-file condition. The procedure for executing this function is depicted in module 2.5.15.

MODULE 2.5.15

```
procedure erase-tape(→result)
    set one to request-size[p]
    write-tape-file-mark( ) → result
    if result less than zero
        then
                exitproc
        else
                backspace-tape-records( )
    endif
    set one to result
endproc
```

Initializing a Tape

When a user mounts a tape on a drive, he or she must initialize the tape for access by the program. The procedure for initializing the tape is depicted in module 2.5.16. The tape is positioned at the load point by the hardware when the user presses the "ONLINE" and "LOAD" switches on the control panel. However, these conditions must be verified by the system itself.

The procedure locates the DCB for the tape drive. If no DCB is found, the specified drive has not been configured in the system and an error code will be

MODULE 2.5.16

```
procedure initialize-tape(→result)
    user-device-name-to-dcb(request-map[p],file-name(pdb))
                                                      → dcb-address
    dcb-address → request-dcb-address[p]
    if dcb-address equals zero
        then
                set er-device-name to event-status[p]
                set er-device-name to result
                exitproc
    endif
    if device-available-bit of device-status[dcb-address] equals zero
        then
                unit-message(em-online, device-name[dcb-address])
                set er-unavailable to event-status[p]
                set er-unavailable to result
                exitproc
```

```
        endif
        request(tape-controller)
        select-tape(drive-number[dcb-address])
        sense-tape-ready(drive-number[dcb-address]) → result
        if result less than zero
            then
                    release(tape-controller)
                    unit-message(em-not-ready, device-name[dcb-address])
                    set er-offline to event-status[p]
                    set er-offline to result
                    exitproc
            else
                    rewind-tape( )
                    clear file-number[dcb-address]
                    clear record-number[dcb-address]
                    clear reel-number[dcb-address]
                    release(tape-controller)
                    release(drive-number[dcb-address])
                    set device-available-bit of device-status[dcb-address]
                    set one to event-status[p]
                    set one to result
        endif
endproc
```

returned to the caller. The procedure checks the device available bit to determine if the tape is on-line. This bit is set when the tape drive channel is opened. If the bit is not set, an error message is printed on the operator's console. Next, the procedure requests access to the tape controller. The physical drive is then selected by the controller and checked for a ready condition. If the tape is not ready, a message is printed on the operator's console. Otherwise, the tape status is initialized in the DCB and the device available bit is set to indicate that the user may access the tape.

Releasing a Tape

Once a user has finished processing a tape, it must be released by the user so that it may be assigned to other users. The procedure for releasing a tape is depicted in module 2.5.17. The user releases the tape by specifying its symbolic name. An invalid device name or a device off-line condition requires no further processing. Otherwise, the procedure obtains access to the physical drive and the tape controller. The tape is rewound and the device is taken off-line. The tape controller is then released.

MODULE 2.5.17

```
procedure release-tape(→result)
    user-device-name-to-dcb(request-map[p],file-name[pdb])
                                                    → dcb-address
        dcb-address → request-dcb-address[p]
        if dcb-address equals zero
            then
                    er-device-name → event-status[p]
                    er-device-name → result
                    exitproc
        endif
        if device-available-bit of device-status[dcb-address] equals zero
            then
                    er-offline → event-status[p]
                    er-offline → result
                    exitproc
        endif
        request(drive-number[dcb-address])
        request(tape-controller)
        take-device-offline( )
        release(tape-controller)
        set one to event-status[p]
        set one to result
endproc
```

Writing an End-of-File Marker

The last function that you may request is the writing of an end-of-file mark on the tape. This signifies the end of a sequence of physical records. The EOF mark itself is treated as another physical tape record. The procedure for executing this function is shown in module 2.5.18. It performs the following steps:

> Obtains access to the device
> Calls the hardware level procedure to write the tape mark
> Checks the status of the operation
> Releases access to the device

MODULE 2.5.18

```
procedure write-tape-file-mark(→result)
    establish-access-to-device( ) → result
    if result less than zero
        then
                exitproc
```

```
        endif
        write-eof( ) → result
        if result equals er-end-of-device
            then
                    set er-end-of-device to event-status[p]
                    exitproc
        endif
        release-device( )
        event-status[p] → result
endproc
```

MODULE 2.5.19

```
procedure write-eof(→result)
    set one to event-status[p]
    tape-write-eof( ) → result
    if result less than zero
        then
                result → event-status[p]
                exitproc
    endif
    sense-end-of-device( ) → result
    if result equals one
        then
                set er-end-of-device to event-status[p]
    endif
    sense-end-of-file( ) → result
    if result equals one
        then
                event-status[p] → result
                clear record-number[dcb-address]
                increment file-number(dcb-address]
                exitproc
    endif
    sense-tape-error( ) → result
    if result equals one
        then
                take-device-offline( )
                er-hardware → event-status[p]
    endif
    event-status[p] → result
    clear record-number[dcb-address]
    increment file-number[dcb-address]
endproc
```

2.5.7   Utility Procedures

A number of utility procedures are required to support the execution of each of the independent tape functions. These procedures are discussed in the following paragraphs.

Establishing Device Access

The tape controller normally can handle up to eight drives, although only one of the drives may be operated at one time. When your process is ready to execute a tape function, it must signal the controller to select the appropriate drive for the operation. However, access to the tape controller and the drive itself must be mediated in a multiprocessing environment. The procedure ESTABLISH-AC-CESS-TO-DEVICE accomplishes this function.

The procedure first checks to see if the device is available by examining the status word in the DCB. If the device available bit is not set, the device has not been initialized. At this point, your process is notified that the device is unavailable. A wait bit in the channel-attributes word dictates whether or not you wait for the device to become available.

Once past this hurdle, your process requests access to a specific drive. As the controller handles only one drive at a time, multiple requests are enqueued on a resource semaphore associated with each drive. When a drive is free, the pro-

MODULE 2.5.20

```
procedure establish-access-to-device(→result)
    request-dcb-address[p] → dcb-address
    request-ccb-address[p] → ccb-address
    if device-available-bit of device-status[dcb-address] equals zero
         then
             if wait-bit of channel-attributes[ccb-address] equals zero
                 then
                     er-unavailable → event-status[p]
                     event-status[p] → result
                     exitproc
             endif
    request(drive-rs-address[dcb-address])
    request(tape-controller)
    select-tape(drive-number[dcb-address])
    set one to event-status[p]
    set one to result
endproc
```

cess must gain access to the tape controller. The controller is also protected by a resource semaphore. Once the process has access to the controller and the tape drive, it issues the tape select command, which locks the controller into the drive. The drive is now able to execute hardware operations.

Releasing a Drive

Once the particular tape operation has been completed, it releases the tape drive to allow other processes access to it. First, the tape controller is released to the next process on the queue. The drive is released to the next user on the queue. The latter step may occur if the tape drive was taken off-line as a result of the previous request.

MODULE 2.5.21

```
procedure release-device
    release(tape-controller)
    if device-available-bit of device-status[dcb-address]
                                                not equal to zero
        then
                release(drive-rs-address[dcb-address])
        endif
endproc
```

Taking a Drive Off-Line

A tape drive may be taken off-line for several reasons. The most common reason is that tape operations are complete and the tape can be dismounted. Another reason for taking a drive off-line occurs when the I/O retry sequence fails and system operator intervention is required. The procedure for taking a drive off-line is depicted in module 2.5.22. When a drive is taken off-line, parameters describing the tape drive status are set to zero in the DCB. The tape is rewound to the load point and a message printed on the operator's console.

Adjusting a Tape's Position

When you open a tape file, the current position may be different from the one requested. The OPEN module must adjust the tape position to the proper file. Since the tape may be moved either forward or backward during this maneuver, a small utility procedure (depicted in module 2.5.23) is used to direct this operation.

MODULE 2.5.22

```
procedure take-device-offline
    request-dcb-address[p] → dcb-address
    if device-available-bit of device-status[dcb-address]
                                                        not equal to zero
        then
            clear device-available-bit of device-status[dcb-address]
            select-tape(drive-number[dcb-address])
            rewind-tape(drive-number[dcb-address])
            clear file-number[dcb-address]
            clear record-number[dcb-address]
            clear reel-number[dcb-address]
            unit-message(em-released, device-name[dcb-address])
        endif
endproc
```

MODULE 2.5.23

```
procedure adjust-tape-position(relative-position, →result)
    relative-position → request-size[p]
    if relative-position greater than zero
        then
            skip-tape-files( )
            if event-status[p] equals er-end-of-file
                then
                set one to event-status[p]
            endif
        else
        negate request-size[p]
            if request-size[p] not equal to zero
                then
                        backspace-tape-files( )
            endif
    endif
    event-status[p] → result
endproc
```

2.6 MASS STORAGE MANAGEMENT

Since the earliest days of computers, it seems that programs have always followed
Parkinson's Law. That is, the programs have always exceeded the memory
available to them. System designers have met this challenge by finding new ways

to store information. In chapter 4 we explore the major approaches to handling this problem. Data storage over the long term did not receive much attention until computers were applied to data processing and file management tasks. Mass storage devices became a necessity and these devices have evolved in complexity over the past two decades. Today, when we refer to mass storage devices we almost always mean disk devices.

Throughout the evolution of computers, hardware has always progressed faster than software design. Improved hardware designs offer exciting advantages to future systems designers. Let us cite two examples. First, many systems treat disks as surface-mode devices, a legacy from single-platter systems. In this mode, software organizes files sequentially on one surface at a time. In fact, since the head assembly moves as a unit, the software could improve access time by arranging files to scan more than one surface at a time.

A second example concerns the multiplicity of mass storage devices—both by number and type—which may exist in a system. Many systems regard the individual mass storage devices as separate entities. Thus directories (see chapter 6) are mapped to disk drives on a one-for-one basis. This approach forces the user to be cognizant of the number and type of drives in the system. In some applications, attention to such detail can waste valuable development time and address space particularly where programmers let it be an overriding concern. Of course, the alternative is to have a global directory spanning all devices. However, loss of the directory device implies total system loss and seems to preclude demountable devices.

Today, many systems are beginning to emphasize a unified approach to mass storage management. Their objective is to focus on the efficient and effective management of mass storage. Each disk is considered as a one-dimensional array of records. For example, on the DEC RL-01 disk drive, there are 10,220 blocks of 512 bytes each. The record size is chosen as the smallest burst of data that can be addressed by the controller at any time. Records are thus numbered from zero to 10219; the disk controller translates the record number to track and block indices. Of course, this approach entails certain restrictions: (1) that the record size should be an integer multiple of the smallest disk sector size, and (2) that to accommodate different transfer rates of different devices, the memory should be able to buffer varying multiples of the basic sector size.

Some Considerations in Mass Storage Management

A unified approach to mass storage management needs to assume certain basic properties, including:

1.   Each device has the same record size, R.
2.   Each device is treated in a uniform manner; differences are isolated in the lowest levels of the device handler.

3. On all devices, the first record is reserved for special purposes (e.g., the boot program and device identifier).

4. A directory of names is allocated on the medium; the directory varies with the size of the device and average file size.

5. A table or vector is provided for tracking available space on the device.

6. A system area may be allocated and indicated in the directory which is subtracted from the space available to the user and can be addressed only by the OS.

We have not observed all these properties in defining our mass storage handlers. However, you will find sufficient hooks on which to hang almost any type of mass storage management system. In this section we address the design of the disk device handler. In section 2.8 we consider the problem of allocating/deallocating space on a mass storage device. You should also refer to chapter 6 for discussions on directories.

2.6.1   The Disk Control Table

The structure of the DCB has been discussed in section 2.1.2. The figure depicting the DCB is reprinted here as figure 2.3. Several features differ from the general discussion of the DCB presented in section 2.1.3.

In the disk handler, only three operations are allowed: READ, WRITE, and UPDATE. Each of these operations has an associated sequence table which describes the steps necessary to complete the request. These tables are depicted in figures 2.4 through 2.6.

READ-TABLE	The simplest operation is to read the disk and complete the request processing.
WRITE-TABLE	When the disk is written, the data are verified by performing read-after-write sequence.
UPDATE-TABLE	The disk is read and the specific words in the block are updated. The disk block is rewritten to the disk and verified.

The next entry that is different is the device record mask. At the device handler level, no buffering is performed for the disk. Rather, any buffering, whether user specified or system temporary, is performed by the I/O manager. Thus the I/O buffer entries are both zero. This is because the memory address supplied to the disk handler may be the address in system or user space. The record mask is set to a value of 255 in order to mask off the low-order device address bits and calculate the block number.

The other major difference is that the disk handler queue is self-contained. The ENTER-INTO-QUEUE, REMOVE-FROM-QUEUE, and EXTRACT-

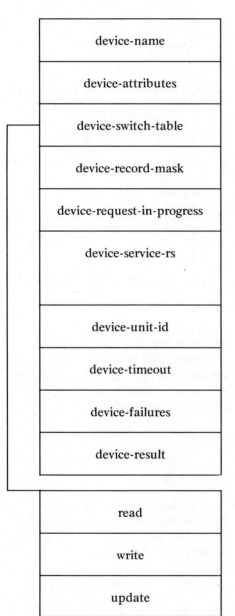

Figure 2.3   Structure of mass storage device control block.

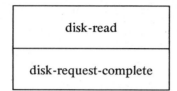

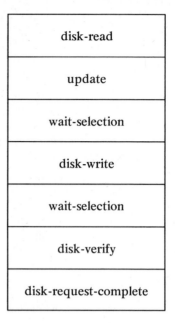

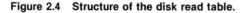

Figure 2.4   Structure of the disk read table.

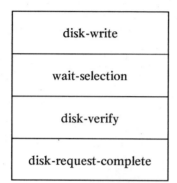

Figure 2.6   Structure of the disk up-
Figure 2.5   Structure of the disk write table.   date table.

FROM-QUEUE entries may or may not be used, depending on the method for sorting disk requests. The disk service queue is double-linked so that if a disk queue entry points to itself, it is readily apparent that it is the only entry in the queue. Although this adds a little bit to system overhead, it offers an extra capability for searching the queue to insert the next request.

2.6.2   The Disk Driver

The disk driver is a continuous process. Once initiated, it executes any requests for disk service that it encounters on the disk queue. The disk driver is normally terminated only when the operator initiates a shutdown procedure of the computer system. The disk driver process is depicted in module 2.6.1.

When the disk driver receives control, it initializes each disk driver that has been configured in the system. Disk initialization generally involves clearing the device state and declaring the device on-line, initializing device-dependent parameters in the DCB, and clearing the device registers.

At completion of initialization, the process suspends itself by calling the scheduler. However, the process control block (PCB) is retained for use by the interrupt handler.

MODULE 2.6.1

```
procedure disk-driver
     for disk-id from 0 to number-of-disks - 1
          do
                    disk-list[disk-id] → dcb-address
                    clear device-state of device-attributes[dcb-address]
                    clear device-request-in-progress[dcb-address]
                    clear device-timeout[dcb-address]
                    clear device-result [dcb-address]
                    disk-failure-count → device-failures[dcb-address]
                    clear-disk(disk-id)
          enddo
     p → disk-process-address
     scheduler( )
endproc
```

2.6.3 Disk Interrupt Processing

The processing of a disk interrupt occurs in two segments: the first reads the status of the disk and re-enables interrupts; and the second processes the interrupt for the user. These routines are depicted in modules 2.6.2 and 2.6.3, respectively.

Disk Interrupt

This procedure, shown in module 2.6.2, is entered directly from the interrupt handler after a disk interrupt has been detected. The procedure saves the value of the program counter and calls INTERRUPT-START to save the state of the control processor. The status information for the disk request is read from the disk controller registers into the appropriate memory locations and the interrupt is processed.

MODULE 2.6.2

```
procedure disk-interrupt
     pc → pcsave
     interrupt-start( )
     disk-process-address → p
     address(disk-device-table) → dcb-address
     read-disk-status( ) → reply
     read-last-disk-address( ) → last-disk-address
     process-interrupt( )
endproc
```

Process-Interrupt

This routine, depicted in module 2.6.3, is called by the interrupt handler to simulate an interrupt. In fact, the interrupt has already occurred and the system has been enabled for the next interrupt. By deferring processing slightly, this approach enhances the real-time service aspects of the OS. Note that all information required to process the interrupt has been saved in the current process control block by INTERRUPT-START.

The sequence of events in processing an interrupt is straightforward.

1. Retrieve the current process address from the DCB. A subprocess is created to execute each disk I/O function, thus allowing a PCB to be dedicated solely for storing device-specific information.

2. The next request, which is a PCB, is fetched from the queue in anticipation of initiating the operation.

3. If a disk error has occurred, a message is printed to the process that was interrupted.

4. If the current request is zero, we return to the process that was interrupted.

5. The next step is to analyze the disk status for the current request. The disk error bits are extracted from the device controller status word. If a mechanical failure of the disk has occurred, the device is marked off-line and the time of failure is stored in the DCB. Otherwise, the error is assumed to be a hardware error consisting of either an abnormal status or a parity error. HARDWARE-ERROR is invoked to attempt a retry of the current request.

6. If the DEVICE-RESULT entry is less than zero, a successful request occurred. The next step in the function sequence is executed. Note that DEVICE-RESULT greater than or equal to one implies that the current request is being retried by the disk handler.

7. Otherwise, a timeout error is assumed to have occurred and HARDWARE-ERROR is called to process it.

MODULE 2.6.3

```
procedure process-interrupt
      pcsave → interrupt-return
      device-request-in-progress[dcb-address] → device-request
      next-cb[device-request] → next-request
      if device-error-code not equal to zero
          then
                  print-error( )
      endif
```

```
    if device-request equals zero
        then
                return-from-interrupt(interrupt-return)
    endif
    and(reply, disk-error-mask) → disk-status
    if disk-status not equal to zero
        then
                clear device-result[dcb-address]
                if disk-mechanical-failure-bit of reply is 1
                    then
                        set device-offline in device-attributes[dcb-address]
                        elapsed-time( ) → device-timeout[dcb-address]
                        return-from-interrupt(interrupt-return)
                endif
                request-device-data[device-request] → disk-io-buffer
                if disk-abnormal-bit of reply not equal to zero
                    then
                            hardware-error(er-abnormal)
                    else
                            hardware-error(er-parity)
                endif
    endif
    if device-result[dcb-address] less than zero
        then
                execution-switch( )
    endif
    clear device-result[dcb-address]
    hardware-error(er-timeout)
endproc
```

Disk-Request-Complete

The last step in each of the disk function sequences consists of cleaning up the current request. The procedure for accomplishing this chore is depicted in module 2.6.4. The procedure sets the number of disk failures into the DCB. It releases the current request from the disk request queue. An entry is also provided in this routine to accommodate cleanup after processing a disk error.

The disk process then examines the status of the disk request queue. If the queue is empty, it clears the current request in the DCB and returns to the interrupted process. Otherwise, it proceeds to select the next request. At this point, of course, we need to know the address of the next request as we have already released the current request's PCB. That is why the address of the next request was fetched in PROCESS-INTERRUPT. We could not predict what the next function step would be, that is, whether we would have to retry the request or proceed to the next one. Thus, in anticipation of this routine, we fetch the next request.

MODULE 2.6.4

```
procedure disk-request-complete
      disk-failure-count → device-failures[dcb-address]

entry disk-request-error:
      release-request(disk-request)

entry select-request:
      if queue-count[dcb-address] not equal to zero
            then
                    disk-select(next-request)
      endif
      clear device-request-in-progress[dcb-address]
      return-from-interrupt(interrupt-return)
endproc
```

2.6.4 Interface from the I/O Manager

The process for executing an I/O function to the disk involves setting up the appropriate parameters in the PCB. Then the PCB must be inserted into the disk request queue. Three modules provide the mechanism for initializing these parameters. Their addresses are stored in the device switch table in the DCB.

Setting Up the Read/Write Function

The steps to execute a read or write function share many common elements after the initial function is determined. The routine for setting up the read function, READ-DISK, is depicted in module 2.6.5 It also contains the common code for the write and update functions.

At the beginning of each routine, the procedure locates the address of the DCB for the specified unit. It then locates the address of the sequence table that directs how a particular function is to be executed.

One entry point common to the read/write functions is labeled READ-OR-WRITE-DISK. This section of code copies the arguments from the procedure list into the PCB. A second entry point, common to all three functions, is noted by the label ISSUE-DISK-IO. At this point, the request is inserted into the disk request queue. The effect of INSERT-REQUEST is to prevent further execution of the process by removing it from the ready-to-run queue. When the disk

I/O function is complete, the status of the request is returned as the result of the procedure.

MODULE 2.6.5

```
procedure read-disk(map, data, size, device-address, unit-number,
                                                      → result)
     address(disk-device-table[unit-number]) → dcb-address
     address(disk-read-table) → request-execution-address[p]
     goto read-or-write-disk

entry write-disk(map, data, size, device-address, unit-number,
                                                      → result)
     address(disk-device-table[unit-number] → dcb-address
     address(disk-write-table) → request-execution-address[p]
     goto read-or-write-disk

entry update-disk(device-address, offset, unit-number)
     address(disk-device-table[unit-number]) → dcb-address
     address(disk-update-table) → request-execution-address[p]
     clear user-map
     offset → request-update-displacement[p]
     device-address → request-device-address[p]
     goto issue-disk-io

read-or-write-disk:
     address(data) → request-device-data[p]
     size → request-number-words[p]
     extract user-map from map
     device-address → request-device-address[p]

issue-disk-io:
     insert-request(dcb-address)
     event-status[p] → result
endproc
```

2.6.5   Selecting and Executing a Disk Request

The disk handler schedules access to the disk as follows. First, when a request is inserted in the disk request queue, it is sorted by the device address. Second, since the structure of the disk request queue changes frequently, the disk handler attempts to optimize usage by selecting the request that minimizes arm movement. The procedure for selecting and executing a disk request is shown in module 2.6.6. It is divided into three parts to make its description easier to follow.

Disk Select

The initial part of the disk selection procedure determines the next request to be executed by the disk handler. The routine is entered with the address of the next request in the disk request queue. The current address of the disk head is read from the disk controller registers, and used to compute the number of words the head would have to move in order to satisfy the request. If DISK-SKIP-COUNT equals zero, the head is properly positioned and the request is initiated.

Otherwise, the routine searches the disk request queue in an attempt to locate a request that minimizes the disk head movement. This is an example of a disk-head scheduling algorithm known as shortest-seek-time-first (SSTF). It is most effective when the length of the disk request queue is short and the dispersion of disk head requests covers the entire disk.

MODULE 2.6.6

```
procedure disk-select(next-request)
    request-sort-key[next-request] → request-previous-key
    read-disk-address(disk-id) → disk-address
    disk-address - request-previous-key → disk-skip-space
    if disk-skip-space equals zero
        then
            goto start-request
    endif
    while next-cb[next-request] not equal to zero
    do
    request-sort-key[next-request] - request-previous-key
                                        → request-previous-key
    request-previous-key - disk-skip-space → disk-skip-space
    if disk-skip-space equals zero
        then
            goto start-request
    endif
    increment disk-skip-space
    if disk-skip-space less than zero
        then
            next-cb[next-request] → next-request
    endif
    enddo
endproc
```

Starting a Request

This code sets the current request address into the DCB.

Selecting the Next Instruction Step

This code selects the next step to be executed for a specific operation. The I/O function sequence tables were depicted in figures 2.4 through 2.6. Each table contains a list of addresses describing how a particular operation is to be executed. At EXECUTION-SWITCH, the procedure selects the next routine for execution.

Functional Routines

There is a functional routine for each possible step in an I/O function sequence. The first of these is READ-DEVICE. It retrieves the device identifier from the DCB and sets the transfer mode of the disk controller to read status. It also clears the last bit of REQUEST-LAST-OPCODE to indicate a normal read from the disk.

Starting the Device

In this code section, the procedure sets up parameters common to all device operations. The real-time clock status is read and stored in the timeout word. This word is used to determine if the device exceeds the expected execution time for the operation. The parameters that are stored in the disk controller registers are the device address from/to which data are to be retrieved/stored, the memory address from/to which data are to be transferred, and the number of words to be transferred.

The pointer to the current step in the I/O function sequence is incremented by one. Finally, the I/O function is initiated by sending a command to the device controller. When the operation is finished, program control returns here and the calling process is notified.

```
start-request:
    next-request → disk-request
    disk-request → device-request-in-progress[dcb-address]

execution-switch:
    request-execution-address[disk-request] → next-function
    call(next-function)
```

```
read-device:
     disk-unit-id[dcb-address] → device-id
     set-read-mode(device-id)

read-or-write-device:
     clear bit0 of request-last-opcode[disk-request]

start-device:
     read-clock( ) → device-timeout[dcb-address]
     request-device-address[disk-request] → device address
     set-device-address(device-address)
     request-device-data[disk-request] → first-memory-address
     set-memory-address(first-memory-address)
     request-transfer-size[disk-request] → word-count
     set-device-count(word-count)
     increment request-execution-address[disk-request]
     start-io-operation(device-id)
     exitproc
```

Writing to a Disk

This section sets up a write operation for the disk. It retrieves the device identifier from the current DCB and sets the transfer mode in the disk controller to
write mode. It then branches to common processing code.

Verifying the Device

This section retrieves the device identifier from the DCB. It sets the transfer
mode of the disk controller to read mode. Bit 0 of REQUEST-LAST-OPCODE
is set to one to indicate that no transfer to the user is expected. The system
verifies that the correct data has been written through a read-after-write
mechanism.

Wait Selection

This section forces the current process to yield access to the disk controller. This
allows another process to initiate an I/O operation.

```
write-device:
     disk-unit-id[dcb-address] → device-identifier
     set-write-mode(device-identifier)
     goto read-or-write-device
```

verify-device:
    disk-unit-id[dcb-address] → device-identifier
    set-read-mode(device-identifier)
    set bit0 of request-last-opcode[disk-request]
    goto start-device

wait-selection:
    increment request-execution-address[disk-request]
    goto select-request
endproc

2.6.6   Disk Request Queue Management

The disk request queue is a list of processes awaiting service by the disk handler. The disk request queue is ordered by increasing disk address. This ordering is extremely responsive to the SSTF algorithm.

The disk I/O operation is a two-stage process. In the first stage, described in section 2.6.5, the parameters for the I/O operation are validated and stored in the PCB of the subprocess that is responsible for executing a given I/O request. Each request is sorted into the disk request queue. INSERT-REQUEST serves as the interface between the I/O manager and the interrupt handler. In this section the two procedures responsible for maintaining the disk service queue are described.

Inserting a Request for Service

INSERT-REQUEST, depicted in module 2.6.7, sorts a disk service request into the disk request queue. It first checks to see if the disk is available for an operation. If the disk is off-line (i.e., unavailable) a timeout error is returned to the caller. The calling process is reactivated with an error code as the event status (see ISSUE-DISK-IO in module 2.6.5).

If the disk is available, the current program counter is stored on the process stack so that execution can resume after the I/O operation is completed. The event status is initialized in anticipation of a successful execution, the disk address is masked to yield a sort key by which the request is inserted into the disk request queue, and the retry count is set to zero since the request is newly initiated.

If the number of requests in the queue is zero, the operation is started immediately. That is, the disk is presumed to be idle. The process links are set so that the queue will be empty when the current process completes execution. This situation may change if another request is inserted while the current operation is in progress.

If the queue is not empty, the list of requests (actually, PCBs linked together) is searched for the appropriate location in which to insert the request. After the insertion is completed, the procedure exits to the scheduler to select the next process for execution. The subprocess has been "blocked" on the disk request queue awaiting service.

MODULE 2.6.7

```
procedure insert-request(dcb-address)
     if device-status of device-attributes[dcb-address]
                                                        equals device-offline
          then
                set er-timeout to event-status[p]
                exitproc
     endif
     get requesting process's PCB → ptemp
     save pc on process stack in PCB
     set one to event-status[p]
     request-device-address[ptemp] & disk-location-mask
                                              → request-sort-key[ptemp]
     clear request-retry[ptemp]
     if queue-count[dcb-address] equals zero
          then
                decrement queue-count[dcb-address]
                ptemp → next-cb[ptemp]
                ptemp → previous-cb[ptemp]
                ptemp → queue-start[dcb-address]
                goto start-request
     endif
     decrement queue-count[dcb-address]
     queue-start[dcb-address] → device-request

next-request:
     if request-sort-key[ptemp] less than
                                         request-sort-key[device-request]
          then
                ptemp → queue-start[dcb-address]
                device-request → next-cb[ptemp]
                ptemp → previous-cb[device-request]
          else
                next-cb[device-request] → device-request
                goto next-entry
     endif
     scheduler( )
endproc
```

Releasing a Disk Request

RELEASE-REQUEST, depicted in module 2.6.8, is called from the interrupt handler at the completion of an disk I/O operation. It removes the current request from the disk request queue and increments the queue counter. The subprocess removed from the queue is reactivated. The bulk of this procedure is concerned with adjusting the disk request queue links.

MODULE 2.6.8

```
procedure release-request(request-address)
     next-cb[request-address] → request-temp
     if request-address equals request-temp
          then
                  clear queue-start[dcb-address]
                  clear queue-count[dcb-address]
          else
                  previous-cb[request-address[ → address-temp
                  address-temp → previous-cb[request-temp]
                  request-temp → next-cb[address-temp]
                  if request-address equals queue-start[dcb-address]
                       then
                                  request-temp → queue-start[dcb-address]
                  endif
                  increment queue-count[dcb-address]
     endif
     activate(request-address)
endproc
```

2.6.7 Disk Service Utilities

The disk is usually the most crucial element in a small computer system. Since memory is usually small, parts of the OS are stored on the disk. A small OS will do well to maintain a constant check on the health of the disk drive, particularly if only one is available. One standard way of performing this validation is to execute, at a fixed interval, a status check process which monitors the health of the disk. The status check procedure is called by the timeout process (see section 7.7.2). This section describes the procedures used to monitor the status of the disk drive.

Checking the Disk Status

The procedure for checking the status of the disk is depicted in module 2.6.9. When this procedure is called, it performs a status check on each disk drive configured in the system. The status checks are:

1. Sense if the disk is "powered up" and set the on-line/off-line status accordingly.
2. Sense if the disk is ready to receive an I/O function.
3. Check to see if the disk has timing problems leading to a disk timeout condition.
4. Sense if the disk controller is ready to process interrupts.
5. If the routine encounters an erroneous condition, clear the disk hardware registers and select the next request for execution.

Obviously, status checks depend on the hardware characteristics of the disk controller and the individual disk drives. This procedure is intended to give you only the flavor for checking the conditions of generic disk drives.

MODULE 2.6.9

```
procedure disk-status-check
      for disk-id from 0 to number-of-disks - 1
            do
                  disk-list[disk-id] → dcb-address
                  sense-power( )
                  device-request-in-progress[dcb-address]
                                                      → device-request
                  sense-disk-ready( ) → result
                  if result equals one
                        then
                              goto check-ready-controller
                  endif
                  if device-request equals zero
                        then
                              set er-hardware to disk-error-code
                              goto get-disk-status
                  endif
                  waiting(disk-io-timeout) → result
                  if result greater than or equal to zero
                        then


      check-disk-status:
                        set one to device-result[dcb-address]
```

```
      get-disk-status:
                        set-read-mode(device-id)
                        read-disk-status( ) → disk-reply
                        read-memory-address( ) → disk-last-core
                        clear-disk(device-id)
                        process-interrupt( )
              endif
              exitproc

   check-ready-controller:
              if device-status of device-attributes[dcb-address]
                        equals device-ready
                  then
                      if device-request equals zero
                        then
                            goto restart-disk
                      endif
                      waiting(disk-io-timeout) → result
                      if result greater than or equal to zero
                        then
                            set er-no-interrupt to disk-error-code
                            goto restart-disk
                      endif
              endif
              waiting(disk-result-time) → result
              if result greater than or equal to zero
                  then
                      set device-startup of device-attributes[dcb-
                        address]
                      if disk-request not equal to zero
                        then
                            goto check-device-status
                      endif

   restart-disk:
              if queue-count[dcb-address] not equal to zero
                  then
                        queue-start[dcb-address] → device-request
                        next-cb[disk-request] → next-request
                        clear-disk(device-id)
                        disk-select( )
              endif
              endif
          endif
      enddo
endproc
```

Sensing Disk Power

A sample routine that senses whether or not the disk is "powered up" is depicted in module 2.6.10. This routine will restart the disk if it determines that it
is powered up. Restarting implies that the disk is in the "startup" mode and on
the next pass should enter into a ready state. If successive tries (noted by DISK-
DOWN-COUNTER) do not find the disk ready, it is declared off-line and an error message is printed on the operator's console

MODULE 2.6.10

```
procedure sense-power
        sense-disk-power(disk-id) → power-status
        if power-status equals one
            then
                    goto disk-running
        endif
        clear-disk(disk-id)

sense-again:
        sense-disk-power(disk-id) → power-status
        if power-status equals one
            then
                    goto wait-and-restart-disk
        endif
        if device-status equals device-offline
            then
                    read-clock( ) → time
                    time - power-msg-frequency → result
                    if result less than zero
                        then
                                exitproc
                    endif
                    increment disk-down-counter
                    if disk-down-counter less than zero
                        then
                        elapsed-time( ) → device-timeout[dcb-address]
                        exitproc
                    endif
            endif
        else
            set device-offline to device-status
                                    of device-attributes[dcb-address]
        endif
        elapsed-time( ) → device-timeout[dcb-address]
```

```
        set er-offline to disk-error-code
        error-message(disk-error-code)
        clear disk-error-code
        exitproc
disk-running:
    if device-status of device-attributes[dcb-address]
                                        equals device-offline
        then
wait-and-restart-disk:
            set device-startup to device-status
                                of device-attributes[dcb-address]
            elapsed-time( ) → device-timeout[dcb-address]
        endif
endproc
```

Processing Hardware Errors

_____

When a hardware error is detected during execution of a disk I/O function, the OS must take steps to ensure that system integrity is maintained. Most systems will attempt to retry a disk I/O function a fixed number of times under the assumption that most hardware errors are transient faults.

In the disk handler, this involves "backing up" the execution sequence to retry a particular execution step. On update, we must specifically back up to the write step before verifying the contents of the disk.

If after a given number of retries, the I/O function results in repeated failures, the current process is released with the hardware error code set as the event status. The next request in the disk request queue is then selected for execution.

MODULE 2.6.11

```
procedure hardware-error(error-code)
    error-code → disk-error-code
    request-device-address[disk-request] → request-address
    disk-unit-id[dcb-address] → unit-number
    error-message(disk-error-code)
    clear disk-error-code
    increment request-retry[disk-request]
    if request-retry[disk-request] equals disk-retries
        then
                disk-error-code → event-status[disk-request]
                if device-failures[dcb-address] greater than or
                                            equal to one
        then
```

```
                    queue-start[dcb-address] → current-request
                    current-request → temp-request
                    next-cb[current-request] → next-request
                    if current-request not equal to disk-request
                         then
                         set er-timeout to
                                        event-status[current-request]
                         release-request(current-request)
                    endif
                    while true
                         do
                             if next-request not equal to
                                temp-request
                                  then
                                  next-request → current-request
                                  else
                                        exitdo
                              endif
                         enddo
                    disk-request-error( )
              endif
              if request-last-opcode[disk-request] less than zero
                    then
                         set − 3 to opcode
                    else
                         set − 1 to opcode
              endif
              increment request-execution-address[disk-request] by
                                                        opcode
              select-request( )
         endif
endproc
```

2.7 MEMORY MANAGEMENT UNIT

In most minicomputer systems, the memory management unit (MMU) is implemented as either a base register machine or a paging machine. The MMU is
usually treated as a peripheral device, although it is accessible only to the OS.
Moreover, the MMU is optional on most minicomputer systems. It usually consists of one or two circuit boards inserted into the computer chassis and coupled
to the memory system by ribbon cables. In this text we have generally assumed
the existence of a page-oriented MMU. In this section we discuss some of the
generic routines necessary to handling this device. The reader is urged to con-

sult the manufacturers' hardware manuals for the specific characteristics of the MMU.

2.7.1   Memory Management Databases

The primary database associated with the MMU is known as the map table. The map table defines the mapping (relationship) between logical pages as perceived by the user process and physical pages accessed by the central processor. Normally, when the system is initialized, a copy of the map table is created in memory and transferred to the MMU hardware registers. The structure of a map table, as utilized in the text, is shown in figure 2.7.

Let us assume that the MMU consists of 16 maps, labeled zero through 15, each consisting of 64 pages of 1024 words. The maximum program size that may be accommodated is 64K words and the total main memory size that can be accomodated is 1024K (= 1M) words. Map 0 is reserved for the OS; maps 1 through 15 are available for assignment to the OS or the user. A process, when it is initiated, is assigned a map by the OS.

The map table reflects the mapping of logical to physical pages. Several logical pages may be assigned to the same physical page (e.g., when several processes are sharing a piece of reentrant code). The number of physical pages is restricted to the number of 1K word blocks of main memory configured in the system. The number of logical pages that can be accomodated is constrained by the size of the map table: in this case, 1024 logical pages.

An entry in the map table corresponds to the index of a physical page in memory. For example,

$$(\text{user-map}(5), \text{logical-page}(13)) \rightarrow \text{physical-page}(27)$$

is one such mapping. Normally, physical pages are allocated sequentially from map 0 for convenience. However, there is no physical reason to constrain the OS in such a fashion. Physical pages can be scattered across all 16 maps.

The Page Resource Monitor

In some minicomputer systems, the workload level may not be sufficient to utilize all of main memory. If the system is dedicated to a fixed set of processes, the total initial process size may be less than the amount of memory represented by the set of physical pages. The excess physical pages would be available to processes for dynamic allocation during execution.

Another motivation for allocating physical pages from a pool is the implementation of a demand-paging algorithm. A program dynamically requests

MAP TABLE

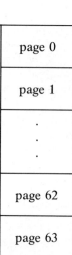

PAGE TABLE

Figure 2.7 Structure of the map table. An entry in the page table is a physical page (range is 0 to 1023).

and releases pages during its execution. Its "working set" of pages will expand and contract in accordance with the properties of its reference string (see section 4.5). As logical pages are released, the associated physical pages become available for allocation to another process.

To manage the global pool of physical pages, we define a resource semaphore PAGE-RS having the standard format described in section 7.10. The set of available physical pages beyond those assigned to the OS is enqueued on this semaphore. Whenever a process needs a physical page, it issues a request against this semaphore. A physical page is extracted from the pool and assigned to the requesting process.

Concept of an I/O Map

In some computer systems, performance is a function of I/O activity and thus, the system is termed I/O bound. In a paging system, I/O operations present a specific problem: ensuring that a logical page which is a source or destination of information for data transfer is not replaced between the time that the I/O operation is initiated and the time that the data transfer is complete. Conversely, the system would like to ensure that a program holding critical resources does not deadlock because it is unable to execute an I/O operation.

An IOMAP is a memory management map dedicated solely to the processing of I/O requests. Two types of pages may be represented in the map: the process data block and a user data page. The purpose of the IOMAP mechanism is to ensure that those pages which are the source or sink of data for an I/O function are always accessible through the MMU when the device is ready to perform the requested operation. Note that it is possible for a system with only a few maps to be unable to address all of memory at one time. A good example is the Data General Nova series, which contains a total of four maps: system, two users, and a data channel map. Together, these four maps are unable to address the total memory of 256,000 words available on a DGC machine. The data channel map serves a corollary purpose to our IOMAP in that it makes pages of memory always accessible for I/O operations.

2.7.2   Memory Management Service Requests

An OS will support several service requests for manipulation of physical pages from a global pool. The first request allows the user to obtain a physical page. The format of the request is:

SYSTEM(GET-PAGE, EVENT-NR)
SYSTEM(VALUE1, EVENT-NR) → PAGE-ID

where   EVENT-NR   is used to signal the user when a physical page is
                                     available
               PAGE-ID   is the index of the corresponding physical page

In a similar fashion, a process may return a physical page to the free page pool with the following request:

SYSTEM (FREE-PAGE, PAGE-ID)

where   PAGE-ID   is the index of the physical page

This page management capability differs from demand-paging, which we will explore in section 4.5. It assumes the user has some knowledge of the program structure and permits the user to control the assignment of logical to physical pages.

In many systems, a process can determine the physical page associated with any of its logical pages. To do so, it issues a PAGE-ID system service request, which is depicted in module 2.7.4.

SYSTEM(PAGE-ID), LOGICAL-PAGE) → PHYSICAL-PAGE

where   LOGICAL-PAGE   is the identifier of the logical page in the process's address space

            PHYSICAL-PAGE   is the identifier of the physical page in the process's memory map

Note that a process can only access logical or physical page identifiers relative to its current memory map. The most common reason for determining a physical page is to remap the logical page assigned to it. Remapping allows a process to change the assignment of a logical page to a physical page. This is normally done when a process wishes to move a data page. To remap a logical page, a process issues the REMAP system service request:

SYSTEM(REMAP, LOGICAL-PAGE, PHYSICAL-PAGE) → RESULT

where   LOGICAL-PAGE   is the identifier of the logical page in the process's space

            PHYSICAL-PAGE   is the identifier of the physical page in the process's current map

            RESULT   is an indicator of the success or failure

MODULE 2.7.1

```
procedure get-page
    request(page-rs) → event-data[p]
    subprocess-ok( )
endproc
```

MODULE 2.7.2

```
procedure free-page
    release(page-rs, physical-page[usp])
    os-exit( )
endproc
```

MODULE 2.7.3

```
procedure remap
    calling-map( ) → user-map
    page-select(user-map, logical-page[usp], physical-page[usp])
    os-exit( )
endproc
```

MODULE 2.7.4

```
procedure page-id
    read-map-table(user-page-id[usp], logical-page[usp])
                                          → return-value [usp]
    set-return-and-exit(1)
endproc
```

MODULE 2.7.5

```
procedure read-map-table(page-id, page, →physical-page)
    extract map-nr from page-id
    page-id + page → map-index
    map-table[map-index] → physical-page
endproc
```

2.7.3   Initalizing the Memory Management Unit

When the OS is booted into memory, the MMU is placed in an inactive status. The OS executes a sequence of startup procedures (see section 7.5) to initalize the system for user program activity. After the system has generated the map table, it must transfer it to the MMU hardware registers and activate the MMU. This function is accomplished by the LOAD-AND-START-MAP procedure (module 2.7.6).

The procedure sets the address and size of the map table to be transferred in the MMU function registers. It then initiates the data transfer via a hardware I/O control instruction. The procedure loops until the data transfer is complete and then checks for an error. If an error occurs during loading of the MMU, the system generates a panic message and halts. As an alternative, the user could dump the map table and status word to the operator's console prior to generating the panic.

Assuming a successful data transfer, the procedure issues the START-MAP command. This command activates the MMU hardware. Every subsequent memory reference is now passed through the MMU, which generates a map fault if a user address is outside the limits specified in the user's process map. In addition, some MMUs also prevent any user from executing privileged instructions—those instructions critical to the integrity of the system which are reserved for OS use. In these cases, the MMU detects the instruction type and generates an illegal instruction trap.

MODULE 2.7.6

```
procedure load-and-start-map
    lock-interrupts( )
    set-map-table-address(map-table-address)
    set-map-table-size(map-table-size)
    initiate-map-load( )
    clear map-ready
    while map-ready equals zero
        do
        sense-map-status( ) → map-ready
        enddo
    sense-map-error( ) → map-status
    if map-status less than zero
        then
        panic('map-load-error⟨0⟩', 0, 0, 0, 0)
    endif
    release-interrupts( )
    start-map( )
endproc
```

2.7.4   Changing the Map Configuration

In all but the most dedicated systems, the configuration of the map table changes as processes enter and leave the system. Whenever a new process is to be scheduled, it must first be assigned a map slot. A group of processes that form a program may be aggregated and assigned one map slot. During processing of system service requests, the process data block (PDB) will be "moved" between user space and system space quite frequently. In this instance, the PDB is remapped into map 0 by selecting an empty page in that map which can be assigned to the PDB. The procedure for selecting a new page is depicted in module 2.7.7.

2.7.5   Moving Data between Maps

Data transfer between the OS and user processes must be accomplished across map boundaries. The protection mechanism prevents direct transfer between maps by user processes. Data transfers are initiated by executing a system ser-

MODULE 2.7.7

```
procedure page-select(map, logical-page, physical-page)
    extract map-table-index from map
    increment map-table-index by logical-page
    map-table[map-table-index] → map-table-entry
    if map-table-entry not equal to zero
        then
        lock-interrupts( )
        set-map-page(map, logical-page, physical-page)
        clear map-status
        while map-status equals zero
            do
            sense-map-status( ) → map-status
            enddo
        sense-map-error( ) → map-status
        if map-error less than zero
            then
            panic('map setup fault⟨0⟩', map, logical-page,
                                            physical-page, 0)
        endif
    endif
    release-interrupts( )
endproc
```

vice request. Under control of the OS, the data are moved from user space to system space (or vice versa).

As mentioned above, the MMU operates in either system state or user state. In system state, all protection mechanisms are disabled. This allows the OS access to any portion of physical memory. However, since the OS, like any other process, can address only 64K words, it must use the MMU to translate user addresses to appropriate physical addresses. Usually, an MMU will operate in a special data transfer mode where the protection mechanism is enabled for one set of addresses only—those residing in user space.

The module for moving data between user and system space is shown in module 2.7.8. This module has entry points for moving data to or from user space. It sets the map state to enable the protection mechanism for the appropriate direction of transfer. Thus, on a transfer from user space, the map state is set to IN-STATE to indicate that each logical address in user space is passed through the protection mechanism. An illegal address in user space will generate a map fault.

The procedure enables the appropriate user map to be used in translating addresses. It then moves the number of words specified between the two maps—map 0 and the user map. Finally, it resets the map state to system state.

The distinction between these states is dependent on the architecture of the

MMU itself. For machines of the PDP-11/70 series, we would have three specific states: kernel, supervisor, and user. We have purposely left the values and explicit meanings undefined so that we do not mislead you when constructing an MMU handler.

MODULE 2.7.8

```
procedure move-from-user-space(map, from, to, number-of-words)
     in-state → map-state
     goto move-data-routine
entry move-to-user-space(map, from, to, number-of-words)
     out-state → map-state

move-data-routine:
     set-map-id(map)
     set-map-state(map-state)
     while number-of-words greater than or equal to zero
     do
     decrement number-of-words
          memory(from) → memory(to)
          increment from
          increment to
          enddo
     set-map-state(system-state)
endproc
```

2.7.6   Map Management Utilities

A few memory map utilities are described in this section. These utilities are used not only by the memory management routines but also by the I/O processing routines.

Selecting a Map

The process of selecting a map involves entering system state to set the current map identifier. If an invalid map is specified, the system prints an error message and terminates the process.

I/O Error Handling

An I/O error is generated when an invalid memory address is specified in an I/O request. IO-ERROR checks the error address against the address of the

MODULE 2.7.9

```
procedure map-select(user-map-number)
    set-map-state(system-state)
    if user-map-number greater than number-of-maps
        then
                error-message(map-error-status)
                error-kill(er-map)
    endif
    set-map-id(user-map-number)
endproc
```

system exit routine. If the error occurred at the end of I/O processing, the map
is set to system state and the routine exits. In this case, an error code has
already been specified as the process status. Otherwise, the error occurred during a data transfer; therefore, a map error is generated.

MODULE 2.7.10

```
procedure io-error(io-error-address)
    if io-error-address equals address(call-os-done)
        then
            increment interrupt-lock-count
            set-map-state(system-state)
            call-os-done( )
    endif
    generate-map-error('I/O error⟨0⟩', io-error-address)
endproc
```

Generating a Map Error

A map error may occur during a data transfer; usually, this error occurs
because a data address exceeds a page boundary. The map status is determined
by reading the hardware registers.

Map status
Map number
Address at which the interrupt occurred
User address data were to be transferred to/from

This information is reported to the operator via a panic message. MAP-
ERROR-ADDRESS is the address of the routine where the error occurred. The
executing process is terminated with the ER-MAP error code.

MODULE 2.7.11

```
procedure generate-map-error(map-error-string, map-error-address)
    if interrupt-lock-count equals zero
        then
        lock-interrupts( )
    endif
    read-map-status( ) → map-error-status
    read-map-number( ) → map-error-number
    read-map-interrupt-address( ) → map-interrupt-address
    read-map-user-address( ) → map-user-address
    set-map-state(system-state)
    panic('map fault⟨0⟩', map-error-address, map-error-status,
                        map-interrupt-address, map-user-address)
    reset process stack
    error-message(map-error-status)
    error-kill(er-map)
endproc
```

Allocating an IOMAP Slot

All IOMAP slots are enqueued on a resource semaphore, IOMAP-RS. The number of IOMAP slots is determined during system initialization (see section 7.5.4). When an I/O request is executed, an IOMAP slot is requested via the semaphore. The REQUEST procedure invokes IOMAP-ALLOCATOR to assign a map slot if any are available. Note that no map slots may be immediately available, as a user process may spawn multiple system processes for I/O that are executed asynchronously from the parent process (e.g., with event number 16).

IOMAP-ALLOCATOR, depicted in module 2.7.12, allocates available slots to all processes in the wait queue. The page associated with the slot is returned to the requesting process. The page replaces the logical page in the process space. The process is activated so that it may execute the data transfer.

2.8 MASS STORAGE ALLOCATION

The space on a mass storage device is usually shared among multiple users. Allocation of this space is a function reserved for the OS. Normally, when a mass storage device is initialized, the OS is the sole owner of the space on the device. As users create files, the OS parcels out this space to each user, who, in turn, becomes its owner. When the user deletes a file, the space is returned to the control of the operating system.

MODULE 2.7.12

```
procedure iomap-allocator
      rs-wait-queue[iomap-rs]  →  rwq
      rs-avail-queue[iomap-rs]  →  avq
      set one to iomap-flag
      while iomap-flag equals one
            do
            if queue-start[rwq] equals zero
                  then
                  if queue-count[avq] equals zero
                        then
                                    exitdo
                  endif
            endif
            remove-from-queue(rwq)  →  iomap-pcb
            remove-from-queue(avq)  →  iomap-page
            iomap-page  →  return-value[iomap-pcb]
            extract logical-page from iomap-page
            extract iomap from iomap-page
            page-select(iomap, logical-page, rs-data-save[iomap-pcb])
            activate(iomap-pcb)
            enddo
endproc
```

   Two types of allocation have been employed in OSs: static and dynamic. In a static strategy, the user declares the total size of the file in the CREATE command. The OS allocates all of the space requested at one time if it is physically able to do so. This strategy is normally used to allocate space for contiguous files. It may also be applied to space allocation for serial and segmented files. However, this places a serious restriction on the ability of serial and segmented files to expand their size. A file can be expanded only if the blocks adjacent to its last block were free, for example, they belonged to the OS. This strategy was often used in early OSs, in certain dedicated real-time systems, and in the less flexible microcomputer floppy disk–based OSs.

   IBM's OS/360 used a variation of the static approach. It divided mass storage space into groups of contiguous blocks. For each group, a dummy file directory entry was created in the Volume Table of Contents (VTOC). Each time that a file was to be created, the OS would search the VTOC for a directory entry with space greater than or equal to the requested size. If the space exceeded the requested size, the excess was "split off" as a new file directory entry.

   Two problems, analogous to memory management policies, affect the static strategy. First, there is a fragmentation of secondary storage. Second, because users often do not know in advance how big their files are going to be, they do not know how much space to request. For example, the relocatable output from compilers is a nonlinear function of the size and characteristics of the source program.

The other approach involves a dynamic allocation strategy. In this strategy, only the exact number of blocks necessary to satisfy the request are allocated from the free space. Several different methods have been used to manage the free space on a mass storage device. Among them are:

Bit Maps.   A contiguous set of disk blocks is reserved on the device when it is initialized. Each bit in this area represents a disk block on the device. The bit has value zero if the disk block is free and value one if the disk block has been allocated to some user. The bit map is not considered part of the allocatable disk space, so its blocks are not represented in itself. The bit map approach makes it rather easy to survey disk space utilization, as one need only count the bits having a value of one and multiply by the block size.

Free Chain.   Another approach is to chain all the free blocks on the disk together in a list. No searching is required to allocate a disk block; it is merely removed from the front of the chain. When a block is deallocated, it is placed at the beginning or end of the chain. This approach requires less main memory for supporting procedures but make it almost impossible to allocate contiguous files.

Free File Map.   One problem with the OS/360 approach was the size of the VTOC when there was a large number of small contiguous areas. Searching the file directory can be an inefficient process. A solution to this problem consists of listing the free blocks in a special file. This file is accessed whenever a block is allocated or deallocated. The list is maintained through normal list manipulation procedures. The choice of a particular method depends on the performance required and the size of the disk. For large devices, the bit map method appears to be more efficient and to require less space on the disk. For floppy disks, the free file map or the free block chain method give adequate performance in relation to the speed of the device and the computer.

2.8.1   Mass Storage Allocation Data Structures

The method described for mass storage allocation is patterned after the bit map method. The bit map method is more complex than either the free chain or free file map methods. By describing it in some detail, you will get a sufficient grasp of its power and efficiency for large devices.

Usually, a contiguous set of blocks is reserved on the disk for a bit map. Rarely is it possible to enlarge a bit map once the device has been initialized. The bit map is usually set up during an independent preparation phase known as disk formatting. For large devices, the implication is that the bit map is laid down on the first few cylinders of each platter.

The number of blocks required for a bit map can be calculated as follows:

Let N be the number of words on the disk

Let b be the number of words per disk block

Let w be the number of bits per data word

Assume that m, b, and w are multiples of 2

Then the number of blocks required is

$$n = \frac{m}{b \times w}$$

As an example, consider the following values: $w = 16$, $b = 256$, and $N = 256$, which yields

$$N = b \times n \times w \rightarrow 1{,}048{,}576 \text{ words}$$

The blocks used to store the bit map are not counted in the allocatable storage on the device.

Accessing the Bit Map

Each mass storage device represents a single entry to the OS. For each device, a system channel is allocated for reading and writing the bit map. The channel is opened during system initialization when the existence of the device is validated.

The number of disk blocks used to store the bit map varies with the size of the device. For most minicomputer systems, the size of the bit map represents a significant percentage of main memory. Thus the bit map for each device is buffered into and out of main memory as necessary.

For each mass storage device, a mass storage allocation table (MSAT) is maintained in memory. The structure of the MSAT is depicted in table 2.6. Each MSAT has a pointer to the memory buffer which contains the current bit map block. Each MSAT also has a pointer to the current word in the buffer at which it is looking. Depending on the type of allocation (e.g., contiguous blocks), the buffer may have to be searched for the appropriate number and distribution of blocks. Other entries in the MSAT are used to track the allocation of blocks to a user.

2.8.2   Mass Storage Functions

A mass storage device that is sharable among multiple users must be treated as a valuable resource. At any time, multiple processes may be requesting alloca-

Table 2.6   Structure of Mass Storage Allocation Table

Mnemonic	Usage
Buffer-address	Pointer to the fixed buffer used in allocation
Allocation-current-address	Current address in the allocation buffer
Allocation-current-count	Current word in the buffer
Allocation-channel	System channel number for this device
Bit-index	Current bit allocation index
Base-address	Current base allocation address
Device-address	Bit map hardare address
Allocation-current-bit	Current bit index in the buffer
Free-storage	Pointer to free space data in the directory's file control block
Use-flag	Word indicating the allocation channel status

tion of file space on the disk. To mediate contention among these processes, the allocation of mass storage space is performed by a system process, MASS-STORAGE-ALLOCATION-PROCESS. Access to the allocation process is controlled by a resource semaphore, MASS-STORAGE-SERVICE.

The mass storage allocation process performs four functions related to the maintenance of disk storage space: allocate space, release space, count the allocated space on a device, and determine the free space in the file system.

Each function request is prepared by an interface procedure and enqueued to a service semaphore, ALLOCATION-PROCESS-SERVICE. The entry placed on the service queue is a subprocess control block (PCB) created by the file manager or I/O manager. The MSA process retrieves service requests from the service semaphore and processes them one at a time.

The Allocation Process

The structure of the MSA process is depicted in module 2.8.1. The MSA process is activated during system initialization. The first activity of the MSA process is the initialization of allocation parameters. The MSA process then enters a continuous loop. Each time it finds a service request enqueued on the service semaphore, it retrieves the request, determines the function, and dispatches control to the appropriate procedure. Once the function is completed, the process is released from the MASS-STORAGE-SERVICE semaphore. This process is shown in figure 2-8.

The functions invoked by the mass storage allocation process are:

1. ALLOCATE-SPACE, which actually allocates space to a user.
2. RETURN-SPACE, which releases allocated space freed by a user.

3. MS-COUNT, which determines the free space available.

4. MS-SUMSPACE, which determines the total mass storage space available on a given device.

2.8.3 Allocating Space

The allocation function consists of two important functions: ALLOCATE and ALLOCATE-SPACE. The procedure ALLOCATE, depicted in module 2.8.2, serve as the interface between the I/O manager, the file manager, and the mass storage storage allocation subsystem. Any system service request that requires additional mass storage space eventually forces an invocation of ALLOCATE. Examples include SEQUENTIAL-WRITE and CREATE.

The ALLOCATE procedure stores the parameters in the PCB, which it then

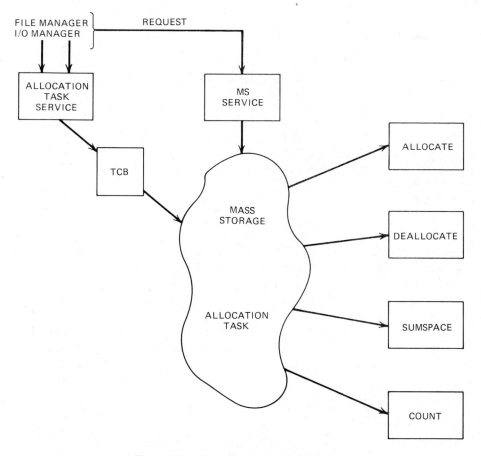

Figure 2.8   Allocation process structure.

MODULE 2.8.1

procedure mass-storage-allocation-process
    initialize-msat( )
    while true
        do
                request(allocation-process-service)
                rs-wait-queue[mass-storage-service] → wait-address
                queue-start[wait-address] → ms-process
                allocation-type[ms-process] → id
                rs-data-save[ms-process] → allocate-function
                case allocate-function of
                    0:   allocate-space( ) → reply
                    1:   return-space( ) → reply
                    2:   ms-count( ) → reply
                    3:   ms-sumpace( ) → reply
                endcase
                reply → event-status[ms-process]
        enddo
endproc

MODULE 2.8.2

procedure allocate(words-needed, unit-number, → base-address)
    words-needed → allocation-size[p]
    unit-number → allocation-type[p]
    release(allocation-process-service)
    request(mass-storage-service, MS-ALLOCATE-FUNCTION)
    allocation-address[p] → base-address
endproc

places on the allocation service queue. It requests MSA service by blocking the current process on the MASS-STORAGE-SERVICE semaphore. This approach does not deadlock the system since a subprocess is created to execute the system service request.

The parameters specified in the ALLOCATE request are the number of words required and the device identifier on which space is to be allocated (if available). The I/O or file manager has already mapped the file name to the appropriate device. Upon completion of the allocation function, the base address of the allocated area is returned to the caller.

Allocation Control

ALLOCATE-SPACE, depicted in module 2.8.3, controls the allocation function. Allocation of mass storage space occurs in two modes: system and user. The mode is indicated by the ID parameter.

MODULE 2.8.3

```
procedure allocate-space(→ result)
    get-sector-number( )
    if id equals zero
        then
                system·space → state
        else
                user-space → state
    endif

allocation-step0:
    next-id → start-id
    if id not equal to zero
        then
                goto allocation-step1
    endif
    goto allocation-step2

allocation-step1:
    next-id → id

allocation-step2:
    if use-flag[id] less than one
        then
                set er-device to result
        else
                get-mass-storage-space( ) → result
    endif
    if state not equal to system-space
        then
                increment next-id
                if next-id equal to number-of-devices
                    then
                            set one to next-id
                endif
    endif
    if result greater than or equal to zero
        then
                insert id into new-address
                new-address → allocation-address[ms-process]
                exitproc
    endif
    case state of
        0:   set one to id
                set user-space to state
                goto allocation-step0
```

```
1:    if next-id not equal to start-id
          then
                    goto allocation-step1
      endif
      clear id
      set 2 to state
      goto allocation-step2

2:    if next-id not equal to start-id
          then
                    goto allocation-step1
      endif

3:    clear allocation-address[ms-process]
      exitproc
   endcase
endproc
```

The system determines whether system or user space is to be allocated. In some small systems, whatever disk space is available is partitioned between the OS and the user. This approach ensures that the system always has some space in which to execute user commands. On many micromcomputer systems, only one floppy disk is available. With limited memory capacity, the OS often stores essential tables and workspaces on the disk until required for processing.

To initialize allocation, the procedure calculates the sector number and number of words to allocate. The allocation state is initialized to the type of allocation requested. The allocation function proceeds as follows:

1. **Step 0.** NEXT-ID marks the device identifier of the device currently available for allocation. This identifier is saved in START-ID in order to prevent looping during the search process. If the type of allocation is user mode, the allocation search begins at the current device. Otherwise, allocation has been requested by the system and proceeds from the system device.

2. **Step 1.** Here we establish the identity of the device to be searched for space.

3. **Step 2.** Allocation takes place in this step. The use flag is checked to determine if the device is available. If not, the caller is notified by a status message containing the appropriate error code. Otherwise, GET-MASS-STORAGE-SPACE is called to acquire mass storage space.

Next, the procedure checks the status of the allocation process. The variable STATE was originally set to the allocation mode. If the allocation was user mode, the variable NEXT-ID is incremented to the next user device. All user devices will be searched for an error code indicating that insufficient space is returned to the caller.

If the result is positive, the address of the newly allocated space is calculated and stored in the subprocess's PCB. The address is composed of the device identifier and the location on disk. If the result is negative, this iteration of the allocation process has failed. If STATE equals SYSTEM-SPACE, an attempt to allocate system space has failed.

The Space Allocation Process

The procedure GET-MASS-STORAGE-SPACE, depicted in module 2.8.4, performs the allocation process in three phases: buffer parameter initialization, bit map searching, and bit map updating.

The allocation process uses a buffer to store a portion of the bit map during the search procedure. The status of a buffer is maintained in workspace provided in the MSA process data block. The structure of the workspace is defined in table 2.7.

When GET-MASS-STORAGE-SPACE is entered, it checks the free storage available for the device against the number of words requested for allocation. Insufficient space for the device will cause an error code to be returned to the caller. The status of the variables associated with the device's current buffer are copied from the MSAT to the workspace. Other temporary variables used in the allocation process are set to zero.

The actual allocation process begins with the initialization of the buffer status variables at START-ALLOCATION. These variables are initialized when the allocation process is begun and each time a new area of the device bit map is read into memory.

A CONTINUE-SEARCH begins a loop that will scan the bit map until a block of space of the appropriate size is located. A word is copied from the bit map buffer. During the search, if a nonzero bit value is detected, there is not enough space at this disk location to satisfy the request. That is, this routine ex-

Table 2.7   Description of Allocation Workspace

Mnemonic	Usage
Top	Address of the current buffer
Allocation-buffer-start	Start address of the current buffer
Allocation-buffer-bit	Start bit in the current buffer
Allocation-buffer-count	Start word in the current buffer
Allocation-buffer-words	Word count in the current buffer
Last-bit	Last bit in the current buffer
Current-device-address	Current device address

its with the address of a block of space ample enough to accommodate the request. Otherwise, it continues to cycle while bumping a pointer through the bit map.

Once the first zero bit is found, the procedure copies the current search location to NEW-ADDRESS, which records the address of the candidate block of space. Whenever the number of allocated sectors equals the number of requested sectors, FINISH-ALLOCATION is invoked to actually assign the block of space.

The request may be so large that several fetches from the bit map are necessary. When this happens, GET-NEW-BUFFER is called to refill the bit map buffer. As a result, all allocation parameters must be reset prior to processing the new buffer contents. RESET-WORKSPACE saves the current allocation state so that one contiguous piece of disk space is allocated per the request size.

MODULE 2.8.4

```
procedure get-mass-storage-space (→result)
     free-storage[id]  fcb-size-address
     if memory(fcb-size-address) less than words
          then
                    set er-space to result
                    exitproc
     endif
     allocation-channel[id] → channel
     bit-index[id] → search-address
     search-address − 1 → search-start
     clear buffer-index
     clear number-of-words
     clear first-sector-found
     clear number-of-allocated-sectors
     buffer-address[id] → top[buffer-index]
     allocation-current-address[id] → start
     allocation-current-count[id] → count
     allocation-current-bit[id] → bit
     device-address[id] → current-device-address

start-allocation:
     count → allocation-buffer-count[buffer-index]
     bit → allocation-buffer-bit[buffer-index]
     start → allocation-buffer-start[buffer-index]

continue-search:
     memory(start) → bit-map
     for bit-id from bit to 0
          do
```

```
                    bit-map & bits[bit-id + 1] → bit-value
                    if bit-value not equal to zero
                          then
                                clear number-of-allocated-sectors
                                clear first-sector-found
                                clear number-of-words
                                reset-work-space( )
                                check-limits(0)
                                goto start-allocation
                    endif
                    if first-sector-found equals zero
                          then
                                increment first-sector-found
                                search-address → new-address
                    endif
                    if number-of-allocated-sectors equals sector-number
                          then
                                increment search-address
                                goto finish-allocation
                    endif
                    check-limits(1)
                    decrement bit-id
              enddo
      if count is less than record-size
            then
                    increment start
                    increment number-of-words
                    set maximum-bit-index to bit
                    goto continue-search
      endif
      get-new-buffer( ) → result
      if result greater than or equal to zero
            then
                    goto start-allocation
      endif
      clear bit-id
      set − 1 to search-address
      set record-size to current-device-address[x]
      clear number-of-allocated-sectors
      clear first-sector-found
      clear number-of-words
      reset-work-space( )
      check-limits(0)
      goto start-allocation
endproc
```

Finishing the Allocation of Space

No space is allocated on the device until the requisite number of sectors have been identified. FINISH-ALLOCATION updates the MSAT parameters and sets the bits in the bit map which correspond to the allocated sectors. The setting of the bits is a straightforward procedure, so I will not belabor it. The key point is that the system continually XORs the new bit value with the old word settings so as not to disturb any previous allocations or inadvertently set a bit for a sector that has not been allocated.

Once all sectors have been marked, the bit map is rewritten to disk. If an error occurs at this point, the system notifies the operator via a console message that a mass storage management error has occurred so that corrective action may be initiated. Incorrect updating of the bit map affects the consistency and integrity of the file system and endangers the validity of any data already on the disk. At this point, the system should probably "panic," so that system recovery procedures may be activated.

Finally, the procedure updates the search parameters for the disk. When the next request is serviced, searching will begin from the address contained in ALLOCATION-CURRENT-ADDRESS[ID].

MODULE 2.8.5

```
entry finish-allocation
     number-of-words → allocation-buffer-words[buffer-index]
     free-storage[id] → fcb-size-address
     memory(fcb-size-address) → number-free-words
     decrement number-free-words by words
     bit-id → last-bit[buffer-index]
     lshift(new-address, sector-shift) → new address
     increment new-address by base-address[id]
     for index from 0 to buffer-index
          do
                    allocation-buffer-words[index] → number-of-words
                    allocation-buffer-start[index] − 1 → start
                    for bit-id from 0 to number-of-words
                         do
                              increment start
                              set − 1 to bit
                              if bit-id equals zero
                                   then
                                             allocation-buffer-bit[index] → bit-number
                                             masks[bit-number + 1] & bit → bit
                         endif
```

```
                              if bit-id equals number-of-words
                                  then
                                      if last-bit[index] greater than or equal
                                                                      to zero
                                          then
                                                  last-bit[index] → bit-number
                                                  xor(masks[bit-number],bit) → bit
                                      endif
                              endif
                              or(memory(start),bit) → memory(start)
                          enddo
                          system(write, 16, channel, top[index], record-size,
                                          current-device-address[index]) → reply
                          if reply less than zero
                              then
                                      issue-ms-error(index, 1)
                                      set one to reply
                          endif
                  enddo
          set last-bit[buffer-index] to bit-id
          reset-workspace( )
          bit → allocation-current-bit[id]
          count → allocation-current-count[id]
          start → allocation-current-address[id]
          current-device-address[buffer-index] → device-address[id]
          set one to reply
          search-address → bit-index[id]
endproc
```

2.8.4   Returning Space to the System

When a user no longer requires space on the mass storage device, it is returned
to system control. Normally, this operation takes place when a file is deleted by
the user. Deallocation of disk space is the converse operation of allocation. It
can use any of the techniques described in the introduction for tracking the
status of mass storage space.

The interface to the mass storage allocation process for deallocation is
depicted in module 2.8.6. Two parameters are required when returning space to
the system: the address of the mass storage area to be released and the size of
the mass storage area to be released.

The address is composed of the device unit number and the hardware location on the device. This address is decomposed into its respective parts: UNIT-
NUMBER and ALLOCATION-ADDRESS[P]. These parameters are stored in

the PCB of the requesting process (remember that this process is really a sub-process created specifically to execute the request for deallocation by the I/O or file managers).

The PCB is enqueued on the ALLOCATION-PROCESS-SERVICE sema-phore by the RELEASE function. As mentioned previously, this semaphore is merely a queue of PCBs waiting to be serviced by the MSA process. MASS-STORAGE-SERVICE is a semaphore containing a queue of service requests. After deallocation is completed, the status of the function is stored in the PCB.

MODULE 2.8.6

```
procedure deallocation(size, address, →result)
    size → allocation-size[p]
    extract unit-number from address
    unit-number → allocation-type[p]
    extract allocation-address[p] from address
    release(allocation-process-service)
    request(mass-storage-service, MS-DEALLOCATE-FUNCTION)
    event-status[p] → result
endproc
```

Returning Space

RETURN-SPACE is the procedure invoked by the MSA process to deallocate sectors on the disk. It uses RETURN-ADDRESS, which identifies the begin-ning of the disk area to be freed, to calculate the number of sectors to be re-leased and the bit map address of the bit corresponding to the first sector.

The code for releasing sectors is encompassed in a large loop. In turn, the system acquires a buffer and reads a segment of the bit map into memory (which may not reference the entire area to be released). If an error occurs dur-ing the read operation, we terminate deallocation and notify the system operator via a console message. We do not proceed further with the dealloca-tion, as it may damage the consistency of the bit map and lead to data integrity violations in the file system. At this point, system recovery procedures should probably be invoked.

The clearing of bits in the bit map is a straightforward procedure which we will not examine in detail. Again, XOR is used to mask the bit map buffer con-tents so that only the specific bits relevant to the released sectors are set to zero. A problem arises when we detect a bit having a value of zero which is supposed to be one. The system must assume this to be an error since it believes the user is trying to return disk space which the user does not own. This step is necessary to protect the integrity of the file system and the validity of other users' data.

Finally, once all the bits are properly marked, RETURN-SPACE updates the bit map on disk and moves to the next segment of space to be released. This process continues until all sectors that were to be released have been marked available in the bit map.

MODULE 2.8.7

```
procedure return-space(→ result)
    get-sector-number( )
    allocation-address[ms-process] → return-address
    if use-flag[id] less than one
        then
                er-deallocate → result
                exitproc
    endif
    return-address - base-address[id] → address-temp
    rshift(address-temp, sector-shift) → bit-address
    extract bmb-address from bit-address
    extract start-bit from bit-address
    and(bmb-address, record-mask) → count
    decrement bmb-address by count
    clear current-sector-index
    clear deallocation-flag
    clear buffer-index
    allocation-channel[id] → channel
    while true
        do
        request(memory-rs, record-size) → return-buffer
        bmb-address → current-device-address[buffer-index]
        system(read, 16, channel, return-buffer, record-size,
                           bmb-address) → current-last-bit
    current-last-bit → result
    if result less than zero
        then
            if result equals er-end-of-file
                then
                        er-deallocate → result
                        issue-ms-error(buffer-index, 3)
                        set − 1 to deallocation-flag
                        goto finish-deallocation
            endif
            issue-ms-error(buffer-index, 2)
    endif
    clear current-buffer-size
    while true
        do
                memory(return-buffer + count) → bit-map-entry
```

```
for current-bit from bit to 0 by − 1
        do
        if current-last-bit greater than or equal to zero
        then
                and(bit-map-entry, bits[current-bit + 1])
                                                → bit
            if bit equals zero
                then
                        er-deallocate → result
                        issue-ms-error(buffer-index, 3)
                        set − 1 to deallocation-flag
                        goto finish-deallocation
            endif
            xor(bit-map-entry, bits[current-bit + 1])
                                                → bit-map-entry
        endif
        increment current-buffer-size
        increment current-sector-index
        if current-sector-index equals sector-number
                then
                    set one to result
                    set one to deallocation-flag
                    bit-map-entry →
                                memory(return-buffer + count)
                    goto finish-deallocation
        endif
        set maximum-bit-index to bit
        bit-map → memory(return-buffer + count)
        increment count
        if count less than record size
                then
                        exitdo
        endif
        enddo
finish-deallocation:
        current-buffer-size →
                                allocation-buffer-words[buffer-index]
        current-last-bit → last-bit[buffer-index]
        return-buffer → top[buffer-index]
        if deallocation-flag equals zero
                then
                    increment bmb-address by record size
                    clear count
                    increment buffer-index
                    exitdo
```

```
                    endif
              enddo
      for temp1 from 0 to buffer-index
          do
          top[temp1] → return-buffer
          if deallocation-flag greater than or equal to zero
                then
                      if last-bit[temp1] greater than or equal to zero
                          then
                          current-device-address[temp1]
                                                      → bmb-address
                          system(write, 16, channel, return-
                                          buffer, record-size,
                                      bmb-address) → result
                          then
                                  issue-ms-error(temp1, 4)
                                  set one to result
                          endif
                          if bmb-address equals device-address[id]
                              then
                                      copy(return-buffer, buffer-
                                          address[id] record-size)
                          endif
                          set one to bit-temp
                              1shift(bit-temp, sector-shift) → bit-temp
                          bit-temp + memory(free-storage[id])
                                          → memory(current-last-bit)
                          endif
              endif
          release(memory-rs, return-buffer)
      enddo
endproc
```

2.8.5   Determining Free Space

A third function associated with mass storage management is the determination of free space available to the system. Normally, this function is done only once—when a particular device is initialized in the system. The number of words returned by this function is used to initialize the FREE-STORAGE parameter in the mass storage allocation table.

The interface procedure for invoking the free space function is depicted in module 2.8.8. Only one parameter is required: the unit number of the device whose free space is to be counted. As described previously, the requesting pro-

cess's PCB is enqueued to the ALLOCATION-PROCESS-SERVICE semaphore and service is requested from the MSA process.

Why is a free space function required in an OS? Because the size and type of
mass storage devices can vary from configuration to configuration. More flexibility is achieved in selecting devices if the space determination function is post-
poned from system generation (when configuration parameters are established)
to actual system operation. Additionally, if one is able to include new devices in
the system without performing a new system generation, it is essential to be able
to determine what new increment of mass storage is available to the users.

The intent of the function described below has been modified from the
foregoing comments. This module may be invoked by the user at any time during the operation of the system. This feature allows the user to inspect a specific
device to determine if enough space is available to create a file of the required
size. On space-limited floppy disks, this feature is extremely useful when planning the distribution of a large number of files.

MODULE 2.8.8

```
procedure get-free-space(unit-number, → result)
    unit-number → allocation-type[p]
    release(allocation-process-service)
    request(mass-storage-service, MS-COUNT-FUNCTION)
    available-space → event-data[p]
    event-status[p] → result
endproc
```

Counting Mass Storage Space

The procedure for determining the available space on a mass storage device is
shown in module 2.8.9. The algorithm used is straightforward. For a given
device, each record in the bit map is read into memory. All bits in the record
that have a zero value are counted. The sum is used to calculate the total space
available on the disk by multiplying the sum by the block size.

MODULE 2.8.9

```
procedure count-space(→ result)
    allocation-channel[id] → channel
    clear available
    clear buffer-address
    request(memory-rs, record-size) → start
    while true
        do
        system(read, 16, channel, start, record-size, buffer-address)
                                                        → result
```

```
            if result greater than or equal to zero
                then
                        if buffer-address equals zero
                            then
                            copy(start, buffer-address[id], record-size)
                        endif
                        start → x
                        for count from 1 to record-size
                            do
                            memory(x)  bit-map
                            for al-bit from maximum-bit-index to 0 by − 1
                                do
                                if bit-map greater than or equal to zero
                                    then
                                            increment available
                                endif
                                lshift(bit-map, 1) → bit-map
                                enddo
                            increment x
                            enddo
                        increment buffer-address by record-size
            endif
            if result equals er-end-of-file
                then
                        lshift(available, sector-shift) → available
                        set one to result
                        exitdo
            endif
            enddo
        release(memory-rs, start)
endproc
```

One way to count bits is shown in the module. It assumes a word where the high-order bit represents the sign of the integer value. By testing the current value of the word BIT-MAP greater than or equal to zero, we know that the high-order bit is zero and that the available space counter should be incremented by one. After each test, we left-shift the bits in the word by one, which moves another bit into the high-order position. This method will work quite well on a central processor that possesses either a logical left- or right-shift instruction.

2.8.6   Determining Disk Space

The fourth function of mass storage management involves the determination of the free space currently available to the user. The amount of free space fluctuates as the user creates and deletes files. It should be noted that the free disk space is a function of the types and sizes of disks (possibly removable) in the system. If a user intends to execute a program that will create a number of new files (or extend existing files), it behooves him or her to determine the disk space available in order to prevent the unfortunate consequence of disk space overflow.

The interface procedure is depicted in module 2.8.10. It merely requests the MSA process to sum the free space available on the currently configured mass storage devices.

The procedure for accumulating the total mass storage free space, MS-SUMSPACE, is depicted in module 2.8.11. For each device in the mass storage allocation table, the procedure verifies that the device is in use. It adds the free storage for that device to the running total maintained in EVENT-DATA[MS-PROCESS], where MS-PROCESS is the address of the PCB for the request being served. When all mass storage devices have been scanned, the value of the EVENT-DATA[MS-PROCESS] reflects the total free space available to the user.

MODULE 2.8.10

```
procedure disk-space
     release(allocation-process-service)
     request(mass-storage-service, MS-SUMSPACE-FUNCTION)
endproc
```

MODULE 2.8.11

```
procedure ms-sumspace(→ result)
     clear event-data[ms-process]
     for index from 0 to ms-devices − 1
          do
          if use-flag[index] not equal to zero
               then
               free-storage[index] → fcb-size-address
               memory(fcb-size-address) → available
               increment event-data[ms-process] by available
          endif
          increment index
     enddo
     set one to result
endproc
```

2.8.7 Initializing the Allocation Parameters

When the OS is initialized, it initiates the mass storage allocation process. One aspect of the initialization procedure is to create the MSAT. The procedure for initializing the MSAT is depicted in module 2.8.12. For each mass storage device, it performs the following operations:

Clears the MSAT entries to zero

Acquires a system buffer to hold bit map segments

Creates a system directory name for the device

Obtains the allocation channel numbers assigned to the device

Opens the channel to the device

Initializes buffer parameters in MSAT entry

Determines available space on the disk

Initializes the free storage variable in the MSAT

Sets the in-use flag for the device in the MSAT

Once the MSAT has been created, this phase of the initialization process is complete. The final step is to notify the system initialization process that the mass storage allocation process is ready to service requests.

MODULE 2.8.12

```
procedure initialize-msat
    clear next-id
    for id from 0 to max-number-of-devices − 1
        do
        clear(mass-storage-allocation-table[id])
        request(memory-rs, record-size) → buffer-address[id]
        make-directory-name(id) → directory-name
        allocation-channel[id] → directory-channel
        system(open, 16, directory-channel, directory-name, 0) → result
        if result less than zero
            then
                panic('ms-allocation<0>', id, directory-channel, result, 0)
        endif
        buffer-address[id] → allocation-current-address[id]
        set maximum-bit-index to allocation-current-bit[id]
        clear allocation-current-count[id]
        clear device-address[id]
        clear bit-index[id]
        directory-channel → allocation-channel[id]
        count-space( ) → result
        if result greater than or equal to zero
        then
                calculate-channel-address(directory-channel) →
                                                        ccb-address
                channel-address[ccb-address] → x
                address(file-directory-free-count[x]) → free-storage [id]
```

```
            available → memory(free-storage[id])
                file-end[x] → base-address[id]
        endif
        result → use-flag[id]
        if result less than zero
                then
                        clear use-flag[id]
        endif
        enddo
    system(post, creating-event-number, creating-process, 1, 0)
endproc
```

2.8.8 Mass Storage Allocation Utilities

Several utilities are required to support the mass storage allocation subsystem procedures. These utilities are described briefly in this section.

Calculating the Sector Number

The caller specifies the number of words to be allocated by the MSA process. This value is resolved into the number of sectors required on the device and the total number of words. Note that ALLOCATION-SIZE may be less than WORDS since the caller does not have to specify a size that is a multiple of the sector size. Excess words in the sector are, of course, wasted. GET-SECTOR-NUMBER (module 2.8.13) performs this operation using logical left and right shifts.

Reading the Bit Map

This procedure (module 2.8.14) performs a random read of the bit map which is specified by CURRENT-DEVICE-ADDRESS. This routine is more of a convenience than anything else, as several procedures need to read the bit map. The only error returned to the caller is an end-of-file condition. Other errors result in the display of a message on the operator's console.

MODULE 2.8.13

```
procedure get-sector-number
    allocation-size[ms-process] + sector-mask → sector-temp
    rshift(sector-temp, sector-shift) → sector-number
    lshift(sector-number, sector-shift) → words
endproc
```

MODULE 2.8.14

```
procedure read-bit-map(→ result)
    system(read-random, 16, channel, start, record-size,
                                    current-device-address[id]) → result
        if result less than zero
            then
                    if result not equal to er-end-of-file
                            then
                                    issue-ms-error(x, 0)
                                    exitproc
                endif
        endif
endproc
```

Checking the Search Limits

When allocating space, the MSA process has to search for an area large enough to accommodate the request. The search will either succeed or fail at the current address. After a search has ended, the limits of the search must be validated. If a failure has occurred (e.g., not enough space), the search parameters are restored in the device table and the search continues (FLAG equals zero). If the search succeeded, the search location is incremented for the next allocation (FLAG equals one). The procedure for checking the search limits is CHECK-LIMITS (module 2.8.15).

Reading a New Buffer

The device allocation bit map is read in fixed-size records. During a search for sufficient space, the search may cross the boundary (although the bit map is logically treated as one continuous record). At this point, the MSA process reserves a new system buffer and reads the next chunk of the bit map. GET-NEW-BUFFER (module 2.8.16) obtains and initializes a buffer, and proceeds to read the next segment of the bit map.

MODULE 2.8.15

```
procedure check-limits(→ result)
    if search-address equals search-start
        then
        if flag equals zero
            then
            set er-space to result
```

```
            reset-work-space( )
            bit → allocation-current-bit[id]
            count → allocation-current-count[id]
            start → allocation-current-address[id]
            current-device-address[x] → device-address [id]
            exitproc
        endif
        increment search-start
    endif
    increment search-address
endproc
```

MODULE 2.8.16

```
procedure get-new-buffer(→result)
    number-of-words → allocation-buffer-words[x]
    clear last-bit[x]
    request(memory-rs, record-size) → start
    increment x
    start → top[x]
    set maximum-bit-index to bit
    set maximum-bit-index to bit-id
    clear count
    clear number-of-words
    current-device-address[x − 1] + record-size
                                    → current-device-address[x]
    read-bit-map( ) → result
endproc
```

Clearing the Workspace

As mentioned above, portions of the MSA process's PDB are used as a work-space for managing the buffers used to search for mass storage space. At the end of the search, whether it ends in success or failure, the workspace must be reinitialized for handling the next request. RESET-WORKSPACE (module 2.8.17) performs this operation for the MSA process. It releases the temporary buffers used in the allocation and adjusts the search parameters to reflect the result of the allocation process.

MODULE 2.8.17

```
procedure reset-workspace
    if buffer-index not equal to zero
        then
```

```
                    address(top[buffer-index]) → top-address
                    copy(top-address, top[0], record-size)
                    buffer[id] + count → start
                    for t1 from buffer-index to 1 by −1
                            do
                                    release(memory-rs, top[t1])
                            enddo
                    clear buffer-index
            endif
            if current-bit equals zero
            then
                    increment count
                    if count greater than or equal to record-size
                            then
                                increment current-device-address by record-size

                                top → start
                                clear count
                                while true
                                        do
                                                read-bit-map( ) → result
                                                if result less than zero
                                                    then
                                                    set −1 to search-address
                                                    clear current-device-address
                                                    else
                                                    exitdo
                                                endif
                                        enddo
                            else
                                increment start
                    endif
                    set maximum-bit-index to bit
            else
                    set current-bit −1 to bit
        endif
endproc
```

3

Process Management

The complexity of an OS is reflected in the difficulties experienced in its design and construction. In order to evaluate a system's design, one must be able to understand its behavior. For most OSs, this task is immense. To cope with the problem, we use a technique known as "divide and conquer" which is described by Horning and Randell [horn73]. In this approach, Horning and Randell argue that the process is the most appropriate unit of decomposition for this technique.

The process concept is a tool for decomposing a discrete event system into components—each of which is separately describable. In general, a process has two aspects: it is a data carrier and it executes actions. The concept of processes has been ingrained in simulation languages for many years, particularly in SIMULA classes.

Once the individual characteristics of devices are masked, they can be treated as resources along with the central processor and the main memory. The basic unit that may compete for the limited number of resources within a computer system is termed a process. Processes may exist in any number within the OS. Nominally, they compete for the most valuable resource of all—a slice of central processor time. This competition generates the requirements for managing processes and scheduling the usage of the central processor. This chapter discusses process management and the various operations involved in scheduling the central processor.

3.1 CONCEPTS OF PROCESS MANAGEMENT

Multiprocessing systems are designed around the concept of maintaining more than one independent process in an active state in main storage (see section 1.4.4). By sharing system resources among multiple active processes, we attempt to reduce the number of idle resources and improve system throughput.

The step from uniprogramming to multiprocessing provides several major benefits. Multiple user processes require a set of system processes to manage resources and provide services. Both user and system processes will share certain code segments, thus realizing memory space savings due to a need for only one copy. By careful statement of resource requirements for both user and system processes, the system resource usage can be optimized to ensure adequate response and maximum throughput. All of these benefits require a more complex system of software and hardware.

3.1.1 Process Types

Our general notion of a process is as a way of conceptualizing and dealing with programs in execution. The process concept allows us to distinguish between static instructions, which occupy a program's memory space, and the sequences of actions they generate when executed.

A program is an executable sequence of instructions that resides in memory (what Dijkstra calls the "rules of behavior"). It is typically produced by compiling one or more source files to produce one or more binary or object files. These object files are collected together with a system library module, and linked to form an executable program. A program, the static entity, contains one or more code paths which are executed by the processes, the dynamic entities. These paths exist because each program's code segment contains one or more conditional, iterative, and/or multiway case selection statements. Two processes may be executing the same code segment but follow entirely different paths through the instructions because of different input data sets.

A program is composed of at least one process (known as the main process). During execution, a process may spawn one or more additional processes leading to the concept of multiprocessing. Multiprocessing is the capability of performing multiple, parallel, and possibly independent activities within a single program.

A process can be viewed as a logically complete, asynchronous locus of control through the address space of a program [denn66]. Each process executes a distinct sequence of instructions during its lifetime. Multiple copies of a process may exist simultaneously, with each copy executing the same set of instructions at varying rates with possibly varying data. The copies of the processes are separated in time or by the operands they use in the instructions.

Our motivation for the process concept is to provide a mechanism for allocating and managing system resources. Among these resources are central processor access, memory space, and mass storage space. Multiprocessing attempts to improve the efficiency of resource utilization by building a queue of demands for all resources. This demand is achieved by having available in memory more than one process waiting for a resource and more than one process ready to use a resource as it becomes available. Concurrent processes are multiplexed among each other's wait-time intervals to ensure continuous "loading" on each resource.

In a single central processor, only one process can have control of the CPU at any one time. Apparent concurrency is achieved because other system resources, notably I/O devices, can be utilized in parallel. This concurrency is justified by applications requirements which are not feasible without exploiting an inherent parallelism. Moreover, one must assume a set of cost–performance increases as the number of active processes grows in relation to the complexity of the application ([baer73, pres75, wats70, wilk68]).

A problem arises in the process concept when one considers the initial allocation of resources. Many system resources are managed by system processes known as resource managers. Clearly, these processes cannot compete for system resources since they control them. Thus a differentiation must be made between system processes and user processes. User processes may compete for system resources via system service requests. System processes are assigned an initial set of resources which they cannot alter. System processes manage the resources of the system. A user process cannot directly spawn another process. Rather, via a system service request, it requests the OS to perform this function on its behalf.

The distinction between user and system processes is often one of convenience for the system designer. They are implemented using a common description, are scheduled by the same module, and share many of the same capabilities. Notable differences do exist.

1. A user process has a PDB for local data storage.
2. A user process may issue a system service request, whereas a system process cannot.
3. A user process may not create another process directly (although indirectly a process is created to service many system requests).
4. User processes may not do direct I/O operations, whereas system processes are able to explicitly perform direct I/O.
5. A user may request and be assigned resources, whereas a system process is usually preassigned a resource or manages one.

Note that certain system processes masquerade as user processes because they must compete for certain system resources. Most notably, the file manager is an exemplar.

3.1.2 Process States

Processes may exist in several states that are related to the utilization of system resources. The following states exist in most systems:

1. **Dormant.** A program is loaded into memory by the system loader but not yet activated for execution. The program has control of one resource—memory—but is not yet ready to be executed.

2. **Ready.** Any process that is resident on the processor scheduling queue such that, in its turn, it could be given control of the central processor (i.e., be ready to run).

3. **Running.** At any instant, the process that has control of the central processor after being dispatched into execution by the scheduler/dispatcher modules.

4. **Waiting.** An executing process that is suspended from execution while awaiting the availability of a specified resource or for completion of another process.

During the course of its lifetime, a process will experience transitions between the states in response to the properties of its instruction sequence, its interaction with other processes, or the action of external agents such as peripheral devices. These transitions are shown in figure 3.1. In many systems, each state may be further subdivided. For example, the waiting state might contain substates labeled memory-wait, file-wait, and device-wait. These subdivisions necessarily increase the size of the support modules, increase the complexity of the system,

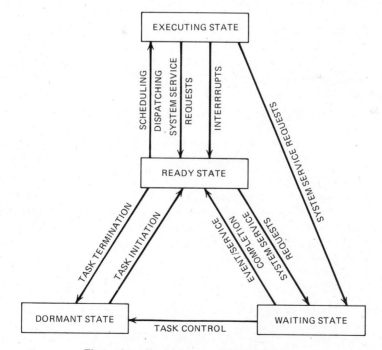

Figure 3.1   Task/process state transitions.

and often require greater system overhead. Most real-time systems tend to simplify the state structure in order to achieve the fastest scheduling and dispatching possible.

The efficiency of an OS can be indirectly measured by observing the distribution of processes over the states. A computer system is termed I/O-bound if many processes are waiting for access to a file or device or the completion of an I/O activity. A computer system is termed compute-bound if many processes are ready to run and very few are waiting for I/O activity. Code built into the OS can take snapshots of the states and thus provide a picture of the operation of the system. Table 3.1 shows one possible sequence of these snapshots.

The explicit system service requests that effect the transition between process states are discussed in subsequent chapters. The affect of interrupts and their relation to device handlers was described in section 2.2.2.

3.1.3 Issues in Process Management

The implementation of a multiprogramming system introduces four classes of problems which are the result of interactions among processes. This section briefly summarizes these four problem classes.

Mutual Exclusion

Mutual exclusion arises from the desire of individual processes to utilize system resources in a conflicting manner. Some resources, such as system modules, are reentrant and can be shared simultaneously among several processes. Others, such as the card reader or line printer, are serially reusable and must be shared sequentially. Mutual exclusion (see section 7.10) involves the locking out of processes from critical sections of code that affect the integrity and structure of the

TABLE 3.1   Snapshots of Process States

Sample Interval	Dormant	Memory Wait	Ready	Channel 1 Usage	Channel 2 Usage	Executing
ϵ_1	Pb, Pd	Pe	Pg	Pa	Pf	Pc
ϵ_2	Pb, Pd	Pe	Pc, Pf		Pg	Pa
ϵ_3	Pb, Pd	Pg	Pe	Pc	Pa	Pf
ϵ_4	Pb, Pd	Pa	Pe, Pg	Pf		Pc
ϵ_5	Pb	Pg	Pd, Pf	Pa	Pc	Pe
ϵ_6	Pc	Pe	Pb, Pg	Pd	Pf	Pa

system. A particularly important example is the updating of the scheduling queue concurrently with the dispatching of a new process.

Synchronization

In a multiprocessing system, many processes depend on other processes for the provision of services. A process may not be able to continue in execution until a specified service is provided, or a process may request a service where its only interest is in being informed of completion of the service. In either case, a process could simply call a subroutine and wait for the request to be completed. However, requests involving slower peripheral devices or requests having long service times can tie up the central processor, to the detriment of system efficiency. Synchronization involves the signaling between two or more processes, using a mutually agreed upon protocol, of the activities of the other. The "signal" is usually implemented as an event that causes the receiving process to take the appropriate action. The management of events in synchronizing processes is described in section 3.4.

Deadlock

The competition for resources among processes may result in a condition known as deadlock, where two processes may not continue in execution until the other one continues. Deadlock arises because the number of units of a given resource is less than the number of processes requesting specified amounts of the resource. A system deadlock occurs when all processes in the system are incapable of further progress in execution. The simplest example occurs where two processes each hold a resource required by the other process and are unwilling to relinquish the resource they own. Several solutions have been proposed for preventing and solving the deadlock problem. A partial solution using resource requests is discussed later in this chapter.

Interprocess Communication

The problems of mutual exclusion and synchronization can be solved in a simple fashion using event management or shared storage. Often, there is a need to communicate more information than just a simple signal of event completion. Exchange of messages between processes involves a complex structure to ensure protection of the processes. Interprocess communication also introduces new problems relative to addressing processes, the existence of receiving processes, and the structure of the scheduler or dispatcher. Interprocess communication is discussed in more detail in section 3.5.

3.2   PROCESS SCHEDULING AND DISPATCHING

One of the most critical resources in any computer system is the central processor. Access to the central processor by any task occurs through the system scheduler/dispatcher modules. This section explores the basic concepts of scheduling and dispatching within the OS, describes the databases necessary to support these functions, and examines the associated functions.

3.2.1   Scheduling versus Dispatching

In many systems, no distinction is made between the scheduling and dispatch-d. ing functions and these operations are usually combined into one module. In real-time systems, it is necessary to distinguish between the two functions. Scheduling is the act of arranging a set of processes in some ordered way according to a well-defined strategy. The SCHEDULER is the module responsible for inserting processes into the "ready-to-run" queue and maintaining the structure of the queue. Dispatching is the operation of selecting a process from the ready-to-run queue and providing it with access to the central processor. The DISPATCHER is the module that removes processes from the ready-to-run queue, establishes their machine state for execution, and transfers control to the process.

3.2.2   Structure of the Scheduler/Dispatcher

The generic structure of a scheduler/dispatcher is shown in figure 3.2. The scheduler is composed of a number of functional modules which perform the operations necessary for process management. Shaw [shaw74] notes that two implementations of the scheduler are possible. The first implementation follows the master or centralized scheduler approach, where the module is integrated into the OS nucleus. Whenever a process is blocked, or an interrupt occurs, the process is placed on the appropriate service queue. The scheduler is entered whenever the process is to be inserted into the ready-to-run queue. The master scheduler implements a systemwide global sharing of the central processor.

An alternative method, known as the shared scheduler, places the scheduling module in the address space of each user program. A process then executes a subroutine call to the scheduler to enter the process onto the ready-to-run queue. As Shaw notes, this scheme allows processes to be scheduled independent of the number of processors. It also allows each program to exercise its own scheduling strategy.

The structure of the scheduler/dispatcher is best described by examining the sample code skeletons. In this example, the following modules provide the scheduling/dispatching functions of the OS:

SCHEDULER	Selects a process
RESUME	Transfers control to an OS process
OS-EXIT	Transfers control to a user process

We need different modules to handle the resumption of process activity because the OS must reactivate the protection mechanisms of the memory management hardware. Since the user process executes in user space, the transfer of control across the hardware map requires a "JUMP TO USER SPACE" instruction. Modules 3.2.1 through 3.2.3 depict the appropriate code skeletons.

The Scheduler

The SCHEDULER selects the next process to be executed. The next process may be either a pending process, placed in a wait state by an interrupt, or a process selected from the ready-to-run queue. The SCHEDULER checks the availability of a pending process and, finding one, selects it as the next process to be executed. If there is no pending process, the next process is selected based on the scheduling algorithm:

No priority.   In this case, the first process on the ready-to-run queue is selected for execution; if the queue is empty, the scheduler cycles until a process is placed on the queue.

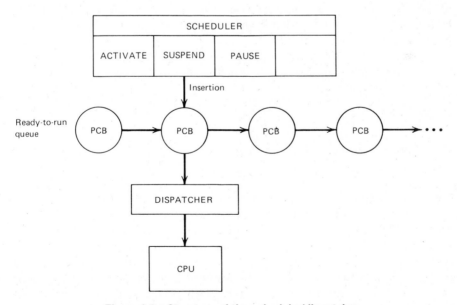

Figure 3.2   Structure of the scheduler/dispatcher.

Priority.   In this case, if the ready-to-run queue is empty, the idle process, having the lowest priority, is executed; whenever a higher-priority process becomes ready, it will preempt the idle process.

A pending process results when an interrupt occurs during the execution of a process. In the two modules below, we assume that we will always attempt to resume the most recently executing process whose control block address is stored in PENDING-PROCESS. Note that PENDING-PROCESS has a value of zero after execution of the system service request. An alternative approach would force the pending process to be rescheduled. The next process on the ready-to-run queue is then selected for execution. Under this scheme, the pending process is not necessarily the next process executed.

The argument for resuming a pending process is often based on the scheduling philosophy. In a time-slice system, resumption allows a process to proceed to the end of its quantum or to the next service request. Thus a process is always rescheduled at a well-defined point in its execution. Alternatively, an interrupt can be thought of as an externally imposed preemption of a process's rights to the processor. After interrupt processing is completed, the processor may be viewed as open to all ready processes. Where a pending process is placed in the ready-to-run determines when it next gets access to the processor.

An interesting case occurs when the OS has no useful work to perform. In a nonpriority system, the dispatcher cycles until a process is made "ready" for execution by an interrupt. In a priority-based system, control is handed to the IDLE-PROCESS. An idle process merely executes a repetitive sequence of instructions in an infinite loop. The idle process possesses the lowest priority in the system. As soon as any process with higher priority becomes "ready," it will be selected for execution. Many systems use the idle process as a means to collect data about system utilization.

P points to the PCB containing the system control information for the process. I defer discussion of this data structure in order to motivate the need for some of its elements.

Resuming Control of a System Process

Two routines are required to return control to processes once a system service request has been executed. These routines are mandated by the nature of the MMU. RESUME (shown in module 3.2.2) returns control to a system process. If the process possesses a data block, events in the data block are updated to reflect completed actions. The return address is retrieved from the process stack; control is transferred to it. Note that resumption merely involves a subroutine call because all system processes (including the file manager) share a dedicated map 0. Figure 3.3 depicts the control transfer activity.

MODULE 3.2.1   (without priority)

```
procedure scheduler
     if pending-process not equal to zero
     then
               pending-process → p
               clear pending-process
               resume ( )
     endif
     remove-from-queue (ready-queue) → p
     if p equals zero
          then
               goto scheduler
     endif
     resume ( )
endproc
```

MODULE 3.2.1   (with priority)

```
procedure scheduler
     if pending-process not equal to zero
          then
               pending-process → p
               clear pending-process
               resume ( )
     endif
     if ready-queue-count equals zero
          then
               address (idle-process) → p
               resume ( )
     endif
     remove-from-queue (ready-queue) → p
     resume ( )
endproc
```

MODULE 3.2.2

```
procedure resume
     if pdb [p] not equal to zero
          then
               pdb-page-select ( )
               update-events ( )
     endif
     unstack the return address from process stack
     call (return-address)
endproc
```

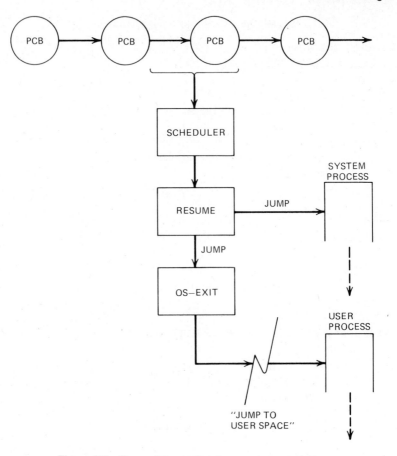

Figure 3.3   Resuming user/system process activity.

Resuming Control of a User Process

OS-EXIT (shown in module 3.2.3) transfers control from the OS to a user process. The system must reestablish the environment of the user process as it was immediately prior to the system service request that enabled the user process to enter the OS. First, the system must release any system overlays that were loaded in order to service the system request. Second, the system service request arguments are popped off the user stack (pointed to by USP). If the process has a data block, the PDB is mapped back to user space. Finally, the CPU registers and status word are restored; the map state is set to user mode; and a "jump to user space" instruction is executed. This sequence of steps returning control to a user process is dependent on the structure of the MMU hardware and the OS architecture.

MODULE 3.2.3

```
procedure os-exit
    stacktop (usp) → function-code
    system-overlay-table [function-code] → overlay-address
    if overlay-address not equal to zero
        then
                system (release-overlay, overlay-address)
    endif
entry os-exit2:
    stacktop (usp) → function-code
    system-table [function-code + 1] → number-of-parameters
    increment usp by number-of-parameters
    if usp greater than or equal to stack-base-address
        then
                address (usp) → usp
                address (stack-area) → usp-limit
                system (error-kill, er-stack)
    endif
    unstack user-return-address from process stack
    unstack user map-nr from process stack
    if map-nr [p] not equal to zero
        then
                pdb-page-select (map-nr [p])
                map pdb back to user space
    endif
    restore registers and CPU status
    set map state to user-mode
    execute 'jump to user space' instruction
endproc
```

3.2.3   Scheduling Algorithms

A variety of scheduling algorithms have been introduced in the literature and implemented in various OSs. Coffman and Denning [coff73] present a detailed mathematical analysis of a number of different scheduling algorithms. In this section, I describe briefly two popular scheduling algorithms and one that I find particularly interesting.

Round-Robin Scheduling

Round-robin scheduling, also known as first in, first out (FIFO), is one of the earliest and simplest scheduling algorithms. Under a FIFO strategy, a process to be scheduled is placed at the end of the ready-to-run queue. Processes are dispatched from the queue by removing the first process in the queue and giving it control of the central processor. Scheduling priority is determined solely by linear position in the queue. The problem with round-robin scheduling is that a process may execute for a long time before relinquishing control of the CPU. In effect, the process "hogs" the CPU to the detriment of other processes' progress. To avoid this problem, each process may be assigned a time quantum (a time slice). This quantum determines the continuous amount of processor time a process may utilize after it has been dispatched. When the time quantum expires, the process will be forcibly rescheduled by the OS. This "time-slice" method is known as a round-robin discipline because the time available is divided evenly among the active processes (t = available time/number of available processes). It is used in various forms by most time-sharing systems supporting interactive terminals. (References include [blat72], [feng79], [free75], [lamp68], and [niel71]).

Priority Scheduling

In priority scheduling, each process is assigned a priority which determines its position in the ready-to-run queue relative to other processes. Priority is an indication of the criticality of a process, that is, its importance to the system. Usually, the process with the lowest priority is called the idle process because it idles or soaks up CPU cycles.

The idea behind a priority scheme is that processes are placed on the ready-to-run queue based on their priority. The process with the highest priority is placed at the head of the queue and it is the first process to be dispatched. One of the design constraints to be decided is the number of priority classes. The number of classes should be selected such that, during execution, bunching of processes in a class does not occur. Standard ranges for priorities vary considerably among OSs. Most minicomputer manufacturers use the range zero to 255 since these values can be conveniently accommodated in 1 byte.

Bernstein and Sharp [bern71] discuss an interesting approach to priority scheduling known as policy scheduling. A user process receives a given amount of service based on the "class" to which it belongs. The process's priority changes dynamically as a function of the difference between the service promised to the user by the policy function and the service he or she actually receives. The implementation of the policy function may be static or dynamic. A static policy function is exemplified by OS/360, which assigns users to job classes based on their declarations of resource requirements. A dynamic policy function is exemplified by the Univac 1100 Series Operating System scheduling algorithm. A user's process migrates among priority classes based on the time it has utilized and the resources it has dynamically acquired.

Adaptive/Reflective Scheduling

Doherty [dohe71] describes a concept known as adaptive/reflective scheduling. Adaptive scheduling embodies a policy for controlling real memory use. Under this policy, limits on the real memory and virtual CPU time are established for each process prior to each dispatch. The memory limit is an estimate of the current working set size derived from the working set size and the direction of change from the preceding time slice. A count is maintained of the number of real memory pages allocated to a process. A time slice for a process is initiated only when enough real memory pages are free to accommodate the predicted working set size. The system adapts to each process's working set size throughout the process's execution.

Reflective scheduling is a policy that provides a variety of processing speeds as functions of each process's working set size. The virtual CPU time limit is established for a process prior to each time slice. It is inversely proportional to the real memory space limit. Processes with large working set sizes are given a minimum time limit in order to improve the productive time of their execution. The effect of this approach is to bias the system in favor of processes that minimize their working set size. These processes have a higher ratio of productive time to overhead time because their virtual time slice is longer and their paging requirements are lower than average. This results in a hierarchy of processing speeds.

Clearly, these policies favor small programs with small execution times and these policies are most effective in interactive environments, where responsiveness must be commensurate with resource utilization. It behooves users in interactive environments to keep their programs small in order to improve their execution times. Experiments by Doherty at IBM have shown that users will adapt to this scheduling approach by restructuring their programs to obtain better responsiveness.

To Preempt or Not

In a priority scheduling system, a problem arises when a process is placed on the ready-to-run queue whose priority is higher than that of the process in execution. This problem can occur when an interrupt signals the completion of an activity that "readies" a process of higher priority, one now ready to proceed in execution. The question to be decided is whether or not to preempt the current process immediately. In a preemption policy, the current process would be forcibly rescheduled and the higher-priority process would be dispatched into execution. Preemption, however, involves process switching costs and additional scheduler logic, and in certain systems may result in severe data management inefficiencies (see thrashing discussion in section 4.5). Shub [shub78] presents a cogent discussion of the costs associated with preemption in a round-robin system.

Shaw [shaw74] describes a selective preemption policy which can be "tuned" to provide efficiency between the extremes of preemption and nonpreemption. Each process is assigned not only a priority but also a pair of flags (u, v) which have the interpretation:

u = 1 if the process may preempt another process; 0 otherwise

and

v = 1 if the process may be preempted by another process; 0 otherwise

Under this scheme, the (u, v) pairs could be tuned through direct observation of the system to the state that yielded the greatest efficiency. Generally, such a tuning process would apply only to system processes and user processes with fixed priorities.

Static versus Dynamic Priorities

Priorities may be assigned to a process according to a static or dynamic algorithm. In the static case, a priority is assigned when the process is created. The priority can be determined in several ways.

1. The priority is the same as the program to which the process belongs.
2. The priority may be calculated from proposed resource usage (such as memory, I/O time, or processor cycles).
3. The priority is based on the estimated running time of the entire program (e.g., optimize shortest jobs first).
4. The priority is based on the type of process independent of the resources it uses.

The problem with static priority assignments is that a proper mix of processes can interact to degrade overall system efficiency seriously. Since the priorities are fixed for the duration of the process's lifetime, corrective measures cannot be taken to adjust system efficiency. The solution is to dynamically assign priorities to a process during execution. This has two aspects: when the process is created, the priority is calculated based on the current behavior of the system; and whenever the process is rescheduled, or when it exhausts a time quantum, the priority is adjusted to reflect its behavior to date.

Many variations on the latter theme have been implemented in several real-time OSs. An interesting scheme that considers multiple resource factors is that used by Univac's 1100 Series Operating Systems [univ73]. A survey of the OS manuals for many minicomputer systems will provide different algorithms.

3.2.4 Databases for Process Management

The scheduling function relies on two major databases: the process control block and the ready-to-run queue.

Operationally, a process is an organizational device for representing information about computations. Each process is composed of a sequence of instructions and some control parameters. The information describing a process, its activation record, is contained in a data structure known as the PCB. A local data storage area, known as the PDB, may be associated with a process. In the PDB are stored the user stack and event vectors. Portions of the PDB are available to the user process to store temporary data. Other portions are restricted exclusively to the OS.

The ready-to-run queue is a list of the processes in the order in which they are to be dispatched into execution. The dispatcher removes the PCB at the head of the queue and assigns control of the CPU to it.

These databases vary in their content and complexity. Different OS implementations keep different information in the PCB. Some systems combine the information in the PCB and the PDB into one control block. The structure of the control block and data block are presented in tables 3.2 through 3.9.

The Base Area of the Control Block

Each control block possesses a base area which is invariant across all processes and each possesses links to the next previous control blocks in the chain. During the lifetime of a process, its control block is resident on a system queue. The identity of this queue is maintained in CURRENT-QUEUE.

System service requests are invoked as functions from the user's process. A request may return a value to the process upon completion of execution. For synchronously executed requests, the function value may be a piece of data relevant to the process's execution. This value is stored in the entry RETURN-VALUE.

A process may have an associated data block which is used for storage of private data (see below). The address of the PDB is stored in the control block since the PDB is mapped between user and system space. The PDB is allocated a page of real memory so that its address is a real memory page index. Some processes do not have blocks and are not allowed to execute system service requests. Nevertheless, processes have a need for a local data workspace. This space is maintained in the control block in the entry PROCESS-DATA.

Most processes have a parent process which created them for a specific purpose. The exceptions are those system processes created during system initialization (see section 7.5). Some system processes (e.g., those created for I/O operations) exist only for a short time; when they have accomplished their mission,

Table 3.2   Process Control Block—Base Area

Mnemonic	Usage
next-cb	Pointer used to link the next PCB to this PCB in the current queue
previous-cb	Pointer used to link this PCB to the previous PCB in the current queue
priority	Current priority of the process (in a priority scheduler only)
return-value	Temporary storage for a value returned from a system module as the direct result of a system service request
current-queue	Identifier of the current queue on which this PCB resides
rs-data-save	Temporary storage for resource semaphore data
pdb-address	Address of a PDB
event-nr	Event number passed from the parent (i.e., creating) process
parent	Identifier of the creating process
event-status	Indicates the status of the current event
event-data	Temporary storage for the value of an event
process-data	Process data workspace (for processes that do not have a PDB)

Table 3.3   Process Control Block—I/O Request Area

Mnemonic	Usage
request-file-address	File address for the current data transfer request
request-map	Identifier of memory map into which the data will be transferred
request-record-type	Indicator of the record type for this request
request-fcb-address	Address of file control block for this request
request-dcb-address	Address of device control block
request-ccb-address	Address of channel control block
request-buffer-address	Address of a buffer used in an I/O request
request-size	Number of words to transfer on this request
request-data-address	Memory address from/to which data are transferred
request-opcode	Function code for system service request
request-ptrs-per-block	Number of segment pointers in SPB
request-ptr-index	Index of pointer in a segment pointer block

they self-destruct. Processes will notify the parent of the success or failure of their actions via an event number. It maintains the identifier of its parent and the event number by which it is to communicate its status in PARENT-ID and EVENT-NR. Two other entries, EVENT-STATUS and EVENT-DATA, are temporary storage locations for the status and value of an event.

Table 3.4 Process Control Block—Overlay Control Area

Mnemonic	Usage
request-overlay-id	Identifier for the current overlay
request-overlay-mode	Mode bits for overlay loading
request-overlay-index	Work cell for overlay index

Table 3.5 Process Control Block—Record Management Area

Mnemonic	Usage
request-lock-address	File address to be locked against access
request-temp-address	Temporary work cell for segmented file searches
request-lock-size	Number of sectors to be locked
request-lock-forward	Address of next process in lock chain
request-lock-back	Address of previous process in lock chain
request-lock-down	Address of next process requesting the same disk sectors

Table 3.6 Process Control Block—Device Request Area

Mnemonic	Usage
request-device-opcode	Device operation code
request-execution-address	Address in memory of current step in a disk function table (see section 2.6.2)
request-device-address	Mass storage device address for current request
request-device-map	Memory map for execution of device request
request-device-data	Address of data area in memory for device request
request-nr-words	Number of words to transfer on this request
request-sort-key	Data value for sorting request in disk service queue
request-last-opcode	Index of last tape operation
request-retry	Number of retries for a disk operation
request-tape-function	Index of direct tape management function

Table 3.7 Process Control Block—Process Stack Area

Mnemonic	Usage
psp	Process stack pointer
pstack	Process stack area

Table 3.8   Process Control Block—Service Request Area

Mnemonic	Usage
map-number	Current map number of user residence
pdb-map-slot	I/O map slot for data transfers to PDB
events-on	Index of initiated events
events-done	Index of completed events
event-chain	Pointer to a list of processes waiting for events to be updated
all-process-link	Pointer to next process in a queue of all processes
delta-time	Number of clock ticks for which the process may be suspended

Table 3.9   Process Data Block

Mnemonic	Usage
user-data[1...128]	Process addressable data
parent-id	PCB address for the process's parent
event-nr	Event number to signal parent when a function is completed by child
data-size	Size of message from parent
data-block[1...128]	Data from parent process
stack-area [1...128]	Storage area reserved for user stack
usp	User stack pointer
usp-limit	Last address available for stack
status[1,...,16]	Status words for events
value1[1,...,16]	First data word for events
value2[1,...,16]	Second data word for events

The Input/Output Request Area

When an I/O request is executed, a system process is created to execute the request. This approach allows the parent process to continue executing independently of the I/O request, which may require substantial time to complete.

The I/O request area contains the parameters relevant to an I/O request. Not all entries are used to execute each request. It is cost-effective, in most systems, to statically allocate a fixed area to hold these parameters rather than dynamically allocate a variable-length data area for each request.

Each I/O request requires a channel. The address of the channel control block (see section 5.3) is determined and stored in REQUEST-CCB-ADDRESS. A channel is associated with a file or device. The control block address is determined and stored in either REQUEST-FCB-ADDRESS or REQUEST-DCB-ADDRESS.

Four entries serve as temporary storage locations. REQUEST-FILE-ADDRESS contains the file address from/to which data are transferred. This address is automatically updated during sequential data transfers. REQUEST-MAP contains the memory map identifier into which the data will be transferred. For block transfers, data are moved directly to the caller's space, so the map number reflects the residence of the caller's process. For record transfers, a disk block is transferred to a system buffer, whose address is maintained in REQUEST-BUFFER-ADDRESS, and the record is extracted.

The Overlay Control Area

A process may be composed of a root segment and one or more overlays. To load an overlay, a process must execute a system service request. A system process is created to locate the overlay on the disk and bring it into memory. Three entries are used to hold overlay information (see section 4.4). REQUEST-OVERLAY-ID contains the identifier of the overlay request by the process. REQUEST-OVERLAY-MODE contains the mode bits specified in the LOAD-OVERLAY request. REQUEST-OVERLAY-INDEX is a work cell for decomposing the overlay identifier and holding the disk address of the overlay.

The Record Mangement Area

A process may issue an I/O request to ready or write a record under conditions that require exclusive access to the record. The system supports a record locking mechanism which guarantees this access in a multiprocessing environment (see section 5.8). The record management area contains parameters relevant to guaranteeing the integrity of the records in this environment. The functions associated with the locking mechanism form a superset of the standard I/O requests.

REQUEST-LOCK-ADDRESS holds the block address of the first disk block in the file, which contains the record to be accessed by the process. A set of sectors must be locked by the system to guarantee exclusive access to the record. REQUEST-LOCK-SIZE specifies the number of sectors to be locked for a given I/O request.

If the disk blocks containing the specified record are already locked against access, the system process created to handle the request is placed on the lock chain to wait until the disk blocks are freed. REQUEST-LOCK-FORWARD, REQUEST-LOCK-BACK, and REQUEST-LOCK-DOWN are entries containing the addresses of other processes in the lock chain. The structure of the lock chain is described fully in section 5.8.1.

The Device Request Area

Each I/O request is eventually resolved into one or more device requests. The device request area holds parameters for constructing and executing device requests and is set up primarily to support disk or tape request execution. REQUEST-EXECUTION-ADDRESS is the current step in a disk function table. REQUEST-DEVICE-OPCODE contains operation codes for non-mass storage devices. REQUEST-LAST-OPCODE contains the last tape operation executed by the system. REQUEST-TAPE-FUNCTION contains the tape function opcode to be executed during direct tape operations.

In general, a disk request requires several parameters. REQUEST-DEVICE-ADDRESS is the physical address where the data reside. This address is calculated by the I/O manager from the logical file address specified by the user. The corresponding memory address is stored in REQUEST-DEVICE-DATA. REQUEST-DEVICE-MAP specifies the memory map that contains the target memory address.

REQUEST-NR-WORDS contains the number of words to be transferred; it is a multiple of the disk sector size. REQUEST-SORT-KEY is used to sort disk service requests on the disk request queue.

The Process Stack Area

Most system processes, such as those created for I/O requests, do not have a PDB. However, they still need a local data storage area in which to maintain a process stack. For these processes, the process stack is located in the PCB and shares the same space as the service request area.

The Service Request Area

User processes can issue system service requests. The service request area holds the parameters that are necessary to service these requests. MAP-NUMBER is the current map in which the process code resides. PDB-MAP-SLOT is an I/O map slot assigned to the PDB for direct data transfers from a device into a PDB.

Three entries control the processing of events. A process may issue up to 15 simultaneous requests by assigning each request an event number. The system keeps track of how many events a process has initiated by setting a bit in the EVENTS-ON entry for each event number associated with a request. Concomitantly, as each event is completed, that event is recorded by setting a bit in the EVENTS-DONE entry. The process can determine how many events are outstanding by taking the logical OR of the EVENTS-ON and EVENTS-DONE entries. The values of the events are updated when the PDB is available. Meanwhile, events that complete have their status and values maintained in event data blocks which are attached to the PCB via the event chain.

ALL-PROCESS-QUEUE is a queue that has every process linked into it. This queue is useful in counting the number of processes in the system. It may also be used for recovery in the event of a system failure when the normal system queues are destroyed. The likelihood that both sets of queues will be destroyed is rather small since ALL-PROCESS-QUEUE is quite stable.

The Process Data Block

The PDB contains the private data for an active process. A PDB is mapped into the low-order addresses of a process's address space. A process may access the low-order 128 (arbitrarily) locations for private data storage. The remaining locations in the PDB are reserved for system private storage associated with the process.

As stated earlier, PARENT-ID contains the PCB address for the process that created the process and EVENT-NR is the event by which the child signals the parent when its mission is completed. The parent may pass to the child a data block up to 128 words in length. DATA-SIZE contains the current length of the data block. These parameters are set up by the system service request PROCESS when it creates a child process.

Each process has an associated stack for processing system service requests. USP points to the current position in the stack. USP-LIMIT is the topmost location of the stack. Its use may be observed in the modules that process system service requests (see section 7.3).

The PDB contains the data areas for storing the status and values of the events that a process may initiate. These are respectively STATUS, VALUE1, and VALUE2.

3.2.5 Scheduler/Dispatcher Functions

The essential characteristic of a multiprocessing system is its ability to orchestrate, if you will, the distinct actions of many processes. In most OSs, there are a variety of functions made available to the user to turn processes on and off, create and destroy processes, or send messages between processes. Underlying these functions are the modules that handle process management, particularly for I/O functions. These are described in the following sections.

Suspending a Process

In the course of execution, a system process may determine that a required resource is not available or that no further work is to be done at the present time. The process may voluntarily suspend execution until it is activated by another process. This procedure places the address of the control block on the process stack. It then calls the system scheduler to activate the next process. The result of this action is that the process is not placed in the ready-to-run queue and is thus inactivated. Figure 3.4 depicts this operation.

Placing the control block address on the process's own stack ensures that the process can be reactivated by merely "resuming" that process. Note that the PCB is not resident on any system queue except the ALL-PROCESS-QUEUE. To reactivate this process, another process must explicitly awaken it via ACTI-VATE(P), where P is the address of the process.

MODULE 3.2.4

```
procedure suspend
     increment psp[p]
     psp[p] → top-of-stack
     p → memory (top-of-stack)
     scheduler ( )
   endproc
```

Deferring Process Execution

During long code sequences, a process may effectively "hog" the central processor. That is, except for interrupts, no other process may be able to access the CPU. To facilitate access to the CPU, a process can voluntarily reschedule itself by "deferring" its execution. The procedure puts the control block address on the process stack. It then requests that it be rescheduled by calling ACTIVATE with its own PCB address. A call to the scheduler selects the next process for execution.

MODULE 3.2.5

```
procedure defer
     increment psp[p]
     psp[p] → top-of-stack
     p → memory (top-of-stack)
     activate(p)
     scheduler( )
   endproc
```

Activating a Process

This procedure places a PCB on the ready-to-run queue. It checks to see if the PCB address is equal to P—the currently executing process. If not, P is entered

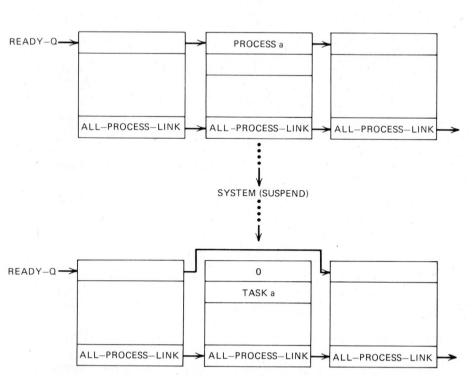

Figure 3.4   How a process is suspended.

onto the ready-to-run queue. If PCB-ADDRESS is equal to P, the process's PCB is already attached to the end of the ready-to-run queue (FIFO scheduling method). A process awakening a suspended process will activate that process with ACTIVATE(PCB-ADDRESS) to place the process on the ready-to-run queue. This procedure is depicted in module 3.2.6.

MODULE 3.2.6

```
procedure activate (pcb-address)
    if pcb-address not equal to p
        then
               enter-into-queue (ready-queue, pcb-address)
    endif
    address(ready-queue) → current-queue [pcb-address]
    endproc
```

Starting a Subprocess

A subprocess is used to perform much of the initalization code necessary to the execution of file and I/O management requests. When a request is processed by the system interface module, it calls START-SUBPROCESS to initialize the subprocess and activate it. EVENT-STATUS[P] is used to hold the address of the subprocess.

When the subprocess has completed, the status of its execution is returned to the parent process. This is accomplished through a module known as SET-SUBPROCESS-STATUS.

Finally, the subprocess must be terminated and its control block returned to the system control block pool. This function is accomplished by the module END-SUBPROCESS. In some cases, the parent process may activate itself as the subprocess (usually, for requests without an event number). END-SUB-PROCESS must check to see if the parent is masquerading as a subprocess:

> If not, then the PCB is released to the PCB pool because the subprocess was created independently of its parent
>
> If so, the event number is marked complete and P is placed on the event chain of the parent so that all events are updated

If P was its own parent, its priority is reduced to that of a normal system process.

The event associated with the process is updated in the process control block. If the process was not executed independently of its parent (EVN not equal to 16), the status of the event is returned to the parent process. Control is returned to the calling process through OS-EXIT.

MODULE 3.2.7

```
procedure start-subprocess
      event-status[p] → subprocess-address
      call(subprocess-address)

entry set-subprocess-status:
      process-status → event-status[p]

entry end-subprocess:
      parent[p] → parent-address
      if parent-address not equal to p
            then
                        event-nr[p] → evn
                        if evn equals zero
                              then
                                    release(pcb-rs, p)
```

```
                    else
                          release(event-rs, evn)
                                event-chain[parent-address] → next-cb[p]
                          p → event-chain[parent-address]
                endif
                scheduler( )
      endif
      decrement priority[p] by subprocess-priority-increment
      event-nr[p] → evn
      event-status[p] → status[evn]
      event-data1[p] → value1[evn]
      event-data2[p] → value2[evn]
      if evn equal to 16
            then
                    event-status[p] → return-value[p]
      endif
      os-exit( )
endproc
```

Checking Event Conditions

When a process is created by another process, it may be executed synchronously with respect to its parent by specifying an event number equal to 16. When a process completes, the associated event number, if any, is checked to determine the appropriate action to be taken. If the event number is not equal to 16, a normal system exit occurs. Otherwise, any overlays are released and the parent process is notified directly of the results of the function.

MODULE 3.2.8

```
procedure event-16-check
      if event-nr[usp] not equal to 16
            then
                    os-exit( )
      endif
      system-overlay-table[function-code] → overlay-address
      if overlay-address not equal to zero
            then
                    system (release-overlay, overlay-address)
      endif
      request (wait-rs)
      status[16] → return-value[p]
      os-exit2( )
endproc
```

Completing Subprocess Initialization

Once a subprocess has been initialized, it must be activated for execution. If an error has occurred during the initialization of the subprocess, the request will be rejected. An error will be denoted by a negative process status. If an error occurred, the process status is reported to the parent and the subprocess is terminated.

P-SETUP-OK is executed when a subprocess has been successfully initialized. The address of the module which executes the service request is retrieved from the switch table and stored temporarily in the event-status. At this point, the subprocess is activated by either of the following:

1. If the parent process is to execute as the subprocess (P = N), the subprocess is called directly. This action is possible because the parent process was in control of the machine at the time the system service request was issued; the subprocess is merely an extension of the parent process's execution. This is used for synchronously executed requests.

2. When the subprocess is independent of the parent, it must be given a life of its own. The event is marked busy. The address of the subprocess is placed on the process stack so that when the process is activated, its PCB is readily available. The parent process is made the pending process while the subprocess becomes the current process. Execution of the user program is then resumed.

MODULE 3.2.9

```
procedure p-setup-done
     if process-status less then 0
          then
                    process-status → error-code
                    if p not equal to n
                         then
                                    release(pcb-rs, n)
                    endif
                    decrement priority[p] by SUBPROCESS-PRIORITY-
                                                        INCREMENT
                    event-error(error-code)
     endif
entry p-setup-ok:
     system-switch-table[function-code + 1] → event-status[n]
     if p equal to n
          then
                    start-subprocess( )
     endif
```

```
entry goto-subprocess:
    mark-event-busy( )
    increment psp[p]
    psp[p] → top-of-stack
    address(event-16-check) → memory(top-of-stack)
    p → pending-process
    n → p
    resume( )
endproc
```

3.2.6   Implementing a FIFO Scheduler

A first in, first out (FIFO) scheduler consists of a linear list of control blocks which form the ready-to-run queue. A PCB is placed on the READY-QUEUE by the ACTIVATE function and removed by the SCHEDULER function. These routines, in turn, call the queue manipulation functions ENTER-INTO-QUEUE and REMOVE-FROM-QUEUE to insert and remove entries from the queue (see section 7.9). For a FIFO scheduling algorithm, these routines take the following form:

1.   ENTER-INTO-QUEUE(READY-QUEUE, PCB-ADDRESS)

When a control block is to be added to the ready-to-run queue, it is placed at the end of the queue. The algorithm is (roughly):

    Set 0 to NEXT-CB[PCB-ADDRESS]

    QUEUE-END[READY-QUEUE] → LAST-PCB-ADDRESS

    PCB-ADDRESS → NEXT-CB[LAST-PCB-ADDRESS]

    PCB-ADDRESS → QUEUE-END[READY-QUEUE]

    increment QUEUE-COUNT[READY-QUEUE]

A more detailed description can be found by examining module 7.9.2.

2.   REMOVE-FROM-QUEUE(READY-QUEUE) → PCB-ADDRESS

When a control block is to be removed from the ready-to-run queue, it is extracted from the front of the queue. The algorithm is (roughly):

    QUEUE-START[READY-QUEUE] → PCB-ADDRESS

NEXT-CB[PCB-ADDRESS] → QUEUE-START[READY-QUEUE]

Set 0 to NEXT-CB[PCB-ADDRESS]

decrement QUEUE-COUNT[READY-QUEUE]

A more detailed description can be found by examining module 7.9.3.

3.2.7 Implementing a General Priority Scheduler

A priority scheduler is implemented by assigning each process a priority. The ready-to-run queue consists of a sorted list of control blocks; the control block at the head of the queue has the highest priority. The process represented by this control block will receive service first. A control block is added to the ready-to-run queue by the ACTIVATE function and removed from the queue by the SCHEDULER function. These routines use ENTER-INTO-PRIORITY-QUEUE and REMOVE-FROM-PRIORITY-QUEUE, respectively, to maintain a priority-ordered queue.

1. ENTER-INTO-PRIORITY-QUEUE(READY-QUEUE, PCB-ADDRESS)

ENTER-INTO-PRIORITY-QUEUE must search the queue for the proper location in which to insert the new control block. The algorithm is (roughly):

QUEUE-START[READY-QUEUE] → PCB-TEMP

while PCB-TEMP not equal to zero

    do

        PCB-TEMP → PREVIOUS-PCB

        if PRIORITY[PCB-TEMP] greater than
                PRIORITY[PCB-ADDRESS]

      then

           NEXT-CB[PCB-TEMP] → PCB-TEMP

      else

          exitdo

     endif

    enddo

if PCB-TEMP equals zero

then

PCB-ADDRESS → NEXT-CB[PCB-TEMP]

increment QUEUE-COUNT[READY-QUEUE]

else

PCB-TEMP → NEXT-CB[PCB-ADDRESS]

PCB-ADDRESS → NEXT-CB[PREVIOUS-PCB]

increment QUEUE-COUNT[READY-QUEUE]

endif

2.   REMOVE-FROM-PRIORITY-QUEUE(READY-QUEUE) → PCB-ADDRESS

Since the READY-QUEUE is sorted with the highest-priority process at the head of the queue, removing a control block from the queue is equivalent to the algorithm used in the FIFO implementation. The algorithm is (roughly):

QUEUE-START[READY-QUEUE] → PCB-ADDRESS

NEXT-CB[PCB-ADDRESS] → QUEUE-START[READY-QUEUE]

clear NEXT-CB[PCB-ADDRESS]

decrement QUEUE-COUNT[READY-QUEUE]

A General Priority Scheme

The algorithms described above represent a simple priority scheme—that is, a single linear list contains all the control blocks. With a large number of active processes, the time spent searching the list can be extensive. Moreover, with this scheme considerable flexibility is allowed in assigning a priority value. In fact, the range of priority values is 0, ..., 32767 since one word is used to hold the priority.

It is inconceivable that any OS will actually require that many distinct priority classes. In fact, most systems restrict the number of distinct priority classes to the range 0, ..., 128 to 0, ..., 256, where the priority value can be accommodated comfortably in 1 byte. This approach may be coupled with an implementation scheme that reduces the system overhead necessary to insert a control block into the ready-to-run queue.

A generalized priority scheme uses a list of 128 (or 256) entries that contain pointers to sublists of control blocks. Within each priority class, the processes having that priority are arranged in FIFO order. Insertion is relatively simple; the system determines in which queue to insert the control block by its priority value, and then calls ENTER-INTO-QUEUE with the address of the queue head. Similarly, removal of a control block means that the system locates the first nonempty sublist and extracts the first control block from it. The routines for performing this generalized priority scheme are presented below.

1. ENTER-INTO-PRIORITY-QUEUE(READY-QUEUE, PCB-ADDRESS)

PRIORITY[PCB-ADDRESS] → PCB-PRIORITY

if PCB-PRIORITY less than 0 or PCB-PRIORITY greater than 255

    then

        return ER-PRIORITY

endif

QUEUE-START[READY-QUEUE] → QHEAD

QHEAD[PCB-PRIORITY] → PCB-TEMP

PCB-ADDRESS → QHEAD[PCB-PRIORITY]

QUEUE-COUNT[READY-QUEUE] → QUEUE-COUNTER

increment QUEUE-COUNT[PCB-PRIORITY]

2. REMOVE-FROM-PRIORITY-QUEUE(READY-QUEUE)
                                        → PCB ADDRESS

QUEUE-COUNT[READY-QUEUE] → QUEUE-COUNTER

for PRIORITY-INDEX from 0 to 255

    do

        if QUEUE-COUNTER[PRIORITY-INDEX] not equal to zero

          then

            exitdo

        endif

    enddo

QUEUE-START[READY-QUEUE] → QHEAD

QHEAD[PRIORITY-INDEX] → PCB-ADDRESS

NEXT-CB[PCB-ADDRESS] → QHEAD[PRIORITY-INDEX]

decrement QUEUE-COUNTER[PRIORITY-INDEX]

In such a fixed priority system, there must always be one process that can be scheduled to utilize the CPU. This process, known as the idle process, has the lowest priority in the OS. By inserting new processes with a priority level greater than 255, we ensure that the system always has a process to schedule.

3.3 PROCESS MANAGEMENT FUNCTIONS

The management of processes is akin to an industrial control problem. One must be able to start and stop processes, communicate with them, and request information about their status. In the multiprocessing environment, a user has (at least) one main process and possibly many subordinate processes active at any one time. In order to accomplish the functions of the program, the user must be able to control the activity of these processes in relation to one another. The control functions provided by the OS in this regard are invoked through system service requests. The following sections describe a set of primitives that might be found in any modern OS.

3.3.1   Assumptions Concerning Process Control

The major issues in process management were discussed briefly in section 3.1.3.
These issues proceed from these fundamental assumptions (see [free75]):

1. We know nothing about the relative speeds of processes. A process is de-
    fined as a sequence of actions that proceed at some rate of execution.
    The activity of a process stops and goes as a function of resource avail-
    ability, algorithm definition, or interaction with other processes. A pro-
    cess can initiate or terminate other processes and, perhaps, find out how
    many of them exist at any instant. Attempting to keep track of each pro-
    cess's status and its current activity poses a tremendous data manage-
    ment problem. Most of a process's execution time would be spent in fol-
    lowing what each of its neighbors (or siblings) was doing. Freeman noted
    that such a situation could lead to a race condition in which the action of
    a process depended on a race in time with one or more other processes
    (like keeping up with the Joneses).

2. The presence of critical sections in a process's instruction sequence poses
    a significant data management problem. Freeman defined a critical sec-
    tion as "a set of instructions in which the result of execution may vary
    unpredictably if variables referenced in the section are changed by other
    processes during its execution." Two processes, arriving at a shared crit-
    ical section at the same time, would attempt to execute and thus gener-
    ate false data for each other. As many portions of the OS exhibit such a
    property (i.e., being critical sections), only one process is allowed to
    utilize a critical section at a time. All other processes must be excluded
    from this instruction sequence and wait their turn.

3. A race condition would lead to inefficient system behavior since each
    process would spend most of its time performing housekeeping chores
    relative to data management. The asynchronicity of parallel processes
    and their variable execution rates can lead to serious problems in algo-
    rithm timing. A process may be ready to execute before the data it needs
    are available. Among multiple parallel processes that are working differ-
    ent aspects of a problem, some form of synchronization is required to as-
    sure correct execution of the algorithm. Synchronization implies that a
    process need only be informed of the completion of one of its neighbors
    and not have to tract its activity. More of its execution time is spent in
    productive work and the race condition is avoided.

Together, the foregoing aspects of process control lead to the following requirements for process management (see [free75]):

1. Parallel processes with shared critical sections must be mutually ex-
    cluded from simultaneous execution of their critical sections.

2. Processes executing outside a shared critical section should not impede or block the access of any other process to the critical section.

3. Processes cannot wait indefinitely for either resources or signals—but while waiting, they should not block the activity of any other process.

These assumptions and their requirements define the basic operations for process management. The number of operations and the flexibility accorded the user vary from system to system, and may depend on the applications environment. A reasonably complete set of operators for process management are discussed in the following sections (compare to Knott's paper [knot74]).

3.3.2 Process Initiation

As essential function of process management is the capability of creating (or spawning) new processes which are entities distinct from the current process. Each new process may be unique entity (executing a separate instruction set) or a "clone" of an existing process (e.g., device handlers for multiple units of a particular device class).

The operation of process creation is performed at two levels. At the user level, you issue a system service request to create and initiate a process. This request has the form

SYSTEM(PROCESS, EVENT-NR, ADDRESS, DATA-SIZE,
DATA-BLOCK → PROCESS-IDENTIFIER

where	EVENT-NR	is used to signal the parent the status of its child
	ADDRESS	is the starting address of the new process
	DATA-SIZE	is the length of a message which the parent may pass to the child
	DATA-BLOCK	is the address of the message
	PROCESS-IDENTIFIER	is the identifier for the new process.

As stated above, the creator of a new process is called the parent and the subordinate process is called the child. Two or more children of the same parent are often called siblings. The parent may specify its relationship to the child via the event number, as follows:

EVENT-NR = 0	Implies that the child is independent of the parent
EVENT-NR = 1...15	Implies that the child signals the parent when it has completed its assigned function
EVENT-NR = 16	Implies that the parent is suspended until the child has completed its assigned function.

A parent may pass a message, whose contents depend on the application, to each child that it creates. The first three words of the message provide the child with some information about its heritage (e.g., who its parent is). The structure of a message block is shown in figure 3.5. Thus, even though a child may execute independently of its parent, it may not be a complete orphan. In fact, at a later time, it may establish communications with its parent.

Initiating a User Process

The procedure for initiating a user process is depicted in module 3.3.1. The OS obtains a control block from the free PCB pool. The PCB address will be returned to the parent as the new process's identifier. Each process has a unique PCB assigned to it so that the set of process identifiers is unique across the system. The OS initializes the new PCB with data pertinent to its function. If the process was created by a user, the user process count is incremented by one. When the user process count goes to zero, the system effectively has no work to do since user processes provide the driving force within the system. The new process is activated for execution by placing it in the ready queue. The event number passed by the parent is marked busy. If the event number was 16, the parent will be suspended until the child completes its execution.

Internal Mechanisms

The creation and initialization algorithms for processes differ in complexity because of the properties each entity possesses. These properties were elucidated in section 3.1.1. The routines for creating and initializing processes within the OS are discussed below. Even though a user cannot create system processes directly, we discuss both types of process creation jointly so that you can compare and contrast the similarities and differences.

parent-id
event-nr
data-size
message (up to 250 bytes)

Figure 3.5   Structure of new process message block.

MODULE 3.3.1

```
procedure process
    create-user-process( ) → pcb-address
    pcb-address → return-value[p]
    process-address[usp] → process-address
    event-number[usp] → event-number
    data-size[usp] → data-block-size
    data-block[usp] → data-block-address
    initialize-user-process(pcb-address, process-address, priority[p],
        event-number, data-block-size, data-block-address,
                                        process-map)
    if priority[p] less than zero
        then
            increment user-process-count
    endif
    activate(pcb-address)
    mark-event-busy( )
    event-16-check( )
endproc
```

System Process Creation

The creation of a system process is straightforward in that it simply requires the allocation of a process control block from the PCB pool. System processes are created only by the OS. The address of the new PCB is returned to the caller.

MODULE 3.3.2

```
procedure create-system-process(→pcb-address)
    request(pcb-rs) → pcb-address
endproc
```

System Process Initialization

A system process is created to perform a specified function. Since it has no data block, its argument stack for calling subroutines is maintained within the PCB. The process's starting address is placed on the stack. The SYSTEM-PROCESS-FLAG in the priority word is set to one to indicate that the process is owned by the system. The event number used to signal the parent and the parent's process identifier are stored in the control block. A system process does not have a process data block, so its address is set to zero.

MODULE 3.3.3

procedure initialize-system-process(pcb-address, starting-address,
                                                                priority-value, event)
    address(pstack[pcb-address]) → psp[pcb-address]
    address(starting-address) → pstack[pcb-address]
    set priority-value to priority[pcb-address]
    set system-process-flag of priority[pcb-address]
    clear pdb[pcb-address]
    clear event-status[pcb-address]
    event → event-number[pcb-address]
    p → parent[pcb-address]
endproc

Creating a User Process

The creation of a user process involves the allocation of a PCB from the resource pool. The address of the PCB is returned to the caller. Next, a PDB is requested from the PDB resource pool. The address of the PDB is stored in the PCB. Finally, an IOMAP slot is requested from the IOMAP resource pool and inserted in the PCB. This procedure is depicted in module 3.3.4.

MODULE 3.3.4

procedure create-user-process(→user-process-address)
    request(pcb-rs) → pcb-address
    request(pdb-rs) → pdb-address
    pdb-address → pdb[pcb-address]
    request(iomap-rs) → iomap-slot
    iomap-slot → pdb-map-slot[pcb-address]
    pcb-address → user-process-address
endproc

Initializing a User Process

The actions necessary to initialize a PCB are shown in module 3.3.5. The first step is to insert the PCB on the ALL-PROCESS-QUEUE, a list of all processes in the system. As a process may move among different queues depending on its state, a single list of all processes is required so that no process is lost due to an error in the system. The SYSTEM-PROCESS-FLAG in the priority word is set to zero to indicate no active events, and the current map number of the process is set to zero. The stack area reserved for system routines is set up in the PCB and the return address is placed on the stack.

Next, the PDB is initialized with data regarding the parent of the processes. The parent's process identifier and event number are placed in the PDB. The data block, if any, is copied from the parent's map space to the PDB. Finally, the user stack area is initialized with the starting address and map number of the program code.

MODULE 3.3.5

```
procedure initialize-user-process(pcb-address, starting-address,
priority, address, size, map, event-number, program-map, data-
                                size, data-block, data-map)
    enter-into-queue(all-process-queue, pcb-address)
    priority → priority[pcb-address]
    set system-process-flag of priority[pcb-address]
    clear event-on[pcb-address]
    clear event-done[pcb-address]
    clear event-chain[pcb-address]
    clear map-number[pcb-address])
    address(pstack[pcb-address]) → psp[pcb-address]
    address(os-exit) → pstack[pdb-address]
    p → process-identifier[pdb-address]
    event-number → event-number[pdb-address]
    data-size → data-block-size[pdb-address]
    copy-from-user-space(data-map, data-block,
            process-data[pdb-address], data-size)
    address(usp-3) → temp-stk-ptr
    address(stack-area) → usp-limit[temp-stk-ptr]
    address(pause) → function[temp-stk-ptr]
    address(starting-address) → return[temp-stk-ptr]
    program-map → map[temp-stk-ptr]
endproc
```

3.3.3   Process Termination

The OS normally provides a variety of methods for terminating the operation of a process. A process may terminate normally because it has completed its as-signed work or abnormally due to an error. It may also be terminated by another process. Processes can be killed in an orderly fashion by specifying their process identifier, eliminating all processes in a priority group, or having each process kill itself. When a process is terminated, it must be removed from all system queues and must relinquish all system resources to their appropriate re-source pools.

The following paragraphs describe the various operations for terminating a process.

Killing a Process

The KILL operation allows a process to terminate itself normally. The logic for the KILL operation is depicted in module 3.3.6. The first step forces the process to wait for all outstanding system requests to complete by waiting for all events. It next removes the process from the ALL-PROCESS-QUEUE and decrements the user process count. If the process is the last user process in the system, a RETURN system service request is issued to place the system in the idle state. Otherwise, the resources for the IOMAP slot, the PDB, and the PCB are released to their respective resource pools. The format of this service request is

    SYSTEM(KILL)

Note that there can be no return from execution of this service request.

MODULE 3.3.6

```
procedure kill
    request(wait-rs)
    extract-from-queue(all-process-queue)
    decrement user-process-count
    if priority[p] less than zero
        then
                if user-process-count equals zero
                    then
                            system(return, 0, pcb-address)
                endif
    endif
    release(iomap-rs, pdb-map-slot[p])
    release(pdb-rs, pdb[p])
    release(pcb-rs, p)
    scheduler( )
endproc
```

Terminating a Process

In a multiprocessing system, the parent process usually creates a number of subordinate processes to perform some of the work in parallel. When the work of the individual processes is complete, each process may terminate itself via the KILL command, or it may be terminated by the parent. A parent may terminate a process for several reasons, the most common of which is that the process's execution goes awry. The TERMINATE command is provided to allow one process to destroy another. The format of this request is

SYSTEM(TERMINATE, EVENT-NR, PROCESS-IDENTIFIER)

where   EVENT-NR   is used to signal the calling process
                                                            when the subordinate process has
                                                            been terminated
            PROCESS-IDENTIFIER   is the identifier of the process to be
                                                            terminated

An error code of ER-PROCESS-IDENTIFIER is returned as the status code of the event if an invalid process identifier is specified as an argument.

The termination request may be invoked locally or globally. In a local fashion, as described above, processes may be terminated only by the parent. In a global fashion, any process may terminate any other process in the system. The issue at hand is one of protection since reserving this function for the parent prevents indiscriminate killing of processes by a process gone berserk. If it is applied in a global fashion, there is no need for a KILL function, as each process is allowed to terminate itself. In any event, a provision should be made for notifying somebody that a process has been terminated.

Deleting Processes by Priority

In a system using a priority scheduler, you may want to terminate all processes executing in a given priority class. For example, an application program creates multiple processes at a fixed priority to service a set of remote user terminals. When the application program is finished, it must delete all processes that it created. It could, of course, terminate each process individually, using its process identifier. A more effective method is to terminate all the processes of a given priority class. The format of this request is

SYSTEM(PRIORITY-KILL, EVENT-NR, PRIORITY)

where   EVENT-NR   is used to signal the caller when all processes at
                                            the specified priority level have been terminated
            PRIORITY   is the specified priority class

The status of the event will indicate the number of processes terminated by this request. You must be careful that the calling process does not have a priority equal to the argument in the request. Of course, the module executing the request can compare the process's priority with the priority-class parameter and reject the request if they are equal.

Aborting a Process

The KILL request allows a process to request normal termination of its execution. However, there are times when a process wants to notify you of an error condition before if terminates. The format of the command is:

SYSTEM(ERROR-KILL, ERROR-CODE)

where ERROR-CODE is the index of an error message to be displayed on the user's terminal

3.3.4   Process Identification

Process identification usually has two aspects: finding out my identity—that is, my process identifier—and finding out the status of another process whose process identifier is already known.

Finding Out My Identity

This procedure, depicted in module 3.3.7, determines the process identifier of the currently executing process. The process identifier, actually the PCB address, is returned as the value of the system call. The format of the request is

SYSTEM(WHO-AM-I) → PROCESS-IDENTIFIER

where PROCESS-IDENTIFIER is the process identifier of the currently executing process

Note that you can do nothing with the process identifier except provide it as an argument to other system requests. It is legitimate to use the PCB address as an identifier because each PCB address is unique within the system.

MODULE 3.3.7

```
procedure who-am-i
     p → return-value[p]
     set-return-and-exit( )
endproc
```

Obtaining the Process Status

The status of a process is indicated by the value of the queue upon which it is currently resident. The identifier of the queue is returned as the value of the system request. The format of the command is

SYSTEM(PROCESS-STATUS, EVENT-NR, PROCESS-IDENTIFIER)
→ STATUS

where   EVENT-NR   is used to signal the caller when the status for the specified process is available

PROCESS-IDENTIFIER   is the identifier of the process whose status is to be determined

STATUS   is an indicator describing the status of the process

An alternative form for expressing status is to assign bits in a status word to represent the queues on which a process might reside. The problem with the "flag" approach is that an erroneous state is easily represented if two or more bits are set. It is difficult to decide to which queue the process should be currently attached—an act usually beyond the ability of the recovery program. With the queue address as the status indicator, there can be no mistake about the queue on which the process resides.

In addition, process status may be determined in either a local or global fashion. In a local approach, the status of processes may be determined only by the parents of those processes. In a global approach, any process may determine the status of any other process. The issue is primarily one of system security.

MODULE 3.3.8

```
procedure process-status
    extract-from-queue(all-process-queue, pcb-address) → result
    if result less than zero
        then
                set result to event-status[p]
                set-return-and-exit( )
    endif
    enter-into-queue(all-process-queue, pcb-address)
    process-identifier[usp] → pcb-address
    current-queue[pcb-address] → return-value[p]
    set one to event-status[p]
    set-return-and-exit( )
endproc
```

3.3.5   Delaying a Process

We have seen that process scheduling can be affected by the completion of events relating to functions initiated by a process. That is, at some point a process runs out of things to do. It then waits for the completion of one or more events that it has previously initiated. As the events are executed asynchronously (by system processes), one cannot predict when they will complete or in what sequence completion will occur. Thus the exact duration of the delay exhibits a random behavior pattern.

In many application system, we must be able to delay a process for a fixed period of time. One example of a periodic request would be to read an environmental sensor every 60 seconds. The process must be able to suspend its activity for exactly 60 seconds, and then regain control of the machine. This capability is provided through the DELAY request, whose format is

SYSTEM(DELAY, EVENT-NR, SECONDS)

where   EVENT-NR   is used to signal the process when the specified period has elapsed

　　　　　　 SECONDS   is the number of seconds to delay

Any number of processes in the system may voluntarily request suspension. The duration of suspension of activity will vary widely from a second or so to several tens or hundreds of seconds. To accommodate control of these processes, the system maintains a list of temporally suspended processes known as the DELAY-QUEUE. Individual PCBs are chained into the delay queue in ascending order. When a process requests suspension, the process with the shortest time remaining until activation appears first in the queue.

General Delay Procedure

The procedure for executing the DELAY request is shown in module 3.3.9. The number of seconds specified by the user is multiplied by the clock rate (i.e., number of ticks per second) to yield the total number of clock ticks the process will be delayed. This value is used to sort the process into an appropriate position in the delay queue. As many independent processes may simultaneously be requesting suspension, the delay queue is protected by a resource semaphore.

Sorting a Process into the Delay Queue

The procedure for sorting a process into the delay queue is depicted in module 3.3.10. The general form of this procedure allows the system to maintain different types of delay queues, yet conform to the standard interface for resource managers. The procedure is straightforward and we will not belabor it. It

MODULE 3.3.9

```
procedure delay
    event-number[usp] → evn
    seconds[usp] * clock-rate → delta-time[p]
    request(delays-rs, p)
    set one to event-status[p]
    end-subprocess( )
endproc
```

MODULE 3.3.10

```
procedure enter-into-delay-queue(address, entry)
    request(delay-ready-rs)
    queue-start[delay-queue] → qptr
    clear previous
    while true
        do
            if qptr not equal to zero
                then
                    delta-time[entry]-delta-time[qptr] → time-delta
                    if time-delta greater than or equal to zero
                        then
                            time-delta → delta-time[entry]
                            qptr → previous
                            next-cb[qptr] → qptr
                    endif
        endo
    if qptr not equal to zero
        then
            delta-time[qptr] - delta-time[entry] → delta-time[qptr]
    endif
    if previous not equal to zero
        then
            entry → next-cb[previous]
        else
            entry → queue-start[delay-queue]
    endif
    qptr → next-cb[entry]
    increment queue-count[delay-queue]
    release(delay-ready-rs)
endproc
```

searches the queue for the appropriate position in which to insert the process based on the number of clock ticks for which the process must wait. The difference in clock ticks that the process must wait (i.e., the additional time this process must wait after the previous process has been activated) is calculated and stored in DELTA-TIME [P]. The number of entries in the queue is incremented by one, and access to the queue is released.

The Delay Process

How does a process become reactivated when its suspension period has expired? By means of the DELAY-PROCESS, which works processes off the DELAY-QUEUE in the following way. It examines the time of the first entry on the queue; it then decrements the number of clock ticks the process must wait and requests a time interrupt at the next clock tick. When the duration of suspension of the first entry reaches zero, the process is activated (placed on the ready-to-run queue). The process then releases control of the delay queue so that possible further additions may be sorted into it.

Note that the DELAY-PROCESS is an infinitely repetitive system process. It is created and activated during system initialization, and continues to execute until the system is shut down. Two resource semaphores are used to control access to the DELAY-QUEUE: DELAY-RS and DELAY-READY-RS. These protect the integrity of the DELAY-QUEUE by allowing either the service request module or the delay process access to it, but only one at a time. This protection is critical since processes sorted out of place in the queue might never get reactivated.

MODULE 3.3.11

```
process delay-process
    request(delay-ready-rs)
    while true
        do
            queue-start[delay-queue] → qpcb-address
            decrement delta-time[qpcb-address]
            if delta-time[qpcb-address] not equal to zero
                then
                    request(time-interrupt)
                else
                    activate(qpcb-address)
                    exitdo
            endif
        enddo
    release(delay-rs)
    repeat
endprocess
```

3.3.6 Changing a Process's Priority

In most OSs, you are given a lot of freedom in managing the flow of work in your program. In a priority-oriented system, the work flow depends on the priorities assigned to different user processes. You are allowed (usually) to change the priority of your process by a relative amount from the base priority assigned by the OS. This scheme prevents you from assigning the highest priorities to all your processes and thus "hogging" the CPU.

The following aspects of priority management are usually implemented:

1. A process is allowed to change its own priority; as a result, it may be rescheduled
2. A process may change the priority of a class of processes all of which are identified as belonging to the same priority group.

The format of the command for changing a process's priority is

SYSTEM(CHANGE-PRIORITY, PROCESS-IDENTIFIER,
DELTA-PRIORITY) → NEW-PRIORITY

where   PROCESS-IDENTIFIER   is the identifier of the process whose priority is to be changed

DELTA-PRIORITY   is the relative amount by which the priority is to be changed

NEW-PRIORITY   is the value of the process's priority

The system returns the value of the new priority to you so that it may be checked against the expected value. Control does not return immediately to the caller. Rather, it is transferred to the scheduler to determine if the effect of the priority change was to force a new process to be dispatched into execution. The value of DELTA-PRIORITY may force the currently executing process to drop below the priority level of other processes. The scheduler is called directly because these processes now become eligible for execution.

3.3.7 Suspending and Awakening a Process

Whenever a process is found on the ready-to-run queue, it is possible for that process to be given control of the CPU. We have seen that a process may voluntarily delay its own execution for a fixed period. We have also seen that a process may permanently remove itself from the system (via KILL). There are instances when you may want to remove a process from the ready-to-run queue but have it retain its data for future execution. With the KILL request this is not possible since both the PCB and the PDB are destroyed.

Most systems provide a set of requests that allow you to suspend and awaken processes. There are several advantages to this approach. First, there is less overhead associated with suspending/awakening a process than with creating/destroying it. Second, the process's data block is preserved even though the process has been rendered inactive. Third, the process can be assigned resources of which it retains control even though it has been suspended. Finally, the process exists—thereby, it can be scheduled immediately, thus avoiding situations where there is not enough memory to accommodate the process if we were to go through the sequence of destroying and then recreating it.

Voluntary Suspension by a Process

A process may voluntarily suspend itself from execution. Once suspended, it can be reactivated only by another process. The format of the command is:

SYSTEM(SLEEP)

The procedure for executing this function is shown in module 3.3.12. The SLEEP function waits for all outstanding events to complete. Although not absolutely necessary, as all data structures remain intact, it guarantees the availability of the PCB/PDB and preserves the integrity of the system. The PCB is then assigned to the SUSPEND-QUEUE until it is awakened by another process. The system scheduler is called to select the next process for execution.

MODULE 3.3.12

```
procedure sleep
    request(wait-rs)
    request(suspend-rs, p)
    clear p
    scheduler( )
endproc
```

Suspending a Process Forcibly

A process may also be suspended by another process in a forcible manner. For example, process A may encounter errors while attempting to read a file. It reports these errors to process B, with whom it is communicating. As process A cannot logically proceed because of the errors, process B decides to suspend A while it investigates the cause of the error. Another example involves a resource monitoring process which you may wish to turn on and off. Yet a third example involves on-line debugging and tracing tools, implemented as processes, which you activate and suspend as necessary.

The format of the request for suspending a process is

SYSTEM(SUSPEND, EVENT-NR, PROCESS-IDENTIFIER)

where   EVENT-NR   is used to signal the process when the specified process has been suspended

             PROCESS-IDENTIFIER   is the identifier of the process to be suspended

The procedure for executing this function is depicted in module 3.3.13. When attempting to suspend a process, SUSPEND must deal with the following cases:

1. **The process does not exist.** The procedure searches the ALL-PROCESS-QUEUE to determine if the process specified by the caller exists. If the process does not exist, an error code of ER-PROCESS-IDENTIFIER is returned to the caller.

2. **The process is active.** If the process exists and is on the ready-to-run queue, it is extracted from that queue and placed on the suspense queue. Note that before a process can be suspended, all of its events must be allowed to complete.

3. **The process is inactive.** One cannot suspend a process that is already inactive (e.g., on the delay queue). It would be inappropriate to return a error code of ER-PROCESS-IDENTIFIER as the process does exist. Rather, we return an indication of its inactive status.

MODULE 3.3.13

```
procedure suspend
    process-identifier[usp] → pcb-address
    event-number[usp] → evn
    queue-start[all-process-queue] → pcb-temp
    while pcb-temp not equal to zero
        do
            if pcb-address equals pcb-temp
                then
                    current-queue[pcb-address] → current-pcb-queue
                    exitdo
                else
                    next-cb[pcb-temp] → pcb-temp
            endif
        enddo
```

```
        if pcb-temp equals zero
            then
                    er-process-identifier → event-status[p]
                    end-subprocess( )
        endif
        if current-pcb-queue equals address(ready-queue)
            then
                    extract-from-queue(ready-queue, pcb-address)
                    while event-on[pcb-address] not equal to zero
                        do
                                request(time-interrupt)
                        enddo
                    request(suspend-rs, pcb-address)
                    set one to event-status[p]
                    end-subprocess( )
        endif
        if current-pcb-queue equals address(suspend-queue)
            then
                    er-process-inactive → event-status[p]
                    end-subprocess( )
        endif
        if current-pcb-queue equals address(delay-queue)
            then
                    er-process-inactive → event-status[p]
                    end-subprocess( )
        endif
endproc
```

Awakening a Process

Once a process has been suspended, it can be reactivated only by another currently active process. The suspended process recovers at the address stored in its control block that reflects the location at which it was executing when it gave up control of the CPU. The format of the command to awaken a process is

SYSTEM(WAKEUP, EVENT-NR, PROCESS-IDENTIFIER)

where   EVENT-NR   is used to signal the caller when the specified process has been reactivated

PROCESS-IDENTIFIER   is the identifier of the process to be reactivated.

The procedure for executing this function is depicted in module 3.3.14. The suspense queue is searched for an entry with a process identifier equivalent to that specified by the caller. If it is found, the process is reactivated. If not, an ER-PROCESS-IDENTIFIER error code is returned to the caller.

MODULE 3.3.14

```
procedure wakeup
    process-identifier[usp] → pcb-address
    extract-from-queue(suspend-queue, pcb-address) → pcb-status
    if pcb-status equals zero
        then
                er-process-identifier → event-status[p]
                end-subprocess( )
    endif
    activate(pcb-address)
    set one to event-status[p]
    end-subprocess( )
endproc
```

3.3.8 Process Scheduling

A common ability of many real-time OSs is the capacity to preschedule a process for execution at a given time. This capability allows you to plan ahead when structuring your workload. You may specify the initiation of certain processes for execution at a later time, without your being physically present.

The basis for scheduling processes is a time-ordered queue of process information. The queue is sequenced in order of ascending time intervals. A system process, SCHEDULE-PROCESS, continually checks the queue to determine if a process should be activated. If so, the process information is removed from the schedule queue, a process is created, and it is placed in the ready-to-run queue.

You request that a process be scheduled for deadline initiation by executing the system service request SCHEDULE, which takes the following form:

SYSTEM(SCHEDULE, HOUR, MINUTE, SECOND, ADDRESS, SIZE, DATA-BLOCK)

where	HOUR	is the hour of day when the process is to be initiated
	MINUTE	is the minute of the day when the process is to be initiated
	SECOND	is the second of the day when the process is to be initiated

ADDRESS	is the starting address of the code segment that will be executed by the process
SIZE	is the size of the data block containing a message passed to the new process from its parent
DATA-BLOCK	is the message to be passed to the new process

The new process will be created independent of its parent since, when it is activated, there is no guarantee that its parent will still be active. This implementation assumes that the process code is resident in memory. The new process is passed a message whose format is depicted in figure 3.5.

Utilizing the information provided by the user, a schedule block is built and inserted into the schedule queue at the appropriate position. The format of the schedule block is shown below.

Mnemonic	Usage
schedule-time	Value of the time when the process is to be initiated
schedule-address	Address of the code segment that will be executed by the process
schedule-size	Size of the message passed to the process
schedule-message	Contents of the message to be passed to the new process.

It is a good idea to limit the size of the schedule block to some power of 2, particularly if the buddy allocation algorithm is being used for allocating memory pools.

The mechanism for implementing the scheduling capability is discussed in the following paragraphs.

Creating a Schedule Block

The procedure for creating a schedule block is shown in module 3.3.15. It is executed when you issue the SCHEDULE system service request. A schedule block is allocated from the memory queue resource pool. The absolute deadline time for the process is calculated and stored in the schedule block. If the deadline time has already occurred, the schedule block is released and the request is ignored. Otherwise, the schedule block is initialized with the pertinent process information and placed on the schedule queue.

MODULE 3.3.15

```
procedure schedule
    request(queue-memory-rs, schedule-size[usp] + 6) → sb-address
    calculate-time(time[usp]) → schedule-time[sb-address]
    if schedule-time[sb-address] less than time-of-day
        then
                release(queue-memory-rs, sb-address)
                os-exit( )
    endif
    schedule-address[usp] → schedule-address[sb-address]
    schedule-size[usp] → schedule-size[sb-address]
    move-from-user-space(schedule-map[usp], schedule-data-block
            [usp], schedule-message[sb-address], schedule-size[usp])
    address(schedule-message[sb-address]) → sm-address
    clear event-nr[sm-address]
    release(schedule-rs, sb-address)
    os-exit( )
endproc
```

Activating a Scheduled Process

SCHEDULE-PROCESS, depicted in module 3.3.16, retrieves elements from the schedule queue and initiates processes at the appropriate time. The process requests access to the schedule queue which it shares with the SCHEDULE procedure. It next retrieves the schedule time from the schedule block at the head of the queue and calculates the time span. If the time span is greater than 10 seconds (value of SCHEDULE-WAIT), it waits for 10 seconds; otherwise, it waits for TIME-SPAN seconds. This operation is repeated until the time-of-day reaches the deadline value for the process to be initiated. A PCB is created and initialized for the new process. The schedule block is removed from the schedule queue and returned to the resource pool. Finally, the process is activated and the process cycles to check the next element.

Note that at any time up to 10 seconds, a new schedule block may be inserted in the queue and will become the next process to be initiated. This scheme accommodates a schedule queue for deadlines up to 24 hours.

3.4 EVENT MANAGEMENT

The synchronization of two processes involves communication between them. The communication may take the form of a "go/no go" signal or it may be a lengthy message. In this section we explore synchronization through the use of

MODULE 3.3.16

```
process schedule-process
    request(schedule-rs)
    while queue-count[schedule-queue] greater than zero
        do
            queue-start[schedule-queue] → sb-address
            schedule-time[sb-address] - time-of-day → time-span
            while time-span greater than zero
                do
                    if time-span greater than or equal to
                        schedule-wait
                        then
                            schedule-wait → delta-time[p]
                        else
                            time-span → delta-time[p]
                    endif
                    request(delay-rs)
                enddo
        enddo
    create-user-process( ) → pcb-address
    remove-from-queue(schedule-queue) → sb-address
    inititalize-user-process(pcb-address, schedule-address[sb-ad-
            dress], user-process-priority, 0, schedule-size[sb-address],
                                    schedule-address[sb-address], 0)
    release(queue-memory-rs, sb-address)
    activate(pcb-address)
    repeat
endprocess
```

event flags, which are a form of go/no go communication. In section 3.5, an expanded discussion of the principles and problems of interprocess communication is provided, with one approach to a general solution.

3.4.1   Concept of an Event

An event is a time-independent operation that occurs within the OS. Events may be initiated directly or indirectly by the user. For example, you issue a READ request and an event is directly initiated. However, internally, the READ request may cause the initiation of other events (indirectly), including the eventual generation of an interrupt. The operation represented by the event may proceed in parallel or in sequence with the initiator. When the event is completed (i.e., the operation is finished), the initiator must be informed of the success or failure of the operation.

In an OS, one or more events can be allowed to occur simultaneously. Each event is assigned a numerical identifier known as the event flag. The number of event flags is determined by the system designer. Each flag requires a certain amount of space to store data values and status words. The number of flags is dependent on the size of the database and the maximum number of independent simultaneous events that you wish to support at one time.

In this example, event flags are integers in the range 0 through 16. These flags are interpreted as follows:

Event Flag	Usage
0	The process created will execute independently of its parent process; no synchronization is possible
1, ..., 15	Normal parallel synchronization between two processes can occur with the parent being notified by the child at the appropriate time
16	The parent is suspended until the child has completed its operation; total synchronization is provided

Associated with each event (except for event flag 0) is a status word and a data value. The status word may be sampled at any time by the initiator to determine how the event is progressing. The status word takes three values:

Status Value	Meaning
< 0	The event terminated in failure and the value of the status word is the system error code
$= 0$	The event is still in progress
> 0	The event was completed successfully and the value of the status word may contain additional information

In addition to the go/no go signal, the subordinate process may also return a one- or two-word data value. The value may be an address, a pointer, or an integer value. The data value is dependent on the particular system service request.

3.4.2   Event Management Operations

In order to motivate the operations for event management, we describe the sequence of actions for synchronizing between two processes:

1. Process A initiates a subordinate process B with event 1.
2. Process A then executes a WAIT(1) until process B has been completed.

3. Process B performs its assigned functions.

4. Upon completion of its operation, process B posts a status and value for event 1.

5. Process A is awakened by the system when the event completion is posted.

6. Process A retrieves the status and value of the event.

This sequence of actions is depicted in figure 3.6.

Each operation is invoked by a system service request. The basic form of event-oriented system service requests takes the form

SYSTEM(FUNCTION, EVENT-NR, . . ., other arguments)

where FUNCTION is the name of the function to be executed, EVENT-NR is the associated event, and the function may require zero or more additional arguments to complete its parameter suite.

Waiting for Event Completion

The WAIT request allows a process to wait for the completion of one or more events before continuing execution. The format of the request is

SYSTEM(WAIT, EVENT-BITS)

where   EVENT-BITS   is a word having one bit set for each event that the process is waiting on

The calling process is suspended until all the specified events have been terminated (i.e., a status has been posted). The system ignores any bits set for events that have not been specified by the caller. If no outstanding events are specified, or all events are already completed, control is returned immediately to the caller. If -1 is specified as the value of EVENT-BITS, all outstanding requests must be posted before the calling process is allowed to resume execution.

MODULE 3.4.1

```
procedure wait
    event-bits[usp] → event-bits
    request(wait-rs, event-bits)
    os-exit( )
endproc
```

Waiting for any Event

A process may also wait for only one of several events to occur. The request takes the format

SYSTEM(WAIT-ONE, EVENT-BITS) → EVENT-NR

where   EVENT-BITS   is a word having one bit set for each event that is to be waited on.

           EVENT-NR   is the number of the event that was completed and which released the process

If more than one event is completed at the time the request is issued, the lowest event number already completed will be returned to the caller.

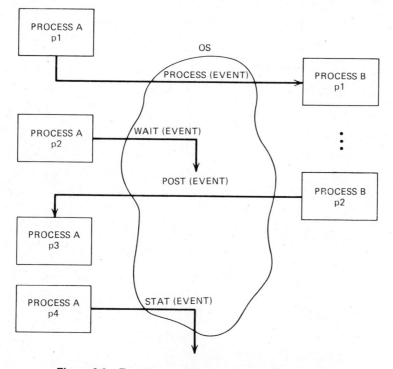

Figure 3.6   Event management—sequence of actions.

MODULE 3.4.2

```
procedure wait-one
    event-bits[usp] → event-bits
    request(wait-one-rs, event-bits)
    os-exit( )
endproc
```

Posting an Event Completion

When a subordinate process has completed its assigned function, it must notify its parent that its work is done. To do so, it posts the status of the event that was used to communicate between the two processes. POST is normally executed at the end of a process, but may be called at any time during the process execution. POST allows the subordinate process to return a status and two data words to the calling process. The format of this request is

SYSTEM(POST, EVENT-NR, PROCESS-ID, STATUS,
DATA-1, DATA-2)

where	EVENT-NR	is used to signal the caller when the subordinate process has completed its work
	PROCESS-ID	is the identifier of the process to be signaled
	STATUS	is the status of the event (see section 3.4.1)
	DATA-1	is the first data word
	DATA-2	is the second data word

MODULE 3.4.3

```
procedure post
    notify(usp, event-nr, process-id, status, event-data)
    set-return-and-exit( )
endproc
```

Receiving an Event Notification

A process must actively request notification of an event from another process. To do so, it issues a RECEIVE system service request. The event in question is marked busy so that a WAIT/WAIT-ONE request may be issued against it. The format of the request is:

SYSTEM(RECEIVE, EVENT-NR)

where   EVENT-NR   is the event number to be marked busy

If the event number is zero, no communication is possible; an error code or the process identifier will be returned to the caller. The event is marked busy and the calling process is suspended if the event number had a value of 16.

MODULE 3.4.4

```
procedure receive
    event-nr[usp] → evn
    if evn equals zero
        then
                set er-event-number to process-status
                set-return-and-exit( )
    endif
    p → return-value[p]
    mark-event-busy( )
    event-16-check( )
endproc
```

Setting the Status of an Event

A process may force the status and value of one of its own events. This capability allows the process to simulate the effect of a subordinate process (which has not been created or has been aborted) by specifying the status and data values that process might have returned to the parent. In addition, the process may force the status and data values to some other value that would normally be returned by the subordinate process. This is useful when the system is attempting to recover from an aborted process that had outstanding events. The format of the request is

SYSTEM(SET-STATUS, EVENT-NR, STATUS, DATA1, DATA2)

where		
	EVENT-NR	is the event whose values are to be set
	STATUS	is the forced value of the event status
	DATA1, DATA2	are the forced values of the event data words

3.4.3   Event Management Databases

The databases supporting event management require several different structures due to the nature of the asynchronous operations. The major structures are:

Event data block in the PDB
PCB event chain blocks

Event resource queue
Event wait resource queues

The Event Data Block

In the PDB associated with each process, storage is allocated for an event data block (EDB). The EDB contains entries for the status and data words for all events numbered 1 through 16 which it stores until the calling process requests these values. Because processes operate asynchronously, a process that created several subordinate processes may not be reactivated until all these processes have completed their functions. These subordinate processes will terminate at different times; their results must be posted to the parent process as they complete their actions. The EDB provides this temporary storage area.

Event Chain Block

Associated with each process is an event chain consisting of event blocks. When a process completes and is ready to post its status and data words to the parent, the parent's PDB may not be available and the subordinate process cannot wait for it. To solve this problem, the NOTIFY procedure creates an event block which is "chained" to the parent's PCB until the parent's PDB is available. The structure of the event block is as follows:

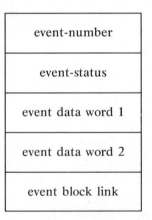

The space for event blocks linked into the event chain is allocated from the free memory pool.

The Event Resource Queue

In a system where event numbers are globally shared, two independent processes may attempt to use the same event. This conflict is resolved through the

MODULE 3.4.5

```
procedure set-status
    event-nr[usp] → evn
    if evn equal to zero
        then
            set er-event-number to process-status
            set-return-and-exit( )
    endif
    status[usp] → status[evn]
    event-data1[usp] → value1[evn]
    event-data2[usp] → value2[evn]
    set one to process-status
    set-return-and-exit( )
endproc
```

use of a resource monitor which allocates events to requesting processes. Whenever a process issues a system service request requiring an event number, the event number is checked for a busy status. If the event number is busy (i.e., it has been allocated), the requesting process is enqueued until the event number is available.

The Event Wait Queues

When a process issues a WAIT or WAIT-ONE request, it is suspended pending the completion of the events specified. The suspended process is enqueued to a resource semaphore (either WAIT-RS or WAIT-ONE-RS as appropriate). When all events have been posted for the process, it is reactivated.

3.4.4   Event Management Utilities

This section describes the basic modules that are required for the event management operations discussed in section 3.4.2.

Event Allocation

The event allocator is depicted in module 3.4.6. This module determines which operation was invoked by the calling process and invokes the appropriate routine to update the event flags. The request is determined by examining the current queue of the calling process.

MODULE 3.4.6

```
procedure event-allocator(rs-address)
    if evn not equal to zero
        then
                set evn-bit in event-done[pcb-address]
                if current-queue[pcb-address] equals address(wait-queue)
                    then
                            wait-allocator( )
                endif
                if current-queue[pcb-address] equals address(wait-queue)
                    then
                            wait-one-allocator( )
                endif
    endif
endproc
```

Wait Allocator

WAIT-ALLOCATOR, depicted in module 3.4.7, updates the event flags in a PCB. The appropriate bit is set in EVENT-DONE. If all specified events are completed, the process is reactivated after clearing the appropriate bits in the event-on and event-done flags.

MODULE 3.4.7

```
procedure wait-allocator
    rs-data-save[pcb-address] → done-bits
    event-done[pcb-address] → event-done-bits
    and(done-bits, event-done-bits) → done-bits-2
    if done-bits equals done-bits-2
        then
        xor(done-bits, event-on[pcb-address]) → event-on[pcb-address]
        xor(done-bits, event-done[pcb-address]) →
                                        event-done[pcb-address]
        activate(pcb-address)
    endif
endproc
```

Waiting for One Event Allocator

WAIT-ONE-ALLOCATOR, depicted in module 3.4.8, reactivates a process whenever any one event for which it has been waiting has completed. The algorithm is much the same as WAIT-ALLOCATOR, with the exception that whereas all flags for completed events are set in EVENT-DONE, only the index of the lowest event completed will be returned to the caller. The user must explicitly check to see if other events have been completed.

MODULE 3.4.8

```
procedure wait-one-allocator
    rs-data-save[pcb-address] → done-bits
    if done-bits not equal to zero
    then
        or(done-bits, event-done[pcb-address]) → bit-temp
        if bit-temp not equal to zero
        then
        lowest-bit(done-bits) → return-value[pcb-address]
        lowest-bit(done-bits) → bit-temp
        bits[bit-temp] → done-bits
        xor(done-bits, event-on[pcb-address]) → event-on[pcb-address]
        xor(done-bits, event-done[pcb-address])
                                    → event-done[pcb-address]
        activate(pcb-address)
        endif
    endif
endproc
```

Marking an Event Busy

MARK-EVENT-BUSY, depicted in module 3.4.9, marks an event busy after it has been allocated to a process. It merely sets the appropriate bit in the EVENT-ON to indicate that the event has been activated by the process.

MODULE 3.4.9

```
procedure mark-event-busy
    if event-nr[usp] not equal to zero
        then
            event-nr[usp] → evn
            or(bits[evn], event-on[p]) → event-on[p]
            clear status[evn]
    endif
endproc
```

Updating a Process's Events

This function updates the event status and values in a process's data block when it becomes available to the OS. The operation, depicted in module 3.4.10, copies the contents of the event chain blocks attached to the PCB to the event data blocks in the PDB. As event chain blocks are emptied, they are returned to the free memory pool.

MODULE 3.4.10

```
procedure update-events(pcb-address)
      event-chain[pcb-address] → event-chain-address
      clear event-chain[pcb-address]
      while event-chain-address not equal to zero
            do
                  event-nr[event-chain-address] → evn
                  event-status[event-chain-address] → status[evn]
                  event-data1[event-chain-address] → value1[evn]
                  event-data2[event-chain-address] → value2[evn]
                  event-chain-address → evn
                  event-block-link[event-chain-address]
                                                        → event-chain-address
                  release(pcb-rs, evn)
            enddo
endproc
```

Setting Up an Event Error Code

EVENT-ERROR, depicted in module 3.4.11, sets an error code as the status of an event. The error code indicates that the subordinate process detected an error while attempting to perform its function. This error code is returned directly to the calling process if the event number was 16, as the caller was suspended awaiting completion of the request.

Notifying a Process of Event Completion

This function, depicted in module 3.4.12, posts the event status after the completion of the event. After the event number is validated, the PDB is mapped into system space. The status and data words for the event are updated according to the values specified by the caller and the event number is released. The effect of this call is to set the appropriate flags in the PCB.

MODULE 3.4.11

```
procedure event-error(error-code)
    event-nr[usp] → evn
    if evn not equal to zero
        then
                error-code → status[evn]
    endif
    if evn equal to 16
        then
                status[evn] → return-value[p]
    endif
    os-exit( )
endproc
```

MODULE 3.4.12

```
procedure notify(usp-temp, event-nr, process-id, status, data1, data2,
→ value)
    process[usp-temp] → px-id
    event-nr[usp-temp] → evn
    if evn not equal to zero
        then
                if evn less than zero or evn greater than 16
                    then
                            set er-event-number to value
                            exitproc
                endif
                page-select(0, pdb[px-id]) → pdb-address
                address(pdb-address[evn]) → evx
                status[usp] → status[evx]
                data1[usp] → value1[evx]
                data2[usp] → value2[evx]
                release(event-rs, evx)
    endif
    set one to value
endproc
```

3.5   INTERPROCESS COMMUNICATION

In a multiprocessing system, processes must be able to exchange data in order
to cooperate on common tasks. The simplest situation involves two processes—
here named P1 and P2. P1 produces and sends a sequence of data, called a

message, to P2. P2, in turn, receives and consumes the messages. Messages, the essential component of interprocess communication, are discrete units of data.

What complicates interprocess communication is the asynchronicity of process execution. That is, either process can proceed at a rate of execution independent of the other process. Conceivably, P1 could produce messages before P2 is ready to consume them. Delaying P1 until P2 is ready to receive a message would require some knowledge on the part of P1 of the status of P2. However, this violates the concept of asynchronicity. To avoid delaying P1, a temporary message storage area should be provided for storing messages until P2 is ready to receive them.

Interprocess communication mechanisms can be classified into two types: shared variables and messages. The shared-variable approach is exemplified by semaphores and events. These mechanisms are usually limited to one or a few words of information storage—a serious constraint. Semaphores are discussed in section 7.10. Events were discussed in section 3.4. Consequently, this section focuses on the more general concepts of message communication.

Interprocess communication (IPC) is subject to two resource constraints: (1) the number of messages produced by the sender cannot exceed the capacity of the storage area, and (2) the receiver cannot consume messages faster than they are produced by the sender.

These resource constraints are enforced by the implementation of a synchronization rule. This rule states that if a sender attempts to place a message in a full storage area, it will be delayed until the receiver has taken another message from the storage area. Furthermore, if the receiver attempts to remove a message from an empty storage area, it will be delayed until the sender places another message in the storage area. Normally, the storage area is wholly contained within main memory. We will see that the first constraint is relaxed when mass storage can be used for additional storage space as in UNIX pipe implementation. The second constraint should never be relaxed (for obvious reasons).

3.5.1   Characteristics of an IPC Facility

There are several characteristics that are deemed essential for implementing an IPC facility. Proposed and actual mechanisms vary considerably, both in general approach and in detail, but all appear to preserve these basic elements. The best delineation of these elements is contained in a report by Sunshine [suns77].

Of major importance in an IPC facility is the range of other processes with which a given process can communicate. Two approaches have been taken to communications: (1) a process may communicate only with processes that have a common ancestor, or (2) any process is a potential communication partner. In either case, a process has to have the ability to learn another process's identity. In most systems, the permanent system processes (e.g., file manager, scheduler) have well-known names. Communication with dynamically created processes requires that the name of the process be available in some common directory.

Any process may have one or more active connections (including, in certain cases, paths to itself). The identity of the participants may not all be known, as in a broadcast message or in a signal affecting a particular class of processes. Knowing the source of a message is important for three reasons. First, it is desirable to sort out the input from different processes. Second, it allows the process to send a reply to a given message. Third, it provides a means of checking the authenticity of a process. Sunshine notes that a single identifier may not serve all three purposes, so multiple identifiers may be required.

Establishment of a connection may require explicit creation (such as binding a link to a process) or paths implicitly associated with processes. Paths may be simplex or duplex, with the latter tending to be of a more complicated order of magnitude. The system may enforce constraints on a communications path. Common constraints include how it is used (i.e., what message types it can pass), frequency of use, and duration of existence.

The authority to communicate, aside from the ability to do so, may be a precious commodity in an IPC facility. The ability to communicate may be associated with the type of name a process possesses, and controlling the acquisition of names can effectively limit the ability to communicate. Authorization must occur before communication can proceed, either when a connection is explicitly opened, or on every message transmission.

Finally, when a process is terminated, all connections to other processes must be clearly closed. Notification of the other process is essential since open-ended communication paths, like dangling participles, are notoriously messy. Cleanup activities must deal with outstanding messages when one of the processes is suddenly aborted.

Resource Allocation

As Sunshine notes, resource allocation is primarily a matter of buffer allocation. Usually, the OS is called on to provide storage space for messages not yet received. Such space may be taken from the process's own data area or from a global pool managed by the OS. Two types of control are necessary. Flow control assures that resources at the source and destination processes are not exceeded. Congestion control assures an equitable allocation of resources among multiple connections so that one process does not dominate the communications system.

Limiting resources is an effective means for controlling the number of messages a process can generate or have waiting when selective reception is allowed. Effective cures include suspending a process, destroying it (a rather drastic action), or deleting messages exceeding a specified age. Where messages may be prioritized, some method is required to bypass normal resource allocation procedures for critical messages.

Functional Capability

At a minimum, any process must be able to both send and receive messages. Variations may be specified for explicit message types such as a reply to a resource request. Some systems include the creation and destruction commands for paths as explicit IPC functions. A broadcast facility is almost always desirable.

Sunshine differentiates commands as blocking or nonblocking. A blocking command imposes lighter synchronizations, so that communicating processes become essentially coroutines. Nonblocking commands allow source and destination processes to operate independently. The latter are substantially more complex and may require the capability of distinguishing the type of command. Blocking commands are said to queue messages in time using standard process suspension facilities. Nonblocking commands require storage space to queue pending messages until a process is ready to receive them.

Several special commands are worthy of consideration. A signal command allows a source process to signify the type of message being sent (e.g., a priority interrupt). A corresponding WAIT command allows a process to wait for a specific signal. The SIGNAL command may also be used to preempt a process's execution and force it to perform a special function. Some systems provide a TEST command to indicate whether signals or messages are available. In any case, send, receive, and test commands can operate sequentially, randomly by message priority, or by selective search.

Receiver Unblocking

In any IPC facility, a receiver will block if no message is ready for it. The receiver is unblocked when the conditions for message reception are satisfied. In a message-oriented system, the presence of a message for consumption satisfies the read request of the receiver. In a stream-oriented system, the receiver unblocks when the exact amount of data has been received.

Messages may be fixed or variable length. In either case, the message is terminated by a special end-of-message character. A message orientation is desirable when messages are of variable length. Stream mode is most appropriate when the data contain indicators that direct their interpretation. Usually, the stream contains a fixed-length header which describes the content and length of the message.

3.5.2   Mailboxes

Our survey of IPC facilities begins with the mailbox mechanism as proposed by Spier [spie73]. Spier examined the requirements associated with defining an

IPC. He then defined the most elementary communication mechanism that satisfied all requirements. Oddly enough, this mechanism is shown to be a single bit.

Spier's single-bit mailbox is capable of transmitting a 1-bit message from a sender to a receiver. The simplest implementation is merely a Boolean variable B which is initialized to a FALSE state. A send operation consists of

```
TRUE → B
```

while a receive operation takes the form

```
WHILE B equals FALSE

DO

REPEAT

ENDDO
```

Unfortunately, this allows the passage of only one message after initialization, as there is no provision for resetting the value of B. Spier makes a simple modification to this mechanism in order to make it reusable. It consists of initializing B to the FALSE state and rewriting the send operation as

```
WHILE B not equal to TRUE

DO

REPEAT

ENDDO

TRUE → B
```

The receiving operation is also modified, as follows:

```
WHILE B equals FALSE

DO

REPEAT

ENDDO

FALSE → B
```

The mailbox mechanism is found in many hardware systems supporting programmed I/O. The 1-bit mailbox is a direct correspondent to the device busy/done flip-flop. A clear example of how this mechanism is employed can be found in *How to Program the Nova Computers* by Data General Corporation [dgc75].

This implementation of a mailbox is restricted merely to conveying information by its own existence. A logical extension is to associate a 1-bit mailbox with a message word, as proposed by Ford and Hamacher [ford77]. The mailbox is then defined as a structure having both a status and a content, as follows:

```
send      WHILE MAILBOX(STATUS) equals FULL
          DO
          REPEAT
          ENDDO
          FULL → MAILBOX(STATUS)
          MESSAGE → MAILBOX(CONTENTS)
receive   WHILE MAILBOX(STATUS) equals EMPTY
          DO
          REPEAT
          ENDDO
          EMPTY → MAILBOX(STATUS)
          MAILBOX(CONTENTS) → VALUE
```

In each of these examples, the mailbox is inaccessible to other processes until the assignment operation is complete. Such a mechanism guarantees that every SEND operation is matched by exactly one RECEIVE operation.

Finally, let us carry the mailbox example to its fullest implementation, for example, a multiword mailbox each with its own status word. We satisfy this last condition of accessibility by implementing the mailbox as a resource semaphore (see section 7.10). The number of slots in the mailbox is merely the number of entries on the AVAIL queue. When the mailbox is completely or partially empty, the next available slot is used to store the message.

We have seen that a one-bit mailbox can be used successfully to implement device-level signals. One further example is in order here. The class of character-oriented devices (such as teletypes and line printers) transfers 1 byte between the device and the CPU at a time. We can consider that each device has a mailbox dedicated to it which is shared by the central processor and the device controller.

From the system point of view, each device can be viewed as executing an internal program of the form (e.g., a line printer)

WHILE QUEUE-COUNT[MAILBOX-QUEUE] not equal to zero

DO

REQUEST(MAILBOX-RS) → NEXTCHAR

PRINT(NEXTCHAR)

ENDDO

and the central processor is buffering characters to the device via its program:

WHILE QUEUE-COUNT[MAILBOX-QUEUE] not equal to 1

DO

REQUEST(PRINT-BUFFER-RS) → NEXTCHAR

RELEASE(MAILBOX-RS, NEXTCHAR)

ENDDO

Ford and Hamacher note that a mailbox mechanism is most efficient when the physical mailbox size is small. This criterion applies to both the contents word and the number of slots in the mailbox. The contents word can be made to handle arbitrarily large messages by implementing a copy routine for assignment to/from the mailbox.

3.5.3 An Alternative Method of Communication

The shared-variable approach to synchronization—semaphores and monitors—relies on the concept of mutual exclusion. Mutual exclusion is a mechanism that forces the time ordering of execution of pieces of code, called critical sections, in a system of concurrent processes. Red and Kanodia [red79] describe an alternative mechanism which is based on observing the sequence of significant events in the course of an asynchronous computation. This is similar to the notion of counter variables proposed by Gerber [gerb77]. Gerber offers a detailed notion of the formalism for counter variables and shows how they solve several examples.

Their approach is based on the definition of two objects: an event count and a sequencer. An event count is an object that tracks the number of events in a particular class that have occurred so far during the execution of a system. An event is a change in the state of some part of the system. A class of events is a set of events that are related to one another, such as machine interrupts.

Reed proposes that we think of an event count as a nondecreasing integer variable. Three primitive operations can be defined for an event count:

ADVANCE(E)   which increases the value of E by 1 (given an initial value of 0)

READ(E)   returns the current value of E directly

AWAIT(E,v)   blocks the process until the value of E reaches v

Associated with event counts is the concept of a sequencer. A sequencer is necessitated by the fact that some synchronization problems require arbitration. That is, some decision must be made on which of several events will be allowed to occur first. The obvious example is access to a shared variable by two processes attempting an update operation. A sequencer is used to order the set of events so that a decision can be made. Event counts alone do not possess this ability to discriminate between events.

A sequencer is also implemented as a nondecreasing integer variable that is initially zero. Red defines only one operation upon a sequencer, TICKET(S). TICKET(S) returns a nonnegative integer value as its result. Reed likens the ticket operation to the automatic machine that orders service in a bakery or a grocery store. The person servicing customers at the counter calls for the customer with the next number in the series. Two uses of the TICKET(S) operation will always give different values. The ordering of values, and thus of events, is dependent on the time ordering of executions of TICKET(S).

Reed shows that a single-producer, single-consumer problem can be solved using event counts (see figure 3.7). Suppose that the producer and consumer must coordinate use of an N-cell ring buffer. The ring buffer is implemented as an array BUFFER[N] whose indices run from 0 to $N - 1$. Two event counts, IN and OUT, are used to synchronize the producer and consumer. Access to the buffer is coordinated by operations on IN and OUT such that the consumer does not read the ith value from the buffer until it has been inserted by the producer, and the producer does not store the $(i + N)$th value in the buffer until the ith value has been removed.

By introducing a sequencer, we can solve the multiple-producer, single-consumer problem (see figure 3.8). Each producer obtains a "ticket" which allows it to insert a message into the buffer. A process merely waits for completion of all producers who have obtained prior tickets. This approach provides for mutually exclusive deposits into the buffer without introducing an a priori sequence constraint on the producers.

3.5.4   Links—A Novel Approach

DEMOS is an OS for the CRAY-1 computer installed at the Los Alamos Scientific Laboratory. Within DEMOS, the designers [bask77] have coalesced all

```
                procedure producer
                   set 1 to I
                   while true
                       do
                              await(out, I − N)
                              buffer[mod(I,N)] ← produce( )
                              advance(in)
                              increment I
                       enddo
                endproc

                procedure consumer
                   set 1 to J
                   while true
                       do
                              await(in, J)
                              consume(buffer[mod(J,N)])
                              advance(out)
                              increment J
                       enddo
                endproc
```

Figure 3.7   Example of event count synchronization (after reed79).

```
        procedure producer
           while true
               do
                     t ← ticket(T)
                     await(in, t)                synchronize with pro-
                                                 ducers
                     await(out, t − N + 1)       synchronize with con-
                                                 sumer
                     buffer[mod(t + 1,N)] ← produce( )
                     advance(in)
               enddo
        endproc
```

Figure 3.8   Example of sequencer to synchronize multiple producers.

communication functions in one mechanism—the link. A link is, conceptually, a path between any two processes and may be passed from one process to another along with a message sent over some other link. A process that creates a link determines its contents and possibly restricts its use. Links are attractive for systems having simple protection mechanisms, such as the single pair of base/limit memory protection registers available in the CRAY-1.

The DEMOS designers believe the following communication functions are essential to OS implementations:

1. System calls, where user processes communicate with the OS that is viewed as a collection of permanent, cooperating processes
2. A process communication mechanism, which provides a way for arbitrary and unrelated processes to communicate with mutual consent
3. A method by which one process can encapsulate one or more processes in support of debugging, monitoring, or simulation exercises

The novel approach proposed by the DEMOS designers is the link. A link permits one process to send messages to another task. It may also be possible to read/write part of the memory of the process to which the message would be sent. A link is a one-way communication path. For two processes to engage in a dialogue, each must have a link to the other.

Each process has associated with it a link table—a list of all active links. A link is identified by a link-id. When a process is created, it is given a set of links by its parents which define its environment. Standard links include the file system, process manager, and the switchboard process.

A link may have an attribute that allows it to move data to or from a specified area within the memory of the target process. In accessing a file, the link to the file system manager allows that process to move data into the requesting process's space. Other attributes dictate whether a process holding a link may duplicate it, pass it to other processes, or use it more than once.

Links come in four flavors: request, resource, reply, and general. Request and resource links are used to send messages that request action from the recipient process. A request link may be destroyed at any time without formal notification of the target process. On the other hand, destruction of a resource link always causes a message to be sent to the target process. Moreover, resource links cannot be passed to another process except by the creator. Reply links are used only once (e.g., to reply to a request from another process). A reply link may carry with it the identifier for any of the other link types. A general link has no restrictions whatsoever but is used only by the switchboard. Any type of link may be passed over a general link.

Primitive communications operations that have been implemented using links are:

1. SEND transmits a specific message to a target process along with an optional link-id. It has two variants:

    (a) DESTROY terminates the link after message transmission.
    (b) DUPLICATE produces a second copy of the link for another process.

2. REQUEST sends a message to a target process over a request or resource link and implicitly creates a reply link.

3. REPLY sends a reply message along with an optional link-id to the requesting process.

4. MOVE reads or writes a block of data through a link.

5. RECEIVE accepts the next incoming message.

6. CALL allows a process to determine if another process exists in the system; it creates a link to that process if it does.

THE DEMOS designers expect the CALL operation to be used heavily within their system. To facilitate its execution, they have implemented a switchboard process to which every other process is connected at creation. When a process wishes to call another process, it directs a message to the switchboard to determine if the process exists. If the process exists, the switchboard creates a link to the target process and passes it back to the caller.

An intuitive understanding of how links should work can best be gleaned from an example. Baskett et al. [bask77] consider the problem of a process P1 attempting to read a file as representative of the class of problems to be addressed by this mechanism. To do so, P1 must engage in the following steps:

1. P1 CALLs the file system manager on its standard link and sends a message containing the file named XFILE and other parameters.

2. A link is created by the kernel and passed to the file system manager.

3. The file system manager receives the message, interprets it, opens XFILE, and creates a resource link to itself.

4. The file system manager sends a reply to P1 on the reply link created by the CALL operation; it passes the identifier of the resource link to P1.

5. P1 becomes ready due to an implicit RECEIVE operation contained in the reply.

6. The reply link is destroyed by the kernel.

7. P1 has two links to the file system: its standard request link and a resource link for XFILE.

8. The file system has no links to P1.

9. P1 uses the resource link for XFILE, specifying the address and size of the buffer in the CALL operation.

10. The file system manager MOVEs data to P1's buffer.

11. The file system manager REPLYs with status information about the data transfer.

12. When P1 is done, it destroys the resource link to XFILE.

13. The resulting message tells the file system manager to close the file.

14. P1 is left with only its standard link to the file system manager.

In summary, links are an attractive vehicle for IPC in computer systems that have limited memory protection mechanisms. The approach taken by the designers is not pure in that it allows several escape hatches. Most notably, the general link allows an escape from the request–reply regime. As implemented, links provide a few primitive operations which can support a wide variety of OS structures.

3.5.5 The UNIX Interprocess Communication Facility

UNIX is an OS for the PDP-11 series computers developed by Ritchie and Thompson [ritc74] at Bell Laboratories. UNIX provides two facilities for supporting interprocess communication: pipes and signals. Signals correspond to the event mechanism that was discussed in the last section. Pipes are essentially files used for data transfer between processes.

Pipes are unnamed (by the user) files used for stream-oriented data transfers between two related processes. A process creates a pipe by a system service request. Pipes may be inherited by one or more of the process's children. The pipe differs from an ordinary UNIX file in several respects. First, pipes are created by their very own system call exclusive of the standard file management services. The system primitive returns two descriptions—one for reading and one for writing. Thus the parent can pass to its descendants the capabilities (and thus the privileges) for reading or writing or both.

Second, pipes have no explicit identifiers other than their descriptors. A pipe ceases to exist when all processes owning a descriptor for it terminate. A process may support only a limited number of pipes—usually up to the maximum number of file descriptors permitted in the system. UNIX provides a limited number of slots in the PCB for file descriptions. This effectively limits the number of files and pipes that may simultaneously be accessed by a process.

Finally, a pipe, unlike a file, is supported by an implicit synchronization mechanism. This mechanism prevents the writer(s) from getting ahead of the reader(s) by more than a fixed number of characters by blocking the writer(s) until the reader(s) catch up. When any reader catches up, the file representing the pipe is truncated to zero length.

A pipe is buffered on three levels. This approach has serious effects on the performance of the IPC mechanism. At the first level, pipes are buffered in system memory. As blocks of system memory are filled, the oldest buffers are written to disk file storage. This corresponds to the transfer of blocks to and from disk through the ordinary file support mechanisms. Finally, if a process writes more than 4096 bytes, the pipe is buffered in time by suspending the process until the readers catch up.

A pipe can be used only between processes with a common ancestor. The ancestor sets up the file description for the pipe and passes it to both subordinate processes. Thereafter, a process may read/write messages from/to the pipe. When a process terminates, the pipe is closed. A process may also voluntarily close a pipe. Writing messages to a pipe when no readers are present results in an error. Reading from a pipe when no writers are present results in an end-of-file condition. Multiple processes may read or write a pipe. However, the identity of the producers is not preserved, so that data from different writers may be interleaved when the consumers read the pipe.

Within UNIX, buffer space for the pipe comes from a common buffer pool. As blocks are written by the producer, they are automatically written to disk file space when the pipe buffers are consumed. As the reader consume data from the pipe, the blocks are read from the disk and passed to the consumer. A producer is blocked when he or she has written 4096 bytes of data, to allow the consumer to catch up. At that point, the disk blocks are freed and the pipe is reset (i.e., the file pointer is reinitialized). An alternative approach is to reset the pipe whenever the consumer catches up with the producer.

A pipe provides only simple data transfer between processes. The READ command blocks until data are available. The WRITE command blocks until the data to be written have been transferred to the system buffer. Unfortunately, there is no mechanism specifying whether or not the data were successfully received by the consumer unless an acknowledgment message is issued.

Creating a Pipe

To create a pipe in UNIX, you must issue the PIPE system call, which has the following format:

```
int file-descriptor[2];
    :
pipe(file-descriptor);
```

Execution of PIPE creates two file descriptors which are used, respectively, for read and write operations on the pipe. A process may read from the pipe using file-descriptor[0] and write to it using file-descriptor[1]. The file descriptors for a pipe are equivalent to those for normal disk files. What sets them apart is that a file attribute flag, FPIPE, is set to denote that the descriptors comprise a pipe.

Using Pipes

Two or more UNIX processes may communicate using pipes. One process, the parent, must have created the pipe originally. Thereafter, whenever it "forks" a child process, that process will know about the existence of the pipes. The reason for this is that UNIX, when creating a new process, duplicates the environment of the parent. So each child has access to all files "opened" by its parent.

To use a pipe, a process issues a UNIX read or write using the respective file descriptors. This allows for apparent full duplex communications between two processes. The protocol of communication is left up to the two processes; that is, it is inherent in the process code. The most likely use of a pipe is sketched out below; the problem, of course, is directing the child to perform specific tasks.

When a new process is created by FORK, it receives control immediately after the system call, as does its parent. The new process can issue an immediate read on the pipe in order to receive instructions about the task it is to perform, or executes an EXEC system call to switch to a new instruction sequence.

After receiving a message through the pipe, the new process can call appropriate subroutines to perform its task. After completing its function, it writes a message to its parent through the pipe and terminates itself. Using the EXEC approach, the new process receives control at the beginning of a new instruction space. It may communicate with the parent through the pipe since all "open" file descriptors are preserved across the transition.

Some Problems with UNIX Pipes

The UNIX implementation of pipes suffers from several problems, one of which concerns the inability of a process to wait for input from multiple sources. When a process issues a READ, it is automatically blocked. An additional facility is required to synchronize input from multiple pipes. The obvious solution is to distinguish between blocking and nonblocking READs on a pipe. A nonblocking READ would allow a process to initiate READs against multiple pipes.

Another problem is that there is no communication between unrelated processes. By changing the pipe implementation, we could preserve the identity of each producer and thus enable each reader to select those processes from which it wishes to receive messages. As an alternative, with each message it receives, the customer would receive the identity of the producing process.

3.5.6   Ports—A Pipe Extension

The implementation of pipes has two serious problems. First, a read on any pipe causes the reading process to go to sleep until the data are available or until the reader is signaled, in which case data may be lost. Thus a process cannot receive inputs from two or more pipes while waiting for the first input from any of them. Second, multiple processes may write to a pipe. The receiving process is unable to tell unequivocally who wrote the message unless a process identifier is implicit in the message.

Rand [zuck77] has developed the port mechanism to solve both these problems. The port mechanism makes it possible to multiplex all the various inputs into a single stream. Moreover, whenever a process writes to a port, the message is preceded by a header containing information identifying the writer and the character count of the message. The header is supplied by the UNIX kernel, so that from the viewpoint of a writer, writing to a port is no different from writing to any other device. Furthermore, the reading process can tell exactly who sent the message.

When a port is created, it is assigned a name and protection information. This action is implemented exactly as if a process were opening a file for writing. To a process, a port can be opened, read, and closed like any other file. Creating a port opens it for reading. Only the creator has read access to it, although its descendants may also be granted read access.

There is a restriction of one reader per port. Unless the individual messages can be directed to a specific reader, having multiple readers serves no apparent purpose and may be as confusing as before. Moreover, if multiple readers were allowed, there would have to be some way to ensure that readers always received complete messages. Once data have been written to a port, the system has only to pass the data onto the reader as called for.

If the creator and its descendants are allowed to read from a port, it is assumed that they will cooperate in its use. Cooperation must be achieved through synchronization by external means, as there is no implicit facility in the port mechanism. One method of synchronization is to use the wait service request available in UNIX.

A port can be regarded by a writing process as an output file that is opened, written, and closed as is an ordinary device. If the message written would overflow the buffering capability, the message is split into several portions, each with its own header. One bit in the header is used to signal an end-of-message condition to the receiving process. It is the reader's responsibility to reconstruct the whole message based on the header information.

Creating a Port

A port is created by issuing a system service request. The format for this request is (using our notation):

SYSTEM(PORT, NAME, MODE, FDS-DATA) → FDR-ID

where   NAME   is the name by which the port may be opened for writing
        MODE   is a word containing the mode indicator
        FDS-DATA   is a two-word array containing the file descriptors for reading and writing
        FDR-ID   is the identifier of the file descriptor for this port

The effect of this request is to create the port and open it for reading. The port will also be opened for writing if a name has been specified. If the name consists of the empty string (e.g., zero), the port cannot be opened by any other process for writing. This situation pertains when one process wants exclusive communication with another process.

The mode bits determine what actions are to be taken when a process reads or writes a port. The following bit settings (assuming a 16-bit word) define what is to occur:

Bit Number	Usage
15	Port is to be opened for reading only
14	Writer's process identifier is supplied to the reader when a message is accepted
7	Write permission of creator
4	Write permission for descendents of creator
1	Write permission for all other users

The creator of a port has complete control over it. The owner of a process (i.e., some user) becomes the owner of the port. Via write permissions, the creator specifies who can utilize the port. In addition, the UNIX superuser may also write to the port. This option is necessary for handling broadcast messages. However, no process, even one owned by the superuser, can open the port for reading except the creator or such descendants to whom it chooses to pass the file descriptor.

Since the UNIX kernel supplies headers for each message written to a port, no writer can forge a header. Thus the reader can rely on knowing what process wrote each message it receives. A possibly malicious writer may write to the port as much and as often as desired in the absence of flow control features. All active writers will be suspended when the combined data from all writers gets ahead of the reader by a fixed format. When the reader catches up, all writers are reactivated at the same priority, and each then has an equal chance to gain access to the port. Therefore, any writer can cause a delay in service but is unable to completely deny access to other processes.

3.5.7   An Interprocess Communication Facility

In previous sections we have examined several techniques for IPC. In UNIX [ritc74], interprocess data are buffered in memory until called for by the receiving process. Eventually, as in-core buffers are filled, interprocess messages are migrated to mass storage. Moreover, all interprocess data are treated as if they were one continuous stream. Even when ports are implemented, they still rely on the pipe mechanism to handle messages.

In the following paragraphs, we examine a simple IPC facility oriented to passing messages between processes. That is, data are transferred between processes in variable-length blocks (although some maximum length is enforced). Furthermore, all messages are buffered in system space, which enables quick and efficient processing. However, this limits the number of messages that can be accommodated in memory at one time.

Using the Interprocess Communication Facility

A process initiates IPC by defining a message queue that will be used to buffer messages between processes. The initiating process then transmits the message queue identifier to the receiving process via the event mechanism. One or more processes may participate in IPC via one message queue. Two or more processes communicate via the message queue by coordinating the sending and receiving of messages through the queue. However, the sending and receiving of messages between two processes is an asynchronous act, necessitating the buffering of messages until they are called for by the receiving process.

The message queue is implemented as a circular queue. Attached to each message is a three-word packet containing the following information:

The identifier of the sending process
The event number specified by the sender when the message was enqueued
The number of words in the message

Defining a Message Queue

The heart of the message transmission facility is a queue which buffers messages until the receiving process calls for them. The procedure for defining a message queue is depicted in module 3.5.1.

A process opens a message queue by invoking the system service request:

SYSTEM(DEFINE-QUEUE, MAX-DEPTH) → QCB-ID

where   MAX-DEPTH   is the maximum number of messages that may
                        be buffered at any one time
          QCB-ID   is the identifier for the message queue

The procedure checks to see if the number of user queues has been exceeded; if so, an error is returned to the caller. MAX-USER-QCBS is a system generation parameter which specifies the number of concurrent queues active in the system. Since queues require memory resources, the system manager needs to limit the number of queues in relation to available memory space.

Each message queue has an associated Queue Control Block which is allocated from system queue memory. A resource monitor is defined to handle reception and allocation of messages from the queue. USER-QUEUE-LIST contains a list of active message queues. This list is searched for an open slot in which to place the new message queue address.

A message queue consists of a memory page that is allocated from the free page set. The page address is placed in the queue list as the address of the message queue. The QCB identifier is returned to the caller for use in sending and receiving messages.

MODULE 3.5.1

```
procedure define-queue
      if nbr-of-user-qcbs greater than or equal to max-user-qcbs
            then
                        set-return-and-exit(er-queue-control-block)
      endif
      increment nbr-of-user-qcbs
      request(queue-memory-rs, qcb-rs-size) → qcb-rs-address
      define-rs(qcb-rs-address, de-qset, de-qset, one-allocator)
      for i from 0 to max-user-qcbs − 1
            do
                        if user-queue-list[i] equals zero
                              then
                                          i → qcb-id
                                          exitdo
                        endif
            enddo
      if i equals max-user-qcbs
            then
                        set-return-and-exit(er-queue-control-block)
      endif
      request(page-rs) → page-number
      page-select(0, empty-page, page-number)
      page-number → user-queue-list[i]
      set-return-and-exit(qcb-id)
endproc
```

Sending a Message

A process transmits a message to another process by issuing a SEND system service request as follows:

```
SYSTEM(SEND, EVENT-NUMBER, QCB-ID, DATA, SIZE)
```

where   EVENT-NUMBER   is used to signal the caller when the message has been received

              QCB-ID   is the identifier of the message queue through which the message will be transmitted

              DATA   is the address of the message to be transmitted to another process

              SIZE   is the length of the message to be transmitted

The procedure for sending a message to another process is depicted in module 3.5.2. Implicit in the act of sending a message is the fact that the message is enqueued until called for by another process.

The procedure validates the message queue identifier via the utility CHECK-QCB-ID. If the caller specifies an invalid identifier, an error will be returned as the value of the event. Next, if the maximum number of messages has been enqueued by the sending process, an error is returned to the caller. The procedure also checks the length of the message to ensure that it does not exceed the maximum message length (given by MAX-DATA-SIZE).

The system requests space within the message queue equivalent to the message size plus the control parameters. QUEUE-FREE-RS manages the space available in the queue. If space is not available, the process blocks until messages have been removed from the queue. The queue page is mapped into system space. The process identifier, event number, and message size are stored as control parameters. The message is copied from user space into the queue page. The queue page pointers are updated, the queue is released, and the event is reserved.

MODULE 3.5.2

```
procedure send-message
    check-qcb-id(qcb-id[usp]) → qcb-address[p]
    if qcb-address[p] less than zero
        then
        event-error(er-queue-control-block)
    endif
    rs-avail-queue[qcb-rs] → avail-address
    if queue-count[avail-address] greater than or equal to max-depth
        then
            event-error(er-queue-depth)
    endif
    if data-size[usp] less than zero
        or data-size[usp] greater than or equal to max-data-size + 1
            then
                event-error(er-size)
```

```
        endif
        request(qfree-rs, data-size[usp] + 3) → result
        if result less than zero
              then
                      set-return-and-exit(result)
        endif
        page-select(0, empty-page, qcb-address[p])
        insert-into-queue(p)
        insert-into-queue(event-nr[usp])
        insert-into-queue(data-size[usp])
        map[usp] → map-temp
        data-block[usp] → address-temp
        adjust-for-pdb(map-temp)
        queue-buffer-size − end → size-temp
        if size-temp less than data-size[usp]
              then
                      if size-temp not equal to zero
                            then
                                    move-from-user-space(map-temp,
                                    address-temp, queue-buffer[end],
                                                       size-temp)
                                    decrement data-size[usp] by size-temp
                                    increment address-temp by size-temp
                      endif
                      clear end
        endif
        move-from-user-space(map-temp, address-temp, queue-
                                    buffer[end], data-size[usp])
        increment end by data-size[usp]
        release(qcb-rs)
        mark-event-busy(event-nr[usp])
        event-16-check( )
endproc
```

Receiving a Message

While SEND-MESSAGE stores all messages on a queue that is shared by one or more processes, ACCEPT-MESSAGE obtains the next message in the queue for the requesting process. The procedure for accepting messages is divided into a preprocessing routine and a retrieval routine (modules 3.5.3 and 3.5.4, respectively).

The format for receiving a message is as follows:

SYSTEM(ACCEPT-MESSAGE, EVENT-NR, QCB-ID, MSG-
ADDRESS)

where   EVENT-NR   is used to signal the caller when the message
                                      has been received
             QCB-ID   is the identifier of the message queue
             MSG-ADDRESS   is the location of the data buffer where the
                                      message will be stored

SETUP-RECEIVE initializes the requestor as a subprocess and validates the
message queue identifier; an error code is returned if the message queue does
not exist. The address of the message buffer is resolved for the special case
where the message is stored in the PDB.

ACCEPT-MESSAGE performs the retrieval of a message from the queue.
The message queue is mapped into the system's empty page to facilitate access.
Access to the message queue is requested. If the queue is active (e.g., another
process is storing/retrieving a message), the caller is suspended until the queue
is available. Next, the procedure determines the parameters of the message.
START reflects the current position in the circular queue (it points to the first
word of the message header). DX thus points to the first word of the message.

The size of the message, including the header packet, is calculated by the
system. Because the queue is circular, certain conditions arise:

1. If the message is completely contained in the queue (SIZE > SIZE-
    TEMP), the message is copied to user space from START to START +
    SIZE inclusive;

2. Or the message may wrap around the end of the queue (SIZE < SIZE-
    TEMP). We first copy from START to the end of the queue buffer (e.g.,
    START + SIZE-TEMP). We then set START to zero and adjust SIZE
    to capture the remainder of the message.

In either case, the space occupied by the message is released to the resource
manager. The receiver is notified that the message is available. Notice that no
check is made on the space available in the receiver's process relative to the
message size.

MODULE 3.5.3

```
procedure receive-message
    page-select(0, empty-page, qcb-address[p])
    request(qcb-rs) → result
    if result less than zero
        then
                set-subprocess-status(result)
```

```
            endif
            start + 2 → dx
            if dx greater than or equal to queue-buffer-size
                  then
                        decrement dx by queue-buffer-size
            endif
            queue-buffer[dx] + 3 → size
            queue-buffer-size - start → size-temp
            if size-temp less than size
                  then
                        if size-temp not equal to zero
                        then
                              move-to-user-space(qmap[p], queue-buffer
                                    [start], qcb-address[p], size-temp)
                              decrement size by size-temp
                              increment qcb-address[p] by size-temp
                              release(qfree-rs, size-temp)
                        endif
                        clear start
            endif
            move-to-user-space(qmap[p], queue-buffer[start], qcb-address[p],
                                                                      size)
            increment start by size
            release(qfree-rs, size)
            subprocess-ok( )
endproc
```

MODULE 3.5.4

```
procedure setup-receive
      check-qcb-id(qcb-id[usp]) → qcb-address[n]
      if qcb-address[n] less than zero
      then
                  p-setup-done( )
      endif
      address[usp] → queue-address[n]
      map[usp] → qmap[n]
      adjust-for-pdb(map[usp])
      p-setup-ok( )
endproc
```

Checking the Queue Depth

A user may want to determine how many messages are waiting in the queue.
The system service request takes the form

SYSTEM(QUEUE-DEPTH, QCB-ID) → QUEUE-COUNT

where	QCB-ID	is the identifier of the queue
QUEUE-COUNT	is the number of messages in the queue or, if negative, the number of unsatisfied requests for messages.

The procedure for determining the queue depth is depicted in module 3.5.5. It is straightforward, so I will not belabor it.

MODULE 3.5.5

```
procedure queue-depth
     check-qcb-id(qcb-id[usp]) → qcb-temp
     if qcb-temp greater than or equal to zero
          then
                    rs-avail-queue[qcb-rs] → avail-address
                    rs-wait-queue[qcb-rs] → wait-address
                    rs-wait-queue[queue-free-rs] → free-wait-address
                    queue-count[avail-address] − queue-count[wait-
                                                   address] → depth
                    depth − queue-count[free-wait-address] → depth
          endif
     set-return-and-exit(depth)
endproc
```

Verifying the Queue Identifier

The QCB-ID is the index of the queue in the user queue list. This index is validated to ensure that the queue has been defined and that the index is converted to the page address of the queue. This procedure, depicted in module 3.5.6, is also straightforward.

MODULE 3.5.6

```
procedure check-qcb-id(qcb-id, →result)
     if qcb-id less than zero
          then
                    set er-queue-control-block to result
                    exitproc
     endif
     if qcb-id greater than or equal to max-user-queues
          then
```

```
                set er-queue-control-block to result
                exitproc
        endif
        if user-queue-list[qcb-id] equals zero
            then
                    set er-queue-control-block to result
                    exitproc
        endif
        user-queue-list[qcb-id] → qcb-address
        page-select(0, empty-page, qcb-address)
        qcb-address → result
endproc
```

Putting an Element in the Queue

A simple little worker routine used to put information packet elements into the circular queue one word at a time. The essential idea is to wrap-around if we come to the end of the queue.

MODULE 3.5.7

```
procedure insert-into-queue(entry)
        if end greater than or equal to queue-buffer-size
            then
                    clear end
        endif
        entry → queue-buffer[end]
        increment end
endproc
```

4

Memory Management

A resource equally as critical as CPU time is main memory. An important trade-off to be made in operating system design concerns the balance between execution time (CPU access) and memory usage (program size). Primary memory is shared between the OS and the users, who are represented by a select set of processes. Sharing of main memory requires that the OS keep track of the amount of memory owned by each process while protecting the integrity of the allocations. In many systems, a user's memory resource needs usually exceed the available physical store. Thus the OS must support a method for both logically extending the memory resource and mapping logical memory to physical memory. This chapter is devoted to exploring the management of main memory. It concentrates on solutions to four basic problems: mapping references, sharing and extending, allocation, and protection of main memory.

4.1 MEMORY MANAGEMENT FUNCTIONS

Modern OSs distinguish between two types of memory: physical and logical. These are also called the physical and logical address spaces, to denote whether the CPU or a user process is generating an address. Physical memory refers to the actual electronic hardware, such as core or semiconductor memory. Logical memory refers to the set of locations or addresses that may be referenced by a program.

The OS, in conjunction with the CPU, usually references physical memory. User processes generate references to a logical memory that is mapped onto the physical memory. Each process believes that its memory starts at location zero and is composed of a set of contiguous addresses. Clearly, if multiple processes are to be resident in memory at once, they cannot all simultaneously own the set of physical addresses from 0 to N. Thus the OS, usually with hardware assistance from the CPU, provides a method for concurrently sharing the physical addresses 0 to N among M processes, so the first aspect of memory management is to map each process's logical memory onto the physical memory at the appropriate time.

One method of mapping logical memory to physical memory is the swapping/chaining technique. Although this technique is simple to implement and can often be used without hardware assistance, it is often not efficient in a multiple-user environment. To accommodate multiple users, and thus realize the economy of scale in multiprogramming systems, the OS must support the sharing of main memory among processes. Sharing complicates the problem of memory management since the OS must decide how to allocate or divide main memory among the available processes that have been selected by the scheduler.

Sharing of main memory introduces another problem—the protection of individual users from each other and of the OS from the users. At the same time, an OS designer may want to allow user processes to communicate with each other. Communication may involve sharing code segments, files, or data. Therefore, the OS must provide a method for protecting a user's information in main memory.

User processes, like many other facets of human activity, seem to obey Parkinson's Law. That is, they always seem to fill the memory allotted to them. The limitation on main memory is due to hardware considerations, such as the number of address bits in an instruction. It is often difficult to expand this limit without reengineering the computer system. Thus OSs may attempt to extend the process's logical memory beyond the maximum physical memory and then map appropriate segments to physical memory as necessary. The process of extending logical memory over physical memory is often called the virtual memory technique.

Memory management, then, consists of five major functions:

Mapping logical memory addresses to physical memory addresses

Sharing physical memory among multiple users

Allocating physical memory among multiple users

Protecting both the OS's and the user's information from one another

Extending logical memory space beyond the maximum physical memory limit

4.1.1 Memory Mapping

The purpose of memory mapping, or more appropriately, address mapping, is to translate the logical addresses into physical addresses. This translation can occur at these distinct times:

1. Absolute translation occurs when a compiler or assembler prepares a program and generates absolute addresses. In many assemblers, the

LOC N instruction sets the current program address to the absolute value of *N*.

2. Static translation occurs when the program is linked to form an executable module. Individual subroutines are collected and assigned addresses relative to some fixed memory address.

3. Dynamic translation occurs when the actual location of the program in physical memory is determined by the OS when the program is loaded. In certain systems, the program may be relocated in physical memory during a break in execution.

Absolution translation was prevalent in early systems when OS techniques were not so sophisticated. Today, some microprocessor systems provide rudimentary OSs using absolute translation. As the microcomputer industry expands, these systems will be replaced by static and dynamic translation. Many commercial minicomputer OSs utilize some variation of static translation. Some of the larger minicomputers, such as the DGC M/600 or the HP-3000, support dynamic translation facilities.

Static and dynamic translation systems differ in the assumptions they make about two aspects of program execution: the ability to predict the availability of memory resources; and the properties of a process's reference string (i.e., the sequence of addresses it generates in retrieving data from memory).

Static translation assumes that the memory resources of a process are well specified after the program is linked. It also assumes that the reference string (e.g., the sequence of addresses referenced by the program) can be determined by preprocessing the program. These assumptions mean that a process cannot expand its data space by requesting additional memory space. Furthermore, in stack-based programs, the stack eventually will reach an upper limit which will force the process to terminate.

Dynamic translation assumes memory resources cannot be totally prespecified. It further assumes that the OS best understands the availability of memory resources and is best able to determine where a program should be loaded. It also assumes that the process reference string is determined only through close observation of the process during execution, and that the data space of the process shrinks and grows as it executes instructions. This pattern varies from one execution to the next and is dependent on the data submitted to the process.

The designer of an OS needs to consider several factors when choosing a method of memory mapping. These factors are described in the following paragraphs.

Hardware Factors

The basic hardware factor to consider is the availability of hardware assistance via a MMU. Static mapping can be implemented without hardware assistance. Dynamic mapping usually requires hardware assistance. A limited form of dynamic mapping can be implemented in computer systems possessing a hardware stack where all memory references are made relative to the stack.

A second factor concerns the impact of address translation on program execution time. In systems using a hardware MMU, additional clock cycles may be added to the execution of each instruction in producing the physical address. The delay is introduced when generating both the next instruction address and the operand address (if it is in main memory). For the PDP-11/70 [dec78] the additional time is 90 nsec for each memory cycle. For the NOVA computers [dgc75] no additional clock cycles are added. The difference is a matter of hardware implementation.

Cost Factors

The first cost factor is the price of a hardware MMU. Current price lists show an average of $5000 for an MMU or approximately 25 percent of the cost of a 65K-byte CPU.

A second cost is introduced by the additional memory requirements of the OS in order to implement a handle for the MMU. The memory requirements may easily approach 2K to 4K bytes of resident code.

The extra clock cycles that may be added by the MMU present a third cost that may affect the design of real-time systems. This cost is subjective in that an application may not be able to use a cheaper processor with an MMU solely because it cannot meet the timing constraints of the application.

Finally, a subjective cost is introduced by the added complexity of the OS when introducing MMU support for dynamic mapping. Addition of MMU support also increases the number of services provided by the OS which are accessible to the user. A survey of the modules provided in this text will demonstrate that the hardware MMU support affects the design of many modules.

Programming Factors

Denning [denn70] notes several factors associated with the development of application programs. These factors rely on the difference between the process's logical memory and the physical memory. While the following factors generally apply to both static and dynamic translation, the benefits derived are greater when dynamic mapping is utilized.

1. Machine independence, which implies that no a priori correspondence exists between logical and physical memory spaces.
2. Program modularity, where separately compiled or assembled modules are not linked together until execution time. It may be possible to dynamically link load modules during execution.

3. List or text processing systems, where the data structures vary in size, shape, and resource requirements during execution.

Denning notes that these factors violate the predictability assumption of static mapping because they depend on whether they are applied immediately before execution or during program execution (i.e., during the linking or the loading phase).

Systems Factors

Denning [denn70] also notes several factors for static versus dynamic mapping which arose from the needs of multiprogramming and time-sharing systems. Generally, the static mapping approach, because of its inflexible assumptions regarding memory availability, cannot satisfy the following objectives:

1. The ability to load a user program into a space of arbitrary size beginning at an arbitrary location.
2. The ability to run a partially loaded program due to the sharing of memory among users.
3. The ability to vary the amount of space in use by a given process.
4. The ability to "relocate" a process anywhere in memory at any time.
5. The ability to begin running a program within certain deadlines.
6. The ability to change system equipment without having to reprogram or recompile.
7. The ability to allocate memory to a user program in noncontiguous portions which may be of fixed or variable size.

Choosing an Approach

The designer must carefully consider the applications environment that will be supported by the OS. A dedicated process control environment may find absolute translation an acceptable solution. A foreground/background partitioned environment, exemplified by DGC's RDOS, is amenable to the static solution. The general-purpose multiprogramming environment, exemplified by HP's MPE 3000, requires dynamic mapping. An astute designer can evaluate which alternative is best for the application environment by examining the trade-off factors associated with each technique (see [gord73]).

4.1.2   Memory Sharing

An implicit function of memory management in a multiprocessing system is the sharing of memory among multiple user's programs and the OS. Sharing of memory poses a significant problem because each user's memory space requirements may be different. User programs may wish to share a common module, such as a subroutine from the FORTRAN library. Of course, all programs share the facilities and services provided by the OS.

The sharing of memory resources can be implemented in several ways. A software module to be shared between two or more programs may be linked into each user program as a separate copy. Alternatively, using a hardware MMU, the software module may be mapped into the logical address space of each user program. Finally, since only one copy of the OS can control the CPU at a time, user programs may serially share the facilities of the OS (such as the system service request processor) via a semaphore mechanism. These modes of sharing memory are explored in other sections of the text.

4.1.3 Memory Allocation

The memory allocation problem is basically viewed as assigning blocks of physical storage to a user process and keeping track of all such assignments in a coherent manner. If the system also supports a virtual memory capability, the problem is compounded by the necessity to track the virtual memory allocations and interact with the mass storage handler. A discussion of virtual memory capabilities is provided in sections 4.4 and 4.5.

Memory allocation in the multiprocessing environment is a decision-making and strategy function. The memory manager must decide where to place a program, allocate the space and load the program into memory. The strategy of placement depends on the memory management methodology used by the designer. The major objectives of an allocation strategy are to be able to place a program anywhere in main memory (dynamic relocation) and to be able to maximize the number of processes in memory that could be ready to run.

The problem of memory allocation is directly related to the problems of extending memory and mapping logical memory to physical memory. The designer must decide whether the logical memory is to be smaller than, equal to, or larger than the physical memory. A second decision is related to memory utilization in that a trade-off exists between the time necessary to manage memory and the efficiency with which memory is utilized.

4.1.4 Memory Protection

In a multiuser environment, user processes must be protected from each other and themselves, and the OS must be protected from user processes. Penetration of another process's address space may be accidental (due to a program error) or it may be deliberately malicious. Protection has two aspects: detecting that a penetration has occurred, and successfully dealing with the pentration so that the target process is not disturbed.

Protection in a strictly software environment is almost impossible to achieve. One method is to use an interpreter to execute all user programs (such as BASIC or APL). In this case, the interpreter monitor allocates pseudo-addresses to all user variables and can check each address prior to referencing the variable. Another method, used by RDOS [dgc75], allocates user memory for code and data above the OS. To penetrate the OS, the program needs to generate negative addresses with large displacements. In assembly language programs, this is relatively easy. In compiler languages, this address is difficult to construct except where negative array subscripts are allowed. Thus a program usually succeeds in destroying itself before it penetrates the OS. The point to be made is that there is no protection in a strictly software system unless all programs are well behaved.

Protection is easily achievable with MMU hardware. It ranges from a simple "no access outside program limits" to sophisticated sharing capabilities. The implementation of a protection mechanism depends on the memory management method selected by the designer. Any general scheme is dependent on dividing memory into fixed (paging)- or variable-length (segmentation) blocks. Each block can be allocated to a user program or to the OS, and may be assigned a protection mode against which the MMU will validate all memory references. Valid references are allowed to retrieve or store data into the memory block. Invalid references detected by the MMU force the initiation of an interrupt so that the CPU can handle the problem.

In most memory protection schemes, four general protection modes can be assigned to a memory block: inaccessible, read/write, read-only, and execute-only. A differentiation between read-only protection, which allows a program to retrieve data from a memory block, versus execute-only protection is made to enforce sharing of data versus sharing of processes. Full read/write protection is required by most OS processes. Subsystems such as utilities or library procedures can be shared by many users and thus are accorded execute-only protection. Usually, the memory allocated to the OS or outside the user's logical address space is marked inaccessible to the program. Inaccessible memory may be made accessible to a program by the OS upon execution of a system service request.

The system designer must take several factors into account in designing a protection mechanism. Obviously, the first factor is the availability of a hardware MMU. The structure of the MMU can restrict the protection scheme or offer a wide variety of choices. A second factor involves the determination of where to protect—in the physical or logical address space. Watson [wats70] believes that protection in the logical address space offers the most flexibility and easiest approach. By comparison, he cites the difficulty of implementing a protection scheme for the IBM System/360, where protection is maintained on physical blocks of memory. A third factor is the cost relative to software/ hardware complexity and time constraints. Protection mechanisms in hardware range from the simple to the complex. Associated with these hardware mechanisms are software schemes having varying degrees of complexity. The combination of hardware and software can impose significant time delays when checking the protection of a given memory block.

4.1.5 Memory Extension

The physical address space on any computer system is directly limited by the number of address bits in an instruction. For example, on Data General Novas, the 16-bit word is treated as a 1-bit indirect address indicator and 15 bits of address. These 15 bits yield a 32K-word address space which must be shared between operating system and user. In most minicomputer systems, the OS averages between 8K and 16K words. Its size is a direct function of its capabilities. OS size can severely limit the flexibility and size of applications programs that can be developed by the programmer and may also limit the number of applications that can be treated using the minicomputer.

The memory address space can be extended in the physical or logical dimensions or both. Physical address space extension requires the assistance of a hardware MMU. Logical address space may be extended using both software and hardware assistance (see [popp77]).

The physical address space is extended by the MMU by providing additional address bits. Each memory address generated by the CPU passes through the MMU before arriving at the memory controller. The MMU attaches additional address bits which were previously specified by the OS. This expanded (or effective) address is passed to the memory controller, which retrieves the indicated word.

In a computer system, the physical address space is referred to as real memory, and the logical address space is often referred to as virtual memory. When real memory is extended by hardware, the relationship between real and virtual memory can be changed in a significant manner. These relationships are depicted below.

RELATIONSHIP BETWEEN REAL AND VIRTUAL MEMORY

	Physical Address Space (R)	
	Normal	Extended
Logical Address Space (V)	$V < R$	$V < R$
	$V = R$	$V = R$
	$V' > R*$	$V > R$
	($V = R$)	

*Simulation of $V > R$; the instantaneous relationship is $V = R$ at any instant.

The logical address space can be extended without hardware assistance by stimulating a larger memory through a technique known as overlaying. Overlaying involves the replacement of a piece of the user's program by another piece—the overlay. Both program pieces share the same set of logical addresses. However, only one piece is assigned at any time during program execution. Overlaying is a method by which the user can overcome main memory limitations. A scheme for implementing an overlay management system is discussed in section 4.4.

Overlaying can be contrasted with the techniques of swapping and chaining which can be used by the OS to overcome main-memory limitations. In swapping, a user divides the application into a number of independent programs and executes it by initiating the first program in the sequence. At any point during program execution the user can request (via an SSR) that the current program be suspended and a new program be executed. When the new program has completed, the old program resumes execution. The two programs communicate with each other by placing data in mass storage files. Under chaining, the old program does not resume execution. Although swapping and chaining are initiated by the user, the mechanics of the operation are under the control of the OS. Swapping and chaining are discussed more fully in section 4.3.

Swapping/chaining are used in the $V < R$ and $V = R$ cases under normal real memory. Overlaying is used to simulate extended memory ($V > R$) in normal real memory. When real memory is extended, the same set of relationships is maintained but the complexity of managing memory increases. Another reason for extending main memory is to acccommodate multiple users. Whereas in many instances the user's virtual memory is less than real memory, the capability exists for $V > R$. The techniques of paging and segmentation can handle both memory allocation to multiple users and the extension of virtual memory.

Paging is a technique whereby both the physical address space and the logical address space are divided into fixed-size units. In real memory these units are known as blocks and in virtual memory as pages. Paging effects a mapping of pages to blocks during execution of a program. However, paging places constraints on the sharing of programs and data and on the ability of data structures to dynamically expand and contract during execution. Another technique, known as segmentation, provides the solution to these problems. It also allows the logical address space contents (i.e., procedures and data) to be dynamically modified during execution. The cost of this flexibility is a concomitant increase in the complexity of the OS software and MMU hardware. Paging techniques are described in section 4.5. A good description of segmentation techniques can be found in [bens72], [orga72], and [wats70].

4.1.6   Memory Management Summary

In summary, memory management in an OS must support the following five basic functions:

Address mapping
Memory sharing
Memory allocation
Memory protection
Memory extension

These functions are performed in a highly interdependent manner. Each solves a problem of memory management but introduces constraints on the whole system. Memory extension encompasses the other four functions as subfunctions when one considers the multiprocessing environment.

The following sections of this chapter examine the memory management functions in greater detail. Both hardware and software implementations are discussed. Sections 4.3 through 4.5 discuss the basic approaches to memory management. The functions of mapping, sharing, allocation, and protection are considered in view of the specific technique.

4.2 DYNAMIC MEMORY ALLOCATION

Within the OS, a free pool of memory is usually set aside to accomodate the temporary needs of various system processes. This memory pool supports temporary system buffers, queue entries, and control blocks for processes. As the OS usually operates in an unmapped mode (i.e., with the MMU disabled), this memory pool represents a contiguous segment that needs to be dynamically allocated to various requestors.

The principles to be discussed in this section also apply to systems that do not support a MMU. In that case, all memory allocation is performed by a software-based memory manager. This section explores the principles of dynamic memory allocation under the assumption of no hardware support. It draws substantially on the work of Denning [denn70].

4.2.1 Placement Policies

The concept of dynamic memory allocation is really a question of implementing a proper placement policy. Allocation is a decision as to where to place a program in memory so that it minimizes wasted space and guarantees that an optimum number of users are accomodated at once. Of course, the implication is that the more users we maintain in memory who are "ready to run," the greater likelihood that we will be able to make efficient use of system resources.

In determining a placement policy, we treat memory as a linear space of m words. Over time, requests for allocation or release of memory blocks will tend to balance out (under an assumption of system equilibrium). However, the memory configuration then displays a checkerboard appearance with holes interspaced among allocated memory blocks. This configuration, varying with time, results from requests of varying size. The objective of a successful memory allocation mechanism is to minimize both the size and number of holes in the memory configuration.

Two important relationships have been derived for replacement policies: the Fifty-Percent Rule and the Unused Memory Rule. The Fifty-Percent Rule was derived by Knuth [knut69]. It assumes a system in equilibrium, that is, one in which allocation and release requests are balanced over a short time interval. (Note that violation of this assumption can lead to a serious deadlock situation.) Briefly, given a system of m words in which n segments are allocated, there will be approximately h holes, where h is equal to $n/2$. This follows from the fact that for a given segment, the space on its right boundary will be a hole for half the time and a segment for the other half. The probability of a hole is $p = 1/2$; for example, the number of segments with holes as right neighbors is $mp = m/2 = h$.

The Unused Memory Rule, described by Denning [denn70], attempts to derive the relationship between the amount of unused memory and the average hole and segment sizes. Again, we assume a system in equilibrium. We also assume the average hole size to be at least $k \times s$, where s is the average segment size ($k > 0$). Then, the fraction of memory f that is unused is given by $f \geq k/(k + 2)$. An application of the Fifty-Percent Rule shows that there are $n/2$ holes in an m-word memory containing n segments. The amount of space occupied by holes is $(m - ns)$ and the average hole size is $x = (m - ns)/h$. Assuming that $x \geq ks$ and performing some algebraic manipulations yields

$$f = \frac{m - ns}{m} = 1 - (n/m)s \geq \frac{k}{k + 2}$$

The impact of these two rules is quite clear. To limit overhead in execution of a placement algorithm, we must be willing to suffer the presence of large holes in the memory configuration. The result is that a fraction of memory is wasted at each instantaneous snapshot of the memory configuration. However, Knuth [knut69] shows that with a large variance in hole sizes, the fraction f can be reduced as low as 10 percent (for $k = 1/4$).

Many algorithms have been proposed for dynamic memory allocation. The following paragraphs explore a few of these algorithms. References include [coff73], [pete77], [shen74], and [tene78].

Best Fit Placement

This algorithm attempts to match the request with a hole that wastes a minimum amount of space. A hole list is maintained which ranks the holes in order of increasing size. Whenever a request is presented to the memory manager, it searches the list for the hole yielding the smallest DELTA as computed by

HOLE-SIZE - NEEDED-SIZE → DELTA

where DELTA is the space remaining beyond the requested size. The objective is to minimize the amount of space wasted with each allocation. In systems that split holes, DELTA is compared to a threshold value to determine whether or not the hole should be split.

First-Fit Placement

This algorithm attempts to find the first hole having enough space to accomodate the request. Holes are maintained in the list by increasing address. The hole-list is searched for the first hole such that

HOLE-SIZE > = NEEDED-SIZE

Usually, no attention will be paid to the amount of wasted space, as the objective is to achieve the fastest allocation of a hole to a request as possible. Unfortunately, this approach results in memory being able to accomodate fewer programs at any time.

Buddy System

The buddy system uses a power-of-2 algorithm to maintain its hole lists. In a given system, each hole will be a power of 2 for 2_i ($i = 1$ to k). The system maintains k hole lists one for each size hole. When an allocation request is submitted, the system calculates the ceiling of the request as the next highest power of 2. That is, for request size s, find minimum j such that ceiling(s) = $2 \times j$.

The system examines the jth hole list for a hole to satisfy the request. If a hole is available, it is removed from the list and assigned to the requesting program. If the list is empty, a hole is removed from the ($j + 1$) list and split into two buddies of size j which are entered into the jth list. A hole is then removed from the jth list and assigned to the requestor. Conversely, two holes on the jth list, which adjoin each other in memory, may be removed and coalesced into a hole which is placed on the ($j + 1$) list.

4.2.2   Implementing a Dynamic Memory Manager

The implementation of a dynamic memory manager is described in this section. It uses a variation of Knuth's Boundary Tagged Allocation Method [knut69].

The memory manager maintains a queue of free memory blocks. The queue header is depicted in figure 4.1. The first five entries form the standard queue header (see section 7.9). QUEUE-BLOCKS represents the number of blocks of free memory in the queue. MEMORY-QUEUE-FORWARD and MEMORY-QUEUE-BACK contain the addresses of the first and last blocks of memory.

Each memory block is tagged by a four-word descriptor known as memory control block (MCB). The MCB is described in table 4.1.

The following paragraphs describe the routines for allocating from the releasing to the memory queue blocks of memory to satisfy users' requests.

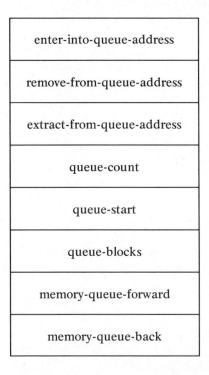

Figure 4.1   Structure of memory queue.

Table 4.1   Description of Memory Control Block

Mnemonic	Usage
previous-size	Size of the previous block in queue after the last allocation
current-size	Current size of the block
forward-link	Pointer to next block in queue
back-link	Pointer to previous block in queue

Note. The latter two entries exist only when the block is resident on the memory queue. Otherwise, when the block is allocated, they contain data. MEMORY-ADDRESS points to the first available data address.

Allocating a Memory Block

A system process requests a free memory block by executing the following statement:

REQUEST(MEMORY-RS, NBR-OF-WORDS) → MEMORY-ADDRESS

When this statement is executed, MEMORY-ALLOCATOR is invoked (module 4.2.1). Processing by the resource management routines has placed the requestor on the WAIT-QUEUE to await servicing by the allocation routine.

MEMORY-ALLOCATOR, at each invocation, attempts to allocate the available free memory to the list of requesting processes. In this simple approach, requestors are placed on the WAIT-QUEUE as they make their individual requests. If the first request cannot be satisfied by the allocator, the procedure exits. No further requests are satisfied until the first waiter has been

MODULE 4.2.1

```
procedure memory-allocator(rs-address)
      set true to queue-flag
      while queue-flag equals true
            do
                  rs-wait-queue[rs-address] → wait-address
                  queue-start[wait-address] → pcb-address
                  if pcb-address not equal to zero
                        then
                        rs-available-queue[rs-address] → available-address
                        rs-data-save[pcb-address] → memory-size
                        extract-from-queue(available-address,memory-size)
                                                      → memory-address
                        if memory-address not equal to zero
                              then
                              memory-address →
                                                      return-value[pcb-address]
                              remove-from-queue(wait-address)
                              activate(pcb-address)
                              else
                                    exitdo
                        endif
                  endif
            enddo
endproc
```

satisfied. Some systems will search the WAIT-QUEUE and attempt to satisfy any requests for which available memory exists. This is a design decision to be weighed carefully, as it has serious impact on scheduling algorithm efficiency.

The mechanics of memory allocation are straightforward. A requestor's PCB is retrieved from the WAIT-QUEUE. If no requests are outstanding, the procedure terminates. Otherwise, the queue is searched for a free memory block corresponding to the requested size. If a free memory block of appropriate size exists, it is assigned to the waiting process and the process is reactivated. The allocation function is repeated until no further allocations can be made.

A word about first-waiter service is in order. Clearly, this will not result in the most efficient allocation scheme, as many processes may be enqueued behind a process that has requested an extraordinary large memory block. An alternative, requiring additional overhead, would sort memory allocation requests by size. This scheme would emphasize the satisfaction of small memory requests over large ones. It is possible that such a scheme would result in more efficient processing of programs that are resident in memory.

Searching the Memory Queue

The memory queue consists of a set of free memory blocks linked in order of increasing size. The list of memory blocks is searched for the first block whose size satisfies the allocation request. The procedure for performing this search is depicted in module 4.2.2.

The allocation size is incremented by two words to provide space for the permanent portion of the MCB. At all times, these two words are transparent to the user. If the allocation size exceeds the current number of free memory words, the procedure is terminated. Otherwise, the queue is searched for a memory block whose size satisfies the request. If the end of the queue is reached, the request is rejected because no free memory block can satisfy the request.

After a free memory block is found, a decision must be made about splitting the block (see figure 4.2). The number of excess words beyond the allocation size, BLOCK-DELTA, is calculated. If BLOCK-DELTA does not exceed the fragmentation threshold, the block is unlinked and returned to the user. The excess words must be regarded as wasted space—at least for this allocation. The fragmentation threshold is a parameter which is defined at system generation time. If the block is to be split, the excess words are extracted from the front of the block. The excess words, including the MCB, remain linked in the queue. A new MCB is constructed in the allocated block. The number of words allocated is used to decrement the free memory count. The address returned to the user is adjusted to point after the MCB. The allocation flag in SIZE is set to one to indicate that this block of memory has been allocated to a user.

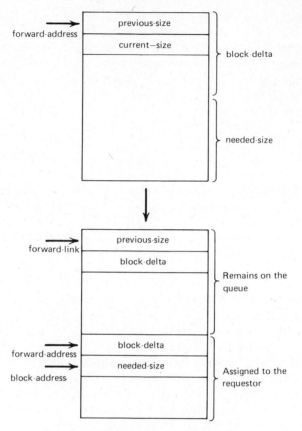

Figure 4.2   Splitting a free memory block.

MODULE 4.2.2

procedure extract-from-memory-queue(q, number-of-words,
                                                                    →block-address)
    number-of-words + 2 → needed-size
    if needed-size greater than or equal to queue-count[q]
      then
          clear block-address
          exitproc
    endif
    queue-start[q] → forward-address
    forward-address → previous-forward-address
    while forward-link[forward-address] not equal to
                                                            previous-forward-address
      do

```
                    forward-link[forward-address] → forward-address
                    if size[forward-address] greater than or equal to
                                                            needed-size
                then
                                exitdo
                endif
          enddo
     if forward-address equals previous-forward-address
          then
                clear block-address
                exitproc
     endif
     size[forward-address] - needed-size → block-delta
     if block-delta less than fragment-size
          then
                unlink(forward-address)
                decrement queue-blocks[q]
          else
                block-delta → size[forward-address]
                increment forward-address by block-delta
                block-delta → previous-size[forward-address]
                needed-size → size[forward-address]
     endif
     decrement queue-count[q] by size[forward-address]
     forward-address + 2 → block-address
     size[forward-address] + forward-address → next-block-address
     set allocation-flag of size[forward-address]
     size[forward-address] → previous-size[next-block-address]
endproc
```

Releasing a Memory Block

A process releases a memory block by executing the statement

RELEASE(MEMORY-RS, MEMORY-ADDRESS)

The procedure for returning a memory block to the free memory queue is depicted in module 4.2.3. MB-ADDRESS is the address of the memory block to be returned to the system.

The procedure calculates the address of the free memory block (remember that the user does not see the first two words). The allocation flag of the block size is cleared to indicate an unallocated block of memory, and the number of free words is incremented by the block size.

Next, the queue is examined to determined if the block can be combined with any free blocks in the queue. If so, these blocks (both fore and aft) are unlinked and combined with the free block. The number of free blocks is decremented by BLOCK-COUNT (this trick really works). The new block is linked into the queue in the appropriate place.

Procedures UNLINK, LINK and COMBINE are used to manage the pointers in the free memory queue.

MODULE 4.2.3

```
procedure enter-into-memory-queue(q, mb-address)
     mb-address - 2 → free
     clear allocation-flag of size[free]
     increment queue-count[q] by size[free]
     set -1 to block-count
     if previous-size[free] greater than or equal to zero
          then
                    decrement free by previous-size[free]
                    unlink(free)
                    combine( )
                    increment block-count
     endif
     free + size[free] → new-free
     if size[new-free] greater than or equal to zero
          then
                    unlink(new-free)
                    combine( )
                    increment block-count
     endif
     decrement queue-blocks[q] by block-count
     size[free] → previous-size[new-free]
     link(free, queue-start[q])
endproc
```

MODULE 4.2.4

```
procedure unlink(block-address)
     back-link[block-address] → previous-block-address
     forward-link[block-address] → next-block-address
     previous-block-address → back-link[next-block-address]
     next-block-address → forward-link[previous-block-address]
endproc
```

MODULE 4.2.5

```
procedure link(block-address, queue-address)
    queue-address → forward-link[block-address]
    back-link[queue-address] → back-link[block-address]
    back-link[queue-address] → back-block-address
    block-address → back-link[queue-address]
    block-address → forward-link[back-block-address]
endproc
```

MODULE 4.2.6

```
procedure combine
    free + size[free] → new-free
    increment size[free] by size[new-free]
    size[free] → previous-size[new-free]
endproc
```

Defining a Free Memory Queue

Initialization of the free memory queue occurs when the OS is booted into memory. The procedure for defining the memory resource semaphore, MEMORY-RS, is depicted in module 4.2.7. The available free memory in the system, as determined by the OS initialization procedure, is declared one contiguous memory buffer and linked into the memory queue. Once processes are activated, this large buffer will be carved into smaller chunks as memory is allocated to satisfy various requests.

MODULE 4.2.7

```
procedure define-memory-rs(rs-address, buffer, buffer-size)
    define-rs(rs, de-queue-set, 0, memory-allocator)
    address(rs-available-queue[rs-address]) → avq
    address(buffer) → buffer-address
    buffer-size - 4 → size[buffer-address]
    size[buffer-address] + buffer-address → next-buffer-address
    size[buffer-address] → previous-size[next-buffer-address]
    set allocation-flag of size[next-buffer-address]
    set allocation-flag of previous-size[buffer-address]
    address(enter-into-memory-queue) →
                                    enter-into-queue-address[avq]
    address(extract-from-memory-queue) →
                                    extract-from-queue-address[avq]
```

```
        clear queue-count[avq]
        clear queue-blocks[avq]
        address(queue-start[avq]) → queue-start[avq]
        queue-start[avq] → memory-queue-forward[avq]
        queue-start[avq] → memory-queue-back[avq]
        enter-into-queue(avq, buffer-address + 2)
endproc
```

4.3 SWAPPING AND CHAINING OF PROGRAMS

The simplest and perhaps the easiest way to extend the logical address space is either to swap or to chain a user's programs. The concept behind swapping/chaining is that a potentially large program is partitioned into a set of independently executable small programs. Then, a user initiates execution of the first program in the sequence. When it completes execution, it either swaps or chains to the next program in the sequence. We differentiate between the two methods as follows:

Swapping. Each program may call another program as if it were a subroutine. When the called program has completed, it returns to its caller, which resumes normal execution.

Chaining. Each program is written in serially executable segments. When a program calls the next segment, it is absolutely overwritten, with no possible return to the caller.

4.3.1 Concepts of Swapping and Chaining

The implementation of a swapping and chaining mechanism is relatively simple. The system either overwrites the current program image in memory, or checkpoints the current image with enough information to reinstate execution when a RETURN command is executed. Swapping was the first method used by OS designers to provide multiprogramming support.

The concepts of swapping and chaining are depicted in figure 4.3. Each time a user chains to a program, the current program is completely overwritten by the code of the new program. Whenever a user swaps a program, the current program is checkpointed to the mass storage system; the new program is located on disk and loaded into memory; and control is transferred to the new program. It is essential to realize that the act of swapping a program consumes disk space, whereas chaining a program does not. This realization places a limitation on the number of consecutive program swaps any one user may execute—often called the "nesting depth." Any user attempting to execute one

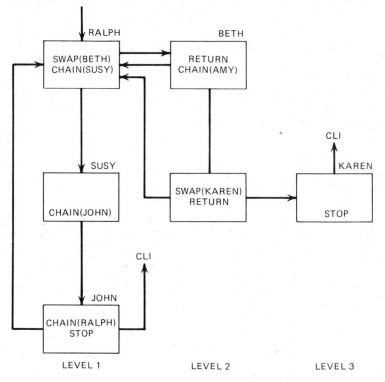

COMMAND LANGUAGE INTERPRETER
(LEVEL ϕ)

Figure 4.3   Swapping versus chaining.

too many program swaps is usually "terminated" and the swaps pace on the disk released.

Notice that the way we arrive at the execution of a user's program is through an EXECUTE command from the Command Language Interpreter (CLI). The CLI is treated as a level-zero program; that is, it is the lowest level at which the user can perform any useful work. Any lower level, of course, would imply that the machine is in a "halted" state. When the CLI swaps to a user program, the nesting depth or level is increased by one; thus RALPH is a level-one user program. Each successive user swap will increment the level until the maximum depth (usually a configurable parameter) is reached. When this occurs, the program is terminated and a system error message is issued to the user. Chaining does not increment the nesting depth since it merely overwrites the current program. Thus a chaining sequence may be (theoretically) infinitely long.

In figure 4.3 we notice that two commands are used to exit from a program. The RETURN command causes the previous program, if any, to be reloaded into memory. Execution continues from the address at which it was interrupted by a SWAP command. Obviously, any program executing at level one which issues a

RETURN command will force the invocation of the CLI. Any program issuing a RETURN request at level $n + 1$ returns to the user program at level n (for $n > 0$). Execution of a RETURN request at level zero results in an error message. Alternatively, the user program can execute a STOP request at any time. A STOP request executed at level n ($n > 0$) forces an immediate return to the CLI (i.e., to level zero). A STOP request issued at level zero forces to terminate the user's session.

Given that a user may swap/chain programs, how do individual program segments communicate data to one another? Clearly, the calling program cannot leave the data in memory since its allocated memory space is completely overwritten by the new program. Thus the two programs must communicate through a mutually agreed upon set of files having predetermined formats. Nominally, multipass compilers operate in exactly this fashion. The first pass of a compiler performs a lexical analysis of the source code and produces a symbol table in a file. The second pass, using both the symbol table and the original source code, generates the intermediate token file. Succeeding passes perform code generation, code optimization, and print the appropriate listings of the program. Each pass would constitute an independent program which creates one or more files to be passed to its successor. A good example of this approach is described in Hansen's articles on his concurrent Pascal compiler [hans73, hans76].

4.3.2 Hardware Considerations

A swapping/chaining approach to memory management may rely on a hardware architecture built around base registers. A base register is a hardware register whose contents are added to each logical address referenced by the program in order to generate a physical address. The key constraint on base register usage is that all memory allocated to a single program must exist as a contiguous block of words. Base registers are configured in several formats:

1. A single base register may exist in the system. This register contains the first physical address assigned to the program. A second register usually contains the length of the program. A physical address is generated as follows:

   c(base register) + c(program length register) → last physical address
   logical address + c(base register) → physical address
   if physical address less than or equal to last physical address
   then do memory reference
   else signal memory address violation

   where c( ) means "contents of."

2. Two base registers may provide additional flexibility. Two base registers containing, respectively, the first and last physical addresses of the program can be used to achieve the same result as in case 1 above. Alter-

natively, the two base registers may contain the starting addresses for independent code and data segments and have associated segment-length registers. In this case, the system determines which base register to use by deciding what type of memory reference is currently in progress.

Both static and dynamic relocation may be accomplished using base registers. With static relocation, a program is initially loaded anywhere in memory and all absolute memory references are resolved. When the program is reloaded from auxiliary storage after swapping, it must be placed in the same location as before. On the other hand, dynamic relocation implies that the program contains no absolute memory references. Thus the values of the base register contents may change each time the program is brought into memory.

There is no apparent advantage to using one base register over two if you are not interested in program sharing. The complexity of the system software is approximately equal for supporting case 1 or 2 above. However, when one considers program sharing, the program must be separable into code and data segments which are both relocatable. Two base registers (as in case 2) are a necessity. The complexity of system software increases because of the need to create two program segments with independent lengths, and to set and maintain the two pairs of registers.

The base register approach encounters several problems. The first problem has to do with the maximum size of the logical address space. Generally, the size of the logical address space is less than or equal to the size of the physical address space. One can simulate a larger logical address space by overlaying portions of a program (as discussed in section 4.4). A second problem concerns memory utilization. When loading a program, the system must find enough contiguous space to hold the entire program. Over time, this may lead to memory fragmentation, which results in decreased performance of the system. One cure, although time consuming, is to perform a compacting operation (also known as garbage collection) on memory in order to yield a contiguous space of the desired size. A third problem concerns access to the base registers themselves. If any type of system integrity is to be maintained, the user program should not be allowed access to the base registers. On the IBM/360 the program could directly access the base registers and, in fact, was required to do so—often with unfortunate consequences. Finally, the system designer should be concerned with the number of base registers if more than two (as in case 2) are available. The more base registers, the more care must be taken in planning the division of a program into pieces assigned to specific base registers. The system also needs to ensure that the instructions of a given program piece reference the correct base register.

4.3.3   Software Engineering Considerations

Although swapping/chaining is the easiest memory management method to implement, careful consideration must be given to the supporting data structures.

The major factors that affect swapping/chaining are described in the following paragraphs.

System Stack Area

When the system swaps out a program, it must save some information about the program so that it may later be reloaded. This information is stored in the system stack area. One stack, usually a system buffer, is dedicated to each user. The number of swaps that a user can perform is dependent on the buffer size and the amount of information to be retained. The first few words of the system buffer will contain information identifying the user.

System Swap Area

A corresponding area is maintained on the mass storage device for holding the images of programs that have been temporarily swapped out. When a program is swapped out, its entire memory space is copied from memory to disk. Care must be taken that the swapping area does not consume all the available disk space. For this reason, most minicomputer systems limit the number of possible swaps to some low integer (e.g., DGC's RDOS has a maximum nesting depth of four). In addition, the system designer must decide whether to maintain individual files for each program swapped out or to store them all in one large sequential file.

Swapping Information

What information needs to be saved when a program is swapped out? Obviously, the system needs the return address at which to resume execution. It also needs to remember the nesting level (i.e., the number of programs previously swapped) if some sort of integrity considerations are to be enforced. And depending on the organization of the swapping area, it will need the program name, the starting address on the disk, and the length of the program.

4.3.4   Swapping/Chaining a Program

The user initiates the swapping or chaining of a program by issuing the EXECUTE system service request. The format of this request is

SYSTEM(EXECUTE, FILENAME, MODE)

where   FILENAME   is the name of an executable file that is to be loaded into memory

              MODE   signifies the action to be taken

Both the OS and the user can issue the EXECUTE command. This command accomplishes one of the following functions, depending on the value of the MODE argument:

MODE = 0   Requests the initial loading of a program by the OS.

MODE = 1   Requests chaining to another program.

MODE = 2   Requests swapping to another program.

The EXECUTE procedure (module 4.3.1) does not actually load the save file. This function is reserved for a low-level system loading routine. Rather, it performs the steps necessary to validate the file and set up the system stack area (if required to do so). When EXECUTE is issued, it retrieves the file name from user space and verifies that the file is executable. Executable files usually have a ".SV" extension if they have been prepared by the system loader. EXECUTE reads the directory portion of the file control block (FCB) onto the system stack. The directory entry contains the information about the file position and size.

The system link editor normally produces files in a contiguous format. In this example, a file cannot be loaded unless it is contiguously organized. This characteristic is required for swapping and chaining systems since the entire program is loaded at one time. Note that the underlying memory management support is independent of the loader format. The system designer may introduce more complexity into the loader format at a corresponding cost in system complexity and overhead.

If the file is organized contiguously, the OS proceeds to load the file into memory. If a SWAP has been requested, the system stack is initialized to reflect the swap parameters. Here the parameters are the return address and the map where the program is loaded. If the number of swap levels has been exceeded, a system stack error is declared. Otherwise, the system stack pointer is incremented by the frame size. The current frame is then initialized. The current file name to be executed is placed in the stack and execution initiated.

MODULE 4.3.1

```
procedure execute
      er-file-name → status
      map[usp] → user-map
      file-name-address[usp] → fnaddress
      adjust-for-pdb(user-map)
      map-string-in(user-map, fnaddress, file-name, MAX-NAME-SIZE)
      check-file-name(file-name) → result
```

```
        if result less than zero
            then
                    execute-error( )
            else
                    set result to status
                    exitproc
        endif
        system(directory-read, 16, file-name, stack) → status
        if status less than zero
            then
                    system(value 1, 16) → value
                    execute-error( )
        endif
        if contiguous-flag of file-attributes[fcb-address] equals zero
            then
                    er-filedata → status
                    execute-error( )
        endif
        file-size[fcb-address] → load-size
        extract load-address from file-start[fcb-address]
        load-save-file( ) → error-code
        if error-code less than zero
            then
                    execute-error( )
        endif
        if mode[usp] equals 2
            then
                    return-address[usp] → stack-return[x]
                    map[usp] → stack-map[x]
                    set true to stack-flag[x]
                    increment level
                    if level greater than or equal to max-levels
                        then
                                er-stack → error-code
                                system-stack-error(error-code)
                    endif
                    increment x by frame-size
        endif
        copy(file-name, stack-file-name[x])
        mode[usp] → stack-mode[x]
        set false to stack-flag[x]
        set − 1 to stack-return[x]
        set − 1 to stack-map[x]
        go-boot( )
endproc
```

4.3.5   Returning from a Program Swap

Once a given program has completed execution, the user may optionally return to the previous program or to the CLI. To return to the previous program, the user issues the RETURN system service request, which has the following format:

SYSTEM(RETURN, STATUS, VALUE)

where   STATUS   is an indication of the success or failure of the swapped
                          program.

            VALUE   is a one-word message conveyed to the caller from the
                          terminated program.

To return from a program swap, the system must restore the environment of the previously executing program. The relevant information was stored in the system stack by EXECUTE prior to loading the current program. The system must inspect the stack for the following conditions:

1. If the stack is empty, an error message must be displayed for the user. This condition occurs in the CLI only if the user has not previously issued an EXECUTE request. It is possible for the user to EXECUTE a new version of the CLI much as you are allowed to recurse copies of the Shell in UNIX [bour78].

2. The stack may have an error flag set during the previous SWAP. Because there is no way to return to the program, the system can only mark the error in the system stack and report to the user when a RETURN is executed. The image of the "swapped" program is stored on disk even though an error occurred, so that a postmortem analysis may be conducted at a later time.

3. The previous program was successfully swapped out. The system obtains the disk address of the swap image, the map where the program is to be loaded, and copies of the PCB/PDB for the process image. The system calls the system loader to reload the program from disk. The system activates the PCB and calls the scheduler. Because the PCB/PDB contain the information to restore the process environment, the program will resume at the instruction after the SWAP request was executed.

4.3.6   Stopping Execution

A user may exit a program by issuing the system service request STOP. It has the following format:

SYSTEM(STOP)

The STOP request has two possible results. If the user is at level zero (e.g., the CLI), the system will terminate the user's job. For any level greater than zero, the system automatically returns to the command language intepreter. Both status and value are set to zero to indicate normal program termination.

4.3.7 Swapping/Chaining Utilities

Two utilities are used by the swapping/chaining modules: EXECUTE-ERROR and LOAD-SAVE-FILE.

Execution Errors

EXECUTE-ERROR is called by the EXECUTE procedure to exit gracefully from erroneous program request. In swapping/chaining, once the EXECUTE module is entered, it opens files necessary to load the requested program. If an error is encountered while verifying the requested program, the system reset and exits gracefully.

MODULE 4.3.2

```
procedure execute-error( )
     system(reset, 16)
     system(set-status, 16, status, value)
     os-exit( )
endproc
```

Loading a Save File

This procedure loads an executable file, such as one with a ".SV" extension, into memory. It first checks the size of the file to ensure that it will fit into one memory map. A memory map consists of 64 1K-byte pages. If the block count in the file exceeds the map size, a file error is reported to the user.

The loading process is straightforward. LOGICAL-PAGE and MEMORY-ADDRESS are set to zero because the map has already been set (in USER-MAP) and the loading process occurs under control of the MMU. That is, MEMORY-ADDRESS is translated by the MMU into a physical address somewhere in memory. To load a file, the system selects a page from the page list, inserts that page into the user map table, and reads data into memory at the physical page location.

4.4 OVERLAY MANAGEMENT TECHNIQUES

The concept of overlaying is intended to increase the effective utilization of memory in a computer system with a fixed memory size. Overlaying is used to

MODULE 4.3.3

```
procedure load-save-file(→ result)
    file-size[fcb-address] + sector-size − 1 → file-size
    extract block-count from file-size
    if block-count − 1 greater than or equal to 64
        then
                er-filedata → result
                exitproc
    endif
    clear logical-page
    clear memory-address
    while logical-page less than block-count
        do
                request-page(page-rs) → physical-page
                page-select(user-map, logical-page, physical-page)
                system(read, 16, user-overlay-channel, memory-address,
                                sector-size, disk-address) → error-code
                if error-code less than zero
                    then
                        if error-code equals er-end-of-file
                            then
                                set 1 to result
                                else
                                        error-code → result
                                endif
                        exitproc
                endif
                increment memory-address by sector-size
        enddo
endproc
```

increase the logical address space available to the user program. Unlike the other memory extension techniques, overlaying does not require any additional hardware support in the central processor–memory complex.

Under the overlay technique, a user program is partitioned into a main segment (the root) and one or more fixed-size segments known as overlays. The root segment is always resident in memory. The overlays are stored on a mass storage device and loaded into memory as necessary. A sequence of overlays that may be loaded into an overlay area (i.e., that portion of memory assigned to a user program and reserved for overlays) is called an overlay group. All of the overlays in an overlay group have the same fixed size. However, different overlay groups may have different fixed sizes.

Nominally, let M be the size of memory allocated to a given user program as determined by hardware constraints. Let R be the size of the root segment.

Then, the area reserved for overlays has a size equivalent to $O = M - R$. We can divide up the memory represented by O among the different overlay groups. For example, one such distribution is (given $M = 32$, $R = 8K$) the following:

Overlay Group	Allocation	Size
0	$\frac{1}{6}O$	4K
1	$\frac{1}{3}O$	8K
2	$\frac{1}{8}O$	3K
3	$\frac{3}{8}O$	9K
Total	O	24K

4.4.1 Characteristic Features of an Overlay System

The structure of generic overlay management has been described in papers by Pankhurst [pank68] and Spacek [spac72]. Every overlay system is dependent on the availability of a relatively fast mass storage system. In general, a user program will utilize several overlays during its execution, and depending on its structure, may use them in sequential or random order. An interactive user executing a program in which each command is serviced by an overlay would certainly not want to wait for a tape to be searched. In that event, swapping and/or chaining, discussed in the preceding section, are more efficient methods of segmenting a large program.

Whenever an overlay is to be loaded, a routine validates the overlay, locates it on disk, and reads it into the appropriate memory area. The overlay loader may exist in one of these forms:

1. As an executive subsystem where a user program issues a system service request to the overlay manager. Since the OS mediates overlay loading, multiple users may share the same overlay file. In addition, other processes in the user's program may be scheduled and executed independent of the overlay loading.

2. Each user program receives a copy of an overlay loading program. This approach is used by Data General's RDOS. In this case, multiple users may be prevented from using the same overlay file. A user program is usually suspended until the overlay load is completed.

Pankhurst notes that overlay systems may be classified by the way in which they organize and load overlays. He gives three classifications:

Automatic. The OS decides how the program should be divided into overlays. Usually, it divides the program into fixed-length blocks based on the physical record length of the mass storage subsystem. Alternatively, it can divide the program along module or subroutine boundaries. Unfortunately, these decisions may yield a program that is executed in an inefficient manner. For this type of system, some hardware support is required. When the program reaches the end of an overlay, it generates a memory fault, which results in the load of a new overlay. Alternatively, the OS replaces each jump to an address outside the overlay by a call to the overlay loader with the address as argument. This approach requires significant intelligence and complexity on the part of the OS, compilers, and linkage editor to bind the program properly into executable form.

Semiautomatic.   The user determines how the program is to be partitioned (perhaps through the use of an overlay specification language), and the OS determines how to load the overlays when required. A good example of this method is that of the Univac 1100 Series Operating Systems. This method tends to be more efficient because the user has some a priori knowledge about the execution path of a program. For example, if control alternates between two overlays in the same group (initially), the programmer may want to split them between two overlay groups to reduce the overlay loading time. Some form of hardware support may still be required to assist the transition between overlays.

Nonautomatic.   The programmer not only chooses how to partition the program into overlays but also must explicitly request an overlay to be loaded. Under this approach, no hardware support is required (although it is optional) and the programming of the overlay manager is much simpler. Conversely, more effort is required from the programmer to structure the program in an efficient manner.

An overlay system may also allocate memory for an overlay area in a dynamic or static manner. In the static approach, each overlay group is assigned to a memory region. Only one member of the overlay group can be resident in memory at any time. An overlay from an overlay group can be loaded only into its preassigned overlay area. The dynamic approach treats memory assigned to the overlay area as a global pool. A request to load an overlay results in a dynamic allocation of a portion of the pool as an overlay area. This allows two overlays from the same group to be loaded at once (although most minicomputer systems prohibit it). When an overlay is exited, the overlay area is released to the global pool.

4.4.2   Concepts of Overlay Management

When a program is partitioned using overlays, the user can represent the program as a tree (see figure 4.4a). The main or root segment is depicted as level zero of the tree. Each overlay that may be called from the root segment is placed at level one of the tree. In most systems, each overlay may invoke further overlays. For example, we could have the following sequence:

EXECUTE MAIN

LOAD A1

LOAD B2

EXECUTE A1

LOAD E2

which results in overlay A1 calling for the loading of overlay E2. Data General's RDOS places a restriction on this approach by requiring that each overlay be loaded from a main program. Thus an error results if an overlay attempts to load another overlay.

In general, an overlay system will prevent an overlay from invoking another overlay at the same level. For example, overlay A3 cannot request execution of overlay C1. Since most systems save return addresses in memory, the overlay may not be able to return properly, resulting in a loss of control. Suppose that A3 could load and call C1. When C1 is executed, it in turn loads and calls A2. A2 is executed and returns to C1, but when C1 returns, A2 occupies overlay area A. C1 may return into the middle of A2 and begin executing haphazardly, thus doing grievous damage to the program's data structures.

Some systems do relax these restrictions somewhat by allowing an overlay to call an overlay at the same level but not able to request its loading. Thus we might have the sequence

EXECUTE MAIN

LOAD A1

LOAD A2

EXECUTE A1

VERIFY C2

EXECUTE C2

where the overlay must verify that the appropriate overlay has been loaded into the overlay area. Note that prior to executing A1, the main program has loaded both A1 and C2.

The discussion above assumed the static method of allocating overlay areas. Under the dynamic approach, each overlay load request would result in the creation of a new overlay area. This approach may lead to a deadlock situation if the depth of the tree is rather extensive. Suppose that the overlay groups have

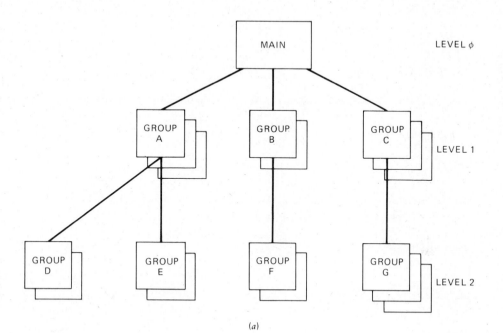

(a)

LO: MAIN

    L1: OVERLAYS A1,A2,A3

        L2: OVERLAYS D1,D2

        L2: OVERLAYS E1,E2

    L1: OVERLAYS B1,B2

        L2: OVERLAYS F1,F2,F3,F4

    L1: OVERLAYS C1,C2,C3

        L2: OVERLAYS G1,G2,G3

END

(b)

Figure 4.4   Representation of an overlayed program.

the following memory requirements: *A*, 2K; *B*, 4K; *C*, 2K; *D*, 2K; *E*, 8K; *F*, 4K; *G*, 6K. If the global pool size is 24K, the following sequence of overlay loads would exhaust the pool:

LOAD B2

LOAD G3

LOAD E1   24K words used

LOAD A1

LOAD F2

Any further request to load an overlay would result in a deadlock situation if the requestor could not proceed in execution.

Virtual Overlays

Data General's RDOS addresses the dynamic overlay problem in a rather unique way. Each system overlay is exactly 256 words in length (equal to one disk sector). System buffers used to store disk block contents temporarily are also 256 words in length. When a system overlay is requested, RDOS allocates a buffer and reads the overlay into it. Each overlay references only data that are local to the overlay or stored in system common tables (e.g., it is reentrant). Moreover, each overlay calls only procedures that are referenced through a system switch table which is permanently resident in memory. A system stack is used to track the procedure calls.

An overlay is virtual in the sense that the buffer can be reallocated once control has left a particular overlay. RDOS allows one overlay to request the loading of another and then to transfer control to it. Should the calling overlay be overwritten in the meantime, RDOS looks up its address on the system stack to reload it. The nesting depth to which system overlays may be invoked is limited only by the number of system buffers.

4.4.3   Structure of the Overlay Manager

In a multiprocessing environment, each overlay area represents a scarce resource. An overlay group, having multiple overlays, can place only one overlay in memory at a time. Access to the overlay area must be mediated among multiple users to prevent one user from writing over another user's overlay. A resource manager controls access to the overlay areas.

For each program which has specified overlays, an overlay file is created by the linkage editor. The overlay table, written as a preamble to this file, contains a description of each overlay group. The overlay table is loaded into memory by the OS when the user program opens the overlay file.

Resource Semaphores

The overlay manager utilizes two resource semaphores to control access to overlays. They are OVERLAY-RS and OVERLAY-LOAD-RS. OVERLAY-RS protects those overlays that have been loaded into memory and are currently in use. OVERLAY-LOAD-RS manages the set of processes waiting for an overlay to be loaded into memory.

Overlay Table/Overlay Control Block

Each user program that has defined overlays has an overlay table associated with it. The overlay table describes the overlay structure of the program. The structure of this table is described in table 4.2. The entries OVERLAY-FILE-ADDRESS through OVERLAY-USE-COUNT of this table are repeated for each overlay group defined in the program and are known as an overlay control block (OCB). Thus the size of the overlay table is calculated as

    NUMBER-OF-OVERLAY-GROUPS * OCB-SIZE + 1 →
    OVERLAY-TABLE-SIZE

where one word at the beginning of the table is used to specify the number of overlay groups. Figure 4.5 shows the relationship of an OCB to the rest of the overlay file.

The OCB contains descriptive information about each overlay group. In an overlay group, there may be up to 256 overlays (an arbitrary limitation). The current overlay of the group has its identifier stored in the right byte of the overlay status word, as shown below.

Each overlay is configured as a multiple number of disk blocks. All overlays within a group have the same size, which is given by the OVERLAY-SIZE. Within any individual overlay, there may be wasted space because the code or data do not fill the overlay. However, this fact must be balanced against the simplicity and flexibility provided by the overlay management technique.

The overlays within an overlay group are stored sequentially and the overlay groups are themselves stored sequentially in the overlay file. The file address of any overlay group, which is maintained in the OCB, is computed as

    OVERLAY-TABLE-SIZE + SUM(OVERLAY-COUNT *
    OVERLAY-SIZE)

Table 4.2   Description of Overlay Table

Mnemonic	Usage
overlay-group-count	The number of overlay groups
overlay-file-address	The address in the overlay file for the first overlay of the group
overlay-memory-address	The memory address where the overlay will be loaded (user space)
overlay-size	The overlay group size
overlay-count	The number of overlays in the group
overlay-parent	The identifier for an overlay that requested the loading of the current overlay
overlay-status	Status information for the overlay group
overlay-use-count	A count of the number of processes concurrently accessing this overlay

for the number of overlay groups. Each OCB also contains the associated logical memory address generated by the linkage editor, where the overlay will be loaded.

When an overlay is requested by a process, its overlay use count is incremented by one. In a multiprocessing system, an overlay cannot be released until its overlay use count goes to zero.

Note that overlays may call other overlays into memory. Normally, the first overlay, loaded by the resident user program, is called the overlay parent. When a child overlay is released, the overlay parent is automatically reloaded into memory.

Two flags are used to mark the status of an overlay group. The LOAD-IN-PROGRESS-FLAG signifies that an overlay has been requested for this area and is currently being loaded by the system. The EXCLUSIVE-USE-FLAG is used to indicate that this overlay is serially reusable.

4.4.4   Overlay Management Functions

The overlay manager supports four functions that allow users to load and release overlays. Each function requires the user to submit an overlay identifier as depicted below. An overlay identifier consists of a group number, corresponding to an overlay area in memory, and an index of an overlay within the group. This section describes the overlay management functions.

Loading an Overlay: Preprocessing

When a process requests the loading of an overlay, it is not known when the process will be reactivated. The reasons for this uncertainty are that loading an

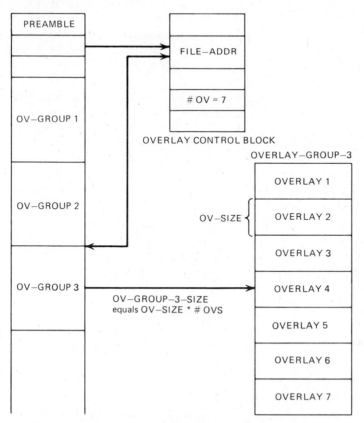

Figure 4.5   Overlay file structure.

STRUCTURE OF OVERLAY STATUS WORD

15	14		7–0

Bit Number	Usage
15	Exclusive use flag
14	Load in progress flag
7–0	Current overlay identifier

STRUCTURE OF THE OVERLAY IDENTIFIER

group-identifier	overlay-number

overlay is a time-consuming process involving a disk read operation, and that the overlay area may be occupied by a different overlay than the one requested. To avoid monopolization of the CPU, the loading of an overlay is performed by a system subprocess and the user process is suspended until the overlay has been made resident in memory.

The procedure for initializing the subprocess is depicted in module 4.4.1. Note that the PCB has been allocated by the system service request processor. This procedure sets the parameters for the overlay loading routine and exits.

MODULE 4.4.1

```
procedure p-load-overlay
    overlay-identifier[usp] → request-overlay-identifier[n]
    mode[usp] → request-overlay-mode[n]
    calling-map( ) → request-map[n]
    request-map[n] → overlay-map
    set-overlay-control-block(request-overlay-identifier[n])
                                        → request-overlay-index[n]
    p-setup-done( )
endproc
```

Loading an Overlay

LOAD-OVERLAY, depicted in module 4.4.2, performs the loading of an overlay. It is invoked by the system service request LOAD-OVERLAY, which takes the following form:

SYSTEM(LOAD-OVERLAY, EVENT-NR, OVERLAY-IDENTIFIER, MODE)

where   EVENT-NR   is used to signal the user when the overlay is available

OVERLAY-IDENTIFIER   is the identifier of the overlay to be loaded

MODE   is the mode in which the overlay is to be loaded

This command reserves a free overlay area and loads the requested overlay if it is not already in memory. If the overlay is in memory, the overlay use count is incremented (subject to the following considerations): (1) the overlay has been marked for exclusive use, and (2) the overlay must be reloaded because the FORCE-NEW-LOAD flag is set.

The FORCE-NEW-LOAD flag marks the overlay as a serially reusable resource because the overlay is not reentrant. Thus a new copy must be loaded each time the overlay is referenced.

MODULE 4.4.2

```
procedure load-overlay
    request(overlay-rs) → overlay-temp
    if overlay-temp less than one
        then
                overlay-temp → event-status[p]
                end-subprocess( )
    endif
    if overlay-temp equal to one
        then
                request(overlay-load-rs)
                end-subprocess( )
    endif
    request-map[p] → overlay-map
    request-overlay-identifier[p] → overlay-identifier
    set-overlay-control-block(overlay-identifier) → overlay
    get-overlay-channel(overlay-map) → ccb-address
    overlay * overlay-size[ocb-address] +
        overlay-file-address[ocb-address] +
                file-start[fcb-address] → read-address
    request-overlay-index[p] → ocb-address
    overlay-memory-address[ocb-address] → memory
    overlay-size[ocb-address] → size
    read-random(group, memory, size, read-address) → result
    if result less than zero
        then
                er-overlay-load → overlay-error-code
        else
                set one to overlay-error-code
    endif
    overlay-error-code → event-status[p]
    release(overlay-load-rs, ocb-address)
    if overlay-error-code less than zero
        then
                release(overlay-rs, overlay-identifier)
    endif
    end-subprocess( )
endproc
```

If the area is in use a request is created and associated with the OCB so that the overlay will be loaded when the area becomes free. By associating an event number with the request, a user process can load more than one overlay before executing any of them. It is the responsibility of the user to ensure that the process does not attempt two loads from the same overlay group. In such a situation, deadlock results, as both overlays will be awaited endlessly.

Initially, the procedure requests to the overlay area (see OVERLAY-ALLO-CATOR). When the overlay area is free, the procedure resumes execution. If OVERLAY-TEMP is less than one, the overlay is already resident in memory and the user process is activated immediately. If OVERLAY-TEMP equals one, the overlay area is in use, so a request is made to load the overlay when the area becomes available.

When the overlay area becomes free, the procedure calculates the address of the overlay in the overlay file. The overlay is loaded directly into memory from the mass storage device. Note that no system buffers are needed since the overlay size is a multiple of the disk sector size. Upon completion of the read request, the result is checked for errors, which will be reported to the user. All users awaiting the loading of this overlay are activated. If an error was detected during loading, the overlay area is marked free.

Releasing an Overlay

When a user process is finished with an overlay, it must release it. This is accomplished by the following system service request:

SYSTEM(RELEASE-OVERLAY, OVERLAY-IDENTIFIER)

where   OVERLAY-IDENTIFIER   is the identifier of the overlay, to be
                                       released

This function releases the specified overlay area. The use count for the overlay group is decremented by one. If the use count is zero, the area is available for allocation to the first pending request. The user process should not attempt to release an overlay from within the overlay itself. Once the overlay area is released, it may be overwritten before a return can be effected to the user procedure. In this case, the system could jump into the middle of a user's overlay, with disastrous consequences.

The procedure for executing this request is depicted in module 4.4.3. It simply marks the overlay area as released (see ENTER-INTO-OVERLAY-AVAIL-QUEUE).

Exiting an Overlay

This function is a special case of releasing an overlay. When the user process exits an overlay, it can return to a specified address in the user program. This function may be called from an overlay since the address at which execution is to continue is specified. The routine does not return to the caller. As the routine does not return, an invalid overlay identifier or address will result in the termination of the process with a system error message.

The format of this command is

SYSTEM(EXIT-OVERLAY, OVERLAY-IDENTIFIER, ADDRESS)

where   OVERLAY-IDENTIFIER   is the identifier of the overlay to be exited

                 ADDRESS   is the address where execution proceeds after the function is completed

The procedure to execute this request is depicted in module 4.4.4. The overlay area is released and control returns to the address specified by the user. An illegal overlay identifier is detected by the resource monitor (see ENTER-INTO-OVERLAY-AVAIL-QUEUE). An illegal address is detected by the MMU.

MODULE 4.4.3

```
procedure release-overlay
    overlay-identifier[usp] → overlay-identifier
    release(overlay-rs, overlay-identifier)
    os-exit( )
endproc
```

MODULE 4.4.4

```
procedure exit-overlay
    overlay-identifier[usp] → overlay-identifier
    release(overlay-rs, overlay-identifier)
    address(usp) → return-address[usp]
    os-exit( )
endproc
```

Retrieving the Next Overlay

Given a priori knowledge about a particular program, a user can structure the overlays in a sequential order. The NEXT-OVERLAY request allows the user to exit the current overlay and retrieve the next overlay in the group. The format of the command to accomplish this function is:

SYSTEM(NEXT-OVERLAY, CURRENT-OVERLAY-IDENTIFIER, NEXT-OVERLAY-IDENTIFIER, MODE)

where   CURRENT-OVERLAY-IDENTIFIER   is the identifier of the
                                                       current overlay

               NEXT-OVERLAY-IDENTIFIER   is the identifier of the
                                                       next overlay to be
                                                       loaded

               MODE   is the mode for loading
                                                       the next overlay

The procedure to execute this function is depicted in module 4.4.5. It releases
the current overlay. It then sets up a request for a LOAD-OVERLAY command. Note that we cannot simply execute a LOAD-OVERLAY command because this routine executes in system space. In this case, REQUEST-MAP
would be overwritten and an attempt would be made to fetch the overlay from
the system overlay file.

MODULE 4.4.5

```
procedure next-overlay
     release(overlay-rs, overlay-identifier[usp])
     p → parent[p]
     set 16 to event-nr[p]
     next-overlay-identifier[usp] → request-overlay-identifier[p]
     mode[usp] → request-overlay-mode[p]
     calling-map( ) → overlay-map
     overlay-map → request-map[p]
     set-overlay-control-block(request-overlay-identifier[p]) → overlay
     overlay → request-overlay-index[p]
     if overlay less than zero
          then
                  system(error-kill, er-overlay-identifier)
     endif
     address(next-overlay-done) → return-address[usp]
     clear map[usp]
     load-overlay( )
next-overlay-done:
     system(status,16) → event-status
     if event-status less than zero
          then
                  system(error-kill, overlay-identifier)
     endif
     os-exit( )
endproc
```

Since the routine does not return to the user, detection of an illegal overlay identifier results in termination of the user process and an error message on the

operator's console. Otherwise, LOAD-OVERLAY is called to bring the overlay into memory. The return address is OS space is set to the routine NEXT-OVERLAY-DONE. This routine determines if the overlay load was successful. If so, return is made to the user process. Otherwise, the user process is terminated.

4.4.5 Overlay Allocation and Release Mechanisms

The allocation and release of overlay areas is controlled by the resource monitor routines. An overlay is allocated as the result of a request against OVERLAY-RS. The overlay area is made available by executing a RELEASE against this same semaphore. This section describes the procedure for allocating and releasing overlay areas.

Allocating an Overlay

The procedure for allocating an overlay area is depicted in module 4.4.6. At eacah pass through the allocation routine, all available areas are allocated at once. If no area is available, the procedure merely exits. The procedure checks to see if any user processes are waiting for an overlay area. If no processes are waiting, the procedure exits.

The allocation routine makes a pass over the wait queue, RS-WAIT-QUEUE, and checks the status of each overlay request. For overlay requests where the overlay is free or the overlay is resident in memory, the process is removed from the queue and activated.

MODULE 4.4.6

```
procedure overlay-allocator(rs-address)
    rs-avail-queue[rs-address] → avq
    queue-count[avq] → qc
    clear queue-count[avq]
    if qc less than zero
        then
                exitproc
    endif
    rs-wait-queue[rs-address] → rwq
    queue-count[rwq] → overlay-wait-count
    if overlay-wait-count is equal to zero
        then
                exitproc
    endif
```

```
        if qc is equal to zero
            then
                    queue-end[rwq] → ov-process
            else
                    queue-start[rwq] → next-process
                    decrement overlay-wait-count
                    while overlay-wait-count greater than or equal to zero
                        do
                                next-process → ov-process
                                next-cb[ov-process] → next-process
                                overlay-status-check(ov-process)
                                decrement overlay-wait-count
                        enddo
        endif
endproc
```

Checking the Overlay Status

The status of the overlay area is maintained in the OCB. Whenever a request to load an overlay is made, the overlay area status must be verified. The procedure to perform the check is depicted in module 4.4.7.

OVERLAY-STATUS-CHECK validates the overlay requested by the user and set up a pointer to an OCB. An invalid overlay causes an error code to be

MODULE 4.4.7

```
procedure overlay-status-check(ov-process)
    request-map[ov-process] → overlay-map
    request-overlay-identifier[ov-process] → overlay-identifier
    set-overlay-control-block(overlay-identifier)
                                            → return-value[ov-process]
    if return-value[ov-process] less than one
        then
                extract-from-queue(rwq, ov-process)
                activate(ov-process)
                exitproc
    endif
    if overlay-use-count[ocb-address] not equal to zero
        then
                if overlay-status[ocb-address] less than zero
                    then
                            exitproc
                endif
```

```
                    if exclusive-use-flag of request-overlay-mode[ov-process]
                        then
                                exitproc
                    endif
                    if force-load-flag of request-overlay-mode[ov-process] not
                        equal to zero
                        then
                                exitproc
                    endif
                    extract overlay-number from overlay-status[ocb-address]
                    if overlay not equal to overlay-number
                        then
                                exitproc
                    endif
                    increment overlay-use-count[ocb-address]
                    if load-in-progress-flag of overlay-status[ocb-address]
                        then
                                clear return-value[ov-process]
                        else
                                set one to return-value[temp]
                    endif
            endif
            set-overlay-control-block(overlay-parent[ocb-address])
                                                                → overlay-temp
            if overlay-temp greater than zero
                then
                        extract nbr-overlay-users from overlay-status[ocb-address]
                            if nbr-overlay-users equals zero
                                then
                                        set er-overlay-id to return-value[ov-process]
                                        extract-from-queue(rwq, ov-process)
                                        activate(ov-process)
                                        exitproc
                            endif
                        increment overlay-use-count[ocb-address]
            endif
            set-overlay-control-block(request-overlay-identifier[ov-process])
            increment overlay-use-count[ocb-address]
            if overlay equals overlay-status[ocb-address]
                then
                        if exclusive-use-flag of request-overlay-mode[ov-process]
                            equals 1
                                then
                                        set exclusive-use-flag of
                                                        overlay-status[ocb-address]
```

```
                    endif
                    if force-load-flag of request-overlay-mode[ov-process]
                       equals zero
                          then
                                clear return-value[ov-process]
                                extract-from-queue(rwq, ov-process)
                                activate(ov-process)
                                exitproc
                    endif
              endif
              set load-in-progress-flag of overlay-status[ocb-address]
              set overlay to overlay-number of overlay-status[ocb-address]
              set ocb-address to return-value[ov-process]
              extract-from-queue(rwq, ov-process)
              activate(ptemp)
        endproc
```

returned to the user and the user process is extracted from the queue and reactivated.

Next, the status of the overlay area is checked. Further checks are made only if the overlay area is in use, that is, if OVERLAY-USE-COUNT is greater than zero. Otherwise, the area is available for the next overlay to be loaded. The following checks are required:

1.   The overlay area has been marked for exclusive use (the EXCLUSIVE-USE-FLAG of OVERLAY-STATUS is set). Allocation is not possible, so we exit.

2.   The user may have requested exclusive use of the overlay. If the area is in use, the system cannot comply with the request.

3.   The user has requested a new copy of the overlay. This request cannot be satisfied even if the appropriate everlay is present when the overlay area is in use.

4.   If the overlay requested is not the current occupant of the overlay area, the request is rejected. If it is, the overlay use count is incremented by one.

5.   Finally, if an overlay is currently being loaded into the overlay area (LOAD-IN-PROGRESS-FLAG > 0), we cannot satisfy the request.

If these tests are passed successfully, the system establishes whether or not the overlay was requested by another overlay (e.g., the overlay parent). If the parent overlay is in use by more than one process (usage count greater than zero), the system cannot satisfy the request since to do so would remove the parent from the overlay area.

Finally, the system establishes the OCB for the requested overlay. The OVERLAY-USE-COUNT for that overlay area is incremented. If exclusive use is requested, the EXLCUSIVE-USE-FLAG is set. If the FORCE-NEW-LOAD-FLAG is set, the system exits to force loading of a new copy of the overlay. Otherwise, the information concerning the current overlay is set in the OCB and the waiting process is activated.

Allocation after Overlay Load

Loading an overlay into memory may take some time, as the size of overlays is variable. An overlay area may be allocated while an overlay load is in progress. However, the system cannot reactivate a process until the read operation has completed. In this case, processes are queued on OVERLAY-LOAD-RS until the load operation has been completed successfully. At that point, all processes waiting for the load operation to complete are activated. Because several overlay areas may be experiencing a "load in progress" concurrently, overlay loading is handled by a resource monitor. The procedure is depicted in module 4.4.8. Referring back to module 4.4.2, we see that once the overlay is loaded, a RELEASE is executed against OVERLAY-LOAD-RS. This results in the execution of OVERLAY-LOADED-ALLOCATOR.

Releasing an Overlay Area

An overlay area is released by executing the RELEASE function upon OVER-LAY-RS. Note that executing this function does not make the overlay area available immediately. In a multiprocessing environment, it usually results in the OVERLAY-USE-COUNT for the overlay area being decremented by one. This is because only one process has freed the overlay while others may still be using it.

The procedure for marking an overlay free is depicted in module 4.4.9. The overlay to be freed is validated and its overlay table address initialized in OCB-ADDRESS by SET-OVERLAY-CONTROL-BLOCK. An invalid overlay results in termination of the procedure. If a user attempts to release an overlay that is not currently loaded, the request is also refused. Finally, if the usage count is zero, the user has tried to release an area that is not in use.

4.4.6 Overlay Management Utilities

Three utilities support the management of overlays. They are presented assuming one system program and one user program. The reader is free to generalize them to multiple user programs at leisure.

MODULE 4.4.8

```
procedure overlay-loaded-allocator(rs-address)
    rs-avail-queue[rs-address] → avq
    queue-count[avq] → ocb-address
    clear queue-count[avq]
    if ocb-address equals zero
        then
            exitproc
    endif
    rs-wait-queue[rs-address] → rwq
    queue-count[rwq] → overlay-wait-count
    queue-start[rwq] → next-process
    while overlay-wait-count greater than or equal to zero
        do
            decrement overlay-wait-count
            next-process → ov-process
            next-cb[ov-process] → next-process
            if ocb-address equals request-overlay-index[ov-process]
                then
                    overlay-error-code → event-status[ov-process]
                    extract-from-queue(rwq, ov-process)
                    activate(ov-process)
            endif
        enddo
    if overlay-error-code greater than or equal to zero
        then
            clear load-in-progress-flag of overlay-status[ocb-address]
        else
            lbyte(overlay-status[ocb-address], − 1)
            clear overlay-use-count[ocb-address]
    endif
endproc
```

Acquiring an Overlay Channel

In this procedure, depicted in module 4.4.10, the overlay channels are maintained in system parameters. As both the OS and the user program have overlay files, separate overlay channels are required. The appropriate channel to use is determined by the program space in which the process executes. If the request is made from map 0, the process is assumed to be part of the OS. Otherwise, a request from any other map is assumed to be a user program. The procedure validates the channel number and verifies that the channel is open and not locked. It sets up both CCB and FCB addresses.

MODULE 4.4.9

```
procedure enter-into-overlay-avail-queue(q, overlay-identifier)
    calling-map( ) → overlay-map
    set-overlay-control-block(overlay-identifier) → overlay-temp
    if overlay-temp less than one
        then
                set − 1 to queue-count[q]
                exitproc
    endif
    if rbyte(overlay-status[ocb-address]) not equal to overlay
        then
                set − 1 to queue-count[q]
                exitproc
    endif
    if overlay-use-count[ocb-address] equals zero
        then
                set − 1 to queue-count[q]
                exitproc
    endif
    decrement overlay-use-count [ocb-address]
    increment queue-count[q]
    rbyte(overlay-status[ocb-address]) → overlay-status[ocb-address]
endproc
```

MODULE 4.4.10

```
procedure get-overlay-channel(overlay-map, →ccb-address)
    if overlay-map not equal to zero
        then
                set user-overlay-channel to ccb-address
        else
                set system-overlay-channel to ccb-address
    endif
    calculate-channel-address(ccb-address) → ccb-address
    if ccb-address less than zero
        then
                set er-overlay-identifier to event-status[p]
                end-subprocess( )
    endif
    if channel-open-flag of channel-attributes[ccb-address]
        then
                set er-overlay-identifier to event-status[p]
                end-subprocess( )
        else
```

```
                if channel-lock-flag of channel-attributes[ccb-address]
                    then
                            set er-overlay-identifier to event-status[p]
                            end-subprocess( )
                endif
        endif
        channel-address[ccb-address] → fcb-address
endproc
```

Retrieving the Overlay Control Block

The procedure SET-OVERLAY-CONTROL-BLOCK is essential to overlay management and, in fact, is the workhorse of all the modules. It is depicted in module 4.4.11. Its purpose is to determine the address of the OCB after validating the overlay.

MODULE 4.4.11

```
procedure set-overlay-control-block(overlay-identifier, →overlay)
        extract group from overlay-identifier
        if group less than one
            then
                    clear overlay
        endif
        if overlay-map is less than zero
            then
                    set system-overlay-table to ocb-address
            else
                    set user-overlay-table to ocb-address
        endif
        if group − 1 greater than overlay-group-count[ocb-address]
            then
                    set er-overlay-identifier to overlay
        endif
        increment ocb-address by group * ocb-size
        extract overlay from overlay-identifier
        if overlay is greater than or equal to overlay-count[ocb-address]
            then
                    set er-overlay-identifier to overlay
            else
                    ocb-address → overlay
        endif
endproc
```

Each overlay identifier is composed of a group identifier and an overlay identifier. The group is validated against the number of overlay groups in the
overlay table. Note that overlay group identifiers begin with 1 in the overlay
identifier, whereas in the table the first group identifier is zero. If the group
identifier exceeds the number of groups defined in the table, an error is
reported to the caller.

Given a valid group identifier, the address of the appropriate OCB is computed by multiplying the group identifier by the OCB-SIZE and adding it to the
base address of the overlay table. The overlay identifier is validated by comparing it to the overlay count for the specific group. If valid, the OCB address is
returned to the caller.

Opening the Overlay File

Before a program can load overlays, it must explicitly open the overlay file. This
function is executed by OVERLAY-OPEN, as depicted in module 4.4.12. It is
requested by the user through the system service request:

SYSTEM(OPEN-OVERLAY, EVENT-NR, OVERLAY-CHANNEL,
OVERLAY-FILE-NAME)

where	EVENT-NR	is used to signal the caller when the overlay file has been opened
	OVERLAY-CHANNEL	is the identifier of the user channel to be assigned to the overlay file
	OVERLAY-FILE-NAME	is the name of the overlay file

The procedure uses the OPEN request to access the file. The system cannot
allow the user to open the file directly since the overlay tabel must be properly
loaded into memory. Any error on opening the file results in a rejected request.
After a successful OPEN, the procedure reads the first word of the file containing the overlay group count. An invalid group count results in a rejection of the
request.

MODULE 4.4.12

```
procedure overlay-open(overlay-channel, overlay-file-name,
                                            → overlay-table-address)
     system(open, 16, overlay-channel, overlay-file-name,
                                            read-overlay-mode)
     if open-result less than zero
          then
               clear overlay-table-address
               exitproc
     endif
```

```
        system(read-sequential, 16, overlay-channel, group-count, 1)
                                              → read-result
    if read-result less than zero
        then
                system(close, 16, overlay-channel)
                clear overlay-table-address
                exitproc
    endif
    if group-count less than one or
        group-count greater than or equal to
                                     MAX-NUMBER-OF-OVERLAYS
        then
                system(close, 16, overlay-channel)
                clear overlay-table-address
                exitproc
    endif
    group-count → group-temp
    request(memory-rs, group-temp * ocb-size) → overlay-table-address
    group-count → memory(overlay-table-address)
    increment overlay-table-address
    memory(overlay-table-address) → overlay-table
    while group-count greater than or equal to zero
        do
                system(read-sequential, 16, overlay-channel,
                                overlay-table, ocb-size) → read-result
                if read-result less than zero
                    then
                        release(memory-rs, overlay-table-address)
                        system(close, 16, overlay-channel)
                        clear overlay-table-address
                        exitproc
                endif
                clear overlay-status[overlay-table]
                increment overlay-table by ocb-size
                decrement group-count
        enddo
endproc
```

The procedure requests a dynamic allocation of memory in which to store the overlay table. The group count is installed as the first word of the table and the overlay table is read into memory one block at a time. This approach is taken to ensure the consistency of the overlay file. Although not explicitly presented here, the integrity of the overlay table could be validated by performing a checksum on each control block and comparing them with values stored in the file. Each block must be loaded and its checksum computed independently to allow for the replacement of overlays within the file.

4.5   PAGE MANAGEMENT TECHNIQUES

In the preceding two sections, we examined two methods for performing memory allocation of a program's logical address space. Under swapping/ chaining, the logical address space of each program was exactly equivalent to its physical address space. Addresses were statically bound during compilation. The program had to be loaded as a single contiguous unit that, despite the usage of base registers, could still lead to memory fragmentation problems. Extension of the logical address space was nonexistent (or nebulous if one insisted upon some traceable relationship between two programs). Overlays provided the user with more flexibility by deferring memory allocation decisions until binding time. The overlay concept allowed the user, figuratively, to extend the logical address space, although literally, at any instant, the logical address space was still equivalent to the physical address space. The program still had to be loaded as a contiguous unit but fixed-length segments could now dynamically be replaced at the user's option. In addition, severe constraints still existed upon who could call or load whom, and the user was generally responsible for the housekeeping. Furthermore, the memory fragmentation problems remained.

The key problem with swapping/chaining and overlays, even with the assistance of base registers, was the fact that it was difficult to utilize main memory efficiently because holes developed between programs. If main memory could be partitioned into fixed-size blocks, suitably small, then the memory fragmentation problem could be uniformly localized. Such a program would also be subdivided into small chunks, known as pages, which could be assigned to corresponding memory blocks. At most, then, the wasted space in memory, when a program was loaded, would be a fraction of one page. Thus memory could be utilized more effectively.

It so happens that the hardware support for page management produces a profusion of other benefits as well as some significant problems. A few of these are:

Dynamic relocation of programs anywhere in memory
Extended protection and sharing mechanisms
Agony over selection of fetch, placement, and replacement algorithms

In this section we explore both the benefits and the problems associated with page management techniques.

4.5.1   Basic Concepts of Paging

In paging, main memory is divided into equal fixed-size blocks usually known as page frames. Each user program is divided into matching size blocks known as pages. One page can reside in a page frame. Pages exist in logical address space, whereas page frames exist in physical address space. As identifiers for pages and page frames are assigned separately, three interesting situations arise as to the relationship between logical address space (LAS) and physical address space (PAS):

1. **LAS < PAS.**   A case that makes use of paging primarily for its increased efficiency in memory utilization. Watson [wats70] discusses an application of this approach for the XDS-940.
2. **LAS = PAS.**   A case that uses paging not only for increased efficiency in memory utilization but also for increased sharing of procedures. An efficient overlay mechanism can be supported via its hardware.
3. **LAS > PAS.**   The case that implements virtual memory and provides the greatest benefits.

In this text we consider paging from the perspective of the last case. The decision to implement case 1 or 2 is usually contingent upon the structure of the MMU and the whims of the OS designer. For example, in designing a system to support a BASIC or APL interpreter, the system designer might choose the approach dictated by case 2 in order to place a bound on the workspace available to each user. Such a user, given an LAS of m pages, would have k pages dedicated to the interpreter and $m - k$ pages for the workspace. This approach would be quite efficient in a time-sharing system.

Identifier Assignment

Pages and page frames are referenced by numerical identifiers that are assigned as follows:

Let p be the size of a page in words (ex: 512).
Let m be the size of main memory in words such that

$$m = n \times p$$
m mod 1024 yields 0
p mod 2K yields 0 and $i \times p = j \times 1024$

That is, main memory is composed of multiples of 1K words. Additionally, each page has a size that is a power of 2, and an even number of pages comprises 1K of memory. The set of integers 0, 1, 2, ..., $n - 1$ comprise the identifiers for the page frames.

Let M be the size of a user's program in words. Then $M = N \times p$, where N is the number of pages required to contain the user's program. The set of integers from zero to $n - 1$ comprise the identifiers for the user's pages. Note that m mod p yields zero is not a requirement. That is, a user's program does not have to fill exactly all the pages required to contain it. The last page may be only partially filled.

As most commercially available minicomputer systems use binary arithmetic, the constraints on page size being a power of 2 are minimal. In fact, most machines possess shift instructions which make the generation of virtual addresses a trivial computation. The constraint on M being a multiple of 1K words is a result of the standardization of memory modules. Recent literature suggests that a size of 8K, 16K, or even 64K might be a more suitable number.

Virtual Address Construction

A virtual address is an address in the logical address space of a user process (usually, where LAS > PAS). All references to logical addresses must be converted to a physical address in main memory. To do so, the system requires the page frame identifier and an offset within the page frame. Thus the system must map from the virtual address to the physical address. Each virtual address is a pair (p, i), where p is the page number in the user process and i is an index into the page (such that $i < w$, where w is the page size).

Consider a machine having a 16-bit word which allows the user to address 64K words. If each page size is 512 words, the logical address space is composed of 128 pages. The page identifier p requires 7 bits and the index requires 9 bits. So the 16-bit word would appear as

page-identifier	word-index

Note that the LAS < PAS case is possible if the MMU supports a word size greater than 18 bits. On the PDP-11/70, each user was restricted to a 64K-byte LAS, whereas the MMU supported up to 128K words. In the DEC VAX-11/780, each user's address space is 2^{32} bytes, and the physical main memory is a maximum of 16 million bytes. The VAX-11/780 uses a 32-bit word having the following construction:

31	30	virtual page id	byte in page

where   bits 31 and 30 are special purpose to VAX/VMS

bits 29–9 select one of 2^{20} pages

bits 7–0 select one of 512 bytes in a page

On a machine with a 16-bit word size, a large virtual address space can be constructed (perhaps artificially) by using two words to represent every memory address. Under such a scheme, the virtual address could appear as follows:

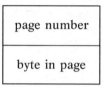

where special precautions would be required to present the virtual address to the OS and the MMU.

Role of the Page Table

One of the benefits of page management is the dynamic relocation of user pages anywhere within memory. Thus page P of the user process may currently reside in page frame p of physical memory. Since multiple users will have their own set of pages, each user program requires a map that shows the relationship between each of its pages and a page frame. In figure 4.6 the virtual address (p, i) is converted to a physical address by looking up the page frame identifier x in the page table. The real address, presented to the memory control unit, is computed by multiplying x by the page size and adding the index i.

It is important to realize that these operations are carried out by the MMU in a fashion that is transparent to the user program. To do so, a copy of a process's page table must be loaded into the MMU. For example, suppose that the MMU has space for 16 memory maps, where each memory map has slots for 64 pages of 512 words each. Map 0 is always dedicated to the OS nucleus. This approach is not feasible for large virtual memory systems, as the cost of the MMU would be exorbitant. Rather, the memory map is retained in memory, and the MMU maintains a pointer to the current user's map. Figure 4.7 depicts the structures for implementing this scheme.

In this scheme the MMU maintains a list of page table addresses for up to n users. A hardware register indicates the current user whose page table is active. The entry in the user map table (in the MMU) is loaded into the hardware page table base register. Each memory address is devolved into its page-identifier and index. The page-identifier is combined with the contents of the page table base register to point to a page table entry. The contents of this entry is the ad-

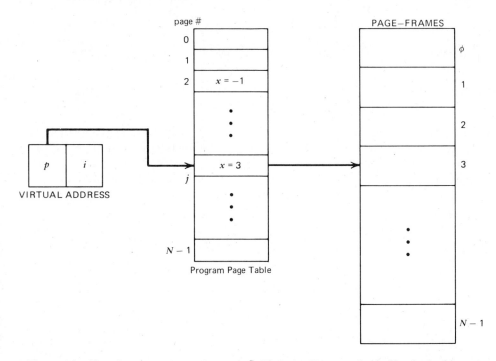

Figure 4.6   Mapping a page to main memory. Virtual address = (*p*, *i*). Physical address — *x* = page-size + *i*. A negative page frame identifier indicates the page is not currently resident in memory.

dress of a page frame in memory. By adding the index to the page frame address we obtain the physical address.

Note that under the general scheme, each page table reference requires an additional memory access to retrieve the page frame address. In the former case, all computations were carried out in the MMU hardware registers. Thus, implementing a large virtual memory may impose additional timing considerations on system overhead and program execution times. The systems designer should be aware of these factors when selecting a philosophy for memory management design.

Additional references that may be consulted include [bobr72], [chu76], [gold74a], [gord73], and [shaw74].

Page Control Bits

Associated with each entry in the page table is a set of control bits. These bits are used to effect the policies for page management. The number and type of bits varies with the MMU. However, the following bits appear to be popular with most hardware designs:

1. **PRESENCE-BIT.**   Specifies whether or not a page is currently resident in main storage
2. **ACTIVITY-BIT(S).**   Measures 'the recent reference activity to the page by replacement policy procedures
3. **CHANGE-BIT.**   Specifies whether or not the contents of the page has been modified since it was loaded into memory

Of these bits, the most important are the PRESENCE-BIT and the CHANGE-BIT. The presence bit is checked on each memory reference by the user program. Should it equal zero, the page has been removed from memory. A page fault interrupt is generated to load the page back into memory. The change bit is used to determine whether a copy of a page must be rewritten to mass storage when the page is replaced in memory. A value of one indicates a modification to the page, thus requiring that it be copied to the disk. In systems where instruction pages (as opposed to data pages) are reentrant, the change bit should never be set.

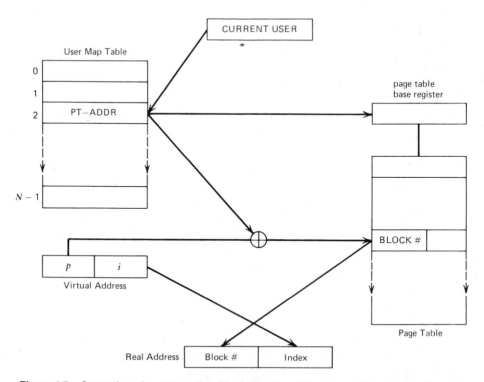

Figure 4.7   General paging structures. Block # is the address in main memory of a page frame (thus no multiplication by page size is required).

4.5.2   Page Management Policies

As Denning [denn70] notes, a virtual memory system is more than a mere mechanism; it includes policies describing how the mechanism is to be used. Generally, three types of policies are considered essential for page management: replacement policies, which determine those pages to be removed from memory; fetch policies, which determine when pages are to be loaded into memory (on demand or in advance of a user request); and placement policies, which determine where pages are to be placed into memory.

Denning notes that replacement and placement policies are complementary under page management. The system uses a replacement policy to determine a set of K pages that can be removed from memory. Those pages to be loaded into memory are then distributed across the empty pages in some fashion. A good algorithm is to distribute them from a linear list built as pages are removed from memory. Fetch policies are significantly more complex, dealing with the problem of predicting which pages to select from the set of pages available to the program which is located on the mass storage device.

Replacement Policies

In considering page replacement policies, we consider the set of pages that could be loaded into memory to be much greater than the set of page frames available to hold them. Now, let x be the page-address stream, that is, the set of pages referenced by a program during execution. Let $x(f)$ be the page referenced at time f. The string $w = x(1), x(2), x(3), \ldots, x(M)$ is often called the page reference string. Let c be the number of page frames currently filled in memory. Then $M(c, t)$ represents the current configuration of the user's program in memory, and $n(c, t)$ is the number of pages in $M(c, t)$.

Consider a reference to page $x(t)$, the current page. Three cases result, depending on the program's current configuration $M(c, t)$:

1. Suppose that $x(t)$ is an element of $M(c, f - 1)$; that is, the current page is resident in memory. No change is required in memory, so $M(c, t - 1) > M(c, t)$. This is known as page change.

2. Suppose that $x(t)$ does not belong to $m(c, t - 1)$. Further, suppose that $m(c, t - 1)$ is less than c; that is, the memory is not completely filled with the program's pages. Then the current page is loaded into memory. Thus $M(c, t - 1) \cup x(t) > M(c, t)$ and $n(c, t - 1) + 1 > m(c, t)$. This is known as page fault.

3. Suppose that $x(t)$ is not a member of $M(c, t - 1)$ and that $m(c, t - 1)$ equals c; then the memory is full and a page must be replaced. Let $y(t)$ be the page selected by the replacement algorithm to be removed from memory. Then $(M(c, t - 1) \text{ remove } y(t)) \cup x(t) > M(c, t)$.

A good page replacement algorithm attempts to make as few page movements between memory and disk as feasible. A number of possible page replacement algorithms have been presented in the literature [coff73, teor72], and some are summarized briefly below.

1. MIN is an algorithm that minimizes the number of page replacements. When replacement is required, MIN examines each page in $M(c, t - 1)$ with respect to its next appearance in M. MIN selects for replacement that page in $M(c, t - 1)$ whose reference is furthest in the future. Clearly, this is impractical since MIN requires exact foreknowledge of future references in the page stream. This knowledge is found only in programs that are relatively static. Since very few programs are static, this future reference string is unpredictable.

2. Least Recently Used (LRU) is a replacement algorithm similar to MIN except that it is backward-looking in the page reference string. LRU looks for the page in W that was mentioned furthest in the past and which is still a member of $M(c, t - 1)$. Studies have shown that LRU algorithms are quite practical in implementation (see [mura80]).

3. Another class of algorithms include FIFO replacement, where the first page loaded is the first page removed. These algorithms move a pointer through the page reference string and remove the next page to which it points in the string. In the worst case, this approach approximates a random replacement algorithm.

The reader interested in an extensive mathematical treatment of paging algorithms is referred to the excellent book by Coffman and Denning [coff73].

4.5.3   A Working Set Model

Suppose that a program occupies $m(t)$ pages at time t. Denning [denn70] defines the space time product across an interval $(t1, t2)$ to be

$$C(T1,T2) = T2 * \overset{T2}{\underset{T1}{SUM}}[M(T) * DT]$$

That is, for the interval $(t1, t2)$, $c(t1, t2)$ represents the total number of pages occupied by the program. Since computer charges are based on time of occupancy and extent of memory used, we can see that $c(t1, t2)$ represents a rough cost of program execution.

Denning proceeds to define the working set $w(t)$ as the smallest collection of pages of a given program that, resident in memory, assure some level of efficiency. The working set concept has intuitive appeal, as Denning shows, in the evaluation of different paging strategies given different types of mass storage devices. It is also useful in determining how to schedule programs to make the most efficient use of system resources. Denning has explored the working set model in considerable detail [denn68, denn72] and with Coffman has explicitly derived an extensive mathematical theory for analyzing the working set [coff73]. This section will explore briefly some of the principles of the working set model.

Principle of Locality

Given a program consisting of a set N of distinct pages, the working set W consists of a subset of these pages at any time. The principle of locality states that the membership of W changes slowly with respect to time. That is, an executing program favors some cluster of addresses in its logical address space over a given time interval. If a program is constructed using structured/modular programming principles, one should be able to see by inspection that a limited number of statements can be executed in a short time. (Consider the modules presented in this text. Many are less than a written page and average about 10 to 20 executable statements. Assuming a 12:1 expansion factor, many of these modules would fill one 256-word page. At 1 μsec per instruction, execution of a module could take from 1 to 2 msec and represent a significant time interval in localized execution.)

Given page i, such that $i < N$, define the reference density of page i as

$$d(i, k) = \text{Prob } (x(k) = i)$$

where $x(k)$ is the page referenced at time k. It is clear that

$$0 \le d(i, k) \le 1$$

$$\Sigma \, d(i, k) = 1 \qquad \text{for} \quad i = 1 \cdots m$$

Using the values $d(i, k)$, we can construct an ordered list of a program's pages by the number of references up to time k. An example of such a list L might be (for a 10-page program):

Index	Page	Reference, k_1	Reference, k_2
1	10	0	0
2	9	0	0
3	1	10	10
4	2	25	25
5	3	100	125
6	8	140	175
7	7	190	230
8	4	215	270
9	6	260	320
10	5	300	400

Suppose that this is an example of L at k_1 and k_2. Since the relative ordering of L has not changed, we can presume that the working set is the same. Now suppose that we had the following ordering at k_2 for indices 6 through 8:

Index	Page	Reference, k_2
6	4	220
7	7	255
8	8	290

The relative ordering of list L has changed between k_1 and k_2. This would imply that the working set has changed between k_1 and k_2.

The principle of locality states that, for long time intervals (k_1, k_2), the relative ordering of $L(k)$ will remain the same or change very slowly. It is difficult to directly measure $d(i, k)$ and equally difficult to predict it by inspection. However, because of the definition of a working set, we need not worry about measurement.

Definition of a Working Set

A working set $w(k)$ for the kth reference is defined as ([denn70])

$$w(k, h) = (I \text{ is an element of } N \text{ such that } I \text{ is an element of } W')$$
where $W' = x(k - h + 1), \ldots, x(k)$ is the page reference string

$$h \geq 1 \text{ is the window}$$
$$i \text{ is a page index}$$

That is, the membership of $w(k, h)$ represents the contents of a backward-looking window of length h which is positioned on the reference string and anchored at $x(k)$. As an example, consider the sequence of page references.

k	0	1	2	3	4	5	6	7	8	9	10
page	p_2	p_1	p_6	p_1	p_3	p_2	p_6	p_4	p_5	p_4	p_5

and an ordering of pages by recency of reference:

$$p_4 \quad p_2 \quad p_5 \quad p_6 \quad p_3 \quad p_1$$

where p_4 is most recently referenced and p_1 is least recently referenced. The working sets for various h are (beginning at $k = 12$):

$W(k, h)$	H
p_4	1
$p_4 \; p_2$	2
$p_4 \; p_2 \; p_5$	3-7

The working set is expected to contain the most useful pages (i.e., the pages with the greatest expectation of being referenced in the future). In terms of $d(i, k)$ since (for $k = 12$) p_2 is an element of $w(k, 7)$ whereas p_1 is not an element of $w(k, 7)$, we expect that $d(2, k) \geq d(1, k)$. We discuss below the selection of an appropriate h.

A Working Set Principle

A working set principle can be stated as follows: A program may execute if and only if its working set pages are currently resident in memory. Furthermore, a page may not be removed from memory if it is the member of a working set of a running program ([denn70]).

The working set exhibits several important characteristics [denn68, denn70]. Suppose that $w(h)$ is the expected working set size. That is,

$$w(h) = \text{expected value } [w(t, h)]$$

Then, Denning [denn68] describes the following properties:

1. Given $h \geq 1$, then $1 \leq w(h) < \min (n, h)$. That is, a program's working set is always one and can be no bigger than the window size or total number of pages in the program. The window size determines the number of pages to be examined in the program reference stream. Thus, at most, there can be h distinct pages ($h \leq M$) or n distinct pages ($m < H$) in the working set.
2. Then, $w(h) \leq w(h + 1)$. That is, the working set increases up to the limit (as prescribed above) over time.

4.5.4 Issues in Page Management

A number of major issues continue to confront the system designer with respect to page management. Many of these issues have arisen from conflicting studies performed on hardware with different characteristics. Others concern apparent flaws in the concept of paging itself. This section explores a few of these issues.

Local versus Global Paging

In a multiprogrammed system, the paging policies can be applied in either a local or a global fashion. In a local paging policy, suitable for the memory map approach described above, main memory is partitioned into workspaces for each program. The number of workspaces may be limited by the MMU architecture or by the OS designer. A paging algorithm is applied independently to each program. In fact, different paging algorithms may be applied to different programs if the OS is sufficiently flexible in design. When a page fault occurs, a replacement will be performed only within the given program's workspace.

Under a global paging policy, one paging algorithm is applied to the total collection of pages belonging to all active programs. While the algorithm treats all pages uniformly, it must recognize which pages belong to which programs. This fact necessitates an additional amount of system overhead. A page fault occurring in any program may cause the replacement of any page in memory. Thus the size of a program's workspace is randomly variable.

Thrashing

Thrashing is a condition that can befall systems managed by the paging technique. It is denoted by excessive overhead in the OS and severe performance degradation in the overall system throughput. Thrashing is the result of a shortage in memory space, and it produces a surplus of processor cycles. This discussion of thrashing is largely drawn from the seminal paper by Denning [denn68].

Thrashing is not due entirely to process behavior but to the lack of understanding about the interaction among process behavior, the paging algorithms, and the capacities of the system hardware. Processes of sufficiently large size will interfere with each other by competing for the same limited main memory resources. Certain paging policies, notably FIFO and LRU, contribute heavily to this competition by forcing global contention among all processes in memory. Moreover, a lack of main memory has serious repercussions in that it increases the likelihood of a missing page for any given process.

The concept of thrashing relies on the fact that the system goes from a period of steady-state efficiency into chaotic movement of pages between storage and main memory. Assume that a process has executed for a virtual time V. During this time, assume further that the missing page probability m has been constant. The expected number of page waits is $V \times m$, each page wait costing one access time T (to the disk). The efficiency of the system, $e(m)$, is defined as follows:

$$e(m) = \frac{\text{elapsed virtual time}}{(\text{elapsed virtual time}) + (\text{elapsed page wait time})}$$

or, symbolically,

$$e(m) = \frac{1}{1 + m \times T}$$

Denning notes that $e(m)$ measures the ability of a process to use the central processor. The change in efficiency is given by the derivative with respect to time T:

$$\frac{d[e(m)]}{dT} = \frac{-T}{(1 + m \times T)^2}$$

For small values of m with $T \gg 1$, the efficiency is sensitive to variations in m. This sensitivity to fluctuations in m for large T is responsible for thrashing.

To demonstrate this effect, Denning proposed a gedanken experiment. Let $(n + 1)$ identical processes exist, of which n are executing in main memory. Assume that each process has a size s, so that main memory size is $M = n \times s$. Let m_0 denote the missing page probability such that $m_0 \ll 1$, and $e(m_0)$ is not much less than 1. On the average, there is sufficient space to hold the most recently referenced pages of each process. The number of active processes is given by

$$ p = \frac{n}{1 + m_0 \times T} $$

By introducing the $(n + 1)$st process, the missing page probability is increased by some factor d. For the simplest case, let all n processes be wholly contained in memory. Loading the $(n + 1)$st process into main memory yields a value for d of $1/(n + 1)$. Note that p decreases as a result because

$$ m_0 \equiv (1 + p)(m_0 + d) $$

Let us assume that $T \gg n \gg 1$. That is, the access time is very large and the number of processes is also large. Denning argues that $d \gg m_0$. If not, the efficiency would be $e(m_0) \ll 1$, which contradicts our assumption about n processes. The corresponding decrease in active processes is

$$ p' = \frac{n + 1}{T + (n + 1) \times m_0 p} $$

such that $p'/p \ll 1$.

Degradation in service is caused by the large access time T, that is, the large speed difference between main memory and the mass storage devices. While one process is waiting for a page to be located and read into memory, other processes continue to execute and eventually page fault. In a typical system, large processes tend to get less space than they require. The space acquired by any one process depends on its structure and execution behavior. Adding more processes to the pot tends to exacerbate the problem.

The solution to thrashing (according to Denning) is twofold. First, ensure a sufficient supply of main memory. Second, use a paging algorithm that isolates a process's page requests by making them dependent only on its current memory holdings. Denning has devised the working set algorithm which is explored below.

To these, we can add two further solutions. First, limit the number of active processes that can be supported by main memory. In the long run, this may be easier than adding more memory or installing a new paging algorithm. Second, use structured programming techniques to enforce the concept of locality, which is assumed only in the working set approach.

Page Size

Page size is a critical factor in the development of a page management system. Page size is influenced by internal fragmentation and the efficiency of page transport operations. Denning notes that it is possible to select an optimal page size that minimizes storage losses. There are offsetting problems. As page size decreases, the likelihood of waste in the process's last page also decreases. However, the size of the program's page table will increase.

Denning has derived an optimal page size result which balances between wasted space (in the last page) and unavailable space (due to the page table). He calculates the optimal page size by assigning costs to losses in memory space. Suppose that p is the average program size and s is the page size. Let c_1 be the cost of losing a word in memory to the table and c_2 be the cost of losing a word to internal fragmentation. Then,

$$c = \frac{c_1}{c_2}$$

$$\text{if } s \ll p, \quad \text{then } s_0 = (2cp)^{1/2}$$

He derives this result in the following way. Let p be an expected value of a random variable for the program size such that

$$p = \text{expected value } [p]$$

Suppose that a program consumes $n = p/s$ pages, where each page has a one-word entry in the page table. The cost per page must be $c_1 \times p/s$. Given $s \ll p$, the expected waste in the last page is $s/2$ with a cost of $c_2 \times s/2$. The total expected cost is

$$\text{expected value } [C/s] = (p/s) \times c_1 + (s/2) \times c_2$$

Using differentiation to compute the minimum, we find the optimal page result mentioned above.

What is a good page size? Most manufacturers constrain the system designer by selecting a hardware-implemented page size of 512 to 2048 words. Batson et al. [bats70] have found that student programs tend to average a few thousand words and that s_0 should be about 50 words.

However, when one considers the time necessary to position the disk heads, the rotational latency, and the time to transfer words from disk to memory, one sees that setup time approximates a time equivalent to transferring 500 words. Selecting a page size less than 500 words implies inefficient use of the disk.

4.5.5   Design of a Page Management System

The system designer must have a detailed knowledge of the MMU and characteristics of the system architecture in order to design a page management system. It is not feasible, within this text's limited space, to describe all the modules necessary to support page management. This section provides a high-level approach to the modules that comprise a page management system.

Setting the Stage

Memory management under paging requires more than just a detailed understanding of the addressing mechanism. The paging philosophy leads to such questions as these:

What happens while a page is being loaded into memory?

How does one control multiple concurrent page requests and releases?

What effect does I/O scheduling have on the satisfaction of page requests and the overall performance of the system?

To answer these questions, one must thoroughly understand the interactions among the scheduling, memory management, and mass storage subsystems. The following description represents a functional scenario of these interactions.

A series of processes are ordered on a ready queue. As main memory space becomes available, the process with the highest priority is assigned a time quantum, $q[i]$, and entered into the run queue. Such processes on the run queue are processed for a burst of time B such that B is less than or equal to $q[i]$. At the end of B seconds of process time, the process is returned to the running queue. The exceptions to this procedure are:

1.   The running time, $t[i]$, of the process exceeds the quantum time ($t[i] > q[i]$), in which case the process is placed on the ready queue with $t[i]$ set to zero.

2.   The process is blocked through execution of a system request.

3.   The process is completed.

4.   A page fault occurs, in which case the process is suspended while the missing page is loaded into memory and then placed on the ready to run queue.

Each process has N pages of M words in its virtual memory space. When a process takes control of the central processor, its virtual memory map is loaded into the MMU's translation registers. When the process loses control of the CPU, the contents of the MMU registers are saved in the processes buffer area. All addressing that the process performs occurs through the MMU. When the process issues a virtual address, if the page exists in memory, the address translation succeeds or a page fault occurs.

Pages will be swapped in and out of memory according to the working set strategy (see section 4.5.3). Pages will be loaded into memory on the demand of the requesting process. When a page is loaded into memory, it is deemed active. Associated with each active page in memory is a counter registering the elapsed processing time of the process since it was last referenced. Every time a page is referenced, the counter is set to zero. If a page is not referenced within the burst B of processing time, the counter is increased by B. When the value of the counter exceeds some system threshold J, the page is released and the page frame is deemed available for reassignment. Available pages exist in the following modes:

1. Immediately available for reassignment
2. In an altered state necessitating swap-out before reuse
3. Queued for swap-out due to alteration

Every process's virtual memory is maintained in complete (total) form on a mass storage device called the paging device. Only its working set ever exists within main memory.

The page manager (a resident system process) manages memory by removing those pages from the working sets that have not been referenced in J seconds. Each page frame thus freed is entered into the available page queue. The page manager keeps track of those pages not currently part of any working set. When a process on the ready queue with a high enough priority has a working set that will fit in memory, the process is entered onto the run queue and its working set size is deducted from the available page frame count. The pages in the process's working set are entered on demand with associated computation of the current working set. If after J seconds of processing, the specified working set size has not been reached, the excess reserved page frames are returned to the available page frame queue by incrementing the page frame count. During processing, when a process requests a page that exceeds its working set size, it is allowed to expand. Otherwise, it is removed from the running list.

A page becomes inactive, and thus available, because it has not been referenced within J seconds and therefore is not a member of the working set, or the process became inactive due to quantum timeout, service blocking, or for exceeding the working set size when no pages were available.

Thus the page manager maintains dynamic working sets for each active process. Each time that a page is to be swapped in on demand, another page may need to be swapped out. The page manager maintains pages on two queues: a swapping queue and an available queue (because they do not require swapping). If a process references a page that has recently been removed from its working set, there is a high likelihood that it is still in memory and attached to one of these queues. If the available page count is nonzero, the requested page can immediately be reassigned to the process.

Role of the Paging Device

In virtual memory systems, a process's address space usually exceeds physical main memory. With multiple processes competing for service, only a relative few of each process's pages may reside in main memory at any time. Thus the set of pages representing a process's address space must be stored on a mass storage device for easy recall.

Originally, the mass storage device was a paging drum—a highly efficient, head-per-track system. The drum was divided into bands called tracks, which were subdivided into equal length sectors. Each sector usually corresponded to one page. Thus hardware architecture often significantly influenced page size. With the advent of high-speed disk subsystems, the need for a specialized paging drum became less apparent.

The performance and organization of paging devices have been given considerable attention in the literature. Most authors assume in their mathematical derivations that it is instantaneously possible to switch from read mode to write mode. That is, after reading (or writing) a given sector, it is possible to switch the status of the heads so as to commence writing (or reading) the next sector with no significant delay. In fact, such an approach is never realizable and most authors' results represent upper bounds on performance. I urge you to consult [foge74] for more detailed descriptions.

Other factors that affect the performance of the page management system include:

Capacity of the paging device (in pages)

Average process size (in pages)

Availability of a dedicated access channel to paging device

Speed of paging device (latency, transfer rate)

Other timing and physical limitations

Organization of I/O queries for device

4.5.6   Page Management Databases

A virtual address, issued by a process, is translated into a real memory address by the MMU. The MMU contains the translation tables necessary to map virtual addresses to physical addresses. The number of pages available to a process usually exceeds the number of blocks in memory. The page manager maintains a table of all the pages in physical memory in order to track the residency of pages for individual processes.

Pages are loaded from the mass storage system to main memory on demand. At times, pages may need to be written out to mass storage. That is, the copy of the page on the disk is to be updated. Neither read nor write is instantaneous, so a backlog of page transfer requests can accumulate. To manage the flow of pages between memory and disk, the page manager maintains several lists which mark the status of each page transfer.

Translation Tables

The translation tables are normally embodied in the MMU. The structure of the MMU is different for each computer manufacturer. Consequently, different information is maintained for the virtual pages. In general, the following registers are provided by most manufacturers in the translation tables:

Mnemonic	Usage
Active-flag	Indicates that the page is currently a member of the process's working set (not always available)
Referenced-flag	Indicates that the page has been referenced by the process during time slice J
Change-flag	Indicates that the page has been modified by the process
Write-protect	Indicates that the page is protected against modification
Block-index	Indicates the physical page address for the virtual page if it is in main memory

An MMU usually contains two or more map tables (at least one each for the system and the user). The map table (or translation memory) stores a copy of the translation table for the active process assigned to that map table. One map table is usually assigned to the OS. Others are assigned to different processes as they are selected for execution by the system scheduler.

When a process is selected for execution, it is assigned a map table by the page manager. The map table is initialized to zeros by the page manager. Then the working set of the process is stored in the map table and the process is dispatched. During execution, entries in the map table are updated as the process demand pages.

When a process is rescheduled by the system, its translation table is unloaded and the map released for assignment to another process. Each page in the working set is released to the available page list for reassignment to other processes.

The Page Table

The page table contains one entry, called a page descriptor, for each physical page in main memory. An entry represents the current status of the page in terms of protection, residency, utilization, and physical location on disk. The following fields usually comprise a page table entry:

Mnemonic	Usage
Page-status	Indicates the current usage of the page (see below)
Write-protect	Indicates that the page is protected against modification when set
Change-flag	Indicates that this page has been altered by some process
Utilization-counter	Indicates the time since the page was last referenced
Lock-flag	Indicates that the page is permanently resident when set
Virtual-page-id	Identifier for the virtual page in the map table
Disk-address	Location on the disk of the image of this page
Read-write-flag	Indicates whether the entry is to be read or written from disk

A physical page may be active in one of four states, as indicated by the value of PAGE-STATUS. The appropriate values for page status are:

Value	Explanation
0	Page is active
1	Page is queued to be swapped out
2	Page is unavailable (i.e., in swap-in or swap-out mode) and may not be accessed
3	Page is available for assignment to some process

A page may be protected against modification by a process. In systems that support reentrant programming, pages will often be identified as belonging to code or data segments. All pages belonging to code segments will have WRITE-PROTECT set to one. The CHANGE-FLAG is used to mark those pages that have been altered by a process. When a page is no longer required in a working set, it will be rewritten to disk if the CHANGE-FLAG is set. The LOCK-FLAG is set to force certain pages to be permanently resident in main memory. In effect, locked pages are never considered as candidates for swap-out when a page must be evicted from memory.

A physical page is linked back to the map table through the VIRTUAL-PAGE-ID fields in order to provide an easy mechanism for updating the map tables. When a page is evicted from memory, the system must update the appropriate map table entry to reflect the absence of that page. The DISK-ADDRESS records the location of the page image on the disk. It is used by the system when a page image must be updated because the page was altered in memory.

Page Manager Workspace

The page manager requires working space to keep track of the pages that comprise the working set of a process. The workspace is composed of additional entries in the PCB as well as dynamically allocated space in the PCB. The following entries are required to augment the standard process data:

Mnemonic	Usage
active-time	Indicates the elapsed processing time since the process was started
quantum	Quantum of processing time allowed to this process
current-ws-size	Current size of the working set for this process
old-ws-size	Working set size at the termination of the last active period
first-virtual-page	First virtual page necessary to activate this process
workset-address	Address of the working set for this process
interval-value	Remaining time in the current burst interval

The value of WORKSET-ADDRESS is an index into the PDB where information about the current working set pages are stored. Each page in the working set has the following information maintained about it: the virtual page identifier, the disk address for the page, and the write protect flag. The number of entries is represented by CURRENT-WS-SIZE.

4.5.7 Page Management Functions

In this section we sketch the primitive functions necessary to implement a page management subsystem based on the working set principle.

The page management subsystem is interrupt-driven in the sense that once a process begins execution, a page manager function will be invoked only upon the occurrence of an interrupt. As a process executes, an instruction is fetched, the appropriate addresses are translated to real memory addresses, and the instruction is executed. At the conclusion of instruction execution, the CPU determines if any interrupts are pending and dispatches to resident code to handle the interrupt. The types of interrupts that relate to page manager activities are:

Interval timer. The burst of time B for this process has expired and the process is placed on the ready-to-run queue.

Page fault. The page requested is not currently resident in memory, so the process is blocked until the page is loaded into memory.

Working set overflow. The process has requested more pages than allowed in its working set, so it is placed on the ready-to-run queue.

Address fault. An illegal virtual address is referenced, which forces the process to be terminated.

Page interrupt. A page has been successfully removed from memory, which necessitates an update of page manager tables.

In the paragraphs below, we describe the procedures that handle these interrupts. Each procedure, in turn, calls other procedures to assist it. We will mention these procedures briefly only by function and let the reader construct them at his or her leisure.

Processing Interval Timer Interrupts

The interval timer is used to count the time allotted to a process for an execution burst. When a process is dispatched, the interval timer is loaded with the burst-time value. At the expiration of this interval, assuming that none of the other interrupts occur, the interval timer generates an interrupt and forces the process to be rescheduled. Selection of the burst-time in a paging system can be a critical factor in the efficiency of the system. Too little time requires considerable system overhead to switch processes. Too much time, combined with an inappropriate working set size, can force the system into a thrashing mode.

The procedure for handling an interval timer interrupt is outlined in module 4.5.1. Note that the quantum of execution may be equal to several bursts. Between bursts a process will not be rescheduled. The simplest case is to set the quantum equal to the burst-time and to make the burst-time relatively long. When the active-time of the process exceeds the quantum of execution, the process is rescheduled.

If the quantum has not expired, the procedure checks to see if it is time to update the working set size. WORKSET-TIME is the number of bursts (normally an even multiple) between calculations of the working set size. The free-count is modified by the change in the working set size. The process is then recycled on the running queue to await its next burst of execution time. Procedure CIRCULATE places the process in the running queue according to preestablished criteria (e.g., priority, first come-first served, etc.).

Processing Page Faults

When a page fault interrupt is detected by MMU, the page-fault procedure is invoked to load the requested page. Because the page is not resident in the translation tables, it is not a member of the current working set and must be introduced by loading the page into memory. The working set size is incremented by one. The interval timer value is stored in the process's workspace until the

MODULE 4.5.1

```
procedure interval-timer-interrupt[process]
    increment active-time[process] by burst-time
    set burst-time to interval-value[process]
    if active-time[process] greater than or equal to quantum[process]
        then
                deactivate(process, ready-to-run queue)
        else
            if active-time[process] less than
                                    (burst-time + workset-time)
                then
                if active-time[process] greater than or equal to
                                                    workset-time
    then
    old-ws-size[process] − current-ws-size[process]
                                            → ws-change
    increment free-page-count by ws-change
    endif
                    endif
                    circulate[process]
        endif
endproc
```

page is loaded into memory. This value is used to reinitialize the interval timer so that the process may complete its burst of execution.

The procedure assumes that the real page is not resident in memory. (Note that it may be resident as a member of a previous working set (see [denn70].) The procedure CHECK-PAGE-TABLE is called to determine if the real page is physically present in memory (described below). The value of the variable SUCCESS indicates the status of the real page.

If SUCCESS equals one, the real page is resident in main memory and is attached to one of the page manager's queues. The page is detached from the queue and added to the list of pages that form the working set of the process. The page descriptor is set to active and restored to the process's map table. If the page was on the available page list, the variables AVAILABLE-PAGE-COUNT and ASSIGNED-PAGE-COUNT are decremented by one. The latter counter tracks the number of real pages assigned to the page manager as opposed to those assigned to various user processes.

If SUCCESS equals zero, the real page is not physically present in memory. The procedure checks to see if there are any pages assigned to the page manager. If there are none, a page must be selected from the process's current working set for replacement. Procedure CANNIBALIZE (not described) selects the appropriate page if the process is the only one (except the system process) that is executing. Otherwise, the process is rescheduled to wait for a page to become available from another user process. The requested page is queued for input while the process waits for it to be loaded, and the appropriate counters are updated.

MODULE 4.5.2

```
procedure page-fault(virtual-page, real-page, process)
    clear success
    increment current-ws-size[process]
    read-interval-timer( ) → interval-value[process]
    if real-page not equal to zero
        then
        check-page-table(real-page, virtual-page, process,
                                    queue-address) → success
        endif
    if success equals one
    then
    detach-page-descriptor(real-page, queue-address,
                                page-descriptor-address)
    decrement free-page-count
    if queue-address equals available-page-list
        then
            decrement available-page-count
            decrement assigned-page-count
    endif
    add-page-descriptor(real-page, process-list[process],
                                page-descriptor-address)
    set one to active-flag[map-buffer-address]
    store-map(virtual-page, map-buffer-address)
    else
        if assigned-page-count equals zero
            then
                if count[ready-queue] less than or equal to 2
                then
                    cannibalize(real-page, process-list[process])
                    decrement current-ws-size[process]
                endif
            else
                deactivate(process, ready-queue)
        endif
        queue-for-input(process, virtual-page)
        decrement assigned-page-count
        decrement free-page-count
    endif
endproc
```

Checking Page Table Entries

This procedure, outlined in module 4.5.3, checks the page table to see if the page indicated by the map table is physically present in memory. The page descriptor is retrieved from the page table. The virtual page is checked to see if it is within the number of virtual pages composing this process. If not, an error (not shown) is generated notifying the system of an illegal address request.

The procedure checks the status of the real page whose address was found in the map table. Two cases result:

> If the real-page corresponds to the requested virtual page and currently has the proper process identifier, it is part of the process's working set and SUCCESS is set to one.
>
> Otherwise, it is not part of the working set and SUCCESS is set to zero.

In addition, it verifies that the page is not currently queued for swapping and thus is unavailable to everybody. If SUCCESS equals one, the address of the queue on which the real page is resident is returned to the caller.

Queueing Pages for Input

If a page was not found to be in memory, the image of the page must be brought into memory from the paging device. The procedure for initializing the descriptor is depicted in module 4.5.4. The following cases must be considered:

1. If a physical page is available to receive the virtual page, its page descriptor is removed from the available page list and initialized with the appropriate information for the virtual page. The request is queued to the swappable-page-list with the read-write-flag set to zero to indicate that the page is to be read. The process is suspended until the page is accessible.
2. If a physical page is not available, the process is enqueued to the page-wait-queue until a physical page is released by another process. The system keeps track of the requested page by storing it in the process data block.

In either case, the procedure removes the first page (if there is one) from the swappable-page-list and enqueues it for swapping (the read-write-flag is set to one). This action ensures that a page will be released by the system and added to the available-page-list.

Note that procedure QUEUE-FOR-INPUT calls a subsidiary procedure REMOVE-TRACE. This procedure (not shown) removes any information from

MODULE 4.5.3

```
procedure check-page-table(real-page, vpage, process,
                                        qaddress, → success)
     vpage → virtual-page
     qaddress → queue-address
     load-page-descriptor(real-page, page-descriptor-address)
     if virtual-page less than max-vp-count[process]
          then
        if page-status(page-descriptor-address) not equal to 2
             then
             if virtual-page equals
                              virtual-page-id[page-descriptor-address]
             then
             if process equals process-id[page-descriptor-address]
             then
                    set one to success
             else
                    clear success
             endif
             endif
          endif
     endif
     if success equals one
          then
             if page-status[page-descriptor-address] equals one
                  then
                       set swappable-page-list to queue-address
                  else
                       set available-page-list to queue-address
                  endif
          endif
endproc
```

the physical page descriptor which may have remained from another process's
map table. We create these linkages between real pages and the virtual pages
they represent only to enhance the flexibility with which the system determines
which real pages belong to which process. Such an approach is not obligatory,
and indeed, is not used on several of the more popular commercial OSs.

Swapping Device Interrupt

When a page has been transferred from the disk to memory, the system is interrupted to complete processing of the transfer. It stores the current register set

MODULE 4.5.4

```
procedure queue-for-input(process, virtual-page)
    if assigned-page-count not equal to zero
    then
        remove-page-descriptor(real-page, available-page-list,
                                        page-descriptor-address)
        decrement available-page-count
        process-id(page-descriptor-address, process) → process-address
        virtual-page-id[page-descriptor-address] → vp-id
        remove-trace(vp-id, process-address)
        clear page-status[page-descriptor-address]
        set virtual-page to virtual-page-id[page-descriptor-address]
        save-write-protect(virtual-page, process)
                                        → write-protect[page-descriptor-address]
        clear change-flag[page-descriptor-address]
        clear utilization-counter[page-descriptor-address]
        process → process-id[page-descriptor-address]
        save-disk-address(virtual-page, process)
                                        → disk-address[page-descriptor-address]
        clear read-write-flag[page-descriptor-address]
        store-page-descriptor(real-page, page-descriptor-address)
        queue-request(real-page)
        suspend(process) else
        deactivate(process, page-wait-queue)
        set virtual-page to desired-virtual-page[process]
    endif
    if first-page(swappable-page-list) not equal to zero
        then
            remove-page-descriptor(real-page, swappable-page-list,
                                        page-descriptor-address)
            set one to read-write-flag[page-descriptor-address]
            store-page-descriptor(real-page, page-descriptor-address)
            queue-request(real-page)
        endif
endproc
```

temporarily so that the process can resume execution from its interruption
point. The cases to be considered, which depend on the direction of transfer,
are:

1. If the page was swapped in, the process waiting for it must be placed on
   the run-queue. The page descriptor is retrieved from the page table and
   information contained therein to set the map table entry, enter the page
   into the process's working set, and place the process on the run-queue.

2.   If the page was swapped out, then the page descriptor is added to the
available-page-list, and the available-page-count is incremented by one.
The page-wait-list is checked to see if any processes are waiting for available pages. If so, the process is removed from the list and its desired virtual page is queued for input.

At the end of page-swap processing, the interrupted process's registers are restored and it resumes execution.

MODULE 4.5.5

```
Procedure swapping-disk-interrupt(page-transfer, page-id, process)
     store-registers(process)
     if page-transfer equals swap-in-mode
     then
          load-page-descriptor(page-id, page-descriptor-address)
          set-map-entry(page-id, page-descriptor-address)
          process-id(page-descriptor-address) → process-address
          process-list[process-address] → current-queue
          add-process(process-address, run-queue)
     endif
     if page-transfer equals swap-out-mode
     then
          add-page-descriptor(page-id, available-page-list,
                                          page-descriptor-address)
          increment available-page-count
          if head[page-wait-list] not equal to zero
               then
                         remove-process(process-temp, page-wait-list)
                         desired-virtual-page(process-temp) → vp-id
                         queue-for-input(process-temp, vp-id)
          endif
     endif
     restore-registers(process)
endproc
```

Deactivating a Process

A process, as we have seen, may be deactivated for several reasons: during page
wait, at the end of a quantum of execution, or because it exceeds the working
set size. Deactivation of a process requires considerable effort on the part of the
OS. All physical pages currently held by the system must be released to the free-
page-list. This involves updating both the process's map table and the page

table. The memory map is released for assignment to another process after its contents are copied to the process's data block.

The procedure to accomplish these operations is sketched in module 4.5.6. The procedure uses the active-time of the process to update the old working set size. Each page in the process's working set is removed from the page table and placed on the available-page-list or swappable-page-list by release-page. The process is removed from the run-queue and placed on the queue specified by the caller (which may be page wait or ready). The process's state vector (e.g., registers, etc.) is stored in the PDB and the next process is fetched from the run-queue and initialized. Note that the queue of real pages previously assigned to the deactivated process are now assigned to the newly initiated process.

Releasing a Page from a Process

A real page is released from a process for two reasons: (1) the process is deactivated, or (2) the page is cannibalized because the working set is full. The status of the page is checked to see if it has been altered. If so, the page is placed on the swappable-page-list and marked unavailable. The counters for free pages and pages assigned to the page manager are incremented by one.

The Page Manager

The page management subsystem is composed of all the modules described in this section. The previous modules are executed in a passive mode; that is, they do not perform their function unless an external event has occurred. This subsystem also includes an active component, the page manager, which is initiated during system initialization.

The page manager performs two operations each time it is executed: (1) it updates the utilization counter for each page in the page table, and (2) it activates a process on the ready list if there is space for its working set.

The outline of the page manager is depicted in module 4.5.8. The page manager scans the page table for resident pages that have not been referenced in the last J seconds (such that the utilization-counter is greater than or equal to J). Any such page is detached from the process with which it is currently associated. The process's working set size is reduced by one and the page is released to the free-space list. The page manager then searches the ready list for porcesses whose working set will fit in main memory. Each process found is removed from the ready list and placed in page-wait status. The first page necessary to initiate processing for that process is queue for input.

MODULE 4.5.6

```
procedure deactivate(process, queue-address)
    active-time[process] → active-temp
    clear active-time[process]
    process-list[process] → current-queue
    if active-temp greater that or equal to workset-time
    then
        if old-ws-size less than current-ws-size[process]
        then
            current-ws-size[process] → old-ws-size[process]
        endif
    endif
    clear current-ws-size[process]
    first-page(current-queue) → next-page
    while next-page not equal to zero
    do
        next page → pageid
        detach-page-descriptor(page-id, page-descriptor-address)
        release-page(page-id, page-descriptor-address)
        forward-link(page-descriptor-address) → next-page
    enddo
    remove-process(process, run-queue)
    add-process(process, queue-address)
    unload-state-vector[process]
    get-next-process(process, run-queue)
    current-queue → process-list[process]
    load-state-vector(process)
    load-interval-timer(interval-value[process])
endproc
```

MODULE 4.5.7

```
procedure release-page(page-id, page-descriptor-address)
    if change-flag[page-descriptor-address] equals one
        then
            add-page-descriptor(page-id, swappable-page-list,
                                        page-descriptor-address)
        else
            add-page-descriptor(page-id, available-page-list,
                                        page-descriptor-address)
            increment available-page-count
    endif
    increment assigned-page-count
    increment free-page-count
endproc
```

```
process page-manager
    for page-id from 0 to max-real-pages
    do
        load-page-descriptor(page-id, page-descriptor-address)
        if page-status[page-descriptor-address] equals zero
        then
            if process-id[page-descriptor-address] not blocked
            then
                increment utilization-counter[page-descriptor-address]
                                        by interval-value(process)
                if utilization-counter[page-descriptor-address] greater
                                        than or equal to workset time
                then
                        process-id[page-descriptor-address]
                                                → process-address
                        increment current-ws-size[process-address]
                        process-list[process-address] → current-queue
                        detach-page-descriptor(page-id, current-queue,
                                                page-descriptor-address)
                    release-page(page-id, page-descriptor-address)
            endif
            store-page-descriptor(page-id, page-descriptor-address)
        endif
    endif
    enddo
    clear working-set-size
    clear failure
    while failure equals zero
      do
            decrement free-page-count by working-set-size
            search-ready-queue(working-set-size, failure,
            process-address)
            if failure equals zero
                then
                        first-request[process-address] → virtual-page
                        detach-process(process-address, ready-queue)
                        queue-for-input(process-address, virtual-page)
            endif
      enddo
endprocess
```

CHAPTER

5

Input/Output
Management

To further remove the user from the physical hardware, and thus virtualize his or her environment, we distinguish between logical and physical views of data. The process should only "see" a logical view. Mapping between this logical view and the physical representation on the peripheral device is the responsibility of the I/O manager (IOM). The IOM furnishes the user with an array of services, all of which are related to the logical structuring of data, but are little related to each other. Some of these services are transparent to the user but, nevertheless, form an essential part of the IOM in relation to device allocation, data staging, performance, and scheduling.

5.1 CONCEPTS OF INPUT/OUTPUT MANAGEMENT

The primary motivation for an IOM is to support the principle of device independence. The diversity of features found in different I/O devices forces programmers to separate I/O services from the remaining program logic. These services are concentrated in the I/O control system (IOCS). The earliest OSs were composed of a simple job monitor and an IOCS. Device independence allowed programmers to recover large investments in code while taking advantage of new or improved capabilities. At the same time, the IOCS allowed a general logical structure to be implemented on the distinct physical structures provided by each device. Thus the user was able to utilize the set of peripheral devices through a standardized interface.

At the hardware level, most I/O devices are locked into a specific hardware connection within the computer. Each device class (or controller) is assigned a unique fixed I/O unit number. Each device requires instructions with device-specific parameters for performing and controlling data transfers. If each program were written to reference hard device addresses, a program would not be able to function unless the device referenced were available. Furthermore, assuring device integrity among two or more users would be extremely difficult.

The scheme for eliminating specific hardware device references involves the establishment of logical names for devices. The IOM was made responsible for resolving the logical-to-physical device connections either prior to execution of the program or during the execution of an I/O request. The latter facility allows dynamic redefinition of logical-to-physical device connections during program execution, a feature that greatly increases the flexibility of the system. This facility has been extended to another level through the use of the logical unit numbers in programming languages such as FORTRAN. Of course, it does not help you much if a device exists which is not of the type initially required by your program. You can safely ignore its existence since it has no impact on your program.

The ability to direct data transfers to devices of different types is an important feature. In minicomputer systems, peripherals constitute the major cost item. In comparison to the CPU and memory, the peripherals generally operate at lower efficiency and utilization. In all but a few number-crunching programs, data transfers to peripheral devices will occupy a disproportionate amount of the resources in any implementation effort. Thus the IOM can provide the user with greater flexibility, peripheral utilization and efficiency, and support device sharing among multiple users by eliminating the subtle differences between files and devices.

5.1.1   Systems Engineering Considerations

The IOM is the first level of the OS with which the user will have direct interaction on a continuing basis. This interaction imposes both user and system design requirements on the IOM.

From the user's point of view, those I/O instructions that are executed should be treated just like any other operation. The user expects to be able to store and retrieve data from secondary storage devices in a specified source format without undue consideration for the physical characteristics of the device. The data formats from unit record peripherals should impose minimum constraints on user programming. References to these storage areas should be made by symbolic names and/or relative addresses. The user expects the system to perform I/O operations efficiently. Finally, the user expects the I/O instructions to be simple and mnemonic.

The impact of device independence on user effectiveness is much more obvious than its impact on equipment effectiveness. The cost of device independence is software design. The efficiency of operation depends on the generality being sought and the structure of the underlying hardware. That is, the cost of integrating a one-of-a-kind device (e.g., a film reader) into the I/O scheme may be more expensive than a procedural scheme for sharing the device. On the other hand, the need to relieve the user from concern about the exact formation of the I/O instruction and its associated device orders may be an overriding consideration. The question to be answered by the software engineer is straightforward: Will the added cost imposed on the system by additional software to handle the device be overcome by a net gain in system performance and efficiency?

The goal of device independence is to provide a package of services that allow programs to substitute devices at execution time without necessitating changes in program code. This goal is supported in three ways in modern OSs: the user is provided with storage location and speed independence through the use of data buffering; data organization on mass storage devices is made independent of the usage sequence of the data through provision of access methods; finally, it should be noted that substitution of two-dimensional devices (such as disks) for linear devices (such as TTYs and line printers) involves a quantum jump in software complexity and user efficiency. The latter capability is most often provided by a spooling mechanism.

5.1.2 Data Management Fundamentals

In OS design, a distinction must be drawn between logical and physical data structures. Physical data structures are represented by the physical devices in the computer system. Logical data structures are organizations of data defined by the programmer. One function of the operating system is to effect the mapping of logical data structures to physical data structures. The latter are well defined by the type of physical device and its controller. The former are also well defined but are affected by the type of OS.

The basic element of I/O management is a datum that represents information about a person, place, or thing to be represented to the computer. Data are presented in many formats: character strings, addresses, numerical values, or instructions. Data items are usually grouped together as a record where the data items bear some relationship to each other (such as the name, sex, and age of a person). A collection of records, given a name, is called a file. Files may be stored on mass storage devices such as disks, drums, or tapes.

Logical data structures are supported by two subsystems in the OS. The record I/O subsystem allows the user to read from or write to a device. It also allows the user to treat a file as a linear (virtual record-oriented) device from/to which records can be retrieved or stored. The management of files as groups of data blocks requires a block or direct I/O subsystem. This subsystem allows the user to specify a disk address from which a fixed-length data block may be retrieved in a random fashion. In most OSs, the user is provided with system service requests to access both subsystems.

In early systems, where data resided on disks and drums, a user specified the absolute addresses. The user also specified the actual physical device number for each device supplying data to the program. Later, users wanted to run the program on multiple data sets. This was especially relevant when the data were located on a mass storage device. In the program, the user specified a logical device known as a channel (not to be confused with hardware channels). When a file is "opened" (i.e., made accessible to the program) a connection is made between the channel and the physical device by the OS. The concept of a channel allows a user to connect to different files (and therefore, different devices) with each program execution.

In multiprocessing systems, several users may attempt to access the same device. For example, two user programs, executing concurrently, attempt to read a record from the card reader. Obviously, only one data set may be in the card reader's hopper at any time. One program would have to wait until the other program had completely read its entire data set. One program could then "tie up" the card reader for a long time. Alternatively, one could provide many card readers where a program would select a card reader and request its data set to be loaded into the hopper. This approach is both time consuming (for the operator) and expensive (card readers are not cheap). However, the idea of multiple card readers (or any record-oriented device for that matter) led to the concept of virtual devices.

A virtual device is a logical concept. The data set on the device is read as it is loaded and stored in a disk file. When the user accesses the device via a channel number, the OS actually connects the program to the file rather than to the device. The user issues read/write requests as if the user were talking to the device, but these are translated into read/write requests to the file system by the OS. One aspect of the virtual device concept is known as the SPOOLing method.

An important aspect of data management is handling the difference in speeds between the CPU/memory and the various peripheral devices. As the CPU is faster than most devices, when a read operation is performed, the CPU usually must wait for the data to become available. Be reading several records ahead of the actual requests, the OS provides a cushion or buffer between the two which serves to increase the efficiency of the system. This anticipatory reading is commonly referred to as buffering. A measure of efficiency results because successive accesses are to records which are already stored in memory. When a buffer is exhausted, another block of data is read from the device.

At the lowest level of data management are the device handlers, which translate logical record requests into physical device operations. Device handlers (discussed in chapter 2) shield the user from the peculiarities of each device by providing a uniform interface for accessing data.

5.2 STRUCTURE OF THE INPUT/OUTPUT MANAGER

An OS must satisfy these objectives in responding to user data management requests:

1. An OS generally supports several types of file organizations (see section 6.2.1). The IOM must be able to handle each file organization in a flexible and versatile manner.

2. A user program may desire to retrieve records in sequences independent of the file organization which improve the efficiency of computation. The IOM must support the basic access methods in a manner that is essentially invisible to the user.

3. Files and devices should be treated in a uniform manner. Device independence is achieved by treating each device as a file from/to which records can be retrieved/stored. The IOM performs the necessary transformations to execute an I/O operation against a file or device.

4. Most OSs allocate mass storage space in a dynamic and automatic fashion. The flexibility and versatility of mass storage–based systems is derived from the fact that they do not have to preallocate the entire file space. Files can contract and expand at the user's whim (given certain integrity constraints). Allocation of file space is performed by the IOM as a result of data management requests from the user.

The mechanisms for satisfying these objectives are buried in the subsystem known as the IOM, which is transparent to the user beyond the level of the system service requests. However, the IOM has the greatest impact on the efficiency of the system and is often the most complex subsystem to be implemented. Proper implementation of the IOM is a major topic in the design of modern OSs.

The IOM is situated between the file manager (see chapter 6) and the device managers (see chapter 2). As mentioned above, a file is a collection of records that can be manipulated by a user program. Once the user has "opened" a file (i.e., made it accessible for I/O), it is the job of the IOM to control all requests for I/O operations against the file.

Madnick and Alsop [madn69] have addressed these questions in a classic paper. They view efficiency as a trade-off between utilization of programmer versus system resources. The IOM, by relieving the programmer of problems associated with formats, organizations, and allocations, allows him or her to concentrate on developing algorithms related to the logical structure of the program. The complexity and availability of mass storage devices and other I/O peripherals is better handled by a common subsystem. This approach obviates the situation where each programmer must worry about the specification of critical parameters. Finally, the uniform interface to files and devices, particularly in high-level languages, enhances the portability of both programs and programmers.

The following paragraphs describe the structure of the I/O subsystem. The terminology is drawn from Madnick and Alsop [madn69], although the hierarchality of the subsystems differs somewhat from their approach. Later sections of the chapter describe the modules and databases for implementing an I/O subsystem.

File Management Interface

To provide a uniform interface to the user, all sources and receivers of data are treated as files. In retrieving data for manipulation, a program must first make the source of data known to the OS. It does so by executing a system service request to open the file. This request results in a search to locate the file, the creation of a file control block (file descriptor), and the initialization of the descriptor for subsequent I/O operations. Conversely, when a program has finished processing a file, it closes the file. The mechanisms and functions associated with file management operations are discussed in chapter 6.

Data Management Operations and Access Methods

Once the data are accessible, a program can retrieve or store data in a file consonant with its algorithm. Access methods allow a program to impose a logical structure on the contents of a file which make the data more amenable to processing. Access methods determine the variations on the basic I/O operations. The program, when it opens the file, may be required to declare the access method it wishes to use, although this may also be implicit in the specific I/O operations executed.

The access method allows the program to store or retrieve a logical record by its position, address, or contents. Modules supporting the access method perform the necessary formatting and buffering operations to ensure that a record is available and in the proper form expected by the program. In addition, access method modules will also perform some of the error handling functions associated with the detection, reporting, and rectification of errors.

File Organization Strategy Modules

Each file is organized on a device in a manner determined by the characteristics of the device. A file organization strategy module (FOSM) is associated with each type of file organization. Its purpose is to map the logical records, as seen by the user, into physical records manipulated by the device. When an I/O operation is executed, the FOSM interprets the request in terms of the target file characteristics.

Whereas access methods are device independent because they deal with logical records, FOSMs are a critical area in the system because they map logical addresses to physical addresses on a device or in memory. What, to an access method, is a logically contiguous virtual method, is a structured and partitioned set of records to the FOSM. To minimize redundancy or unnecessary I/O, the FOSM will usually incorporate a buffering capability. Buffers provide a way of speeding up access to the data by a program at the expense of additional complexity in the management software.

Device Strategy Modules

The logical I/O request issued by the program is passed through the filter determined by the FOSMs. It is converted to physical I/O commands by the device strategy modules (DSMs). Within a DSM, the basic operations of read or write, allocate or deallocate, and control are handled depending on the particular characteristics of that device. The DSM also handles synchronization of requests from two or more programs attempting to access the same device. The DSM generates and passes to the I/O control system a sequence of I/O commands to be executed which will satisfy the I/O request. It also manages space allocation for mass storage devices. DSMs were examined in detail in chapter 2.

A DSM may handle two different types of requests—read/write records and allocate/deallocate records—although the latter are commonly reserved for mass storage systems. A DSM must necessarily consider the physical characteristics of a device, so a system needs DSMs for almost every class of device.

Input/Output Control System

At the lowest level of the I/O subsystem are the modules that execute the I/O commands. Each device handler also controls error processing, device diagnostics, and other housekeeping chores. Included in the I/O control system is the interrupt manager and any specialized I/O routines. The most common device handlers and the interrupt manager were discussed in chapter 2.

5.2.1   Channels—A Pipeline to the Program

A channel represents a pipeline from the program to a specific file or device. When you request access to a file by opening it, you specify a channel number, which is used in subsequent I/O requests, to identify the file or device. The use of a channel number provides device independence. Data may be read from a card reader during the first execution of a program by assigning a channel number to the card reader. Subsequently, data may be read from a disk file by assigning this same channel number to the disk file. The following sequence of statements provides an example:

. . .

assign(2, $ttyin)

read(2) filename

. . .

assign(10, filename)

do i = 1,1000

read(10) data(i)

. . .

1000 enddo

Associated with each channel is a descriptor known as the channel control block (CCB). Each time a channel is assigned, a CCB will be created and initialized. The structure of the CCB is discussed in section 5.2.2. A channel is a logical name for a file or device. When a channel is assigned, it is linked to the file or device descriptor for which it is a pseudonym. The IOM routines use this link to determine how to execute each I/O request.

Global versus Local Channels

Channels may be assigned according to a global or local algorithm. In a global scheme, the OS defines a fixed number of channels. A program competes for channels as follows:

1. A program may request the system to allocate a free channel for it. If no channels are free, it is placed in a suspended state until a channel becomes free.

2. Alternatively, a program may guess a channel number and specify it in an I/O request (usually an OPEN command). If the channel is free, it is assigned to the program. If the channel is busy (allocated), the system will either suspend the program or return a status word indicating that the channel is busy. The former approach is not preferable because the program may succeed in locking up the entire system. The latter approach allows the program to make another guess if the first attempt fails.

In a global scheme, the number of channels must be fixed so that each user knows the range of channel numbers from which a choice may be made (case 2), or from which the user may be assigned a number (case 1). Only one CCB will be needed per channel since all CCBs are maintained in system space.

In a local scheme, each user has his or her own set of channel numbers and each channel has its own control block. These channels may be mapped onto a set of system channels (e.g., see DGC's FORTRAN IV implementation) or independently linked to the FCB in system space. The possible cases are:

1. Each user, when linking a program, declares a fixed contiguous sequence of channels from a set of integers (1, ..., N). Any channel number greater than N will be recognized as erroneous and treated appropriately.

2. Alternatively, a user can randomly specify a channel number from the range of positive integers. The CCBs are searched to determine if the channel already exists. If not, that channel is initialized for the user; otherwise, an error code can be returned. This scheme allows a much larger set of channels to exist in the system.

In the local scheme, a CCB will exist for each user channel. CCBs from several users may now be linked to the same device or file. This could create a potentially dangerous conflict of interest in the event that multiple I/O operations are allowed. The modules for I/O management will suffer a corresponding increase in complexity. The system described in the text assumes a fixed number of channels, specified at system generation time, which are allocated on a global basis.

Number of Channels

In either case, you always face a crucial problem: How many channels are enough? Too few channels will force processes to wait until a free channel is available. Too many channels may consume scarce primary storage through preallocated CCBs. Another problem concerns allocation of channels to the OS (see below). In most systems, the workload changes frequently; so do the requirements for the number of channels. Thus a good argument can be made for allowing users to declare the number of channels required when execution of a program is initiated. In many real-time systems the number of channels is known beforehand and a system can be generated containing exactly the requisite number of channels. In this case, a good argument is made for fixed global allocation of channels.

When the global scheme is implemented, the system administrator can tune the system for the appropriate number of channels by observing the number of processes waiting for a free channel. Such observation must be done under conditions of repeatable workloads. The number of channels is increased or decreased by setting the appropriate parameter when performing a system generation.

System versus User Channels

The OS, just like the user, requires channels for communicating data to and from the external world. The problem the designer faces is whether the OS should compete with the users for channels or whether it should have a set of dedicated channels. In part, the solution depends on the degree of modularity with which the OS will be implemented.

If the OS were to compete for channels with user processes, a system process waiting for a channel could lead to a deadlock situation. This could result if a user process held a channel and requested a system service. If the service module required a channel, it would block while waiting for a channel to become available. At the same time, a user process would block while waiting for the system service to be completed. Thus a deadlock situation could occur.

In a local scheme, such deadlocks would not occur, as the OS, when it execute its startup code, would declare the number of channels to perform its functions. The number of channels would have to be tuned over a period of time to ensure that scarce primary storage space is not wasted on CCBs that are never used.

If the OS is implemented in hierarchical fashion, high-level system processes could be viewed as "superusers." In this case, these system processes could legitimately compete with user processes for channels in the global scheme or declare the number of channels they require in a local scheme. Most OSs effect a compromise between dedicating a few channels to the most critical system processes and requiring the rest to compete for channels.

5.2.2   Channel Control Block

Each channel is described by a CCB which contains information about its current status. When a channel is assigned, the CCB is allocated from free memory space. When a channel is connected to a file or device, the CCB is initialized with the characteristics of the file or device. When the channel is released, the CCB is returned to the free memory pool. The definition of a CCB is provided in table 5.1.

5.3   BUFFER MANAGEMENT

The concept of a buffer implies a temporary holding cell to be used during I/O operations. Buffers are required to solve the impedance mismatch between the speed of the central processor and the speed of the I/O devices. Buffering is also used to solve the mismatch between the logical record size requested by the program and the physical record size supported by the device. The latter approach

Table 5.1 Description of a Channel Control Block

Entry	Usage
channel-attributes	A group of bits that define the status and access modes of the channel
channel-address	A pointer to a FCB or DCB to which the channel is connected
channel-outbuffer-rs	A pointer to the resource semaphore which allocates output buffers (if defined) for this channel
channel-inbuffer-rs	A pointer to the resource semaphore which allocates input buffers (if defined) for this channel
channel-sequential-rs	A pointer to the resource semaphore which controls sequential access to data in a multiprocessing environment
channel-save-address	A temporary location for storing the physical device address when the channel is opened for sequential input
channel-next-read-address	The physical device address for the next data record to be read from the file or device
channel-use-count	A count of the number of tasks using the channel in a multiprocessing environment

is also known as blocking of data. The use of buffering is a technique for improving the efficiency of utilization of the central processor.

5.3.1 How Buffering Works

Initially, when you specify buffering on an I/O channel, the system must set up a pool of buffers. When you request a READ function on device, a buffer is procured from the system and a physical record is read into it. Each time you issue a read request, data are extracted from the buffer according to the logical record specifications and delivered to your process's storage area. When the contents of the buffer are exhausted, it is returned to the system.

When you request a WRITE function, a buffer is procured from the system, and the logical record is moved from your process's storage area into the buffer. Subsequent WRITE requests add data to the buffer until it is completely full. At this point, the system writes the contents of the buffer to the file as a physical record and allocates another buffer to you.

When I/O operations on a channel are terminated, the system releases the buffers associated with the channel to free memory. For input, any data left in the buffer can be simply ignored since you never requested them. On output, since buffering is transparent to you, the system must "flush" the buffers. That is, it must ensure that their contents are properly written to the file or device before the channel can be closed. The reason for this is that you, when you issue a WRITE request, expect the data to be available.

5.3.2   Buffer Allocation Schemes

Various buffering techniques have been developed for supporting I/O management. Three common methods used to provide buffering services are the buffer pool, circular buffering, and ping-pong buffering.

Buffer Pools

In a buffer pool, a set of buffers is allocated from free memory space. The size of each buffer is equivalent to the physical record size. Associated with each buffer is a control block containing status information and pointers. The control blocks are maintained in a linked list. When a buffer is allocated, the buffer represented by the first free control block is assigned to the user. Linked lists may be maintained by several different algorithms. You should consult Knuth's Fundamental Algorithms [knut69] for descriptions of the basic list maintenance algorithms.

Buffer pools have several advantages over the other two allocation schemes. First, the number of buffers is relatively unlimited. Buffers may be added or subtracted from the pool using dynamic requests. Second, buffers may be allocated to both input and output from the same pool. As an alternative, separate pools may be established. This, of course, presumes that the physical record size is the same for both input and output records. Finally, buffers may be allocated from the pool in either a local or global fashion. Under global management, a common pool is established for all user channels opened by a specific program. Buffers are allocated to each channel as needed to satisfy an I/O request. Under local management, each process sets aside sufficient space to accommodate its buffer pool.

Circular Buffering

In circular buffering, buffer space equivalent to a multiple of several physical records is allocated in free memory. Two pointers are required to track the allocation of buffers, IN and OUT. Two other pointers, START and END, respectively, contain the initial and final addresses of the buffer. A separate buffer must be established for output as well as input.

The pointers are initialized such that START = IN = OUT. As data are received from the device, the IN pointer is incremented. When the program requests data from the buffer, the OUT pointer is incremented. Normally, the

OUT pointer will track (i.e., follow) the IN pointer around the buffer (see figure 5.1). When the IN pointer reaches END, it is reset to START, allowing subsequent data to wrap around the end of the buffer. Similarly, when OUT reaches END, it is reset to START and also wraps around the end of the buffer. The system must observe two restrictions in this scheme. First, if IN > OUT, then OUT cannot exceed IN − 1. Second, if OUT > IN, then IN cannot exceed OUT − 1. If either of these conditions were allowed to occur, the user would by trying to read data not yet gathered from the device.

Ping-Pong Buffering

Ping-pong buffering represents one of the simplest schemes for managing buffers. It is relatively efficient for I/O systems with a low frequency of activity. Generally, two buffers are allocated for input or output. While one buffer is being filled or emptied by the system, the user is simultaneously accessing the other buffer. When the user has filled or emptied a buffer, the system automatically switches him or her to the other buffer. In effect, user requests "ping-pong" back and forth between the two buffers. Because only two buffers are used, the system must be able to fill or drain the buffer not in use faster than the user finishes with the other buffer. Otherwise, the user might be delayed in performing I/O operations while the system fills or empties a buffer.

5.3.3 Buffer Management Data Structures

The buffer manager requires two data structures to control the allocation of buffers to user processes. These are the Buffer Control Block and the Buffer Manager Control Block.

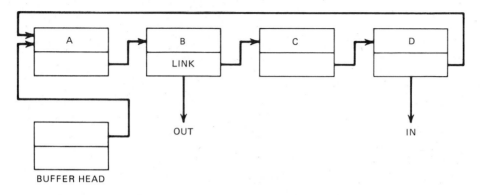

Figure 5.1 Circular buffering illustration.

The Buffer Control Block

Each buffer allocated to an I/O channel has an associated Buffer Control Block (BCB). The structure of the BCB is shown in table 5.2. If n buffers are to be allocated to a channel, space for n control blocks is allocated contiguous to the buffer manager control block.

In the system described herein, up to four buffers can be assigned for either input or output functions on the channel. This limit is artificial but appears to work well in practice—even under a moderate level of multitasking. Of course, the number of buffers to be assigned depends strongly on the size of the buffer, the frequency of I/O operations, and the number of tasks concurrently accessing a particular channel. For a detailed analysis of how to determine the number of buffers, the reader should consult Everling [ever75].

A buffer is allocated in multiples of one or two memory blocks (again, an arbitrary limitation). The logical buffer size, as specified by the user, may be less than the physical size. This information is stored in the BUFFER-DATA-SIZE entry.

The BUFFER-PAGE represents the physical memory page on which the buffer was allocated. The BUFFER-LINK entry is required for these reasons:

1. The number of real memory pages usually exceeds the number of virtual memory pages any program, including the OS, can see at once.

2. The OS can only view a limited number of buffers mapped into its address space. BUFFER-LINK provides a pointer to a buffer mapped into the OS's address space.

3. Since only limited space is available for addressing current buffers, BUFFER-PAGE is used to select a buffer to be mapped into the OS address space.

When a buffer is mapped out of system address space, it is not lost. Rather, it is merely inaccessible to the OS. By swapping buffers in and out of system space

Table 5.2 Description of Buffer Control Block

Mnemonic	Usage
buffer-link	A link to the buffer
buffer-data-size	Logical data size of the buffer
buffer-page	Index of the real memory page that contains the buffer
buffer-status	Information regarding the status of the buffer
buffer-data-address	The current data address in the file associated with this buffer

as necessary, the designer avoids fancy tricks needed to access outside the normal address limits.

Last but not least, it is often important to retain on the device a "memory" of where the data came from. BUFFER-DATA-ADDRESS is used only for mass storage devices. It provides a convenient entry for tracing an error location. The BCB is displayed in figure 5.2.

The Buffer Manager Control Block

A buffer manager is created for the input and/or output function on a channel. Associated with the buffer manager is the Buffer Manager Control Block (BMCB), which is shown in table 5.3. The BMCB contains two resource semaphores, BUFFER-RS and BUFFER-IO-RS. BUFFER-RS monitors the allocation of buffers to user processes that access the channel. BUFFER-IO-RS monitors the allocation of buffers to the device handler for emptying or filling the buffer. Buffers circulate between these two semaphores during normal operations.

The buffer manager needs to know the number of buffers assigned to it. This

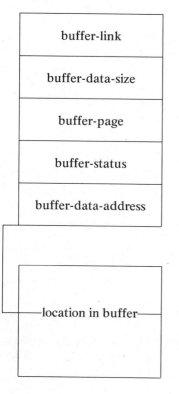

Figure 5.2   Structure of the buffer control block.

Table 5.3   Description of the Buffer Manager Control Block

Mnemonic	Usage
buffer-io-rs	Address of the resource semaphore for controlling buffer allocation to the device handler
buffer-rs	Address of the resource semaphore controlling allocation of buffers to the IOM
buffer-io-map	The IO-MAP slot allocated to buffers for I/O operations
buffer-current	Index of the current buffer at the head of the AVAIL queue
buffer-count	Number of buffers assigned to this manager
buffer-physical-size	Physical size of the buffer
buffer-index	Index of the current data word in the buffer

count is maintained in the BUFFER-COUNT entry. One way to check if a buffer is not lost is to verify that

QCOUNT[RS-AVAIL-Q[BUFFER-RS]] + QCOUNT[RS-AVAIL-Q[BUFFER-IO-RS]]

is equal to BUFFER-COUNT. If not, a buffer has been misplaced. It can be easily recoverd by checking the entries on the AVAIL queues against the BCB addresses.

Only one buffer is processed by the buffer manager at any time when responding to user requests. The address of the buffer's BCB is maintained in BUFFER-CURRENT. A pointer to the current data word in the buffer is maintained in BUFFER-INDEX. This pointer is updated by the size of the user's request, REQUEST-SIZE[P], whenever a read or write operation is executed.

5.3.4   Management of Buffering Operations

The OS manages buffering of I/O operations in response to user requests. To do so, two resource semaphores are maintained by the system which effect communication between the IOM routines and the buffer manager. These are BUFFER-RS and BUFFER-IO-RS, which support the following functions:

BUFFER-RS   Controls the allocation of buffers at the IOM interface with the user process

BUFFER-IO-RS   Controls allocation of buffers at the buffer manager interface with the device handler

The routine for effecting the actual filling or draining of a buffer, BUFFER-IO-PROCESS, is the same for input or output. However, the manner in which buffers flow between the two resource semaphores differs. These differences between input and output operations are discussed in the following paragraphs.

Input Buffering

On input, all buffers are initially queued to BUFFER-IO-RS. When the buffering process is initiated, it requests a buffer from this resource, fills the buffer
with data by executing a "read device" request, and releases the buffer to
BUFFER-RS. It continues to fill buffers in this manner until it is blocked on the
resource semaphore due to the unavailability of a buffer. When the user issues a
READ request, data are extracted from the first buffer linked to BUFFER-RS.
When the buffer is empty, the buffer is released to BUFFER-IO-RS by the IOM
for refilling. This sequence of events is shown in figure 5.3.

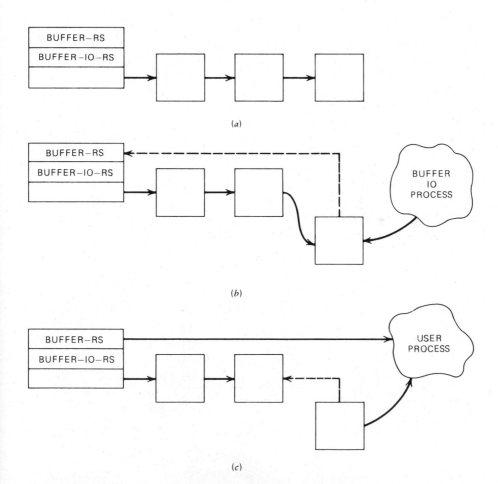

Figure 5.3   Input buffer management. (a) Initial buffer setup; (b) System fills buffer and
releases; (c) User empties buffer and releases for refilling.

Output Buffering

On ouput, all buffers are initially enqueued to BUFFER-RS. When the buffering process is initiated, it blocks on BUFFER-IO-RS, which has no enqueued buffers. The user executes one or more WRITE requests which fill the buffer. The buffer is released by the IOM to BUFFER-IO-RS. The buffering process, sensing the presence of a full buffer, executes a "write device" operation to empty the buffer. The buffer is then returned to BUFFER-RS to await refilling. This sequence of events is shown in figure 5.4.

Independent Processing

In this scheme, separate copies of the buffering process exist for input and output operations. Thus there is no conflict between operations at the user interface. By circulating buffers between resource semaphores, it shields the user

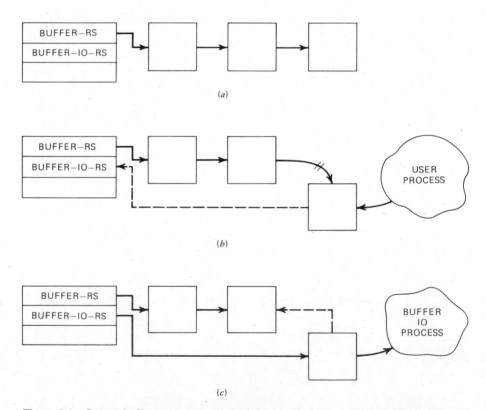

Figure 5.4   Output buffer management. (a) Initial buffer setup. (b) User fills buffer and releases it. (c) Buffer is emptied and released for refilling.

process from the speed of the I/O device. It also guarantees the user process either a continual supply of data on input or a continual repository for output. This state is assured in a priority-based system by the fact that the buffering process is assigned a higher priority than any associated user processes.

5.3.5 The General Buffer Process

The structure of the general buffer process is shown in module 5.3.1. This code skeleton applies equally well to input or output operation. The buffering process can be activated in one of the following ways:

1. If automatic buffering is specified when the file is created or the device configured, whenever a user opens a channel to the file or device, buffer processes will be initiated for input, output, or both.

2. The user may activate buffering on a channel at any time after it has been opened to a file or device by executing the BUFFER-CHANNEL request.

The buffering process, for either input or output, continues to execute until the channel is closed by the user. The process may block on a resource semaphore because no buffer is available on which it may operate.

In making a pass through its instruction sequence, the process must first retrieve the address of its BMCB. It requests a buffer from BUFFER-IO-RS with which it will execute the appropriate I/O function. If no buffers are available, the process blocks on the resource semaphore. Parameters in the BCB and the BMCB are used to set up the actual device I/O operation. The process then executes the appropriate I/O function to fill or empty the buffer. Since the routine is merely an OS module, it is called directly from the buffering process. Upon return, it sets the status of the operation, updates the file address, and releases the buffer for processing by the user. It then repeats the sequence of instructions again.

5.3.6 Allocating a Buffer

A buffer is allocated when the program executes a READ or WRITE request or one of the buffer management requests. If no buffers are available, the process is blocked on the wait queue of the associated resource semaphore. When a buffer appears on the available queue, the process is reactivated. This fact may lead to a seeming contradiction unless one remembers that the allocation routine is called by both the ENTER-INTO-QUEUE and the REMOVE-FROM-QUEUE functions (see section 7.9).

The buffer allocator (module 5.3.2) determines if a buffer indeed is available. If not, the routine exits immediately; this suffices to handle the

MODULE 5.3.1

```
process buffer-io-process
      buffer-manager[p] → bmcb-address
      buffer-io-rs[bmcb-address] → io-rs-address
      request(io-rs-address) → request-buffer-address[p]
      request-buffer-address[p] → buffer-address
      buffer-page[buffer-address] → page-identifier
      extract io-map from request-data-address[p]
      request-map[p] → buffer-map
      page-select(buffer-map, io-map, page-identifier)
      buffer-physical-size[bmcb-address] → request-size[p]
      clear buffer-status[buffer-address]
      call-os-function(io-function[p]) → buffer-data-size[buffer-address]
      if buffer-data-size[buffer-address] not equal to zero
            then
            buffer-data-size[buffer-address]
                                               → buffer-status[buffer-address]
            clear buffer-data-size[buffer-address]
      endif
      request-file-address[p] → buffer-data-address[buffer-address]
      release(buffer-rs[bmcb-addr], buffer-address)
      repeat
endprocess
```

REMOVE-FROM-QUEUE routine. If buffers (at least one) are available, the procedure selects a process to be activated. When activating the process, if there is no current buffer, a new buffer is allocated and the index into the buffer is set to zero. Otherwise, the current index into the buffer is used to satisfy the I/O function.

The I/O function code is used as an index to determine which I/O module to invoke. These routines are discussed in the next section. If a user tries to perform an OPEN function on a channel that is already open, an error code is returned. Normally, a program cannot get this deep into the system without determining the CCB address. Therefore, the process must have already opened the channel

MODULE 5.3.2

```
procedure buffer-allocator(rs-address)
      while true
            do
            rs-available-queue[rs-address] → available-address
            rs-wait-queue[rs-address] → wait-address
```

```
            if queue-count[available-address] not equal to zero
                then
                if queue-count[wait-address] not equal to zero
                    then
                    if buffer-current[rs-address] not equal to zero
                        then
                        queue-start[available-address]
                                        → buffer-current[rs-address]
                        clear buffer-index[rs-address]
                    endif
                    buffer-index[rs-address] → data-address
                    buffer-current[rs-address] → buffer-address
                    queue-start[wait-address] → pcb-address
                    page-select(0, empty-page,
                                        buffer-page[buffer-address])
                    case request-opcode[pcb-address] of
                        read: buffer-read-record( )
                            exitcase
                        write: buffer-write-record( )
                            exitcase
                        next-buf: next-buffer( )
                                exitcase
                        flush-buf: flush-buffer( )
                                exitcase
                        open: activate-waiter(er-function)
                    endcase
                    else
                        exitdo
                endif
                else
                    exitdo
            endif
        enddo
endproc
```

5.3.7   Executing an I/O Function under Buffer Management

A process has issued an I/O request with a channel under buffer management. How does the system execute the I/O request? The type of request is identified by the I/O function code in the PCB. Each type of I/O function has an associated routine to perform that function. In addition, the system provides two buffer management functions that allow a process to control the sequencing of I/O functions.

Reading from a Buffer

The procedure for reading a record from a buffer is depicted in module 5.3.3. This procedure transfers data from system space to user space in accordance with a read request. If a buffer is exhausted, it will be released to the I/O resource semaphore for refilling. Note that if a buffer does not contain the required data, the procedure exits to the allocation routine, which assigns the next available buffer.

The amount of data remaining in the buffer is calculated by subtracting BUFFER-INDEX from BUFFER-DATA-SIZE (the logical data size of the buffer). If the balance is less than or equal to zero, the buffer status is returned to the process as an error code. The condition will normally occur, for example, when an end-of-file has been detected or an error occurs in filling the buffer. Next, if the record type of the request is fixed length, the balance in the buffer is compared to the requested record size. If the remaining data are insufficient to satisfy the request, the buffer is released and the procedure exits (to the allocator for the next buffer). DELTA is initialized to the requested record size for subsequent updating of buffer parameters.

FIND-RECORD-SIZE is invoked to determine the record size. For a fixed-length record, DELTA has already been set. The problem arises when you expect a string of characters (of unknown length) terminated by a null byte. This routine steps through the buffer looking for a null byte and sets DELTA accordingly. If DELTA equals zero, the buffer is released and the procedure exits. If DELTA is not zero and less than the balance (i.e., you have not run off the end of the buffer), the data record is copied to the process's space. The number of words transferred is returned as the value of the event. This operation is important, as for fixed-length records, it confirmes the size of the record, and for variable-length records, it informs the process of the exact length of the record (it may be needed for further processing).

The buffer index, which is a pointer to the current data element in the record, is updated by DELTA (e.g., the record length). If the buffer is exhausted, it is released to the I/O resource semaphore. Finally, the process is reactivated with the data in hand.

MODULE 5.3.3

```
procedure buffer-read-record
     buffer-data-size[buffer-address] − buffer-index[buffer-address]
                                                          → balance
        if balance less than or equal to zero
            then
            buffer-status[buffer-address] → delta
```

```
            clear buffer-status[buffer-address]
            release-input-buffer( )
            activate-waiter(delta)
            exitproc
      endif
      if request-record-type[pcb-address] equals fixed-record-type
            then
            if balance less than request-size[pcb-address]
                  then
                  release-input-buffer( )
                  exitproc
            endif
            else
                  if balance greater than or equal to
                                            request-size[pcb-address]
                        then
                              request-size[pcb-address] → delta
                        else
                              balance → delta
                  endif
                  request-record-type[pcb-address] → record-type
                  find-record-size(data-address, record-type, delta) → delta
                  if delta less than balance
                        then
                              if delta equals zero
                                  then
                                    release-input-buffer( )
                                    exitproc
                              endif
                  endif
                  request-data-address[pcb-address] → user-data-address
                  request-map[pcb-address] → user-map
                  move-to-user-space(user-map, data-address,
                                            user-data-address, delta)
                  buffer-data-address[buffer-address] +
                        buffer-index[rs-address] → event-data[pcb-address]
                  increment buffer-index[rs-address] by delta
                  if buffer-index[rs-address] equals
                                      buffer-data-size [buffer-address]
                        then
                              release-input-buffer( )
                  endif
            endif
            activate-waiter(delta)
endproc
```

Writing a Record to a Buffer

The procedure for writing a record to a buffer is depicted in module 5.3.4. Once a buffer has been completely filled, it is released to the I/O resource semaphore to be written to the file. The status of the buffer is checked and if it is negative, an error has occurred in writing out the previous contents of the buffer. This indicates an end-of-file condition (on a contiguous file) or an I/O error at the device handler level. The error condition is returned to the process.

The amount of space remaining in the buffer is calculated. If the record size is greater than the remaining space, the buffer is released and the procedure ex-

MODULE 5.3.4

```
procedure buffer-write-record
     buffer-status[rs-address] → delta
     if delta less than zero
          then
          buffer-physical-size[rs-address] →
                                        buffer-data-size[buffer-address]
          clear buffer-status[rs-address]
          activate-waiter(delta)
          exitproc
     endif
     buffer-index[rs-address] + request-size[pcb-address]
                                                  → location-in-buffer
     if location-in-buffer greater than or equal to
                                buffer-data-size [buffer-address]
          then
               pad-and-release-buffer( )
          exitproc
     endif
     request-map[pcb-address] → user-map
     request-data-address[pcb-address] → user-data-address
     move-from-user-space(user-map, user-data-address,
               data-address, request size[pcb-address])
     increment buffer-index[rs-address] by request-size[pcb-address]
     buffer-data-size[buffer-address] − buffer-index[rs-address] → delta
     if delta equals zero
          then
          pad-and-release-buffer( )
     endif
     activate-waiter(delta)
endproc
```

its. Upon return to the allocator, a new buffer will be allocated to satisfy the request. Otherwise, the record is copied from user space into the buffer. The buffer index is updated to reflect the number of words transferred from the process. If the buffer space is exhausted, it is released to the I/O resource semaphore. In any event, the process is then reactivated.

Obtaining the Next Buffer

An OS provides buffer management for I/O requests in order to isolate a process from the physical functions of the device. Nevertheless, the user may possess a priori knowledge about the input data, and certainly does so about the data. This knowledge may permit the user to exercise a certain amount of control over I/O operations. Therefore, it is incumbent upon the buffer manager to allow a process to skip the remaining contents of a buffer if it has no use for it.

On input, the buffer manager allows a process to skip to the next buffer in the input sequence via the NEXT-BUFFER command. The format of this command is

SYSTEM(NEXT-BUFFER, EVENT-NR, CHANNEL)

where   EVENT-NR   is used to signal when the next buffer is available for reading

CHANNEL   is the number of a channel which has been opened for buffered input

The procedure for executing the next buffer command is depicted in module 5.3.5. If the status of the buffer is negative, the process is activated immediately

MODULE 5.3.5

```
procedure next-buffer
    if buffer-status[buffer-address] not equal to zero
        then
            clear buffer-data-size[buffer-address]
            activate-waiter(buffer-status[buffer-address])
        else
            if buffer-index[rs-address] not equal to zero
                then
                release-input-buffer( )
            endif
            activate-waiter(1)
    endif
endproc
```

and notified of an error condition. Otherwise, the buffer is released to be re-
filled. Note that the buffer is not released if it is empty. An empty buffer results,
of course, from an end-of-file or device error condition which was captured
above. After the buffer is released, the process is reactivated.

Flushing a Buffer

The corresponding operation, on the output side, is to allow a process to force
out a partially filled buffer. When the buffer is flushed, the remaining data
space is filled with zeros (as the buffer is not cleared when it is written out), indicating null values. The format of the command is

> SYSTEM(FLUSH-BUFFER, EVENT-NR, CHANNEL)

where   EVENT-NR   is used to signal when the buffer has been padded
    and released

              CHANNEL   is the number of a channel that has been opened
    for buffered output

The procedure for flushing a buffer is depicted in module 5.3.6. A buffer is
flushed only if it is not empty. Excess space is padded with zeros before the buffer is released to the I/O resource semaphore. Your process is reactivated with a
successful event status.

MODULE 5.3.6

```
procedure flush-buffer
    if buffer-index[rs-address] not equal to zero
        then
                pad-and-release-buffer( )
    endif
    activate-waiter(1)
endproc
```

5.3.8 Buffer Management Utilities

Three utility modules support the implementation of the buffer manager. They
are described in the following paragraphs.

Padding and Releasing a Buffer

When a process has filled an output buffer, it is released to BUFFER-IO-RS for
eventual writing to the device. A buffer is determined to be filled when (1) you

flush the buffer, and (2) the current request size plus the buffer index would exceed the physical size of the buffer.

In either event, the remaining space beyond BUFFER-INDEX in the buffer is padded with zeros. This is a precautionary measure, as buffers are usually not cleared when allocated from BUFFER-RS (although they could be). At this point, the buffer is removed from the AVAILABLE queue and released to BUFFER-IO-RS. The process that waited for the write or flush operation to complete is reactivated. The procedure for padding and releasing a buffer is depicted in module 5.3.7.

MODULE 5.3.7

```
procedure pad-and-release-buffer
    buffer-physical-size[rs-address] − buffer-index[rs-address] → size
    clear memory(data-address) for size words
    remove-from-queue(rs-available-queue[rs-address])
    release(buffer-io-rs[rs-address], buffer-address)
    clear buffer-current[rs-address]
endproc
```

Releasing an Input Buffer

Unlike an output buffer, when an input buffer is exhausted, it can just be thrown away. That is, it is released to BUFFER-IO-RS for refilling. An input buffer is exhausted when the current request size plus the buffer index would exceed the logical data address in the buffer, you request the next buffer, or you close the channel.

The procedure for releasing an input buffer is depicted in module 5.3.8. Note that the status of the buffer is checked immediately for an error. If no error has occurred, the buffer is removed from the AVAILABLE queue and released to BUFFER-IO-RS. The current buffer index in the resource semaphore is cleared. If an error occurred, the buffer will not be released.

The difference in treatment of errors is significant. As you have not issued a read request, an error while reading must wait for treatment until you actually request the data. The error can be handled immediately once you are notified of its existence. On output, as the physical write operation to the device may be delayed until well after the logical write operation occurred, you are notified much later of its occurrence. Error handling of a write error can be significantly more difficult. The onus of correction resides with you.

Activating a Waiting Process

Normally, a process will block on an event number while waiting for an I/O operation to complete. Once the operation is done, the status is reported (whether failure or success) to the process, which is removed from the WAIT queue and reactivated. The procedure for activating a waiting process is depicted in module 5.3.9.

For your protection, your process is not removed from the WAIT queue until the operation is complete. Suppose that the current buffer cannot accommodate the request. Then the next buffer must be allocated from the AVAILABLE queue (and, in fact, none may be available). If your process was removed from the WAIT queue at the same time the buffer was allocated, it could receive no data or just garbage. Furthermore, while allocating another buffer, the phasing of records to processes may be thrown out of sequence in a multiprocess environment. And, of course, your process is supposed to be oblivious to the operations of the buffer manager.

MODULE 5.3.8

```
procedure release-input-buffer
     if buffer-status[buffer-address] equals zero
         then
                 remove-from-queue(rs-available-queue[rs-address])
                 release(buffer-io-rs[rs-address], buffer-address)
                 clear buffer-current[rs-address]
         else
                 clear buffer-data-size[buffer-address]
                 clear buffer-index[rs-address]
     endif
endproc
```

MODULE 5.3.9

```
procedure activate-waiter(status)
     status → event-status[pcb-address]
     remove-from-queue(rs-wait-queue[rs-address])
     activate(pcb-address)
endproc
```

5.3.9 Defining a Resource Semaphore for Buffering

Buffering on a channel is handled by a pair of resource semaphores—one for input and one for output. The general principles of resource management are described in section 7.10. The procedure for defining a buffering resource, which has some unique features, is depicted in module 5.3.10. Setting up a buffering semaphore is a dynamic procedure that minimizes the drain on memory resources until space for buffers is actually required.

The first step in defining a buffer resource semaphore is to validate the number of buffers for the I/O mode. If the number of buffers is zero, no buffering is required and the appropriate buffer attribute bit is cleared.

The second step is to create a buffering process. A PCB allocated and initialized with the address of BUFFER-IO-PROCESS. The space required for the semaphore and control blocks is calculated and allocated from the free memory pool. Information regarding the buffer space, the channel, and the file is stored in the PCB. A buffer page and an IO-MAP slot are requested from the system and initialized.

The third step sets up the address of the actual I/O routine that reads or writes the device. Depending on whether a file or device is being buffered, the I/O routine switch list yields the appropriate address. The resource semaphore is initialized in the BCB.

The next step is to allocate the buffers themselves. Note that for a serial file, space is allocated only for the data file. The buffer allocation process operates as follows:

Store address of BUFFER-PAGE in control block

Compute physical buffer size

Initialize buffer status

On input, link the buffers to the allocator associated with the device handler

On output, link the buffers to the allocator associated with the IOM

If more buffers are to be set up, step to the next control block and allocate another page

Repeat until all buffers are initialized

Note that the pages allocated are in the buffer process space, not in your space. Remember that each process can have a full complement of pages and it is up to the OS to manage them within the allowed memory limits. The final step consists of initializing the information relative to the current buffer and I/O operation.

MODULE 5.3.10

```
procedure define-buffer-rs(number-of-buffers, inout-flag)
    if number-of-buffers equals zero
        then
        if inout-flag greater than or equal to zero
            then
            clear inbuffer-flag of channel-attributes[ccb-address]
            else
            clear outbuffer-flag of channel-attributes[ccb-address]
        endif
    endif
    request(pcb-rs) → buffer-pcb-address
```

initialize-process(buffer-pcb-address, buffer-io-process,
                                    system-io-priority, 0)
buffer-rs-size + (number-of-buffers * buffer-cb-size) → buffer-size
request(memory-rs, buffer-size) → bcmb-address
bcmb-address → parent[buffer-pcb-address]
buffer-size → request-size[buffer-pcb-address]
buffer-size → buffer-physical-size[bcmb-address]
ccb-address → request-channel-address[buffer-pcb-address]
fcb-address → request-fcb-address[buffer-pcb-address]
request(page-rs) → buffer-page
request(io-map-rs, buffer-page) → buffer-io-map[bcmb-address]
extract io-map-number from buffer-iomap[bmcb-address] →
                                    request-map[buffer-pcb-address]
extract from buffer-iomap[bcmb-address] →
                                    request-data-address[buffer-pcb-address]
if device-channel-flag of channel-attributes[ccb-address]
                                                    not equal to zero
      then
      channel-address[ccb-address] → address-of-channel
      device-switch-address[address-of-channel] →
                                                    switch-address
      else
      address(file-switch) → switch-address
endif
if inout-flag less than zero
      then
      increment switch-address by address(file-or-device-read-next)
      bmcb-address → channel-inbuffer-rs[ccb-address]
      buffer-pcb-address → inbuffer-process
      else
      increment switch-address by address(file-or-device-write-next)
      bmcb-address → channel-outbuffer-rs[ccb-address]
      buffer-pcb-address → outbuffer-process
endif
memory(switch-address) → io-function[buffer-pcb-address]
buffer-address + buffer-rs-size → bcb-address
define-rs(buffer-rs[bmcb-address], de-queue-set, de-queue-set,
                                    buffer-io-allocator)
define-rs(buffer-io-rs[bmcb-address], de-queue-set, de-queue-set,
                                    one-allocator)
number-of-buffers → buffer-count[bmcb-address]
clear nbufs
while true
      do
      buffer-page → buffer-page[bcb-address]

```
                    if device-channel-flag of channel-attributes[ccb-address]
                                                          equals zero
                    then
                    if serial-flag of file-attributes[fcb-address] equals zero
                         then
                              buffer-physical-size[bmcb-address] − 2 →
                                                    buffer-data-size[bcb-address]
                         else
                              buffer-physical-size[bmcb-address] → buffer-
                                                    data-size[bcb-address]
                    endif
               endif
               clear buffer-status[bcb-address]
               if inout-flag less than zero
                    then
                    release(buffer-io-rs[bmcb-address], bcb-address)
                    else
                    release(buffer-rs[bmcb-address], bcb-address)
               endif
               if nbufs less than buffer-count[bmcb-address] − 1
                    then
                    increment nbufs
                    increment bcb-address by buffer-cb-size
                    request(page-rs) → buffer-page
               endif
          enddo
          clear buffer-current[bmcb-address]
          clear buffer-index[bmcb-address]
     endproc
```

5.4 ACCESS METHODS

The IOM represents another level of functional abstraction between a process
and the system hardware. At this level, we distinguish between the logical and
the physical organization of data on mass storage and peripheral devices. The
physical organization of data is represented by one of the file organization
strategies described in section 6.2. The logical organization is represented by
the access methods surveyed in this section and described in detail in sections
5.5 through 5.7.

What is an access method? Basically, it is a collection of modules that define
a given logical view of data. The role of the access method is to further enhance
the independence of a process from the hardware. The access method modules,
in conjunction with the buffer manager, define the bulk of the IOM. A variety

of different access methods exist: random, sequential, and stream I/O are presented in this text. The amount and kind of information specified for an I/O service will depend on the access method. Each access method provides a different degree of sophistication.

5.4.1   Basic versus Queued Access Methods

A major differentiation in access methods consists of the basic versus the queued access method. A basic access method is just that: a bare-bones control mechanism that allows you to generate a direct operation on a device. In a basic access method, your process is required to provide all necessary services associated with blocking and buffering records, and with synchronizing access to the device. An example of a basic access method is the set of modules that implement the tape management functions described in section 2.5.

The queued access method converts each request for a logical record (via its logical address) to a physical record. In the process, the access method may have to block or unblock logical records from physical records. The queued access method may also provide buffering services for you on sequential requests. The queued access method supports synchronizing operations, error analysis, and error reporting. The access methods discussed in detail in sections 5.5 through 5.7 are representative of this class of access methods.

5.4.2   Sequential Access Method

Perhaps the simplest method of accessing a collection of records is in sequential order (see figure 5.5). When a file is opened, the current record number is set to zero. Every read request results in the fetch of the next record from the file, after which the record number is incremented by one. Given the current record number, you can move forward or backward in the file one record at a time. Some systems also allow you to skip forward or backward over a block of n records with one request. This feature should be familiar to you through the FORTRAN READ, REWIND, and BACKSPACE commands.

The sequential access method (SAM) is rooted in the historical predecessors to modern automatic data processing systems. The earliest data processing systems were card-oriented, and still later, magnetic tape–based systems. A clerk began at the start of a file, read each record until the appropriate one was located, and stored, retrieved, or updated data on that record. A key aspect of this approach was that individual records could not be detected visually. The process was time consuming and each new access had to begin anew at the start of the file.

The advent of magnetic tape systems improved the efficiency of data processing shops. All data records were placed in sorted sequence on a master tape. Another tape containing the update transaction in sorted sequence was also

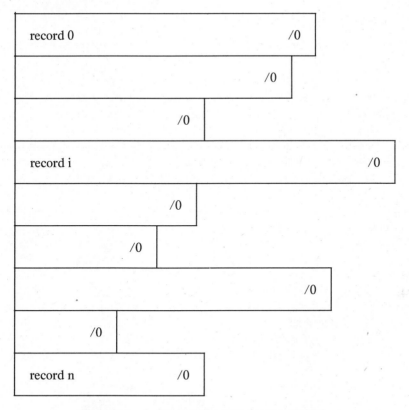

Figure 5.5   A sequential/stream access method.

prepared. A process read an update transaction, scanned the master tape until the matching record was found or the location where the record should be, and then updated or inserted the record while writing it to a new master tape.

SAM is quite practical when processing single transactions. It is easily understood because it imposes a minimum amount of effort on the user in formulating a retrieval request. It applies uniformly to a wide range of I/O devices: cards, printers, tapes, and mass storage disk drives (although these simulate the former devices). It is intended to satisfy all but the most specialized requirements for data processing and, in most circumstances, does so very efficiently. SAM minimizes both main storage requirements and CPU time requirements. It has its greatest utility in computer systems which are heavily employed for static records management.

A variant of the SAM is known as the stream access method because data are read in a stream. This method is used throughout UNIX [ritc74] to move data. Each record is assumed to consist of a string of characters terminated by a null byte. The length of each record may vary in the file. The address of the next record is always the current position in the file after the last read, write, or I/O pointer movement.

Relationship to File Organizations

In chapter 6 we examine methods for physically organizing files on mass storage devices. We shall examine the contiguous, serial, and segmented organizations. At this point we wish to determine how SAM relates to these types of file organization. Although it is not obvious now, the SAM can be used with each of these organizations.

A contiguous file consists of a set of consecutive disk sectors. Both sequential and stream access methods can be utilized with a contiguously organized file. Records are consecutively placed in the file. In this organization only, the system could allow records to cross sector boundaries.

Sequential access and serial organization are effectively the same method applied to the logical and physical storage regimes, respectively. Both are the simplest methods for storing and retrieving large amounts of data where the time to access the next record is important but time to process the entire file is not critical. This combination is most efficient because the logical and physical record sizes are known, the blocking factor is known, and most programs will move through the file in the forward direction only. The system can perform lookahead fetching of disk sectors in anticipation of process requests and thus minimize the time a process waits for the next record.

Sequential access can also be used with a segmented file organization, although this is the least efficient combination. Primarily, this results from the fact that every logical record must first be "looked up" in the segment pointer block in order to locate the segment data block. Consequently, there may be a delay in reading a segment data block if the blocking factor is small. In some cases, this may double the execution time for the program.

5.4.3   Indexed Sequential Access Method

Searching a sequential file can be a laborious process. Often, the collection of records has at least one field by which each record can be uniquely identified. This field is known as the record key. Rather than reading through all the records looking for the value of the key, we can build an index of keys and record addresses. In the index, keys are arranged in lexicographical order; that is, if key K[j] is greater than key K[i], record R[j] will appear after record R[i] in the file. Thus, we arrive at the indexed SAM.

The structure of an indexed sequential file is depicted in figure 5.6. Each entry in the index is composed of a key/address pair. The keys K[i] can be sorted in either ascending or descending sequence. Each address is the location of a record in the file. Records can be placed in the file in two ways. If for each K[j] > K[i], then ADDRESS[j] > ADDRESS[i], the file is called an indexed sequential file. If the addresses are randomly ordered, the file is called an indexed random file.

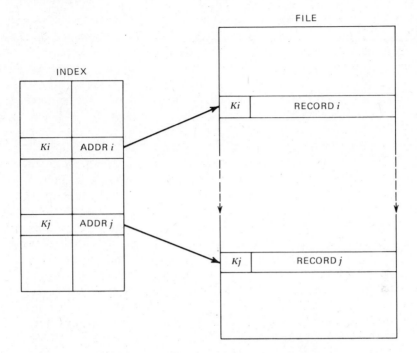

Figure 5.6   Indexed sequential access method.

The indexed sequential access method (ISAM) received a large measure of popularity (or notoriety) from early IBM System/360 implementations. Essential to the ISAM approach are four concepts: keys, key-to-address transformations, prime data areas, and overflow data areas. Each record in the file has a key by which it is uniquely identified. Records are stored in an area known as the prime data area. The determination of where in the prime data area to store a record is accomplished by the key-to-address transformation—an algorithm for locating a record given its key. In some systems, several keys map to the same address. This necessitates an overflow data area where additional records after the first are stored. A more detailed exposition of these principles can be found in [lefk69], [mart73], and [wied77].

ISAM can support both random and sequential processing—a fact that we will examine briefly below. It is advantageous in that it requires relatively little planning and analysis in advance of creating the file. For this reason, when indexed sequential organizations are used, many files are created in indexed random format, as we are not particularly concerned with the addresses of records but only their accessibility by key fields.

An ISAM file possesses two major disadvantages. First, the access method modules tend to be quite large and complex. The OS has to process both the key index and the prime data area where actual records are stored. Depending on the key-to-address transformation, an area whose subtlety should not be overlooked [lum71], additional data areas for handling overflow records will also require substantial management. Second, the performance of ISAM is moderate at best for individual record processing and deteriorates as the file naturally expands. This is due to the fact that the index must still be sequentially accessed and manipulated.

Three functions should be considered in deciding whether or not to implement an indexed SAM: file loading, sequential processing, and random processing. File loading is the process of initializing a file with a collection of records while creating the key indices. Two major problems may arise in loading a file. First, the initial collection of records may have such a wide distribution of keys that the file is only sparsely populated, thus resulting in a significant waste of space in the prime data area. Second, presenting records in their key sequence is essential. A random ordering would make it impossible to predict where records would be stored in the prime data area and, of course, require extensive manipulation of the key index. If records are stored out of sequence, subsequent file processing requests could produce baffling results.

You may wish to retrieve sequentially against an indexed file. The key index would be little used for an indexed sequential file, and an absolute necessity for an indexed random file. Performance would vary widely depending on how records were stored in the prime data area. Sequential processing may also include a restricted update capability limited to the modification of existing records in place. New records cannot be added, nor can the length of an existing record be changed, without a massive reshuffling of the key index and, possibly, the prime data area as well. Under sequential processing, file reorganization may be required to insert new records or modify existing ones. It is difficult to know when reorganization should take place, as it depends on the layout of the prime data area and how the key-to-address transformation is affected. The process of reorganization may be time consuming and may have to be accomplished at inopportune times.

The value of an indexed organization of data is most apparent when performing individual transactions in any order. Random retrieval is a powerful capability and may be all that is required. In fact, many systems will sacrifice performance in other functional areas so as to optimize retrieval efficiency. Deletion and update in place are equally easy to perform (as long as one does not update the key field). The most difficult operation to perform is random insertion. The major problem that plagues us is the reshuffling of the prime data area. Again, performance is dependent on whether records are deposited in the prime data area in a random or sequential fashion.

5.4.4 Random Access Method

A random access method (RAM) is one in which the addresses of the records in the file are arranged in a random fashion. It always implies a fixed record size (i.e., the logical record size is equivalent to some multiple of the physical record size) because the data are transferred directly to/from the user process data area. Moreover, the record address specified by the user process is used to calculate directly the location of the record in the file. RAM provides a user process with the greatest flexibility since it imposes no a priori knowledge about the structure of the data or their content upon the user process. Rather, interpretation of the data is explicitly left up to the user process.

Two implementations of the RAM have been supported by many OSs. For convenience, I will name these the general and restricted RAMs. For the general RAM, the logical record size is equivalent to a variable number of bytes. Here, the physical record size is the byte (or an even multiple of bytes). This implementation has been featured in systems that support byte-addressable mass storage devices (such as the Univac FH1732 drum). The restricted RAM commonly found in many minicomputer systems requires the physical record size to be equivalent to one disk sector.

The concept of random access is based on an address generation algorithm that computes the mass storage address from the record key (whether from only the record index or based on the contents of the record itself). This approach contrasts with SAM, wherein the location of the record is simply determined by the position of the key in relation to preceding and succeeding keys. In many mainframe systems, the address generation algorithm takes the form of a hashing algorithm [lum71].

Most minicomputer systems implement random access through a technique known as self-indexing or direct addressing. A self-indexing key is one where the key is the address on the mass storage device where the record is stored. Self-indexing is viable when:

1. One physical record is stored in each device storage location (sector).
2. The range of keys is similar to the range of device addresses.
3. Keys in the file are consecutive without clusters or gaps formed by the addition or deletion of keys.

To implement this technique, the keys are equivalenced to the addresses of file blocks. For the moment, let us assume that logical record size is equivalent to physical record size. Then each logical record (e.g., a file block) occupies one disk sector. The range of keys is limited by the number of disk sectors per mass storage device (e.g., an RL-01 has 10,220 disk sectors). Thus the keys are consecutively ordered from zero to 10,219. To retrieve any logical record in a file, we merely give its address, which is its block number in the file.

Random accessing implies that a user may issue a sequence of logical record keys which are randomly distributed. This approach allows the user considerable flexibility in both populating a file with data and retrieving data from that file. Figure 5.7 depicts an instance of random access.

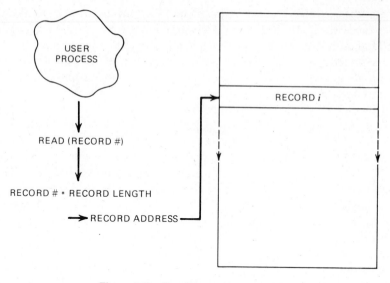

Figure 5.7 Random access method.

Relationship to File Organization

Again, let us jump ahead a bit and mention that there are three types of physical file organizations: contiguous, serial, and segmented (see chapter 6). How does random accessing relate to these types of file organization? Clearly, RAMs can be used efficiently with contiguously organized files since space for each file is a sequence of consecutively arranged disk sectors.

Random access is not normally used with serially organized files because the desired file block must be located by following the pointers from the first block in the file. This necessitates reading every block in the file up to and including the desired block, and may require that the entire file be inspected (on the average, one-half of the pointers must be inspected [wied77]). Moreover, each successive access must always begin anew at the start of the file.

Random access can be used with segmented files. Contrast this with the contiguous organization and you will see that it is a limited example of the address generation algorithm because the file block address is transformed into an explicit device sector address by lookup through the segment pointer blocks.

5.5 THE INPUT/OUTPUT MANAGER INTERFACE

A major objective for the IOM is to ensure device independence. When a process issues an I/O request, that request should be executed independently of the target peripheral. One way to ensure treatment is to mask the actual device operations by localizing them in the device handler (or device strategy modules). With this approach, the system treats each device as a psuedofile that can be manipulated as are other user files. Of course, certain device characteristics impose some restrictions on file operations for a given device. Thus the line printer, referenced as psuedofile "lpt0", can be opened only for output.

The IOM, consisting of the access methods, buffer manager, and channel management routines, implements this uniform interface to files and devices. The IOM's job is to transfer data records between user processes and data files. Prior to effecting the data transfer, appropriate tables must be prepared for the access method routines. This section discusses the set of modules that provide the first-level interface between the user process and the IOM.

5.5.1 Executing an I/O Request

To execute an I/O operation, you issue a system service request with an I/O function as the primary argument. The system service request is processed by the user interface modules as described in section 7.3. Once the requested function has been validated and the arguments set up on the user stack, an IOM module is called to perform the function.

Each I/O request has an associated event number and channel number. The IOM interface must do several things in preparing for I/O function execution:

1. Validate the channel number supplied by the user process and locate the channel control block.
2. Determine whether direct or buffered I/O will be used to transfer the data.
3. Validate the parameters for the I/O request in relation to the current status of the channel.
4. Determine whether the request refers to a file or device; assign the address of the appropriate execution routine.
5. Create and initialize the system subprocess that will execute the request.

These functions of the IOM are discussed in the following sections, with the exception of system subprocess creation. As noted in section 7.5, each system service request having an event number has a system subprocess created to execute that event. A subprocess is created to ensure that the calling process is not blocked if the request cannot be satisfied immediately (as, for example, when the specified disk sectors are blocked by another process). The mechanics for creating the subprocess are explained in chapter 3. Initialization of the subprocess parameters is performed by the IOM routines.

5.5.2   The I/O Request Switch Table

An essential database required by the IOM is the I/O request switch table. This table contains the addresses of the processing routines for each type of I/O request. This table is initialized during system generation when the OS modules are linked together to form an executable program. The principle of relocatability requires independent modules. Thus the IOM cannot have a priori knowledge of where the modules reside in physical memory.

The structure is depicted in figure 5.8. There is one entry for each valid I/O request that may be issued by the calling process. Entries for the OPEN and

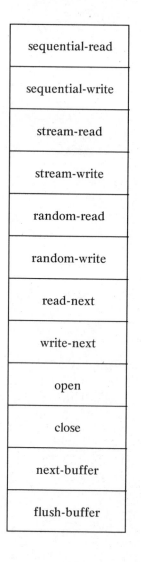

Figure 5.8   Structure of the I/O request switch table.

CLOSE functions are included in the table. Although these functions are discussed in chapter 6 under file management, they actually straddle the boundary between I/O and file management, as they establish the link between a process and a file. Similarly, you are able to directly control two buffering functions using a priori knowledge about your data, although general management of buffers operates transparently.

5.5.3   Initial I/O Function Processing

A certain amount of preprocessing is required prior to the execution of an I/O request. This activity has certain benefits:

1. Erroneous arguments can be detected and rejected without a significant investment in processing the request. This reduces system overhead and eliminates the need for "backing out" of request execution when an error is discovered.
2. By splitting the I/O request processing into setup and execution phases, the system can better stage I/O processing amont multiple users. This contributes to the enhancement of the degree of multiprocessing.

Each function listed in the switch table has an associated preprocessing routine which is explained in the following sections.

Reading/Writing a Sequential Record

The routines for preprocessing the sequential read/write functions are depicted in modules 5.5.1 and 5.5.2, respectively. The address of the routine to execute the function is stored in the REQUEST-OPCODE entry of the subprocess control block. When the subprocess executes the function, the module address is readily available. For sequential I/O, the length of the record is specified by the caller. The user map, which specifies the memory map where the process resides, is determined by the system. The data address is retrieved from the

MODULE 5.5.1

```
procedure p-read-sequential
     address(sequential-read) → request-opcode[p]
     fixed-record-type → request-record-type[p]
     get-address-map-size( )
     get-channel-address(read-protect-flag) → ccb-address
     p-setup-ok( )
endproc
```

```
procedure p-write-sequential
    address(sequential-write) → request-opcode[n]
    fixed-record-type → request-record-type[n]
    get-address-map-size( )
    get-channel-address(write-protect-address) → ccb-address
    p-setup-ok( )
endproc
```

stack and stored in the PCB. The address of the CCB is determined and protection bits are checked for the file. Any errors due to invalid file status will cause the I/O request to be rejected. If preprocessing is successful, the subprocess is scheduled for execution by placing it on the READY queue.

Reading or Writing a Stream

The routines for preprocessing the stream read/write functions are depicted in modules 5.5.3 and 5.5.4, respectively. The sequence of operations is similar to that of the routines described above. The essential difference occurs in the requirement to size the input or output record. A stream record is a variable-length sequence of characters terminated by a null byte. On input, the user is allowed to specify the maximum number of characters to be read. If no maximum is specified (SIZE less than zero), the default stream record size is assigned for the request. On output, the number of characters in the stream record (including the null character) is counted and assigned to the data transfer size.

Two problems are noted here which the designer should address in his or her design. First, on input, what is the result if no maximum is specified and no default is assigned? Clearly, data will be transferred until a null character is detected. Given no a priori knowledge about the data, it is possible for input data to exceed the size of the allocated buffer and overflow other variables and portions of the program. Second, on output, if you forget to terminate a stream with a null character, the system continues to fetch characters until a null character is detected. This may result in fetching of garbage from the user space which again may exceed the available buffer space.

Preprocessing Buffer Requests

These routines, depicted in modules 5.5.5 and 5.5.6, preprocess the functions for flushing and getting the next buffer. The address of the execution routine is stored in the operation code. These functions do not require size or address in-

MODULE 5.5.3

```
procedure p-read-stream
    address(stream-read) → request-opcode[n]
    stream-record-type → request-record-type[n]
    get-address-map-size( )
    get-channel-address(read-protect-flag) → ccb-address
    size-input-record( )
    p-setup-ok( )
endproc
```

MODULE 5.5.4

```
procedure p-write-stream
    address(stream-write) → request-opcode[n]
    stream-record-type → request-record-type[n]
    get-address-map-size( )
    get-channel-address(write-protect-flag) → ccb-address
    size-output-record( )
    p-setup-ok( )
endproc
```

formation since no transfer of data takes place under control of the user. It is necessary, however, to check the channel attributes to ensure that buffering has been established for the channel. If no buffering is active, an error code is returned to the calling process and the request is rejected. Otherwise, the process is scheduled for execution by placing it on the READY queue.

Initializing Tape Functions

This routine (module 5.5.7) preprocesses the direct tape management functions (see section 2.5). Preprocessing of a tape function has two aspects: (1) you may open or close a channel to a tape file in the normal way, and (2) you may execute certain control functions without the benefit of the CCB.

The preprocessing routine determines if the tape function exists in the latter class. If so, it must set up the DCB for the request directly. It accesses the tape name in user space (pointed to by SIZE[USP]), searches the device list, and returns a pointer to the DCB. If the DCB address is zero, an invalid device name was specified, and the request is rejected with an error code. Otherwise, the value of the size parameter is copied from user space into the process block. This approach seems to contradict the normal processing of parameters but is required by the fact that, for tape functions, the size parameters serve a double purpose. Thus a pointer, rather than the actual value of the parameter, is placed on the stack by the system service request processor. The system deter-

MODULE 5.5.5

```
procedure p-flush-buffer
    address(flush-buffer) → request-opcode[n]
    get-channel-address(write-protect-flag) → ccb-address
    if outbuffer-flag of channel-attributes[ccb-address] equals one
        then
                p-setup-ok( )
        else
                er-function → process-status
                io-setup-error( )
    endif
endproc
```

MODULE 5.5.6

```
procedure p-next-buffer
    address(next-buffer) → request-opcode[n]
    get-channel-address(read-protect-flag) → ccb-address
    if inbuffer-flag of channel-attributes[ccb-address] equals one
        then
                p-setup-ok( )
        else
                er-function → process-status
                io-setup-error( )
    endif
endproc
```

mines the CCB address, retrieves the DCB address and places it in the PCB, and verifies that the device is available for manipulation. A timeout error will result if the device is not available.

5.5.4   Establishing the Control Blocks

The second step in setting up an I/O request is to establish and validate the control blocks. Each I/O request requires both a CCB and a FCB or DCB. The CCB address is calculated from the channel number supplied by the user and is used to retrieve the DCB address. The routines to perform the validation of the control blocks are described below.

MODULE 5.5.7

```
procedure p-tape
     tape-function[usp] → request-tape-function[n]
     if request-tape-function[n] less than TAPE-FUNCTION-WITH-DCB
          then
               move-from-user-space(map[usp], size[usp], request-
                                                          size[n])
          else
               user-device-name-to-dcb(map[usp], size[usp]) →
                                                          request-size[n]
               if request-size[n] equals zero
                    then
                         er-device-name → process-status
                         p-setup-done( )
               endif
     endif
     get-channel-address(0)
     request-channel-address[n] → ccb-address
     channel-address[ccb-address] → tape-dcb
     tape-dcb → request-dcb-address[n]
     if device-available-flag of device-attributes[tape-dcb] equals one
          then
               p-setup-ok( )
     endif
     er-timeout → process-status
     io-setup-error( )
endproc
```

Calculating the Channel Address

This routine (module 5.5.8) calculates the address of the channel control block (CCB-ADDRESS), given the channel number. Channels are allocated globally in this system. Thus the channel number specified in the request must be checked to see if it is a dedicated system channel. System channels have a negative value. If not, an invalid channel number is returned to you.

If the channel number is positive, it is validated against the number of defined user channels. An invalid channel number error code is returned to you if the channel number exceeds the number of defined channels. The channel number is used to calculate the CCB address. CCB-address resolution is depicted in figure 5.9.

```
procedure calculate-channel-address(channel-number, → ccb-address)
      if channel-number less than zero
          then
          if absolute(channel-number) greater than
                                        number-of-system-channels
              then
                      set er-channel-number to ccb-address
                      exitproc
          endif
          else
          if channel-number greater than number-of-user-channels
              then
                      set er-channel-number to ccb-address
                      exitproc
          endif
      endif
      increment channel-number by number-of-system-channels
      address(channel-table) + channel-number → channel-slot
      memory(channel-slot) → ccb-address
endproc
```

Initializing the Control Block Pointers

GET-CHANNEL-ADDRESS (module 5.5.9) sets up the addresses of the CCB and DCB in the subprocess responsible for executing the I/O request. The address of the CCB is calculated using the specified channel number. If the CCB-ADDRESS is less than zero, the request is rejected because the channel was not defined at system generation.

Given a valid channel number, the procedure checks to see if the channel has been opened to a file. A channel may be opened but locked; this indicates that a reset operation is under way. The result is to treat the channel exactly as if it were closed. An error code is returned to you and the request is rejected.

The protection bits are validated against the read/write attributes for the channel. If a conflict is detected, a protection violation error code is returned to the caller and the request is rejected. Otherwise, the procedure sets up the control block addresses and increments the channel use count by one.

Each time an I/O request is issued, the channel attributes are validated relative to the protection bits. Although this increases system overhead, it also provides an extra measure of security within the system. The ability to modify the protection attributes, once a channel has been opened, is not explicitly implemented. Nothing prevents the user from modifying the system to allow, for

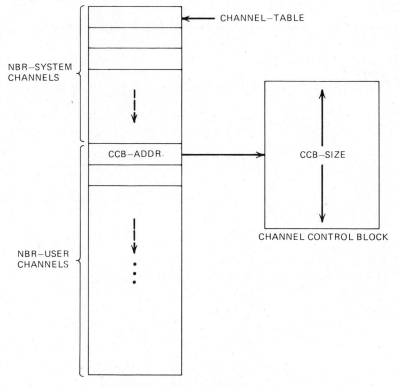

NBR—SYSTEM
CHANNELS

NBR—USER
CHANNELS

CHANNEL—TABLE

CCB—ADDR.

CCB—SIZE

CHANNEL CONTROL BLOCK

Figure 5.9 CCB—address resolution.

example, dynamic specification of exclusive access to a channel for a specified period of time.

MODULE 5.5.9

```
procedure get-channel-address(protection-flags, →ccb-address)
    channel[usp] → channel-number
    calculate-channel-address(channel-number) → ccb-address
    if ccb-address less than zero
        then
            set er-channel-number to process-status
            p-setup-done( )
    endif
    if channel-open-flag of channel-attributes[ccb-address] equals one
        then
            if channel-lock-flag of channel-attributes[ccb-address]
                                                        equals one
```

```
                        then
                                set er-channel-closed to process-status
                                p-setup-done( )
                        endif
                endif
                if protection-flags of channel-attributes[ccb-address]
                                                        not equal to zero
                        if write-protect-flag of channel-attributes[ccb-address]
                                                        not 0
                                then
                                        set er-write-protect to process-status
                                else
                                        set er-read-protect to process-status
                                endif
                                p-setup-done( )
                endif
                ccb-address → request-channel-address[n]
                channel-address[ccb-address] → request-dcb-address[n]
                increment channel-use-count[ccb-address]
        endproc
```

5.5.5   Establishing the Procedure Address

The third step in setting up an I/O request is to determine the procedure for handling the data transfer. There are three possible I/O cases: buffered, direct file, and direct device.

The routines described below determine the type of I/O requested and set up the procedure address for executing the request accordingly.

Direct or Buffered Input

This routine (module 5.5.10) determines whether or not buffered input is to be used for data transfer. If so, the process is placed on the channel input buffering semaphore to await servicing. When the process's turn arrives, the appropriate procedure is determined and executed. Otherwise, the request is executed directly.

Direct or Buffered Output

A complementary routine to the previous one, this module determines whether or not buffered output is to be used for the data transfer. If buffered output has been specified, the process is placed on the output buffering semaphore; else the request is executed directly.

MODULE 5.5.10

```
procedure direct-or-buffered-input
     request-ccb-address[p] → ccb-address
     if inbuffer-flag of channel-attributes[ccb-address] equals one
          then
                    request(channel-inbuffer-rs[ccb-address])
                    io-exit( )
     endif
     direct-input-output( )
endproc
```

MODULE 5.5.11

```
procedure direct-or-buffered-output
     request-ccb-address[p] → ccb-address
     if outbuffer-flag of channel-attributes[ccb-address] equals zero
          then
                    direct-input-output( )
     endif
     request(channel-outbuffer-rs[ccb-address])
     io-exit( )
endproc
```

Direct Input and Output

Direct input and output occurs when a disk block (or multiple thereof) has been requested by a process. The system first locates the explicit address of the routine that will execute the I/O function. This routine is invoked to perform the I/O after validation.

MODULE 5.5.12

```
procedure direct-input-or-output
     get-procedure-address( ) → io-function-address
     if io-function-address less than zero
          then
                    io-function-address → process-status
                    io-error-exit( )
     endif
     call(io-function-address)
     io-exit( )
endproc
```

Locating the Procedure Address

The system must locate the address of the procedure that will explicitly execute the I/O request. Files and devices differ in their treatment of how to effect a data transfer. At this time, however, we must finally couple the subprocess to the data transfer routine. Delaying the coupling until this point has preserved the uniformity of the interface to the user. In coupling to a file access method, we can defer checking of parameters and file status until the access method is invoked. But in coupling to device handlers (e.g., direct output), the decision to execute the I/O request based on the device status must be made immediately. The decision may be viewed as a primitive allocation algorithm. We allow access to the device only if it is available. The objective, of course, is to separate the allocation decision from the management of the device.

In GET-PROCEDURE-ADDRESS (module 5.5.13), to determine if the address of a device handler should be fetched, we examine the value of DEVICE-CHANNEL-FLAG in the device attributes. If this bit is set, direct device linkage is indicated. The user is not allowed to manipulate a direct access device (e.g., a disk), as these devices are shared by multiple users. If the DEVICE-AVAILABLE-FLAG is not set, the device has "timed-out" and is not accessible to the user. Otherwise, the address of the device procedure is retrieved from IO-TABLE-ADDRESS. Alternatively, if DEVICE-CHANNEL-FLAG is zero, a channel has been opened to a file and the file procedure table is stored in IO-TABLE-ADDRESS. In figure 5.5 the operation code of the I/O request serves as an index into the table. Each entry in the table is the address of the appropriate system module for processing the particular request.

All that remains is to check the procedure address value and determine if the I/O request is valid for the file or device. A value of -1 indicates an invalid function which results in an error code being returned to the user.

5.5.6   Determining Record Size

In processing an I/O request, it is important to set up the proper record size for the data transfer. Two routines are used to determine the record size as described below. Such a determination is essential to ensure the accuracy of data transmission between the system and the external device. On input, without a default record size, the system could overwrite vital user or system data. On output, the system could collect garbage beyond the end of the record that the user intended to output.

Sizing an Input Record

SIZE-INPUT-RECORD, depicted in module 5.5.14, validates the size of the input record. If the input record type is FIXED-RECORD-TYPE, processing

MODULE 5.5.13

```
procedure get-procedure-address(→io-function-address)
     request-dcb-address[p] → dcb-address
     device-attribute[dcb-address] → device-attributes
     if device-channel-flag of device-attributes equals one
          then
                    if direct-access-flag of device-attributes equals one
                         then
                                   set er-function to io-function-address
                                   exitproc
                    endif
                    if device-available-flag of device-attributes equals zero
                         then
                                   set er-timeout to io-function-address
                                   exitproc
                         else
                                   device-switch-address → io-table-address
                    endif
          else
                    address(file-switch-address) → io-table-address
     endif
     memory(io-table-address + request-opcode[p] →
                                                            io-function-address
     if io-function-address less than zero
          then
                    set er-function to io-function-address
     endif
endproc
```

defaults to the SIZE-OUTPUT-RECORD routine. If the record is STREAM-RECORD-TYPE, the stream default size is used as the expected record length.

Sizing an Output Record

This routine, depicted in module 5.5.15, uses the record type to set the request size parameter. If the record type is FIXED-RECORD-TYPE, the procedure checks either the DCB or the FCB for the size of the physical or logical record. If neither control block has a defined size, the default fixed size is assigned to the size parameter. If the record type is STREAM-RECORD-TYPE, a procedure is called to count the number of characters in the string (up to and including the null character). The number of characters returned is the minimum of the actual character count or the maximum stream record length. The number of characters is assigned to the size parameter.

MODULE 5.5.14

```
procedure size-input-record
    if request-record-type[n] equal to fixed-record-type
        then
                size-output-record( )
                exitproc
    endif
    if request-record-type[n] equal to stream-record-type
        then
            if request-size[n] less than zero
                then
                        stream-default-size → request-size[n]
            endif
    endif
endproc
```

5.5.7   I/O Preprocessing Facilities

A number of utility routines support the preprocessing of I/O requests. These routines are discussed in the following paragraphs.

Setting the Basic Parameters

The basic parameters to be set for any data transfer are the size of the request, the address where the data are to be stored, and the user map in which the address resides. GET-ADDRESS-MAP-SIZE, depicted in module 5.5.16, initializes these parameters in the PCB. If the I/O request was issued with the address located in the PDB, the PDB must be mapped into system space in order to receive the data.

I/O Error Handling

IO-ERROR-EXIT (depicted in module 5.5.17) is a focal point for processing errors resulting from preprocessing I/O requests. The variable PROCESS-STATUS contains the status of the function after preprocessing and it is used to set the event status field for the I/O request. When an error occurs, the channel is not assigned, so the channel use count must be decremented by one.

Decrementing Channel Use

This routine, depicted in module 5.5.18, performs the single function of decrementing the channel use count. Because this operation is performed by

MODULE 5.5.15

```
procedure size-output-record
    if request-record-type[n] equals fixed-record-type
        then
                request-channel-address[n] → ccb-address
                if device-channel-flag of
                            channel-attributes[ccb-address] equals one
                    then
                        request-dcb-address[n] → dcb-address
                        device-record-size[dcb-address] → size-of-record
                    else
                        request-fcb-address[n] → fcb-address
                        file-record-size[fcb-address] → size-of-record
                endif
                if size-of-record not equal to zero
                    then
                            size-of-record → request-size[n]
                            exitproc
                endif
                fixed-default-size → request-size[n]
    endif
    if request-record-type[n] equals stream-record-type
        then
                size-of-record → rsize
                request-data-address[n] → data-loc
                map-string-in(request-map[n], data-loc, rsize,
                                                    stream-max * 2)
                size-of-record → request-size[n]
    endif
endproc
```

several routines in the IOM, it seems appropriate to provide a common routine
for all subsystems to use.

MODULE 5.5.16

```
procedure get-address-map-size
    size[usp] → request-size[n]
entry get-address-and-map:
    calling-map( ) → request-map[n]
    data-address[usp] → request-data-address[n]
    adjust-for-pdb(request-map[n])
endproc
```

MODULE 5.5.17

procedure io-error-exit
    process-status → event-status[p]
io-exit:
    decrement-channel-use(p)
    end-subprocess( )
endproc

MODULE 5.5.18

procedure decrement-channel-use(p)
    request-ccb-address[p] → ccb-address
    decrement channel-use-count[ccb-address]
endproc

5.6 RANDOM ACCESS METHODS

The concept of random access has been discussed in section 5.4. This section discusses the implementation of the RAM through a set of functional modules.

5.6.1 Random Read

The RANDOM-READ request allows a user to transfer data from an arbitrary location in a segmented or contiguous file. The format of the request is:

SYSTEM(RANDOM-READ, EVENT-NR, CHANNEL, ADDRESS,
                        NR-WORDS, FILE-ADDRESS)

where		
EVENT-NR	is used to signal the caller when the request has completed
CHANNEL	is the number of the channel that has previously opened for input
ADDRESS	is the location in the user process to which data will be transferred
NR-WORDS	is the number of words to transfer on this request
FILE-ADDRESS	is the address of data in the file

This request combines both aspects of the general RAM and the restricted random block access method. This is accomplished by examining the file address specified by the user process and the following cases result.

1. If the request size is an even multiple of the disk block size and the file address is aligned with a disk block boundary, the disk block will be transferred in its entirety to the address in the process space. The statements to calculate these values are

MODULUS(NR-WORDS, DATA-BLOCK-SIZE) → TEMP1
MODULUS(FILE-ADDRESS, DISC-SECTOR-SIZE) → TEMP2

Both TEMP1 and TEMP2 must be zero for the RAM to operate in block mode.

2. If either of the two conditions above does not hold, the general RAM is used. The system assigns a buffer equivalent to the data block size for the data block containing the required data. The data are extracted from the buffer and transferred to the calling process; the system buffer is then released.

Note that the buffer used here is not under the control of the buffer manager. It is strictly temporary space allocated by the IOM to hold a disk block while the data record is extracted. It is released as soon as the data have been transferred to the calling process.

Initializing the Read Request

The procedure for initializing the random read request is depicted in module 5.6.1. We first initialize the subprocess that executes the request. Common initialization functions are performed by a utility module START-READ-WRITE. If the parameters for the read request are successfully validated, the procedure exits.

If you attempt to read past the end of the file, the procedure calculates the new request size based on the current file size. REQUEST-FILE-ADDRESS is the logical index into the file. If you attempt to read beyond the end of file (i.e., REQUEST-FILE-ADDRESS + REQUEST-SIZE greater than FILE-END), an error code is returned to the user and the request is rejected.

A successful exit from SETUP-READ via P-SETUP-OK causes the subprocess to be scheduled for execution. However, an exit via P-SETUP-DONE will usually be accompanied by an error code and the request will be rejected.

Validating the Read/Write Parameters

A common routine is used to validate the parameters for a read/write request. START-READ-WRITE, depicted in module 5.6.2, checks for a valid address; an address less than zero forces the rejection of the request. An error code is returned to the user. The system invokes routines to set up the request

```
procedure setup-read
     start-read-write(read-protect-flag) → read-status
     if read-status greater than or equal to zero
          then
                    p-setup-ok( )
     endif
entry read-eof-check:
     file-size[fcb-address] − request-file-address[n] → request-size[n]
     if request-size[n] greater than or equal to one
          then
                    p-setup-ok( )
          else
                    er-end-of-file → process-status
                    decrement-channel-use(n)
                    p-setup-done( )
     endif
endproc
```

parameters for address, memory map, and transfer size in the PCB. It locates
the CCB and validates the protection bits for the channel. Finally, it verifies
that a random request is valid for this channel. Random requests are valid only
for segmented or contiguous files. Thus if the file type is serial, an invalid status
will be returned from the RANDOM-CHECKS routine.

```
procedure start-read-write(protection-flags, →result)
     file-address[usp] → request-file-address[n]
     if file-address[usp] less than zero
          then
                    set er-file-address to process-status
                    p-setup-done( )
     endif
     get-address-map-size( )
     get-channel-address(protection-flags)
     random-checks( ) → result
endproc
```

Executing a Read Request—First Stage

The execution of a read request is performed at two levels of control. Procedure
READ, depicted in module 5.6.3, completes the initialization by determining

the actual physical device address for the request. It invokes DO-READ to control the data transfer. After the read operation has completed, it sets the event status to reflect a successful completion. A successful read will return to you the number of words transferred from the file to user space.

Executing a Read Request—Second Stage

The second stage in the execution of a read request affects the data transfer between the file and your process. DO-READ, depicted in module 5.6.4, adjusts the device address and request size to the nearest block boundary. If the device address is not equal to zero, the system allocates a buffer and temporarily loads the appropriate block into it. The requested words are extracted from the buffer and moved to user space for processing. If the read request size is a multiple of the disk sector size, the data are transferred directly to user space.

MODULE 5.6.3

```
procedure read
    find-device-address( ) → device-address
    if device-address less than zero
        then
                io-exit( )
    endif
    do-read( )
    if event-status[p] greater than or equal to zero
        then
                request-size[p] → event-status[p]
    endif
    io-exit( )
endproc
```

5.6.2   Random Write

The RANDOM-WRITE request allows you to transfer data from your process to an arbitrary location in a segmented or contiguous file. The format of the request is:

SYSTEM(RANDOM-READ, EVENT-NR, CHANNEL, ADDRESS,
                                  NR-WORDS, FILE-ADDRESS)

where   EVENT-NR   is used to signal the caller when the request
                                        has completed

CHANNEL	is the number of the channel that has previously opened for output
ADDRESS	is the location in your process from which the data will be retrieved by the system
NR-WORDS	is the number of words to be written
FILE-ADDRESS	is the address in the file where the data are to be written

This request combines both aspects of the general RAM and the restricted block access method. The conditions for determining which method to utilize have been described in section 5.6.1.

MODULE 5.6.4

```
procedure do-read
    adjust-address-and-size( ) → device-status
    if device-status not equal to zero
        then
                read-buffer( ) → result
                if result less than zero
                    then
                            exitproc
                endif
                request-buffer-address[p] → bufaddr
                request-data-address[p] → dataddr
                move-to-user-space(request-map[p], bufaddr, dataddr,
                                                    request-size[p])
                release(memory-rs, request-buffer-address[p])
        else
                read-user( )
    endif
endproc
```

In executing a RANDOM-WRITE request, you should be aware of two conditions. First, if the write request should exhaust the available disk space in a contiguous file, an error code will be returned to the process. As the size of a contiguous file is fixed when it is created, the size cannot be dynamically expanded by write requests. Second, the system cannot allow the process to issue write requests that would create holes in a file. That is, when writing a record, either the record space must already exist in the file or it you must specify the next available but unwritten address in the file.

Initializing a Write Request

The procedure for initializing a write request has a format similar to that for the read request and is depicted in module 5.6.5. The routine START-READ-

WRITE is invoked to set up the address, map, and size parameters as well as to locate the address of the CCB. The channel attributes are checked to ensure that the file is not write-protected. The only special case to be checked is that the process is not attempting to write beyond the limits of a contiguous file. If the file address to be written exceeds the size of the contiguous file, the request will be rejected.

MODULE 5.6.5

```
procedure setup-write
      start-read-write(write-protection-flag) → write-status
      if write-status greater than or equal to zero
           then
                   p-setup-ok( )
      endif
entry write-check:
      if contiguous-flag of file-attributes[fcb-address] equals zero
           then
                   p-setup-ok( )
      endif
      set er-file-address to process-status
      decrement-channel-use(n)
      p-setup-done( )
endproc
```

Executing a Write Request—Stage 1

The procedure for executing a write request consists of two levels of control. The first level, depicted in module 5.6.6, is complex because it must handle the situation where a write request forces the extension of a segmented file. WRITE computes the address of the last word to be written under the current request and compares this address to the current file size. If the address is less than the file size, the procedure calls DO-WRITE to perform the data transfer.

When the address to be written is greater than the file size, the system attempts to extend the file space to cover the request. First, it must request exclusive access to the file in order to extend it. When access is granted, the procedure checks the current size of the file. It is possible that another process has reduced the size of the file prior to access being granted for this request. Note this can only occur for segmented files. In this case, exclusive access is terminated and an error returned to the caller.

If the requested file address is less than the allocated size of the file, the system determines the physical device address. Otherwise, it proceeds to allocate the segment pointer blocks and segment data blocks to satisfy the request. Errors may occur if an erroneous device address is calculated or the required allocation cannot be made.

Let us assume that each of the previous steps has been successful. We must perform one last function—updating the file directory to reflect the newly extended file. Once this has been accomplished, we calculate the physical device address and perform the data transfer.

The routines REQUEST-FILE-ADDITION and RELEASE-FILE-ADDITION, described in section 5.8, are used to lock the segment pointer blocks so that the logical file space extension may be examined. This action guarantees that no other process will attempt to simultaneously extent the same file as all other processes will be enqueued to one lock chain.

MODULE 5.6.6

```
procedure write
     request-fcb-address[p] → fcb-address
     request-size[p] − 1 + request-file-address[p] → write-address
     if write-address greater than or equal to file-size[fcb-address]
          then
                request-file-addition( )
                if file-size[fcb-address] not equal to request-file-
                                                        address[p]
                     then
                           set er-file-address to process-status
                           release-file-addition( )
                           io-exit( )
                endif
                if request-file-address[p] less than
                                         file-allocated-size[fcb-address]
                     then
                           find-device-address( ) → device-address
                           if device-address less than zero
                                then
                                device-address → process-status
                                release-file-addition( )
                                io-exit( )
                           endif
                     else
                           allocate-segmented( ) → result
                           if result less than zero
                           then
                           set result to process-status
                           release-file-addition( )
                           io-exit( )
                           endif
                endif
                increment file-size[fcb-address] by request-size[p]
                directory-update( ) → result
```

```
                  if result less than zero
                      then
                              result to process-status
                              release-file-addition( )
                              io-exit( )
                  endif
                  release-file-addition( )
          else
                  find-device-address( ) → device-address
                  if device-address less than zero
                      then
                              io-exit( )
                  endif
      endif
      do-write( )
      io-exit( )
endproc
```

Executing a Write Request—Second Level

DO-WRITE, depicted in module 5.6.7, performs the data transfer at the second level of execution of a write request. If the physical device address is not located on a sector boundary, the system allocates a buffer, copies the user data into the buffer, and exits. If the write address is aligned on a sector boundary, it performs the write operation directly from user space. In either case, the disk sectors to be written will be "locked" before the operation is performed. After the operation, these sectors are released from "lock" status.

5.6.3   Address Operations for Random Requests

The essential feature of the random request is that a process may specify any valid address in the file. The logical file address must be converted to a physical device address in order to perform the data transfer operation. To do so, the logical file address is used to locate a segment pointer block (SPB). Within the SPB are addresses of the segment data blocks (SDBs) corresponding to the physical device addresses. Once a physical device address is located, it must be aligned along a sector boundary so that the disk controller can perform the read or write.

Finding the Device Address

FIND-DEVICE-ADDRESS, depicted in module 5.6.8, determines the physical device address for the read/write request. Since a random request may be ex-

MODULE 5.6.7

procedure do-write
    adjust-address-and-size(device-address) → device-address
    if device-address not equal to zero
        then
            lock-request( )
            read-buffer( ) → result
            if result greater than or equal to zero
            then
            request-buffer-address[p] → bufaddr
            request-data-address[p] → dataddr
            request-map[p] → user-map
            request-size[p] → rqst-size
            move-from-user-space(user-map, dataddr, bufaddr,
                                            rqst-size)
            write-buffer( )
            endif
        else
            lock-request( )
            write-user( )
    endif
    free-request( )
endproc

MODULE 5.6.8

procedure find-device-address (→ result)
    if contiguous-flag of file-attributes[fcb-address] not equal to zero
        then
            file-start[fcb-address] + request-file-address[p]
                                → block-number
            request-size[p] → request-lock-size[p]
            set device-address to result
            exitproc
    endif
    calculate-block-number(request-file-address[p]) → block-number
    calculate-pointers-per-block( )
    calculate-pointers-per-block( )
    file-start[fcb-address] → spb-address
    while block-number greater than or
        equal to request-pointers-per-block[p]
        do
        decrement block-number by request-pointers-per-block[p]
        set request-pointers-per-block[p] to block-size

```
                    increment spb-address by block-size
                    read-random(0, spb-data, 2, request-temp-buffer) → result
                    if result less than zero
                    if result less than zero
                         then
                         set result to event-status[p]
                         exitproc
                    endif
                    spb-data → spb-address
                    enddo
               calculate-data-offset(request-file-address[p])
               increment sdb-address by data-offset
               data-offset + request-size[p] − data-block-size → device-address
               if device-address greater than or equal to zero
                    then
                         decrement request-size[p] by device-address
               endif
               request-size[p] → request-lock-size[p]
               set device-address to result
endproc
```

ecuted against either a contiguous or segmented file, we have the following two cases:

Contiguous File. In a contiguous file, all disk blocks are sequentially allocated from the initial block. To calculate the physical device address, the logical block number is added to the address of the first disk block. The request size is set as the lock request size (for READ-LOCK or WRITE-RELEASE operations). If the requested address aligns with a disk sector boundary, a zero result (i.e., no offset) is returned.

Segmented File.   In a segmented file, locating the device address is a two-step process. First, the target logical block number is calculated given the file address. Then the system calculates the number of pointers per block, since the SPB size may vary. It searches the sequentially linked SPBs for the appropriate one. The FILE-START entry points to the first SPB. Each SPB is read in turn until the SPB containing the pointer to the data block is found. The data offset in the data block are calculated and added to the SDB address to yield the physical device address.

Calculating the Pointers per Block

To locate a SDB, the system must calculate the number of pointers per SPB. This number varies with the size of the pointer block. Each pointer is assumed to consume two words (for a 16-bit machine). The last two words of any SPB are used to store a pointer to the next SPB as they are accessed in a sequential manner.

Calculating Data Block Sizes

In like fashion, the SDB size is determined by the system before it can access the data. The data block size is stored as a field in the allocation data word, which is an entry in the file control block. The value of this field is the number of disk sectors composing the data block. Multiplying this value by the number of words per disk sector yields the data block size in words.

Calculating the Block Number

Given the data block size and the address of the first word to be retrieved, the system calculates the block number to retrieve through simple division. This routine is used throughout the IOM, so deserves its own module.

MODULE 5.6.9

```
procedure calculate-pointers-per-block
      file-allocation-size[fcb-address] → allocation-data
      extract pointer-block-size from allocation-data
      (pointer-block-size * sector-size)/2 → request-pointers-per-block[p]
      decrement request-pointers-per-block[p] by 2
endproc
```

MODULE 5.6.10

```
procedure calculate-data-block-size(→data-block-size)
      file-allocation-data[fcb-address] → allocation-data
      extract data-block-size from allocation-data
      data-block-size * sector-size → data-block-size
endproc
```

MODULE 5.6.11

```
procedure calculate-block-number(address, →result)
      calculate-data-block-size( ) → data-block-size
      address/data-block-size → result
endproc
```

Adjusting the I/O Parameters

A file address may begin at any location in the file. This address may not correspond to a disk sector boundary. Because the disk controller can only access
fixed-size sectors, the system must adjust the address and size parameters for
the request to the nearest disk sector boundary address and size. The routine for
accomplishing this adjustment is depicted in module 5.6.12.

   If the address is aligned with a sector boundary and if the size is a multiple of
the sector size, the routine merely exits. For a nonaligned file address, the lock
address (used to prevent concurrent accesses) is masked with a record mask.
This mask is equivalent to the disk sector size. The request size is masked to
yield a multiple of the number of sectors to be retrieved. For example, suppose
that the lock address is 124633 (octal) and the request size is 1146 (octal). With
a sector size of 400 words (octal), the adjusted parameters for the lock address
and lock size are equal to 124400 and 1400, respectively.

MODULE 5.6.12

```
procedure adjust-address-and-size(→ result)
    request-lock-address[p] → lock-address
    if request-lock-size[p] & record-mask equals zero
        then
                clear result
                if lock-address & record-mask equals zero
                    then
                            clear result
                            exitproc
                endif
        endif
    lock-address & record-mask → request-lock-address[p]
    request-lock-size[p] & record-mask → request-lock-size[p]
    increment request-lock-size[p] by sector-size
    set one to result
endproc
```

5.6.4   Allocating New Segments in a File

In segmented files, the file may be dynamically expanded by writing a new
record at the end of the file. A new SDB may have to be allocated to accommodate the new record. As a side effect, a new SPB may also be allocated if the
previous pointer block has been completely filled. The procedure for allocating

a new SDB is depicted in module 5.6.13. A new segment is allocated only when a process executes a request extending the file.

To allocate a new SDB, the system must calculate its SPB identifier (SPB-ID). The SPB-ID is stored in the PCB to preserve the reentrancy of the procedure. Because the mass storage allocation process (see section 2.8) is an independent process, there may be a significant time interval between the time a request is made for space allocation and the time the request is satisfied. During this period, other processes may also request new segments for their files. Making the segment allocator reentrant preserves the essential parallelism of processing.

After the SPB-ID is calculated, the system determines whether a new SPB must be allocated. When a segmented file is created (see section 6.5), the first SPB is allocated and initialized immediately. A new SPB will be allocated only when the current pointer block has been filled.

To allocate a new SPB, the system performs the following steps:

1. It allocates disk space sufficient to accommodate the new SPB. If the allocation fails, the write request is rejected and the process is notified by an error code.

2. The FILE-START and FILE-END entries point to the beginning and end of the segment indices, respectively (not to the first and last words in the file). We attempt to read and write the new SPB to ensure that it is accessible. Why? If the segment index is a contiguous space, we may have exceeded the maximum file size.

3. If all goes well, the system updates the FCB. The directory entry is updated by the IOM during final processing of the I/O request.

Whether or not a SPB is allocated, under most conditions a new SDB will be allocated. Again, a request is made to the MSAP to provide sufficient space for the data block. An allocation failure causes the request to be rejected and the process to be notified via an error code. The address of a new SDB, successfully allocated, is inserted into the SPB at the appropriate location.

Finally, the system updates the file directory entry to reflect the expanded size of the file. This step is not performed until all allocations have been successfully completed. If the machine were to halt at this point, the system could recover by comparing the file size with the segment pointers. It would then determine whether a successful expansion had taken place.

MODULE 5.6.13

```
procedure allocate-segmented(→result)
     file-size[fcb-address] → file-size
     calculate-block-number(file-size) → number-of-data-blocks
     calculate-pointers-per-block( )
     modulus(number-of-data-blocks,request-pointers-per-block[p])
                                    → request-pointer-index[p]
```

```
            if request-pointer-index[p] greater than zero
                then
                        if file-size[fcb-address] not equal to zero
                            then
                                    request-pointers-per-block[p] + 1 → block-size
                                    allocate(block-size, 0) → event-data1[p]
                                    if event-status[p] less than zero
                                        then
                                                event-status[p] → result
                                                exitproc
                                    endif
                                    block-size + file-end[fcb-address]
                                                                    → spb-address
                                    read-random(0, spb-data, 2, spb-address)
                                                                        → result
                                    if result less than zero
                                        then
                                                exitproc
                                    endif
                                    event-data[p] → spb-data
                                    write-random(0, spb-data, 2, spb-address)
                                    if result less than zero
                                        then
                                                exitproc
                                    endif
                    endif
                                    event-data[p] → file-end[fcb-address]
            endif
            allocate-file-block( ) → spb-address
            if event-status[p] less than zero
                then
                        event-status[p] → result
                        exitproc
            endif
            request-pointer-index[p] + file-end[fcb-address] → spb-address
            write-random(0, spb-data, 2, spb-address)
            if result less than zero
                then
                        exitproc
            endif
            calculate-data-block-size( ) → data-block-size
            increment file-allocated-size[fcb-address] by data-block-size
            request-size[p] → request-lock-size[p]
            clear result
endproc
```

MODULE 5.6.14

```
procedure allocate-file-block(→block-address)
    file-allocation-data[fcb-address] → allocation-data
    extract device-code from allocation-data
    calculate-data-block-size( ) → data-block-size
    allocate(data-block-size, device-code) → block-address
endproc
```

5.6.5   Random Access Utilities

A number of utility procedures are required to support the management of random access requests. These procedures are described in this section.

Checking for Random Access

RANDOM-CHECKS, depicted in module 5.6.15, verifies that the file organization is amenable to random access. At the same time, it initializes the FCB and CCB addresses for the other preprocessing routines. The procedure verifies that the channel has been opened to a file and that the file is not a serially organized

MODULE 5.6.15

```
procedure random-checks(→result)
    request-fcb-address[n] → fcb-address
    request-channel-address[n] → ccb-address
    if device-channel-flag of channel-attributes[ccb-address] not  equal
                                                               to zero
            then
            if serial-flag of file-attributes[fcb-address] not equal to zero
                then
                        er-function → status
                        decrement-channel-use(n)
                        p-setup-done( )
            endif
            else
                    set er-function to status
                    decrement-channel-use(n)
                    p-setup-done( )
        endif
        file-size[fcb-address] − request-file-address[n] + request-size[n] →
                                                                result
endproc
```

file. If either of these conditions fails, the random request is rejected; otherwise, the logical address in the file is calculated. By this approach, we determine if we are attempting to read past the end of the file.

Reading and Writing Buffers

The system must read an entire disk sector even though the amount of information you requested is less than the entire disk sector size. In this event, the system allocates a temporary buffer, reads the disk sector into the buffer, extracts the required data, and releases the buffer. The procedures for reading and writing temporary system buffers are depicted in modules 5.6.16 and 5.6.17, respectively. They are used to update disk blocks where only a portion of the disk block is to be rewritten. For example, the SPBs of a segmented file are updated each time a new segment is allocated. Note that we cannot use the system buffer manager, as it executes at a higher level of control than the IOM.

MODULE 5.6.16

```
procedure read-buffer(→result)
    request-lock-size[p] → read-size
    request(memory-rs, read-size) → buffer-address
    read-random(0, buffer-address, read-size,
                                    request-lock-address[p] → result
    result → event-status[p]
    if result less than zero
        then
                release(memory-rs, buffer-address)
    endif
endproc
```

MODULE 5.6.17

```
procedure write-buffer-(→result)
    request-buffer-address[p] → buffer-address
    request-lock-size[p] → write-size
    write-random(0, buffer-address, write-size,
                                    request-lock-address[p]) → result
    result → event-status[p]
    release(memory-rs, buffer-address)
endproc
```

5.7   SEQUENTIAL ACCESS FUNCTIONS

The concept of a sequential access method (SAM) has been discussed in section 5.4. This section explores the implementation of the SAM through a detailed examination of the functions provided by IOM. Note that many of the functions used here are common to all I/O functions and have been described in section 5.6.

5.7.1   Sequential and Stream Reads

The SEQUENTIAL-READ function transfers a specified number of words from a system buffer or directly from a file to the user program. The mode of transfer is dependent on the mode of the channel at the time the read is initiated. The format of the command is

SYSTEM(SEQUENTIAL-READ, EVENT-NR, CHANNEL, ADDRESS, NR-WORDS)

where   EVENT-NR   is used to signal the caller when the data transfer is complete

CHANNEL   is the identifier of a channel that has been opened for input

ADDRESS   is the location in the user process where the data are to be stored

NR-WORDS   is the number of words to be read

The status of the event number should be examined to determine if an error occurred during the read operation. A positive status indicates the actual number of words transferred to the process.

The STREAM-READ function takes the same format as the SEQUENTIAL-READ request with the exception that the NR-WORDS is absent. Instead, as each character is copied to user space, it is examined for a null value. When a null character is detected, the transfer is complete, and the number of characters transferred is passed to the process as the event status. The NR-WORDS parameter is interpreted as the maximum number of words to transfer if a null character is not detected. The system requires a maximum transfer size for a stream read as the possibility exists that data could overflow the intended buffer.

Reading a Record Sequentially

The procedure for executing the SEQUENTIAL-READ request is depicted in module 5.7.1. The actual read operation is performed by the module DO-

READ discussed in section 5.6. This routine serves to setup the parameters necessary to complete the operation.

Initially, the procedure requests access to the channel through CHANNEL-SEQUENTIAL-RS. By using this semaphore, the system ensures that records in the file are dispatched on a first come, first served basis to requesting processes. There are certain reasons for this approach:

1. When sequentially reading a record, each request specifies the number of words to be read. Thus the next record address can be calculated only after the current request is satisfied.

2. In a similar but more serious vein, a stream counts characters during execution. Thus the system never knows the next read address until a complete stream record has been read.

Once the process has been granted access, the next record address in the file is calculated. If this address is less than zero, the request is rejected. A serial file is

MODULE 5.7.1

```
procedure sequential-read
     request-channel-address[p] → ccb-address
     request(channel-sequential-rs[ccb-address])
     find-next-read-address( ) → result
     if result less than zero
          then
               io-exit( )
     endif
     if request-size[p] is greater than block-balance
          then
               increment-next-read-address(block-balance)
               find-next-read-address( ) → result
               if result less than zero
                    then
                         io-exit( )
               endif
     endif
     request-size[p] → request-lock-size[p]
     do-read( )
     increment-next-read-address(request-size[p])
     request-size[p] → event-status[p]
     request-file-data[p] → event-data[p]
     release(channel-sequential-rs[ccb-address])
     io-exit( )
endproc
```

accessed in blocks whose size is specified when the file is created. If the request attempts to cross the block boundary, the next block address in the file is determined, and the record addess calculated. At this point, an invalid read address would indicate that block pointers have been corrupted or the end of the file had been reached.

Once the parameters for the read operation have been set, the actual read request is performed. The channel address is incremented by the record size. You are notified of the size of the record that has successfully been read. Finally, the process releases control of the channel.

Incrementing the Next Read Address

After a record has been sequentially read, the logical address in the file (maintained in the CCB) is incremented by the size of the record just read. The only time we need to be careful is when we are accessing a serial file. In this case, if we reach the end of the data block, we must update the channel address (logical file address) by two words in order to retrieve the pointer to the next block. The procedure to increment the channel address is depicted in module 5.7.2.

MODULE 5.7.2

```
procedure increment-next-read-address(size)
     increment channel-next-read-address[ccb-address] by size
     if serial-flag of file-attributes[fcb-address] not equal to zero
        then
        calculate-data-offset(channel-next-read-address[ccb-address])
        if data-offset + 2 equals data-block-size
             then
                    increment channel-next-read-address[ccb-address]
        endif
     endif
endproc
```

Determining the Next Read Address

Determining the next read address in a file is a procedure dependent on the organization of the file. While finding the next address to read, the procedure validates and sets up the parameters in the PCB for the read operation. This procedure is depicted in module 5.7.3.

Initially, we compute the balance of the file, that is, the number of words remaining in the file. Remember that the file address specified is actually the in-

MODULE 5.7.3

```
procedure find-next-read-address(→result)
    channel-next-read-address[ccb-address] → request-file-address[p]
    file-size[fcb-address] − request-file-address[p] → file-balance
    if file-balance less than or equal to zero
        then
            set er-end-of-file to result
            set er-end-of-file to event-status[p]
            release(channel-sequential-rs[ccb-address])
            exitproc
    endif
    if contiguous-flag of file-attributes[fcb-address] not equal to zero
        then
            find-next-contiguous-address( ) → result
            exitproc
    endif
    calculate-data-offset(request-file-address[p])
    if data-offset equals zero
        then
            if channel-next-read-address[ccb-address] not equal to zero
                then
                    if serial-flag of file-attributes[fcb-address]
                                                        not equal to zero
                        then
                            find-next-serial-address( ) → result
                        else
                            set request-size[p] to size-of-request
                            increment size-of-request
                            if size-of-request greater than or
                                                equal to data-block-size
                                then
                                    set er-size to result
                                    set er-size to event-status[p]
                                    release(channel-sequential-rs[ccb-address])
                                    exitproc
                            endif
                            find-next-segmented-address( ) → result
                            if result less than zero
                                then
                                    exitproc
                            endif
                    endif
            endif
    endif
endif
```

```
    if segmented-flag of file-attributes[ccb-address] not equal to zero
      then
        if channel-save-address[ccb-address] not equal to zero
          then
          find-next-segmented-address( ) → result
          if result less than zero
              then
                      exitproc
          endif
        endif
    endif
    file-size[fcb-address] − request-file-address[p] → file-balance
    data-block-size − data-offset → block-balance
    if serial-flag of file-attributes[fcb-address] not equal to zero
      then
        decrement block-balance by 2
    endif
    if block-balance greater than or equal to file-balance
      then
        set file-balance to block-balance
    endif
    data-offset + channel-save-address[ccb-address] →
                                        request-lock-address[p]
    set one to result
endproc
```

dex of a word in the file. If the file balance is less than or equal to zero, the request exceeds the file size and is rejected. At the same time, access to the channel is also released.

If a valid file address is confirmed, further processing depends on the file organization. Individual routines perform the calculations for each file type. These are

FIND-NEXT-CONTIGUOUS-ADDRESS (module 5.7.4)
FIND-NEXT-SERIAL-ADDRESS (module 5.7.5)
FIND-NEXT-SEGMENTED-ADDRESS (module 5.7.6)

Calculating the next read address for a contiguous file is straightforward since all disk blocks are adjacent. However, the calculation becomes complicated when one considers the serial or segmented file organizations. First, the system calculate the data offset in the current data block of the requested data. If the data offset is zero, and the next channel address is not zero, a new data block must be read. Next come the housekeeping chores. The system computes the balance of data left in the block and the balance of data remaining in the file.

For serial files, of course, two words are subtracted for the pointer to the next data block. If the file balance is less than the block size, the file size becomes the new block balance. This computation ensures that the system does not access erroneous data remaining in the block from previous users. Finally, the new read address is calculated and stored in REQUEST-LOCK-ADDRESS.

Determining a Contiguous File Address

The procedure for determining the next contiguous address is depicted in module 5.7.4. Because contiguous files are treated as one large block, the file balance becomes the block balance (i.e., what is left to read in the file). The file size, naturally, becomes the data block size. The current file address is the offset in this "large" data block. The new address to be read (stored in RE-QUEST-LOCK-ADDRESS) is just the current channel address (a physical disk address) plus the data offset.

MODULE 5.7.4

```
procedure find-next-contiguous-address(→result)
     request-fcb-address[p] → fcb-address
     file-balance → block-balance
     file-size[fcb-address] → data-block-size
     request-file-address[p] → data-offset
     data-offset + channel-save-address[ccb-address] →
                                          request-lock-address[p]
     set one to result
endproc
```

Determining the Next Serial Address

The procedure for determining the next serial address is depicted in module 5.7.5. The system first checks if the calling process's request will cross a data block boundary. If the request size plus one is greater than the data block size, the request is rejected, as the system does not permit splitting records across data blocks. Otherwise, the data block size is decremented by two and added to the channel save address. This yields the address of the next data block to be read into memory.

Determining the Next Segmented Address

This procedure (depicted in module 5.7.6) relies upon FIND-DEVICE-AD-DRESS to calculate the next segment address based on the pointer block size

MODULE 5.7.5

procedure find-next-serial-address(→result)
    request-ccb-address[p] → ccb-address
    request-size[p] → size-of-request
    increment size-of-request
    if size-of-request greater than or equal to data-block-size
        then
             set er-size to result
             set er-size to event-status[p]
             release(channel-sequential-res[ccb-address])
             exitproc
    endif
    decrement data-block-size by 2
    channel-save-address[ccb-address] + data-block-size →
                               request-lock-address[p]
endproc

and the number of pointers per block. FIND-DEVICE-ADDRESS (see module 5.6.8) sets up the next read address in REQUEST-LOCK-ADDRESS. This address is stored as the current physical disk address in the CCB. The reason we break out these steps into a separate module is that they are invoked from FIND-NEXT-READ-ADDRESS more than once.

MODULE 5.7.6

procedure find-next-segment-address(→result)
    find-device-address( ) → result
    if result less than zero
        then
             result → event-status[p]
             release(channel-sequential-rs[ccb-address])
             exitproc
    endif
    request-lock-address[p] → channel-save-address[ccb-address]
endproc

Adjusting the Size Parameters

On a sequential read, the user may only read to the end of the data block. No read request is allowed to cross a data block boundary. Thus if the size of the request is greater than the number of words remaining unread in the data block, the request size is adjusted to reflect data balance. This procedure is depicted in module 5.7.7.

MODULE 5.7.7

```
procedure adjust-sequential-read-size
     if request-size[p] greater than block-balance
          then
                  block-balance → request-size[p]
     endif
     request-size[p] → request-lock-size[p]
     adjust-address-and-size( )
endproc
```

5.7.2   Sequential And Stream Writing

_____

The SEQUENTIAL-WRITE function transfers the specified number of words
to a file or system buffer. The mode of transfer is dependent on the mode of the
channel. The format of the request is

SYSTEM(SEQUENTIAL-WRITE, EVENT-NR, CHANNEL, ADDRESS,
NR-WORDS)

where	EVENT-NR	is used to signal the process when the data transfer is complete
	CHANNEL	is the identifier of a channel that has been opened for output to a file
	ADDRESS	is the location in the user process from which the data will be taken
	NR-WORDS	is the number of words to be written

The status of the event number should be examined to determine if an error occurred on the write operation. A positive value indicates the number of words
transferred to the file.

The STREAM-WRITE function has the same format as the sequential write
function. However, under the STREAM-WRITE operation, writing terminates
when a null character is encountered in the data stream. NR-WORDS is interpreted as the maximum number of words to transfer if a null character is not
found. Otherwise, the procedures to process these two requests are the same.

Writing a Sequential Record

_____

Writing a sequential record requires consideration of two factors: the file
organization and the padding of data blocks.

The former factor is important in calculating the file parameters whereas the
latter determines how to fill a data block when the remaining space is inade-

quate for the current request. Both factors have an impact on the allocation of new file blocks when the file must be expanded during the write operation. The procedure for executing a sequential write function is depicted in module 5.7.8.

This procedure calls START-SEQUENTIAL-WRITE to set up the file address, request size, and block address parameters. If an error is detected, the request will be rejected. If the file type does not indicate a segmented file, a serial data block has already been allocated. The status of the serial data block is verified.

If the file is segmented, the system determines whether or not to allocate a new data block. A data offset of zero indicates that a new block should be allocated. If the block balance is less than zero, the current data block is padded with zeros and released. A new data block is allocated by the PAD-SEG-MENTED procedure. We also set the file and lock address, calculate the physical device addresses, and proceed to execute the write function.

If the file is serially organized, a balance of fewer than two words (required for the pointer to the next data block) forces the data block to be padded with zeros and a new data block to be allocated (by PAD-SERIAL). The file address and lock address parameters are set in the PCB and the procedure executes the function.

MODULE 5.7.8

```
procedure sequential-write
    start-sequential-write( ) → write-size
    if write-size less than zero
        then
            io-exit( )
    endif
    data-block-size − data-offset → block-balance
    if segmented-flag of file-attributes[fcb-address] not equal to zero
        then
            if data-offset equals zero
                then
                    allocate-segmented( ) → block-address
                    if block-address less than zero
                        then
                            exit-sequential-write( )
                    endif
                else
                    if block-balance less than zero
                        then
                            pad-segmented( ) → block-address
                            if block-address less than zero
                                then
                                    exit-sequential-write( )
                            endif
                    endif
            endif
```

```
                    endif
               file-size[fcb-address]  →  request-file-address[p]
               file-size[fcb-address]  →  request-lock-address[p]
               find-device-address( )  →  device-address
               if device-address less than zero
                    then
                              exit-sequential-write( )
               endif
          else
               if block-balance less than 2
                    then
                              pad-serial( )  →  block-address
                              if block-address less than zero
                                   then
                                             exit-sequential-write( )
                              endif
               endif
               file-end[fcb-address] + data-offset  →
                                             request-file-address[p]
               request-file-address[p]  →  request-lock-address[p]
          endif
          request-size[p]  →  request-lock-size[p]
          do-write( )
          increment file-size[fcb-address] by request-size[p]
          exit-sequential-write( )
endproc
```

Starting a Sequential Write Request

START-SEQUENTIAL-WRITE, depicted in module 5.7.9, performs the setup chores for the SEQUENTIAL-WRITE request. If the file is contiguously organized, the request is rejected as a contiguous file cannot be expanded. Otherwise, the procedure requests permission to add a record to the file. FILE-ADD-RS is a resource semaphore which is used to mediate multiple concurrent extensions to a file.

Calculating the Data Offset

This procedure, depicted in module 5.7.10, performs these functions:

1. Determines the data block size based on the file organization
2. Computes the data offset in the data block from the specified address
3. Computes the remaining space in the current data block

Exiting the Sequential Write Function

This procedure, depicted in module 5.7.11, performs these functions:

1. Updates the file entry in the directory to reflect the new file size
2. Signals a successful write by returning the size parameter
3. Releases FILE-ADD-RS so that other requests may proceed

Finally, the procedure executes a normal I/O exit request.

MODULE 5.7.9

```
procedure start-sequential-write(→ result)
    request-fcb-address[p] → fcb-address
    if contiguous-flag of file-attributes[fcb-address] not equal to zero
        then
                set er-function to event-status[p]
                set er-function to result
                exitproc
    endif
    request(file-add-rs[fcb-address])
    file-size[fcb-address] → request-file-address[p]
    calculate-data-offset(request-file-address[p])
    set one to result
endproc
```

MODULE 5.7.10

```
procedure calculate-data-offset(address)
    calculate-data-block-size( ) → data-block-size
    modulus(address, data-block-size) → data-offset
    data-block-size − data-offset → block-balance
    decrement block-balance by request-size[p]
endproc
```

MODULE 5.7.11

```
procedure exit-sequential-write
    directory-update(fcb-address)
    file-size[fcb-address] → event-data[p]
    release(file-add-rs[fcb-address])
    io-exit( )
endproc
```

5.7.3   Sequential I/O Utilities

Several routines are required to support the execution of sequential I/O functions. They have been collected in this section under the general heading of utilities.

Finding the Record Size

FIND-RECORD-SIZE determines the record size of stream data to be written to a file. Stream data consist of variable-length records terminated by a null character. To update the directory entry on disk properly, the system must know the size of the record just written to the disk. It counts the characters in the data stream until a null character is encountered. The maximum length is provided as a safety check on the searching algorithm. If the user forgets to place a null byte at the end of the stream, the algorithm could conceivably search all of memory. This would potentially cause a map fault by attempting the access beyond the process's limits. The routine is depicted in module 5.7.12.

MODULE 5.7.12

```
procedure find-record-size(record, maximum-length, →result)
      2 * maximum-length → record-length
      define-string(string-address, record, record-length)
      set two to record-count
      while get-character-and-decrement(string-address,
                                  record-length-error) not equal to zero
            do increment record-count
            enddo
      record-count/2 → result
      exitproc
record-length-error:
      increment record-length
      record-length → result
endproc
```

Padding Data Blocks

You may attempt to write a logical record that exceeds the balance of the current data block. When this occurs, a new data block must be allocated to contain the logical record. However, the space remaining in the current data block must be dealt with. The system cannot leave it as it is, as it may contain garbage from previous users. A read operation performed later in the life of the file might pick up this garbage and erroneously interpret it as valid data. This could cause the program to crash, produce erroneous results, or do unexpected things. To prevent such problems, the system carefully pads the data block with well-known data.

Two schools of thought exist in this regard. One argues that the last word in the previous record should be repeated throughout the remainder of the block, as certainly this is valid data. The other argues that the remainder of the block should be filled with null characters. The approach you take depends on the philosophy espoused for the system. We opt for the latter method, as null characters are easy to recognize and are also terminators for stream data. Thus any attempt to read past the last data stream in a block would result in a null character. As this null character occurs before the end of the file, we would interpret a null character as terminating a zero-length record and thus signaling a switch to the next data block.

Padding a Serial File Data Block

The procedure for padding the data block of a serial file is depicted in module 5.7.13. The procedure performs the following steps:

1. Sets up the file address and request size parameters.
2. Adjusts the lock address and size to the device boundaries. If the request size does not exactly correspond to a physical block, the disk block is read into a system buffer.
3. Allocates the next file block and establishes it as the end of the file.
4. Calculates the address in the buffer where padding begins and pads with zeroes the remaining words in the buffer. The number of words to pad is stored in REQUEST-LOCK-SIZE.
5. The new block address is stored in the last two words of the buffer.
6. The file size is updated by the request size.
7. The buffer, if any, is written to disk and released.
8. The offset in the current file block is set to zero and the procedure exits.

Padding a Segmented File Data Block

The procedure for padding a segmented file data block is depicted in module 5.7.14. It sets up the size parameters in the PCB for the read request and calculates the device address. It adjusts the lock address and request size to a block boundary. If an entire block is not to be written, the block is read into a system buffer for further processing. The address (END-OF-BLOCK-AD-DRESS) where padding will commence is calculated. The procedure then clears

MODULE 5.7.13

```
procedure pad-serial(→result)
    block-balance → request-size[p]
    block-balance → request-lock-size[p]
    file-end[fcb-address] + data-offset → request-lock-address[p]
    request-lock-address[p] → request-file-address[p]
    adjust-address-and-size( ) → result
    if result not equal to zero
        then
                read-buffer( ) → result
                if result less than zero
                    then
                    exitproc
        endif
    endif
    allocate-file-block( ) → file-end[fcb-address]
    if event-status[p] less than zero
        then
                event-status[p] → result
                exitproc
    endif
    extract offset from request-file-address[p]
    request-buffer-address[p] + offset → pad-address
    clear from pad-address for request-lock-size[p] words
    request-buffer-address[p] + request-lock-size[p]
                                        → end-of-block-address
    decrement end-of-block-address by 2
    file-end[fcb-address] → memory(end-of-block-address)
    increment file-size[fcb-address] by request-size[p]
    write-buffer( )
    clear data-offset
    event-status[p] → result
endproc
```

the specified area (whose size is given by BLOCK-BALANCE). The buffer is written and released. The file size is updated to reflect the newly padded block. Finally, a new block is allocated for the next write request.

5.8   AN INPUT/OUTPUT PROTECTION MECHANISM

Earlier in this chapter, we discussed the need for protecting records within a file when it is accessed by multiple processes. As each process may be executing

```
procedure pad-segmented(→ result)
    block-balance → request-size[p]
    block-balance → request-lock-size[p]
    find-device-address( ) → result
    if result less than zero
        then
                exitproc
    endif
    adjust-address-and-size( ) → result
    if result not equal to zero
        then
                read-buffer( ) → result
                if result less than zero
                    then
                            exitproc
                endif
    endif
    extract offset from request-file-address[p]
    request-buffer-address[p] + offset → pad-address
    clear beginning at pad-address for request-lock-size[p] words
    write-buffer( )
    increment file-size[fcb-address] by request-size[p]
    allocate-segmented( )
    event-status[p] → result
endproc
```

read and write functions on the file, each function request must be checked to ensure noninterference with other requests. At the same time, a process may be allowed to bypass the protection mechanism and directly read or write a record in the file. Thus the philosophy is to provide a mechanism that enforces protection but requires a user to determine the standards for its usage in his or her program.

The protection mechanism we will describe is based on the concept of the "lock-list." The lock-list concept reserves disk sectors for exclusive use by a process. The respective disk sectors are placed on a list associated with a semaphore which is attached to the FCB. Other processes requesting the same or a subset of the disk sectors already reserved are suspended and enqueued on the resource semaphore pending completion of any activity. The protection mechanism requires two resource semaphores: FILE-ADD-RS, which provides a lock-list for adding data to a file, and FILE-MODIFY-RS, which provides a lock-list for updating a file.

The appropriate semaphore is selected by the IOM when it processes a read or write request. If a write request would expand the extent of the file, the request is enqueued to FILE-ADD-RS. However, if the file address specified in the write request already exists, the request is enqueued to FILE-MODIFY-RS. A read request is always enqueued to FILE-MODIFY-RS since it will be rejected only if the file address does not exist.

Three specific functions are provided for utilizing the protection mechanism:

READ-LOCK	Reads data beginning at the specified address and locks the respective sectors against further access
WRITE-RELEASE	Writes data to previously locked sectors and releases them for access by other processes
UNLOCK	Releases locked sectors without the necessity of writing data to them

These functions and their implementation are described in the following sections. In general, they execute as if they were random requests for I/O. However, they possess an additional feature in that the system always checks to see that the locations referenced by the function are available for reading or writing by the program before actually proceeding with the request.

5.8.1 Reading and Locking Disk Sectors

The READ-LOCK function performs random access input from a segmented or contiguous file. Before the read operation is executed, the file's lock-list is inspected to determine if the specified sectors are locked against access. If the sectors are locked, the request is either deferred or rejected until the sectors are released. The action to be taken depends on the mode of the channel.

When the request is honored, a lock entry is created and associated with the file's lock-list. Once the lock entry is created, subsequent READ-LOCK operations on the channel will be deferred or rejected. Only other READ-LOCK operations are affected. Normal random access read and write functions are not validated against the lock-list. The format of the READ-LOCK request is

SYSTEM(READ-LOCK, EVENT-NR, CHANNEL, NR-WORDS, FILE-ADDRESS)

where	EVENT-NR	is used to signal the process when the read operation is complete
	CHANNEL	is the number of a channel previously opened for input
	ADDRESS	is the address of the process buffer that will receive the data
	NR-WORDS	is the size of the request
	FILE-ADDRESS	is the address of the data in the file

Two data values are returned as a result of the completion of the READ-LOCK request. The event status contains either an error code or the actual number of words transferred to the process. If the READ-LOCK request is successful, the event value contains the lock descriptor word that must be used in subsequent WRITE-RELEASE or UNLOCK requests.

Reading and Locking: Preprocessing

A READ-LOCK request forces a process to be suspended until the specified sectors are accessible. As you may want to continue processing, a subprocess is created to handle the execution of the request. P-READ-LOCK, depicted in module 5.8.1, initializes a subprocess for execution of the READ-LOCK request. The subprocess is given a higher priority than the process issuing the request to ensure early execution of the request and also to enable the requestor to block waiting for completion of the function.

When the subprocess is first activated (at START-SUBPROCESS), it retrieves the procedure address from the EVENT-STATUS entry. In this case, the address of READ-LOCK has been placed therein.

START-READ-WRITE is invoked to initialize the I/O parameters and to check the protection flags. If the setup was successful, control is transferred to the subprocess (see section 3.2.5). A result less than zero indicates that the specified address exceeded the physical size of the file. The procedure computes the request size and verifies that the address does not exceed the file size. A

MODULE 5.8.1

```
procedure p-read-lock
    event-nr[usp] → evn
    create-system-process( ) → n
    initialize-system-process(n, start-subprocess, priority[p] + 2, evn)
    address(read-lock) → event-status[n]
    start-read-write(protection-flags) → result
    if result greater than or equal to zero
        then
            go-to-subprocess( )
    endif
    file-size[fcb-address] − request-file-address[n] → request-size[n]
    if request-size[n] greater than or equal to one
        then
            p-setup-ok( )
        else
            io-setup-error(er-end-of-file)
        endif
endproc
```

valid request size causes the request to be executed, whereas an invalid size forces the request to be rejected.

Reading and Locking a Record

READ-LOCK reads a specified record and locks the corresponding sectors on the disk against further access. READ-LOCK establishes the device address of the record via FIND-DEVICE-ADDRESS. An invalid device address will cause rejection of the request. The request parameters are aligned with a disk sector boundary. The following cases result on a READ-LOCK:

1.   The request is not an exact multiple of the disk sector size. If the lock reject flag of FILE-ATTRIBUTES is set, the system rejects the request because one or more users may be modifying overlapping segments of the specified record area.

2.   The system requests access to the specified sectors via FILE-MODIFY-RS. LOCK-FLAG determines the eventual disposition of the request. If the physical sectors are already locked and LOCK-FLAG equals 0, the request is rejected immediately; otherwise, the subprocess is enqueued on the lock chain until the sectors are released.

READ-LOCK invokes either READ-BUFFER or READ-USER to transfer data from disk to user. The main difference between them is that READ-BUFFER assumes that only a portion of the disk block is required by the user. However, the whole sector must be read into memory. Therefore, READ-BUFFER temporarily acquires a system buffer, reads the disk sector, and extracts the record for the user. The parameters for extraction are located in the PCB. READ-USER merely copies the information directly to the user space. In either case, a successful read causes the record size to be returned as the event status, and the process identifier as the lock identifier.

MODULE 5.8.2

```
procedure read-lock
    find-device-address( ) → result
    if result less than zero
        then
            io-error-exit(result)
    endif
    request-fcb-address[p] → fcb-address
    if lock-reject-flag of file-attributes[fcb-address] not equal to zero
        then
            clear lock-flag
```

```
        else
                set one to lock-flag
        endif
        adjust-address-size( ) → result
        if result not equal to zero
                then
                        if lock-flag equal to zero
                                then
                                        io-error-exit(er-lock)
                        endif
                        request(file-modify-rs[fcb-address], lock-flag) → result
                        if result less than zero
                                then
                                    io-error-exit(result)
                        endif
                        read-buffer( ) → result
                        if result less than zero
                                then
                                        exitproc
                        endif
                        request-map[p] → user-map
                        request-data-address[p] → dataddr
                        move-to-user-space(user-map, request-buffer-address[p],
                                                dataddr, request-size[p])
            else
                        clear request-buffer-address[p]
                        request(file-modify-rs[fcb-address], lock-flag) → result
                        if result less than zero
                                then
                                        io-error-exit(result)
                        endif
                        read-user( ) → result
                        if result less than zero
                                then
                                        exitproc
                        endif
        endif
        request-size[p] → event-status[p]
        notify(p, event-nr, parent, event-status, event-data)
        if request-buffer-address[p] greater than zero
                then
                        release(memory-rs, request-buffer-address[p])
        endif
endproc
```

5.8.2   Writing and Releasing Sectors

WRITE-RELEASE performs random access output and releases the locked sectors. If other requests are pending on the locked sectors, they will be activated when the WRITE-RELEASE function is completed. You must specify the lock descriptor that was returned by a successful READ-LOCK request. This lock descriptor identifies the entry in the lock-list associated with the previous READ-LOCK request.

Both the READ-LOCK and WRITE-RELEASE requests allow you to specify the number of words to be transferred to/from mass storage. It is possible for you to specify a lesser number of words when writing to the disk than were read from the disk under the READ-LOCK operation. The write request may also include words that were not covered by the previous READ-LOCK operation, and for this reason the entire data block must be reserved until the WRITE-RELEASE request is completed.

The format of the WRITE-RELEASE request is

SYSTEM(WRITE-RELEASE, EVENT-NR, CHANNEL, ADDRESS, NR-WORDS, FILE-ADDRESS, LOCK-ID)

where	EVENT-NR	is used to signal the process when the WRITE-RELEASE request has been completed
CHANNEL	is the number of the channel opened for output
ADDRESS	is the address of the process buffer from which the data will be taken
NR-WORDS	is the number of words to be transferred
FILE-ADDRESS	is the address in the file where data are to be written
LOCK-ID	is the lock descriptor from the previous READ-LOCK

Writing and Releasing a Record

The procedure for writing and releasing a record is shown in module 5.8.3. WRITE-RELEASE is executed directly because the relevant sectors should already be locked. However, substantially more checking must be done because the disk sectors may have been locked by a different process. First, WRITE-RELEASE initializes the write parameters via START-READ-WRITE. The system decrements the channel usage count because START-READ-WRITE

procedure write-release
    p → n
    start-read-write(write-protection-flag)
    decrement-channel-use(n)
    lock-identifier[usp] → n
    event-nr[usp] → event-nr[n]
    p → parent[n]
    request-ccb-address[n] → n-ccb-address
    request-ccb-address[p] → p-ccb-address
    if n-ccb-address not equal to p-ccb-address
        then
            p-setup-done(er-lock-identifier)
    endif
    request-fcb-address[n] → n-fcb-address
    request-fcb-address[p] → p-fcb-address
    if n-fcb-address not equal to p-fcb-address
        then
            p-setup-done(er-lock-identifier)
    endif
    request-file-address[p] → p-file-address
    request-file-address[n] → n-file-address
    if p-file-address less than n-file-address
        then
            p-setup-done(er-lock-identifier)
    endif
    n-file-address + request-size[n] → n-size
    p-file-address + request-size[p] → p-size
    if n-size less than p-size
        then
            p-setup-done(er-lock-identifier)
    endif
    request-map[p] → request-map[n]
    request-lock-address[n] → lock-address
    request-file-address[p] + request-size[p] → new-lock-address
    if record-mask & new-lock-address equals zero
    then
        if request-buffer-address[n] not equal to zero
           then
               release(memory-rs, request-buffer-address[n])
               clear request-buffer-address[n]
        endif
    endif
    extract offset from request-file-address[p]

```
            extract sector-address from request-file-address[p]
            if request-buffer-address[n] − 1 less than zero
                then
                        request-file-address[p] − sector-address +
                            request-lock-address[n] → request-buffer-address[n]
                        if request-buffer-address[n] equals zero
                           then
                                    decrement request-data-address[n] by offset
                           else
                                request-file-address[p] →
                                                            request-file-address[n]
                                request-size[p] → request-size[n]
                        endif
                else
                        request-file-address[p] − sector-address → delta
                        move-from-user-space(request-map[p],
                                request-data-address[p], request-buffer-address[n]
                                                    + delta, request-size[n])
                        increment request-lock-address[n] by delta
                        request-buffer-address[n] + delta →
                                                        request-data-address[n]
                        clear request-map[n]
            endif
        request-size[p] + offset + record-mask → request-lock-size[p]
        do-write( )
endproc
```

assumes that it is preparing for subprocess execution. Then it verifies the calling
process identifier against the process identifier that locked the specified sectors
(as one process can pass a lock identifier to another process).

A process is not allowed to write-and-release sectors if any of the following
conditions hold:

1. The channels on which the disk sectors were locked are different.
2. The file control blocks are different.
3. The current process attempts to release only a portion of the locked area,
   including a subarea not locked by the original process.
4. The area to be released does not correspond to the area that was originally
   locked.

If the request successfully passes these checks, the current process is allowed to
modify and release a subarea of the locked sectors. Most of the code is used to set
up the new lock parameters for the case in which only a segment of the lock area
is to be released. Data are copied from user space into a buffer when the disk sec-

tors to be modified do not correspond to disk sector boundaries. From here, writing proceeds normally via a call to DO-WRITE that is also responsible for releasing the sectors after writing.

5.8.3   Unlocking Disk Sectors

The UNLOCK request allows a process to release data sectors without performing a write operation. Any read or write requests pending on the locked sectors are activated by the unlock function. The format of the request is

SYSTEM(UNLOCK, LOCK-ID) → ERROR

where   LOCK-ID   is a lock descriptor returned by a previous READ-LOCK

             ERROR   is a possible error code

MODULE 5.8.4

```
procedure unlock
    unlock-identifier[usp] → n
    if current-queue[n] not equal to zero
        then
                set-return-and-exit(er-lock-identifier)
    endif
    request-fcb-address[n] → fcb-address
    release(file-modify-rs[fcb-address], n)
    decrement-channel-use(n)
    release(pcb-rs, n)
    set-return-and-exit(1)
endproc
```

5.8.4   Lock-List Initialization Procedures

A lock-list is a list of processes that are blocked in execution while awaiting access to one or more sectors of a physical record. Elements are inserted into or removed from the lock-list when a system process performs a request or release operation upon the resource semaphore FILE-MODIFY-RS. Four procedures are required to manage the lock-list.

Inserting a Process into a Lock-List

A process is inserted into the lock-list when a REQUEST operation is issued against the semaphore FILE-MODIFY-RS. This operation takes the form

REQUEST(FILE-MODIFY-RS[FCB-ADDRESS], LOCK-FLAG)

where if LOCK-FLAG has the value zero, the request will be rejected if the physical record is already locked. Otherwise, the process is placed on the lock-list associated with the channel specified in the READ-LOCK request. The procedure for inserting a process into a lock-list is depicted in module 5.8.5. The argument LOCK-LIST-ADDRESS is the address of the lock-list for the specified channel. The argument ENTRY is the value of LOCK-FLAG.

ENTER-INTO-LOCK-QUEUE initially checks the status of the lock-list. If it is empty, (i.e., FIRST-ELEMENT equals zero), the process is inserted as the

MODULE 5.8.5

```
procedure enter-into-lock-queue(lock-list-address, entry)
      clear request-lock-down[p]
      address(queue-start[lock-list-address]) → lock-queue-head
      queue-start[lock-list-address] → first-element
      if first-element equals zero
            then
                  clear return-value[p]
                  lock-queue-start(p)
                  exitproc
      endif
      request-lock-back[first-element] → first-element
      request-lock-address[p] → first-ms-address
      first-ms-address + request-lock-size[p] − 1 → last-ms-address
      clear start-level
      search-lock-list( ) → insert-level
      insert-level → return-value[p]
      if insert-level not equal to zero
            then
                  if entry equals zero
                        then
                              set er-lock to return-value[p]
                              exitproc
                  endif
      endif
      if current-element equals zero
      then
                  lock-queue-start(p)
            else
                  lock-queue-insert(p, current-element)
      endif
endproc
```

first element of the queue. A value of zero returned by the procedure indicates that the lock has been established.

If the lock-list is not empty, ENTER-INTO-LOCK-QUEUE searches for the appropriate location in the queue in which to insert the process. The list is ordered by the value of the first mass storage address to be referenced in the request. Multiple tasks may be blocked awaiting access to a single mass storage address, so the procedure develops depending sublists for these processes. The procedure invokes SEARCH-LOCK-LIST to determine where a process is to be inserted into the list. INSERT-LEVEL is the nonzero depth in a group of processes if the process is already present in the list. This depth is set by the procedure to indicate the task is already blocked for those disk sectors.

Next, ENTER-INTO-LOCK-QUEUE checks to see if the request should be rejected. If INSERT-LEVEL is greater than zero and ENTRY equals zero, a lock error code is returned by the procedure. The requested lock will not be established. Finally, the process is inserted into the list at the location given by CURRENT-ELEMENT and is established as either the first process to lock the specified sectors (via LOCK-QUEUE-START) or the most recent process to do so (via LOCK-QUEUE-INSERT).

Upon return from the REQUEST, the event status will contain one of the following values, indicating the state of the process:

<0 An error occurred; the process is not suspended
$=0$ Lock is established and ready for I/O
>0 Process in lock-list and blocked

Removing a Process from the Lock-List

When a disk sector becomes accessible, any processes blocked against it must be reactivated. The entry describing the disk sector is removed from the lock-list by the RELEASE operation on the semaphore FILE-MODIFY-RS. This operation takes the form

RELEASE(FILE-MODIFY-RS[FCB-ADDRESS], LS-ADDRESS)

where   LS-ADDRESS   is the mass storage address of the disk sector

The procedure for removing one or more processes from the lock-list is depicted in module 5.8.6. The argument LOCK-LIST-ADDRESS is the address of the lock-list for the channel specified in the WRITE-RELEASE request. The argument ENTRY is the mass storage address for the disk sector. The procedure invokes ADJUST-LIST to extract the entry for the physical record. The current process is allowed to continue execution after the extraction has been performed.

MODULE 5.8.6

procedure remove-from-lock-queue(lock-list-address, entry)
    address(queue-start[lock-list-address]) → lock-queue-head
    clear start-level
    adjust-list(entry)
    clear return-value[p]
endproc

Lock-List Allocation

The REQUEST/RELEASE operations have two results: the lock-list is manipulated to insert or remove a process, and the current process is informed of the result.

    LOCK-ALLOCATOR determines how to handle the current process. If the result of the operation was less than or equal to zero, the process is reactivated. Otherwise, the process will have been blocked on the list. You should consult section 7.10 for detailed explanation of REQUEST/RELEASE functions.

MODULE 5.8.7

procedure lock-allocator(rs)
    if return-value[p] less than or equal to zero
        then
            activate(p)
    endif
endproc

5.8.5   Lock-List Manipulation Procedures

A lock-list is a two-dimensional queue consisting of a list of elements identifying disk sectors with which are associated PCBs. A PCB is attached to a list when the process is blocked awaiting access to the disk sectors. The following functions are required to manipulate the lock-lists for insertion, searching, and adjustment of PCBs:

ADJUST-LIST	Removes an element and closes up the ranks
SEARCH-LOCK-LIST	Identifies the location in which to insert a new list element
FREE-LOCK-LIST	Removes all elements associated with a particular channel

Adjusting the Lock-List

When an element is removed from the lock-list, the remaining elements must be redistributed in the chain because the first element may have included succeeding elements as subsets which now assume an identity of their own.

The procedure for adjusting the lock-list is ADJUST-LIST, which removes the specified element from the lock-list. If this process was the only process blocked against that mass storage address, the procedure exits gracefully. LOCK-QUEUE-EXTRACT manipulates the pointers for relinking the list elements.

Other processes may have been blocked against the same mass storage sectors whose first sector was specified by ENTRY in REMOVE-FROM-LOCK-QUEUE. If so, these processes, which may have sectors to lock of varying length, must be distributed across the chain based on the first sector address. REQUEST-LOCK-DOWN points to the first such process enqueued to a given mass storage location. At this point the system also checks to see if this was the last entry in the circular list and sets the pointer to the first entry in the list.

ADJUST-LIST computes the area that was locked by adding the lock size to the first sector address. SEARCH-LOCK-LIST finds the location in which to insert the first sublist. This sublist is inserted into the lock chain in its entirety. Each sublist in the list is also inserted into the lock chain in the appropriate position.

In figure 5-10, PCB-11, PCB-12, and PCB-13 are entries in the sublist. Each PCB may also be the head of a deeper sublist. Therefore, the sublists whose heads are PCB-11, PCB-12, and PCB-13 will migrate to positions in the primary lock chain.

Searching the Lock-List

When an insertion is to be made in the lock-list, the specific location must be found by scanning the entries in the chain. The search always starts from the first entry. The procedure for searching the lock-list is depicted in module 5.8.9. First, the system determines if the list is empty. If so, the procedure exits with the CURRENT-ELEMENT equal to zero. In this case (as we saw in ENTER-INTO-LOCK-QUEUE), the PCB is inserted as the only entry in the queue.

When the lock-list consists of multiple entries, we need to search the lock-list for the appropriate position at which to insert the PCB. The search parameters, START-MS-ADDRESS and LAST-MS-ADDRESS, bound the area on the mass storage device that was locked. Each entry in the lock-list has its first and last addresses compared with these two bounds. This isolates the position in which to insert this process.

If the process is to be inserted at the beginning or end of the lock-list, the

MODULE 5.8.8

```
procedure adjust-list(entry)
    entry → removed-element
    lock-queue-extract(removed-element)
    request-lock-down[removed-element] → current-process
    current-process → first-process
    if first-process equals zero
        then
                exitproc
    endif
    while true
        do
        request-lock-forward[removed-element] → first-element
        if search-element not equal to zero
            then
                if first-element equal to memory(lock-queue-head)
                    then
                            request-lock-back[first-element] →
                                                    first-element
                endif
        endif
        request-lock-forward[current-process] → first-ms-address
        lock-queue-head → save-queue-head
        request-lock-address[current-process] → first-ms-address
        first-ms-address + request-lock-size[current-process − 1 →
                                                last-ms-address
        search-lock-list( ) → insert-level
        if current-element equals zero
            then
                    lock-queue-start(current-process)
            else
                    lock-queue-insert(current-process, current-element)
        endif
        if insert-level equals zero
            then
                    activate(current-process)
        endif
        if next-process not equal to first-process
            then
                    next-process → current-process
                    save-queue-head → lock-queue-head
        endif
    enddo
endproc
```

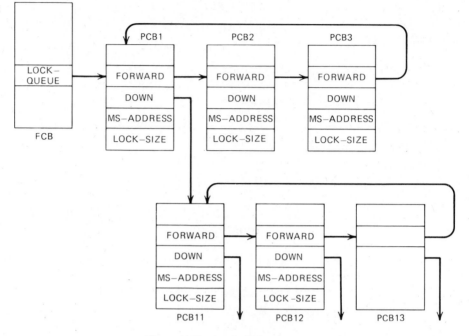

Figure 5.10   Lock chain structure.

procedure exits. Otherwise, it searches the sublist to find at what depth the new PCB should be inserted. Note that multiple sublists may exist horizontally and vertically below the primary lock-list. The limiting factor that precludes any further insertions at a deeper level is the size of one disk sector.

MODULE 5.8.9

```
procedure search-lock-list(→ insert-level)
      clear lock-identifier
      start-level → insert-level
      if memory(lock-queue-head) equals zero
            then
                    clear current-element
                    set current-process to removed-element
                    set one to select-element
                    exitproc
      endif
      first-element → current-element
      while true
            do
                    request-lock-address[current-element] → start-ms-address
```

```
                start-ms-address + request-lock-size[current-element]
                                            → last-ms-address
            while last-ms-address less than start-ms-address
                do
                if current-element equals memory(lock-queue-head)
                    then
                            increment lock-identifier
                            request-lock-back[current-element] →
                                                    current-element
                            exitproc
                endif
                request-lock-back[current-element] → current-element
                enddo
            enddo
        if start-ms-address greater than last-ms-address
        then
                    exitproc
        endif
        increment insert-level
        address(request-lock-down[current-element]) → lock-queue-head
        memory(lock-queue-head) → current-element
        if current-element not equal to zero
            then
                    request-lock-back[current-element → current-element
        endif
endproc
```

Releasing Elements from the Lock-List

Multiple processes may share access to a file—a situation that necessitates the locking mechanism. Some or all of these processes may have opened the file on different channels. At any time, a task may close a channel to a file. When this event occurs, other processes blocked on the file via the same channel must be removed from the lock-list and activated with the error code ER-CHANNEL-CLOSE. If a task issued a RESET command, all channels would be closed and the lock-list emptied.

FREE-LOCK-LIST (module 5.8.10) removes all PCB from the lock-list associated with a specified channel. FREE-LOCK-LIST is usually invoked by the CLOSE request or the RESET request. It requires two arguments:

RS-ADDRESS	Address of the semaphore in the FCB
CHANNEL	Identifier of the channel on which the file was opened

MODULE 5.8.10

```
procedure free-lock-list(rs-address, channel)
    address(workspace) → stack-address
    clear current-level
    rs-wait-queue[rs-address] → rwq
    address(queue-start[rwq]) → lock-queue
    memory(lock-queue) → last-element
    request-lock-back[last-element] → current-element
    if last-element not equal to zero
        then
entry check-down:
            while true
                do
                address(request-lock-down[current-element])
                                                → down-element
                if memory(down-element) not equal to zero
                    then
                    copy(lock-queue, stack-address,3)
                    increment stack-address by 3
                    increment current-level
                    down-element → lock-queue
                    memory(lock-queue) → last-element
                    request-lock-back[last-element]
                                                → current-element
                else
                exitdo
            endif
            enddo
entry check-element:
            request-ccb-address[current-element] → ccb-address
            if current-level equals zero
                then
                    if current-queue[current-element]
                                                not equal to zero
                    then
                        goto continue-search
                    endif
            endif
            lock-queue → lock-queue-head
            adjust-list(current-element)
            if current-level equals zero
                then
                request-ccb-address[current-element] → ccb-address
                decrement channel-use-count[ccb-address]
```

```
                    release(pcb-rs, current-element)
                    else
                    er-channel-close → return-value [current-element]
                    activate(current-element)
               endif
     endif
entry continue-search:
     if current-element not equal to last-element
          then
                    request-lock-back[current-element] → current-element
                    goto check-down
          else
               decrement current-level
          if current-level greater than or equal to zero
                    then
                         decrement stack-address by 3
                         copy(stack-address, lock-queue, 3)
                         goto check-element
               endif
     endif
endproc
```

The procedure uses a workspace, which may be part of the PDB, to store information about the position and depth in the lock-list. The algorithm consists of scanning the lock-list for each entry which utilizes the specified channel. At each entry in the primary level, the search descends to all subentries to determine if any of these also have use of the channel. The pointers for each level are stored in the workspace because as processes are found that use the specified channel, they are immediately activated with ER-CHANNEL-CLOSE as the result of the function.

Whenever a process is removed from the lock-list, any processes at a lower depth are immediately redistributed throughout the chain. If the lock-list has grown to a considerable depth and length, the process of scanning all entries and redistributing sublists may consume a large portion of time.

5.8.6 Lock Queue Utilities

Two procedures are used to simplify the locking and freeing of a file: LOCK-REQUEST and FREE-REQUEST. These routines are used by the IOM. Their intent is self-evident.

Three procedures are used to directly manipulate the lock queue: LOCK-QUEUE-START, LOCK-QUEUE-INSERT, and LOCK-QUEUE-EXTRACT. LOCK-QUEUE-START enters an element into an empty lock-list. LOCK-

QUEUE-INSERT enters the current element after the specified entry and adjusts the chain pointers. LOCK-QUEUE-EXTRACT removes an entry from the lock-list and adjusts the chain pointers.

MODULE 5.8.11

```
procedure lock-request
        request-fcb-address[p] → fcb-address
        request(file-modify-rs[fcb-address], p)
endproc
```

MODULE 5.8.12

```
procedure free-request
      request-fcb-address[p] → fcb-address
      release(file-modify-rs[fcb-address], p)
endproc
```

MODULE 5.8.13

```
procedure lock-queue-start(current-element)
      current-element → request-lock-forward[current-element]
      current-element → request-lock-back[current-element]
      current-element → lock-queue-head
endproc
```

MODULE 5.8.14

```
procedure lock-queue-insert(new-element, current-element)
      request-lock-forward[current-element]
                                    → request-lock-forward[new-element]
      new-element → request-lock-forward[current-element]
      request-lock-forward[new-element] → fwd-element
      request-lock-back[fwd-element] → request-lock-back [new-element]
      new-element → request-lock-back[new-element]
      if lock-identifier not equal to 0
          then
                 new-element → lock-queue-head
      endif
endproc
```

MODULE 5.8.15

```
procedure lock-queue-extract(current-element)
    request-lock-forward[current-element] → fwd-element
    if fwd-element − current-element equals zero
        then
            clear lock-queue-head
        else
            request-lock-back[current-element] → back-element
            back-element → request-lock-back[fwd-element]
            fwd-element → request-lock-forward[back-element]
            if back-element − lock-queue-head equals zero
                then
                    fwd-element →lock-queue-head
            endif
    endif
endproc
```

CHAPTER

6

File Management

Just as main memory is shared among multiple users, secondary storage must also be shared among users. Sharing is accomplished through allocation of physical blocks of a disk drive or tape reel to a particular user. Within this space allocation, data are represented as a named, possibly protected, collection of records known as a file. Each user, of course, wishes to manage independently a private portion of the disk. User isolation is accomplished by assigning a directory—that is, a catalog or index of personal files. At the same time, a user may wish to share some of these files with other users while restricting them to a particular type of access.

A second aspect of file management concerns the provision of a means of accessing the files. Accessibility involves opening (linking a program to a file) and closing (unlinking a program from a file) of files. Associated with accessibility is the concept of efficient utilization of available user space. An OS usually supports several methods of file organization which provide different degrees of access efficiency. This chapter describes the design of a file management subsystem as a collection of available services. The file management subsystem usually represents the highest level of data management that is normally supported by the OS.

6.1 CONCEPTS OF FILE MANAGEMENT

A file management system can be simple or complex. It may provide a few simple services necessary to a specific application, or a sophisticated range of functions for solving a variety of data management problems. To design a file management system, the system designer must be cognizant of the major concepts associated with file management.

6.1.1 Motivation for a File System

A file is a collection of related information on which is imposed a structure specified by its user. The file is known and addressable by the file name. Examples of files are the text of a program to be compiled, an executable load module, or the ticket and seat reservation information for an airline flight. A file is usually composed of subunits known as records, which in turn are composed of data items or fields. The data stored in files represent information about entities in the real world.

Why do we need files? Several motivations for file systems are easily mentioned. First, and perhaps foremost, the file system is used to overcome the limitations on the size of main memory. The data to be manipulated by the process usually exceed the immediate capacity of main memory. File space on mass storage devices provides a convenient way to hold the data until they are needed by the process.

Given that we can store information, it makes sense to be able to store it between executions of a program (as most programs are run over and over again). The file system provides a method for organizing data so that we can retrieve them when we want them, yet be assured that they are available at any time. Long-term storage of data is an essential feature of modern OSs.

The mass storage devices on which data are stored possess fixed physical characteristics. Often, the physical organization of data is unsuited for usage by a program. This is particularly true when many programs may manipulate the same data. The file, as a logical concept, may be viewed differently by each program. The file system performs the translation of logical characteristics to physical characteristics.

Finally, the file system provides a set of services that enables the user to manipulate the data as necessary to accomplish the work. One such service is the protection of data from access by other users. The file system should also protect the user from accidental hardware failures by giving the capability to "back up" data. Another service allows multiple users to share a single copy of a file. This service is motivated by the need to improve equipment effectiveness by maintaining only a single copy of frequently used programs or data on the mass storage devices. The mass storage device is usually the most expensive hardware component of the computer system. The file system allows multiple users to share a single device at low cost.

File systems can be simple or complex. Their nature depends on the variety of applications and the environment in which the computer system will be used. For an interactive, general-purpose system, the following constitutes a minimal set of intrinsic requirements [wats70]:

1. Each user should be able to create, delete, and change files.
2. Each user may have controlled access to other users' files.

3. Each user may control what types of access are allowed to the user's files.
4. Each user should be able to restructure the user's files in a form appropriate to his problem.
5. Each user should be able to move data between files.
6. Each user should be able to back up and recover the user's files in case of damage.
7. Each user should be able to access the user's files by a symbolic name.

The next few sections explore some of these requirements in greater detail.

6.1.2 Volume Sharing and File Directories

Modern mass storage devices provide anywhere from 5 up to 600 Mbytes of data storage in one volume. It is inconceivable to expect that each user should have a private volume, as their cost runs from $100 to $500. Moreover, the efficiency of the computer system would be seriously degraded if the number of users were limited by the number of volumes that could be accommodated on the system at one time. The file system provides a method for volume sharing known as the file directory.

The file directory is a list of all the files that belong to a single user. In fact, the file directory is usually itself a file. As users, like files, come and go, the OS must be able to maintain a list of the current user directories. This list is often known as the master file directory (MFD) and is also a file itself. The location of the MFD must always be known in order to access the volume contents. On most systems, it is placed on the first few cylinders of the first disk platter. Thus the MFD is assigned a unique, fixed allocation of space near the beginning of the volume.

The MFD is transparent to the user. It is accessible only by the OS and usually only through special access methods. If a user wants to access a file, the name of the file must be specified to the OS. The file manager searches the MFD for the location of the user's directory, and then searches the user's directory for the location of the file. The entry in the file directory is usually an abbreviated form of the FCB.

In figure 6.1, note that two users have utilized the same file name, ABC. This does not pose a conflict, as the user directories are independent of each other. Within the file system, all user directory names must be unique within a given volume. Furthermore, within a user directory, all user file names must be unique. Thus, to access a given file, we specify its system-path-name, which is a concatenation of the names of all directories forming the access path to the file. The system-path-name is a unique road map to any file managed by the OS. An example of a system-path-name is VOL1: USER2: ABC.

In a system with multiple devices, the user may have to specify the volume name as well, as there could also be a file named ABC in the directory USER2 on VOL2. The specification of the volume name is the result of the file space

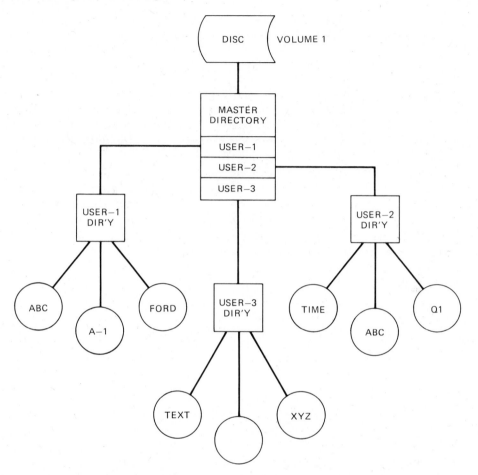

Figure 6.1 Structure of file directories.

allocation strategy. File space may be allocated using either a global or local strategy. In a global strategy, the file manager considers all mass storage devices as providing a single contiguous file space. Allocation of a file to a volume may be independent of the user. There is only one MFD, as there is only one file space.

In a local strategy, each volume is treated as a single file space. Each volume has its own MFD. File space allocation requires the user to specify on which volume a file should be placed. The local strategy requires a simpler algorithm than the global strategy. It also allows a removable volume capability as each volume carries its own MFD with it. This capability allows the potential file space to be extended to the limit of the number of available volumes rather than the number of disk drives. Implementing a removable volume capability under a global strategy usually requires special rules that violate the uniformity and symmetry of the file management system.

Subdirectories versus Partitions

In most minicomputer systems, a directory is usually associated with a single volume such as a disk pack. The disk pack must be shared among multiple users in a manner that allows each user flexibility in naming and creating files. Two approaches to allocating space on a volume have been used: subdirectories and partitions. To understand these concepts, the reader must realize that the directory represents all the allocatable space available on the disk. The system has to parcel this space among the various users.

Both subdirectories and partitions are named subdivisions of the allocatable space on the disk. The difference between them is that the partition is a fixed allocation of disk blocks, whereas the subdirectory may expand and contract as necessary. The subdirectory name becomes another entry on the access path to the file. In figure 6.1, the subdirectories are USER-1, USER-2, and USER-3. Subdirectories are discussed further in section 6.9.

6.1.3   File Characteristics

Each file is uniquely different from every other file in the system. At a minimum, this difference is forced by the fact that no two files may have the same name (within a user directory). Other characteristics serve to further distinguish files.

File Name

Each file is given a name. The name is usually represented as a string and should be representative of the contents of the file. File names, in most minicomputer systems, vary from 1 to 12 characters in length. The file name can usually be composed of letters, numbers, and certain special characters, generally beginning with an alphanumeric character. One exception is a file name that represents a system device as a psuedofile. These names may begin with the character "$" in order to identify them as psuedofiles.

Examples of valid file/device names are

$LPTO	Indicates line printer unit 0
FORTCOM	Indicates the FORTRAN compiler
TESTDATA	Could indicate a set of user test data

File Extension

A problem arises when naming files by the method described above. Suppose that a user has a program for computing the gas mileage of his or her car that is stored in a file named FINDMILEAGE. The user wants to compile this program to create an object module, and link/load it with other subroutines and system library modules to create an executable element. Each successive file would have to be given a different name, even though they all relate to the same program. The proliferation of names, particularly for users with many files, would make the housekeeping chore of remembering what one has extremely difficult.

To solve this problem, a file name is usually extended by appending two or three characters that specify the usage of the file. The extension is optional, although most system programs will automatically insert the proper extension for any files that they may create. The OS usually recognizes a standard set of extensions, but the user is free to create new ones. Among the common extensions are:

Extension	Meaning
DR	Directory/subdirectory file
FR	FORTRAN source module
OL	Overlay library
SV	Executable program
LB	User library of relocatable object modules

The extension is usually separated from the file name by a period. The separation character is based on the whim of the designer. Examples include:

FORTRAN.LB To indicate the FORTRAN Library
SYSTEM.SV To indicate an executable version of the OS

For example, using FINDMILEAGE, we would have a FORTRAN source file labeled FINDMILEAGE.FR. This file would be compiled into a relocatable binary labeled FINDMILEAGE.RB. Then we would link this binary with modules from the FORTRAN library FORTRAN.LB to produce an executable program called FINDMILEAGE.SV.

File Attributes

A file is further distinguished by a set of attributes specifying its type, protection, and buffering mode. Bits in the FILE-ATTRIBUTES word (see figure 6.2) indicate which attributes are set. When a copy of a file's directory entry is printed on the terminal, letters are used to indicate the attributes that are set. The list of attribute letters and their possible meanings might include:

Attribute	Meanings
P	Permanent file (may not be altered)
D	Directory file
C	Contiguous file
S	Segmented file
L	Serial file
E	Link entry file
W	Write-protected file
R	Read-protected file
O	Output buffering standard
I	Input buffering standard
K	Reject lock sequences
X	Execute only file

The usage of these attributes according to file types is discussed in later sections of this chapter.

File Type

The type of file refers to its organization and usage. The types and organizations provided depend on the environment in which the system will be used. However, certain standard types exist. These are enumerated briefly below and described in the text.

Type	Usage
Directory	Holds FCBs which describe other files
Link entry	Serves as a logical pointer to an existing file in the current or another directory
Segmented	Provides a random access file structure that can have unlimited size
Contiguous	Provides one contiguous block of storage that supports fast direct access
Serial	Provides a sequential organization that may expand in an unlimited fashion

6.1.4   File Management—The File Control Block

The effective management of files requires several databases. The primary database is the file control block (FCB), which describes the characteristics of the file. Its structure is shown in table 6.1.

15–11	10–6	5–0

Bit Numbers	Usage
15–14	Device class on which file is stored
10–6	Pointer block size
5–0	Data block size

Figure 6.2 Structure of the allocation data word.

Table 6.1 File Control Block Structure

Entry	Usage
file-name	Name of the file
file-extension	Two-character extension specifying file type
file-attributes	Attributes of the file
file-link-name	Name of the target file for a link entry
file-start	Physical disk address of the first file block
file-allocation-data	Information about disk allocation
file-size	Size of the file
file-end	Physical disk address of last file block
file-directory-free-count	Number of free words in a directory
file-create-date	Date when the file was created
file-create-time	Time when the file was created
file-buffer-size	Buffer size for automatic buffering
file-record-size	Size of the physical record
file-directory-address	Address of the file directory entry
file-use-count	Count of the number of users
file-allocation-size	Initial size of the file
file-modify-rs	Address of the semaphore controlling updates
file-add-rs	Address of the semaphore controlling extensions

Each file is given a name that has a string representation of the name is composed of 1 to 10 characters (although this is an arbitrary decision). The type of file is qualified by adding a two-character extension to the file name, as described in section 6.1.3. Each file is distinctively characterized by its file attributes. The structure of the attribute word is shown in table 6.2.

Depending on the file type, the file manager may determine where the begin-

Table 6.2   Structure of the File Attributes Entry

Bit Number	Usage
15	Write protect flag
14	Read protect flag
13	Permanent file flag
12	Lock reject flag
11	Output buffering flag
10	Input buffering flag
9	Channel lock flag
8	Channel open flag
7	Immediate close flag
5	Device channel flag
4	Directory file flag
3	Link file flag
2	Segmented file flag
1	Contiguous file flag
0	Serial file flag

ning and end of the file are located on disk. FILE-START and FILE-END, respectively, contain the addresses of the first and last disk blocks on the file. Because disk blocks assigned to a segmented file may be scattered all over the disk, these entries reflect the addresses of the first and last segment pointer blocks instead (see section 6.2.3).

Every file has a size. For contiguous files, this size is permanently fixed when the file is created. For serial files, the size is initially zero but increases as records are added to the file. The same fact holds true for segmented files, with one basic difference. A segmented file may also decrease in size as records are deleted from the file. That is, a user process may decide to release disk blocks assigned to a segmented file. FILE-SIZE contains the current file size in each case.

Each file has its creation date and time recorded in the FCB. This allows the system to keep track of the age of a file system where the contents of the file undergo substantial modification. Some systems allow files to be selectively deleted based on their age.

Two important entries are the buffer size and the record size. If a file is marked for automatic buffering, FILE-BUFFER-SIZE specifies the size of the buffer to be allocated when the file is opened by a user process. The record size specifies the physical size of the record for the file (see figure 6.3).

The entries FILE-NAME through FILE-RECORD-SIZE represent the file directory entry—that portion of the FCB which is stored on disk for the lifetime of the file. When a file is opened by the user, the file directory entry is read into

15–14	13–12	11–0

Bit Numbers   Usage

15–14	Number of output buffers to allocate
13–12	Number of input buffers to allocate
11–0	Physical record size

Figure 6.3   Structure of FILE-RECORD-SIZE.

memory and additional information appended to form the FCB. This additional information is used by the file manager to control access to the file.

The additional information consists of the file directory entry address, the use count for the file, and the resource semaphores which control additions and modifications to the file's contents. FILE-DIRECTORY-ADDRESS contains the address of the file directory entry on disk. Whenever the file is expanded, both the FCB and the file directory entry are updated. This approach attempts to ensure the most accurate reflection of the file's current status. FILE-USE-COUNT merely keeps track of the number of users concurrently accessing the file. When the number of users goes to zero, the FCB is deleted from memory. FILE-MODIFY-RS and FILE-ADD-RS are resource semaphores used to monitor and control concurrent updates and additions to the file when the appropriate system calls are utilized (see section 5.8).

6.1.5   File Protection

In any OS, a large number of files need to be managed and associated with user processes when requested. If individual copies of a file were maintained for each user, the required file space would quickly exceed the mass storage capacity of the system. Thus it is imperative that the operating system support a file sharing capability and a corresponding file protection capability. In file sharing, multiple users are allowed to open the file and read or write from the file in apparently simultaneous fashion. Support for record sharing has been discussed in section 5.8.

The second capability, file protection, involves the notion of control over reading, writing, and accessing the file's contents. The user wants to be able to protect data from being tampered with by others. Most systems implement a limited form of file protection. The problem is that adequate file protection requires a trade-off between the overhead associated with data structures and program code and the degree of protection to be provided to the user. Protection, as it applies to privacy and security, is currently a significant problem in OS design. The designer must be aware of different methods of implementing a file protection system in order to determine which one meets the requirements of the specific environment.

Components of a File Protection System

A file protection system has four components:

Objects to be protected: for example, files
Types of access to files that will be allowed
Individuals who can access files
Procedures that implement file protection

In a file management system, each file has an owner, the individual who creates the file by specifying its name and location. If the owner decides that the file can be shared with other users, who they are and in what manner they can access the file must be specified. File protection procedures to implement these capabilities can be designed using global or local methodologies. What is important is that the protection procedure be able to authenticate the user.

Types of Access to a File

A number of different types of access can be defined for a file system. Usually, some special access privileges are provided that depend on the structure of the OS. A generic list of access privileges commonly cited in the technical literature includes:

READ access   User is given permission to read all or part of a file into his or her own environment. User can then process and manipulate the data according to specific requirements.

UPDATE access   User is given permission to modify the contents of all or a portion of the file.

WRITE access   User cannot only update the contents of the file but may also add new records to it, thus extending its size.

DELETE access   User is given the capability to delete the file itself. In systems using files for interprocess communication, deletion of a file would indicate that the message had been received.

EXECUTE access   User is given the privilege of using the file to perform a specific function without the ability of reading it and seeing how it accomplishes its task.

CHANGE access   User is given the privilege of modifying the attributes of a file. Normally, this privilege is reserved for the file owner.

A user who does not possess any of these privileges is not allowed to access the file in any way. The owner of the file normally possesses all privileges except the EXECUTE privilege. Other types of access privileges are frequently encountered, including the ability to copy data records from a file and the ability to determine the existence of a file without accessing its contents. It should be noted that the complexity of the file protection system increases in direct proportion to the number of access privileges to be supported and the way in which they interact.

Password Protection

The simplest method of authenticating a user for access to a file is to give him or her the "key" to the file. The key generally takes the form of a password associated with a particular access privilege. A password system can be implemented either globally or locally. On a global scale, one password is associated with each type of access privilege. Each user who can exercise a particular access privilege is told the password for that privilege. When assigning a file, the user submits the passwords for each privilege to be exercised. The problem with this approach is that the more users who know the passwords, the greater likelihood that an unauthorized user will find them out.

The implementation of password protection on a local basis involves an access list maintained with each file. Entries on the list, created and maintained by the owner, consist of user identifiers and passwords. One password usually suffices to allow a user to exercise all access privileges. Each user identifier has a different password associated with it. Note that if a password is compromised in this approach, only one user is inconvenienced, whereas many users must be notified when the password is changed in the previous approach.

The cost of implementing the global approach is relatively low. If each password consisted of six characters, at most 36 characters would be reserved in the directory file entry. The local approach, on the other hand, requires 12 characters per user identifier with no apparent limit on the number of users who might be permitted to use the file (assuming that each user identifier and each password requires six characters). The access list might be organized as a sequence of disk blocks associated with the directory file entry. Figure 6.4 demonstrates one such structure. Note that the validation procedure must fetch the access control list and search it each time a user requests the file. For many users, this may require multiple disk accesses and lengthy search times.

Maintenance of an access control list can be a difficult problem. Changing the password involves searching the list for the proper entry. The password is then replaced and the access control list updated on the disk. When deleting a

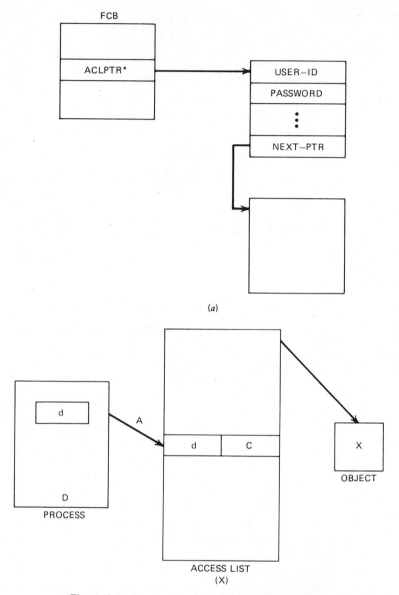

Figure 6.4   An access control list implementation.

user, the entry is filled by zeros. Of course, if that were the only entry in that block, the system must compact the access list. When adding a new user identifier, the system may have to allocate another disk block and link it to the current list. All of these operations require a complex set of utilities, thus increasing both the size and complexity of the OS.

Process issues action A for object x

System obtains c by searching access list for d

    If A is enabled by c, do the action

    Otherwise, return an error

The Access Matrix

A variation on the access control list is known as the access matrix. Two approaches to the access matrix can be implemented. In the first, a list is kept of the valid user identifiers that may access the file. Associated with each user identifier is an access word specifying the valid access privileges for that file. Each access privilege is specified by a bit set to one in the access word (see figure 6.5).

A second approach that establishes a unique relationship between a pair of users is described by Colin [coli71]. A matrix of user identifiers is created that relates a user's access privileges to every other user's files. The entry in the matrix consists of a user access word (UAW) whose bits specify the privileges that a user may exercise with respect to the other users' files. Whenever access is requested to the user's own files, the UAW contains all bits set to one.

Both methods require significant storage requirements but allow considerable flexibility in the protection system.

Design Principles for a Protection Mechanism

The issue of information protection is large enough to occupy a book by itself. Indeed, a well-thought-out tutorial on information protection has been published by Clark and Redell [clar75]. Nevertheless, this topic is too important to leave without mentioning key design principles for protection mechanisms. These principles are extracted from an excellent paper by Saltzer [salt74].

Producing a protection mechanism that will guarantee the security and integrity of information to date has proven impossible. The degree to which protection is engendered by the software is a function of cost. The frequency and

	F1	F2	F3	F4	F5	F6 . . . .
U1			(r, w)			
U2		(e)		(r)		(c, d)
U3	(r, w)				(e, c, d)	
⋮						

Files

Figure 6.5   Structure of an access matrix. Note: the legend is r = read, w = write, e = execute, c = create, de = delete.

complexity of access control decisions that must be made are important variables in the cost of protection. With these facts in mind, let us survey the design principles suggested by Saltzer:

1. **Economy of mechanism.** Keep the design as simple and concise as possible; it is easier to inspect and less costly to execute.

2. **Defaults.** An acccess decision should be made on the basis of granting permission rather than excluding it. A protection scheme specifies when access is made; the default is lack of access.

3. **Mediation for all objects.** Simply, every access to every object must be authorized.

4. **Open design.** Every user should know what the rules are and how they are applied.

5. **Least privilege.** Every process should execute using the least set of privileges necessary to accomplish its function.

6. **Least common mechanism.** Minimize the amount of mechanism common to more than one user (note that this argues against global passwords and the personal privilege passwords for each user).

7. **Psychological acceptability.** Each and every user must be convinced that the mechanism works and is easy to use, and thus can apply the protection mechanisms routinely and correctly.

Recently, attempts have been made to design and implement secure OSs that ensure absolute protection. These systems are just now being delivered for test and evaluation; therefore, it is to early to tell if their approaches will be successful. If you are interested in more information on these topics, consult [bers79], [lind76], [mcca79], [mill76], [pope74c] and [pope79].

6.2 FILE ORGANIZATION

The physical organization of the file depends on the physical characteristics of the device. Most devices are treated as sequential files, where records are accessed in a linear order. This approach is typical of all unit record devices and most magnetic tape systems. One exception is the LINCtape or DECtape system, where users may randomly access blocks on the tape. By comparison, disk storage devices offer tremendous flexibility in organizing files. The surface of a disk platter is arranged in a series of diminishing-radius concentric circles known as tracks. Each track is further subdivided into sectors. The minimum quantity of information usually transferred in a disk system is one sector. However, in some head-per-track disk systems, the disk is word-addressable.

Physical records can be stored anywhere on disk. For reasons of efficiency in seeking and transferring data, every attempt is made to locate related physical records in contiguous sectors or on parallel platters in the same track. The allocation of space on the disk is handled by the mass storage allocation task described in section 2.8. In most minicomputer systems, a physical record is fixed equivalent to the sector size by the disk controller. This approach simplifies the handling of disk requests and space allocation. If a physical record were composed of several sectors, the device handler would have to search the volume free space table to determine where to store the next physical record. This operation adds considerable complexity to the device handler algorithm as well as significant overhead in processing a disk request. It can also lead to fragmentation of the space on a given platter and to wasted space in a physical record if the logical record does not exactly correspond in size.

The structure of the disk allows the file management system to organize files in three different ways: serial, contiguous, and segmented. Each organization possesses different performance characteristics and limitations. These methods of organization are explored in the next few sections.

6.2.1   Serial File Organization

A serial file consists of blocks linked in sequential order. Figure 6.6 depicts a serial file organization. Normally, a serial file is implemented using a single link from one block to the next. Double links have also been used to speed up access. Knuth [knut69] discusses several algorithms for accessing linked lists and their associated performance features. (Note that his discussion must be modified by a parameter that characterizes the disk access time.)

Access in a serial file is relatively fast; one can retrieve either the previous block or the next block from the current block. To find a given record, the file must be searched block by block from the beginning of the file until the appropriate entry is found.

The following cases should be considered in processing a serial file:

1. **One physical block per logical record.**   Only one block needs to be read into memory at one time. The logical record may be updated in place by overlaying the old data with the new data. Insertion of a new logical record is relatively easy, as the system merely acquires another physical block and adjusts the pointers (see figure 6.7).

2. **Several physical blocks per logical record.**   To retrieve the entire logical record, all physical blocks must be read into memory. Time needed to retrieve a logical record depends on the number of physical blocks because each block must be read and its pointer inspected to find the next block. Adding a new logical record is relatively easy, as the system acquires the requisite number of blocks and adjusts the pointers of the first and last blocks (see figure 6.8).

3. **Several logical records per physical block.**   Once a block is read into memory, the file manager must extract the logical record from those

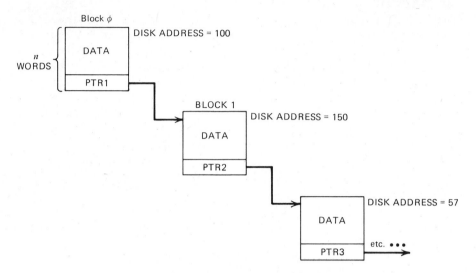

Figure 6.6   Serial file organization.

stored in the block. Adding a new logical record is difficult because, if the block is full, one or more current residents must be displaced to the new block. Usually, a logical record is not split across blocks under this scheme. A significant amount of block space can be wasted in accommodating displaced records (see figure 6.9).

Accessing a record in a serial file requires, on the average, that half the blocks be read and examined. Thus

$$\text{average blocks read} = \sum_{i=1}^{n} \frac{i}{n} = \frac{1}{2}(1+n)$$

which is reduced to $n/2$ for $n \gg 1$, where n is the number of blocks in the file.

The time to read this number of blocks is

$$\text{fetch time} = \frac{n}{2} \cdot \frac{\text{block size}}{\text{transfer rate}}$$

To obtain the next logical record, two cases exist:

Case 1.   If logical records are ordered on some key, then

$$\text{next fetch time} = \frac{\text{block size}}{\text{transfer rate}}$$

as the system uses the pointer to access the next block.

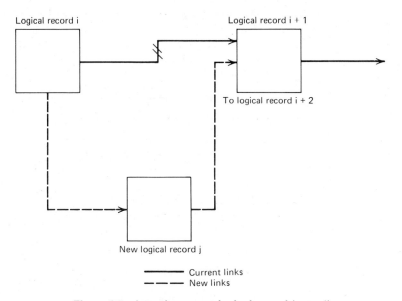

Figure 6.7 Inserting a new logical record (case 1).

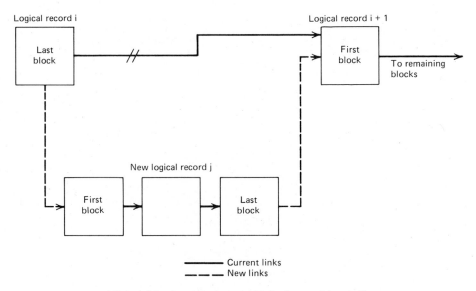

Figure 6.8 Inserting a new logical record (case 2).

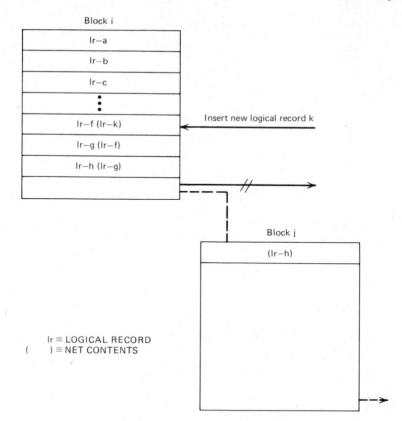

Figure 6.9   Inserting a new logical record (case 3).

Case 2.   If logical records are scattered throughout the file

$$\text{next fetch time} = \frac{n}{2} \cdot \frac{\text{block size}}{\text{transfer rate}}$$

as the file will have to be searched in its entirety.

Both Wiederhold [wied77] and London [lond73] discuss other parameters of serial file organization performance. You may also wish to consult [ibm79], [lefk69], and [robe70].

6.2.2   Contiguous File Organization

A contiguous file consists of a set of physical blocks located in a contiguous space on a disk. Figure 6.10 shows the organization of a contiguous file. This organization provides a rigid structure that yields the fastest access to data. The

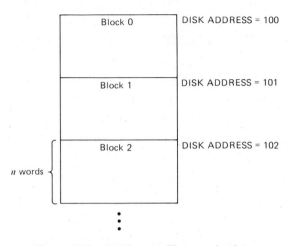

Figure 6.10   Contiguous file organization.

size of the contiguous file is permanently fixed at creation time; it cannot be expanded but may be reduced in size. The major drawback is that a contiguous file cannot always be created on a heavily loaded device because the requisite number of disk blocks may not be available.

Accessing a record in a block is relatively simple. Given the record number r and the record length l, one computes the block address b as

$$b = \frac{l \times r}{\text{block length}}$$

which may then be used to directly retrieve the block. As no pointers need to be followed, this organization provides fast access to data.

A replacement of record r is quite easy; it is merely overlaid by accessing the appropriate number of blocks. The same three cases apply for contiguous files as described for serial files in section 6.2.1. Insertion of a new record is quite difficult. On the average, the system might have to move half the records in the file by length l in order to make room for the new record (see figure 6.11). Insertion of a new record will fail if, in moving records, the last record would be moved beyond the end of the file.

6.2.3   Segmented File Organization

A segmented file, also called an indexed file, consists of a sequential index containing the addresses of the respective data blocks. This organization, which attempts to overcome the access problem of serial files, is depicted in figure 6.12. The index provides a measure of random access and a means for easily handling additions to the file.

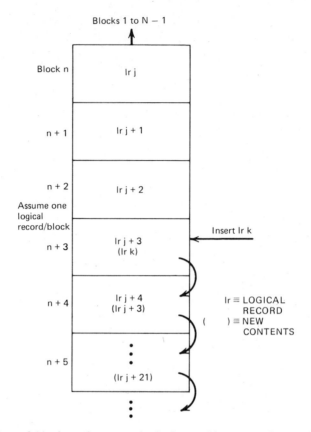

Figure 6.11   Inserting a new logical record into a contiguous file.

The index is constructed as a set of segment pointer blocks (SPBs) and may be organized in either a serial or contiguous manner. In a contiguous approach, the maximum size of the file is known (e.g., one disk volume), and the appropriate number of index blocks is allocated accordingly. In the serial approach, the size of the file is unlimited (and may exceed a disk volume). However, searching through a serial index poses problems similar to a serial file search.

Each SPB contains n entries or pointers to data blocks, and possibly a pointer to the next index block. Consider a disk volume having 512 byte sectors. If a segmented file, consisting of "file-size" words is to be created, the number of index blocks is computed as follows:

$$\text{number of pointers} = \frac{\text{file size}}{\text{block size}}$$

$$\text{number of index blocks} = \frac{\text{pointers} \times \text{pointer size}}{\text{block size}}$$

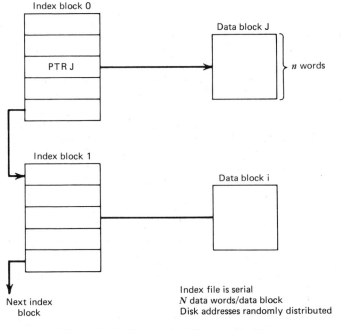

Figure 6.12   Segmented file organization.

The pointer to a disk block must be large enough to accommodate the entire range of mass storage devices.

Retrieving a record in a segmented file requires two disk accesses (in the worst case). First, the address of the index block is computed and read. Then the address of the data block is retrieved from the index block and the data block read into memory. Insertion of a new record follows the cases depicted in figures 6.7 through 6.9.

6.3   STRUCTURE OF THE FILE MANAGER

Three approaches can be taken in executing file management functions. The first approach requires a process to wait after it has executed a file management request. This approach leads to inefficiencies in applications where the program interacts with multiple files simultaneously. For example, if program P requires a record from file A and a record from file B, the following sequence is executed:

.

.

.

read(A)

wait for read to complete

.

.

.

read(B)

wait for read to complete

process records from A and B

.

.

.

A second approach assumes that all file management functions can be performed in parallel with the process's computations. Thus a process would issue requests to read A and B, and then continue with its processing until it needed A and B. This approach would be accomplished by the following sequence of actions:

read(A, event-for-A)

read(B, event-for-B)

.

.

.

execute further instructions

.

.

.

wait(event-for-A and event-for-B)

process records from A and B

.

.

.

Each of the read requests would result in the creation of an independent sub-process to perform the read function. When a subprocess is complete, it posts the result of the read as the status of its event. In the meantime, the application process continues to execute until it needs records A and B. Of course, this scheme will not work if the contents of record A include a pointer used to locate record B.

Any sequence of file management functions could be executed in parallel (up to the limit of available event numbers) as long as they do not interfere with each other. In most complex application programs, the inherent parallelism of this approach would result in greater efficiency.

The third approach represents a hybrid of the previous two methods in that it assumes that some file management functions result in independent processes, and some require the process to wait until completion of the request. This approach is utilized by many OSs for minicomputers.

In this section we examine the general approach: that all file management functions are performed in parallel with the user's application process.

6.3.1   The File Manager

The file manager exists as an independent OS application process. It is created and initiated during system startup. Usually, only one file manager exists in a system. However, the structures to be described do not preclude the possibility of having two or more file managers concurrently active. Indeed, in a system that is heavily I/O-bound, multiple file managers may increase the efficiency of handling file management requests.

A user process requests a file management function through the SYSTEM interface (see section 7.3). Each request results in a system queue entry (SQE) that is entered onto the work queue of the file manager process. Some preprocessing of the arguments is performed during the creation of the SQE. If arguments are determined to be invalid, the request will be rejected and the appropriate error code will be returned as the status of the event.

The file manager process retrieves system queue entries from its work queue and executes the function described therein. It may execute the function by calling the function directly as a subroutine or by creating a subprocess to execute the request and passing to it the SQE.

Upon completion of the file management function, the result is posted to the caller as the event status.

System Queue Entry Characteristics

A SQE is constructed by the preprocessing routines from the arguments submitted in the system service request and it contains all the information necessary to perform a file management function. The structure of an SQE is shown in figure 6.13 and table 6.3. This form of SQE accommodates all possi-

system-queue-function-address
system-queue-pcb-address
system-queue-event-number
system-queue-size
system-queue-channel
system-queue-attributes
system-queue-mode
system-queue-file-name
system-queue-allocation-size
system-queue-number-of-output-buffers
system-queue-number-of-input-buffers
system-queue-buffer-size
system-queue-file-type
system-queue-buffer-address
system-queue-open-mode
system-queue-new-file-name
system-queue-buffer-map

Figure 6.13   Structure of the system queue entry.

Table 6.3   Structure of a System Queue Entry

Mnemonic	Usage
system-queue-function	Function code of the file management function to be performed
system-queue-pcb	Address of the caller's PCB
system-queue-event	Event number used to control the function
system-queue-size	Size of the SQE
system-queue-channel	Channel number to be used in executing the function
system-queue-file-type	Indicator of the file type
system-queue-attributes	Copy of the attributes word from the argument list
system-queue-date	Date to be set for the file
system-queue-mode	Copy of the mode bits from the argument list
system-queue-file-name	Copy of the file name from the argument list
system-queue-allocation-size	Copy of the file name from the argument list
system-queue-new-file	Copy of the file name from the argument list
system-queue-open-mode	Copy of the mode bits from the argument list
system-queue-nr-in-bufs	Number of input buffers to be allocated for this file
system-queue-buffer-map	Index of user's map
system-queue-nr-out-bufs	Number of output buffers to be allocated for this file
system-queue-buffer-size	Size of buffers to be allocated

ble data items, but only those required for a specific function are initialized during argument preprocessing. The size of an SQE varies with the type of function to be performed, as each function requires a different set of arguments. Each SQE is composed of a basic data set to which is attached function-specific data. The size of an SQE is easily computed using the following guidelines:

SYSTEM-QUEUE-BASE	equ 6
SYSTEM-QUEUE-FILE-NAME-SIZE	equ 6
SYSTEM-QUEUE-CREATE-SIZE	equ SYSTEM-QUEUE-BASE + SYSTEM-QUEUE-FILE-NAME-SIZE + 1
SYSTEM-QUEUE-OPEN-SIZE	equ SYSTEM-QUEUE-CREATE-SIZE
SYSTEM-QUEUE-FILE-DATA-SIZE	equ SYSTEM-QUEUE-OPEN-SIZE
SYSTEM-QUEUE-DIRECTORY-READ-SIZE	equ SYSTEM-QUEUE-FILE-DATE-SIZE

SYSTEM-QUEUE-CHANNEL-BUFFER-SIZE	equ SYSTEM-QUEUE-BASE + SYSTEM-QUEUE-FILE-NAME-SIZE + 3
SYSTEM-QUEUE-FILE-BUFFER-SIZE	equ SYSTEM-QUEUE-CHANNEL-BUFFER-SIZE
SYSTEM-QUEUE-DELETE-SIZE	equ SYSTEM-QUEUE-CREATE-SIZE − 1
SYSTEM-QUEUE-FILE-ATTRIBUTE-SIZE	equ SYSTEM-QUEUE-DELETE-SIZE
SYSTEM-QUEUE-RENAME-SIZE	equ SYSTEM-QUEUE-BASE + SYSTEM-QUEUE-FILE-NAME-SIZE * 2
SYSTEM-QUEUE-CLOSE-SIZE	equ SYSTEM-QUEUE-BASE
SYSTEM-QUEUE-RESET-SIZE	equ SYSTEM-QUEUE-BASE − 1
SYSTEM-QUEUE-LINK-SIZE	equ SYSTEM-QUEUE-RENAME-SIZE
SYSTEM-QUEUE-UNLINK-SIZE	equ SYSTEM-QUEUE-BASE + SYSTEM-QUEUE-FILE-NAME-SIZE

The File Manager Process

The file manager process is depicted in module 6.3.1. The file manager requests the first SQE from its work queue (named SYSTEM-RS). It retrieves the appropriate values and looks up the function address and its overlay address (in this example, all file management functions are treated as overlays). The file manager requests the overlay to be loaded via LOAD-OVERLAY. It then calls the function as a subroutine. Each function will set the event status during its execution. Upon return to the mainline code, the result is posted to the user process. The overlay is released and the SQE block returned to the memory pool. The file manager then cycles to execute the next request.

Two additional modules support the file manager process: FILE-MGR-LOG and FILE-MAINTENANCE-OK. These are depicted in modules 6.3.2 and 6.3.3.

FILE-MGR-LOG writes a file directory entry back to disk after a file has been updated. Remember that the directory entry was read into memory in order to create a FCB. Changes in the FCB must also be reflected in the file directory entry.

FILE-MAINTENANCE-OK is a convenient entry point for setting the status of the function.

Note that each file management function is performed sequentially, although to the user they appear to be performed in parallel. One variation that can increase efficiency is to initiate multiple file managers. A second variation involves the creation of a system process for each file management function similar to the way in which I/O management requests are handled (see section 5.5.1). To implement such a capability, I could replace the line

```
call(function-address)
```

by the following sequence of instructions:

```
system-queue-event[fmb-address] → evn
create-system-process( ) → ftcb-address
initialize-system-process(ftcb-address, function-address, 0,
      evn, 0, system-queue-size[fmb-address], fmb-address, 0)
activate(ftcb-address)
```

I would also delete the following lines from the file manager process and place a copy of them into each function module:

```
system(post, event-nr, tcb-address, status, data1)
system(release-overlay, overlay-address)
release(system-memory-rs, fmb-address)
```

The following is the code for the file manager. Note that the SQE is pointed to by FMB-ADDRESS (which stands for file manager block).

MODULE 6.3.1

```
process file-manager
    request(system-rs) → fmb-address
    system-queue-pcb[fmb-address] → pcb-address
    system-queue-function[fmb-address] → function-code
    file-mgr-process-switch-table[function-code] → function-address
    file-mgr-process-overlay-table [function-code] → overlay-address
    system(load-overlay, 16, overlay-address, 0) → status
    if status greater than or equal to 0
        then
            call(function-address)
    endif
```

```
entry file-maintenance-post:
     system(post, event-nr, pcb-address, status, data1)
     system(release-overlay, overlay-address)
     release(system-memory-rs, fmb-address)
     repeat
endprocess
```

MODULE 6.3.2

```
procedure file-mgr-log
     directory-write(directory-record, directory-address)
     goto file-maintenance-post
endproc
```

MODULE 6.3.3

```
procedure file-maintenance-ok
     set one to status
     goto file-maintenance-post
endproc
```

The File Manager—PDB Workspace

The file manager requires a workspace to hold local data during the processing of a request. This workspace is allocated in the PDB in order to preserve the reentrancy of the file management procedures. Data in the workspace are, of course, accessible to all procedures invoked by the file manager to satisfy any request. The structure of the file manager workspace is described in table 6.4.

6.3.2   File Manager Databases

The file manager uses the function code from the SQE to look up the function address and the overlay address for the function module. This facility requires two tables. The first table is the process switch table, which contains the addresses of each file management function module. It is defined as follows:

```
file-mgr-process-switch-table of
     address-of-channel-buffer,
     address-of-close,
     address-of-create,
     address-of-delete,
     address-of-directory-read,
     address-of-file-attributes,
     address-of-file-buffer,
     address-of-file-date,
```

Table 6.4   Structure of the File Manager's Workspace

Mnemonic	Usage
file-mgr-pcb-address	Address of the user's PCB
file-mgr-event-nr	Event number by which the user will be signaled upon completion of the function
file-mgr-function	Function code
file-mgr-channel	Channel number attached to the file (if any)
file-mgr-file-type	File type work cell
file-mgr-attributes	Attributes work cell
file-mgr-data	Data work cell
file-mgr-mode	Mode work cell
file-mgr-file-name	File name work cell
file-mgr-extension	File name extension work cell
file-mgr-allocation-size	Allocation size work cell
file-mgr-buffer-map	Map index for buffers
file-mgr-nr-in-buffers	Number of input buffers
file-mgr-new-file-name	New file name work cell
file-mgr-nr-out-buffers	Number of output buffers
file-mgr-buffer-size	Work cell for buffer size
file-mgr-status	Event status
file-mgr-data1	Data value 1 for event
file-mgr-data2	Data value 2 for event
file-mgr-directory-address	Address of directory file entry
file-mgr-directory-entry	Space for creating a file directory entry

```
            address-of-link,
            address-of-open,
            address-of-rename,
            address-of-reset,
            address-of-unlink,
        end
```

where the addresses are resolved when the executable version of the OS is prepared by the linker/loader.

The second table is the process overlay table, which contains the overlay addresses for each function module. It is defined as follows:

```
        file-mgr-process-overlay-table of
            overlay-address-of-open,
            overlay-address-of-close,
            overlay-address-of-create,
```

```
            overlay-address-of-delete,
            overlay-address-of-directory-read,
            overlay-address-of-file-modify,
            overlay-address-of-file-modify,
            overlay-address-of-file-modify,
            overlay-address-of-create,
            overlay-address-of-open,
            overlay-address-of-file-modify,
            overlay-address-of-close,
            overlay-address-of-delete,
    end
```

where several functions may be combined into one overlay.

An additional table, FILE-MGR-SQE-SIZE-TABLE, contains the SQE sizes for each function according to the definitions given in section 6.3.1. The preprocessing routines use this table to allocate memory for a SQE. It is defined as follows:

```
        file-mgr-sqe-size-table of
            system-queue-channel-buffer-size,
            system-queue-close-size,
            system-queue-create-size,
            system-queue-delete-size,
            system-queue-directory-read-size,
            system-queue-file-attributes-size,
            system-queue-file-buffer-size,
            system-queue-file-date-size,
            system-queue-link-size,
            system-queue-open-size,
            system-queue-rename-size,
            system-queue-reset-size,
            system-queue-unlink-size,
    end
```

6.3.3   File Manager—System Queue Routines

Several routines support the initialization of an SQE for the file manager. These routines are depicted in modules 6.3.4 through 6.3.7.

Initializing an SQE

SYSTEM-QUEUE-SETUP acquires a block of memory of sufficient size to accommodate the SQE. It uses the FILE-MGR-SQE-SIZE-TABLE, indexed by the function code, to determine the proper SQE size. It then initializes the common base entries from the user stack arguments. The common entries are the function code, the process identifier, the size of the SQE, and the event number for the request.

MODULE 6.3.4

```
procedure system-queue-setup(→sqe-address)
    function[usp] → function-code
    file-mgr-sqe-size-table[function-code] → sqe-size
    request(system-memory-rs) → sqe-address
    function-code → system-queue-function[sqe-address]
    sqe-size → system-queue-size[sqe-address]
    p → system-queue-pcb[sqe-address]
    event-nr[usp] → system-queue-event[sqe-address]
endproc
```

Completing an SQE

SYSTEM-QUEUE-END is called at the completion of preprocessing for a file management function. It places the SQE on the file manager's work queue and marks the event associated with the request busy. Finally, it calls EVENT-16-CHECK to determine if the calling process should be suspended. The calling process is suspended if it specified event number 16, as this event number indicates that the process will await the completion of the file management function.

MODULE 6.3.5

```
procedure system-queue-end
    release(system-rs, sqe-address)
    mark-event-busy( )
    event-16-check( )
endproc
```

Error Handling for SQE Preprocessing

SYSTEM-QUEUE-ERROR is called to process an error that has been detected during SQE initialization. When an error is detected, the SQE block will be returned to the memory pool. EVENT-ERROR is called to set the event status to the error code and notify the user.

MODULE 6.3.6

```
procedure system-queue-error(error-code)
    release(system-memory-rs, sqe-address)
    event-error(error-code)
endproc
```

Initializing a File Name for an SQE

SYSTEM-QUEUE-FILE-SETUP is called when a file name is required as an argument to the function. It calls SYSTEM-QUEUE-FILE-READ (not shown) to copy the file name string from user space into the SQE.

MODULE 6.3.7

```
procedure system-queue-file-setup(→sqe-address)
    system-queue-setup( ) → sqe-address
    system-queue-file-read(filename, system-queue-file-name
                                                [sqe-address], 0)
endproc
```

6.3.4 File Manager—Preprocessing Routines

The preprocessing routines for the file management function are depicted in module 6.3.8. The method of preprocessing is straightforward. Essentially, each routine will:

1. Allocate SQE block
2. Initialize SQE baseline information
3. Copy specific arguments from the user stack to the SQE block as required by each function
4. Place the SQE block on the file manager's work queue
5. When necessary, process error by freeing SQE block

Each of the submodules is self-explanatory. The reader may correlate the preprocessing code with the formats for the system calls presented later in this chapter.

MODULE 6.3.8

```
procedure p-create
    system-queue-file-setup( ) → sqe-address
    file-type[usp] → system-queue-file-type[sqe-address]
```

        allocation-size[usp] → system-queue-allocation-size[sqe-address]
        system-queue-end( )

entry p-delete:
entry p-unlink:
        system-queue-file-setup( ) → sqe-address
        system-queue-end( )

entry p-rename:
entry p-link:
        system-queue-file-setup( ) → sqe-address
        system-queue-file-read(filename, system-queue-new-file, 0)
        system-queue-end( )

entry p-file-attributes:
        system-queue-file-setup( ) → sqe-address
        attributes[usp] → system-queue-attributes[sqe-address]
        system-queue-end( )

entry p-open:
        system-queue-setup( ) → sqe-address
        channel[usp] → system-queue-channel[sqe-address]
        mode[usp] → system-queue-open-mode[sqe-address]
        system-queue-file-read(filename, system-queue-file-name, 1)
        system-queue-end( )

entry p-close:
        system-queue-setup( ) → sqe-address
        channel[usp] → system-queue-channel[sqe-address]
        system-queue-end( )

entry p-channel-buffer:
        system-queue-setup( ) → sqe-address
        channel[usp] → system-queue-channel[sqe-address]

entry channel-buffer-end:
        nr-in-buffers[usp] → system-queue-nr-in-buffers[sqe-address]
        nr-out-buffers[usp] → system-queue-nr-out-buffers[sqe-address]
        buffer-size[usp] → system-queue-buffer-size[sqe-address]
        system-queue-end( )

entry p-file-buffer:
        system-queue-file-setup( ) → sqe-address
        goto channel-buffer-end

entry p-directory-read:
    system-queue-file-setup( ) → sqe-address
    buffer-address[usp] → system-queue-buffer-address[sqe-address]
    map[usp] → map-nr
    adjust-for-pdb(map-nr)
    map-nr → system-queue-buffer-map[sqe-address]
    system-queue-end( )

entry p-reset:
    system-queue-setup( ) → sqe-address
    system-queue-end( )

entry p-file-date:
    system-queue-file-setup( ) → sqe-address
    date[usp] → system-queue-date[sqe-address]
    time[usp] → system-queue-time[sqe-address]
    system-queue-end( )
endproc

6.3.5   File Management Functions

A file management facility provides support for system files as entities rather than for individual data records within files. The number of functions and their action depends on the designer and the environment for which the OS is designed. A minimum set of functions is listed in table 6.5.

These functions require a complex set of modules to accomplish their tasks. Each function is discussed in the remaining sections of this chapter. Other functions are provided by various manufacturers' OSs. A detailed analysis of each function (in the manner above) is not possible. Rather, a summary of some of the more popular functions and their options is provided in the following paragraphs. The reader is referred to the manufacturers' literature for more detail on function and implementation.

Appending One File to Another

In general, the APPEND command will concatenate two files to form a new file. The contents of the two source files are not altered. A format for this request might appear as

SYSTEM(APPEND, EVENT-NR, A-FILE, B-FILE, NEW-FILE, NEW-FILE-TYPE)

where   EVENT-NR   is used to signal the caller when the new file has been created from the two source files

A-FILE   is the name of the first source file
B-FILE   is the name of the second source file
NEW-FILE   is the name of the file to be created
NEW-FILE-TYPE   is the type of a file to be created

Appending files is a useful method for reorganizing a file where no such explicit command exists. The contents of the file B are inserted into the new file directly after the contents of file A. The length of the new file is given by

FILE-SIZE[FILE-A] + FILE-SIZE[FILE-B] → FILE-SIZE[NEW-FILE]

The organization of the new file is specified by the file type. Care must be taken when specifying a contiguous file as the type of the new file, as there may not be enough available space on mass storage to accommodate it. In most systems, one or both of the source files may be empty (FILE-SIZE equals 0).

A basic algorithm for the APPEND request would include:

Validate nonexistence of NEW-FILE-NAME

Create a file of specified type with NEW-FILE

Open NEW-FILE

Table 6.5   File Management Functions

Name	Function
CREATE	Add a new file to the system directory
DELETE	Remove a file from the system directory
RENAME	Change the name of a file in the system directory
FILE-ATTRIBUTES	Set the attributes of a file
FILE-BUFFER	Set the default parameters for a file buffered on input and/or output
OPEN	Create a logical path between a user and a file or device
CLOSE	Terminate a logical path between a user and a file or device
CHANNEL-BUFFER	Set up buffering on a channel that has been opened in buffer prep mode
DIRECTORY-READ	Read the directory information for a specified file
DIRECTORY-SPACE	Allow the user to determine the amount of available disk space on a given device
LINK	Create a logical path from one file to another
UNLINK	Remove a logical path to a file
FILE-DATE	Change the date/time field of a file

Open FILE-A

Copy contents of FILE-A to NEW-FILE

Close FILE-A

Open FILE-B

Copy contents of FILE-B to NEW-FILE

Close FILE-B

Close NEW-FILE

Copying One File to Another

The COPY command duplicates the contents of the input file in the specified output file. Under DGC's RDOS, this command has the mnemonic XFER. It allows you to copy a file anywhere, including to a device. Thus, under RDOS, the PRINT command is treated as an implicit XFER to the line printer: for example,

PRINT FILE-A is the equivalent to XFER FILE-A $LPT

In DEC'S IAS, you are allowed to change the organization of the resultant file. For example, you may issue the command

$COPY/CONTIGUOUS DK2:OLDFILE.MAC DKO:OLDFILE.DAT

which creates a contiguous file on disk volume DK0. In addition, for contiguous files, a new allocation parameter may be specified, thus effectively increasing the size of the file. A general format for this request might be

SYSTEM(COPY, EVENT-NR, SRC-FILE, NEW-FILE, FILE-TYPE, SIZE)

where	EVENT-NR	is used to signal the caller when the new file has been created
	SRC-FILE	is the name of the file to be duplicated
	NEW-FILE	is the name of the duplicate file to be created
	FILE-TYPE	is the type of the new file
	SIZE	is an optional parameter specifying the number of blocks to be allocated if the new file is to be a contiguous file

Erasing a File

_____

This command allows you to discard the contents of a file but retain its entry in the system directory. Its operation should be compared to RENAME, which discards the old name but keeps the contents, or DELETE, which discards both the name and the contents of the file. A format for the call might be

SYSTEM(ERASE, EVENT-NR, FILE-NAME)

where   EVENT-NR   is the event used to signal the caller when the file
                           has been erased
           FILE-NAME   is the name of the file to be erased

The process of erasure depends on the type of file. For contiguous files, the system may merely write zeros (or some null data) throughout the file. For serial and segmented files, the system would release the data blocks. For segmented files, the pointer blocks would also be released. In the latter cases, the entries FILE-SIZE, FILE-START, and FILE-END would all be set to zero. A file that has been declared permanent cannot be erased.

Printing a File

_____

Most systems provide a user with the capability to obtain a complete listing of the contents of a file either on the line printer or on the user's terminal. The format of the command is

SYSTEM(PRINT, EVENT-NR, FILE-NAME, DEVICE-NAME,
OPTIONS)

where   EVENT-NR   is used to signal the caller when the file has
                           been printed on the device
           FILE-NAME   is the name of the file to be printed
           DEVICE-NAME   is the name of the device on which the file is
                           to be printed
           OPTIONS   are device specific or formatting information
                           for printing the file

6.4   CREATING AND LINKING A FILE

_____

Before a file can be used to store data, it must be created on mass storage or linked to a file that already exists. Creating a file involves the allocation of space for the file and the specification of file characteristics. On the other hand, when linking to a file, you are merely creating a logical path to a file that already exists. The format for the CREATE requeset is

    SYSTEM(CREATE, EVENT-NR, FILE-NAME, FILE-TYPE,
    ALLOCATION-SIZE)

where		
	EVENT-NR	is used to signal the caller when the file has been created
	FILE-NAME	is the name to be assigned to the file
	FILE-TYPE	is the type of file to be created
	ALLOCATION-SIZE	is a type-dependent parameter related to file size

The allocation size parameter is determined as follows:

File Type	Allocation Size Parameter
CONTIGUOUS-FILE	Number of disk blocks comprising the file
SERIAL-FILE	Number of disk blocks comprising a physical record
SEGMENTED-FILE	Left byte contains the number of disk blocks comprising one segment pointer block; right byte contains the number of disk blocks comprising a segment data block

The format of the LINK request is

    SYSTEM(LINK, EVENT-NR, LINK-FILE-NAME, TARGET-FILE-NAME)

where		
	EVENT-NR	is used to signal the caller when the link entry has been created
	LINK-FILE-NAME	is the name of the pointer file to be created
	TARGET-FILE-NAME	is the name of the file pointed to be the link entry

We discuss both the CREATE and LINK commands together because they produce the same result: the creation of a system directory entry for a new file. They differ in that under CREATE, the entry describes the actual file characteristics, whereas under LINK, the entry just points to an already existing file.

6.4.1   General File Creation Procedure

When you issue the CREATE command, the file is created in your local directory. An error will result if you attempt to create a file with the name of a file
that already exists or with a name having an illegal syntax. The file name is
specified as an string terminated by a null character. An illegal file name may
occur if you provide an illegal format (e.g., a number as the first character) or
an invalid extension (you cannot create a directory file with this command). An
error may also result if the file directory has no slots in which to place the new
FCB.

The procedure for the CREATE command is depicted in module 6.4.1. It is
invoked by the file manager to perform the creation of a file. The SQE, which
has been retrieved from the system queue, is pointed to by FMB-ADDRESS.
When creating a file, the system searches the file directory to determine if a file
already exists with the specified name and extension. If such a file is found
(DIRECTORY-RECORD-ADDRESS > 0), you will be notified via the error
code ER-CREATE.

The system checks to see if you have specified a file type. If not, the system
will create the file using the default file type (SEGMENTED-FILE) which was
specified during system generation. The default should be selected by the
designer with careful consideration for the environment. A default of
CONTIGUOUS-FILE is not recommended, as there may not be enough
available space on the disk after some period of operation. Disk space tends to
become fragmented (but still manageable) over the lifetime of the system. A
critical program, attempting to create a file, would fail if no disk space were
available when the default is CONTIGUOUS-FILE.

When a new file is created, the system initializes a copy of file directory entry.
Since CREATE is a subroutine of the file manager, it can use that process's
PDB as a workspace. The workspace required by CREATE is described in table
6.6. The file directory entry is pointed to by NEW-FCB-ADDRESS.

Routines are invoked by file type to perform the specific calculations
necessary to allocate space for each file. These modules also initialize the file
directory entry with the appropriate information (see section 6.4.2). If an illegal
file type is specified, it is captured at this point, and you are notified by the error
code ER-TYPE. An error resulting from the setup routines forces the request to
be rejected.

The system obtains space for the file by invoking the mass storage allocation
process (see section 2.8). ALLOCATE returns the address of the first disk block
in the file on the specified device. The system copies the starting address to the
ending address only if the file is not contiguously organized.

Finally, the time/date information and default values for buffer and record
sizes are inserted into the file directory entry. A copy of the file directory entry is
then inserted into the file directory by the module WRITE-NEW-DIREC-
TORY-RECORD.

Table 6.6   CREATE/LINK—PDB Workspace

Mnemonic	Usage
new-fcb-address	Space to initialize the FCB for the file to be created or linked
device-type	Device type and unit number on which the file is to be created (for systems with multiple types of mass storage devices
allocation-size	Number of words/blocks to allocate on the device (type dependent)
pointer-size	Size of the SPBs for a segmented file
segment-size	Size of the SDBs for a segmented file

MODULE 6.4.1

```
procedure create
    search-directory(file-name[fmb-address]) →
                                            directory-record-address
    if directory-record-address greater than or equal to zero
        then

    endif
    if file-type[fmb-address] equals zero
        then
                default-file-type → file-type[fmb-address]
    endif
    copy(file-name[fmb-address], file-name[new-fcb-address],
                                            file-name-size)
    if allocation-size[fmb-address] equals zero
        then
                default-data-size →allocation-size[fmb-address]
    endif
    device-type → file-allocation-data[new-fcb-address]
    case file-type of
        segmented-file:     setup-segmented( ) → result
                            exitcase
        contiguous-file:    setup-contiguous( ) → result
                            exitcase
        serial-file:        setup-serial( ) → result
                            exitcase
    else
        set er-type to status
        file-maintenance-post( )
    endcase
    if result less than zero
        then
```

```
                set result to status
                file-maintenance-post( )
        endif
        allocate(allocation-size, device-type) → file-start[new-fcb-address]

        if file-type not equal to file-contiguous
                then
                        file-start[new-fcb-address] → file-end[new-fcb-address]
        endif
        if event-status[p] less than zero
                then
                        event-status[p] → status
                        file-maintenance-post( )
        endif
        clear file-buffer-size[new-fcb-address]
        set default-record-size to file-record-size[new-fcb-address]
        date( ) → file-create-date[new-fcb-address]
        dbsec( ) → file-create-time[new-fcb-address]
        write-new-directory-record( )
endproc
```

6.4.2   File Creation Strategies

Depending on the type of file to be created, the allocation size is interpreted in different ways. Consequently, three modules are used by the system to initialize the size and allocation data in the file directory entry.

Setting Up a Contiguous File

The module for initializing a contiguous file is depicted in module 6.4.2. It sets the contiguous flag in the file attribute entry. The allocation size, representing the number of disk blocks to be allocated, is shifted by the number of bits encoding the disk sector size in order to compute the total file size. This value is stored in FILE-SIZE. The true size of the file is found by

$$\text{number of disk blocks} \times \text{disk sector size} = \text{total file size}$$

Setting Up a Serial File

The routine for setting up a serial file is depicted in module 6.4.3. It sets the serial bit of the file attributes entry. The allocation size specifies the number of

MODULE 6.4.2

procedure setup-contiguous(→ result)
    set contiguous-flag of file-attributes[new-fcb-address]
    set lshift(file-mgr-allocation-size[fmb-address], sector-size) to
            data-block-size of file-allocation-data[new-fcb-address]
    file-mgr-allocation-size[fmb-address]
                                   → file-size[new-fcb-address]
    file-mgr-allocation-size[fmb-address]
                       → file-allocation-size [new-fcb-address]
    clear result
endproc

disk blocks that will comprise one physical record. The module, as described, allows up to 64 blocks per physical record (approximately 32K bytes). This limitation is due to the track size on most disks provided for minicomputer systems (i.e., 64 sectors of 512 bytes each). If more than 64 blocks are specified, the error code ER-SIZE is returned and the request is rejected. The allocation size is stored in the DATA-BLOCK-SIZE field of the FILE-ALLOCATION-DATA entry. The file size is initialized to zero and as records are added to the file, the file size will be incremented by the IOM. It is important to note that space will be allocated for a serial file in chunks of $n \times 512$ bytes, where n is the number of disk blocks in a physical record.

MODULE 6.4.3

procedure setup-serial(→ result)
    set serial-flag of file-attributes[new-fcb-address]
    if file-mgr-allocation-size[fmb-address] greater than 64
        then
                set er-size to result
                exitproc
    endif
    set file-mgr-allocation-size[fmb-address] to data-block-size of
            file-allocation-data[new-fcb-address]
    clear file-size[new-fcb-address]
    clear result
endproc

Setting Up a Segmented File

The routine for setting up a segmented file is depicted in module 6.4.4. It sets the segmented bit in the file attributes entry. From the allocation size, it retrieves the segment pointer and segment data size values. The structure of the allocation size word is

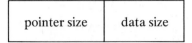

pointer size	data size

This module allows one SPB to consist of up to 32 disk blocks (approximately 16K bytes). This limitation is an arbitrary one based on the characteristics of disks designed for minicomputer systems. As stated earlier, each data segment can consist of up to 64 disk blocks (approximately 32K bytes). If either of these values is zero, the system defaults (normally 1/1) will be used. The file allocation data word is initialized to the sizes of the SPB and SDB. The file size is set to zero. As records are added to the file, the file size will be incremented by the IOM. The allocation size is set to the value of one SPB, as this amount of storage will be immediately allocated when the file is created.

MODULE 6.4.4

```
procedure setup-segmented (→result)
      set segmented-flag of file-attributes[new-fcb-address]
      extract pointer-size from file-mgr-allocation-size[fmb-address]
      if pointer-size equals zero
            then
                        default-pointer-size → pointer-size
      endif
      if pointer-size greater than max-pointer-size
            then
                        set er-size to result
                        exitproc
      endif
      extract segment-size from file-mgr-allocation-size[fmb-address]
      if segment-size equals zero
            then
                        default-segment-size → segment-size
      endif
      if segment-size greater than max-segment-size
            then
                        set er-size to result
                        exitproc
      endif
      lbyte(pointer-size, file-allocation-data[new-fcb-address])
      rbyte(segment-size, file-allocation-data[new-fcb-address])
      pointer-size * sector-size → allocation-size
      clear file-size[new-fcb-address]
      clear device-type
      clear result
endproc
```

6.4.3 General Link Creation Strategy

The LINK command is grouped with the CREATE command, as they both establish new files. However, the LINK procedure results only in the establishment of a "pointer FCB" that contains the name of the target file. The routine for executing the LINK request is depicted in module 6.4.5.

The system searches the directory and determines if the target file exists. If the file does not exist, error code ER-NOFILE is returned. You are not allowed to link to a nonexistent file, but on some systems this restriction may be relaxed. If the file exists, a file directory entry is created that contains a pointer to the target file. The link entry flag is set in FILE-ATTRIBUTES to indicate that this is a link entry. Finally, the file directory entry is written to the disk.

6.5 DELETING AND UNLINKING A FILE

The converse operation to creating/linking a file is known as deleting/unlinking. Deletion is the process by which the system reclaims disk space at the behest of the user. Unlinking is the process of destroying a logical path to the target file. The formats for deleting/unlinking a file are equivalent:

    SYSTEM(DELETE, EVENT-NR, FILE-NAME)

    SYSTEM(UNLINK, EVENT-NR, FILE-NAME)

where   EVENT-NR   is used to signal the caller when the file has been deleted or unlinked

          FILE-NAME   is the name of the file

MODULE 6.4.5.

```
procedure link
    search-directory(file-name[fmb-address]) →
                                        directory-record-address
        if directory-record-address less than or equal to zero
        then
                set er-nofile to status
                file-maintenance-post( )
        endif
    copy(file-name[fmb-address], file-link-name[new-fcb-address],
                                        file-name-size)
    set link-entry-flag of file-attributes[new-fcb-address]
    write-new-directory-record( )
endproc
```

6.5.1   General File Deletion Procedure

The routine for deleting a file is depicted in module 6.5.1. The system verifies that the file exists and may be deleted. Before a file can be deleted, it must be closed by all processes. Moreover, the file to be deleted may not be a link entry (that is what UNLINK is for) and it may not be a permanent file.

Next, the system must determine whether the file has any space allocated to it. If not, the system merely removes the file directory entry from the system directory. This step is not as frivolous as it seems; many files are created without ever being populated by data.

If a file has space allocated to it (FILE-SIZE not equal to zero), the system invokes a deallocation routine, depending on the file type, to release the space. An invalid file type results in an error code.

The file deletion procedure utilizes a workspace which is stored in the file manager's PDB. The structure of this workspace is described in table 6.7.

6.5.2   Specific File Deletion Strategies

Each file organization requires a specific deletion strategy which returns allocated space to the OS. These strategies are discussed in the paragraphs below.

Deleting a Contiguous File

The routine for deleting a contiguous file is depicted in module 6.5.2. In a contiguous file, all the space is colocated on disk. Thus, to deallocate this space, we

Table 6.7   Delete/Unlink—PDB Workspace

Mnemonic	Usage
pointer-blocks	Number of pointer blocks currently used in the file
block-number	Current block number on the disk
file-total	Total amount of file space released
spb-size	Size of a segment pointer block
sdb-size	Size of a segment data block
next-segment-address	Disk address of next segment in the file
answer-flag	Temporary cell for communicating between modules
current-segment- address	Current segment address in the file
spb-address	Disk address of the current SPB
spb-buffer	Buffer to hold the current SPB

MODULE 6.5.1

```
procedure delete
    find-closed-file( )
    check-not-link-entry( )
    check-not-permanent-file( )
    if file-size[fcb-address] equals zero
        then
                zero-directory( )
                exitproc
    endif
    extract file-type from file-attributes[fcb-address]
    case file-type of
        segmented-file:   delete-segmented( )
                          exitcase
        contiguous-file:  delete-contiguous( )
                          exitcase
        serial-file:      delete-serial( )
                          exitcase
    else
        set er-delete to status
        file-maintenance-post( )
    endcase
endproc
```

need to call the MSAP only once to release all the space in the file. DEALLO-CATE returns a flag that informs us whether or not the deletion was successful. If not, a message is printed on the system console informing the operator that an executive-level error has occurred. This error indicates a problem with the space allocation map for the disk volume and affects the integrity of the file system.

If the deallocation terminated successfully, the directory record is cleared and the number of free slots for FCBs in the directory is incremented by one.

Deleting a Serial File

The routine for deleting a serial file is depicted in module 6.5.3. To delete a serial file, the chain of data blocks must be followed and each data block released to the system individually. Pursuing this chain involves reading each data block and retrieving the pointer to the next block. The end of the file is reached when the next data block pointer is zero.

The initial step requires decoding the data block size which is stored in the allocation data entry and which represents the number of disk blocks comprising one physical record. Next, the address of the first data segment is retrieved

MODULE 6.5.2

```
procedure delete-contiguous
     file-size[fcb-address] → file-size
     file-start[fcb-address] → file-start
     deallocate(file-size, file-start) → answer-flag
entry clear-directory:
     if answer-flag less than zero
          then
                    error-message(delete-error)
     endif
entry zero-directory:
     clear(file-mgrdirectory-record[pdb])
     increment file-directory-free-count[directory-fcb-address]
     directory-write(file-mgrdirectory-record[pdb], directory-address)
     file-maintenance-post( )
endproc
```

from the FCB. If the current segment address is zero, the file is empty. Therefore, the procedure notes a successful deletion and clears the directory entry.

The algorithm for deleting a block requires the system to read the data block
into memory, compute the next segment address, and release the data block
pointed to by the current segment address. Two checks are maintained: the first
merely involves checking the next block pointer for zero as this indicates the end
of the file. A second check involves counting the number of words released and
comparing this value with the file total. In this way, the system ensures that it
does not release any more space than is currently allocated to the file. Whenever
the end of the file is found, the directory entry is cleared and the status returned
to the caller.

The following computation develops the pointer to the next segment:

$$\text{current-segment-address} + \text{sdb-size} - 2$$

Note that this computation is independent of SDB-SIZE.

MODULE 6.5.3

```
procedure delete-serial
     extract sdb-size from file-allocation-data[fcb-address]
     sdb-size * sector-size → sdb-size
     file-start[fcb-address] → current-segment-address
     if current-segment-address equals zero
          then
                    set one to answer-flag
                    clear-directory( )
```

```
        endif
        clear file-total
        read-direct(spb-buffer, current-segment-address)
        while file-total less-than file-size[fcb-address]
              do
                      current-segment-address + sdb-size − 2
                                                    → next-segment-address
                      deallocate(sdb-size, current-segment-address)
                            →answer-flag
                      if answer-flag less than zero
                          then
                                  clear-directory( )
                      endif
                      increment file-total by sdb-size
                      read-direct(spb-buffer, next-segment-address)
                                                    → answer-flag
                      if answer-flag less than zero
                          then
                                  clear-directory( )
                      endif
                      set next-segment-address to current-segment-address
              enddo
        set one to answer-flag
        clear-directory( )
endproc
```

Deleting a Segmented File

The routine for deleting a segmented file is depicted in module 6.5.4. To delete
a segmented file, the system must access each segment pointer block and release
each data segment for which a pointer exists in the SPB.

The first step consists of extracting the segment pointer and segment data
block sizes from the file allocation data. The total space released is initialized to
zero and the address of the first SPB retrieved from the file control block.

Each SPB is read into memory. An index steps through the SPB releasing
each data segment in turn. When the SPB is exhausted, it is released to the free
space pool. Note that this system treats the SPBs as a serially organized file.
Suppose that the SPB size is four blocks. The total number of bytes is 2048.
Then the SPBs are contiguous areas of 2048 bytes, and there may be any
number of them chained together. This allows for unlimited file expansion (up
to the maximum capacity of the disk).

Each data segment is released by the DEALLOCATE routine. The index
pointer is incremented by two to get the address of the next SPB. The amount of

MODULE 6.5.4

```
procedure delete-segmented
      extract sdb-size from file-allocation-data[fcb-address]
      sdb-size * sector-size → sdb-size
      extract pointer-block-size from file-allocation-data[fcb-address]
      pointer-block-size * sector-size → spb-address
      clear file-total
      file-start[fcb-address] → spb-address
entry start-block-read:
      clear block-number
      spb-address → next-segment-address
entry read-next-block:
      increment block-number
      clear index
      read-direct(spb-buffer, sector-size, spb-address) → answer-flag
      if answer-flag less than zero
            then
                  clear-directory( )
      endif
      while file-total less than file-size[fcb-address]
            do
                  if block-number not equal to pointer-blocks
                        then
                              if index equals sector-size
                              then
                              increment spb-address by sector-size
                              goto next-read-block
                              endif
                        else
                              if index equals sector-size − 2
                              then
                              spb-buffer[index] → spb-address
                              deallocate(spb-size, next-segment-address)
                              goto start-block-read
                              endif
                  endif
                  deallocate(sdb-size, spb-buffer[index])
                  increment index by 2
                  file-total + sdb-size → file-total
            enddo
      deallocate(spb-size, next-segment-address) → answer-flag
      clear-directory( )
endproc
```

file space released is incremented by the data segment size. This latter mechanism ensures that the system releases only as much space as has been allocated to the file. Finally, the last SPB is released and the directory entry is cleared.

6.5.3 General File Unlinking Procedure

The routine for unlinking a file is depicted in module 6.5.5. It checks to see that the link entry is closed. If so, and if the specified file is a link entry, the directory entry is erased. Otherwise, you have tried to apply the UNLINK command to a data file resulting in a system error.

MODULE 6.5.5

```
procedure unlink
    find-closed-file( )
    if link-entry-flag of file-attributes[fcb-address] not equal to zero
        then
                zero-directory( )
    endif
    er-function → status
    file-maintenance-post( )
endproc
```

6.6 FILE MODIFICATION ROUTINES

Several commands are provided that allow you to modify the attributes of a file. In the system presented here, four commands are considered.

6.6.1 Renaming a File

The RENAME command allows you to change the name of a file while preserving its contents. The format of the command is

SYSTEM(RENAME, EVENT-NR, OLD-FILE-NAME, NEW-FILE-NAME)

where	EVENT-NR	is used to signal when the file has been re-named
	OLD-FILE-NAME	is the current name of the file
	NEW-FILE-NAME	is the replacement name for the file

The routine for executing the RENAME command is depicted in module 6.6.1. This routine checks the active file list and the system directory for a file bearing the same name as the new file name. If one is found, an error is returned, as you are not allowed to rename a file to an existing file name.

To rename a file, it must be closed, not a link entry, and not a permanent file. If these conditions are met, the system copies the new file name into the directory record and rewrites that entry onto disk.

MODULE 6.6.1

```
procedure rename
    search-file-list(file-mgr-new-file-name[pdb]) → result
    if result not equal to zero
        then
                search-directory(file-mgr-new-file-name[pdb]) → result
                if result not equal to zero
                    then
                            set er-create to status
                endif
    endif
    find-closed-file( )
    check-not-link-entry( )
    check-not-permanent-file( )
    copy(file-mgr-new-file-name[pdb], file-mgr-directory-record[pdb],
                                            file-name-size)
    directory-write(file-mgr-directory-record[pdb], directory-address)
    file-maintenance-post( )
endproc
```

6.6.2 Setting the File Attributes

The FILE-ATTRIBUTES command allows you to set the attributes of a file. It has the following format:

```
SYSTEM(FILE-ATTRIBUTES, EVENT-NR, FILE-NAME,
ATTRIBUTES)
```

where   EVENT-NR   is used to signal when the attributes have been established for the file

FILE-NAME   is the name of the file

ATTRIBUTES   is a word containing a bit set for each attribute to be established for this file

The attributes that may be set by this request include read/write protection, permanent file status, and the lock reject bit.

The routine for executing the FILE-ATTRIBUTES command is depicted in module 6.6.2. The execution of this command is straightforward; the system sets those bits in the attributes word as specified by you. A file's attributes may be set only when the file is closed. As a link file points to another file, attributes may not be set for it. To set the attributes the system masks off all those flags that do not correspond to attributes. Then the attributes are masked out in the fiie attributes word while preserving the other characteristics of the file. Finally, the new attributes are set in the file attributes word.

The approach taken here is markedly different from that utilized in DGC's RDOS [dbc75]. RDOS allows you to set individual attributes at any time through the use of the CHATR command. The user is also allowed to specify attributes for a link entry.

MODULE 6.6.2

```
procedure file-attributes
    find-closed-file( )
    check-not-link-entry( )
    and(file-mgr-attributes[pdb], attribute-mask)
                                        → file-mgr-attributes[pdb]
        complement(attribute-mask) → com-attribute-mask
        and(com-attribute-mask, file-attributes[fcb-address])
                    → com-attribute-flags
        or(com-attribute-flags, file-attributes[fcb-address])
                    → file-attributes[fcb-address]
    directory-write(file-mgr-directory-record[pdb], directory-address)
    file-maintenance-post( )
endproc
```

6.6.3 Setting the File Buffers

The FILE-BUFFER command allows you to establish the default parameters for buffered I/O for any file. The format of the command is

    SYSTEM(FILE-BUFFER, EVENT-NR, FILE-NAME, NR-IN-
    BUFFERS, NR-OUT-BUFFERS, BUFFER-SIZE)

where		
	EVENT-NR	is used to signal when the buffering parameters have been established
	FILE-NAME	is the name of the file for which the parameters are to be set
	NR-IN-BUFFERS	specifies the number of input buffers
	NR-OUT-BUFFERS	specifies the number of output buffers
	BUFFER-SIZE	is the size of the buffer

The routine for executing the FILE-BUFFER command is depicted in module 6.6.3. The system determines that the file is closed and not a link entry. Then it validates the number of buffers for I/O. The system designer should establish a limit defined by a system parameter.

Next, the buffer size is validated against the system limits. The buffers should be a fixed number of disk blocks. In this module, one or two disk blocks are the explicit limits, although you may want to parameterize the size according to some other rule (e.g., ten 80-character records similar to the input one expects from a teletype/CRT). Finally, the values for the buffer size and the number of I/O buffers are stored in the FCB.

MODULE 6.6.3

```
procedure file-buffer
    find-closed-file( )
    check-not-link-entry( )
    check-number-of-buffers(file-mgr-nr-in-buffers[pdb]) → result
    if result less than zero
        then
                set er-size to status
                exitproc
    endif
    check-number-of-buffers(file-mgr-nr-out-buffers[pdb]) → result
    if result less than zero
        then
                set er-size to status
                exitproc
    endif
    if file-mgr-buffer-size[pdb] not equal to sector-size
        or file-mgr-buffer-size[pdb] not equal to sector-size * 2
        then
                set er-size to status
                exitproc
    endif
    file-mgr-buffer-size[pdb] → file-buffer-size[fcb-address]
    set-buffers(file-buffer-size[fcb-address], file-mgr-nr-in-buffers[pdb],
            file-mgr-nr-out-buffers[pdb]) → file-buffer-size[fcb-address]
    directory-write(file-mgr-directory-record[pdb],    directory-address)
    file-maintenance-post( )
endproc
```

6.6.4   Setting the File Date

The FILE-DATE command allows you to set the creation date and time for a file. The date is determined by the system when the file is created. The format of the command is

SYSTEM(FILE-DATE, EVENT-NR, FILE-NAME, DATE, TIME)

where   EVENT-NR   is used to signal when the date and time are established in the FCB

            FILE-NAME   is the name of the file for which date/time are to be set

            DATE   is the current date

            TIME   is the time in seconds

The routine for executing the FILE-DATE command is shown in module 6.6.4 The file must be closed before the date and time are set.

MODULE 6.6.4

```
procedure file-date
    find-closed-file( )
    file-mgr-date[pdb] → file-creation-date[fcb-address]
    file-mgr-time[pdb] → file-create-time[fcb-address]
    directory-write(file-mgr-directory-record[pdb], directory-address)
    file-maintenance-post( )
endproc
```

6.6.5 Supporting Cast

There are three supporting routines that are used quite frequently to checks the attributes of files.

Checking for a Closed File

Before a file's attributes can be modified, the file must be placed in a quiescent state. The routine to verify this state is depicted in module 6.6.5. It searches the active file list for the name of the file. Any file appearing in the active file list has been opened by some user. If it has, the file management command cannot be satisfied and an error is returned. Next, the routine verifies the existence of the file by searching the system directory. If the file does not exist, the directory record pointer returned is less than zero, and an error code will be returned to the caller.

Checking for a Permanent File

A file that has been declared permanent cannot have certain attributes changed. This routine, depicted in module 6.6.6, verifies that the permanent file bit is not set in the attributes word. If it is, an error code is returned.

MODULE 6.6.5

procedure find-closed-file
  search-file-list(file-mgr-file-name[pdb]) → directory-record-address
  if directory-record-address not equal to zero
    then
      set er-file-open to status
      file-maintenance-post( )
  endif
  search-directory(file-mgr-file-name[pdb]) →
               directory-record-address
  if directory-record-address not equal to zero
    then
      directory-record-address → status
      file-maintenance-post( )
  endif
endproc

MODULE 6.6.6

procedure check-not-permanent-file
  if permanent-file-flag of file-attributes[fcb-address]
                 not equal to zero
    then
      set er-permanent to status
      file-maintenance-post( )
  endif
endproc

Checking a Link Entry

Certain file management commands do not apply to link entries. This routine,
depicted in module 6.6.7, verifies that the link entry bit of the file attributes
word is not set. If it is, an error is returned.

MODULE 6.6.7

procedure check-not-link-entry
  if link-entry-flag of file-attributes[fcb-address] not equal to zero
    then
      set er-link to status
      file-maintenance-post( )
  endif
endproc

6.7   OPENING A FILE OR DEVICE

As mentioned previously, a process refers to a file or device by a channel number. The file or device is a physical entity to which data may be stored or from which data may be retrieved. The channel number represents a pseudoname for the file or device that effectively allows a process file or device independence.

Before a process can execute I/O operations against a file or device, it must first establish a conduit along which data can travel. Effectively, this conduit is a logical connection between the CCB and the FCB or DCB. The operation of establishing the conduit is known as "opening the file."

Opening a File

To open a file, the process issues the OPEN system service request. When the OPEN request is completed, the specified channel number will be associated with the file or device. This channel number is used in subsequent I/O requests to identify the specific file or device to be accessed. A channel number may be associated with only one file or device at any time, thereby uniquely identifying it. However, a single file or device may have multiple channel numbers associated with it, effectively representing, multiple users. The format of the OPEN system service request is

SYSTEM(OPEN, EVENT-NR, CHANNEL, FILE-NAME, MODE)

where	EVENT-NR	is used to signal the caller when the channel has been established to the file or device
	CHANNEL	is the number of the channel to be used in subsequent I/O operations
	FILE-NAME	is the name of the file or device to be opened
	MODE	specifies the data access rights and type of buffering

You specify the channel number that you wish to associate with a particular file or device. If the channel number is in use (see section 5.3), you are forced to wait until the channel is released. Alternatively, you may request that the system allocate any free channel for you by specifying a -1 as the channel number. The system locates a free channel, if one is available, allocates it to you, and returns the channel number as the status of the event.

You may also specify the data access mode for subsequent I/O requests. You may request that the file or device be read- or write-protected by setting the appropriate bits in the mode word. These bits are "ANDed" with the protection bits specified in the file attributes word. You are only allowed those access rights set in the attributes word. The following table shows the data access rights to a file after it has been opened.

ALLOWED USER DATA ACCESS RIGHTS

Access requested (R/W)	File or device attributes (R/W)			
	0/0	0/1	1/0	1/1
0/0	0/0	0/1	1/0	1/1
0/1	0/1	0/1	1/1	1/1
1/0	1/0	1/1	1/0	1/1
1/1	(irrelevant—no access)			

where 0 = access allowed
      1 = access rejected

A 1-flag in the access mode indicates that you wish to protect the file against that type of access. No user ever willingly opens a file with $R/W = 1/1$, as this implies that no I/O operations can be performed against this file.

You may also specify automatic buffering for the channel. You do so by setting either or both of the INBUFFER/OUTBUFFER flags in the mode word. If zero is specified for these bits, the system uses the default parameters specified in the FCB. If you specify buffering, and no defaults are set, you must execute a BUFFER-CHANNEL request to set up buffering for the channel (see section 5.3.4 for a discussion of buffering). When you specify automatic channel buffer, the system sets the CHANNEL-LOCK-FLAG in CHANNEL-ATTRIBUTES. It does so to prevent you from issuing I/O requests other than SEQUENTIAL-READ or SEQUENTIAL-WRITE. The reason for this action is that the system needs to keep proper track of the pointers that record the location in the file, whatever its physical organization. With automatic buffering, these pointers are managed by the buffer manager (see section 5.3) although they are maintained in the FCB. A different type of I/O request would circumvent the control exercised by the buffer manager.

Setting Up Channel Buffering

As noted above, you may open a channel with automatic buffering in effect. If no defaults exist, you must specify buffering parameters via the BUFFER-CHANNEL request. The format of this command is

SYSTEM(BUFFER-CHANNEL, EVENT-NR, CHANNEL,
NR-IN-BUFFERS, NR-OUT-BUFFERS, BUFFER-SIZE)

where		
	EVENT-NR	is used to signal when buffering has been established for the channel
	CHANNEL	is the number of the channel for which buffering is to be established
	NR-IN-BUFFERS	is the number of buffers to be allocated to input
	NR-OUT-BUFFERS	is the number of output buffers to be allocated
	BUFFER-SIZE	is the size of the buffers to be allocated

You may establish buffering for either input or output or both. The number of buffers may vary from one to four, although this is an arbitrary limitation. The size of the buffers may be either one or two disk blocks (again, an arbitrary limitation). To establish different buffer sizes for input and output, you must issue two BUFFER-CHANNEL request.

6.7.1   A General Open Procedure

The general open procedure for files or devices is displayed in module 6.7.1. The first step is to validate the channel number. In the system presented here, channel numbers are allocated globally (see discussion in section 5.3.3) across the user population. If the channel number is a −1, the system finds a free channel for you. The address of the CCB is calculated from the channel number. A channel already in use or an invalid channel number yields an error code which is returned to you.

The next step is to associate the channel with the specified file or device. A simple test is performed to determine which routine to invoke. It is assumed that a file has an extension. Thus if FILE-MGR-EXTENSION is nonzero, the channel is to be associated with a file. Otherwise, the system will associate the channel with a device. In most systems, a more comprehensive check is performed on the name of a file since greater flexibility is allowed in naming files. Furthermore, if links are created to a device (e.g., PRINTER for LPT0), it is not immediately clear to the system how to open the channel.

Upon return from one of the opening procedures, the channel pointer (CHANNEL-ADDRESS) is checked for an error code. A positive value indicates that the channel is associated with a file or DCB. The OPEN-FLAG of the channel attribute word is set. If you indicated automatic buffering, the channel lock bit is set as well. The channel number is returned as the status of the event. Finally, buffer processes are activated if automatic buffering was specified.

The process of opening a file or device requires a complex sequence of functions to be performed. This general procedure appears relatively simple because it defers much of the work to support modules (see sections 6.7.3 through 6.7.5). Particular attention should be paid to the opening and closing of files since the mechanics of this process are often overlooked in more theoretical books on operating systems.

MODULE 6.7.1

```
procedure open
     file-mgr-channel[pdb] → open-channel
     if open-channel equals − 1
          then
               find-free-channel( ) → open-channel
     endif
     calculate-channel-address(open-channel) → ccb-address
     if ccb-address less than zero
          then
               set ccb-address to status
               exitproc
     endif
     if channel-attributes[ccb-address] not equal to zero
          then
               set er-channel-use to status
               exitproc
     endif
     if file-mgr-extension[pdb] not equal to zero
          then
               open-file-channel( ) → channel-address[ccb-address]
          else
               open-device-channel( ) → channel-address[ccb-address]
     endif
     if channel-address[ccb-address] less than or equal to zero
          then
               channel-address[ccb-address] → status
               exitproc
     endif
     set channel-open-flag of channel-attributes[ccb-address]
     if buffer-mode of file-mgr-open-mode[pdb] not equal to zero
          then
               set channel-lock-flag of channel-attributes[ccb-address]
     endif
     open-channel → status
     activate-buffer-processes( )
endproc
```

6.7.2 Opening a File Channel

The procedure for opening a file channel is shown in module 6.7.2. A cursory glance shows that each type of file organization requires special attention for certain types of access. In addition, you will note the interplay of many system data structures in establishing the channel.

The first step in opening a file channel is to locate the FCB and bring it into memory. If the file does not exist, or the number of links exceeds the nesting depth, an error results. Next, the attributes specified in the FCB are masked with the open mode bits to form the channel attributes. The protection bits of the channel are set for $R/W = 1/1$ mode as described above. If so, and the file use count is zero, a mode error is returned to you. Next, the type of file (given by FILE-FLAGS) is extracted from the file attributes word and inserted into the channel attributes word. This operation is a matter of convenience that improves the efficiency of I/O operations.

Next, the system set up the buffers for the channel. The parameters for the number of buffers and their sizes are derived from the default values found in the FCB as they were specified when the file was created. Note that they may be zero.

Next, the protection mechanisms are defined for the file, depending on its organization. Several cases are possible:

1. During a write operation on contiguous or segmented files, individual disk blocks must be locked against multiple writes. This protection is guaranteed by defining a resource semaphore (FILE-MODIFY-RS), which mediates these operations (see section 5.8).

2. During a write operation, as data are added to a serial or segmented file, new disk blocks may have to be allocated from mass storage and linked into the file structure. To guarantee protection, a resource semaphore (FILE-ADD-RS) is defined to mediate addition of new disk blocks to the file. Note that contiguous files have a fixed size and cannot be extended.

3. During read operations, multiple processes may request reads with different addresses in the file. Each user needs to be able to save the user's current location in the file. Multiple processes issuing read requests on the same channel (shared by these processes) would cause conflicts unless these read operations are synchronized. This protection is guaranteed by defining a resource semaphore that sequences read operations on the channel.

Depending on file organization, the current address in the file is initialized in the CHANNEL-SAVE-ADDRESS. This address specifies where the next I/O operation will begin using the selected access method.

Finally, the FILE-USE-COUNT is incremented by one and the FCB address returned to you.

MODULE 6.7.2

```
procedure open-file-channel(→result)
    find-or-build-fcb( ) → fcb-address
    if fcb-address less than zero
        then
                fcb-address → result
                exitproc
    endif
    set-buffer-and-protection-flags(file-attributes[fcb-address]) →
                        channel-attributes[ccb-address]
    if protection-flags of channel-attributes[ccb-address] greater
                                            than zero
        then
                if file-use-count[fcb-address] equals zero
                    then
                            extract-from-queue(all-file-queue, fcb-address)
                            release(memory-rs, fcb-address)
                endif
                clear channel-attributes[ccb-address]
                set er-mode to result
                exitproc
    endif
    extract file-flags from file-attributes[ccb-address]
    set file-flags of channel-attributes[ccb-address]
    open-buffering(file-record-size[fcb-address],
                        file-buffer-size[fcb-address])
                    → result
    if result less than zero
        then
                exitproc
    endif
    if write-protection-flag of channel-attributes[ccb-address]
                                            equals zero
        then
                if serial-flag of file-attributes[fcb-address] equals zero
                    then
                            if file-modify-rs[fcb-address] equals zero
                                then
                                        request(memory-rs, lock-rs-size)
                                            → file-modify-rs[fcb-address]
                                        lock-rs-set(file-modify-rs[fcb-address])
                            endif
                endif
```

```
                    if contiguous-flag of file-attributes[fcb-address]
                                                           equals zero
                    then
                         if file-add-rs[fcb-address] equals zero
                            then
                            request(memory-rs, count-rs-size)
                                          → file-add-rs[fcb-address]
                            define-binary-rs(file-add-rs[fcb-address])
                         endif
               endif
          endif
          if read-protection-flag of channel-attributes[ccb-address]
                                                           equals zero
               then
               request(memory-rs, count-rs-size)
                              →channel-sequential-rs[ccb-address]
               define-binary-rs(channel-sequential-rs[ccb-address])
               clear channel-next-read-address[ccb-address]
               if segmented-flag of file-attributes[fcb-address]
                                                      not equal to zero
               then
                    if file-size[fcb-address] equals zero
                       then
                         set −1 to channel-save-address[ccb-address]
                       else
                           ccb-address → request-channel-address[p]
                           fcb-address → request-fcb-address[p]
                           clear request-file-address[p]
                           find-device-address( )
                           request-lock-address[p]
                              → channel-save-address[ccb-address]
                    endif
               else
               file-start[fcb-address] → channel-save-address
                                                       [ccb-address]
          endif
     endif
     increment file-use-count[fcb-address]
     fcb-address → result
endproc
```

6.7.3   Opening a Device Channel

The procedure for opening a device channel is shown in module 6.7.3. The
system validates the device name by searching the list of devices configured in

the system. If the device name is not found on the list, an error is returned to you.

The device attributes are masked with the open mode flags to create the channel attributes word. If the channel is both read- and write-protected, a mode error is returned. Otherwise, the channel is associated with the device.

Buffering is initiated for the device based on parameters found in the DCB. These parameters are set when the device is configured into the system.

Finally, a device initialization routine is called to prepare the device for I/O operations.

MODULE 6.7.3

```
procedure open-device-channel(→result)
    search-device-list(file-mgr-file-name[pdb]) → dcb-address
    if dcb-address equals zero
        then
                set er-device-name to result
                exitproc
    endif
    set-buffer-and-protection-flags(device-attributes[dcb-address])
                        → channel-attributes[ccb-address]
    if protection-flags of channel-attributes[ccb-address] equal zero
        then
                clear channel-attributes[ccb-address]
                set er-mode to result
                exitproc
    endif
    set device-channel-flag of channel-attributes[ccb-address]
    device-record-size[dcb-address] → dr-size
    device-buffer-size[dcb-address] → db-size
    open-buffering(dr-size, db-size) → result
    if result less than zero
        then
                exitproc
    endif
    device-switch-address[dcb-address] → open-type
    file-or-device-open[open-type] → open-address
    if open-address greater than zero
        then
                call(open-address)
    endif
    dcb-address → result
endproc
```

6.7.4   General Channel Buffering Procedure

The general procedure for establishing channel buffering parameters is depicted in module 6.7.4. The first step is to validate the channel number by checking for a CCB. If none is allocated, the channel is either not in use or has not been configured into the system. An error code is returned to the user.

Next, the channel number is checked to see if it is open and locked. If so, the channel is already in use and buffering parameters may not be set for it. ER-CHANNEL-USE is returned to the user.

Then the size of the buffer is validated, based on the channel association. For files, a buffer may consist of one or two disk blocks. For devices, the buffer may be any size less than two disk blocks. This latter approach accommodates the variable-size unit record devices. If the size is not valid, ER-SIZE is returned to the user.

Finally, the system defines the resource semaphores to control buffering and activates the buffer processes for the files.

6.7.5   Support Routines for Opening a Channel

Two routines are used to support the opening of a file. The first finds a free channel for the user. The second builds or locates a copy of the FCB in memory.

Finding a Free Channel

The routine for locating a free channel is depicted in module 6.7.5. It allocates a channel from the global pool of CCBs maintained by the OS. The routine searches the user channel list for a channel number whose CCB-ADDRESS is zero. If such a channel is found, the channel number is returned to the caller. Unassigned channels have not been allocated a CCB, thus providing an easy means for checking for a free channel.

Finding or Building a File Control Block

When opening a channel to a file, the system must verify its existence and access to a FCB. The routine to perform these two functions is displayed in module 6.7.6. In opening a file, the system must be aware of the existence of link entries and be capable of threading the link list to the target file. This threading is performed to a level of four links. An error code will be returned to you if this limit is exceeded.

To open a channel, the system first searches the active file list to determine if

MODULE 6.7.4

```
procedure buffer-channel
     calculate-channel-address(file-mgr-channel[pdb]) → ccb-address
     if ccb-address less than zero
          then
                    set er-channel-number to status
                    exitproc
     endif
     if channel-open-flag of channel-attributes[ccb-address] equals one
          and channel-lock-flag of channel-attributes[ccb-address]
                                                                  equals one
          then
                    set er-channel-use to status
                    exitproc
     endif
     channel-address[ccb-address] → fcb-address
     if device-channel-flag of channel-attributes[ccb-address]
                                                                  equals zero
          then
                    if file-mgr-buffer-size[pdb] not equal to sector-size
                         and file-mgr-buffer-size[pdb]
                                                  not equal to sector-size * 2
                         then
                                   set er-size to status
                                   exitproc
                    endif
          else
                    if file-mgr-buffer-size[pdb] less than zero
                         or file-mgr-buffer-size[pdb]
                                                  greater than sector-size * 2
                         then
                                   set er-size to status
                                   exitproc
                    endif
     endif
     file-mgr-buffer-size[pdb] → channel-buffer-size
     define-buffer-rs(file-mgr-nr-in-buffers[pdb], − 1)
     define-buffer-rs(file-mgr-nr-out-buffers[pdb], 0)
     clear channel-lock-flag of channel-attributes[ccb-address]
     activate-buffer-processes( )
endproc
```

MODULE 6.7.5

```
procedure find-free-channel(→channel-number)
    number-of-user-channels − 1 → channel-number
    while channel-number greater than or equal to zero
        do
            calculate-channel-address(channel-number) →
                                                            ccb-address
            if ccb-address greater than or equal to zero
                then
                    if channel-attributes[ccb-address] not
                                                        equal to zero
                        then
                            decrement channel-number
                        else
                            exitproc
                    endif
            endif
        enddo
endproc
```

the file has been opened previously by another user. This step is necessary since the other user may have locked the file for exclusive use. If it is not found on the active file list, a search is made in the system directory. If not found there, the file does not exist; an error code is returned to you.

When a FCB is found in the directory, it is read into memory by SEARCH-DIRECTORY. As the directory entry is a subset of the FCB, a full FCB is allocated from the free memory pool, initialized with the directory information, and the new FCB is entered onto the active file list. For serial and segmented files, the size of the physical record is computed and stored in the allocation data entry. The address of the new FCB is returned to the caller.

MODULE 6.7.6

```
procedure find-or-build-fcb(→result)
    clear link-count
    while true
        do
            search-file-list(file-mgr-file-name[pdb]) → fcb-address
            if fcb-address not equal to zero
                then
                    exitproc
            endif
            search-directory(file-mgr-file-name[pdb]) → fcb-address
            if fcb-address less than zero
```

```
                    then
                            exitproc
                endif
                while link-entry-flag of file-attributes[fcb-address]
                                                    equals one
                        do
                        increment link-count
                        if link-count greater than or equal to MAX-LINKS
                                then
                                        set er-no-file to result
                                        exitproc
                        endif
                        file-name-size → fn-size
                        copy(file-link-name[pdb], file-mgr-file-name[pdb],
                                                            fn-size)
                        enddo
            enddo
        request(memory-rs, fcb-size) → fcb-table
        clear(fcb-table,fcb-size)
        copy(file-name[fcb-address], file-name[fcb-table],
                                            directory-record-size)
        fcb-table → fcb-address
        file-mgr-directory-address[pdb] →
                                    file-directory-address[fcb-address]
        enter-into-queue(all-file-queue, fcb-address)
        file-size[fcb-address] → file-allocated-size[fcb-address]
        if contiguous-flag of file-attributes[fcb-address] equals zero
            then
                    fcb-address → request-fcb-address[p]
                    calculate-data-offset(file-size[fcb-address]) → data-offset
                    if data-offset not equal to zero
                            then
                            file-size[fcb-address] − data-offset +
                                data-block-size → file-allocated-size[fcb-address]
                    endif
            endif
        fcb-address → result
endproc
```

6.7.6   Support Routines for Channel Buffering

Two routines are used to initialize buffering on a channel. The first validates the buffering parameters and the second initiates the buffer processes.

Parameter Validation

The OPEN-BUFFERING routine, depicted in module 6.7.7, initializes the parameters for buffering on a channel. For each mode, it defines the resource semaphore that controls the allocation of buffers. The number of buffers is specified in the CCB. Buffering is initiated for a mode only if the appropriate bit has been set in the attributes word.

Activating Buffer Processes

The routine for activating the buffer processes is depicted in module 6.7.8. A process is activated if and only if the buffer process parameter for that mode contains the address of the process. The processes themselves are discussed in section 5.3.

The activation of buffer processes is treated separately because buffering may be activated at any time after a file has been opened. Thus you could open a file, read a few records (say, descriptor information), and then activate buffering for the remainder of the I/O operations on the file. In fact, the number of buffers to allocate may be contained in the descriptor records.

6.8   CLOSING AND RESETTING FILES

Once you have completed I/O operations against a file, you must close it. When a file is closed, certain parameters describing the file are updated in the directory. The CLOSE request destroys the association between the channel number and the file/device to which it was attached and thus makes the channel available for allocation to another user. A special variant of the CLOSE request is the RESET request. The RESET request proceeds to close all open channels allocated to a process. It is called when a process terminates normally or is aborted in order to ensure a tidy environment. The user may also issue the RESET request at any time. The format of the CLOSE command is

    SYSTEM(CLOSE, EVENT-NR, CHANNEL)

where   EVENT-NR   is the event used to signal the caller when the
                         CLOSE operation has completed
           CHANNEL   is the number of the channel to be closed

The format of the RESET command is

    SYSTEM(RESET, EVENT-NR)

where   EVENT-NR   is used to signal the caller when all channels have
                             been closed

6.8.1   The General Close Procedure

The general procedure for closing a file or device channel is depicted in module
6.8.1. In closing a channel, the system must wait until all I/O operations on the

MODULE 6.7.7

```
procedure open-buffering(record-size, buffer-size, →result)
    clear input-process
    clear output-process
    clear channel-inbuffer-rs[ccb-address]
    clear channel-outbuffer-rs[ccb-address]
    if outbuffer-flag of channel-attributes[ccb-address] not equal to zero
          then
                  extract number-of-output-buffers from record-size
                  define-buffer-rs(number-of-output-buffers, 0)
    endif
    if inbuffer-flag of channel-attributes[ccb-address] not equal to zero
          then
                  extract number-of-input-buffers from record-size
                  define-buffer-rs(number-of-input-buffers, − 1)
    endif
    set one to result
endproc
```

MODULE 6.7.8

```
procedure activate-buffer-processes
     if inbuffer-process not equal to zero
          then
                  activate(inbuffer-process)
                  set inbuffer-flag of channel-attributes[ccb-address]
     endif
     if outbuffer-process not equal to zero
          then
                  activate(outbuffer-process)
                  set outbuffer-flag of channel-attributes[ccb-address]
     endif
     set one to result
endproc
```

channel have been completed by any subordinate processes. This also involves ensuring that all buffers have been properly written to the file before it is closed.

The first step is to validate the channel number. The system verifies that the channel has been assigned and is currently open. If both these conditions are not met, an error code is returned to the caller. The channel is then locked against further access and buffering is terminated. The system then waits for all channel activity to cease by placing the file management process on the DELAY-QUEUE. After channel activity has ceased, all buffers (if any were allocated), and the CCB are released to the memory pool.

MODULE 6.8.1

```
procedure close
    calculate-channel-address(file-mgr-channel[pdb]) → ccb-address
    if ccb-address less than zero
        then
                ccb-address → status
                exitproc
    endif
    if channel-open-flag of channel-attrbutes[ccb-address] equals zero
        then
                set er-channel-close to status
                exitproc
    endif
    start-close( )
    while channel-use-count[ccb-address] not equal to zero
        do
                request(delay-rs, delay-time)
        enddo
    finish-close( )
    set one to status
    file-maintenance-post( )
endproc
```

6.8.2   The General Reset Procedure

The general procedure for resetting all channels is depicted in module 6.8.2. This procedure is shown for the global user environment, where all user channels are allocated from a global pool. Extension to the concept of local channel pools is straightforward.

The procedure for resetting all channels follows closely from that for closing a single channel. However, it attempts to close all open channels in parallel, as this is more efficient in terms of system operations. The RESET operation could be conducted sequentially and be written as follows:

```
            for index from 0 to nr-user-channels − 1
                do
                    system(close, event-nr, index)
                enddo
```

MODULE 6.8.2

```
procedure reset
    clear open-count
    set channel-number to zero
    while channel-number less than number-of-user-channels − 1
        do
        calculate-channel-address(channel-number) → ccb-address
        if channel-open-flag of channel-attributes[ccb-address]
                                                not equal to zero
            then
                    start-close( )
                    increment open-count
        endif
        enddo
    if open-count equals zero
        then
                set one to status
                file-maintenance-post( )
    endif
    clear channel-number
    while channel-number less than nr-user-channels − 1
        do
        calculate-channel-address(channel-number) → ccb-address
        if channel-attributes[ccb-address] not equal to zero
            then
                if channel-use-count[ccb-address] equals zero
                    then
                            finish-close( )
                            decrement open-count
                endif
        endif
        enddo
    while open-count not equal to zero
        do
                request(delay-rs, delay-time)
        enddo
    set one to status
    file-maintenance-post( )
endproc
```

The intent behind closing all the channels is to reset the I/O subsystem to a naive state. If the RESET operation were to proceed sequentially as outlined above, some process could attempt to open a channel that had just been closed. To circumvent such a problem, additional logic and indicator flags would have to be introduced into the channel handling mechanisms.

The first step in resetting of the I/O environment consists of starting close operations on all channels. If no channels are open, a successful return is made to the caller. Next, the system cycles over all open channels. If a channel usage count is zero, the close completion procedure is executed. It then delays for 1 second and recycles to examine remaining channels. This procedure is repeated iteratively until all channels are closed.

6.8.3 Support Routines for Closing a File

There are several procedures that perform the bulk of the work in closing a channel.

Initiating Close Operations

The procedure to initiate close operations on a channel is depicted in module 6.8.3. The channel is locked to preclude any further access by any other processes. If the channel is attached to a file, any processes enqueued to one of the resource semaphores are terminated with error codes. The semaphore control blocks are released to the free memory pool and all buffer processes that have been active for the channel are terminated.

Terminating Buffer Processes

The procedure to terminate buffer activity on a channel is depicted in module 6.8.4. This procedure checks to see if a resource semaphore is defined for either input or output buffering. If a resource semaphore is defined, FREE-BUFFERING is invoked to release the buffers and deactivate the resource semaphore. On output, all buffers must be flushed before they may be released. Buffers must be flushed (and not simply thrown away) because the process has emitted the data with the expectation that they will be stored on the file or device. With regard to input buffers, these may be safely thrown away. They represent data the process did not expect to receive and will not use.

Freeing the Output Buffers

The procedure for releasing the buffers attached to a channel is depicted in module 6.8.5. The procedure waits for all buffer activity to cease. The wait queue consists of a list of processes waiting to execute an I/O function using

MODULE 6.8.3

```
procedure start-close( )
    set channel-lock-flag of channel-attributes[ccb-address]
    channel-address[ccb-address] → fcb-address
    if device-channel-flag of channel-attributes[ccb-address] equals zero
        then
            if file-modify-rs[fcb-address] not equal to zero
                then
                    free-lock-chain(file-modify-rs[fcb-address], ccb-address)
            endif
    endif
    close-buffering( )
endproc
```

MODULE 6.8.4

```
procedure close-buffering
    channel-outbuffer-rs[ccb-address] → rs-address
    if rs-address not equal to zero
        then
                system(flush-buffer, event-nr, file-mgr-channel[pdb])
                free-buffering(rs-address)
    endif
    channel-inbuffer-rs[ccb-address] → rs-address
    if rs-address not equal to zero
        then
                free-buffering(rs-address)
    endif
endproc
```

buffering. No new I/O requests may be initiated because the channel is locked when the CLOSE request is issued. When I/O activity has completed, the buffer-io-process PCB is released to the free PCB pool.

Finishing the Close Request

The procedure for finishing the closing of a channel is depicted in module 6.8.6. The procedure verifies that the resource semaphore for sequential access I/O was defined for this channel. If so, the resource semaphore control block is released to the free memory pool. The procedure then calls the appropriate routine to close a file or device.

MODULE 6.8.5

```
procedure free-buffering(rs-address)
    buffer-io-rs[rs-address] → buffer-io-address
    while remove-from-queue(rs-wait-queue[buffer-io-address])
                                                    not equal to zero
        do
            close-delay( )
        enddo
    remove-from-queue(rs-wait-queue[buffer-io-address]) →
                                                    buffer-address
    release(pcb-rs, buffer-address)
    while remove-from-queue(rs-available-queue[buffer-io-address])
                                                    not equal to zero
        do
            remove-from-queue(rs-available-queue[buffer-io-address])
                                                    → buffer-address
            release(page-rs, buffer-page[buffer-address])
        enddo
    while remove-from-queue(rs-available-queue[rs-address]) not
                                                    equal to zero
        do
            remove-from-queue(rs-available-queue[rs-address]) →
                                                    buffer-address
            release(page-rs, buffer-page[buffer-address])
        enddo
    release(io-map-rs, buffer-iomap[rs-address])
    release(memory-rs, rs-address)
endproc
```

MODULE 6.8.6

```
procedure finish-close
    channel-sequential-rs[ccb-address] → rs-address
    if rs-address not equal to zero
        then
            release(memory-rs, rs-address)
    endif
    if device-channel-flag of channel-attributes[ccb-address]
                                                    not equal to zero
        then
            close-device( )
        else
            close-file( )
    endif
    clear(ccb-address, ccb-size)
endproc
```

Closing a File

The procedure for closing a file is depicted in module 6.8.7. It decrements the usage count of the file. If no other processes are using the file, the resource semaphores for modifying and adding records (if defined) are released. The FCB is extracted from the active file list and returned to the free memory pool. In effect, the file is no longer known to the system.

MODULE 6.8.7

```
procedure close-file
     decrement file-use-count[fcb-address]
     if file-use-count[fcb-address] equals zero
          then
                    file-modify-rs[fcb-address] → rs-address
                    if rs-address not equal to zero
                         then
                                   release(memory-rs, rs-address)
                    endif
                    file-add-rs[fcb-address] → rs-address
                    if rs-address not equal to zero
                         then
                                   release(memory-rs, rs-address)
                    endif
                    extract-from-queue(all-file-queue, fcb-address)
                    release(memory-rs, fcb-address)
     endif
endproc
```

Closing a Device

The procedure for closing a device is depicted in module 6.8.8. Because each device possesses different characteristics, a special procedure must be called to terminate operations on that device. This routine is accessed through the device's switch list.

MODULE 6.8.8

```
procedure close-device
     device-switch-address[fcb-address] → ds-address
     file-or-device-close[ds-address] → close-address
     if close-address greater than zero
          then
                    call(close-address)
     endif
endproc
```

6.9   DIRECTORY MANAGEMENT FUNCTIONS

The file management system supports a function for reading the directory entry for a file. This allows the user to retrieve information relative to the structure and attributes of the file. The format for the directory inquiry is

SYSTEM(DIRECTORY-READ, EVENT-NR, FILE-NAME, DIRECTORY-BUFFER)

where		
	EVENT-NR	is used to signal the caller when the directory information is available
	FILE-NAME	is the name of the file for which information is to be retrieved from the directory
	DIRECTORY-BUFFER	is a buffer provided by the user in which the information will be stored

The data returned in the directory buffer correspond to the entries in the FCB (table 6.1) labeled FILE-ATTRIBUTES through FILE-RECORD-SIZE.

6.9.1   Reading a Directory Entry

The procedure for reading a system directory entry (SDE) is depicted in module 6.9.1. The procedure determines if the specified entity is a file or a device. If it is the latter, the device name is converted to the DCB address and the contents of the DCB returned to the user. Otherwise, it is a file. The active file list is searched first on the chance that the file may already be open. If such is not the case, the system then searches the system directory for an SDE for the file. If no SDE exists, an error code indicating that the file does not exist is returned to the user.

6.9.2   Directory Management Utilities

When a file is to be located, the system looks for the FCB or the DCB associated with the file. The FCB may be found on either the active file list or in the system directory. The DCB will be found in the system device list. Three routines are used to locate the FCB.

Searching the Device List

The procedure for searching the system device list is depicted in module 6.9.2. It locates the address of the DCB if the device has been configured into the system. The user-specified device name is compared with the device names in

MODULE 6.9.1

```
procedure directory-read
    if file-mgr-extension[pdb] equals zero
        then
        user-device-name-to-dcb(0, file-mgr-file-name[pdb]) →
                                            dcb-address
        copy(dcb-address, file-mgr-directory-buffer[pdb],
                                    directory-record-size)
        set dcb-address to event-status[p]
        else
            search-file-list(file-mgr-file-name[pdb]) → fcb-address
            if fcb-address is equal to zero
                then
                    search-directory(file-mgr-file-name[pdb]) →
                                            directory-address
                    directory-address → event-status[p]
                else
                    fcb-address → event-status[p]
            endif
    endif
endproc
```

MODULE 6.9.2

```
procedure search-device-list(device-name, →dcb-address)
    set one to dcb-address
    address(system-device-list) → sd-address
    while dcb-address not equal to zero
        do
        memory(sd-address) → dcb-address
        compare-arrays(device-id, device-name[dcb-address],
                                    device-name-size) → result
        if result not equal to zero
            then
                    increment sd-address
            else
                    exitproc
        endif
        enddo
    set er-device-name to dcb-address
endproc
```

the list. When a match is found between names, the system copies the appropriate information to the directory buffer in the process data block. If no device is found, an error code is returned to the user.

Searching the File List

The procedure for searching the active file list is depicted in module 6.9.3. The active file list, known as ALL-FILE-QUEUE, contains an FCB entry for each file currently open in the system. The procedure searches the list comparing the user-specified file name with the FCB file name. If a match is found, the address of the FCB is returned to the caller. Otherwise, the caller is notified that the file does not exist.

MODULE 6.9.3

```
procedure search-file-list(file-name → fcb-address)
     queue-start[all-file-queue] → fcb-address
     while fcb-address not equal to zero
          do
          compare-arrays(file-name, file-name[fcb-address],
                                             file-name-size) → result
          if result equal to zero
               then
                         exitproc
          endif
          next-fcb[fcb-address] → fcb-address
          enddo
     clear fcb-address
endproc
```

Searching the System Directory

The procedure for searching the system directory is shown in module 6.9.4. The system directory is searched in a linear fashion. Each block of the system directory is read into memory and the SDEs are examined for a match with the user-specified file name. This procedure reads one disk block at a time from the system directory, starting at logical block zero of the directory. SEARCH-BASE tracks the progress of the search through the system directory.

The procedure sets up the parameters for the search. It then examines each directory entry in a block, comparing the user-specified file name with the file name in the SDE. If a match is found, it copies the system directory information to the caller's directory buffer (which has been mapped into system space) and sets up a pointer to this buffer in DIRECTORY-RECORD-ADDRESS. If no match is found, it increments the pointer in the block and continues the search.

If the block is exhausted, the directory address is updated and the next block read. When SDE-ADDRESS becomes negative, it is checked for an end-of-file indicator. If this is true, a no-file condition is signaled. Otherwise, an error occurred in reading the system directory and an error message is sent to the operator's console.

MODULE 6.9.4

```
procedure search-directory(file-name, →directory-record-address)
    clear search-base
    clear sde-address
    while sde-address greater than or equal to zero
        do
        system(read, 16, directory-channel, directory-search-
            address, sector-size, search-base) → sde-address
        directory-search-address → sx
        sx + sde-address − directory-record-size → search-limit
        while search-limit greater than or equal to sx
            do
            copy(sx, temp-file-name, file-name-size)
            compare-arrays(file-name, temp-file-name,
                                        file-name-size) → result
            if result equals zero
            then
            directory-record-size → dr-size
                copy(sx, file-mgr-directory-record[pdb], dr-size)
                sx − directory-search-address +
                            rq-lock-address[p] → rq-lock-address[p]
                address(file-mgr-directory-record[pdb]) →
                                        directory-record-address
                exitproc
            endif
            increment sx by directory-record-size
            enddo
            increment search-base by sde-address
            enddo
    if sde-address not equal to er-end-of-file
        then
            error-message(directory-error)
    endif
    set er-nofile to director-record-address
endproc
```

6.9.3   Directory Update Utilities

The three utility functions described below support the creation and updating of directory records

Updating a Directory Entry

The procedure for updating SDE is shown in module 6.9.5. Whenever a file attribute is modified, or data are added to the file, both the FCB and the SDE must be updated. The contents of an SDE (which form the basis for the FCB) are rewritten to the directory. This operation is straightforward, as the FCB contains the address of the SDE.

MODULE 6.9.5

```
procedure directory-update(fcb-address)
    random-write(0, file-name[fcb-address], directory-record-size, file-
                                directory-address[fcb-address])
endproc
```

Writing a New Directory Record

The procedure for writing a new directory record is depicted in module 6.9.6. This procedure checks the directory for an empty slot in which to insert a new SDE. If no slots are available, the system will append the SDE to the end of the directory file. A count of free slots is maintained in the FCB associated with the system directory is searched for the location of that slot. A free SDE slot has a file name consisting of a string of blanks. Appending a new SDE may involve the allocation of another disk block. As this procedure is part of the file manager, it merely invokes the IOM to execute the appropriate write function.

Writing a Directory Record

The procedure for writing a directory record is shown in module 6.9.7. This procedure is used to fill an empty slot in the system directory. The new directory record is located in the file manager's PDB. It must be adjusted to the IOMAP slot prior to writing. ADDRESS is the address of the directory address for the SDE. This procedure is segregated because it is used by other file manager routines.

MODULE 6.9.6

```
procedure write-new-directory-record
    if file-directory-free-count[directory-fcb-address] not equal to zero
        then
            decrement directory-free-count[directory-fcb-address]
            search-directory(free-file) → directory-record-address
            if directory-record-address greater than or equal to zero
            then
                directory-write(new fcb-address, directory-address[fmb])
                exitproc
            endif
    endif
    system(sequential-write, 16, directory-channel, new-fcb-address,
                                              directory-record-size)
    system(status, 16)
endproc
```

MODULE 6.9.7

```
procedure directory-write(record, address)
    clear rmap
    adjust-for-pdb(rmap)
    random-write(rmap, record, directory-record-size, address)
endproc
```

6.9.4   Additional Directory Functions

In section 6.1.3 we discussed the sharing of a volume through use of directories. The flexibility of the directory concept is enhanced by allowing the space to be subdivided into partitions and subdirectories. At system initialization, only one directory exists per mass storage device—the master volume directory. Other directories and partitions are created at the behest of the system manager. This section looks at some of the functions required to support enhanced directory management.

Subdirectories Revisited

A directory serves as an index to the files contained on a disk volume. A subdirectory serves as an index for some mutually exclusive subset of the total collection of files on the volume. The subdirectory entry itself is a file in the directory. A subdirectory may expand or contract in size as files are created and deleted within its area. A special case of the subdirectory known as the partition is allocated a fixed size of disk space at the time it is created and usually represents a contiguous portion of the volume.

An example illustrates the difference. The system manager must share disk space among eight users. Suppose that the disk volume contains a total of 10 Mbytes of space, of which 2 Mbytes are allocated to various system files. The system manager can divide the remaining space (equal to 8 Mbytes) in one of the following ways:

1. He or she could create eight disk partitions of 1 Mbyte each. This guarantees a fixed amount of file space to each user. However, the user is limited to exactly that amount of file space.

2. He or she could create a disk partition of 8 Mbytes and create eight subdirectories within it. This allows any user to allocate and release as much file space as can be used. However, users are limited to the total space of the partition and may not encroach on system file space.

Creating a Subdirectory

Two commands are usually available for the creation of subdirectories: CREATE-DIRECTORY and CREATE-PARTITION. The syntax of the commands is identical except for the size parameter associated with the partition request. The format of these commands is

```
SYSTEM(CREATE-DIRECTORY, EVENT-NR, DIRECTORY-NAME)
SYSTEM(CREATE-PARTITION, EVENT-NR, PARTITION-NAME,
SIZE)
```

where	EVENT-NR	is used to signal the caller when the directory or partition has been created
	DIRECTORY-NAME PARTITION-NAME	is the name of the directory or partition that is to be created
	SIZE	is the number of disk blocks to allocate

A directory name must have an extension .DR to indicate that it is a directory file. Directory files are modifiable only by the OS and may be created only by the OS. When allocating a partition, the size parameter is specified in multiples of disk sectors. Partitions are usually created with a minimum fixed size; Data General's RDOS requires that a partition be allocated a minimum of 64 disk blocks (equivalent to 16K words).

Referencing a Directory

When a user job is activated in the system, the user must set up the environment in which it can execute. One aspect of this procedure is to "make known" the directory containing the files to be accessed by the process. Associated with the procedure of "knowing" a directory is the concept of a default directory.

Consider how a user would reference a file. All directory names necessary to uniquely identify that file would be specified. This is called a path name. In figure 6.1, the structure of a multilevel directory is shown. To reference the file TEXT, the user must specify the path as VOL1:USER3:TEXT. It is important to specify the volume directory name since the system may be configured with multiple volumes. Requiring that the path name be specified each time the user wishes to reference a file is not only tedious but is prone to errors and an increase in user overhead.

Suppose that the user were able to specify the name of a directory to which all file references would default unless the path name were explicitly provided with the file name. This is the concept of the "local" directory. In order to specify the local directory, the SET-DIRECTORY command is provided. The format of this command is

SYSTEM(SET-DIRECTORY, PATHNAME)

where   PATHNAME   is the name of the directory the path consisting
                             of necessary to identify a unique local directory

Thus if the owner of the TEXT file wanted to establish a local directory, the path name would be specified as VOL1:USER3. Any future file reference would cause the directory USER3 to be searched. If the user specified the file name TIMETABLE (referring to figure 6.1), an error would result, as that file does not exist in directory USER3.

Releasing a Directory

Directories, like files, may outlive their usefulness. At some point, the system manager will need to remove a directory from the system. A specific command, REMOVE-DIRECTORY, is provided for this purpose. The format of this command is

SYSTEM(REMOVE-DIRECTORY, DIRECTORY-NAME)

where   DIRECTORY-NAME   is the name of the directory to be
                                   removed

When releasing a directory, the system must ensure that the directory is completely empty. As the directory is a file, this can be ascertained by verifying the file size or examining the number of SDE slots in the directory FCB. If it is empty, the directory's SDE would be removed from the parent directory and the space released to the system.

7

The User Interface and Utilities

An interactive computer system is designed to help you solve problems quickly and easily from a terminal. From the terminal, you talk to the system and tell the computer what you want it to do. The medium through which you talk to the system is known as the OS command language. This command language defines the user environment, which is the set of things you can and cannot do with the computer. An OS module, known as the Command Language Interpreter (CLI), translates your commands into sequences of internal system service requests and executes them. When the work is completed, the CLI tells you if the results were successful, and if not, why not.

The objective of user management is to configure the environment to provide you with exactly the capabilities you need to meet the differing requirements of your work. In a multiuser system, you should be isolated from every other user so that you do not interfere with the work being done by other users of the system.

A small computer system usually has a small number of users. Configuring the user environment consists of three distinct tasks:

1. Devising an appropriate command language that allows you to manipulate the objects supported by the OS; such objects include devices, files, and processes.

2. Generating a specific version of the OS for a given set of hardware resources to supply and support an adequate number of objects.

3. Loading the OS into the computer and initializing its data and control structures so that the computer system can do useful work for you.

In this chapter we explore the implications of each task on the OS design process. The most emphasis will be given to the structure and facilities provided by the OS command language, because this aspect of the user environment is most frequently and directly experienced by you. System generation is infrequently performed but is extremely important to the performance and efficiency of the computer system. However, system generation is usually aided by a dialogue between you and a special program that allows you to select from a menu of features. This simplistic approach minimizes the effort you must expend to create a new version of the OS. Finally, installing an OS, a process known as "booting," is straightforward and requires little more effort than answering a few questions about the external environment of the computer system.

7.1 STRUCTURE OF THE USER ENVIRONMENT

A small computer system may have one or more users simultaneously doing work, or a number of users who sequentially share the system. In either case, the OS has to keep track of what objects belong to which user and how much of each system resource each has used. Together, these two aspects of the user environment dictate the need for a coherent structure applicable to both the single-user and multiuser environments. The features of one such structure are described in the following paragraphs.

7.1.1 An Overview of the User Environment

When you talk to the OS, you tell it to perform a specific processing request. The OS performs—or executes—the request for the user and presents the results. If the request failed, it attempts to tell you as completely and concisely as possible the reason for the failure. You may then repeat the process by telling it to perform another request. This sequence, known as interactive or conversational processing, continues until you have performed all the work you have to do. This sequence is commonly known as a work session or terminal session, as commands are entered through a terminal device. If several users can do conversational processing at one time, each user converses with the OS and receives responses from it simultaneously.

The process by which you make yourself known to the OS is called "logging on," during which process the OS validates your identity. It takes this opportunity to create the common control and data structures necessary to monitor your actions and process your requests, as well as determining which privileges you enjoy and what restrictions must be enforced against you.

The problem of identifying a user exists whether the system supports single or multiple users. Commonly, each user is assigned a user identifier, which may be a number or an alphanumeric character string. Whenever you log onto the system, you identify yourself with your user identifier. Some systems reinforce this process of authentication by requiring a password to be entered at the same time. User identifier/password pairs are an effective means of verifying that you are allowed to access the system.

When you have logged onto the system, you are furnished with a workspace (which can be thought of as a scratchpad or temporary area for storing and manipulating data). The concept originated with implementations of APL but has been carried over to the general conversational environment. The workspace exists, of course, only as long as you are logged onto the system. Usually, the size of the workspace expands and contracts as you put data into or remove data from it.

Most users need a place to permanently store data between terminal sessions. Again, borrowing terminology from APL implementations, this place is called a library. Each user will have at least one such library allocated when the user identifier is assigned. In a library, a user saves files, each identified by its file name, which may contain data, programs, or other commands. In fact, a library is really a special instance of a directory (or subdirectory) which you read about in chapter 6.

There usually exists a set of public libraries that hold data and programs accessible by all users. Examples of such libraries are the OS utility programs, the system configuration parameters, and the FORTRAN subroutine library. These libraries are usually provided by the computer vendor as part of the system software, or by the installation manager.

As mentioned above, you do all your work through the medium of the OS command language. There are commands that allow you to do any number of things: create a file; add to, delete, or edit a file; run a program or list the files in your workspace. One such command is very special—it allows you to exit the computer system gracefully (also known as "logging off").

At the end of a terminal session, when you have completed all your work, you log off the system. Once you have logged off, you may no longer issue any commands or access any of the files in your libraries. At this time, your workspace is destroyed, together with any files it contained. The terminal becomes inactive until another user logs onto the system.

This narrative has given a brief overview of the user environment. In the following sections we examine the supporting concepts in more detail before delving into command language issues.

7.1.2   User Profiles

A user profile services to delineate the resources available to, and features exercisable by, a given user. Through the profile, individual users may be assigned exactly those capabilities that satisfy the work requirements. A profile will vary in size and complexity according to the amount of detail to be specified about a user. At a minimum, the following items of information are found in a profile:

1. A user identifier that identifies the user and private library
2. A password used to validate the user's identity
3. Whether or not the user is manager of a group library
4. An optional list of group library names to be shared among several users
5. Maximum sizes for the user's workspace and private library
6. An optional limit on the amount of system time the user may consume
7. An optional log-on message informing the user about the system environment
8. An optional list of restricted commands for this user

In any system, one user generally stands out above the rest. This user is variously known as the "superuser" or the "system manager" and is allowed to execute a set of privileged commands that affect the configuration of the system. The two most common superuser functions are the ability to create, modify, or analyze a user profile, and the ability to generate a new version of the OS. Where configuration parameters may be set dynamically, this function is reserved for the superuser. One such example is the ability to add or drop a peripheral from the OS resource set at any time as long as it is not the primary system device. The superuser also has the capability to cancel peremptorily any user's session for any number of reasons, although most often it is exercised because the user attempts to perform an unauthorized function.

7.1.3   Workspaces

A workspace is assigned when you log onto the computer system. As stated earlier, a workspace is a temporary area where one stores data and programs during a terminal session. If you want to keep data or programs permanently (or indefinitely), you must save them in a library to that you have access. The workspace, then, is a collection of files which disappears when you sign off the system.

A workspace may be allowed to grow to an arbitrarily large size or it may be restricted a specific number and type of files. Obviously, the worst such restriction is one program and one data file extant at any one time. Because this unnecessarily limits the flexibility of interactive users, most system designers choose a happy medium somewhere between the two extremes. This design point is a function of several system parameters.

One such parameter is the size of main memory. Although an ideal situation would be to keep the entire workspace in main memory, the size of some programs and data files, coupled with the number of such files, will clearly exceed main memory capacity. Another factor is the number of users (usually small) that the system is designed to support at one time. Thus the workspace is usually maintained on mass storage with only those files of most immediate interest to the user held in main memory at once. Swapping a file to or from mass storage is transparent to the user except for some small delay.

When you sign onto the system, you are usually given a clean or empty workspace. Some systems allow the specification of a default workspace, which, in reality, is a user library stored on disk. The user library, under the default procedure, is automatically copied into your workspace. Although such an approach is time consuming, it provides you with greater flexibility in managing your data.

Let us assume that you have an empty workspace. To accomplish any work, you need to be able to create files in it—whether they contain data or programs does not matter. Once you have done some work, you need to be able to find out exactly what you have in the workspace. Thus you must be able to list the contents of the workspace—either in their entirety or by specific file type.

You can create files in several ways. You may use the system text editor to define a data file or the source code for a program module; you may load a file from the libraries to which you are permitted access; or you may run a program that creates the file as a result of its actions. One such program is a language compiler that translates the source text of a program module into object code. Another is a user program that (possibly) processes some input data and generates an output data file.

Analogous to the creation of a file is the aspect of removing files from a workspace. You may specifically delete one file by name or you may wipe the slate clean by erasing the entire contents of the workspace. Variations on this theme allow selective deletion of files by type, age, or comparison of file names with some skeleton format. An associated concept does not physically delete a file but allows the user to remove it to a "safe place"—that is, to save it in a library where either one file or the whole workspace may be stored.

Last, but not least, you may execute a program contained in your workspace. A feature provided in most systems is the ability to make a file that is actually a list of system commands. In effect, this provides you with a command-level macro capability. For the stout of heart, some systems will allow you to submit programs for execution in a background mode (also known as the batch stream) where no further interaction with the user is required.

7.1.4   Libraries

Libraries are places where files are more or less permanently stored between user terminal sessions. They have three flavors: private, group, and public. A private library is meant to be used by one user and, in general, is solely accessible by the user with the matching user identifier. Within this library, a user can create, modify, and delete files as desired. In some instances a user may wish to share a particular file with another user. To do so, the primary user specifies the particular secondary user, the particular file, and the access privileges which that secondary user will enjoy with respect to the file (see section 6.1.2 for a discussion of file sharing).

A group library contains a set of files accessible by a specified group of users. Generally, this group is a subset of the larger user population. A user is permitted to access a group library if the library name is mentioned in the user profiles. Management of the group library may be approached from two viewpoints: all group users can do all things to all files, or only one user can do all things to all files. The latter case is considered to be a restricted group library, and the former case is an unrestricted group library. In the restricted case, the group library administrator may create, modify, and delete files, whereas other users are restricted to listing the library contents and reading (copying) a file from the library.

A public library is one that is accessible to all users of the system. Public libraries are administered by the system manager, who has the responsibility for installing them, and creating, modifying, or deleting files within them. The users of the system are only permitted to list the contents of public libraries and to read (copy) specific files into their own workspaces. Things usually stored in public libraries are object modules of system subroutines, executable versions of system processors, and standard system data files such as the configurable system parameters.

There is no magical aura associated with the three-way division of libraries. It merely happens to be a convenient way to enforce access privileges on collections of files. What matters is how one views the library concept in the user environment. To summarize:

1.   Each user usually has one and only one private library associated with his or her user identifier.
2.   Each user may have access to one or more group libraries for those groups of which the user is a member.
3.   Each user has access to all public libraries.

7.2   OPERATING SYSTEM COMMAND LANGUAGE

The primary linkage between you and the OS is the command language (also known as the OSCL). Its unique feature is that every user is obligated to employ it in order to establish initial communication with the computer system. What constitutes an OSCL varies from vendor to vendor. This section describes some of the factors to be considered in designing and implementing an OSCL for a computer system.

An OSCL Background

Computer users have, by and large, always been willing to argue for and about the languages they use to solve problems. At the beginning, there was raw machine language—a messy pattern of ones and zeros. This was superseded by assembly language, which removed the annoyance of machine language coding. Assemblers performed the clerical work of translating symbolic instructions into patterns of ones and zeros.

The next step up was provided by higher-order procedure-oriented languages such as FORTRAN, COBOL, and so on, which were implemented by a compiler. The exact code produced by the compiler was not important as long as it implemented the algorithm embodied in the procedure. In addition, there also arose a class of problem-oriented languages, such as GPSS, where the user describes the basic rules and data structures, but basic algorithms are intrinsic to the system.

A counterpoint to this development has been the evolution of command languages. In the beginning, there were no OSs; therefore, there were no command languages. With the development of the first batch monitors, the user had a choice of a few things to do and, simple command languages were developed to allow specifications to be made. These languages were modeled on assembly systems because, after all, they assembled a user's job into a coherent processible whole. And that is where command language development has been stuck for the past 20-odd years. Some attempts have been made to move to a procedural language [code71], but few have succeeded. The most successful procedural language has been Burrough's Work Flow Language, which is modeled after ALGOL 60 and is an inherent part of the Master Control Program.

Some Basic Definitions

A command language is the language by which a user addresses the system and indicates the task to be performed. A command language possesses both syntax and semantics. The syntax specifies what can be legally stated in the language and the semantics specifies what it means (i.e., what will happen when each command is executed by the system).

A command system is the entire complex of modules, data structures, and statements that form the interface between the user and the system. The interface is more complex than just the command language. It includes such things as the control characters, by which a terminal user may delete characters, create macros, or do substitution of parameters into a command. An important aspect of the command system is the form and content of the response language that conveys information to the user.

Basic Questions about Command Language

When setting out to design a command language and, by implication, its command system, the designer needs to decide several basic questions. These questions, posed by B.C. Shearing [simp74], fall into five categories: lexical, syntactic, scope, semantics, and defaults.

Lexical matters concern the physical characteristics of the language at the character-by-character level. A key question is the set of characters on which the language is based. The choice is between the minimal set of characters as defined by FORTRAN, the compromise approach taken by PL/1, or the open approach of ALGOL, where lexical details are left to the implementer. Another key question concerns the metasymbols—the characters that have special meaning to the command system and thus are usable in data and programs only with care. The third major consideration is the significance to be given to delimiters. Other factors include whether or not the language is free-format, block-structured, supports multiline statements, and has a prompt character.

Syntactic considerations concern the form statements should take, the structure of the language, the manner in which control can be modified, procedures or macros handled, and parameters passed to them. A key aspect of structure is the distinction between declarative and executable statements and what must be declared. Another question is what facilities are provided for control (e.g., for testing, jumping, etc.). The next syntactic question relates to the provision of macros and cataloged procedures. Finally, the designer needs to consider the concepts of variables, and if programs can receive and return values of such variables.

The scope of the control language concerns the facilities that must be supported and those that are optional. Currently, enormous variations exist among control languages because of hardware and OS characteristics. It is unclear if we should insist on a minimal kernel of functions or constrain them to be concentric across specified subsets. Semantics is a critical aspect of command system design, as it concerns the meaning of standard verbs in the language. Equally important is whether or not there should be universal names and meanings for certain inevitable principles and devices. The obvious example is OS/360's SYSIN and SYSOUT, for the input and output devices, respectively. Another critical aspect concerns the provision for error handling and reporting rules, and if the system should exit to the user for dealing with certain types of errors. Other considerations include editing, file labeling, and the provision of a trapdoor facility to permit handling of oddball things that always seem to occur.

The final area concerns defaults—the general policies to be adopted when the user leaves certain things unsaid. The system must make an assumption about what the user means—an assumption chosen to reflect the most common use of the facility. Two key aspects of default handling should prevail: that simple jobs are really simple and that interactive use is practical. Default decisions will vary based on user characteristics, installation policies, and the computer system configuration.

The Overall Approach

We view an OSCL as a set of operators or functions which define for the user the capabilities of the computer system at the terminal interface. We can think of the OSCL as another abstract machine that serves to hide the gross features of the OS. It provides the means by which the user gets work done, by which resources are acquired in order to do useful work, and by which information is communicated to the system. A command language may be relatively small, such as System/360 Job Control Language, or it may be relatively big, like DGC's RDOS or Univac's 1100 Series Executive Control Language.

The design of the command language and its associated processor, the CLI, is often put off until the last minute. In many cases, a command language "just happens." As a result, command languages are often tangled constructs that serve to confuse the user attempting to utilize the system efficiently. Lest one be seduced into designing and implementing an elegant and powerful command language, a warning is well heeded [boet69]. Boettner comments that the command language is the user's window to the system and cannot be independent of it. It does no good to produce a beautiful command language if the system behind it is no good. One must design the OS and command language together.

This section is a synopsis of earlier work performed by the author [kais75]. In it we discuss three sets of criteria appropriate to the design of OSCLs and an extensive analysis of command language design. Other explorations of the problems associated with command language design can be found in [boet69], [oscl73], [sibl76], and [unge74].

7.2.1   User Design Criteria

The systems designer, in developing an OSCL, must consider the human engineering factors associated with the end user. The user's perception of the command language and the ease or difficulty of use will affect subsequent behavior in communicating with the system. An inadequate design can lead to confusion and ineffiency on the part of the user. Let us survey some of the criteria that are important from the user's point of view.

Simplicity

The command language should appear simple, masking the peculiarities of the hardware and giving the user confidence when stating job requirements. The average user should require a minimum of OSCL statements to accomplish the work at hand, and there should be several levels of complexity, so that a user may begin with a "starter" set of commands and follow a natural learning path to the sophistication of the full command set. System/360 Job Control Language (JCL/360) is a good example of how not to design an OSCL. JCL/360 is plagued by a lack of simplicity and few commands, requiring a user to submit many boring details about the work that are better left as options. In many cases, the user does not care about the myriad possibilities and merely specifies the system defaults. The moral of JCL/360 is that fewer commands do not automatically imply simplicity.

Conciseness or Brevity

There are two aspects to this criterion: what the user has to say to the system and what the system has to say to the user. The amount of what is to be said depends on the environment. In a batch environment, users should be able to say as little or as much as they please in describing their work. Because users are absent in both time and space from the execution of the work, a verbose response is preferable in order to aid the analysis of errors. JCL/360 usually requires gross amounts of information to run a single program. Contrast this command language with the batch environment supported by many minicomputer systems.

In an interactive environment, the user engages in a one-on-one dialogue with the system and it is in the user's interest to minimize the amount of information that must be specified in a command. For example, some systems require a user to specify only enough characters to identify a command uniquely [boet69]. Responses to the user should be as brief but noncryptic as possible. In any event, the user should always have the option of obtaining more information from the system. This criterion argues for many commands, each with a well-defined purpose, that have few options with well-known default values; but not so many commands that purposes and actions begin to conflict (e.g., consider the TSO commands [boet69]).

Uniformity or Symmetry

The command language should look the same whether submitted from a batch or interactive environment. The syntax of a command should be uniform; commands performing similar functions should have parameters appearing in the same relative positions. The semantics of the command should be symmetric; it should work for all data types for which the command would be logically feasible. In particular, the superuser should differ only from normal users in that he or she is capable of exercising an additional set of privileged commands.

Ease of Reading

A command language should be easy to read, as one should be able to comprehend what one has written about one's work. An aspect of this criterion is parameterization of the command, two common forms of which are keywords and position sequences. Keyword parameters are better than position parameters because names are better mnemonic than sequence positions, particularly when one wants to omit a specific parameter. This format can lead to excessive verbosity in the command syntax. Thus most systems utilize a mixture of positions for required parameters and keywords for optional values.

The types of parameters should be isolated from each other and, in any case, relatively few in number. Selection of parameter names is equally important as the selection of command names. The name should indicate the specific effect the parameter has on the function performed by the command. Command names that refer to different functions should not sound too much alike. Boettner [boet69] cites the TSO/360 commands CORRECT, REVISE, and UPDATE, which sound as though they do the same sort of things but, in fact, perform quite differently from each other.

Error Detection and Prevention

The command language should be designed to minimize the possibility of the user doing accidental damage to the user's own or another's environment. Drastic things should be done only by explicit commands and should require a secondary confirmation from the user before proceeding. A good example is the command to remove files from a library. Many minicomputer systems will request a "yes" or "no" confirmation from each user before a file is explicitly deleted from the system.

Errors detected by the system should be reported to the user. Several levels of error notification make it easier to decide which errors are reported immediately and which are delayed to the end of the program. In any event, the level of notification is closely associated with the severity of action taken by the OS in response to the error. Levels of notification may run from a simple warning about a syntax fault to termination of the user's program when it threatens system integrity.

Flexibility

A command language should not and cannot be all things to all users. Simple features such as macros and procedures can allow the user to extend the language in a straightforward manner. New commands should be easily incorporated into the environment. Most minicomputer systems treat the majority of commands as the names of executable programs. To add a new command implies, in most cases, the implementation of a new program in the system library. The command language should also accomodate changes in the hardware configuration without requiring the user to learn new patterns of behavior. Thus introduction of a new tape drive should require the user to learn only a new mnemonic for it (such as MT0) rather than a new command. Optimum flexibility is achieved where individual users can execute only a specific subset of the total commands available in the system. In fact, normal users execute a restricted set of commands that are exercisable by the superuser.

Reassurance

The command language should provide the user with reassurance; that is, the user should receive a response to every command and this response should state exactly the function being performed for the user. Another reassurance is to prompt the user for the next command. Many interactive systems have a limited buffering capability that allows the user to type ahead in the command stream if the user knows what he or she wants to do. At the same time, the user must be assured that any command sequence entered in advance can be canceled if the current command fails in execution.

Reassurance also involves informing the user of the running environment. This allows the user to know how the command that was entered will be interpreted by the system. The simplest case is for the CLI to print a prompt character when it is expecting a command and nothing otherwise. Systems that are heavily subsystem-oriented may select different prompt characters for each subsystem. DEC's RSX-11M OS uses a right-angle bracket followed by an abbreviated version of the subsystem's name (e.g., >PIP for the peripheral interchange processor).

7.2.2   Structural Criteria

Structural criteria relate to the syntactic and semantic factors that govern decisions regarding the physical structure of the language. Structural design decisions are relatively inflexible. Once the command language is set into implementation, major design changes to the structure are difficult, if not prohibitively expensive, to make. Structural design decisions should be made after consideration of the human engineering factors. As an OSCL is a major communications medium between the users and the OS, it structure should be designed to accommodate the user. This section examines several criteria to be considered in the design of OSCL structures.

Extensibility

An OSCL should offer a capability for extending the capabilities provided by the base command language. Two types of extensibility are possible: macro generation and procedure definition. Macro generation may be implemented in either a static or dynamic sense. Under JCL/360, a user may define and catalog a procedure skeleton. When a procedure is invoked, any parameters are replaced using arguments from the //PROC statement before the command sequence is executed. Most minicomputer systems allow for indirect addressing of files containing command sequences. For example, Data General's RDOS allows

    FORTRAN/A/X/P/L @COMPILEFILES@

which would be expanded to

    FORTRAN/A/X/P/L MAIN1

    FORTRAN/A/X/P/L SUB1

    FORTRAN/A/X/P/L SUB2

if the file COMPILEFILES contained the respective filenames.

Some command languages currently allow dynamic replacement of parameters in an OSCL skeleton at execution time. This feature is useful where the parameter values depend on the results of previously executed OSCL statements. However, the level of sophistication required of the user is often that of a system programmer. In addition, the overhead associated with maintaining this environment is sufficiently high to discourage it on all but the largest systems. Two cases worthy of note are IBM's VM/CMS EXEC processor and the UNIX shell ([ritc74, bour78]).

In contrast to parameter replacement, an OSCL procedure capability would act as a subroutine call to a separate group of OSCL statements. The only command language to offer such a capability is Burrough's Work Flow Language, which is based on ALGOL. In part, this capability is derived from the fact that the entirety of the Burrough's Master Control Program is also written in a variant of ALGOL, so the interface is relatively clean and simple. One last point to be made is that there appear to be no requirements for recursion or sophisticated loops in the command languages. It is generally anticipated that users would utilize a procedure capability to create new commands within their workspace.

File Specification

An important aspect of OSCL communication is the specification of a file and its binding to a task. Files can be assigned to a process in either a static or dynamic manner. In a static system, all file specifications are made in OSCL statements prior to the invocation of the program. JCL/360 provides a good example of this mechanism. Alternatively, files can be assigned dynamically through execution of OS service requests. Although we prefer the latter approach, specification and assignment of files at the OSCL interface should remain a viable option for the user.

Process Parameterization

Another important aspect of OSCL communication is the concept of process parameterization. Questions arise in this regard as to what types of parameters are required, when they are to be specified, and what their scope of action is.

The first question distinguishes between positional and keyword parameters. A positional parameter has a specific mandatory occurrence in the argument list. A keyword parameter is usually a keyword equated with a value. Our previous goal of simplicity suggests that the number of positional parameters be kept to a minimum (usually one or two). Optional arguments should be specified by keyword parameters where well-known defaults are assumed. The choice of a keyword should be a name meaningful to the user that naturally describes the condition it represents.

Another question arises from the distinction between global versus local parameters. A global parameter would describe a characteristic of the environment, whereas a local parameter would be specific to a given command. Some global parameters may be initialized by the user and others may only be inspected for their values. For global parameters, defaults are assumed by the system until the user defines the parameter. This approach allows considerable flexibility in the specification of the user environment at the expense of a few extra OSCL statements.

Control Structures

The functional power and complexity available to an OS user are heavily influenced by the OSCL. A system that is more sophisticated than its users is unlikely to be very popular. On the other hand, a system where users and designers interact closely is usually quite responsive to user needs. To facilitate a system's usage, the OSCL should support a few simple control structures, such as conditional branching and execution, value assignment to parameters, and iterative execution. In addition, a macro replacement or procedure capability would extend the user's control over the local environment. A particularly attractive model of an OSCL is the Job Description Language for the George 3 OS provided by International Computers, Ltd [cutt70].

7.2.3   System Design Criteria

A command system can take one of two formats. In the first place, it may be an integral component of the OS, such as JCL/360. It also may be a separate processor that reorganizes arguments passed from users into acceptable formats and calls the appropriate system services. This latter approach is exemplified by DGC's RDOS Command Language Interpreter. In fact, the CLI executes as a user program. This approach is exemplified by the UNIX shell processor, which provides a monitor environment for the user [ritc74].

A command language, to the user, is one definition of an OS's functional capabilities. A function available at the OSCL level should be available at the system service request interface (although not necessarily vice versa). The antithesis of this approach is diffusivity, where services at the command language level are different from the executive services. This property makes it difficult to integrate new functions into the system. Other criteria have an impact on the design of the command system. This section examines these criteria from the system as opposed to the user viewpoint.

Command Invocation

The environment in which a command language is to be used is of primary importance. Some systems are primarily batch-oriented, such as OS/360 and GECOS-III. Their command languages reflect a view where the job or session is treated as a complete self-containing algorithm except for certain logical linkages. Flexibility is extremely limited because of the number of commands necessary to run a program. Other systems are more conducive to interactive or time-sharing environments. By far the most recent successful phenomenon has been the emergence of UNIX, licensed by Western Electric. In many cases, each command is really a program, and therefore the distinction is more apparent than real. There are a few commands that must be executed immediately by the command system. Integrity considerations prevent their execution from being entrusted to a load module.

One should also be cognizant of certain special environments where the command language is embedded in a monitor subsystem. Good examples are BASIC and APL.

In designing a command system, one is tempted to survey other OSs and compare their respective features. The designer should be careful not to compare apples with oranges. Problems arise from these factors:

1. Each system has different functional capabilities; there may be no functional equivalents in other systems.
2. Some systems have commands for explicit functions that are deemed implicit by other systems.

Classification of Commands

In some command systems, as in many programming languages, commands are often classified as declarative or executable. Declarations are static or dynamic, and may be local or global in scope. Executable commands result in the initiation of a program, whereas declarative commands may set an environmental parameter (such as an execution time limit). The methods for classifying commands vary from vendor to vendor. Boettner [boet69] describes one such taxonomy based on the entities manipulated by the commands. Weegenaar [weeg74] proposes a scheme based on the types of operations to be performed by the system.

Environmental Control

The major issue in environmental control is the (non)existence of a control character. Kaisler [kais75] has examined this issue in some detail. The possible cases for environmental control are summarized as follows:

No Control Character.   The state of the machine is in either user or mode. In system mode, the OS is prepared to accept command language statements, whereas in user mode, it is prepared to accept data. Transition from user to system mode is accomplished by program termination or hitting a special "attention" key on the terminal. This approach restricts the user to one process at a time, as there is no way of directing input to a particular process. If data are misplaced, the system will reject the input or attempt to execute a load module by that name.

One Control Character.   Each command is preceded by a control character through which the system recognizes commands; all other input is treated as data and passed to the current user program (if any). This restricts the capability for supporting parallel processes by requiring a complex mechanism to direct data streams.

Two or More Control Characters.   In this approach, one control character is used to specify command language statements and the other to communicate with the command system during execution of user programs. Thus multiple processes can be implemented at the command level, as the second control character can be used to direct data to a particular process. It allows commands to be issued at any time during a user's interactive session. However, the increased complexity often requires greater sophistication of the users.

Clearly, the number of control characters is a critical factor in command system design. If affects the complexity of the system in both structure and content. The designer needs to take into account the purpose of the OS and the sophistication of the users when considering an implementation approach.

Default Handling

Each command should have a number of well-known, well-defined defaults for the optional variables. When no defaults are available, the user must specify a tremendous amount of detail for every program. If too many details are required, the user may commit errors of omission that are corrected by the system without telling the user what action was taken.

Almost all mainframe systems offer a minimal set of defaults relating to scope and specification of the user environment. The simplest defaults are none at all; that is, the system makes no assumptions about what the user will do. This approach is taken by many minicomputer OSs.

Default handling can be implemented at two levels. At the first level, the system manager assigns default values to certain classes of users that define their global environment. Each user should be able to dynamically specify local default values as long as they do not override parameters for the class. Each user also should be able to determine exactly what defaults are currently set for the environment by interrogating the OS.

Error and Contingency Handling

A command system must be able to handle errors arising from commands issued by the user. The action the system takes when an error is detected depends on its severity. Local errors occur when the user has failed to satisfy some condition associated with the invocation of a command (bad control character, too few arguments, etc.). Supervisory control implies that contingencies are detected and reported back to the user via status codes. The system takes no action unless the error threatens the integrity of the system. In most minicomputer systems, error handling is left to the user based on this approach. In supervisory control, execution is closely monitored and the system exercises strict control and handling of errors and contingencies. This latter approach is exemplified by such interpretive subsystems as BASIC and APL.

In the command language, at least two facilities should be provided for contingency handling. The first facility consists of the status codes returned from each system service request. The second facility consists of a capability for directing program control based on the value of the status code. The GEORGE 3 system [cutt70] for the ICL 1900 series provides a condition test that allows the user to skip commands based on the status code.

7.2.4   Some Further Thoughts on the Command System

The previous sections have explored many of the basic concepts necessary for the design of an effective command language. At this point, let us explore a few implementation-dependent issues.

Commands are recognized and handled by an OS module known as the CLI, which monitors a user's terminal until the command is typed into the system by the user (we shall say typed even though commands may also be read from a file, e.g., a macro capability). The CLI examines the command, verifies its syntax, and determines how to execute it.

Commands may be of two types: intrinsic and extrinsic. An intrinsic command is one that, because of its inherent function, cannot be executed as a user process and must therefore be executed directly by the OS in a synchronous manner. The obvious example is the command by which a user signs onto the system, as no useful work can be done until the user has been properly recognized. By default, extrinsic commands are any commands that can be executed as a user process. Most commands fall into this category, including the command to log off the system.

A user might be able to type a command in two ways. First, by typing the whole command statement at once, whereupon the CLI immediately takes over to analyze and execute the command. Or just the command name may be typed, whereupon the CLI queries the user for the remaining arguments (if any). This latter approach is particularly useful in systems that cater to unsophisticated users and provides a sound basis for implementing a "helping hand" service. Some systems go even further by requiring a user to type only enough characters to identify a command uniquely. MTS (see [boet75]) has successfully used this approach to satisfy several environments.

Another aspect of command execution is strongly dependent on the syntax required to invoke a user program. In some systems, there exists an explicit RUN or EXECUTE command that must be used to execute any user program. The CLI need only recognize a restricted list of names, which are the things it knows how to do (from the system designer's viewpoint). Any command name not on the list is treated as an invalid command and responded to with an appropriate error message. Alternatively, the CLI accepts anything (a name, that is) as a command and processes it in one of three ways:

1. The command name is looked for on the list of intrinsic commands that the system executes directly. If found there, it is executed immediately provided that all the right arguments have been specified.

2. The command name is that of an extrinsic command (e.g., a program name). These commands can be treated in three ways:

    (a) The system initially searches the user's workspace to see if there exists an executable file with the same name. If so, the file is loaded and executed after being passed the argument list.

    (b) The system may also search a user library or a set of group libraries; the same result occurs.

    (c) The system finally searches any public libraries for an executable file the same name; the same result occurs.

3. If neither of the foregoing conditions is met, an error is declared and an appropriate error message is issued to the user.

Under this approach it is best to keep the number of intrinsic commands to a minimum, as they are executed synchronously and are usually resident modules of the OS. However, this is not as serious a matter as it seems, as the CLI itself can be made to be a process that executes for the user. Thus major portions of the CLI are removed from memory when they are not required by the user.

7.3 SYSTEMS COMMUNICATIONS: SYSTEM SERVICE REQUESTS

The second major linkage between the user and the OS occurs through system service requests. The OS has created an environment in which the program executes and it imposes the restriction that the set of services common to all users, such as file management, are privileged operations. Access to these services is provided through a formal mechanism known as the system service request. This mechanism also has been known as a supervisor call, system call, or executive request.

The mechanics of the system service request (SSR) are relatively straightforward. Essentially, it is a "trapdoor" that allows the user to have a function performed by the OS on the user's behalf. The implementation of the SSR is usually dependent on the computer architecture; that is, a specific hardware (or software) instruction is executed to notify the OS that a service is required. The instruction may result in a software interrupt fielded by the OS. It then executes the necessary instructions to switch the context from user space to OS space. Generally, arguments are passed in CPU registers or in a list pointed to by the contents of one of the CPU registers. The OS fetches the arguments, validates and interprets them, and proceeds to execute the requested function.

The following paragraphs discuss two general implementations of the SSR. The first, utilized by Data General on the Nova series computers, is strictly a software interface. The second, utilized by DEC on the PDP-11 family, is a combination hardware/software interface. In both implementations, certain conventions need to be observed to ensure proper communication of information and to preserve system integrity.

System Request Processing: Data General

A user communicates with the RDOS system via a software linkage. A request is identified by a system command word. The structure of the RDOS command is

.SYSTM

command-word

error-routine-address

⟨next instruction; e.g., a normal return⟩

The .SYSTM instruction is assembled as an indirect subroutine call to the routine whose address is stored in memory address 15. The address is reserved by the vendor for storing the location of the routine that processes all SSRs in RDOS. This routine processes the request and calls the appropriate OS procedure to execute it. Arguments are passed in accumulators (e.g., CPU registers) AC0, AC1, and A2. Accumulator AC3 contains a pointer to the user's program stack.

Two types of return are possible upon completion of a system request. If an exceptional condition is detected, program control is transferred to a user-specified error-processing routine. The error code is returned to the user in accumulator AC2. Otherwise, program control resumes at the next normal instruction in the user's program. Note that the command word and the error routine address are considered to be part of the same instruction. Results of the system request will be returned in the accumulators (usually accumulator AC0). Consult the RDOS reference manual for a more detailed description of this mechanism [dgc75].

This approach is simple in implementation and works very well in a small operational system. Because it is totally a software artifact, the possibility exists for the user to subvert the system by providing false or misleading information. However, RDOS assumes that its users are both honest and cooperative. Thus this method is efficient for small computer systems without memory management and protection hardware.

System Request Processing: Digital Equipment's PDP-11

System requests are accomplished by four instructions in the PDP-11: TRAP, EMT, IOT, and BPT. These instructions are used differently by various OSs, and indeed, perform differently on different machines. Each instruction, when executed, is processed in essentially the same way.

Traps are, effectively, interrupts generated by the software rather than the hardware. When a trap occurs, the current Program Counter (PC) and Program Status Word (PSW) are pushed onto the processor stack. A trap vector containing the new PC and PSW is used to load the respective registers. The PC contains the address of the trap-handling routine (similar to hardware interrupt handling, as discussed in chapter 2). Upon completion of trap handling, the routine issues an RTT (Return from Trap) instruction to restore the calling process's environment.

EMT and TRAP are general instructions for invoking special services by interrupting the current process. EMT (Emulator Trap) is used extensively by DEC software to invoke OS services. By convention, TRAP is used to invoke special user services and differs only in its trap vector address. BPT is usually used to invoke special debugging routines and therefore is assigned a separate vector address. IOT is used in OSs where DEC wishes to differentiate between I/O services and other system services.

DEC software is written so that system services are coded in user programs as macros. The assembler expands these macros using appropriate macro library definitions. When the macro is expanded, the end result is to issue either an EMT or IOT instruction. Argument list addresses are passed on register R0.

7.3.1 Database for the System Request Mechanism

The SSR mechanism requires three tables for effecting the proper interface between the user and the OS: the system entry point table, the system call descriptor table, and the system switch table.

The system entry point table contains an address for each function implemented in the system. Undefined functions should have their addresses set to a negative constant (such as −1) by the system linker during the system generation process. Each SSR is identified by a function code that is used as an index into the table to validate the request.

The system call descriptor table contains two important entries necessary for copying the argument list and setting up the system stack. A stack is used because each SSR may have a variable number of arguments, ranging from zero to no more than 10. The first entry is the address of the parameter stacking routine. The second entry is the number of words to be reserved on the system stack, including a status word returned to the user at the completion of the request.

The system switch table determines how a SSR will be executed. Three types of requests are provided, where the type is determined by the first entry in the table. An entry of −1 indicates a synchronous request; the result of the request is returned as the value of the SYSTEM call. An entry of zero indicates that the request is executed immediately; the result is returned as the value of the status word. An address (i.e., an entry greater than zero) indicates that the request is to be enqueued to a system resource monitor that executes the function asynchronously; the result is returned as the value of the associated event. The second entry in the table is always the address of the actual module that performs the function.

7.3.2 System Request Processing: General Comments

The execution of a SSR requires processing in both the user space and system space. The amount of processing is dependent on the OS structure. In the examples provided in previous chapters, all the processing was performed in OS space. In this description the system stack is set up in user space and then mapped into OS space. This approach relieves the OS of processing, which must be performed synchronously by a resource monitor.

The basic algorithm for system request processing is as follows:

.set up the system stack in the PDB
.copy request parameters onto the stack
.execute the "jump to system space" instruction

in system space:
.map the PDB into system space
.retrieve the function code from the system stack
.using the system switch table, jump to the function module
.upon function completion, set the status word in the system stack
.map the PDB back to user space
.return to user space

in user space:
.check the status word for request completion
.retrieve any values returned by the function

The merits of this approach are obvious. Only one user can enter system space at a time by executing the "jump to system space" instruction. Depending on the number and type of arguments, parameter stacking can be a lengthy process (requiring several machine cycles) compared to remapping the PDB. The validation of individual arguments is performed by the module executing the request. Even if the user were to submit an erroneous argument (perhaps maliciously), its effect is felt only in user space because of the protection provided by the mapping hardware.

7.3.3   System Request Processing: User Space

The system request processing in user space falls into two categories: setting up arguments and calling the function, and checking the status word and retrieving results. The generic structure of a SSR is

SYSTEM(FUNCTION, PARAM1, PARAM2,..., PARAMn)→
RETURN-VALUE

The procedure for processing a system call is depicted in module 7.3.1. Figure 7.1 shows the code segment structure and the stack area in the PDB. Figure 7.2

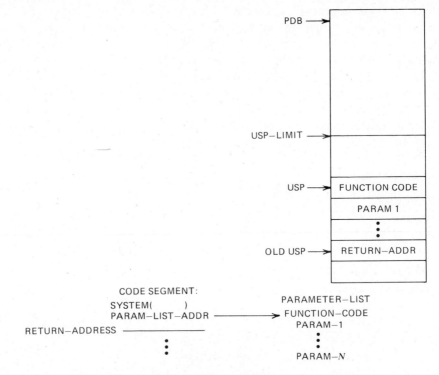

Figure 7.1   System service request processing: user space.

shows excerpts from the system call descriptor table and the parameter stacking routines.

When the user executes a SSR, the procedure SYSTEM, loaded from the system library and linked with the user's program, is entered. SYSTEM retrieves the function code, FUNCTION-CODE, from the parameter list that is pointed to by the PLA (the Parameter List Address). The function code is validated against the range of values (0,...,number of SSRs). An invalid function code results in FUNCTION-CODE being set to zero. A zero FUNCTION-CODE will force a transfer to a function known as DUMMY (at entry 0 of the table) that merely sets an error code and exits to the user.

Next, a stack frame is allocated in the PDB using the second value of the entry in the SYSTEM-CALL-TABLE. If the stack exceeds the maximum stack size, the process will be terminated by a call to ERROR-KILL after resetting the stack pointers. An alternative strategy would be to reset the stack pointer to OLDUSP and treat the request as a dummy function with the appropriate error status. The former approach is necessary for the real-time environment, whereas the latter serves quite well in a general-purpose system.

Next, the parameter stacking routine address is retrieved from the SYSTEM-CALL-TABLE. The routine is invoked to load parameters onto the stack by their type. Finally, the return address and the function code are placed on the system-call-table:

⋮

/ / some function

parameter stacking routines:

double-string-address:
        memory(parameter-list-address) → atemp
        memory(atemp) → memory(usp)
        memory(parameter-list-address + 1) → atemp
        memory(atemp → memory(usp + 1)
        increment parameter-list-address by 2
        increment usp by 2
        jump to string address

string-address:
        memory(parameter-list-address) → atemp
        memory(atemp) → memory(usp)
        increment parameter-list-address
        increment usp by 2
        jump to string-address
        . . .

address:
        parameter-list-address → memory(usp)
        . . .

Figure 7.2   Parameter stacking demonstration.

stack. The "jump to system space" instruction is executed to force a software interrupt and initiate processing in system space.

Upon return from the execution of the SSR, the user can examine the return value to retrieve the result of the function. For synchronous/asynchronous requests, the status of the event flag specifies the result of the request. User processing after SSR completion is described in section 7.3.5.

MODULE 7.3.1

procedure system(function, parm-1,. . .,parm-n, return-value)
    increment usp
    memory(parameter-list-address) → function-code
    if function-code less than zero
        or function-code greater than MAX-SSR
        then
            clear function-code

```
    endif
    usp − 2 → oldusp
    system-call-table[function-code + 1] → frame-size
    oldusp − frame-size → usp
    if usp less than usp-limit
        then
                address(usp) → usp
                address(stack-area) → usp-limit
                system(error-kill, er-stack)
    endif
    system-call-table[function-code] → parameter-stacking-routine
    call(parameter-stacking-routine)
empty:
    address(return-value) → memory(oldusp)
    function-code → memory(usp)
go-to-system:
    execute hardware 'jump to system space' instruction
```

Parameter List Processing

Parameters to a function generally have either a value or an address of a value. Values may be further subdivided into single- or double-word values or character strings. A double-word value may represent either a double-precision integer or a floating-point value. To load a parameter on the stack, the value is retrieved from the parameter list (indexed by the PLA) and pushed onto the stack. The pointers PLA and USP are incremented appropriately.

In this example we have assumed that for single- and double-word parameters, the value in the parameter list is the address of the parameter. This assumption follows the normal conventions of most compilers. Further, we only copy the requisite number of parameters for the system call by placing the number of words and their description in the SYSTEM-CALL-TABLE. This saves one word in the parameter list and serves as a further integrity check.

7.3.4   System Request Processing: System Space

A user process requests system service, which allows it to gain access to OS functions. This access is obtained by executing a "jump to system space" instruction that forces a software interrupt of the central processor. The interrupt routine for executing a SSR is entered to execute the request. SSR execution involves several distinct steps:

Set appropriate protection status for system space
Access the PCB

Validate the function request and initialize the PCB

Set up return and exit information

Execute the request

Set data into the PCB

Return to the user

Establishing System Mode

When system space is entered via an interrupt, the first task is to set the execution mode to system mode. In most systems, system mode disables certain software checks that prevent the user from executing privileged instructions. The OS must also reset the state of the memory management unit to indicate that system space is to be accessed. The MMU retains the previous state information after an interrupt. In most MMUs, transition to the system mode allows the OS to execute some subset of the privileged instructions (such as setting the MMU or I/O instructions).

Another task that the system must perform is to save the CPU context. Most minicomputers have only one set of CPU registers (exceptions are the PDP-11 and the MODCOMP IV). The contents of these registers generally remains the same after a software interrupt. To effect a graceful return to the user, the current contents of the registers are saved in the PCB before the system proceeds to execute the request.

Initiating the Request

After saving the CPU context, the OS retrieves the function call and argument list. These data are transferred from user space to system space to prevent any violations of system security and integrity. The SSR function is validated by the OS, and the individual arguments for each function are validated by the system module that executes that function. Additional data required to perform the function are gathered and added to the argument list. The return address of the user process is placed in the user's PCB.

Executing the Request and Returning to the User

Assuming a valid function, the appropriate system module will be called to execute the function. Upon completion, the result of the function is stored in the PCB. At this point, two options exist: the OS may return directly to the previously executing process, or the OS may place the process on the READY queue and call the system scheduler.

The former method has been used in some real-time systems to ensure that processes get immediate response to service requests. It does not guarantee equal service to each process. This approach is destined to fail when a process is heavily computer-bound. The latter approach is widely used, as a process gives up control of the CPU when it issues an SSR. At that point it is equivalent to other processes and must wait its turn. In priority systems, a higher-priority process may have become ready and would thus be scheduled ahead of the previous process. This method assures a more equitable distribution of CPU resources among user processes.

A Detailed Example

The module for processing a SSR in system space is depicted in module 7.3.2. A detailed discussion of this module will help in clarifying the steps to be taken in linking from a user program into the OS.

MODULE 7.3.2

```
procedure os-enter
      initialize map-state to os-mode
      save cpu registers in user's PCB
      save machine status in user's PCB
      p → psave
      map user's PDB to system space
      map user's usp to system space
      get request code and store in function-code
      if function-code less than zero
            or function-code greater than max-ssr-code
            then clear function-code
                  call(xnone)
      endif
      clear map-nr[pcb-address]
      if system-switch-table[function-code] not equal to zero
            then
                  event-nr[usp] → event-number
                  if event-number less than zero
                        or event-number greater than MAX-EVENT
                        then
                              psave → p
                              er-event-number → process-status
                              set-return-and-exit( )
                        else
                              bits[event-number] → event-number-bit
```

```
                              and(event-number-bit, event-on[p]) →
                                                    evn-temp
                          if evn-temp not equal to zero
                                  then
                                          request(wait-rs, event-number)
                              endif
            endif
        endif
        system-switch-table[function-code] → function-type
        if function-type less than one
              then
                    system-overlay-table[function-code] →
                                                    overlay-address
                    if overlay-address not equal to zero
                          then
                          system(load-overlay, 16, overlay-address) →
                                                    pstatus
                          if pstatus less than zero
                                then
                                        set-return-and-exit( )
                          endif
                    endif
                    system-switch-table[function-code + 1] →
                                                    function-address
                    call(function-address)
              endif
        if event-nr[usp] not equal to 16
              then
                    request(pcb-rs) → n
                    address(pstack) → psp[n]
                    address(start-subprocess) → pstack[n]
                    p → parent[n]
                    increment priority[n] by 2
                    clear pdb[n]
                    clear event-status[n]
              else
                    p → n
                    p → parent[n]
                    increment priority[n] by 2
        endif
        event-nr[usp] → event-nr[n]
        system-switch-table[function-code] → function-address
        call(function-address)
    endproc
```

When the user enters the OS via a system service request, the first procedure is to set the MMU to system state. Next, it saves the environment of the user's process in its PCB and maps the PDB into system space. This step makes the contents of the PDB directly accessible to the system routines. The system then validates the service function; illegal function requests merely return to the user with an error code.

Next, the system checks for an event number associated with this function. If a valid event is found, the system verifies that the event number is available. If not, the process is suspended until the event number becomes free. The function request is then validated for its type. A type of less than one indicates that the function resides in a system overlay. The overlay loader is invoked to bring the function code into memory. Note that the process could be suspended at this point because the overlay area is already occupied.

If the function type is greater than one, the function requires preprocessing to set up its arguments. The value of the function type is the address of the preprocessing routine. If the event number is not equal to 16, an asynchronous porcess will be created to service this function request and the preprocessing routine performs this chore. Otherwise, the function will be invoked directly for execution.

7.3.5   System Service Request: User Space Revisited

Upon completion of a SSR, control normally reverts to the user process. Execution of the request may result in either success or failure. Successes are easily dealt with as the information requested, if any, is presented as the value of the system function or as event data. If a failure occurs, the OS attempts to supply as much information as possible regarding the error. The notable exception to this rule is when the failure results in the termination of the process.

In this text, the following methods are provided for returning information to the user:

1. A SYSTEM function argument assumes a new value as, for example, in the RANDOM-READ request storing data into a user-specified buffer.
2. The result of executing the SYSTEM function may be the value of the function itself.
3. An asynchronous event has been completed, whereupon the event status and event value words are used to convey appropriate information to the creating process.

The first method is well understood, as it is merely the implementation of the argument passing/return mechanism of subroutines (which, in effect, is what the SYSTEM routine really is). The second method is also well understood, as most programming language functions return a single value on one of the CPU registers (or at the top of the stack). By treating the SYSTEM function as just another user-invoked function, we obtain the benefits of subroutines and functions. The third method, however, is an artifact of our implementation of processes and events. Thus it deserves further consideration.

The invocation of certain SSRs causes the OS to create an asynchronous process to execute them. The user specifies an event number that becomes the medium of communication between the requesting process and the serving process. A serving process (or another process) may return three words of information to the requestor: the status of the event and two data words. Dedicated space in the PDB is used to store the values of the status and data words until the requestor calls for them.

When the user issues a SSR which requires an event number, its status is set to zero. When the request is completed, the status of the event is set to the completion code (as explained below). The values of one or both of the data words will be set according to whether or not that function returns additional information to the user. Of course, these values depend on the nature of the specific request.

Three functions have been provided to allow the user to access the event data.

Obtaining the Event Status

The STATUS request (module 7.3.3) provides access to the status for the specified event. Any event number may be specified, as no checking is done to determine if the event has actually been used in a previous system call. If an illegal event number is specified, an error code will be returned to the user. The format of the STATUS request is

SYSTEM(STATUS, EVENT-NR) $\rightarrow$ EVENT-STATUS

where   EVENT-NR   the event number whose status is requested
           EVENT-STATUS   the value of the event's status word

The interpretation of the event status was explained in section 3.4.3. To summarize, the meaning of the status word values is

$$< 0 \qquad \text{Error code}$$
$$= 0 \qquad \text{Request is incomplete}$$
$$> 0 \qquad \text{Request was successfully completed}$$

Any of the system error codes may be returned by the OS as the status of the specified event. However, the error code ER-EVENT-NUMBER has the particular meaning that an erroneous event number was specified in the STATUS request. It behooves the user to check the value of the event status carefully upon completion of each STATUS request.

To check if an event has been used, the system must examine the EVENT-ON entry in the PDB. The code to determine if an event has been activated consists of:

```
pdb[p] → pdb-address
if bits[event-number] & event-on[pdb-address] equals zero
     then
               set er-event-unused to return-value[p]
               exitproc
endif
```

Obtaining the Event Data Values

An SSR may return two additional words of information. The values returned are a function of the particular system request and have no general meaning. The format of the calls is

SYSTEM(VALUE1, EVENT-NUMBER) → VALUE-1

SYSTEM(VALUE2, EVENT-NUMBER) →VALUE-2

where　　　EVENT-NUMBER　　　the event number whose value is requested
　　　　　　VALUE-1　　　　　　　are the data values returned by the system
　　　　　　VALUE-2

MODULE 7.3.3

```
procedure status
     event-nr[usp] → event-number
     if event-number less than one
          or event-number greater than or equal to MAX-EVENT
          then
                    set er-event-number to return-value[p]
          else
                    status[event-number] → return-value[p]
     endif
endproc
```

7.4 SYSTEM CONFIGURATION AND GENERATION

An OS, as provided by a vendor, is a collection of modules and utilities that must be configured into a usable system. The process of tailoring this set of

MODULE 7.3.4

```
procedure value1 or value2
    event-nr[usp] → event-number
    if event-number less than one
        or event-number greater than or equal to MAX-EVENT
        then
            set er-event-number to return-value[p]
        else
            value1[event-number] → return-value[p]
    endif
endproc
```

modules to meet the local physical constraints and performance requirements of a specific hardware configuration is known as system generation. System generation involves establishment of system configuration parameter values, the compilation of system module parameters using these configurations, and linking the system modules into an executable program.

7.4.1   Motivation for System Generation

An OS provides a range of services in relation to the combination of hardware and software resources that can be configured in the computer system. Given a set of physical resources (e.g., disks, memory, tapes, etc.), the user is provided with a set of executive software modules with which to make the best possible use of these resources. The set of physical resources available with most computer systems can be integrated in a variety of tantalizing ways. Providing unique sets of modules for each configuration is a physical impossibility. What we do, as software engineers, is to tailor a set of general purpose modules to a specific hardware configuration.

System generation allows the user to select from a menu of available services those elements required for the specific installation. This selection must not exceed the physical resources and yet must meet performance requirements. The degree to which these two apparently conflicting aims are satisfied is a true measure of the flexibility of the system generation process.

One last point is in order here: the process of system generation should be no mean feat. That is, it should not be an exhausting costly chore. It should not require an intimate knowledge of the executive functions performed by the OS and it should provide guidance to the user when selecting the services and specifying the values of configuration parameters.

7.4.2   Software Engineering Considerations

As software engineers, the basic problem with which we are faced is quite simple: how to map executive software modules onto available system resources in order to minimize the cost/performance ratio. The following techniques have been used to perform this mapping.

1. **Overlay techniques.**   Almost every system uses overlays for managing services and software resources. A major exception is the UNIX OS, which provides no facility whatsoever for overlays. Overlay techniques suffer from two limitations:

   (a)   Overlays reduce performance in the executive and must be limited to infrequently used services or those that may be overlapped with other activities.

   (b)   Some functions cannot be overlaid due to module interactions and the sequence of operations to be performed.

2. **Code tailoring.**   A specific set of services is selected through conditional assembly and conditional linking, which provides a precise method for tailoring a system to the user's requirements. This approach allows us to build a minimal system. It is particularly useful for generating real-time systems requiring high performance.

3. **Dynamic configuration.**   The OS has the capability to react to changing user requirements by adapting its configuration in an efficient manner. The complexity and performance trade-offs engendered by this approach make it infeasible for real-time systems. However, DEC's RSX-11M has used this approach quite successfully in providing a general-purpose OS

The code tailoring method is used in almost every system to some degree. Code tailoring has two components: conditional assembly and conditional linkage. Conditional assembly uses configuration parameters to determine what source code is to be compiled and assembled into binary modules. Values for the configuration parameters are retrieved from the template file. In conditional linking, we choose among a variety of modules to be linked and loaded into an executable program. For example, the system would conditionally load a device handler for a fixed or moving-head disk, depending on how the user answered the system generation dialogue. Both DGC's RDOS and DEC's RSX-11M use system generation dialogues to configure their OSs. The reader will find DEC's system generation process to be quite lengthy and complex, and requiring substantial knowledge of the OS when compared to DGC's straightforward though somewhat terse dialogue.

The conditional assembly/linkage approach presents the user with several problems:

1. A lengthy generation time may ensue due to recompilation of all modules affected by a change in a configuration parameter.
2. The process may result in a multiplicity of systems to meet different requirements, thereby complicating maintenance.
3. This approach will encourage nonmodular systems while making it easier to insert new functions.
4. The cost to test, validate, and verify a newly generated system may be quite high.

7.4.3   System Configuration Parameters

During the system generation process, the system manager sets the values of configuration parameters that determine how many and what type of resources will be included in the system. Specifying the values of the configuration parameters is an art in most systems. The influence of these parameters on interacting processes often determines the efficiency the system. Moreover, selection of appropriate values requires both an intimate understanding of system internals as well as a feeling for their effect on the system. Table 7.1 lists the parameters (in no apparent order) and constitutes a base set of parameters one might find in an OS. These parameters are used in code skeletons throughout the text.

7.5   SYSTEM INITIALIZATION

Without software, a computer system is just a collection of bare hardware. To do something useful with the computer system, we must initialize the OS program. This step is called "initial program load" or "booting." The term "booting" is derived from bootstrap and it is exactly what an OS does: hoists itself into memory by its own bootstraps. Once the system is loaded into memory, it performs a variety of initialization operations which prepare it to accept user requests. These operations allow the OS to validate its environment in terms of its hardware configuration, create the system queues and resource pools, and activate the system processes.

7.5.1   The Bootstrap Procedure

The procedure for booting an OS has been greatly simplified since the early days of minicomputers. At one time, the user was required to toggle in the

Table 7.1   System Configuration Parameters

Parameter	Usage
pdb-page	Virtual page which contains the PDB; it is directly addressable by a process
pdb-user-space	Number of words available to the user in the PDB
number-of-events	Number of distinct simultaneous events
page-size	Size of the page
pdb-stack-size	Size of the stack used to hold SSR arguments; it is the remaining space after subtracting the user space and event storage
clock-frequency	Rate at which the system clock is updated
max-user-qcbs	Maximum number of user message queues
number-user-maps	Number of memory maps allocatable to user processes
number-user-channels	Number of user channels available for I/O
number-user-processes	Number of simultaneous user processes
number-system-processes	Number of simultaneous system processes
memory-size	Number of memory blocks available in the system
number-memory-pages	Number of physical memory pages ($2 \mid \times \mid$ memory-size)
number-fixed-io-slots	Number of page slots dedicated to I/O
number-io-maps	Number of memory maps dedicated to I/O
number-maps	Number of memory maps in use
first-io-map	First memory map dedicated to I/O
directory-channel	Channel number for I/O on system directory
error-channel	Channel number for transmitting error messages to the system console
system-overlay-channel	Channel number for loading OS overlays
user-overlay-channel	Channel number for loading user overlays
process-stack-size	Stack size for a process
idle-process-priority	Priority for the idle process
user-process-priority	Priority for a user process
system-process-priority	Priority for the system process
user-io-priority	Priority for user process performing I/O
system-io-priority	Priority for a system process performing I/O

bootstrap code via the console switches. This program, usually 10 to 20 instructions, read the first sector of track 0 on a disk drive or the first block off a magnetic tape. The disk or tape was referred to as the "boot" device.

Today, minicomputers store the bootstrap routine in a ROM chip which is physically located on the CPU board. The bootstrap routine is activated by a console switch which reads the ROM chip contents into memory and executes the routine. For example, on the PDP-11/34 console, the operator would depress the "CONTROL" and "BOOT" switches simultaneously to invoke the bootstrap program. A consequence of this action is to execute the bootstrap routine immediately.

The result of executing the bootstrap is to load a block from the boot device. The data loaded from the boot device are a more complex initialization program. Usually, this routine queries the operator for the file name containing an executable version of the OS. The routine searches the device directory (if disk) and loads the contents of the file into memory. Once the program has been successfully loaded, control is transferred to it to initialize the OS.

7.5.2   Initializing the Operating System

The system boot procedure loads the base OS modules into memory. Control is transferred to the procedure INITIALIZE-SYSTEM, which is depicted in module 7.5.1. This procedure sets up the idle process and activates it. The idle process gains control of the CPU whenever there is no useful work for the OS to perform. The procedure then calls a sequence of initialization modules to establish the OS data bases and validate the environment.

MODULE 7.5.1

```
procedure initialize-system
      address(idle-process) → p
      initialize-system-process(p, os-idle, 0, 0)
      decrement psp[p]
      initialize-system-queues( )
      initialize-system-resources( )
      initialize-system-processes( )
      lock-interrupts( )
      initialize-clock( )
      enter-into-queue(ready-queue, p)
      scheduler( )
endproc
```

7.5.3   Initializing The System Queues

The routine for initializing the system queues calls the setup routine for the queue. Some system queues use the standard setup routines, whereas others, such as the priority queue, require special setup routines because of their inherent structural variation.

INITIALIZE-SYSTEM-QUEUES creates a set of buffers to hold system error messages. These buffers hold system-level error messages generated as the result of a fatal error in the system. This procedure also initializes the channel table and space for user queues and control blocks.

MODULE 7.5.2

```
procedure initialize-system-queues
     priority-queue-set(ready-queue)
     all-process-queue-set(all-process-queue)
     fifo-queue-set(error-free-queue)
     address(error-buffer-space) → emb-address
     for j from 1 to number-error-buffers
          do
                    enter-into-queue(error-free-queue, emb-address)
                    increment emb-address by error-buffer-size
          enddo
     (total-channels-1) * ccb-size → channel-table-size
     clear(channel-table, channel-table-size)
     clear number-user-queues
     clear(user-queue-list, max-user-queues)
     fifo-queue-set(all-file-queue)
     enter-into-queue(all-file-queue, directory-fcb-address)
endproc
```

7.5.4 Initializing System Resources

The next step is to initialize the system resource semaphores, which control access to resource pools and critical systems processes. This procedure is depicted in module 7.5.3. The resource semaphores to be initialized are:

system-rs
system-memory-rs
pcb-rs
delay-ready-rs
delay-rs
schedule-rs
time-interrupt
error-rs
mass-storage-service
allocation-process-service
lpt-access
tti-access
tto-access

tty-access
tape-controller
tty-input-rs
tty-output-rs
tty-outbuf-rs
overlay-rs
overlay-load-rs

This procedure calls three routines to initialize the memory management hardware and associated pools.

INITIALIZE-PAGE-RS | Sets up a free memory pool of pages not reserved by the OS.
INITIALIZE-IOMAP-RS | Allocates the proper number of I/O map slots
INITIALIZE-MAP | Sets up the number of maps that were used during the system generation.

Next, the routine assigns unallocated pages on map 0. Map 0 is reserved for the OS. These pages provide expansion space for OS tables. Finally, the system allocates an I/O map slot for accessing the system directory. This I/O map slot is used to read blocks from the directory file when searching for a file entry.

MODULE 7.5.3

```
procedure initialize-system-resources
      define-rs(system-rs, deque-queue-set, deque-queue-set,
                                              one-allocator)
      define-memory-rs(system-memory-rs, system-process-space,
                              system-process-free-space)
      initialize-buffer-rs(pcb-rs, pcb-space, number-user-processes,
                                              pcb-size)
      initialize-buffer-rs(pcb-rs, pcb-space, number-systems-processes,
                                              pcb-size)
      define-rs(delay-ready-rs, deque-queue-set, count-queue-set,
                                              one-allocator)
      define-rs(delay-rs, delay-queue-set, count-queue-set,
                                              one-allocator)
      define-rs(schedule-rs, fifo-queue-set, schedule-queue-set,
                                              schedule-allocator)
      define-rs(time-interrupt, deque-queue-set, count-queue-set,
                                              interrupt-allocator)
      define-rs(error-rs, deque-queue-set, error-queue-set, one-allocator)
      define-rs(mass-storage-service, deque-queue-set,
                              count-queue-set, one-allocator)
```

```
define-rs(allocation-process-service, deque-queue-set,
                              count-queue-set, one-allocator)

address(channel-table) → ct-address
define-binary-rs(channel-sequential-rs[ct-address])
address(directory-fcb) → directory-fcb-address
define-binary-rs(file-add-rs[directory-fcb-address])
define-binary-rs(lpt-access)
define-binary-rs(tti-access)
define-binary-rs(tto-access)
define-binary-rs(tty-access)
define-binary-rs(tape-controller)
define-rs(tty-input-rs, deque-queue-set, character-queue-set,
                                          one-allocator)
define-rs(tty-output-rs, deque-queue-set, character-queue-set,
                                          one-allocator)
define-rs(tty-outbuf-rs, deque-queue-set, count-queue-set,
                                          one-allocator)
define-rs(overlay-rs, deque-queue-set, overlay-available-queue-set,
                                          overlay-allocator)
define-rs(overlay-load-rs, deque-queue-set,
                   overlay-loaded-queue-set, overlay-loaded-allocator)
rs-available-queue[tty-outbuf-rs] → avq
character-queue-maximum → queue-count[avq]
lock-rs-set(file-modify-rs[directory-fcb-address])


initialize-page-rs( )
initialize-iomap-rs( )
initialize-map( )


for j from first-free-memory-page to max-map-pages
     do
          request(page-rs) → page-address
          select-page(map-zero, j, page-address)
          select-page(first-iomap, j-iomap-offset, page-address)
     enddo
request(page-rs) → directory-search-page
request(iomap-rs, directory-search-page) → directory-search-map
extract directory-search-address from directory-search-map
extract directory-search-map from directory-search-map
memory-size-free-memory-start → free-memory-size
     define-memory-rs(memory-rs, free-memory-start, free-memory-size)
endproc
```

7.5.5 Initializing System Processes

The next step is to initialize the system processes and activate them. Each process is allocated a control block and inserted into the system ready queue. The processes to be initialized are:

INITIALIZATION-PROCESS	Activates the system service processes
DELAY-PROCESS	Controls the time suspension of other processes
SCHEDULE-PROCESS	Controls the deadline scheduling of potential processes
DISK-DRIVER	Services all disk requests
TTY-INPUT-PROCESS	Services the console terminal on input
TTY-OUTPUT-PROCESS	Services the console terminal for output
TIMEOUT-CHECK-PROCESS	Checks the list of devices for timeout conditions

MODULE 7.5.4

```
procedure initialize-system-processes
    create-user-process( ) → pcb-address
    initialize-user-process(pcb-address, file-maintenance-process,
                                system-process-priority, 0, 0, 0, 0, 0)
    activate(pcb-address)
    disk-initialization( )
    create-user-process( ) → pcb-address
    initialize-user-process(pcb-address,
        mass-storage-allocation-process, system-process,
                                priority, 0, 0, 0, 0, 0,)
    activate(pcb-address)

    overlay-open(system-overlay-table, system-overlay-channel,
                                system-overlay-file)
    create-user-process( ) → pcb-address
    initialize-user-process(pcb-address, loaderuser-process-priority,
                                0, 0, 0, 0, 0,)
    set one to user-process-count
    activate(pcb-address)

    create-system-process( ) → pcb-address
    initialize-system-process(pcb-address, delay-process,
                                system-io-priority, 0)
```

```
    activate(pcb-address)

    create-system-process( ) → pcb-address
    initialize-system-process(pcb-address, schedule-process,
                                        system-io-priority, 0)
    activate(pcb-address)

    create-system-process( ) → pcb-address
    initialize-system-process(pcb-address, disk-driver,
                                        system-io-priority, 0)
    activate(pcb-address)

    create-system-process( ) → pcb-address
    initialize-system-process(pcb-address, tty-input-process,
                                        system-io-priority, 0)
    activate(pcb-address)

    create-system-process( ) → pcb-address
    initialize-system-process(pcb-address, tty-output-process,
                                        system-io-priority, 0)
    activate(pcb-address)

    create-system-process( ) → pcb-address
    initialize-system-process(pcb-address, timeout-check-process,
                                        system-io-priority, 0)
    activate(pcb-address)
endproc
```

7.5.6   System Initialization Utility Routines

The system initialization procedures require utility routines to set up the system data structures. These routines are discussed in the following paragraphs.

Initializing the Page Semaphores

Once the resident OS modules have been allocated a fixed set of pages, the remaining pages are queued to a resource semaphore. Pages are allocated by the resource semaphore on demand by user processes. The resource semaphore is set up during system initialization by the INITIALIZE-PAGE-RS routine. PAGE-RS is maintained as a bit queue (see section 7.6.3), where the high-order bit of a page is set to indicate that the page is available.

The number of memory pages is calculated during the system generation and established as a system parameter. The 64 pages allocated to the operating system (map 0) are subtracted from the total to yield the number of pages available to user processes. The number of pages available to users becomes the value of the queue counter.

The bad page table is defined during the system generation process. Many systems have a means whereby a memory exerciser is executed which determines the status of all pages in memory. Those pages that generate storage/retrieval errors are entered into a bad page table, which is stored on disk or printed for the operator. Pages found in the bad page table are extracted from the queue and are not available for allocation to users.

MODULE 7.5.5

```
procedure initialize-page-rs
     define-rs(page-rs, deque-queue-set, 0, flagged-allocator)
     rs-available-queue[page-rs] → avq
     set-bit-queue(avq, page-bits, number-memory-pages,
                                     page-in-convert, page-out-convert)
     set( − 1, page-bits[4], number-memory-pages/16-4)
     number-memory-pages-64 → queue-count[avq]
     set page-available-flag of pdb-page
     release(page-rs, pdb-page)
     address(bad-page-table) → bpt-address
     clear i
     while bpt-address[i] not equal to 0
          do
                extract-from-queue(avq, bpt-address[i])
                increment i
          enddo
endproc
```

Initializing the IOMAP-RS

IOMAPs are memory maps dedicated to facilitating direct communication between user processes and devices. An IOMAP page is used to hold a PDB so that data may be read/written directly from/to the device. The number of IOMAPs is defined at system generation, based on the number of concurrent user and system processes that can exist in the system. One map slot is reserved for each process and the total number of map slots divided by 64 yields the number of IOMAPs to be reserved. Although one map slot is defined per process, a process may utilize more than one map slot at a time.

IOMAP-RS, like PAGE-RS, is maintained as a bit queue. In reality, each IOMAP slot is equated with a memory page. When a process is ready to I/O, the page containing the target data address is remapped via the IOMAP slot.

IOMAP slots are allocated and controlled by the OS, so that, in effect, the process's data page belongs to the OS for the duration of the I/O operation.

MODULE 7.5.6

```
procedure initialize-iomap-rs
    define-rs(iomap-rs, deque-queue-set, 0, iomap-allocator)
    rs-available-queue[iomap-rs] → avq
    set-bit-queue(avq, iomap-bits, number-io-maps * 64,
                              iomap-in-con-vert, iomap-out-convert)
    set( - 1, iomap-bits, number-iomaps * 4)
    number-iomaps * 64 → queue-count[avq]
    and(address(free-memory-start), page-size) →
                                        free-memory-base
    rshift(free-memory-base, 9) → first-free-memory-page
    first-free-memory-page - iomap-offset - max-user-queues
                                        → first-queue-page
    1shift(first-queue-page, 9) + first-iomap → iop-address
    for ib from first-queue-page to max-map-pages
        do
                extract-from-queue(avq, iop-address)
                increment iop-address by page-size
        enddo
endproc
```

Initializing a Memory Map

As mentioned previously, a memory map contains 64 page slots. The number of maps to be activated in the system is specified at system generation time. When the OS is bootstrapped, the MMU must be initialized. The map table always contains an image of the hardware MMU. To initialize the MMU, the map table is cleared. Each page entry in the map table is marked free; and the page index for the first 64 real pages are identified for map 0. The map table is then loaded into the MMU and it is activated, which will then mediate all subsequent memory references.

Initializing a Pool Semaphore

A pool is a contiguous memory area containing multiple buffers of a predefined length. The number of buffers of a given type is specified at system generation. One pool is particularly important to the system: PCB-RS, which contains the buffers to be allocated for user or system process control blocks.

MODULE 7.5.7

```
procedure initialize-map
      number-maps * 64 → total-pages
      clear(map-table, total-pages)
      for page-index from 0 to 63
            do
                  set page-available-flag of map-table[page-index]
            enddo
      load-and-start-map( )
endproc
```

INITIALIZE-POOL-RS, depicted in module 7.5.8, defines a resource sema-phore to control a buffer pool. It initializes the semaphore's available queue with a list of the addresses of buffers contained in the pool.

MODULE 7.5.8

```
procedure initialize-pool-rs(rs-address, space, count, size)
      define-rs(rs-address, deque-queue-set, deque-set, one-allocator)
      count → limit
      size → buffer-size
      address(space) → buffer-address
      for cx from 1 to limit
            do
                  release(rs-address, buffer-address)
                  increase buffer-address by buffer-size
            enddo
endproc
```

Initializing the Delay Queue

This procedure initalizes the DELAY-QUEUE for the OS. It is included here rather than in chapter 3 because it is called only during system initialization. Note that we only have to define the input routine for the queue as the DELAY request inserts PCBs into the queue but never removes them; this action is per-formed by DELAY-PROCESS.

Initializing the Scheduling Queue

This procedure initiizes the scheduling queue in a like manner to the delay queue. As above, the SCHEDULE request only inserts into the queue, whereas the SCHEDULE-PROCESS removes from the queue.

MODULE 7.5.9

```
procedure delay-queue-set(queue-address, → size)
    fifo-queue-set(delay-queue)
    address(enter-into-delay-queue) →
                            enter-into-queue-address [delay-queue]
    fifo-queue-size → size
endproc
```

MODULE 7. 5. 10

```
procedure schedule-queue-set
    fifo-queue-set(schedule-queue)
    address(enter-into-schedule-queue) →
                            enter-into-queue-address[schedule-queue]
    fifo-queue-size → size
endproc
```

7.6   OPERATING SYSTEM DATABASES

It should be apparent at this point that the OS is largely based on tables (or databases). In truth, one must say that an OS is driven by the contents of these tables in the sense that they direct what actions it will take (where these actions are encompassed by the system modules). The nature of the OS is further defined by system parameters and system constants. System parameters serve to modify a specific instance of an operating system by describing its internal and external environment. Parameters are variable in the sense that they can be assigned different values as the environment changes. Any specific environment is described by a (possibly) unique set of parameters. System constants, on the other hand, define fixed features of the environment; those that are generally immutable because of the system hardware.

This section collects, in one place, descriptions of all the system tables, parameters, and constants that have been used in the text. Its purpose is twofold. First, it gives the reader a view of the OS from a data architecture approach. It describes why data values were chosen and system structures defined as they were. Second, it will serve as a convenient reference if the meaning of a particular database escapes you when reading the other sections of the text.

7.6.1   System Databases

A system database may consist of one or multiword tables, the content of which may change slowly or rapidly with time. Thus efficient structures are an important aspect of OS design. Considerable effort must be devoted to defining OS data structures to ensure high system performance.

System Switch Table

The system switch table is used to define the processing of system service requests. An entry in the system switch table consists of two values: a preprocessing indicator and the address of a module that executes the request.

A SSR comes in two flavors: synchronous and asynchronous. Asynchronous requests require an event number and may require preprocessing of arguments. An asynchronous request is executed independently of the caller, although with an event number equal to 16, it may be executed while the caller is suspended. A synchronous request is always executed while the caller is suspended.

The preprocessing entry may take on three values, as follows:

−1   Indicates that this system request has an event number but no system process associated with it

0   Indicates that this system request requires neither an event number nor a system process

⟨address⟩   Indicates that this system request requires both an event number and a system process. The address is that of the system module that preprocesses the request and initializes the system process

The definition of the system switch table is as follows:

system-switch-table of

0,	none,
−1,	channel-buffer,
−1,	close,
−1,	create,
−1,	delete,
−1,	directory-read,
−1,	file-attributes,
−1,	file-buffer,
−1,	file-date,
−1,	link,
−1,	open,
−1,	rename,
−1,	reset,
−1,	unlink,

0,	clock-frequency,
0,	date,
0,	define-qcb,
p-delay,	delay,
p-dequeue,	dequeue,
0,	error-kill,
0,	error-message,
0,	execute,
p-flush-buffer,	flush-buffer,
0,	free-page,
p-setup-ok,	get-page,
p-setup-ok,	get-character,
0,	kill,
0,	kill-qcb,
p-load-overlay,	load-overlay,
p-next-buffer,	next-buffer,
0,	next-overlay,
0,	page-id,
0,	pause,
0,	put-character,
0,	post,
0,	queue-depth,
−1,	queue,
p-read-lock,	read-lock,
p-sequential-read,	direct-or-buffer-input,
p-read,	read,
−1,	receive,
0,	remap,
0,	return,
0,	release-overlay,
0,	schedule,
0,	set-date,
0,	set-status,
0,	set-time,
0,	status,
0,	stop,
0,	system-id,
p-tapef,	tape-function,
−1,	process,
0,	who-am-i,
0,	time,
0,	unlock,
0,	value−1,
0,	value−2,
0,	wait,

$$
\begin{array}{ll}
\text{p-write,} & \text{write,} \\
-1, & \text{write-release,} \\
\text{p-sequential-write,} & \text{direct-or-buffer-output,}
\end{array}
$$

The Standard Device List

The standard device list contains entries for each device configured in the OS during the system generation process. Entries in the table point to the function tables associated with each device class.

STANDARD-DEVICE-LIST of

TTY-DEVICE-TABLE,

LPT-DEVICE-TABLE,

MAGNETIC-TAPE-TABLE,

$\vdots$

CARD-READER-TABLE,

7.6.2   System Pointers and Base Addresses

An OS requires pointers to keep track of the dynamic entities in the system. Usually, these pointers are available to any system module and may be changed by any of these modules. A second set of global parameters consists of the base addresses for system tables and data structures. Usually, these base addresses are assigned static values when the OS is booted into memory.

Current Process Pointer

The address of the PCB for the currently active process is stored in P.

Subprocess Pointer

The OS may create a subordinate process in response to a SSR. The address of the PCB for the subordinate process is stored in N during its initialization.

Clock Variables

The OS updates the system time with each interrupt of the real-time clock. Four variables comprise the system clock: MILLISECOND, SECOND, MINUTE, and HOUR. Their usage is obvious.

Calendar Variables

The OS also maintains a calendar that tracks the day of the month of the year. Four variables support the calendar functions: DAY, MONTH, YEAR, and DAY-OF-YEAR. The DAY-OF-YEAR variable is used to calculate a time entry for the file control block. During continuous operation, these variables will be updated appropriately as each 24-hour period elapses.

Address of Directory File Control Block

Many systems maintain a single directory for small disk volumes. This is particularly true of floppy disk–based systems. In these systems, the volume directory is treated like a file. Usually, its FCB is read from disk and remains permanently resident while the computer system is in operation. The address of the system directory's FCB is stored in DIRECTORY-FCB-ADDRESS.

7.6.3   System Resources

An operating system can provide either static or dynamic allocation of system resources. Dynamic allocation involves the assignment of a resource from a general pool of resources units. In general, each resource pool is controlled by a resource monitor implemented as a semaphore and a set of procedures. Among the basic resource pools are:

PCB-RS
: Contains a set of PCBs for system and user processes. The number of PCBs determines the number of active processes at any time in the system.

PAGE-RS
: Contains a list of free pages in system memory. The set of pages is those pages in memory after pages have been allocated to the OS.

IOMAP-RS
: Contains a set of IOMAP slot identifiers. An IOMAP slot identifier is a page identifier. Pages in IOMAPs are assigned to processes for remapping the PDB so that data may be transferred directly to/from the PDB.

SCHEDULE-RS
: Contains a set of blocks that are used to schedule future processes by a specified deadline. The number of blocks determines the number of processes that may be prescheduled.

7.6.4   System Process Queues

System processes, during their lifetimes, are resident on a variety of queues that record the status of the process. The queues vary with the primitives implemented in the OS. Among the basic queues are:

ALL-PROCESS-QUEUE | One entry for each system and user process that is currently active. A process is entered onto the queue when it is created and removed from the queue when it is terminated, aborted, or killed.

READY-QUEUE | One entry for each process that is active and ready-to-run. This queue is usually a simple linear list, although the structure may be modified to support a priority structure.

DELAY-QUEUE | One entry for each process that has requested a time delay in execution. The queue is sorted by the duration of the delay requested by each process.

SCHEDULE-QUEUE | A queue containing entries for each potential process, for example, one that will be initiated at some future time. The queue is sorted by deadline (i.e., the specified time that a process must be initiated and activated).

7.7   OPERATING SYSTEM UTILITIES

The "unsung heroes" of an OS are its utility modules. System utilities provide a set of common services to the major subsystems of the OS and are almost never accessible by the end user. They are often endowed with special privileges to increase their efficiency and performance. The trade-off, of course, is the execution of well-defined utility modules versus system security and integrity.

This section will strike you as being a little eclectic in its approach. It is precisely so because utilities never seem to form an integrated subsystem. The designer usually shoehorns them in wherever they will fit best. In fact, what is one OS's utility could very well be another's subsystem. On the other hand, although utility modules are not very well integrated in one place, they do serve as an integrating or binding agent in the OS, as every other module seems to depend on them.

7.7.1   Concepts of Utilities

The opening paragraphs of the chapter hinted at what we consider to be the real nature of system utilities. It is useful to clarify this approach in relation to other notions held over from first- and second-generation systems. Classically, a utility was a stand-alone program loaded by the user to perform a specific function. For example, most minicomputer systems still treat the diagnostic programs as stand-alone utilities. Why? Because they performed a function that the user generally preferred not to do. As OSs evolved, utilities became those "miscellaneous things" that the vendor provided gratis with the computer system. In many cases, this practice persists today. Immensely popular was the sort/merge utility—a separate program independently executed by the user on a specially prepared file. Equally popular was a program called the text editor, which allowed a user to enter and modify the source text of program modules. Other variations have included things such as program development aids, file management aids, and a host of optional modules that enhanced the capabilities of the bare-bones OS.

In general, a utility was considered to be any general-purpose program that performed a common function. The operative words are general-purpose and common. A callous system designer would interpret the word "utilities" to mean "afterthoughts." There was nothing glamorous or exciting about designing and writing a utility; indeed, it was often viewed as a tedious chore which detracted from the task of building complex subtle pieces of code that formed the nucleus of the OS.

Our viewpoint of utilities differs somewhat from the classic view. To us, utilities are the glue that interconnects the basic subsystems of an OS into a coherent whole. Features such as the text editor and the sort/merge capability are merely programs—whether provided by user or vendor is often immaterial, as they execute in exactly the same way. What approach, then, should we take to the concept of utilities? And more important, what are the basic utilities that should be provided in the nucleus of any OS? These questions are addressed in this chapter.

Utilities: Extensions to the Physical Machine

The operative words that we stressed in the definition of a utility were general-purpose and common. Think on these words for a minute:

General-purpose implies usefulness in a variety of different situations.

Common implies a characteristic that is widely and publicly used.

How do these concepts relate to the instruction set of a machine? To the central processing unit? By and large, the instruction set of the CPU is composed of those operations that were found to be the most useful in performing computations. The standard instruction set varies little from machine to machine. In addition, most manufacturers will add a set of esoteric instructions to their CPU architectures that are supposed to enhance the performance by making it easier to execute certain types of computations.

In a similar fashion, almost every OS relies on a well-defined subset of operations for its implementation. These operations may be thought of as extensions to the physical architecture of the machine. In general, it is more cost-effective to implement these operations in software than in hardware, particularly where the operations require variable-length operands or distinctly different formats for certain applications. In either case, almost every module of the operating system will depend on these extended instructions—a distinct commonality. Thus the low-level modules, which serve a general purpose and are common to most subsystems, are utilities. They really are extensions to the physical architecture of the machine that make it more amenable to OS implementation.

What are the implications of utilities? First, they are not, except in rare cases, available to user programs but rather are solely used by the OS. Second, because they are used by almost every subsystem, they must have a uniform interface and provide a standard service. The exact effect of a particular implementation of a utility depends on (at least) one of its arguments. Third, the effect of a utility must be well defined, although not in as strict a sense as a hardware function. A modicum of flexibility is both desirable and necessary when one level removed from the physical electronics. Finally, utilities must be efficient in their operation, as they will be executed many times over by the OS.

A Survey of Utilities

There is a common set of utilities that forms the foundation of every OS. We will examine several members of this set in the remaining sections of this chapter. In addition, depending on the specific purpose of the OS, there are utilities that cater solely to the achievement of that purpose. Often, what constitutes a utility is more the whim of the designer that the result of any formal rule about OS design. Just so, the following paragraphs describe some views about what should or should not be included in the utility set.

A common, if not essential, feature of most OSs is a clock/calendar mechanism. This feature allows the system to discern the sequencing of events and mark the passage of time if for no other reason than historical accuracy. Implementations vary, although in most systems there is a dependency on a real-time clock based on an oscillating crystal. You cannot implement an effective real-time OS without a clock facility.

A vestigial feature remaining from early generation OSs is the memory dump capability. In early systems, when a program "blew up," the user was left with little recourse but to dump the entire contents of memory and then laboriously examine it off-line. A dump simply consisted of a listing of each memory cell and its value at the time the program crashed. The listing contained both the OS and user programs, as there was no feasible way to separate the two. The contents of the CPU registers were also dumped for inspection. In many cases, the user got a program dump at program termination whether or not it was wanted. Some users, particularly those wedded to batch submissions, swear by memory dumps as the only was to debug a program.

A data structure familiar to every programmer is the character string. Peculiarly enough, manufacturers have not been able to design hardware that can effectively handle these beasts at the instruction level, and it is usually left to the OS to provide some sort of string-handling capability. Two aspects of string handling are important: converting from character to internal binary representation, and editing and formatting of character strings.

Errors can occur at any time, in any place, and to any program—the OS not excepted. Good error management involves the timely reporting of the probable cause along with whatever ancillary information is available in order to enable the user to diagnose the problem. An integrated error management facility, linked to every system module, is a necessary feature in modern OSs.

The advent of multiprogramming systems gave rise to the phenomenon of waiting in line, queueing, as it were. Early-generation systems never experienced this behavior, as they executed requests in a strictly sequential fashion. Queues (or lists, if you prefer) are a fundamental aspect of modern OSs. Through efficient queue management, the potentially scarce resources of the system can be shared in a nearby optimal fashion.

A seminal paper by Dijkstra [dijk68] defines a concept for managing access to resources known as a semaphore. The concept and its variations are the basis for every modern OS. The extent to which semaphores can be used in system design is unlimited. The trade-off is the overhead necessary to manage the associated data structures that support the semaphore. The system described in the text makes extensive and varied use of semaphores to control many aspects of system operation.

All of the foregoing capabilities are utilities. In effect, they form the structural foundation upon which the OS is built. Let us compare and contrast some things that classically have been considered utilities. In our view, of course, they are merely enhanced user programs. Examples are text editors, library editors, program debugging tools, and relocatable loaders. Granted, all these software units are general purpose in nature and common to all users. However, they are distinguished by several characteristics. First, they are accessible to all system users without restriction. Second, they stand alone in execution; that is, they depend on the OS for services such as I/O. Finally, the OS does not rely on these units during execution; the user does. It is convenient for manufacturers to provide them because they use them in much the same way as users to develop the system software.

With these distinctions in mind, the remaining sections of this chapter examine the structure and implementation of several basic OS utilities. By no means is this a definitive set, as that depends on the specific nature of the OS.

7.7.2 Clock and Calendar Management

Most OSs regularly maintain a time-of-day clock and a yearly calendar. The system time and date are set by the operator during system initialization. The system time is maintained by the OS by monitoring the real-time clock. This section describes the functions necessary to maintain the system clock and calendar.

Setting the Time

At system startup, the operator sets the system time through a console command. This procedure, depicted in module 7.7.1, verifies the arguments for the hour, minute, and second of the time. The request is rejected if any of the arguments exceeds the appropriate range of values.

MODULE 7.7.1

```
procedure set-time
    if hour[usp] less than zero or
        xhour[usp] greater than or equal to 24
        then
            set-return-and-exit(er-time)
    endif
    if minute[usp] less than zero or
        minute[usp] greater than or equal to 60
        then
            set-return-and-exit(er-time)
    endif
    if second[usp] less than zero or
        second[usp] greater than or equal to 60
        then
            set-return-and-exit(er-time)
    endif
    lock-interrupts( )
    hour[usp] → hour
    minute[usp] → minute
    second[usp] → second
    clear millisecond
    calculate-time(hour, minute, second) → time-of-day
    release-interrupts( )
    set-return-and-exit(1)
endproc
```

To set the system time, we have to lock interrupts to prevent the time from being updated due to a real-time clock interupt (as interrupt processing would take precedence). The procedure also calculates the time-of-day in seconds since midnight for use as an event marker. It then releases interrupts so that the real-time clock can update the system time.

Retrieving the Date

The user is allowed to retrieve the date through a system service request. The format of this request is

    SYSTEM(DATE, DAY, MONTH, YEAR)

The procedure is depicted in module 7.7.2.

MODULE 7.7.2

```
procedure date
      map[usp] → user-map
      move-to-user-space(user-map, day, uday[usp])
      move-to-user-space(user-map, month, umonth[usp])
      move-to-user-space(user-map, year, uyear[usp])
      move-to-user-space(user-map, day-of-year, day-of-year[usp])
      os-exit( )
endproc
```

Real-Time Clock Routines

The real-time clock is managed by two routines: the clock initialization (module 7.7.3) and the interrupt handler (module 7.7.4). The initialization routine sets the clock interrupt interval and starts the clock. This procedure is part of the system initialization code that is executed only when the OS is booted or re-started after a crash.

The CLOCK-INTERRUPT routine is called each time an interrupt is generated by the real-time clock. The interrupt handler immediately reinitializes interrupts and releases any processes waiting on the time queue. The millisecond counter is incremented to reflect the expiration of a "clock tick." This example is set for milliseconds. The reader is free to adjust the example to fit his or her own needs. You are forewarned, however, that interrupts occurring faster than 1 msec generally consume large amounts of system overhead. If the millisecond counter reaches 1000, the procedure increments the system time. The scheduler is then called to dispatch the next task.

MODULE 7.7.3

```
procedure initialize-clock
    enable-clock( )
    set-clock-cycle(10 * clock-interval)
    start-clock( )
endproc
```

MODULE 7.7.4

```
procedure clock-interrupt
    start-interrupt( )
    release(time-interrupt)
    read-clock( ) → last-time
    increment millisecond by clock-interval
    if millisecond greater than or equal to 1000
        then
        clear millisecond
        increment second
        increment time-of-day
        if second greater than or equal to 60
            then
            clear second
            increment minute
            if minute greater than or equal to 60
                then
                clear minute
                increment hour
            endif
        endif
    endif
    scheduler( )
endproc
```

Checking for Timeouts

Many processes in the system await input from another process. The failure of the input to arrive is critical to the integrity of the system. If the waiting process holds scarce system resources (such as memory), a system deadlock may eventually result. The system cannot terminate the process, as it does not know if and when the input will arrive. If inputs are queued, the queue may fill up and cause a system crash because no process is available to service it. A good example of such a process is a user terminal that services user commands. If the user decides to leave the terminal, the process may wait forever.

Most systems institute a timeout checking process that measures the time between inputs. The system sets a threshold for the time interval between inputs. If an input does not arrive within the specified time, the system can take corrective action. As each process has different timeout requirements, the system cannot watch each one.

Usually, a timeout checking process is established for each class of processes to be watched by the system. For example, one process would monitor the activity of all processes that serve user terminals. The timeout process cycles through a checklist, calling each procedure in turn. The procedure takes whatever action is necessary, including canceling the process if its timeout threshold has been exceeded. The timeout procedure is depicted in module 7.7.5. Note that the procedure calls the checking procedure at intervals based on a system parameter TIMEOUT-COUNT.

MODULE 7.7.5

```
process timeout-check
    for t from 1 to timeout-count
        do
        request(time-int)
        enddo
    clear t
    while timeout-checklist[t] greater than or equal to zero
        do
        timeout-checklist[t] → check-address
        call(check-address)
        increment t
        enddo
    repeat
endprocess
```

Miscellaneous Clock Functions

Two procedures provide quick access to values related to clock management.

Clock-Frequency	Retrieves the clock frequency specified at system generation
Calculate-Milliseconds	Returns the elapsed time in milliseconds since the real-time clock was last inspected by the system

MODULE 7.7.6

```
procedure clock-frequency
    set-return-and-exit(clock-frequency)
endproc
```

MODULE 7.7.7

```
procedure calculate-milliseconds(delta)
    read-clock( ) → current-time
    last-time – current-time → delta
endproc
```

7.7.3   Editing and Conversion Utilities

The process of moving data between the I/O devices and the computer system often requires the application of editing and conversion routines to reformat the data. The algorithms for many of these routines are well-known to every programmer. Generally, these routines are incorporated into the systems library very early on in the system development process.

Data Conversion Routines

The data conversion routines consist of the subroutines called at the I/O interfaces to convert to/from the binary representation used internally by the central processor. Among the conversion routines required by the OS are:

BINOCT/OCTBIN	Conversion between octal and binary
BINDEC/DECBIN	Conversion between decimal and binary
BINHEX/HEXBIN	Conversion between hexadecimal and binary

String Management Package

A primary form of communication between module in the OS is messages. These are usually composed of one or more strings and need to be constructed by the users, edited, and passed between modules. String management poses a problem in small systems because message length can vary over a wide range and the number of active message can easily exceed the memory space available for message handling.

An approach that has been successfully used in a real-time system is described in this section. Each string is based on a two-word packet which consists of two pointers: a pointer to the first character in the string and a pointer to the first character past the end of the string. The user module must provide the packet area, the string buffer and the maximum size of the string (which is the size of the buffer). Figure 7.3 depicts the string management data structure.

This string management package supports eight functions for defining and constructing strings. The algorithms for these functions are depicted in modules 7.7.8 through 7.7.15. The eight functions are:

define-string	Defines a string by initializing the string packet
string-size	Returns the current size of the string
get-character-and-increment	This function retrieves the first character of the string and increments the pointer
get-character-and-decrement	Retrieves the last character from the string and decrements the pointer
write-character-and-increment	Inserts a character at the end of the string and increments the pointer
write-character-and-decrement	Adds a character at the beginning of the string and decrements the pointer
copy-string	Copies one string onto the end of another
remove-blanks	Removes trailing blanks from a string

MODULE 7.7.8

```
procedure define-string(string, buffer, size)
    address(buffer) → btemp
    lcycle(btemp, 1) → string[1]
    lcycle(btemp, 1) → string[2]
    lcycle(btemp, 1) → string[3]
    size * 2 → string[4]
endproc
```

MODULE 7.7.9

```
procedure string-size(string, → string-size)
    string[2] – string[1] → string-size
endproc
```

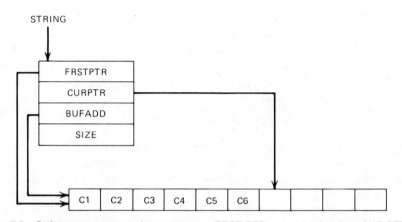

Figure 7.3 **String management data structure. FRST PTR = start of string; CUR PTR = current end of string; BUF ADD = address of string buffer; SIZE = buffer size.**

MODULE 7.7.10

```
procedure get-character-and-increment(string, empty, → character)
    string[1] → char-address
    if char-address greater than or equal to string[2]
        then
            goto address(empty)
        else
            increment string[1]
            get(char-address) → character
    endif
endproc
```

MODULE 7.7.11

```
procedure get-character-and-decrement(string, empty → character)
    if string[1] greater than or equal to string[2]
        then
            goto address(empty)
        else
            string[2] → char-address
            char-address - 1 → string[2]
            get(char-address) → character
    endif
endproc
```

MODULE 7.7.12

```
procedure write-character-and-increment(string, character)
    string[2] → char-address
    increment string[2]
    put(char-address, character)
endproc
```

MODULE 7.7.13

```
procedure write-character-and-decrement(string, character)
    decrement string[1]
    string[1] → char-address
    put(char-address, character)
endproc
```

MODULE 7.7.14

```
procedure copy-string(fromstr, tostr)
     string-size(string) → stsize
     while stsize greater than zero
          do
                    get-character-and-increment(fromstr, strdone) → char
                    write-character-and-increment(tostr, char)
          enddo strdone:
endproc
```

MODULE 7.7.15

```
procedure remove-blanks(string)
     while get-character-and-decrement(string, rtbempty)
                                                       not equal to blank
          do
          enddo
     increment string[1]
rtbempty:
endproc
```

7.8 ERROR MANAGEMENT

In describing this sample OS, I have attempted to follow most of the basic structured programming rules. It is often assumed that in structured programs that can be proven correct, errors will not be a problem. Unfortunately, the state of the art in program correctness offers us no assurance about verifying programs of the complexity of modern OSs. Thus you, as a system designer, must take precautions to detect and handle errors within the system.

For a minute, assume that the modules you have just written could be proven correct. Even though they are correct, Parnas and Wurges [parn77] suggest that undesired events will occur at run time. In part, the concept of correctness is based on the idea that structured programming is a means of eliminating error. That is, each subprogram is assumed always to perform correctly. Moreover, each program composed of such subprograms is written under the assumption that it itself will never behave incorrectly.

Parnas and Wurges suggest the following justifications that render this assumption false.

1. Even the best "structured programmers" occasionally err; if they are good, the error will not be in any obvious way.
2. The computers we use do fail and, in so doing, may cause the program to fail by changing code or data or both.

3. In practice, programs undergo periodic maintenance that may surface errors that had not appeared before.

4. Incorrect or inconsistent data may be supplied to the system.

Parnas distinguishes between an error and an undesired event. To him, an error is something that should be detected and corrected (which implies substantial knowledge about the system). On the other hand, an undesired event is one that includes all events that result in a deviation from the normal behavior of the system. Therefore, you not only detect undesired events, you also handle them (as correction is really more a debugging function). No general algorithm exists for recovery from undesired events, and we are not presumptuous enough to suggest that we have discovered one. Nor will we belabor the distinction between error and undesired event much further, as it only yields to greater confusion.

Thus what follow in this section are some thoughts on error handling where the error is an undesired event. We do suggest some thoughts on program organization (e.g., the OS architecture) and guidelines for anticipating the types of errors that might occur.

7.8.1 Error Handling

Errors are a fact of life in computer programming. The more complex the program, the greater the number of errors. No OS can be truly said to be without error although, existing errors may be undetected (for the present). When you update the OS, you potentially induce new errors. The emerging art of software science suggests that as a program gets older, it gets better. That is, errors in the software are found and eliminated or corrected. However, this same discipline also tells us that as the number of errors gets smaller, they also get harder to find, and that the mean time to find the next error, given you just found one, increases. This is not an encouraging result, as it virtually implies that we will never find the last error in a program. This is not as bad as it seems, however, if we have designed a robust system that can suffer the presence of (undetected) errors and still accomplish useful work.

Let us assume that the input data to a program is correct. In our case, the program is the OS and the data are user programs or command language statements. There are several types of error that are internal to the system as the user sees it: hardware, software, and programming. Hardware errors are fairly rare in most recent machines and are easily detected, as a program will produce obviously incorrect results and may not execute at all. Moreover, many machines can correct simple errors (such as memory parity), or degrade gracefully when the error cannot be corrected. The nemesis of many installations is the intermittent hardware error that is extremely difficult to detect and requires considerable hardware/software skills and patience to track down.

Software errors are also usually rare in a production system, but when they occur they are extremely difficult to detect. These errors are generally a result of bad system design or poor implementation choices. They are not noticed in normal system operation but occur when the system is unduly stressed. As such, they are intermittent and may occur as the result of unusual loading factors (e.g., two programs issuing I/O calls in a particular sequence).

Most numerous are programming errors, although this category really encompasses systems and operating errors as well. Programming errors can be divided into the following classes:

1. Appreciation errors, where the designer failed to read or comprehend the specification thoroughly before starting work.
2. Logic errors, which imply failure in "thinking through" the problem at a detailed level.
3. Coding errors, which can be subdivided into:

   (a) Syntax errors resulting from a failure to understand language constructs and statements.
   (b) Structural errors resulting from erroneous interaction of statements or faulty design of data structures.
   (c) Semantic errors resulting from failure to understand what a language statement does for you.

The purpose of this section is to say considerably more about error handling than you would normally find in an OSs text. We shall examine some of the factors that influence the occurrence of errors and suggest one method for checking an OS for errors.

7.8.2 Principles for Error Handling

Structured design has been advocated as a means for eliminating errors in programs. Whereas the assumption may work well in the design environment, operational systems are subject to errors due to machine failure or inconsistent data that may not have been adequately considered in the program code. Moreover, the program—because of its structured design—is assumed to be inherently immune to failure. Because structured programs are built on abstract machines implemented by lower-level modules, it is further assumed that one can postpone decisions on error checking to the abstract machine level.

In practice, this is rarely the case, and substantial error checking must be incorporated at every level. Reasonably so, because in a hierarchically structured system, each lower level must function without the knowledge of what the upper levels have done. Moreover, where lower levels can be used by a variety of upper-level modules, possibly implemented by several individuals, one must maintain continual vigilance.

It is hard to quantize the principles of error handling, as many of them are specific to the OS. Nevertheless, a few general principles emerge—largely as a result of structured programming. The first concerns the compartmentalization of knowledge about the system as a result of structured programming. Although an error may occur at a lower level of the system, operating without any knowledge of upper levels, it is the case that the information required to deal appropriately with the error is at a higher level. Therefore, appropriate data must be reflected to the next higher level for the error to be handled properly. However, this higher-level module must also be able to "encapsulate" the error and prevent it from damaging other subsystems.

The second principle concerns who will detect errors that violate system specifications. Parnas [parn77] suggests that it be the responsibility of the abstract machine, that is, that each level of the system detect errors occurring relative to its functions. When an error occurs, the machine calls or "traps" to a special error-handling routine. In principle, this preserves the concept of information hiding, so that error routines have only as much knowledge as necessary to deal with the error. Unfortunately, the size of the OS and the overhead required to provide this mechanism grow considerably (see the example in Parnas's paper). A judicious compromise is required to determine where error handling mechanisms are to be placed.

The problem mentioned above yields a third principle: module specifications must anticipate errors. Parnas calls these "abstract errors," in the sense that one prepares for those most likely to occur. Clearly, you cannot test for every error at every level. Experience with program verification systems has shown that the code to verify correctness can easily double or triple the size of a module. Thus errors to be checked and when to check for them are two of the most critical judgments you will make in designing systems.

Error handling must be cognizant of the fact that errors can propagate in two directions: upward and downward. An upward-propagating error is the result of a failure in a mechanism that was used properly or the reflection of an error detected at some lower level. A downward-propagating error is usually the result of inconsistent or incorrect data passed from above. Such errors must be reflected back to the previous level, as the lower-level module usually does not (and possibly should not) have sufficient knowledge to determine what was meant. When a level receives a report of an error below, it may attempt to recover from the error or report it to the next higher level.

Upon detecting an error in a structured system, the error must be reflected up to the next level in the hierarchy, where it is corrected, or if proper information is lacking, reflected to the next level. At each level, the error-handling routines have the responsibility for restoring the abstract machine state to one consistent with the specifications. This process of unraveling the sequence of module calls provides no information as to where the error occurred, in keeping with the principle of information hiding.

Not much has been said here about recovery and diagnostic policies, and probably should not be. In many cases, these are installation dependent or deisgner dependent; no generic model exists. However, this approach has several advantages (after [parn77]):

1. Each error-handling procedure is written at the level where the knowledge exists to handle the error properly according to the specifications.

2. The system can evolve toward increased reliability without major revisions. Error-handling routines start off in a primitive fashion, perhaps printing no more than their name and the erroneous register contents. As development progresses, routines handling errors that occur more frequently are replaced with sophisticated diagnostic routines.

3. Limited use of the "trap" mechanism simplifies debugging when a system is integrated by many programmers. No one individual knows the details of the whole system. When a bug appears, it may be a difficult job assigning responsibility for analysis. Even the printing of the module name in which it occurred is a great help in clarifying where to search for the error.

7.8.3   A Look at the Types of Errors

Endres [endr75] discusses errors and their causes within systems programs. He performed his work while testing IBM's DOS/VS release 28. We discuss his results because they demonstrate certain generic classes of errors of which you should be cognizant when designing a system.

Endres believes the search for the causes of programming errors must be conducted on several levels. He defines the cause of error as the discrepancy between the difficulty of the problem and the adequacy of the means applied (i.e., what should have been different for the error not to have occurred). He distinguishes the following causes of error.

Technological
Organizational
Historic
Group dynamic
Individual
Other

The prevention of error is all of those measures that are capable of reducing the discrepancy. Endres notes that there are always two ways to reduce the discrepancy: either increase the tools applied to solve a given problem, or modify the process so that the available tools are more suitable.

Endres examined the types of errors discovered during the testing of DOS/VS. He classified these errors into different groups and attempted to determine some error factors for each class. The following tables present the major factors of error discovered by Endres and his colleagues.

MACHINE CONFIGURATION AND ARCHITECTURE

Different device types and device features
Device-specific properties with variations in error treatment
Availability and clarity of hardware documentation
Central or decentralized handling of I/O devices

DYNAMIC BEHAVIOR AND COMMUNICATION BETWEEN PROCESSES

Representation of process information in the system unprotected
Structuring of the process hierarchy
Descriptions of interfaces and communications areas between processes
Standardized routines not suitable
Description techniques for dynamic events
Descriptions of resources and their properties
Centralized or decentralized handling of resource allocation and supervisor functions

SYSTEM FUNCTIONS

Quality of specifications
Clarification of exception conditions
Generalization versus specialization of functions
System versus user functions
Self-discipline in implementing one's own "bright ideas"

INITIALIZATION

Automatic adaptation of operators
Parameter specifications unclear
Forced initialization is missing
Initialization performed at wrong time

ADDRESSABILITY

Extension of symbolic addressing
Extension of address space
Delineation of address spaces for each process
Overwriting of code in data areas

REFERENCE TO NAMES

Syntax of names

Qualification of names in a reference path

Associative addressing of tables

Mixup of system constants

7.8.4 Error Considerations in Module Design

When a module is specified, you should be aware of the limitations on the way that module can handle errors and what types of errors you should expect to occur. The following paragraphs describe some major considerations to bear in mind when specifying and constructing modules.

A module, obviously, must be aware of limitations on parameters that are presented to it by upper levels. Any piece of software has a limited range of values with which it can cope, whether it be disk addresses, process identifiers, or whatever. An error should be reported if the range of values is exceeded by the current parameter value. Sometimes, run-time checks may be eliminated if compile-time checks are sufficient to weed out incorrect values.

Certain modules are responsible for storing information about the state of the system and thus have an inherent capacity limitation. No software to date has been able to guarantee infinite storage, and so should report an error when its capacity is exceeded. An important facet of design is the ability to predict when such an error will occur (i.e., to determine available capacity). The QUEUE-COUNT entry for several of the resource monitors described throughout the text is one such mechanism.

Many modules are explicitly designed to provide information about the state of the system. It is possible that information will be requested before it is created or after it has been deleted from a data element. An error should be specified for all such conditions. Inspection of the event management routines in section 3.4 will show a particularly difficult case. When an event is created, a value must be assigned to the event status that indicates an incomplete event. Failure to observe this convention will result in requesting processes interpreting the contents of the event status in an erroneous fashion.

In a hierarchically structured system, the order in which certain operations are conducted may place restrictions on module design. Casual reasons for this approach include efficiency, ease of implementation, or enhanced capability of detecting errors. An obvious example is one in which the file manager requires that a file be opened before it can be read or written. Another concerns the reading of data blocks in a segmented file before they have actually been written. A basic approach is to check for the existence of certain conditions before proceeding with the remainder of the module's functions.

A common class of programming errors has been recognized that results in strange actions by the system. An example concerns the user's attempt to open a file that has already been opened. Few systems, assuming a benign user environment, would think to check for this condition. Alternatively, some systems provide this condition as a way of checking if a file is already open. Using the unlikely action as means for encoding special operations (such as exits to the debugger) is dangerous. When users become dependent on them, they can defeat the specifications of the module by providing an abnormal entry or exit. Strange actions can be both annoying and confusing to the user. We suggest that it is simpler to report an error and provide the user with an alternative means for detecting such a condition.

It is apparent that misinformation supplied by a higher level may violate one or more error checks. It is usually not feasible to provide multiple error indications, so the designer must establish some priority for reporting errors. Generally, priority will be influenced by the sequence of operations, although the designer may choose to report a different error on the basis of one or more errors reported from below. An essential concept here is that the set of error checks is sufficient to cover all possible errors. That is, if none of the error checks applies, the change specified as the result of invoking a module can be accomplished without violating any module limitations. Furthermore, the fact that no error is reported should guarantee that the value of the function (if any) will not be undefined.

Finally, it should be apparent that reporting an error due to violation of limitations is simpler to detect than one that results from the failure of a resource mechanism. In most cases, no accurate information is available to determine what happened, as the user has neither access to nor understanding of the internals of the system. Rather, we must present the user with a classification of the error that focuses attention on a particular piece of software. Some failures may be so catastrophic that explicit information is not available or is readily obscured. Nevertheless, the system must attempt to classify the error as explicitly as possible in order to restrict the pieces of software or data that caused the error.

In summary, proper handling of errors requires a systematic approach to error handling in all parts of the system. At the very beginning, the designer will have to write the specifications for handling errors in the system. Moreover, this must start at the lowest levels of the system or else redundancy and failure to detect and report errors will result.

7.8.5 An Approach for Testing Operating Systems Designs

This section is based on papers by Linde [lind75] and Attanasio et al. [atta76] that discuss the penetration of OSs. Such penetration ranges over a variety of scenarios, from students beating the system through concerted acts of industrial espionage. Linde has constructed an attack strategy known as the Flaw Hypothesis Methodology that, based on detailed knowledge of an OS, attempts to assess its vulnerabilities.

The Flaw Hypothesis Methodology, as described below, has been used to successfully attack and penetrate several existing OSs. From this experience, Linde and his colleagues have been able to define generic sets of OS flaws and attacks. Linde suggests that many of these flaws may be characteristic of other OSs. The current emphasis on computer security and privacy of data as required by law and government regulation has led to attempts to retrofit current OSs as well as design new systems that are proveably secure. For microcomputer OSs, the impact of security and protection mechanisms may overwhelm performance considerations. However, for large minicomputer systems operating in interactive multiuser environments, such mechanisms are a necessity.

The Flaw Hypothesis Method provides us with an approach to considering OSs specifications from the viewpoint of error analysis. Clearly, an OS that has errors in it also possesses vulnerabilities, as these same errors bear the brunt of a penetrator's attacks. Determining where the penetrator might attack a system provides us with a good guideline for developing error checks, analyzing subsystem interfaces, data structure details, and error-handling services.

The Flaw Hypothesis Methodology requires several stages.

1. Knowledge of the system control structure
2. Generation of an inventory of suspected flaws
3. Confirmation of flaw hypotheses
4. Generalization of underlying systems weaknesses for which the flaw represents a specific instance.

Knowledge of the system control structure is an obvious requirement for conducting a penetration effort. This information can be obtained by careful analysis of the system manuals. From this study, security objects (disks, files, passwords) that are protected by system control objects (the file catalogs, installation management techniques, etc.) can be identified. A security object may also be, recursively, a system control object protecting itself. During system design, you can list the objects to be protected and the objects for controlling protection. From these lists you can develop a conceptual representation of the control structure in the system.

The next step is to generate a set of flaws—points of attack in the system control structure. A flaw hypothesis consists of one or more attack strategies on a control object and is usually weighted by priority and probability of success. For existing systems, the penetrator can study system code listings in order to analyze exact methods of attack. The designer will have to pursue the analysis more abstractly—usually from the functional design and system specifications.

The next step is flaw hypothesis confirmation. This may be accomplished by either gedanken (thought) experiments or live tests. A successful penetration consists of an interloper capturing a control object, working up the control structure, and finally seizing supervisory control of the system. Live tests can ascertain if the flaw actually exists (it may result from inadequate documentation). For the designer, the confirmation tool is through testing the system specification must be examined for incongruities and contradictions.

The final step is flaw generalization, whereby the set of confirmed flaws is analyzed for generic weaknesses. Weaknesses are categorized by functional area such as scheduling, access control, and so on. The results of these studies can be applied to correcting flaws in existing systems, if possible, or modifying the design in new systems.

As mentioned above, this approach to testing and verifying the design of an OS can lead to a more secure correct system. Where a team of individuals is designing the system, one person may be assigned from the outset to play devil's advocate and attack the design. Preliminary penetration analysis in the early stages of development and implementation may lead to fewer software errors and less debugging time later.

Linde and his colleagues have identified a set of generic system functional flaws from the various systems they have successfully penetrated. In addition, they have identified a set of successful attack strategies. Some of these flaws and attacks provide an initial guide to using the Flaw Hypothesis Methodology.

GENERIC FUNCTIONAL FLAWS

Authentication. The user must be able to confirm that the OS and hardware are what they purport to be. There is no systemwide scheme for hardware components to identify each other or software modules to check the revision or identity of each other.

Documentation. Documentation may be written in a complex manner or be deficient in critical areas.

Error detection. Protection mechanisms may be disabled as a result of an error, and not reset after appropriate actions are taken.

Implementation. A well-thought-out design and specification may be defeated by a bad implementation. Decisions may be deferred to the implementor, who may not follow the specifications or check all conditions.

Implicit trust. Module X assumes module Y's parameters are correct because module Y is a system process.

Implied sharing. The system stores data or pointers or references user's parameters in the user's address space because memory is in critical demand.

Legality checking. User parameters may not be checked adequately; in particular, unusual or extraordinary parameter values may not be anticipated.

Parameter passing mechanisms. It is safer to pass a parameter's value in a register than a pointer to that parameter. Passing by reference can lead to an implied sharing weakness, as the parameters may not be moved out of the user address space before legality checking occurs.

Passwords. Passwords for various control objects may be easy to guess, made up of a limited set of characters, or a restricted syntax.

Priority.   Many systems modules are given supervisor privileges to facilitate access to certain system tables. The more modules operating in supervisor state, the greater the chance for penetration and the weaker the system.

Residue.   Information may be made available to the penetrator through poor housekeeping practices and system design carelessness.

Utilities.   The design of utilities is often not pursued with as much care as is that of the rest of the system. Utilities are often included in a system without adequate checking or control.

GENERIC ATTACK STRATEGIES

Asynchronous processes.   Multiple processes overlapping each other's execution attempt to change parameters that have been legally checked but not yet used.

Browsing.   A search by an authorized or unauthorized user for privileged information in the computer system.

Clandestine code.   Patch code containing trapdoors is submitted for repairing the OS or a utility program error.

Denial of access.   A program is written to usurp a preponderant share of the system's physical resources—the ultimate goal is to deny legitimate users access to resources in a timely manner.

Error inducement.   A program written to cause deliberate errors so that the subsequent state vector may contain system information.

"NAK" attack.   The user generates an asynchronous interrupt of an executing process, which then allows the user to perform an operation before resuming the processing. During this interrupt, the system may be left in an unprotected state.

Operator spoof.   Attempts are made to circumvent installation management procedures or operator actions that can compromise the security of the system.

Trojan Horse.   The planting of an entry point or trapdoor in the OS that allows subsequent unauthorized access to the system. It also refers to malicious side effects of functions that are executed correctly.

Unexpected operations.   The invocation of seldom-used system primitives or marcos in an unusual manner which takes advantage of system weaknesses.

Unexpected parameters.   The submission of unusual or illegal parameters in a supervisor call which attempts to circumvent the system's legality checking procedures.

7.8.6   System Error Code Summary

Throughout this text, various error codes have been specified in the modules that have depicted the core for individual functions. This section summarizes these error codes and provides a brief description of what each means.

Mnemonic	Meaning
er-abnormal	An abnormal state has been detected for a mass storage disk drive.
er-address	An illegal memory address has been specified in a system call. Usually, the memory address is outside the user's allocated memory space.
er-channel-close	A specified channel is closed to I/O operations. I/O operations cannot be performed without an open channel.
er-channel-use	The channel requested is in use by another process. This error occurs when one process attempts to open a channel previously opened by another process.
er-create	A process has attempted to create a file with a name equivalent to that of an existing file.
er-deallocate	A process has attempted to return disk space to the system that has not been marked allocated to any user.
er-lock	A process has attempted to reference a locked sector on a channel having a mode set to reject requests for locked areas.
er-lock-id	A process has specified an invalid lock identifier when attempting to write-and-release or unlock disk sectors.
er-memory	The system has detected insufficient memory to perform the requested function.
er-mode	A process has specified an invalid mode in loading an overlay or opening a channel.
er-offline	The system has detected a device off-line when responding to a system service request.
er-overlay-identifier	A process has specified an illegal overlap identifier when attempting to load or release an overlay.
er-permanent	A process has attempted to alter a permanent file.
er-read-protect	A process has attempted to access a device, file, or channel that is protected against reading.

er-size

A process has specified an invalid size in a system service request. The interpretation of the error is dependent on the specific request.

er-space

The system has detected insufficient disk space while attempting to create a contiguous file.

er-process-id

A process has specified an illegal process identifier while attempting to perform a process-related function.

er-time

A process has specified an invalid time component while attempting to set the system clock or schedule a process for execution.

er-timeout

The system has detected a timing failure while accessing a device. This error is returned only after the system has attempted the number of retries specified in the device control block and determines that it is not a transient phenomenon.

er-file-type

A process has specified an illegal file type while attempting to create a file.

er-unassigned

A process has referenced memory as a parameter in a system service request that has not been assigned to the process.

er-write-protect

A process has attempted to access a device, file, or channel that has been protected against writing.

7.9   QUEUE MANAGEMENT

A foundation of modern OS design is the management of queue structures. Within the multiprocessing system, a large number of resources are available for allocation to any of these processes and a process will usually get the first available resource unit from the pool when it requests one. Conversely, if no resource units are available, the process must wait (in an orderly fashion) until a unit is released by another process. Several processes may then be waiting for a resource unit. The classic example is a set of processes waiting to utilize the central processor—the scheduling queue.

Both aspects of this process–resource dichotomy rely on waiting and, furthermore, waiting in line—a queue. Knuth [knut69] provides a generic definition and description of queue structures and operations: a queue is a linear list for which all insertions are made at one end of the list; all deletions (accesses) are made at the other end. The best example of such a queue is the round-robin queue for processor scheduling discussed in section 3.3. Unfortunately, in OSs, the management of queues is not such a simple task. The corresponding structures become more complex as the number and variety of queues proliferate.

A. C. Shaw, in his excellent book, *The Logical Design of Operating Systems*, describes a generalized queue structure that allows uniform treatment of queue elements regardless of queue organization and usage. This approach (with several modifications) is used as the basis for the queue structures shown below. In this section the basic structure and algorithms for implementing a generalized queue management facility are described. Variations are imposed by different requirements of functional modules within the OS. These are discussed as appropriate.

7.9.1   Structure of the Generalized Queue

Each queue in an OS requires a descriptor for its structure. In the generalized queue structure, the descriptor is implemented as a queue header—a five-word block of information to which is attached unique queue descriptors and a list of elements. A queue header is composed of five (or possibly six) items.

ENTER-INTO-QUEUE-ADDRESS	Address of a routine that inserts elements into the queue
REMOVE-FROM-QUEUE-ADDRESS	Address of a routine to remove elements from the queue
EXTRACT-FROM-QUEUE-ADDRESS	Address of a routine that searches for a given element in the queue, and removes it from the queue
QUEUE-COUNT	Tally of the number of elements in the queue
QUEUE-START	Pointer to the first element in the queue
QUEUE-END	For double-ended queues, pointer to the last element in the queue

Two basic linking mechanisms for queues exist: first-in, first-out and double-end. In single-link queues, there exists a pointer to the first element in the list. Each element contains a pointer to its successor with the exception of the last element, whose pointer is either zero or may be the address of the first element in the queue (a circular queue). Double-linked queues provide more flexibility in information retrieval with a concomitant increase in processing time and storage requirements. The reader is referred to [knut69] for an extensive discussion of list and queue structures and algorithms.

7.9.2   Generalized Queue Operations

The generalized queue structure depicted in figure 7.4 supports the basic operations on queues described in Knuth [knut69] and Shaw [shaw74]. These operations are:

INITIALIZE	Construct a queue header and initialize its entries
INSERT	Insert an element into the queue
REMOVE	Delete an element from the queue
EXTRACT	Search for an element in the queue and, if found, remove that element
COUNT	Determine the number of elements in a queue

A variation on the EXTRACT operation is merely to scan the queue to determine if an element is entered therein. This operation would be useful in implementing an access control system where a variable number of capabilities exist, and the presence or absence of a specific capability must be determined. Other operations might include SPLIT, which divides a single queue into two independent queues, and JOIN, which combines two queues into one. These operations are easily implemented using the basic operations mentioned above. Accurate descriptions of how to implement them are found frequently in the literature, particularly in Knuth.

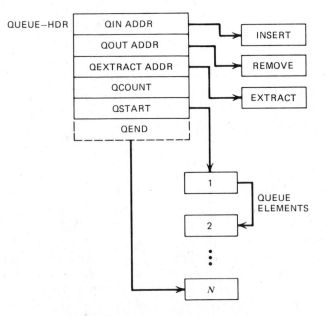

Figure 7.4   Generalized queue header.

7.9.3   Queue Management Functions

Each type of queue is supported by a set of modules corresponding to the basic operations on the queue. In addition, a set of generalized interfaces is provided so that any module does not need to know the exact calling sequence for each queue type. Each module of the queue management system is discussed in the following paragraphs.

Manipulating Queues—General Interfaces

In module 7.9.1 are depicted the basic routines for accessing queue structures. These interfaces allow the caller to insert, remove, extract, and count the elements in the queue. In effect, the generic interfaces merely transfer control to the address of the routine responsible for handling that function. Note that different queue structures will have different routines associated with these functions, as the essence of the queue is embedded in the queue modules.

MODULE 7.9.1

```
procedure enter-into-queue(q, entry)
    enter-into-queue-address[q] → insert-address
    call(insert-address)
    exitproc

entry remove-from-queue(q)
    remove-from-queue-address[q] → remove-address
    call(remove-address)
    exitproc

entry extract-from-queue-(q, entry)
    extract-from-queue-address[q] → extract-address
    call(extract-address)
    exitproc

entry queue-count(q, → count)
    queue-count[q] → count
endproc
```

Inserting an Element into a FIFO Queue

A FIFO queue is characterized by the fact that its elements are linked together by a single link. Moreover, elements are inserted only at the beginning of the queue. The insertion of an element is depicted in figure 7.5. The address of the new element becomes the value of the queue header; the queue count is incremented by one.

MODULE 7.9.2

```
procedure enter-into-fifo-queue(q, entry)
      queue-start[q] → next-cb[entry]
      entry → queue-start[q]
      increment queue-count[q]
endproc
```

Removing an Element from a FIFO Queue

To remove an element from a FIFO queue, we take the element pointed to by the queue header (see figure 7.6). The new value of the queue header becomes

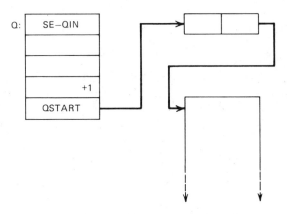

Figure 7.5   Single-ended queue insertion.

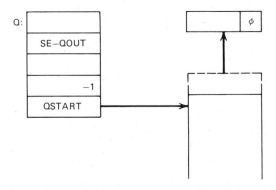

Figure 7.6   Single-ended queue removal.

the next element in the queue. This element is pointed to by the link entry of the first element. If the queue is empty, a zero value will be returned to the caller. Otherwise, the element count within the queue is decremented by one.

MODULE 7.9.3

```
procedure remove-from-fifo-queue(q, → element)
    queue-start[q] → element
    if element not equal to zero
        then
                decrement queue-count[q]
                next-cb[element] → queue-start[q]
                clear next-cb[element]
    endif
endproc
```

Extracting an Element from a FIFO Queue

A very common operation performed on many queue structures is the removal of an element from within the queue. This operation cannot be performed by REMOVE-FROM-QUEUE since its responsibility is merely to remove the first element of the queue. A special function, EXTRACT-FROM-QUEUE, searches the queue for the specified element. If found, the element is removed from the queue and the element count is decremented by one. If not found, the routine returns a value of zero to the caller.

MODULE 7.9.4

```
procedure extract-from-fifo-queue(q, entry, → fifo-current)
    queue-start[q] → fifo-current
    clear fifo-previous
    while fifo-current not equal to zero
        do
                if fifo-current not equal to entry
                    then
                            fifo-current → fifo-previous
                            next-cb[fifo-current] → fifo-current
                endiff
        enddo
    decrement queue-count[q]
    if fifo-previous not equal to zero
        then
                next-cb[fifo-current] → next-cb[fifo-previous]
        else
                next-cb[fifo-current] → queue-start[q]
    endif
endproc
```

Initializing a FIFO Queue

Initializing a queue structure merely consists of inserting the addresses of the queue manipulation routines into the queue control block. This function is a dynamic one, as queues can be created and destroyed by the OS at will. Note that the addresses of the queue manipulation routines are available after the OS has been link-edited into an absolute module.

MODULE 7.9.5

```
procedure fifo-queue-set(q, → fifo-queue-size)
    address(enter-into-fifo-queue) → enter-into-queue-address[q]
    address(remove-from-fifo-queue) → remove-from-queue-address[q]
    address(extract-from-fifo-queue) → extract-from-queue-address[q]
    clear queue-start[q]
    clear queue-count[q]
endproc
```

Inserting an Element into a Double-Ended Queue

Insertion of an element into a double-ended queue involves the updating of both the backward and forward pointers. A further test is involved to check if the queue is empty. In this case, the element inserted becomes both the first and last element of the queue. Otherwise, an element will be inserted at the end of the queue. Figure 7.7 depicts this operation.

MODULE 7.9.6

```
procedure enter-into-double-ended-queue(q, entry)
    clear next-cb[entry]
    if queue-end[q] not equal to zero
        then
        queue-end[q] → element
        entry → next-cb[element]
    else
        entry → queue-start[q]
    endif
    entry → queue-end[q]
    increment queue-count[q]
endproc
```

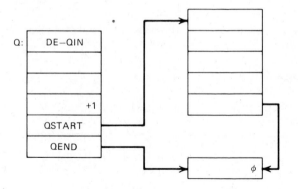

Figure 7.7   Double-ended queue insertion.

Removing an Element from a Double-Ended Queue

The procedure to remove an element from a double-ended queue is similar to that for the FIFO queue. The element to be removed is taken from the front of the queue. If the queue is empty, a value of zero is returned to the caller. Otherwise, the element count is decremented by one, and the first element in the queue is returned to the caller. If the element removed is the only element in the queue, both the forward and backward pointers are set to zero. This operation is shown in figure 7.8.

Extracting an Element from a Double-Ended Queue

Extracting an element from a double-ended queue is the most complex operation to be performed in queue manipulation. Usually, the element to be removed

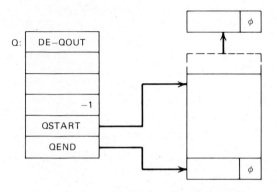

Figure 7.8   Double-ended queue removal.

MODULE 7.9.7

```
procedure remove-from-double-ended-queue(q, → element)
    queue-start[q] → element
    if element not equal to zero
        then
                decrement queue-count[q]
                next-cb[element] → queue-start[q]
                clear next-cb[element]
                if queue-start[q] equals zero
                    then
                            clear queue-end[q]
                endif
    endif
endproc
```

is located somewhere in the middle of the queue. Thus two sets of pointers must be adjusted in order to "link" around the element to be removed. One also must be careful to check the boundary conditions for the queue. That is, if the element is extracted from the front or back of the queue, special processing is required.

MODULE 7.9.8

```
procedure extract-from-double-ended-queue(q, entry,
                                    → double-ended-current)
    queue-start[q] → double-ended-current
    clear double-ended-previous
    while double-ended-current not equal to zero
        do
                if double-ended-current not equal to entry
                    then
                        double-ended-current →
                                            double-ended-previous
                        next-cb[double-ended-current] →
                                            double-ended-current
                endif
                decrement queue-count[q]
                if double-ended-previous not equal to zero
                    then
                        next-cb[double-ended-current] →
                                    next-cb[double-ended-previous]
                        if next-cb[double-ended-previous] equals zero
                            then
                            double-ended-previous → queue-end[q]
```

```
                              endif
                    else
                              next-cb[double-ended-current]  →  queue-start[q]
                              if queue-start[q] equals zero
                                    then
                                              clear queue-end[q]
                              endif
                    endif
              enddo
endproc
```

Initializing a Double-Ended Queue

The procedure for initializing a double-ended queue is exactly the same as for FIFO queues. Only one additional pointer needs to be initialized to zero.

MODULE 7.9.9

```
procedure double-ended-queue-set(q,  →  double-ended-queue-size)
      address(enter-into-double-ended-queue)  →
                                              enter-into-queue-address[q]
      address(remove-from-double-ended-queue)  →
                                              remove-from-queue-address[q]
      address(extract-from-double-ended-queue)  →
                                              extract-from-queue-address[q]
      clear queue-count[q]
      clear queue-start[q]
      clear queue-end[q]
endproc
```

7.9.4   Counting Queues

In an OS, there are many instances where one needs to maintain a count of the resources or objects that are being manipulated. The count of characters in an output buffer is an example. A counting queue is often associated with a resource semaphore managing a limited number of resources. For example, one needs a count of all processes in the system or the number of processes awaiting service from the mass storage allocator.

The queue header for a counting queue consists of the first four elements of a standard FIFO queue. Only three operations are defined for a counting queue: insertion, deletion, and initialization. Insertion increments the queue count;

deletion returns the current value of the counter and decrements the counter by one; and initialization sets up the counting queue structure.

Inserting into a Counting Queue

Procedure ENTER-INTO-COUNTING-QUEUE handles insertions into a counting queue. Insertion merely means that the internal counter is incremented by one. Although not explicitly shown, the designer may want to check for overflow of the counter value. This test would be useful in situations where recursive or runaway functions are likely to occur. Another possible modification is to declare a maximum value and generate an error indication when that value is exceeded.

MODULE 7.9.10

```
procedure enter-into-counting-queue(q, entry)
     increment queue-count[q]
endproc
```

Removal from a Counting Queue

Procedure REMOVE-FROM-COUNTING-QUEUE retrieves the current value of the queue counter. If the value is greater than or equal to one, the value is decremented by one. A possible modification to this routine would have the OS generating an error if the caller ever tried to decrement the queue count below zero.

MODULE 7.9.11

```
procedure remove-from-counting-queue(q, → element)
     queue-count[q] → element
     if element greater than or equal to one
          then
                decrement queue-count[q]
     endif
endproc
```

Initializing a Counting Queue

Procedure SET-COUNTING-QUEUE initializes a counter queue. The value of the counting queue is originally set to zero. Note that the extraction and removal functions obtain an identical result when applied to a counting queue. A possible modification to this routine would allow the user to specify a value as the initial value for the counting queue.

MODULE 7.9.12

```
procedure set-counting-queue(q,  → count-queue-size)
    address(count-enter-into-queue) → enter-into-queue-address[q]
    address(count-remove-from-queue)  →  remove-from-queue-address[q]
    address(count-remove-from-queue)  →  extract-from-queue-address[q]
    clear queue-count[q]
endproc
```

This implementation of counting queues has the counting function performed in ascending sequence. If suitable hardware instructions for DECREMENT AND TEST FOR ZERO are available, the designer may want to implement the counting function in descending sequence.

7.9.5   Bit Queues

Frequently, OSs are developed around fixed-size objects that can be allocated to any process. One need know only that a particular object has been allocated from the set. Housekeeping chores relative to who "owns" the object and its return to the system are usually performed using space within the object itself. For these types of resources, the bit queue technique provides a fast easily managed allocation scheme.

The bit queue technique relies on a one-to-one correspondence between bits in a word and the objects in a resource class. For example, two possible applications are the allocation of disk blocks and the allocation of memory blocks.

Data General's RDOS uses bit maps for disk block allocation. Depending on the size of the disk, the first n blocks of the disk contain a bit map specifying which blocks have been allocated and which blocks are free. This bit map is not accessible to the user but is maintained exclusively by the operating system. A similar scheme could be used to allocate memory blocks.

The bit queue consists of a seven-element queue header which is defined as follows:

```
QUEUE-HEADER of
ENTER-INTO-BIT-QUEUE-ADDRESS,
REMOVE-FROM-BIT-QUEUE-ADDRESS,
EXTRACT-FROM-BIT-QUEUE-ADDRESS,
QUEUE-COUNT,
QUEUE-BITS-ADDRESS,
INPUT-CONVERT,
OUTPUT-CONVERT
```

Nominally, one counts the bits in a word from left to right. That is, the leftmost bit is presumed to be bit zero. It is also useful to be able to address the bits in a backward sequence. To facilitate this procedure, we define an index

```
REVERSE-BITS =
0100000
040000
020000
010000
04000
02000
01000
0400
0200
0100
040
020
010
04
02
01
```

The standard queue operations are defined for bit queues and are described in the following paragraphs.

Inserting an Element into a Bit Queue

A bit queue is composed of n words corresponding to the queue size. Insertion consist of setting the appropriate bit corresponding to the entity to be allocated. To perform this operation, the system needs to locate the word in the bit queue corresponding to the entry. As the number of bits per entry will vary with the queue, INPUT-CONVERT is called to calculate the address of that word. Setting the bits corresponds to ORing a string of ones into the word.

Removing an Element from a Bit Queue

Removal of an element from a bit queue consists of setting the appropriate bits to zero. Most of this code is used to calculate the address of the word containing the specified bits and create the mask for clearing the proper bits. Some systems contain instructions that will automatically set a string of bits to zero or one while

MODULE 7.9.13

```
procedure enter-into-bit-queue(q, entry)
    input-convert[q] → input-address
    call(input-address, entry) → element
    decrement element
    if element greater than or equal to zero
        then
                queue-bits-address[q] + rshift(element, 4)
                                              → bit-queue-address
                memory(bit-queue-address) → temp1
                and(element, 017) → temp2
                reverse-bits[temp2] → temp3
                or(temp1, temp3) → memory(bit-queue-address)
                increment queue-count[q]
    endif
endproc
```

counting them. For example, the Data General Eclipse has such an instruction, which was included expressly for handling bit allocation/deallocation of memory and disk blocks.

MODULE 7.9.14

```
procedure remove-from-bit-queue(q, → element)
    clear element
    decrement queue-count[q]
    if queue-count[q] less than zero
        then
                increment queue-count[q]
        else
                queue-bits-address[q] → bit-temp
                while memory(btemp) equals zero
                    do
                            increment element by 16
                            element → atemp
                            increment btemp
                    enddo
                btemp → bit-queue-address
                while atemp greater than or equal to zero
                    do
                            lcycle(atemp, 1) → atemp
                            increment element
                    enddo
```

```
            and(element, 017) → temp1
            reverse-bits[temp1] → temp2
            memory(bit-queue-address) → temp3
            xor(temp2, temp3) →  memory(bit-queue-address)
            increment element
            output-convert[q] → output-address
            call(output-address, element) → element
        endif
endproc
```

Extracting an Element from a Bit Queue

MODULE 7.9.15

```
procedure extract-from-bit-queue(q, entry, → element)
    input-convert[q] → input-address
    call(input-address, entry) → element
    decrement element
    and(element, 017) → etemp
    queue-bits-address[q] + rshift(element, 4) → bit-queue-address
    memory(bit-queue-address) → temp1
    reverse-bits[temp1] → temp2
    if and(temp1, temp2) equals zero
        then
            clear element
        else
            xor(temp1, temp2) → memory(bit-queue-address)
            decrement queue-count[q]
            entry → element
    endif
endproc
```

7.10 SEMAPHORE MANAGEMENT

Another key principle that characterizes modern OSs is the use of the semaphore concept to control synchronization of interacting processes. This concept was first proposed by E.W. Dijkstra in the early 1960s and a discussion of the semaphore concept, considerations for implementation, and application to cooperating processes is found in his seminal paper [dijk68].

Dijkstra described semaphores as nonnegative integer variables. Two operations are defined for semaphores:

P   Decrement the semaphore by one, if possible. If the semaphore is zero, it cannot be decremented and the process invoking the operation waits until it is possible to decrement the semaphore.

V   The semaphore is incremented by one in a single instruction that prevents the semaphore from being accessed by any other process except the one executing the operation.

The P and V operators have only recently appeared widely in hardware instruction sets. One of the earliest machines to implement the P/V operators was the Univac 1108. The Univac 1108 provides two instructions that allow a process to implement a crude binary semaphore capability: TEST-AND-SET and CLEAR-TEST-AND-SET. Both instructions were indivisible in the sense that they could not be interrupted.

7.10.1   Solving Mutual Exclusion Using Semaphores

The use of semaphores allows the implementation of a straightforward solution to the problem of mutual exclusion. As mentioned in section 3.1, mutual exclusion involves allowing one of n processes to execute a critical section of code completely before any other process may execute it. The solution allows n processes to operate in parallel in an asynchronous fashion.

Let S be a binary semaphore having the value of 0 or 1. S serves the function of a simple lock upon the critical code segment. When $S = 0$, some process is executing its critical segment. Since only one process can decrement S to 0, mutual exclusion of all other processes is guaranteed. On the other hand, as Shaw [shaw74] notes, mutual blocking is not possible because processes attempting to execute the critical segment will be performed sequentially when $S = 1$.

Figure 7.9 depicts an example solution. Each process is assumed to perform an iterative function with a variable time frame. Note that a process must perform a V operation after leaving its critical segment.

7.10.2.   Semaphores as Resource Counters and Synchronizers

A semaphore can serve two functions in producer/consumer situations. First, it may be a resource counter tracking the production and consumption of resources. Second, it may be a synchronizer coordinating between the production and consumption of resources. A process consumes a resource by performing a P operation on the semaphore associated with it and produces a resource by performing a V operation on the same semaphore. In the implementation of the semaphore, a counter is decremented with each P operation and incremented with each V operation. The counter is initialized to the number of resources available. When resources are unavailable, a process can be placed on a queue to

Program P

.

semaphore S

.

set S to 1

/

/ Process P1:

/

P1:   P(S)

    execute critical segment

    V(S)

    .

    goto P1

    . . .

/

/ Process Pn:

/

Pn: P(S)

    execute critical segment

    V(S)

    .

    goto Pn

End of Program   **Figure 7.9 Mutual exclusion via semaphores.**

wait. As resources are released, the first process on the queue is awakened and given control of the resource.

Dijkstra's original papers on semaphore operations ([dijk65, dijk68]) discuss the problem of synchronization. His example concerns two processes using a single resource such as buffer storage. One process produces an output record and puts it in the next available buffer, where it is retrieved by an I/O process and printed.

Buffer storage consist of N equal-sized buffers, where each buffer is capable of holding one record. The two processes can be easily synchronized using three semaphores.

EMPTY-BUFFER	The number of empty buffers
FULL-BUFFER	The number of full buffers
BUFFER-SEMAPHORE	A mutual exclusion semaphore for buffer operations

The code segment for the two processes is shown in figure 7.10. The buffer operations ADD-TO-BUFFER and TAKE-FROM-BUFFER are protected as critical sections. This protection is required by the fact that buffers are usually linked on an available space list. If the system is generalized to multiple producers and consumers, mutual exclusion is necessary to protect the buffer operations code segments. This is exactly the case encountered in a multiprogramming system, where multiple interactive users are currently executing.

7.10.3   Semaphore Support for Interprocess Communications

The scheme described in section 7.10.2 can be generalized to provide message communications between two processes. The procedures are complicated by the fact that each process may initiate either one-way or two-way messages. Shaw [shaw74] describes an explicit case for *n* processes communicating with a terminal user. He suggests there are four types of communication:

Process-to-User	One-way communication requiring a reply
Process-to-User-to-Process	Requires the user to respond to the original message with an acknowledgment
User-to-Process	A one-way message from the user to some process (or perhaps all processes)
User-to-Process-to-User	The user queries a process and awaits an answer

Up to this point, the code segments resemble those described in section 7.10.2. Shaw, however, complicates the situation by imposing additional constraints on the communication processes. First, the communications link between the process and the user is half-duplex in nature. Second, the user may press an "attention" button to gain priority within the communications system. This priority is necessary, as the next message sent by the user may result in termination of one or more processes. Finally, user messages are routed to the appropriate process through use of a message interpreter.

   The solution described by Shaw requires a synchronization semaphore for each process. The user communicates with the message interpreter through another semaphore. The message interpreter transmits/receives messages to/from individual processes. In effect, Shaw has shown that the multiple interprocess communication problem can be reduced to a series of one-to-one communications.

Semaphores EMPTY-BUFFER, FULL-BUFFER,
                              BUFFER-SEMAPHORE
initialize EMPTY-BUFFER to N
           FULL-BUFFER to 0
           BUFFER-SEMAPHORE to 1

procedure P(S),..... S − 1 → S, endproc
procedure V(S),..... S + 1 → S, endproc

procedure main-process
      produce an output record
      p(empty-buffer)
      p(buffer-semaphore)
      add-to-buffer( )
      v(buffer-semaphore)
      v(full-buffer)
endproc

procedure I/O-Process
      p(full-buffer)
      p(buffer-semaphore)
      take-from-buffer( )
      v(buffer-semaphore)
      v(empty-buffer)
      print record
endproc

procedure I/O-Process

      p(full-buffer)

      p(buffer-semaphore)

      take-from-buffer( )

      v(buffer-semaphore)

      v(empty-buffer)

      print record

endproc

Figure 7.10   Example of process synchronization by semaphores.

7.10.4   Resource Semaphore Database

Each resource semaphore is composed of a resource control block and two queues: the wait queue and the availability queue. The resource control block has the following structure:

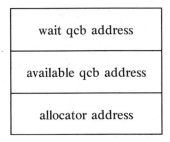

| wait qcb address |
| available qcb address |
| allocator address |

The wait QCB and available QCB addresses point to the queue control blocks (see section 7.9) for lists of processes waiting for resources and lists of available resources, respectively. The allocator is a routine that assigns resources to waiting processes in some prescribed format. Two examples are shown in modules 7.10.3 and 7.10.4. An allocator routine provides a mechanism for controlling the manner in which resources are assigned to processes. In addition, if data transformation, validation, and verification or other services are required, these can be encoded in the allocator to be effected as resources are assigned to waiting processes. Examples of special allocators have been described in previous chapters.

7.10.5   Resource Semaphore Operations

The two primary semaphore operations are request and release. These functions correspond to the P and V operations described by Dijkstra in his classic paper. However, the implementation of these operations has been substantially augmented to provide an efficient queueing mechanism when the demand exceeds the supply.

Requesting a Resource

A process requests a resource by executing the REQUEST procedure and specifying the appropriate resource semaphore. Optionally, a process may include data that are to be stored in the queue or that describe the nature or amount of resource to be allocated. Implementation stores the identifier of the current process in the wait queue of the semaphore and sets the current queue of the process to the wait of the semaphore. It then calls the resource allocator to allocate any available resources to those waiting in the queue. This approach simplifies processing as, on the average, we expect that a process will have to wait in the queue for some period of time before a resource is available. For those times when a resource is immediately available, the time necessary to first insert and then immediately retrieve a process from the queue is negligible compared to the period that the process might wait.

MODULE 7.10.1

```
procedure request(rs-address, data, → rs-value)
     data → rs-data-save[p]
     rs-wait-queue[rs-address] → rwq
     enter-into-queue(rwq, p)
     rs-wait-queue[rs-address] → current-queue[p]
     call(rs-allocator[rs-address], p)
     if current-queue[p] not equal to ready-queue
          then
                scheduler( )
     endif
     return-value[p] → rs-value
endproc
```

Releasing a Resource

A process releases a resource by executing the RELEASE procedure and specifying the appropriate resource semaphore. The process is required to specify the units of the resource to be released; this varies with the type of resource. Again, the resource identifiers are first stored on the available queue. Then the resource allocator is called to allocate resources to those processes waiting for resources. This approach is taken under the assumption that there is a general case where resources will remain on the queue for periods of time substantially longer than the time necessary to insert them into the queue.

MODULE 7.10.2

```
procedure release(rs-address, data)
     stack(rs-address)
     rs-avail-queue[rs-address] → rsa
     enter-into-queue(rsa, data)
     stack-top( ) → rs-address
     call(rs-allocator[rs], rs)
     unstack( )
endproc
```

Allocating One Resource Unit

ONE-ALLOCATOR, depicted in module 7.10.3, is used to allocate one unit of a resource. It is executed when a REQUEST operation on a resource semaphore is performed. It checks to see if there are processes waiting for resources and if there are available resources to allocate. If these tests fail, the procedure exits immediately. The process that issued the REQUEST is enqueued on the wait queue before the allocator is invoked. This approach simplifies subsequent processing.

If there are waiting processes and resources to allocate, ONE-ALLOCATOR will assign all of the available resources to the waiting processes. If there are more resources than processes, resources are allocated to all other processes. If more processes are waiting than resources are available, allocation continues until the current supply of resources is exhausted.

Each process removed from the wait queue is reactivated with the identity of the allocated resource assigned to it. The wait and available queues are advanced to the next element.

MODULE 7.10.3

```
procedure one-allocator(rs-address)
     rs-wait-queue[rs-address] → rsw
     rs-avail-queue[rs-address] → rsa
     while queue-start[rsw] not equal to zero
             & queue-count[rsa] greather than or equal to one
         do
             remove-from-queue(rsw) → poa
             remove-from-queue(rsw) → return-value[p]
             activate(poa)
             rs-wait-queue[rs-address] → rsw
             rs-wait-queue[rs-address] → rsa
         enddo
endproc
```

Conditional Resource Allocation

FLAGGED-ALLOCATOR, depicted in module 7.10.4, is a general allocator that determines whether a resource may be allocated. When invoked, FLAGGED-ALLOCATOR satisfies all outstanding resource requests from the resource availability queue. The process that issued the REQUEST has been attached to the end of the wait queue. FLAGGED-ALLOCATOR locates this process by retrieving the last element of the queue (stored in QUEUE-END). The process provided a flag with the request, which indicated if it wanted to wait for the resource.

Now, if the wait queue is empty, the process's request has been satisfied, and the further action is moot. If the queue is not empty and the flag is zero, the process will wait its turn for a resource. However, if the flag is one, the process is not willing to wait. It is extracted from the queue and reactivated immediately. A return value of zero indicates that no resource has been assigned to the process.

MODULE 7.10.4

```
procedure flagged-allocator(rs-address)
     rs-wait-queue[rs-address] → rsw
     rs-available-queue[rs-address] → rsa
     while queue-count[rsw] not equal to zero
             and queue-count[rsa] not equal to zero
          do
             remove-from-queue(rsw) → pfa
             remove-from-queue(rsa) → return-value[pfa]
             activate(pfa)
             rs-wait-queue[rs-address] → rssw
             rs-avail-queue[rs-address] → rsa
          enddo
          queue-end[rsw] → pfa
          rs-data-save[pfa] → wait-flag
          if queue-count[rsw] not equal to zero
                  and wait-flag not equal to zero
             then
                  extract-from-queue(rsw, pfa) → pfa
                  clear return-value[pfa]
                  activate(pfa)
          endif
endproc
```

Defining a Resource Semaphore

DEFINE-RS initializes a resource semaphore control block, thus defining a resource semaphore. RS is the address of the resource semaphore control block. The addresses of the wait QCB and available QCB, respectively, are stored in resource control block as follows. To RS, add the size of the resource semaphore control block; the new address is the address of the wait QCB. INITIALIZE-WAIT-QUEUE is invoked to set up the wait queue; it returns the size of the wait QCB. The size of the wait QCB is added to RSW to give the address for the available QCB. INITIALIZE-AVAIL-QUEUE is invoked to set up the available queue. The address of the allocation routine is stored in the appropriate location. This approach is used because a resource semaphore may use different queue types for its wait and available queues. These queue types have different sizes; this information is known only when the resource control block is set up.

MODULE 7.10.5

procedure define-rs(rs, initialize-wait-queue, initialize-avail-queue,
                                                                allocator)
    rs + rs-size → rs-wait-queue[rs]
    rs-wait-queue[rs] → rsw
    init-wait-queue(rsw) + rsw →rs-avail-queue[rs]
    if address(initialize-avail-queue) not equal to zero
       then
            rs-avail-queue[rs] → rsa
            initialize-avail-queue(rsa)
    endif
    address(allocator) → rs-allocator[rs]
endproc

MODULE 7.10.6

procedure define-binary-rs(rs)
    define-rs(rs, deque-queue-set, count-queue-set, one-allocator)
    release(rs)
endproc

7.10.6 Semaphore Performance Problems

Semaphores exist to coordinate the use of fixed sets of resources by multiple processes. When too many processes demand a resource, processes will be enqueued on the semaphore. As a resource is released, requests are granted on a first come, first served basis. The phenomenon we witness is that transactions are "bumping into" or conflicting with one another—a natural occurrence where concurrent processing is allowed. Assuming one unit of resource, if a process holds that unit for an extended duration, other processes will "convoy" behind that process; that is, faster moving processes soon bump into slower ones.

The convoy phenomenon gives rise to these interesting statistics concerning resource semaphores:

1.   The duration D for which the semaphore is held
2.   The interval I between successive requests of a resource by a process
3.   The collision cross section C of the semaphore (the percentage of time that a request is granted immediately)

A resource semaphore can be characterized as low traffic or high traffic. A high-traffic semaphore is one that is frequently accessed (i.e., the interval between requests is small). In an N-process, M-resource system, where N is much greater than M, the semaphore queue may contain up to $N - M$ processes. Let D be 200 microseconds and I be 1000 microseconds; then C is 2. Suppose that $N - M$ is greater than or equal to 5. We have the following situation:

Let $P1$ (a process) hold semaphore S with $M = 1$ and $N = 6$

Processes $P2$, ..., $P6$ are scheduled and request S immediately; because S is busy, $P2$, ..., $P6$ wait for it

When $P1$ awakes, it executes and releases after 2000 μsec

$P2$ is granted S by the resource monitor

$P1$ executes 800 μsec and requests ST; however, S is busy, so $P1$ is enqueued on S

The problem is that if $N - M$ is greater than I/D, $P1$ almost always finds the resource busy when it next requests it. On the average, not all these processes are going to be dispatched before $P1$ requests S again. The system enters a thrashing state, where much of the CPU time will be dedicated to context switching. If the time to switch contexts is approximately D or larger, a convoy builds on S. This idealized case has assumed that all processes are identical with respect to I and D. In actual systems, I and D vary considerably over the set of processes. Moreover, a process, while holding S, may enter a wait state on another semaphore S'. This action magnifies the actual duration D by some variable factor. In this way, the convoy length can begin to approach $N - M$.

The obvious solution to the problem is to attempt to minimize the duration of a high-traffic semaphore. This involves implementing a protocol for process design that forbids blocking when a high-traffic semaphore is held (say, for I/O or page fault). Another strategy suggests that we reduce traffic on a semaphore by changing the granularity of the resource. This approach may just postpone the problem to another semaphore.

A critical issue in semaphore management is associated with the concept of granting requests in first come, first served order. One approach is to grant requests in random order under the theory that every process will eventually get served. As an alternative, the system might awaken all processes (at a point before the resource request) and let them mutually contend for the resource. Neither approach appears reasonable in a priority-based system. A final approach suggests tracking the values of I and D much as one tracks a process's working set. One then grants requests on the basis of shortest duration. Suffice it to say that this problem is an open research area to which the reader is invited to apply his or her talents.

A

Structure of the Program Design Language

The modules presented in the text have been written in a pseudocode known as the Program Design Language (PDL). This language allows the designer to concentrate on specifying the functional design of the module without being constrained by syntactic forms. The PDL is not compiled. As it is similar syntactically to many popular programming languages, the code skeletons presented herein may be readily understood by any user who has experience in high-level procedure-oriented languages.

Several benefits may be derived from using a PDL to specify a functional design. The major benefit is the ability to concentrate on the logical solution to the problem. As a side effect, it allows easy writing and changing of programs, as modifications to program logic can be checked out before they are actually executed. Finally, the code skeletons are easy to read and understand and correspond in appearance to the programs found on many computer systems.

PDL has no formal rules for constructing its statements. Rather, it attempts to express program logic in natural English prose. Variables are defined as needed; the names of variables may be any length as long as they express the usage of the variable. For example, the variable SECTORS-PER-TRACK can be used to specify different fixed- or moving-head disk sizes in the computer system.

Three types of structures can be defined in the PDL. A table of values can be specified by enclosing its index pointer(s) in square brackets. An example might be

DISPATCH-TABLE from 1 to 100

.
.
.

CURRENT-PROCESS-ID → DISPATCH-TABLE [I]

A complex structure that is composed of a group of variables or tables can also be defined. The group may be referenced as an entire entity (QUEUE-HEADER) or by it individual elements (ENTER-INTO-QUEUE-ADDRESS). An example of a complex structure is the queue control template:

```
queue-header of
    enter-into-queue-address,
    remove-from-queue-address,
    extract-from-queue-address,
    queue-count,
    queue-start
```

The other type of structure is the code structure known as a procedure. Each procedure is identified by a name; it may require an optional list of arguments enclosed in parentheses. A procedure definition is enclosed in the keywords PROCEDURE ... ENDPROC. A procedure is called by name and followed by its optional argument list. An example is

```
Procedure Select-Task(Task-List)


    .
    .
    .


(procedure body defined here)


    .
    .
    .


Endproc
```

and a call to this procedure would appear as

SELECT-TASK(DISPATCH-TABLE)

The procedure-body is composed of statements describing the actions to be performed. In the PDL, considerable latitude is allowed in expressing operations and logic. A mixture of English prose and arithmetic symbolism will be used, as appropriate, to convey the meaning of the operations to be performed. The first type of statement is the sequence statement, which describes an action that is immediately followed by the next sequential statement. The sequence statement contains verbs such as ADD, SUBTRACT, SORT, and procedure calls, or it may be composed of arithmetic operators. Examples are:

ADD 1 TO FILE-BLOCK-COUNT

READ(FILE-NAME,NR-BLOCKS,ERROR-FLAG)

PROCESS-TIME + IS − TIME*2 → PROCESS-TIME

Binary decisions are represented by the IF ... THEN ... ELSE construct. In its most general form, it is used to describe one of two sets of actions that will take place depending on the state condition. The action sets may be any collection of PDL statements, such as nested IFs, sequence statements, procedure calls, and so on. The general syntax of the IF ... THEN ... ELSE construct is:

IF p

THEN f

ELSE g

ENDIF

where p is the predicate or condition list and f and g are lists of actions to be performed when p is true or false, respectively. An example is

IF END-OF-FILE is true

THEN set flag equal to one

ELSE read next record

ENDIF

Two types of repetitive control structures for looping under prescribed conditions are provided in the PDL. The DO WHILE statement evaluates the predicate and performs the set of actions until the predicate value is false. The PERFORM UNTIL, similar to the COBOL constructs, evaluates the predicate and performs the set of actions until the predicate value becomes true. The syntax of these two statements is

WHILE p   PERFORM UNTIL p

DO f   f

ENDDO   ENDLOOP

The CASE statement is used to simulate a branch table. It may be an efficient and effective alternative to multiple levels of nested IF ... THEN ... ELSE statements. The CASE statement selects one of *n* action sets based on the value of an evaluated expression. The syntax of the CASE statement is

CASE p OF

    V1: f1

       exitcase

    V2: f2

       exitcase

    Vm: fn

  else fe

ENDCASE

where there is an explicit exit from the CASE statement after the execution of the action set. A CASE statement may possess a default action that is performed if none of the explicit cases is selected.

Finally, an unconditional branch statement allows a transfer of logic flow to any labeled statement. Labels may be attached only to the start of a statement. Thus transfer of logic cannot be to the THEN clause of an IF ... THEN ... ELSE statement, into the loop of a DO WHILE, or to any of the specific cases of the CASE statement. An example is

       GO TO LABEL1

   LABEL1: IF p

         THEN f

         ELSE g

         ENDIF

The following two situations are illegal:

  GO TO LABEL2   GO TO LABEL3

  DO WHILE p   CASE P OF

LABEL2: statement   LABEL3: V3 f3

ENDDO   ENDCASE

Within any of the statement constructs, other statements can be nested to any level. Nested statements are indented to improve the readability of the design. Nesting is used only to the extent that it does not increase the complexity of the design or violate the principles of structured and modular programming.

B

Implicit System Functions

The instruction sets of commercially available central processors vary considerably in the number and type of instructions that they possess. In a similar manner, various programming languages support different sets of intrinsic functions for performing basic logical or relational operations. To remain hardware or language independent, a number of operators used in this text have been cast as functions. The user is free to implement them in a manner that optimizes the characteristic use of a specific machine. This appendix summarizes the set of operators as they are used in the text.

RCYCLE (WORD, NBITS)

This function performs a right circular shift of the bits in a word. Bits shifted out of the right end of the word are entered into the left end of the word. NBITS represents the number of bits to right shift modulo the word size.

LCYCLE (WORD, NBITS)

This function performs a left circular shift of the bits in a word. Bits shifted out of the left end of the word are entered into the right end of the word. NBITS represents the number of bits to left shift modulo the word size.

RSHIFT (WORD, NBITS)

This function performs a logical right shift of the bits in a word. As each bit is shifted out of the right end of the word, a corresponding zero bit is entered into the left end. NBITS represents the number of bits to right shift modulo the word size.

LSHIFT (WORD, NBITS)

This function performs a logical left shift of the bits in a word. As each bit is shifted out of the left end of the word, a corresponding zero bit is entered into the right end. NBITS represents the number of bits to left shift modulo the word size.

OR (A, B, RESULT)

This function performs a logically inclusive OR on a bit-by-bit basis of the contents of words A and B. The corresponding bit in the result is set according to the following table:

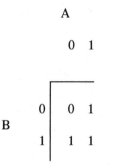

AND (A, B, RESULT)

This function performs a logical AND on a bit by bit basis of the contents of words A and B. The corresponding bit in the result is set according to the following table:

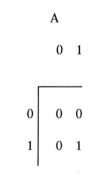

XOR (A, B, RESULT)

This function performs a logical exclusive OR on a bit by bit basis of the contents of words A and B. The corresponding bit in the result is set according to the following table:

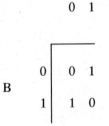

MEMORY (ADDRESS)

This function has the double connotation of indicating both retrieval from and storage into a memory cell according to its position in an assignment statement. If the function is on the left-hand size of an assignment statement, it indicates the source of a value.

ADDRESS (variable/constant name)

This function returns the address of a variable or constant as its value. It may be implemented as a hardware instruction or as a pointer to the constant or variable.

CALL(ADDRESS)

This function performs a subroutine jump to the routine at the specified address. It is normally implemented as an indirect jump through another address.

References

aber73

Abernathy, D.H., et al. Survey of Design Goals for Operating Systems. *Operating Systems Review,* Vol. 7, no. 1, 1973.

abra73

Abrahams, P. A Compiler Writer's Wishbook for Operating Systems. *SIGPLAN Notices,* Vol. 8, no. 9, 1973. This paper defines some of the features of an operating system that the compiler-writer could use to simplify the job. Two key areas which the author feels should be emphasized are file maintenance and system reliability and recovery.

akko74

Akkoyunlu, E., et al. Interprocess Communication Facilities for Network Operating Systems. *IEEE Computer,* Vol. 7, no. 6, 1974. This paper discusses the problems of communication facilities among multiple processes in computer networks. The authors survey some interprocess communication mechanisms reported in recent literature, including Farber's DCS and Walden's concepts. A specific implementation, SBS at Stony Brook, is described in detail. SBS's communications mechanism relies on process ports and data ports to effect interaction among processes.

albr76

Albrecht, H. R., and K. D. Ryder. The Virtual Telecommunications Access Method: A Systems Network Architecture Perspective. *IBM Systems Journal,* Vol. 15, no. 1, 1976. This article discusses VTAM, which supports teleprocessing requirements in a virtual storage environment. The components of VTAM are described in detail, particularly as they relate to SNA.

alex64

Alexander, C. *Notes on the Synthesis of Form.* Harvard University Press, Cambridge, MA, 1964.

ande76

Anderson, D.R. Data Base Processor Technology. *NCC 1976,* Vol. 45. AFIPS Press, Arlington, VA. This paper discusses the concept of offloading database management operations to a separate processor. This concept imposes certain constraints on system design because of system architecture considerations.

anzi75

Anzinger, G., and A.M. Cadal. A Real-Time Operating System with Multiterminal and Batch/ Spool Capabilities. *Hewlett-Packard Journal,* Vol. 27, no. 4, 1975. This article describes HP's RTE-II real-time executive for its 2100 series computer systems. RTE-II is an advanced version of a previous system which features real-time measurement and control capabilities and program development aids. RTE-II supports priority scheduling of concurrent processes as well as a foreground/background partitioned environment.

arno74

Arnold, J.S., D.P. Casey, and R.H. Mckinistry. Design of Tightly-Coupled Multiprocessing Programming. *IBM Systems Journal,* Vol. 13, no. 1, 1974. This article describes five aspects of programming support for multiprocessing hardware. This support includes facility locking, service management, CPU affinity, dispatching, and alternative CPU recovery. The authors discuss the rationale for implementation of such services.

asak75

Asaki, H., et al. Resource Sharing and Scheduling in OS7. *Proceedings of the 2nd USA–Japan Computer Conference, Tokyo,* 1975. This paper describes the resource sharing function for OS7—the operating system for the HITAC 8700/8800. This function supports allocation of resources in a multiprogramming, multiprocessing, virtual memory environment. Schemes for managing various resources, such as processors, memory, and programs, are presented.

atta76

Attanasio, C.R., P.W. Markstein, and R.J. Phillips. Penetrating an Operating System: A Study of VM/370 Integrity. *IBM Systems Journal,* Vol. 15, no. 1, 1976. This article discusses a methodology for discovering OS design flaws as an approach to learning system design techniques that may make it possible to enhance data security. A team was formed to explore the penetration of VM/370. The methods and results of this penetration study are described in some detail.

atwo73

Atwood, J.W. I/O Supervision in the Project SUE Operating System. *IEEE Computer,* Vol. 6, no. 11, 1973. This paper describes an I/O supervisior for the IBM 360. Project SUE is attempting to construct a reliable and understandable OS for the System/360. The I/O supervisor is based on levels of hierarchy that attempt to correct some of the problems with the System/360 architecture.

ausl73

Auslander, M.A., et al., Functional Structure of IBM Virtual Storage Operating System. *IBM Systems Journal,* Vol. 12, no. 4, 1973. This series of articles discusses the trade-offs, options, and objectives behind the architectural features related to the implementation of a virtual storage OS. In particular, the influences of a dynamic address translation mechanism on OS technology are discussed.

aver75

Averitt, W. Real-Time Executive System Manages Large Memories. *Hewlett-Packard Journal,* Vol. 27, no. 4, 1975. This article describes the dynamic memory mapping feature of HP's RTE-III system for its 2100 series computers. RTE-III is a multipartition, real-time, multiprogramming system supporting up to 256K words of memory.

bach73

Bachman, C.W. The Programmer as Navigator. *CACM,* Vol. 16, no. 11, 1973. Bachman's Turing Award Lecture emphasizes the role of programmers as navigators in database information space. The programmer must learn the "rules of the road" in order to avoid conflicts with other programmers. In complex table-driven operating systems composed of interacting processes, the general principles discussed here can also be applied.

baec72

Baecker, H.D. Garbage Collection for Virtual Memory Systems. *CACM,* Vol. 15, no. 11, 1972. This paper evaluates four methods for garbage collection where pages are allocated from free space lists.

baer73

Baer, J.L. A Survey of Theoretical Aspects of Multiprocessing. *ACM Computing Suverys,* Vol. 5, no. 1, 1973. This article looks at several features of the multiprocessing environment. Among them are additional instructions needed to support multiprocessing and extensions to high-level languages. The latter part of the paper deals with theoretical models of multiprocessing systems and an appendix attempts to classify existing multiprocessing systems.

bail74

Baily, J.H., J.A. Howard, and T.J. Szczygielski. The Job Entry Subsystem for OS/VS1. *IBM Systems Journal,* Vol. 13, no. 3, 1974. This article discusses an extended job management facility for a virtual storage operating system. It provides both SPOOLing and job scheduling services.

balk74

Balkovich, E., L. Presser, et al. Dynamic Memory Repacking. *CACM,* Vol. 17, no. 3, 1974. This paper discusses the conditions under which dynamic repacking of main memory can reduce the fragmentation of memory. Repacking is shown to be beneficial only if the system is operating below saturation level.

ball73

Ballard, A., and D. Tsichritzis. Systems Correctness. *SIGPLAN Notices,* Vol. 8, no. 9, 1973. This paper discusses several problems and considerations necessary to prove the correctness of a system. The authors' method rests on the precise statement of properties, assumptions, and decisions relating to the system design. They feel that attempting to prove a system correct aids in the understanding of the system's operation.

balz71

Balzer, R.M. Ports—A Method for Dynamic Interprogram and Job Control. *SJCC 1971,* AFIPS Press, Vol. 38, Arlington, VA.

barr71

Barron, D.W. *Computer Operating Systems.* Chapman & Hall, London, 1971. This book describes the general principles underlying OS design for multiprogrammed systems.

barr74

Barron, D.W. Job Control Languages and Job Control Programs. *The Computer Journal,* Vol. 17, no. 3, 1974. This paper discusses some aspects of job control languages. Emphasis is on the problem of having to program in JCL in order to communicate with the computer. Suggestions for improving the human engineering of JCLs are proposed with explicit examples.

bask76

Baskett, F., and A.J. Smith. Interference in Multiprocessor Computer Systems with Interleaved Memory. *CACM*, Vol. 19, no. 6, 1976. This paper analyzes memory interference caused by several processors simultaneously using several memory modules.

bask77

Baskett, F., et al. Task Communications in DEMOS. Proceedings of the 6th ACM Symposium on Operating System Principles. *Operating Systems Review*, Vol. 11, no. 5, 1977.

bats70

Batson, A., Ju, S., and Wood, D. Measurements of Segment Size. *CACM*, Vol. 13, no. 3, 1970.

baue76

Bauer, H.R., G.D. Thomas, and J. Van Baalen. A Multiprogramming Operating System for the TI980A. *Proceedings of ACM 76*, Houston, TX, 1976. This paper discusses variations on several versions of a multiprogrammed OS developed by students at the University of Wyoming. The systems were written in a structured assembly language based on a model suggested by Madnick & Donovan. It demonstrates that a reasonable OS for a small computer can be developed in a few months' time.

beiz71

Beizer, B. *The Architecture and Engineering of Digital Computer Complexes*. Plenum Press, New York, 1971. This two-volume work attempts to survey the entire range of computer system technologies at a level appropriate to an advanced senior undergraduate course. The book ranges from simple discussion to complex mathematical formulae. This work is quite readable and is recommended for managers desiring a technical introduction to computer systems.

bela69

Belady, L.A., and C.J. Kuehner. Dynamic Space Sharing in Computer Systems. *CACM*, Vol. 12, no. 5, 1969.

bela79

Belady, L.A. Evolved Software for the 80's. *IEEE Computer*, Vol. 12, no. 2, 1979. In this essay on how to reach a better balance between free innovation and disciplined construction of software, the author encourages the experimental approach in software engineering coupled with a modifiable and configurable software inventory.

bell71

Bell, G., and A. Newell. *Computer Structures: Readings and Examples*. McGraw-Hill, New York, 1971.

belp73

Belpaire, G., and J.P. Wilmotte Semantic Aspects of Concurrent Processes. *SIGPLAN Notices*, Vol. 8, no. 9, 1973. This paper examines the nature of parallel processes and how one describes their interactions in a dependent environment. The authors introduce a language of events and a set of D-operations (D for dependence) that they claim demonstrates the correctness of solutions in concurrency problems. The paper is theoretical and appears incomplete but contains several interesting concepts.

bens72

Bensoussann, A., C.T. Clinger, and R.C. Daley. The Multics Virtual Memory: Concepts and Design. *CACM,* Vol. 15, no. 5, 1972. The Multics Virtual Memory is based on the segmentation principle. Each segment is potentially sharable and carries its access privileges with it. The implementation of the virtual memory principle on the Honeywell 645 processor is described.

bern71

Bernstein, A.J., and J.C. Sharp. A Policy-Driven Scheduler for a Time-Sharing System. *CACM,* Vol. 14, no. 2, 1971. This paper discusses a policy function that specifies the amount of service of a user process that belongs to a class as a function of time. Priority changes dynamically as a function of the difference between the service promised to the user by the policy function and the service he actually receives.

bers79

Berson, T.A., and G.L. Barksdale. KSOS—Development Methodology for a Secure Operating System. *AFIPS Proceedings, NCC 1979,* Vol. 48.

birr78

Birrel, A.D., and R.M. Needham. Character Streams. *Operating Systems Review,* Vol. 12, no. 3, 1978. This paper discusses the facility for handling streams of continuous characters that are input to an OS. The stream is considered as a file buffer where the systems designer must make decisions about character codes, record structures, and carriage control characters.

bjor75

Bjork, L.A., Jr. Generalized Audit Trail Requirements and Concepts for Data Base Applications. *IBM Systems Journal,* Vol. 14, no. 3, 1975. The concept of generalized audit trails is discussed relative to system integrity, recovery, and security requirements. The types of information to be retained in the audit trail are described and different types of audit assumptions for the DB/DC environment are introduced.

blak77

Blake, R.P. Exploring a Stack Architecture. *IEEE Computer,* Vol. 10, no. 5, 1977. This article discusses one of the most recent stack machines—the HP-3000. The author presents a tremendous amount of information on the optimal design of a stack machine. For OS designs, some insights are provided on features used in computers which directly execute high-level language programs.

blas79

Blasgen, M. et al. The Convoy Phenomenon. *Operating Systems Review,* Vol. 13, no. 2, 1979. This article describes a phenomenon in which many processes queue up on a short-term lock associated with a protected object. The authors note the impact on performance and propose several possible solutions.

blat72

Blatny, J., S.R. Clark, and T.A. Rourke. On the Optimization of Performance of Time-Sharing Systems by Simulation. *CACM*, Vol. 15, no. 6, 1972. This paper discusses the variations in systems parameters that can be used to optimize performance of the system. The paper notes the trade-offs in selecting system features, such as scheduling algorithms, size of memory, supervisor overhead, and CPU speed. The paper uses as a basic measure of performance the mean cost of delay for all jobs.

bobr72

Bobrow, D.G., et al. TENEX: A Paged Time Sharing System for the PDP-10. *CACM*, Vol. 15, no. 3, 1972. This paper describes the set of goals used to develop and implement the TENEX system. TENEX is designed to support a powerful multiprocessing large memory virtual machine. The goals for TENEX are those which are important for any time-sharing machine.

boet69

Boettner, D.W. Command Languages for General Purpose Computer Systems. Unpublished Notes, University of Michigan Computer Center, 1969. These notes present the author's opinion of the state of command language development. He felt it was about time to say the obvious about command language design and proceeded to do so in a pithy, direct, and informal style.

boet75

Boettner, D.W., and M.T. Alexander. The Michigan Terminal System. *IEEE Proceedings*, Vol. 63, no. 6, 1975. This paper discusses the Michigan Terminal System (MTS), a general-purpose OS for the System/360 computers. MTS is one of the few successful alternatives to OS/360, and perhaps the only one to be oriented to providing efficient response in a time-sharing environment.

bos81

Van den Bos, J., . Plasmeijer, and J. Stroel. Process Communication Based on Input Specifications. *ACM TOPLAS*, Vol. 3, no. 3, 1981. The authors model process communication on a production rule system. Each input triggers a specific action inside the process where the input/action association is given by a set of production rules. Inputs not in the rule set are rejected.

bour78

Bourne, S.R. The UNIX Shell *Bell System Technical Journal*, Vol. 57, no. 6, 1978.

braw68

Brawn, B.S., and F.G. Gustavson. Program Behaviour in a Paging Environment. *AFIPS Proceedings, FJCC 1968*, Vol. 33.

bris75

Bristol, E.H. On the Real-Time Supervisory Operating System of the Future. *Proceedings of the 1975 IFAC/IFIP Workshop on Real-Time Programming*, Cambridge, MA, August 1975. This paper discusses concepts of supervisory operating systems for distributed computer systems. The author advocates a distributed approach to virtual resources and "contracts" between applications programs and the OS for resource support.

broo75

Brooks, F.P., Jr. *The Mythical Man-Month: Essays on Software Engineering.* Addison-Wesley, Reading, MA, 1975.

brow72

Brown, D.T., R.L. Eibsen, and C.A. Thorn. Channel and Direct Access Device Architecture. *IBM Systems Journal,* Vol. 11, no. 3, 1972. This article discusses the system dependence on channel and DASD architecture for the 360/370 series computers. Proposals for an interface that provides efficient service and satisfactory system performance are described. The solution, a block multiplexor channel with sector addressing of devices, is described in detail with reference to specific performance parameters.

brow75a

Brown, R.R., J.L. Elshoff, and M.R. Ward. The GM Multiple Console Time Sharing System. *Operating Systems Review,* Vol. 9, no. 4, 1975. The authors discuss their experience in developing an unorthodox time-sharing system for supporting large numbers of graphics users. Among the major design principles were implicit I/O by virtual memory reference and dynamic loading of modules during execution.

brow75b

Brown, R.R. MCTS Customer Task Environment. *Operating Systems Review,* Vol. 9, no. 4, 1975. This paper describes the user environment of GMR's time-sharing system. Key problems addressed by this environment include support for numerical analysis computations, high interaction rates for graphics terminals, and flexible, safe, and secure access to large volumes of on-line data. The paper surveys the design decisions necessary to support these functions.

bulm77

Bulman, D.M. Stack Computers: An Introduction. *IEEE Computer,* Vol. 10, no. 5, 1977. This article discusses the basic ideas of stack architecture and surveys machines based on stacks or with interesting stack features. The impact of programming languages is discussed in some detail.

camp68

Campbell, D.J., and W.J. Heffner. Measurement and Analysis of a Large Operating System during Development. *AFIPS Proceedings, FJCC 1968,* Vol. 33. This is a classic paper on the instrumentation and performance analysis of an OS. It discusses what types of data to collect and the types of analysis that can be performed on that data. A survey of measurement techniques is also provided.

cana74

Canaday, R.H., R.D. Harrison, et al. A Back-End Computer for Data Base Management. *CACM,* Vol. 17, no. 10, 1974. A DBTG-type database is implemented on a small computer dedicated to the data management function. The authors believe it to be an economically feasible approach particularly for sharing databases among multiple systems.

chan76

Chandrsekaran, C.S., and K.S. Shankar. Towards Formally Specifying Communications Switches. *Trends and Applications 1976: Computer Networks,* IEEE 76CH1143-7C. This paper attempts to derive requirements for the specification and design of a family of communication switching systems (CSS). The requirements are correlated with an abstract machine definition of a CSS. This approach is quite useful in developing an abstract machine methodology for OS design.

cher79

Cheriton, D.R., et al. Thoth, a Portable Real-Time Operating System. *CACM,* Vol. 22, no. 2, 1979. This paper describes an operating system which is designed to be portable over a large set of machines. It is implemented in a high-level language that provides a standard interface to all applications programs. Thoth encourages the design of applications programs at networks of communicating processes by providing efficient interprocess communication primitives.

chi81

Chi, Chao S. Higher Densities for Disk Memories. *IEEE Spectrum,* Vol. 18, no. 3, 1981. This article briefly examines some of the factors that are producing and will produce higher density disk memories in the near future. Factors include improved coding techniques and new head technology leading to higher track densities.

chu76

Chu, Y. Evolution of Computer Memory Structure. *NCC 1976,* Vol. 45. AFIPS Press, Arlington, VA. This paper discusses the memory structure of some typical computers from the viewpoint of software needs. The organization of memory and the functions available often affect OS design. The Burroughs B1700, B5500, and B6700 represent explicit configurations where OS design is affected by hardware structure.

ciel79

Ciepielewski, A. *CS User Guide.* Dept. of Telecommunications and Computer Systems, Royal Institute of Technology, Stockholm, TRITA-CS-7903, 1979. CS is a high-level language for writing sequential programs using concurrent execution of several activities. It is based on C and incorporates many of the features of MODULA.

clar73

Clark, B.L., and J.J. Horning. Reflections on a Language Designed to Write Operating Systems. *SIGPLAN Notices,* Vol. 8, no. 9, 1973. The authors discuss their experiences in developing systems programming languages for Project SUE. The authors emphasize that the language has two functions: to effect communication among people (e.g., system designers) and to prevent cleverness in the construction of systems (which seems to result in more errors). The system programming language is based on Pascal.

clar75

Clark, D.D., and D.D. Redell. *Protection of Information in Computer Systems.* IEEE Computer Society, 75CH1050-4, 1975.

code71

Code, Inc. *Standardized Job Control Language.* NTIS, AD-742542, 1971. This report summarizes the concepts of the standardized job control language. SJCL was formulated to offer the user a consistent method for describing the desired operating environment necessary for performing a given collection of programming tasks. It attempts to relieve the user of any responsibility for computer-dependent specifications. To the author's knowledge, SJCL was never implemented or tested.

coff72

Coffman, E.G., M.J. Elphrick, and A. Shoshani. System Deadlocks. *Computing Surveys,* Vol. 4, no. 1, 1972.

coff73

Coffman, E.G., and P.J. Denning. *Operating Systems Theory.* Prentice-Hall, Englewood Cliffs, NJ, 1973.

coli71

Colin, A.J.T. *An Introduction to Operating Systems,* American Elsevier, New York, 1971.

colo76

Colon, F.C., R.M. Glorioso, et al. Coupling Small Computers for Performance Enhancement. *NCC 1976,* Vol. 45, AFIPS Press, Arlington, VA. This paper discusses a specific implementation of coupled microprocessors that form a cluster. Processors are differentiated by the functions they perform. The structure of the interprocessor controller (IPC) imposes certain design constraints on the OS.

conw72

Conway, R.W., W.L. Maxwell, and H. L. Morgan. On the Implementation of Security Measures in Information Systems. *CACM,* Vol. 15, no. 4, 1972. This paper presents a security mechanism as a matrix of decision rules where the x–y indices are processes and data items. This approach could be useful in dedicated, real-time operating systems.

cott76

Cotton, I., R.P. Blanc, and M. Abrams. *Computer Networks.* Institute of Electrical and Electronic Engineers, New York, 1976.

cour75

Courotis, P.J. Decomposability, Instabilities, and Saturation in Multiprogramming Systems. *CACM,* Vol. 18, no. 7, 1975. This paper discusses a model of dynamic behavior and performance of computing systems. The model is based on a technique of variable aggregation and the concept of nearly decomposable systems. The objective is to identify unstable regimes of operations and critical computing loads that can lead to saturation. (See also *corrigendum, CACM,* Vol. 20, no. 2, p. 99, 1977.)

cutl76

Cutler, D.N., R.H. Eckhouse, Jr., and M.R. Pellaquini. The Nucleus of a Real-Time Operating System. *Proceedings of ACM 76,* Houston, TX, 1976. This paper presents an overview of a real-time OS nucleus for the RSX-11M system. It discusses the interrupt mechanisms and management of system resources. The design goals for RSX-11M are described, including an 8K-byte nucleus supporting a multiprogramming user environment.

cutt70

Cuttle, G., and P.B. Robinson, Eds. *Executive Programs and Operating Systems.* Mac-Donald, London, 1970.

daki75

Dakin, R.J. A General Job Control Language: Language Structure and Translation. *The Computer Journal,* Vol. 18, no. 4, 1975. This paper develops the structure of a common interface language for accessing the facilities of a variety of operating systems. It discusses major features of a control language such as the generalization of function calls and limiting the scope of assignments.

dala75

Dalal, Y.K. More on Selecting Sequence Numbers. *Proceedings of the SIGCOMM/SIGOPS Interprocess Communication Workshop. Operating Systems Review,* Vol. 9, no. 3, 1975. This paper extends the ideas and issues described in [toml75]. The author refutes several ideas proposed in that paper and discusses various alternative schemes to replace resynchronization. An interesting scheme is proposed whereby the system remembers the last sequence number used in the communication between two entities.

dec78

Digital Equipment Corporation. *PDP-11/70 Processor Handbook. PDP-11 Peripherals Handbook.* Maynard, MA 1978.

denn65

Dennis, J.B. Segmentation and the Design of Multiprogrammed Computer Systems. *Journal ACM,* Vol. 12, no. 4, 1965.

denn66

Dennis, J.B., and E.C. VanHorn. Programming Semantics for Multiprogrammed Computations. *CACM,* Vol. 9, no. 3, 1966. The authors describe a set of meta-instructions essential to writing programs in multiprogrammed computer systems. These instructions relate to parallel processing, program debugging, and the sharing among users of memory segments.

denn68

Denning, P.J. Thrashing: Its Causes and Prevention. *AFIPS Proceedings, FJCC 1968,* Vol. 33. This classic paper shows how inefficiencies in paged multiprogramming systems result from thrashing. A description of the working set algorithm is provided as a potential solution. The paper also recommends three-level memory hierachies consisting of main memory, bulk or extended memory, and mass storage.

denn70

Denning, P.J. Virtual Memory. *Computing Surveys,* Vol. 2, no. 3, 1970. This seminal paper studies, from a theoretic viewpoint, the problems associated with automatic storage allocation in a virtual memory.

denn72

Denning, P.J., and S.C. Schwartz. Properties of the Working Set Model. *CACM,* Vol. 15, no. 3, 1972. This paper discusses the properties of the program's working set $w(j, t)$ at time t. Relations among several factors affecting working set size are discussed as they are derived from both time-averaged and ensemble-averaged definitions. An efficient algorithm for estimating the average working set is described.

denn74

Denning, P.J. Is It Not Time to Define Structured Programming? *Operating Systems Review,* Vol. 8, no. 1, 1974.

denn75

Denning, P.J., and S.C. Graham. Multiprogrammed Memory Management. *IEEE Proceedings,* Vol. 63, no. 6, 1975. This paper provides a theoretical approach to discussing the critical factors in system processing efficiency for paging systems. The authors show that working set policies can provide the lowest paging rates and highest processing efficiency.

denn76

Denning, P.J. Fault-Tolerant Operating Systems. *Computing Surveys,* Vol. 8, no. 4, 1976. Denning discusses four architectural principles for designing error-tolerant operating systems. These four principles are process isolation, resource control, decision verification, and error recovery and are all related to "capability-domain" architectures. Implementation methods are discussed for various situations.

denn79

Denning, P.J., J.C. Browne, and J.L. Peterson. The Impact of Operating Systems Research on Software Technology. In *Research Directions in Software Technology,* P. Wegner and J. Dennis, Eds. MIT Press, Cambridge, MA, 1979.

denn80a

Denning, P.J., and T. D. Dennis. On Minimizing Contention at Semaphores. *Operating Systems Review,* Vol. 14, no. 2, 1980. Denning provides a method for reducing semaphore contention by utilizing a tagged memory. It relies on the principle of locking the individual semaphores rather than the programs that manipulate them.

denn80b

Denning, P.J. Working Sets Past and Present. *IEEE Transactions on Software Engineering,* Vol. SE-6, no. 1, 1980. Denning argues forcefully for the view that no cheaper nonlookahead memory policy will be found than in the working set approach. He claims that it yields optimal multiprogrammed memory management at no greater cost than other common dispatchers.

depi75

D'epinay, T.L. A New Method of Constructing and Using Real-Time Operating Systems. *Proceedings of the 1975 IFAC/IFIP Workshop on Real-Time Programming,* Cambridge, MA, August, 1975. This paper discusses some abstract methods for describing the construction and utilization of real-time operating systems. The method appears to be useful in the design phase.

dgc75

Data General Corp. *Data General Communications System,* No. 014-000070-00. *How to Load and Generate Your Nova-Line RDOS System,* No. 093-000188-00. *RDOS Command Line Interpreter Manual,* No. 093-000146-00. *Real-Time Disk Operating System Reference Manual,* No. 093-000075-07. *Extended Relocatable Loaders,* No. 093-00080-03. DGC, 1975.

dgc78

Data General Corp., Southboro, Mass. Introduction to the Advanced Operating System, 069-000016. AOS Library File Editor, 093-000198. AOS Macroassembler Reference Manual, 093-000192. LINEDIT Text Editor User's Reference Manual, 093-000218. AOS Debugger and Disk File Editor, 093-000195. AOS SPEED Text Editor, 093-000197.

dick74

Dickey, S. Distributed Computer Systems. *Hewlett-Packard Journal,* Vol. 26, no. 3, 1974. This article describes the HP-9700 series distributed systems. The 9700 systems are composed of a central data processing system coupled with one or more satellite minicomputer systems dedicated to specific tasks such as data collection, laboratory automation, process control, or automatic testing. These systems feature transparent communications among processes in different systems, including remote file access and system services.

dijk68

Dijkstra, E.W. Cooperating and Sequential Processes. In *Programming Languages* (NATO Advanced Study Institute), F. Genuys, Ed. Academic Press, New York, 1968. This seminal paper describes Dijkstra's concept of semaphores and their utilization in the synchronization of cooperating processes. A discussion of the problems of deadly embrace is presented with the solution using the banker's algorithm. Implementation strategies for the P and V operators are also presented.

dijk71

Dijkstra, E.W. Hierarchical Ordering of Sequential Processes. *Acta Informatica,* Vol. 1, no. 2, 1971. Dijkstra describes a resource sharing concept based on secretaries and semaphones. The secretaries, akin to Hoare's monitors, are used to implement a synchronous virtual machine.

dion80

Dion, J. The Cambridge File Server. *Operating Systems Review,* Vol. 14, no. 4, 1980. The Cambridge File Server attempts to hide the physical characteristics of disk storage, such as block sizes and timing constraints, without imposing excessive restrictions on the use of this storage. The Cambridge File Server supports multiple filing systems that coexist on the same machine.

dodd69

Dodd, G.G. Elements of Data Management Systems, *Computing Surveys,* Vol. 1, no. 2, 1969. A description is given of basic types of data management techniques as well as the relation of each to the hardware on which it is used. These basic elements can be used as building blocks to describe and build more complex data management systems.

dohe71

Doherty, W.J. *The Effects of Adaptive Reflective Scheduling.* IBM Research Report RC3672, Yorktown Heights, NY, 1971. This paper describes a concept known as adaptive reflective scheduling. Adaptive scheduling effectively manages memory by dynamically following the working set size of a program. Reflective scheduling is based on the programmer's modifying program structure to effect the performance. Doherty suggests that the memory and time trade-off is as important with virtual memory as it is with real memory.

dono75

Donovan, J.J., and S.E. Madnick. Hierarchical Approach to Computer Systems Integrity. *IBM Systems Journal,* Vol. 14, no. 2, 1975. Security is an important factor if the programs of independent and possibly error-prone or malicious users are to coexist in the same computer system. This article discusses a hierarchically structured OS incorporating a virtual machine monitor that provides better software security than the classical multiprogramming approach. The authors claim that this system can be obtained by exploiting existing software resources.

endr75

Endres, A. An Analysis of Errors and Their Causes in Systems Programs. *IEEE Transactions on Software Engineering,* Vol. SE-1, no. 2, 1975. This paper discusses the detection of program errors during the internal testing of DOS/VS. The author provides a generic classification of error types and their possible causes. This information is used to draw conclusions concerning the most effective methods for detection and prevention of errors

ensl79

Enslow, P.E. Languages for Operating System Description, Design and Implementation. *AFIPS Proceedings, NCC 1979,* Vol. 48.

eswa76

Eswaran, K.P., J.N. Gray, et al. The Notions of Consistency and Predicate Locks in a Database System. *CACM,* Vol. 19, no. 11, 1976. This paper discusses shared databases under an assumption of consistency constraints in the data. The basic premise is that transactions must lock logical rather than physical subsets of the database. An implementation of predicate locks on logical subsets is discussed.

ever75

Everling, W. *Exercises in Computer Systems Analysis,* 2nd ed. Lecture Notes in Economics and Mathematical Systems, Vol. 65. Springer-Verlag, Berlin, 1975.

fabr73

Fabry, R.S. Dynamic Verification of Operating System Decisions. *CACM,* Vol. 16, no. 11, 1973. Modern operating systems make many decisions that are transparent to the users. In real-time systems, dynamic consistency checking can lead to enhanced reliability at modest additional cost. This paper discusses the types of decisions to be made and how they can be checked. The checking algorithm is different from the decision algorithm in each case.

fabr74

Fabry, R.S. Capability-Based Addressing. *CACM,* Vol. 17, no. 7, 1974. This paper describes the use of capabilities in implementing an addressing scheme. The advantage of capabilities used as addresses is that their interpretation is context independent. This may provide a superior method for the basis of protection in operating systems.

faga76

Fagan, M.E. Design and Code Inspections to Reduce Errors in Program Development. *IBM Systems Journal,* Vol. 15, no. 3, 1976. This paper discusses a method for formal inspection of design and code. The objective is to reduce the number of errors detected at each stage of the development process through a mechanism that verifies the design and code. Criteria for each development stage are discussed and related to operations performed in that stage.

farb75

Farber, D.J., and K.C. Larson. Network Security via Dynamic Process Renaming. *4th Data Communications Symposium,* IEEE 75CH1001-7, 1975. This paper describes a scheme for interprocess communication that uses an addressing mechanism based on process addressing. It is shown that security is achieved by dynamic process renaming using mutually agreed upon algorithms. However, such a scheme places a significant burden on system overhead when resolving address references to processes.

fein73

Feinroth, Y., E. Franceschini, and M. Goldstein. Telecommunications Using a Front-End Minicomputer. *CACM,* Vol. 16, no. 3, 1973. This paper discusses the embedding of telecommunications I/O within an OS. A front-end minicomputer is used to provide remote access to a large-scale computer.

feng79

Feng, T., and C.P. Hsieh. *Modelling and Resource Allocation of Linearly Restricted Operating Systems.* RADC TR-79-311, Griffiss AFB, New York, 1979.

ferr74

Ferrari, D. Improving Locality by Critical Working Sets. *CACM,* Vol. 17, no. 11, 1974. This paper discusses a technique for improving program locality via restructuring. It is particularly useful though not optimum in working set systems.

flor72

Flores, I. *Peripheral Devices.* Prentice-Hall, Englewood Cliffs, NJ, 1972.

foge74

Fogel, M. The VMOS Paging Algorithm. *Operating Systems Review,* Vol. 8, no. 1, 1974. This article discusses the paging algorithm used in the VMOS system provided by Sperry-Univac for the Series 70 machines. The algorithm implements a working set model and this paper presents the decision rules for such implementation.

ford76

Ford, W.S., and V.C. Hamacher. Low Level Architecture for Supporting Process Communication. *British Computer Journal,* Vol. 20, no. 2, 1976.

fran79a

Frank, G.R., and C.J. Theaker. The Design of the MUSS Operating System. *Software—Practice and Experience,* Vol. 9, pp. 599–620, 1979.

fran79b

Frank, G.R., and C.J. Theaker. MUSS—The User Interface. *Software—Practice and Experience,* Vol. 9, pp. 621–631, 1979.

fras72

Fraser, A.G. On the Interface between Computers and Data Communications Systems. *CACM,* Vol. 15, no. 7, 1972. This paper discusses the problems encountered in specifying the requirements for a computer–communications system interface.

free75

Freeman, P. *Software Systems Principles.* Science Research Associates, Palo Alto, CA, 1975.

frie73

Friedman, F.L., and V.B. Schneider. A Systems Implementation Language for Small Computers. Proceedings of the SIGPLAN/SIGOPS Interface Meeting, *SIGPLAN Notices,* Vol. 8, no. 9, 1973. The authors discuss a few features of a systems implementation language developed at Purdue University. The language was intended to be a kernel for a family of languages into which assembler-coded modules of small OSs could be decompiled. The main objective was to design a machine-independent language which would eventually allow OSs to be transported among different machines.

fry76

Fry, J.P., and E.H. Sibley. Evolution of Data Base Management Systems. *Computing Surveys,* Vol. 8, no. 1, 1976. This paper deals with the history and definition common to database technology. It delimits the objectives of database management systems and discusses trends and issues in database technology.

full74

Fuller, S.H. Minimal Time-Processing Drum and Disk Scheduling Disciplines. *CACM,* Vol. 17, no. 7, 1974. This paper compares the minimal total processing time (MTPT) versus shortest latency time first (SLTF) scheduling disciplines. It is shown that MTPT is preferable for intracylinder disk scheduling.

gain72

Gaines, R.S. An Operating System Based on the Concept of a Supervisory Computer. *CACM,* Vol. 15, no. 3, 1972. This paper describes an OS organized as a small supervisor and a set of independent processes. The primitives of the system may be viewed as a "supervisory computer."

gain78

Gaines, R.S., and N.Z. Shapiro. Some Security Principles and Their Application to Computer Security. *Operating Systems Review,* Vol. 12, no. 3, 1978. This paper examines some general concepts of computer security and attempts to identify the underlying concepts of computer security. The authors note that security is a synergistic group of procedures working together and thus is a systems problem where no single security mechanism is used in isolation.

garn80

Garnett, N.H., and R.M. Needham. An Asynchronous Garbage Collector for the Cambridge File Server. *Operating Systems Review,* Vol. 14, no. 4, 1980.

gele73

Gelenbe, E. The Distribution of a Program in Primary and Fast Buffer Storage. *CACM,* Vol. 16, no. 7, 1973. This paper is geared to evaluations of cache memories interfaced between the CPU and main memory. However, it has applicability to minicomputer systems with small main memories and large nonexecutable semiconductor disks.

gerb77

Gerber, A.J. Process Synchronization by Counter Variables. *Operating Systems Review,* Vol. 11, no. 4, 1977. This paper discusses a method for synchronizing processes. Synchronization conditions are expressed in terms of counters incorporated into the definitions of data objects shared by several synchronous processes. Several examples are presented for the classic synchronization problems.

glad75

Gladney, H.M., et al. An Access Control Mechanism for Computing Resources. *IBM Systems Journal,* Vol. 14, no. 3, 1975. This paper discusses the architecture of an access control mechanism for managing database resources. The objectives of the subsystem are described and the architecture is presented from the user viewpoint. The major objectives are authorization, integrity, and security. The implications for OS design are thoroughly explored.

gold73

Goldberg, R.P. Architecture of Virtual Machines. Workshop on Virtual Computer Systems, Harvard University, March 26–27, 1973.

gold74a

Goldberg, R.P. Survey of Virtual Machine Research. *IEEE Computer,* Vol. 7, no. 6, 1974. This paper surveys research in the field of virtual machines and how such systems are implemented. The principles of virtual machine design are discussed for several examples that have been reported in the literature. The basic conclusion (at that time) is that virtual machines are practically realizable.

gold74b

Goldberg, R.P., and R. Hassinger. The Double Paging Anomaly. *NCC 1974,* Vol. 43. AFIPS Press, Arlington, VA. Certain page replacement algorithms can cause more page faults as the size of memory increases. Conversely, stack algorithms do not exhibit this behavior. This paper investigates the dynamics of double-paging (i.e., running the paged OS/VS2 under a paged virtual machine monitor, VM/370). Increases in virtual memory size without corresponding increases in real memory can lead to significant increases in page faults.

gold74c

Gold, D.E., and D.J. Kuck. A Model for Masking Rotational Latency by Dynamic Disk Allocation. *CACM,* Vol. 17, no. 5, 1974. This paper discusses algorithms for masking the rotational latency of a disk or drum. It further discusses anticipating I/O scheduling for restricted classes of programs. Latency may be masked using a small amount of buffer memory.

good75

Goodenough, J.B. Exception Handling: Issues and Proposed Notation. *CACM,* Vol. 18, no. 12, 1975. This paper discusses the features a programming language needs to handle exceptional conditions in an orderly and reliable manner. It shows how deficiencies in current approaches can be remedied.

gord73

Gordon, R.L. The Impact of Automated Memory Management on Software Architecture. *IEEE Computer,* Vol. 6, no. 11, 1973. This paper argues for increased programmer efficiency by removing constraints imposed by conventional storage system architectures. This is accomplished by automatic memory management of virtual memory.

gord75

Gordon, R.L., and R. Howbrigg. Systems of Cooperating Schedulers. *Proceedings of the 1975 IFAC/IFIP Workshop on Real-Time Programming,* Cambridge, MA, August, 1975.

This paper reviews implicit and explicit scheduling methods for computer resources. The authors discuss an OS based on a hierarchy of cooperating schedulers. This approach is particularly relevant to the design of "layered" OSs.

gors78

Gorski, J. A Modular Representation of the Access Control System. *Operating Systems Review*, Vol. 12, no. 3, 1978. This paper discusses a definition and implementation of an access control system from a formalistic viewpoint. The idea of an access control module that enforces protection policies is described and specified.

grah75

Graham, R.M. *Principles of Systems Programming*. John Wiley & Sons, New York, 1975. This book examines some of the principles of systems programming which the author notes is one of the most challenging and complex areas of computer science. He notes that it is a field which encompasses many specialties. This is an introductory text that is eminently readable.

habe72

Habermann, A.N. Synchronization of Communicating Processes. *CACM*, Vol. 15, no. 3, 1972. This paper describes a synchronization mechanism for proving correct communications of processes. Certain aspects of processes, such as message buffers and interprocess communications, are discussed as examples. The basic primitives are discussed in some detail.

habe73

Habermann, A.N. Integrated Design. *SIGPLAN Notices*, Vol. 8, no. 9, 1973. This paper discusses several features of a systems programming language that could be useful during the design, analysis, and documentation/description phases of OS implementation.

habe76a

Habermann, A.N., L. Flon, and L. Cooprider. Modularization and Hierarchy in a Family of Operating Systems. *CACM*, Vol. 19, no. 5, 1976. This paper describes the design philosophy used in the construction of an OS family. Members of this family can share much software as a result of modular design.

habe76b

Habermann, A.N. *Introduction to Operating Systems Design*. Science Research Associates, Palo Alto, CA, 1976.

haml73

Hamlet, R.G. Efficient Multiprogramming Resource Allocation and Accounting. *CACM*, Vol. 16, no. 6, 1973. The general problem of allocating resources in a multiprogramming system is discussed. It is noted that the principle of unfairness can be applied in the interests of efficiency. The problem of accounting for resource usage is discussed in the multiprogramming environment.

haml76

Hamlet, R.G. High-Level Binding with Low-Level Linkers. *CACM*, Vol. 19, no. 11, 1976. A scheme for improving the linking of programs is described. This scheme provides for detecting inconsistent usages among separately compiled modules.

haml80

Hamlet, R.G., and R.M. Haralick. Transportable Package Software. *Software—Practice and Experience,* Vol. 10, no. 1, 1980. This paper suggests a kernel of routines that interface to the peculiar operating system of each machine. The kernel provides sophisticated but standard operating system interfaces. Using this approach, applications packages, which are machine independent, may be developed, thus enhancing transportability and ease-of-use.

hans70

Hansen, P.B. The Nucleus of a Multiprogramming System. *CACM,* Vol. 13, no. 4, 1970.

hans72a

Hansen, P.B. Structured Multiprogramming. *CACM,* Vol. 15, no. 7, 1972. This paper discusses a proposal for a structured representation of multiprogramming in a high-level language. A combination of critical regions and event variables enables the programmer to control scheduling of resources among competing processes to any degree desired. The concepts are useful both in operating systems and user programs.

hans72b

Hansen, P.B. A Comparison of Two Synchronizing Concepts. *Acta Informatica,* Vol. 1, no. 3, 1972.

hans73

Hansen, P.B. Concurrent Programming Concepts. *ACM Computing Surveys,* Vol. 5, no. 4, 1973. This article describes language features that support multiprogramming based on event queues, semaphores, and monitors. It suggests two principles for a choice of language concepts and discusses these principles with detailed examples.

hans74

Hansen, P.B. A Programming Methodology for Operating Systems Design. *IFIPS Proceedings,* North-Holland, New York, 1974.

hans76

Hansen, P.B. The SOLO Operating System. *Software—Practice and Experience,* Vol. 6, no. 2, 1976.

hans78a

Hansen, P.B. and J. Staunstrup. Specification and Implementation of Mutual Exclusion. IEEE Trans. on Software Engineering, Vol. SE-4, no. 5, 1978.

hans78b

Hansen, P.B. Distributed Processes: A Concurrent Programming Concept. *CACM,* Vol. 21, no. 11, 1978.

hans80

Hanson, D.R. A Portable File Directory System. *Software-Practice and Experience,* Vol. 10, pp. 623–634, 1980. This paper describes a machine independent method for specifying a file. The portable directory system facilitates uniform usage of portable software. It supports a hierarchical directory structure similar to that found in UNIX.

hari78

Haridi, S. *The Use of SIMON in Multiprocess Based Programs.* Dept. of Telecommunications and Computer Systems, Royal Institute of Technology, Stockholm, TRITA-CS-7805, 1978.

harr76

Harrison, M.A., and W.L. Ruzzo. Protection in Operating Systems. *CACM,* Vol. 19, no. 8, 1976. This paper presents a model of protection mechanisms in a computer system. It attempts to determine whether objects can be accessed in given situations (i.e., acquire rights to the object). There are cases where the accessing problem cannot be decided to be safe.

hart77

Hartmann, A.C. *A Concurrent Pascal Compiler for Minicomputers.* Lecture Notes in Computer Science, Springer-Verlag, New York, 1977.

heck77

Heckel, P.G., and B.W. Lampson. A Terminal-Oriented Communication System. *CACM,* Vol. 20, no. 7, 1977. This paper describes a small computer–concentrator network whose objective is to service a large number of terminals efficiently. Problems of local echoing, error detection, and multiplexing are discussed.

hedi79

Hedin, A. *NILSON—An Interactive Package with Conversational Facilities for the PDP-11.* Dept. of Telecommunications and Computer Systems, Royal Institute of Technology, Stockholm, TRITA-TTS-7901, 1979.

heim78

Heimbigner, D. Writing Device Drivers in Concurrent Pascal. *Operating Systems Review,* Vol. 12, no. 4, 1978. Concurrent Pascal performs all I/O through an intrinsic procedure called IO. IO links directly to the device driver through the vector address passed as an argument. This approach makes it possible to define a generic schema to which all device drivers can be adapted. The author describes the features of this generic structure and two examples of device drivers for PDP-11 peripherals.

hell75

Hellerman, H., and T.F. Conroy. *Computer System Performance.* McGraw-Hill, New York, 1975.

hind75

Hinds, J.A. An Algorithm for Locating Adjacent Storage Blocks in the Buddy System. *CACM,* Vol. 18, no. 4, 1975. This paper describes a simple scheme for determining the location of a storage block relative to other blocks in a buddy storage allocation system.

hoag79

Hoagland, A.S. Storage Technology: Capabilities and Limitations. *IEEE Computer,* Vol. 12, no. 5, 1979. The author examines the state of the art in storage technology. He concludes that although recent advances have increased the size and speed of competing technologies, disk technology will remain the primary mass storage media for the remainder of the century.

hoar68

Hoare, C.A.R. Record Handling. In *Programming Languages* (NATO Advanced Study Institute), F. Genuys, Ed. Academic Press, New York, 1968. This paper describes the basic principles of record-handling management within a file system. The efficiency of techniques for generation, accessing, and discrimination in general record-handling systems is presented. Specific examples from languages that allow explicit declaration of records are used to demonstrate the basic principles.

hoar72

Hoare, C.A.R., and R.H. Perrot, Eds. *Operating Systems Techniques.* Academic Press, New York, 1972. This book contains the proceedings of an international seminar on operating systems held at Queen's University in Belfast in 1971. The papers relate to specific topics of OS design for both commercial and university/research environments.

hoar74

Hoare, C.A.R. Monitors: An Operating System Structuring Concept. *CACM,* Vol. 17, no. 10, 1974. This paper develops the concept of monitors proposed by Brinch-Hansen. Monitors are resource managers that manage a collection of data and procedures. An OS can be structured as a collection of monitors.

hoff77

Hoffman, L.J. *Modern Methods for Computer Security and Privacy.* Prentice-Hall, Englewood Cliffs, NJ, 1977.

holt73

Holt, R.C., and M.S. Grushow. A Short Discussion of Interprocess Communication in the SUE/360 Operating System. *SIGPLAN Notices,* Vol. 8, no. 9, 1973. This paper briefly discusses the interprocess communication and synchronization scheme used in the SUE operating system. The scheme is based on access to facilities (processes) through the use of primitive operations implemented by the kernel.

holt75

Holt, R.C. Structure of Computer Programs: A Survey. *IEEE Proceedings,* Vol. 63, no. 6, 1975. This paper classifies reasons for dividing large computer programs into parts. The mechanisms for program composition are discussed along with techniques for folding programs to meet memory constraints. This paper provides a good introduction for readers interested in program structure concepts.

horn73

Horning, J.J., and B. Randall. Process Structuring. *ACM Computing Surveys,* Vol. 5, no. 1, 1973. This paper discusses several methods for structuring complex processes, two of which are process combination and process abstraction. Basic topics of OS design such as concurrency, synchronization, multiprogramming, and interpreters are discussed relative to these approaches.

howa73

Howard, J.H., Jr. Mixed Solutions to the Deadlock Problem. *CACM,* Vol. 16, no. 7, 1973. This paper emphasizes a mixture of detection, avoidance, and prevention mechanisms as providing effective and practical solutions to the deadlock problem.

hsia75

Hsiao, D.K. *Systems Programming: Concepts of Operating and Data Base Systems.* Addison-Wesley, Reading, MA, 1975.

hunt80

Hunt, J.G. Interrupts *Software—Practice and Experience*, Vol. 10, no. 2, 1980. This paper summarizes a philosophy for interrupt handling and examines it in light of the PDP-11 architecture. The author notes all interrupts should be handled by dedicated processes. He then suggests some additional architectural features which are likely to improve interrupt handling by providing a unified interface.

ibm78

International Business Machines Corp. *Introduction to IBM Direct-Access Storage Devices and Organization Methods.* Poughkeepsie, 1978

ibm79

IBM Corp. *Operating Systems in a Virtual Machine,* GC20-1821, 1979.

inte76

Interdata, Inc. *Data Communications Applications Guide.* Publication 29-468, Oceanport, NJ, January 1976. A handy-dandy little guide that discusses Interdata's approach to providing an integrated hardware/software capability for data communications.

jamm77

Jammel, A.J., and H.G. Stiegler. Managers vs. Monitors. *IFIP Proceedings*, North-Holland, New York, 1977. This paper examines conflicts arising from implementations of the monitor concept. A manager concept is proposed that mediates multiple accesses to a given resource. This approach solves the problem of nested monitors arising from stepwise refinement.

jans81

Janson, P.A. Using Type-Extension to Organize Virtual-Memory Mechanisms. *Operating Systems Review*, Vol. 15, no. 4, 1981. This paper examines a representation of virtual memory mechanisms using an object-based approach to simplify procedures and data structures. The virtual memory mechanism consists of a set of type manager modules implementing abstract information containers.

jone75

Jones, A.K. and W.A. Wulf. Towards the Design of Secure Systems. *Software—Practice and Experience*, Vol. 5, no. 4, 1975.

jone77

Jones, A.K. The Narrowing Gap between Language Systems and Operating Systems. *Proceedings of IFIP 1977*, Vol. 7, Montreal, Quebec, 1977.

kais75

Kaisler, S.H. The Design of Operating Systems Command Languages. Master's thesis, Dept. of Computer Science, University of Maryland, 1975.

katz70

Katzan, H., Jr. Operating Systems Architecture. *SJCC 1970*, AFIPS Press, Vol. 36. Arlington, VA. This paper discusses some basic OS properties that affect the architectural design. Among these properties are access methods, utilization of resources, scheduling, and performance considerations. The impact of these properties on the different types of OSs and, in particular, on storage and processor management is examined.

katz73

Katzan, H., Jr. *Operating Systems: A Pragmatic Approach*. Van Nostrand Reinhold, New York, 1973.

keed79

Keedy, J.L. On Structuring Operating Systems with Monitors. *Operating Systems Review*, Vol. 13, no. 1, 1979. This paper considers whether Hoare's monitor proposal for OS structuring could be applied usefully in the design of substantial OSs. Attention is drawn to problems that might arise in resource scheduling, synchronization, and process scheduling.

kern79

Kernighan, B.W., and J.R. Mashey. The UNIX Programming Environment. *Software—Practice and Experience*, Vol. 9, pp. 1-15, 1979.

kern81

Kernighan, B. and L. Masinter. The UNIX Programming Environment. *IEEE Computer*, Vol. 14, no. 4, 1981. UNIX provides an environment where complex tools are built from simple, single-function components. Many operating systems do some things well, but spend a substantial fraction of their resources interfering with the user. UNIX diverges in that it does many things well, and those it doesn't are not particularly obstructive to the user.

kess77

Kessels, J.W. An Alternative to Event Queues for Synchronization in Monitors. *CACM*, Vol. 20, no. 7, 1977. This paper discusses a P/V-operation primitive as an alternative to implementing monitors. The problem is discussed with an example using the readers/writers problem.

kimb75

Kimbleton, S.R., and G.M. Schneider. Computer Communications Networks: Approaches, Objectives, and Performance Considerations. *Computing Surveys*, Vol. 7, no. 3, 1975. This paper discusses major issues in the design of computer communication networks. A discussion of message, circuit, and packet-switching techniques is presented and these technologies are evaluated. A rationale and factor analysis for implementing a packet-switching network is described in detail.

kimb76

Kimbleton, S.R., and R.L. Mandell. A Perspective on Network Operating Systems. *NCC 1976*, Vol. 45, AFIPS Press, Arlington, VA. The design of a network operating system (NOS) is discussed in terms of the functions it provides and its role as a mediating agent in a resource sharing network. Differences between the NOS and the host OS are identified, and the interaction between the two systems is explored.

knot74

Knott, G.J. A Proposal for Certain Process Management and Intercommunication Primitives. *Operating Systems Review*, Vol. 8, no. 4, 1974. This paper describes a set of interrupt-based primitives for process control and intercommunication. Detailed examples of the primitives are also provided.

knut69

Knuth, D.E. *The Art of Computer Programming: Fundamental Algorithms*. Addison-Wesley, Reading, MA, 1969. The first volume of a series that will eventually encompass many of the facets of computer systems and information processing technology. This book is the standard reference work on the fundamental information structures currently in use. Many of the algorithms appearing in this book are used in various forms in the text as the basis for primitive OS functions and services.

knut74

Knuth, D.E. Computer Programming as an Art. *CACM*, Vol. 17, no. 12, 1974. Knuth's Turing Award Lecture examines the nature of computer programming as an art form versus a science. His paper is particularly important when one remembers that we continually refer to the "art of system programming."

kosi73

Kosinski, P.R. A Data Flow Language for Operating Systems Programming. *SIGPLAN Notices*, Vol. 8, no. 9, 1973. This paper describes a graphical programming language for examining data flow in a computation. Programs are constructed through function definition and composition, and are based on primitive operations. This approach has great utility in OS design and implementation because it enhances the understanding of the system's structure.

kuro75

Kurokawa, T. New Marking Algorithms for Garbage Collection. *Proceedings of the 2nd USA-Japan Conference*, Tokyo, 1975. This paper describes two new marking algorithms for garbage collection that feature small working storage and high-speed execution. A comparison for the time and storage requirements for both algorithms is presented.

kurz75

Kurzban, S., T.S. Heines, and A.P. Sayers. *Operating Systems Principles*. Petrocelli/Charter, New York, 1975. This text provides a high-level introductory look at some of the components of operating systems. Examples are drawn for several systems. In many cases, treatment of important topics is rather cursory. This text is noteworthy for its discussion of operating system command languages and symbol binding, and the system development process.

lamp68

Lampson, B.W. A Scheduling Philosophy for Multiprocessing Systems. *CACM*, Vol. 11, no. 5, 1968.

lamp69

Lampson, B.W. Dynamic Protection Structures. *AFIPS Proceedings, FJCC 1969*, Vol. 35.

lamp73

Lampson, B.W. A Note on the Confinement Problem. *CACM*, Vol. 16, no. 10, 1973. This paper explores the problem of confining a program during its execution so that it cannot transmit information to any program except its caller.

lamp74

Lampson, B.W. Protection. Proceedings of the 5th Princeton Symposium on Information Sciences and Systems, *Operating Systems Review*, Vol. 8, no. 1, 1974. Lampson describes abstract models that reflect the properties of most existing mechanisms for enforcing protection or access control. He also explores the properties of existing systems in terms of these models.

lamp76a

Lampson, B.W., and H.E. Sturgis. Reflections on an Operating System Design. *CACM*, Vol. 19, no. 5, 1976. This paper details the experience gained in attempting to develop a general-purpose multiaccess OS. The system featured capabilities for protection and a layered approach to system construction. A solution to problems with the memory hierarchy structure is discussed; these problems resulted from the positions of disks and ECS in the hierarchy on the CDC 6400.

lamp76b

Lamport, L. The Synchronization of Independent Processes. *Acta Informatica*, Vol. 7, no. 1, 1976.

lamp80

Lampson, B.W., and D.D. Redell. Experience with Processes and Monitors in MESA. *CACM*, Vol. 23, no. 2, 1980. When monitors are used in real systems of any size, a number of problems arise that have not been adequately dealt with: the semantics of nested monitor calls; the various ways of defining the meaning of wait; priority scheduling; handling of timeouts; aborts; and other exceptional conditions. This paper describes some approaches to solving these problems using a language known as MESA which was developed at XEROX PARC.

laue75

Lauesen, S. A large, Semaphore-Based Operating System. *CACM*, Vol. 18, no. 7, 1975. This paper describes the internal structure of a large OS as a set of cooperating sequential processes. The processes synchronize by means of semaphores and extended semaphores. The system is shown to be free of "deadly embrace" constraints.

laue78

Lauer, H.C., and R.M. Needham. On the Duality of Operating System Structures. Proceedings of the 2nd International Symposium on Operating Systems, IRIA, 1978, *Operating Systems Review*, Vol. 13, no. 2, 1979. This paper notes that OSs may be placed in one of two rough categories: message oriented or procedure oriented. The former consists of a small static number of big processes with an explicit message communication system while the latter has a large rapidly changing number of small processes and a process synchronization mechanism. This paper argues that these are duals of each other.

lefk69

Lefkovitz, D. *File Structures for On-Line Systems.* Spartan Books, Baltimore, MD, 1969.

levi81

Levin, G.M. and D. Gries. A Proof Technique for Communicating Sequential Processes. *Acta Informatica*, Vol. 15, no. 2, 1981. This text describes a set of rules for showing total correctness for communicating sequential processes in the absence of deadlocks. Sufficient conditions are given to show that a program is deadlock-free.

lieb77

Liebowitz, B.H., and J.H. Carson. *Distributed Processing.* Institute of Electrical and Electronic Engineers, Inc, New York, 1977. A tutorial on distributed processing which assembles a vast collection of papers, categorizes them, and augments the categories with minimal commentary. It is useful in that several of the papers are not widely available prior to reproduction in this text.

lind75

Linde, R.H. Operating Systems Penetration. *NCC 1975*, AFIPS Press, Arlington, VA. This paper discusses an approach known as the Flaw Hypothesis Methodology for assessing OS vulnerabilities to penetration. Based on this methodology, several strategies for successfully attacking an OS are discussed. It is suggested that application of this methodology during OS design would aid in validation of the system structure.

lind76

Linden, T.A. Operating System Structure to Support Security and Reliable Software. *Computing Surveys*, Vol. 8, no. 4, 1976. This paper focuses on two concepts for implementing secure and reliable software: small protection domains and extended-type objects. These concepts encourage modular software structures. An implementation approach based on the concept of capabilities is discussed.

lind79

Lindgard, A. P—A Time-sharing Operating System for Laboratory Automation. *Software—Practice and Experience*, Vol. 9, 1979. P is an OS supporting laboratory automation and interactive computer used on a multiprogrammed RC4000 computer. The emphasis has been on the ability to write process control programs in an HLL. The OS is used to run control and data collection programs for a variety of experiments. Laboratory automation programs can be started and removed dynamically, and may even be restarted after system failure.

lion78

Lion, J. An Operating System Case Study. *Operating Systems Review*, Vol. 12, no. 3, 1978. This paper describes a case study approach for teaching a course on operating systems. The system chosen for study is the UNIX system. The criteria were a nontrivial system, a capability for hands-on experience, and average students.

lisk72

Liskov, B.H. The Design of the Venus Operating System. *CACM*, Vol. 15, no. 3, 1972. This paper describes an experimental multiprogramming system for a small computer. The system was designed to evaluate the effect of machine architectures on the complexity of software. In particular, portions of the system are implemented as microprograms.

list76

Lister, A.M., and K.J. Maynard. An Implementation of Monitors. *Software—Practice and Experience*, Vol. 6, no. 3, 1976.

lock68

Lockemann, P.C., and W.D. Knutsen. Recovery of Disk Contents after System Failure. *CACM*, Vol. 11, no. 8, 1968.

lond73

London, K.R. *Techniques for Direct Access*. Auerbach, Philadelpia, 1973.

luca71

Lucas, H.C., Jr. Performance Evaluation and Monitoring. *Computing Surveys*, Vol. 3, no. 3, 1971. The purposes for monitoring and evaluating the performance of computer systems are extensively described in this excellent survey paper. Eight different techniques are examined and rated for suitability of use in evaluating and analyzing performance.

lum71

Lum, V.Y., P.T. Yuen, and M. Dodd. Key-to-Address Transformation Techniques—A Fundamental Study on Large Existing Formatted Files. *ACM*, Vol. 14, no. 4, 1971.

lum75

Lum, V.Y., M.E. Senko, et al. A Cost Oriented Algorithm for Data Set Allocation in Storage Hierarchies. *CACM*, Vol. 18, no. 6, 1975.

lyck78

Lycklama, H. and D.L. Bayer. The MERT Operating System. *Bell System Technical Journal*, Vol. 57, no. 6, 1978.

lync74

Lynch, H.W., and J.B. Page. The OS/VS2 Release 2 System Resources Manager. *IBM Systems Journal*, Vol. 13, no. 4, 1974. This article discusses the Systems Resources Manager of OS/VS2. This component attempts to solve three problems: distributing resources across the workload, optimizing resource usage, and coordinating the decisions of independent resource utilization algorithms. The goals and methods for achieving centralized resource allocation are described in terms of SRM.

mack74

Mackinnon, R.A. Advanced Function Extended with Tightly Coupled Multiprocessing. *IBM Systems Journal*, Vol. 13, no. 1, 1974. This article discusses the concept of tightly coupled multiprocessors using shared memory. A single copy of the OS is shared between two IBM 370s and manages both real and virtual storage. Work is directed to one of the CPUs via the job entry subsystem. Both processors are able to access all I/O devices depending on their channel configurations.

madn69

Madnick, S. E., and J.W. Alsop II. A Modern Approach to File System Design. *AFIPS Proceedings, SJCC 1969*, Vol. 34. This paper presents a generalized model for the design of sophisticated file management systems. This model is based on the concepts of hierarchical modularity and virtual memory. An example is given where each level of the model is elaborated in terms of an assumed environment.

madn74

Madnick, S.E., and J.J. Donovan. *Operating Systems*. McGraw-Hill, New York, 1974.

maeg79

Maegaard, H., and A. Andreasan. REPOS: An Operating System for the PDP-11. *Operating Systems Review*, Vol. 13, no. 3, 1979. This paper describes an OS for low-end PDP-11 computers that serve as concentrators and batch stations for a large host mainframe. These computers have no mass storage and very little memory (e.g., 8K or 16K words). The system is written in Pascal.

mann76

Mann, W.F., S.M. Ornstein, and M.F. Kraley. A Network-Oriented Multiprocessor Front-End Handling Many Hosts and Hundreds of Terminals. *NCC 1976*, Vol. 45. AFIPS Press, Arlington, VA. This paper discusses the design of a front-end computer in terms of systems requirements and issues regarding hardware configuration selection, communications protocols, and flow control.

mant79

Manthey, M.J. A Model for and Discussion of Multi-Interpreter Systems. *CACM*, Vol. 22, no. 5, 1979. An interpreter introduces yet another "machine" between the physical hardware and the user. Interpreters are often slow and large programs. Depending on the language to be interpreted, an interpreter may place special demands on the system resources and services. The author examines the features of a computer system necessary to support a multi-interpreter environment.

mart73

Martin, J. *Design of Man–Computer Dialogues*. Prentice-Hall, Englewood Cliffs, NJ, 1973.

mcca79

McCauley, E.J., and P.J. Drongoski. KSOS—The Design of a Secure Operating System. *AFIPS Proceedings, NCC 1979*, Vol. 48.

mcge73

McGeachie, J.S. Multiple Terminals under User Program Control in a Time-Sharing Environment. *CACM*, Vol. 16, no. 10, 1973. This paper discusses the multiple-terminal communication facility available on Dartmouth's TSS.

mcge77

Mcgee, W.C. The Information Management System IMS/VS. *IBM Systems Journal*, Vol. 16, no. 2, 1977. This issue of the *IBM Systems Journal* discusses IBM's approach to an integrated database management/data communications facility. This approach is embodied in

IMS/VS for System/370 family of computers. This issue describes the general structure and operation for the database/data communication facilities provided by IMS/VS. It is helpful to the system designer in that it can provide a feel for some of the higher-level applications programs that must be supported by an OS.

mcin74

McIntire, R.E. Powerful Data Base Management Systems for Small Computers. *Hewlett-Packard Journal*, Vol. 25, no. 11, 1974. This article describes the HP IMAGE database management system for its 2100 and 3000 series computer systems. IMAGE is a schema-oriented DMBS which provides programming language interfaces as well as a user-oriented query language.

mcke76

Mckeag, R.M., and R. Wilson. *Studies in Operating Systems*. Academic Press, London, 1976. This book reprints studies of four major operating systems whose development had profound effects on the state of the art. The four systems are Burrough's B5500 MCP, CDC Scope 3.2, T.H.E. Multiprogramming System, and the Cambridge University Titan Supervisor. Each study addresses fundamental implementation techniques in a manner that allows a comparative analysis of these diverse systems.

mcph74

McPhee, W.S. Operating System Integrity in OS/VS2. *IBM Systems Journal*, Vol. 13, no. 3, 1974. This article discusses a variety of system integrity problems and their general solution. In particular, techniques used in OS/VS2 are discussed as specific examples. The impact of system integrity support on overall system performance is also addressed.

mill76

Millen, J.K. Security Kernel Validation in Practice. *CACM*, Vol. 19, no. 5, 1976. This paper discusses a security implemented for the PDP-11/45. A security kernel is a hardware and software mechanism that enforces access controls within a computer system. Proving that a security kernel is indeed "correct" is a difficult process but can be simplified by some assumptions as the author has demonstrated.

mill78

Miller, R. UNIX—A Portable Operating System. *Operating Systems Review*, Vol. 12, no. 3, 1978. This paper discusses the methods used to move the UNIX system from a PDP-11 to an Interdata 7/32. It was found that the UNIX System was portable to another system with some difficulty. However, the idea of portable OSs written in high-level languages has been shown to be tractable.

mills76

Mills, D.L. An Overview of the Distributed Computer Network (DCN). *NCC 1976*, AFIPS Press, Arlington, VA. This paper describes a multicomputer network implementation at the University of Maryland. The network is composed of several PDP-11s and two large Univac 1100 Series machines. DCN emphasizes interprocess communication, resource sharing, and a distributed architecture of capabilities.

mills77

Mills, P.M. Control Functions for a Multiprocessor Architecture. *Operating Systems Review*, Vol. 11, no. 1, 1977. This paper examines known techniques in the control of execution of processes in a multiprocessor/multiprogramming environment. It also discusses a framework of control routines for controlling the concurrent execution of processes.

more74

Moreira, A., C. Pinhero, and L.F. D'elia. Integrating Data Base Management into Operating Systems—An Access Method Approach. *NCC 1974*, AFIPS Press, Vol. 43. Arlington, VA. Generally, database management systems have implemented as utility software executing under supervision. In many cases, functions of the OS are extensively duplicated in both the DBMs and the OS. The authors describe an approach for integrating the two concepts that yields an efficient standardized data management capability.

morg74

Morgan, H.L. Optimal Space Allocation on Disk Storage Devices. *CACM*, Vol. 17, no. 3, 1974. This paper discusses some of the fractors affecting the allocation of file space when the on-line storage space is less than the amount required by users. These factors drive decisions as to which files are permanently resident and which files must be demountable.

morr77

Morris, D., G.R. Frank, and C.J. Theaker. Machine-Independent Operating Systems. *IFIPS Proceedings*, North-Holland, New York, 1977. This paper describes work toward a machine-independent OS for the Manchester University MU5 computer family. The objective is to minimize the description of the target machine into a few modules. The rest of the system depends on the virtual machine presented by these modules. Independence is obtained by rewriting only a few modules, assuming that the system is written in a suitable high-level language.

mura80

Muramatsu, H. and H. Nogishi. Page Replacement Algorithms for Large-Array Manipulation. *Software—Practice and Experience*, Vol. 10., no. 3, 1980. This paper shows that the Least Recently Used (LRU) method, the most frequently used page replacement algorithm, may not be suitable for large-array manipulation. The authors provide a solution that distinguishes between instruction fetch and operand fetch, noting that these have completely different patterns. The solution handles the two reference strings in optimal fashion and thus preserve the utility of the LRU method.

need75

Needham, R.M., and M.V. Wilkes. Domains of Protection and the Management of Processes. *Computer Journal*, Vol. 12, no. 2, 1975.

niel71

Nielsen, N.R. An Analysis of Some Time-Sharing Techniques. *CACM*, Vol. 14, no. 2, 1971. Nielsen examines the effectiveness of certain time-sharing techniques via a simulation model. The objective is to determine the best method for implementing a time-sharing system given a B6500 architecture.

oppe68

Oppenheimer, G., and K.P. Clancy. Considerations for Software Protection and Recovery from Hardware Failures in a Multiaccess, Multiprogramming Single Processor System. *AFIPS Proceedings, FJCC 1968*, Vol. 33. This paper is a good tutorial on the subject of recovery of information on a mass storage device. The authors discuss almost every aspect of preserving information and how to use it in recovery.

orga72

Organick, E.I. *The MULTICS System: An Examination of its Structure*. MIT Press, Cambridge, MA, 1972. This book represents the essential definitions of Multics from a systems designer's viewpoint. It offers one of the earliest and most thorough descriptions of the segmentation technique in a computer system.

oust80

Ousterhout, J.K., D.A. Scelza, and P.S. Sindhu. Medusa: An Experiment in Distributed Operating System Structures. *CACM*, Vol. 23, no. 2, 1980. Medusa is a distributed OS for the Cm* multimicroprocessor and is an attempt to capitalize on the architectural features of Cm*. The OS is partitioned into disjoint utilities that communicate with each other via messages.

pank68

Pankhurst, R.J. Program Overlay Techniques. *CACM*, Vol. 11, no. 2, 1968. This paper examines the general features of program overlay techniques. It discusses programming techniques as a function of machine hardware and other system features. A specific example is described for a multiprogrammed CDC6600.

parm72

Parmalee, R.C., et al. Virtual Storage and Virtual Machine Concepts. *IBM Systems Journal*, Vol. 11, no. 2, 1972. This article reviews the concepts of virtual machines and discusses several early implementations. It considers the virtual machine system, CP-67, to show how some implementation problems were corrected.

parn72

Parnas, D.L. On the Criteria to Be Used in Decomposing Systems into Modules. *CACM*, Vol. 15, no. 12, 1972. A seminal paper that discusses modularization as a mechanism for improving the flexibility and comprehensibility of systems designs.

parn75

Parnas, D.L., and D.P. Siewiorek. Use of the Concept of Transparency in the Design of Hierarchically Structured Systems. *CACM*, Vol. 18, no. 7, 1975. This paper deals with the design of hierarchically structured programming systems. The emphasis is on requiring programmers to work with an abstraction of the real machine. The object is to make levels below the direct base machine transparent to the user.

parn77

Parnas, D.L., and D. Wurges. Response to Undesired Events in Operating Systems. *Proceedings of IFIP77*, Vol. 7, Montreal, Canada, 1977.

pate80

Patel, A. and M. Purser. Systems Programming for Data Communications on Minicomputers. *Software—Practice and Experience*, Vol. 10, no. 2, 1980. This paper discusses some of the issues in supporting data communications on minicomputers when the communications systems is more complex than point-to-point or multidrop lines. The authors discuss special considerations for external interfaces, internal structures, and loading and through-put from a system programming viewpoint.

paul80

Pauli, W., and M.L. Soffa. Coroutine Behaviour and Implementation. *Software—Practice and Experience,* Vol. 10, pp. 189–204, 1980. This paper investigates coroutines—a scheme for retentive control. It explores the literature concerning coroutines. It also investigates the spaghetti stack as a viable data structure for managing run-time storage when coroutines are used.

pete73

Peterson, W.W., T. Kasami, and N. Tokura. On the Capabilities of While, Repeat, and Exit Statements. *CACM,* Vol. 16, no. 8, 1973. This paper discusses some of the principles of well-formed programs using sequence control statements as found in PDL.

pete77

Peterson, J.L., and T.A. Norman. Buddy Systems. *CACM,* Vol. 20, no. 6, 1977. This paper describes two algorithms for implementing a class of buddy systems for dynamic storage allocation. The problem of fragmentation for buddy systems is discussed in detail.

piep75

Piepmeier, W.L. Optimal Balancing of I/O Requests to Disks. *CACM,* Vol. 18, no. 9, 1975. This paper determines a policy for efficient allocation and utilization of a set of disk drives with different characteristics. Each disk drive is represented by a queuing model.

pirk75

Pirkola, G.C. A File System for General-Purpose Time-Sharing Environment. *IEEE Proceedings,* Vol. 63, no. 6, 1975. This paper discusses the file system for the Michigan Terminal System (MTS). An overview of some of the external facilities provided to users for manipulating files is described. Particular emphasis is placed on the sharing of files among multiple users.

pope74a

Popek, G.J. Protection Structures. *IEEE Computer,* Vol. 7, no. 6, 1974. This paper describes the concepts of protection as they apply to the problem of computer security. Basic protection mechanisms that have been proposed in the literature are described. Finally, General strategies for increasing the reliability of protection facilities are discussed.

pope74b

Popek, G.J., and R.P. Goldberg. Formal Requirements for Virtualizable Third Generation Architectures. *CACM,* Vol. 17, no. 3, 1974. The authors describe the requirements for a third-generation computer system that can support virtual machines. Their objective is to give sufficient conditions for testing if a given architecture can support a virtual machine.

pope74c

Popek, G.J., and C.S. Kline. Verifiable Secure Operating System Software. *NCC 1974,* AFIPS Press, Vol. 43. Arlington, VA. Security is a "weak link" phenomenon as the old cliché about the chain points out. Whereas many systems have claimed to be secure, none has yet been found to be absolutely reliable. This paper describes some of the concepts associated with the idea that an OS can be proven secure. In particular, the system under construction relies on isolation and limited time sharing to provide a secure environment.

pope79

Popek, G.J., et al. UCLA Secure Unix. *AFIPS Proceedings, NCC 1979,* Vol. 48.

popp77

Poppendieck, M, and E.J. Desautels. Memory Extension Techniques for Minicomputers. *IEEE Computer,* Vol. 10, no. 5, 1977. This article presents a tutorial on the methods used for extending the physical address space of minicomputers. These methods include index mapping, memory bank switching, and extended core memory treated as a fixed-head swapping disk.

pres75

Presser, L. Multiprogramming Coordination. *ACM Computing Surveys,* Vol. 7, no. 1, 1975. This paper presents a tutorial on the coordination of parallel activities in a computer system. It discusses the coordination primitives of Dijkstra and presents several examples of increasing complexity that involve extensions to the original primitives.

prie73

Prieve, B.G. Using Page Residency to Select the Working Set Parameter. *CACM,* Vol. 16, no. 10, 1973. The working set parameter j is used to determine the pages in a process's working set. This paper examines Denning's arguments and modifies the model to improve the selection of the time interval j.

prie76

Prieve, B.G., and R.S. Fabry. VMIN—An Optimal Variable-Space Page Replacement Algorithm. *CACM,* Vol. 19, no. 5, 1976. This paper discusses the criteria for comparing variable space page replacement algorithms. It discusses an optimum page replacement algorithm called VMIN which is based on removing a page from the working set as determined by its cost of encountering a page fault.

raim76

Raimondi, D.L., et al. LABS/7—A Distributed Real-Time Operating System. *IBM Systems Journal,* Vol. 15, no. 1, 1976. This article describes a hierarchical distributed OS that provides facilities for attaching multiple System/7s to a host 370. LABS/7 supports multiprogramming and multitasking. It provides a communication facility for interfacing with the host.

rand75

Randall, B. System Structure for Software Fault Tolerance. *IEEE Transactions on Software Engineering,* Vol. SE-1, no. 2, 1975. This paper discusses a method for structuring complex computing systems to provide fault tolerance. The method depends on recovery blocks and conversations between subsystems to keep all components aware of the status of their neighbors.

ravn80

Ravn, A.P. Device Monitors. *IEEE Transactions on Software Engineering,* Vol. SE-6, no. 1, 1980. A driver is the part of an I/O system used for processing an I/O request for a specific channel or device. This paper discusses the interaction between the CPU and the channel through Hoare's monitor concept. An implementation using hardware interrupt facilities is presented through extensions to the PDP-11 concurrent Pascal.

redd76

Reddi, S.S., and E.A. Feustal. A Conceptual Framework of Computer Architecture. *Computing Surveys,* Vol. 8, no. 2, 1976. This paper discusses the concepts, definitions, and ideas of computer architecture. It is suggested that architectures can be viewed as composed of three components: physical organization, control and a flow of information, and representation, interpretation, and transformation of information. Design problems and trade-offs for several architectures are discussed.

rede80

Redell, D., et al. Pilot: An Operating System for a Personal Computer. *CACM,* Vol. 23, no. 2, 1980. The Pilot OS provides a single-user, single-language environment for higher-level software on a powerful computer. Its features include virtual memory, a large "flat" file system, streams, network communication facilities, and concurrent programming support. These facilities are similar to corresponding facilities provided in large multiuser systems.

reed79

Reed, D.P., and R.K. Kanodia. Synchronization with Event Counters and Sequencers. *CACM,* Vol. 22, no. 2, 1979. The authors propose a new synchronization mechanism that allows processes to control the relative order of events directly, rather than by using mutual exclusion to protect manipulation of shared variables. A formal definition of the mechanism is given and augmented by several examples.

retz75

Retz, D.L. Operating System Design Considerations for the Packet-Switching Environment. *NCC 1975,* AFIPS Press, Vol. 44. Arlington, VA. This paper discusses design requirements for a host OS used in an ARPANET-type environment. The major purpose of these HOSs is to manage computing rather than communication resources. Modifications to an HOS required by the packet-switching environment are described and analyzed.

retz76

Retz, D.L., and B.W. Schafer. The Structure of the ELF Operating System. *NCC 1976,* AFIPS Press, Vol. 45. Arlington, VA. This paper describes the structure of the ELF OS for the DEC PDP-11 series computers. ELF is a multiprogrammed OS used in diverse research applications at various sites on the ARPANET. ELF provides multiuser terminal access to remote interactive systems.

ritc74

Ritchie, D., and K. Thompson. The UNIX Time-Sharing System. *CACM,* Vol. 17, no. 7, 1974. This paper discusses a general-purpose, multiuser, interactive OS for the DEC PDP-11 computers. UNIX provides many features often found on larger OSs and has found extremely wide acceptance in the military community.

robe70

Roberts, D.C., *Final Report on a Study of File Organizations.* Informatics, Rockville, MD, 1970.

rodr73

Rodriguez-Russell, J. Empirical Working Set Behaviour. *CACM,* Vol. 16, no. 9, 1973. This paper discusses the behavior of working set algorithms and presents some empirical results.

rueb75

Rueb, W., and G. Schrott. Nested Interrupts and Controlled Preemptions to Satisfy Priority Real-Time Schedules. *Proceedings of the 1975 IFAC/IFIP Workshop on Real-Time Programming,* Cambridge, MA, August, 1975. This paper discusses the problem of handling a variety of interrupts in a real-time system. The objective of the real-time OS is to execute interrupt service routines and tasks in a manner that guarantees the satisfaction of requirements of external processes. A consistent approach to scheduling for this problem is considered.

sala76

Salako, A. File Organization and Disk Scheduling for Minicomputer Systems. *Trends and Applications 1976: Micro and Mini Systems,* IEEE 76CH1101-5C, Gaithersburg, MD, 1976.

salt74

Saltzer, J.H. Protection and the Control of Information Sharing in Multics. *CACM,* Vol. 17, no. 7, 1974. This paper describes the design of mechanisms to control the sharing of information in the Multics system. The key principles of access control lists, hierarchical control, identification/authentication of users, and primary memory protection are discussed.

samm71

Sammet, J.G. A Brief Survey of Languages Used in Systems Implementation. *SIGPLAN Notices,* Vol. 6, no. 9, 1971. This article surveys some of the features of high-level languages used for systems implementation. Several popular languages are briefly described. Future trends are examined, including the concept of an OS writing system similar to compiler writing systems.

saxe75

Saxena, A.R., and T.H. Bredt. A Structured Specification of a Hierarchical Operating System. *SIGPLAN Notices,* Vol. 10, no. 6, 1975.

saye71

Sayers, A., Ed. *Operating Systems Survey.* Petrocelli/Charter, New York, 1971.

sche70

Scherr, A.L., and D.C. Larkin. Time-Sharing for OS. *AFIPS Proceedings, FJCC 1970,* Vol. 37. This paper discusses the objectives of the Time-Sharing Option (TSO) for the System/360 OS. The design principles for general-purpose time sharing within the OS framework are discussed.

schn74

Schneiderman, B., and P. Scheuermann. Structured Data Structures. *CACM,* Vol. 17, no. 10, 1974. This paper discusses a system for arbitrary linked list structures that provides sufficient execution-time protection. Its basic operations can be incorporated into the OS at the utility level for user support.

schr72

Schroeder, M.D., and J.H. Saltzer. A Hardware Architecture for Implementing Protection Rings. *CACM,* Vol. 15, no. 3, 1972. This paper describes the hardware processor mechanisms for implementing rings of protection. The hardware provides for automatic validation of references across many boundaries. The hardware concept provides an effective protection mechanism for both user and system programs.

selw70

Selwyn, L.L. Computer Resource Accounting in a Time-Sharing Environment. *SJCC 1970,* AFIPS Press, Vol. 36. Arlington, VA. A managerial problem in the computer time-sharing environment is accounting and charging for resource usage. This involves the development of a pricing policy for various types of services performed by the system. The author discusses the implications of these policies on the design of measurement and collection systems that gather the data to drive the accounting function.

senk77

Senko, M.E. Data Structures and Data Accessing in Data Base Systems: Past, Present and Future. *IBM Systems Journal,* Vol. 16, no. 3, 1977. This paper surveys a broad range of commercial and research database systems. Common characteristics of these systems are discussed. Many DBMSs have their roots in older filing systems. The categories of hierarchic, network, and relational models are discussed with an emphasis toward deriving a common set of capabilities.

shat78

Shatzer, R. Distributed Systems/1000. *Hewlett-Packard Journal,* Vol. 29, no. 7, 1978. This article discusses DS/1000, a software system that allows the user to interconnect HP-1000 computer systems in a variety of configurations. DS/1000 also allows the user to access HP-3000s via DS/3000 to take advantage of their superior capabilities. DS/1000 operates with HP's RTE-III multiprogramming OS for the HP-21MX computer systems.

shaw74

Shaw, A.C. *The Logical Design of Operating Systems.* Prentice-Hall, Englewood Cliffs, NJ, 1974. This is an excellent book describing OS principles with an emphasis on multiprogramming systems. The author examines the logical organization and interactions of the components of an OS. It is a good introductory text which can be read as a precursor to the current text.

shen74

Shen, K.K., and J.L. Peterson. A Weighted Buddy Method for Dynamic Storage Allocation. *CACM,* Vol. 17, no. 10, 1974. The buddy method allows block sizes of 2^k for storage allocation. This new method allows block sizes of 3×2^k with less memory policy for various types of services performed by the system. The authors discuss the implications of these policies on the design of measurement and collection tools that gather data to drive the accounting function.

shor75

Shore, J.E. On the External Storage Fragmentation Produced by First-Fit and Best-Fit Allocation Strategies. *CACM,* Vol. 18, no. 8, 1975.

shub78

Shub, C.H. Preemption Costs in Round Robin Scheduling. *Proceedings of the ACM National Conference,* 1978. This paper examines round-robin scheduling with preemption costs for both a uniprocessor and a multiprocessor configuration. The effective level is approximated from a formula based on actual load; overhead parameters are derived from simulation results.

simo62

Simon, H.A. The Architecture of Complexity. *Proceedings of the American Philosophical Society,* Vol. 106, no. 6, 1962. This paper is not concerned with computer systems but rather addresses the concept of complexity. The basic ideas in this paper should be read and understood by any systems designer attempting a complex systems development.

simp74

Simpson, D., et al. *Job Control Languages—Past, Present and Future.* NCC Publications, London, 1974. This book is a volume of proceedings from a one-day conference organized by the British Computer Society on Job Control Languages. Key papers are presented on (then) state-of-the-art developments in the United Kingdom.

smed75

Real-Time Concepts and Concurrent Pascal. *Proceedings of the 1975 IFAC/IFIP Workshop on Real-Time Programming,* Cambridge, MA, August, 1975. This paper discusses some of the concepts and features required of a real-time programming language. Examples are given showing the usage of concurrent Pascal in the real-time environment.

smlt80

Smith, A.J. Multiprogramming and Memory Contention. *Software—Practice and Experience,* Vol. 10, no. 3, 1980. The author uses a random walk over possible partitions of memory to model memory contention and calculate throughput under multiprogramming. He finds that small programs with compact working sets run with less interference than larger, more diffuse programs.

souc76

Soucek, B. *Microprocessors and Minicomputers.* Wiley, New York, 1976. This text is a comprehensive reference book on microprocessor design and microcomputer systems development, programming, and interfacing. It draws on the author's many years of experience in the computer field.

spac72

Spacek, T.R. A Proposal To Establish a Pseudo-Virtual Memory via Writable Overlays. *CACM,* Vol. 15, no. 6, 1972. This paper presents some ideas on overlay system design for extending memory available to a program. These techniques are particularly useful in microprocessor systems that have no hardware assists for memory management.

spie69

Spier, M.J., and E.I. Organick. The Multics Interprocess Communication Facility. *Proceedings of the 2nd ACM Symposium on Operating Systems Principles,* 1969.

spie73

Spier, M.J. Process Communication Prerequisites or the IPC Setup Revisited. *Proceedings 1973 Sagamore Conference on Parallel Processing.* Syracuse University, Syracuse, NY, 1973.

spie74

Spier, M.J. A Critical Look at the State of Our Science. *Operating Systems Review,* Vol. 8, no. 2, 1974.

stee75

Steele, Guy L., Jr. Multiprocessing Compactifying Garbage Collection. *CACM,* Vol. 18, no. 9, 1975. This paper discusses garbage collection for the simple case of two processors. It examines the requirements for interprocess communication and interlocks and attempts to optimize efficiency of the list processor while the other processor performs garbage collection.

stie78

Stiefel, M.L. Superminis: What's in a Name? *Mini-Micro Systems,* Vol. 11, no. 6, 1978.

ston81

Stonebraker, M. Operating Systems Support for Database Management. *CACM,* Vol. 24, no. 7, 1981. This paper examines operating system services which may be used to support data base management functions. The author draws upon his extensive experience in implementing INGRES under UNIX.

suns76

Sunshine, C.A. Factors in Interprocess Communication Protocol Efficiency for Computer Networks. *NCC 1976,* AFIPS Press, Vol. 45. Arlington, VA. This paper emphasizes the efficiency of communications between processes in a distributed processing environment. Performance is discussed in terms of protocol policies, flow control, buffering acknowledgment, and operation. The author shows that efficiency is required not only at the transmission level but also at the communications level.

suns77

Sunshine, C. *Interprocess Communication Extensions for the UNIX Operating System: I. Design Considerations.* RAND Corporation, R-2046/1-AF, Santa Monica, CA, 1977.

tene78

Tenenbaum, A., and E. Wilder. A Comparison of First-Fit Allocation Strategies. *Proceedings of the ACM National Conference,* 1978. This paper presents two modifications of the first-fit algorithm given by Knuth. They are compared under two measures of efficiency: average allocation search time and memory utilization efficiency.

teor72

Teorey, T.J., and T.B. Pinkerton. A Comparative Analysis of Disk Scheduling Policies. *CACM,* Vol. 15, no. 3, 1972. This paper examines several scheduling policies for movable-head disks. The performance criteria of expected seek time and waiting time are evaluated. The possibilities of implementing a two-policy algorithm are discussed with relation to input loading conditions.

thea79a

Theaker, C.J., and G.R. Frank. MUSS—A Portable Operating System. *Software—Practice and Experience,* Vol. 9, pp. 633–643, 1979.

thea79b

Theaker, C.J., and G.R. Frank. An Assessment of the MUSS Operating System. *Software—Practice and Experience,* Vol. 9, pp. 657–670, 1979.

thom75

JSYS Traps—A TENEX Mechanism for Encapsulation of User Processes. *NCC 1975,* AFIPS Press, Vol. 44. Arlington, VA. This paper describes a mechanism by which a process can control the virtual machine seen by other processes. Using this mechanism a process can "encapsulate" the execution environment of another process. The mechanism operates by allowing one process to monitor selected system calls and take appropriate actions. Its application as a general-purpose OS facility is evaluated.

tibb76

Tibbels, H.F. A Structure for Interprocess Communication in a Data Communications Handler. *Proceedings of ACM 76,* Houston, TX, 1976. This paper discusses a method for controlling transfers between processes in a communications handler. A single queue structure is used to coordinate parallel time-independent operation of attached processes.

toml75

Tomlinson, R.S. Selecting Sequence Numbers. Proceedings of the SIGCOMM/SIGOPS Interprocess Communication Workshop, *Operating System Review,* Vol. 9, no. 3, 1975. The author discusses a technique for selecting and synchronizing sequence numbers used to identify messages transmitted between two entities. He shows that sequence numbers can be chosen such that both entities can be synchronized completely. Sequence numbers, in fact, are related to the accumulated byte total transmitted from one entity to another.

trap69

Trapnell, F.M. A Systematic Approach to the Development of System Programs. *SJCC 1969,* AFIPS Press, Vol. 34. Arlington, VA. This paper discusses some principles for predicting cost and time for the development of large programming systems. The main theme of the paper is to urge detailed and explicit planning of all phases of the development project. Trapnell draws from his experience in managing the OS/360 development project to explicate some lessons for the reader.

turt80

Turton, T. The Management of Operating System State Data. *Operating Systems Review,* Vol. 14, no. 2, 1980; reprinted from *Quaestiones Informaticae,* Vol. 1, no. 4, 1979. Turton proposes a new method for managing OS state data based on the relational database concept. A central service routine manages all shared state data.

unge74

Unger, C., Ed. *Command Languages.* American Elsevier, New York, 1974.

vanl76

Van Leer, P. Top-Down Development Using a Program Design Language. *IBM Systems Journal,* Vol. 15, no. 2, 1976. This paper describes work performed at McDonnell-Douglas Automation Co. in the selection and evaluation of programming tools. The PDL used in the text is adapted from one presented in the paper.

wald72

Walden, D.C. A System for Interprocess Communication in a Resource Sharing Network. *CACM,* Vol. 15, no. 4, 1972. One of the best papers on mechanisms for interprocess communication. It introduces the concept of process ports.

walk80

Walker, B.J., R.A. Klemmerer, and G.J. Popek. Specification and Verification of the UCLA Unix Security Kernel. *CACM,* Vol. 23, no. 2, 1980. Data Secure Unix, a kernel structured OS, was constructed to develop procedures by which OSs can be shown to be secure. This paper discusses the specifications and verification experience in producing a secure OS.

wass79

Wasserman, A.I., and C.J. Prenner. Toward a Unified View of Data Base Management, Programming Languages, and Operating Systems—A Tutorial. *Information Systems,* Vol. 4, pp. 119-126, 1979. This paper identifies some common concepts in programming languages, database management, and operating systems.

wats70

Watson, R.W. *Timesharing System Design Concepts.* McGraw-Hill, New York, 1970.

weeg74

Weegenaar, W.J., and D. Wielenga. Towards a Generalized Command Language for Job Control. In [unge74].

weiz81

Weizer, N. A History of Operating Systems. *Datamation,* January, 1981.

wett80

Wettstein, H., and G. Merbeth. The Concept of Asynchronization. *Operating Systems Review,* Vol. 14, no. 4, 1980. The authors develop the concept of asynchronization in a systematic manner. They explore the underlying data structures as well as the operations upon them.

whee74

Wheeler, T.F., Jr. OS/VS1 Concepts and Philosophies. *IBM Systems Journal,* Vol. 13, no. 3, 1974. This article discusses the key facilities of supervisor and job scheduling functions in a virtual storage OS. These facilities include system initiation, page management, I/O supervision, and job entry subsystems.

whit76

White, J.E. A High-Level Framework for Network-Based Resource Sharing. *NCC 1976,* AFIPS Press, Vol. 45. Arlington, VA. This paper discusses the design considerations for the construction of generalized distributed systems within a resource sharing computer network. The impacts on local host OSs are identified with a general model of data types and processes.

wied77

Wiederhold, G. *Database Design.* McGraw-Hill, New York, 1977. Although this book purports to discuss database design, over 50 percent of the text is concerned with file system organization and design. The first six chapters are recommended reading for any OS designer because they represent a succinct survey and analysis of existing major file system techniques.

wilh76

Wilhelm, N.C. An Anomaly in Disk Scheduling: A Comparison of FCFS and SSTF Seek Scheduling Using an Empirical Model for Disk Accesses. *CACM,* Vol. 19, no. 1, 1976. This paper discusses disk accesses and the efficiency of FCFS over SSTF scheduling. This efficiency is the result of a lower mean queue length for access requests per disk.

wilk68

Wilkes, M.V. *Time-Sharing Computer Systems.* MacDonald, London, 1968.

wilk73

Wilkes, M.V. The Dynamics of Paging. *Computer Journal,* Vol. 16, no. 1, 1973.

wirt77

Wirth, N. Modula: A Programming Language for Modular Multiprogramming. *Software— Practice and Experience,* Vol. 7, no. 2, 1977.

wood73

Woods, C.M. An Example in Synchronization of Cooperative Processes. *Operating Systems Review,* Vol. 7, no. 3, 1973.

wulf71

Wulf, W., et al. Reflections on a Systems Programming Language. *SIGPLAN Notices,* Vol. 6, no. 9, 1971. This paper discusses BLISS, a language in active use at Carnegie-Mellon University, which is used for OS development and implementation. A critical evaluation of the language is presented.

wulf74

Wulf, W., A.K. Jones, et al. HYDRA: The Kernel of a Multiprocessing Operating System. *CACM,* Vol. 17, no. 6, 1974. This paper describes the HYDRA design philosophy. The philosophy is based on the notion of generalized resources. Emphasis is on expandability and security.

wulf75

Wulf, W. Reliable Hardware/Software Architecture. *IEEE Transactions on Software Engineering,* Vol. SE-1, no. 2, 1975. This paper discusses the problem of reliability in a hardware/software system and the strategies that can achieve reliability.

yohe74

Yohe, J.M. An Overview of Programming Practices. *Computing Surveys,* Vol. 6, no. 4, 1974. This paper discusses the nature of "good programming." Programming is taken to mean the entire process of communication between human beings and computers. The author divides the process into nine tasks that are described in detail. This paper should be read prior to beginning the development of an OS as it offers insight into the kinds of features really required by users.

zuck77

Zucker, S. *Interprocess Communication Extensions for the UNIX Operating System II: Implementations.* Rand Corporation, R-2064, Santa Monica, CA, 1977.

Index